GLOBAL ANTI-TERRORISM LAW AND POLICY

SECOND EDITION

Edited by

VICTOR V. RAMRAJ

MICHAEL HOR

KENT ROACH

AND

GEORGE WILLIAMS

CAMBRIDGE UNIVERSITY PRESS
Cambridge, New York, Melbourne, Madrid, Cape Town,
Singapore, São Paulo, Delhi, Tokyo, Mexico City

Cambridge University Press
The Edinburgh Building, Cambridge CB2 8RU, UK

Published in the United States of America by Cambridge University Press, New York

www.cambridge.org
Information on this title: www.cambridge.org/9781107014671

© Cambridge University Press 2012

First edition published 2005
Second edition published 2012

Printed in the United Kingdom at the University Press, Cambridge

A catalogue record for this publication is available from the British Library

Library of Congress Cataloguing in Publication data
Global anti-terrorism law and policy / [edited by] Victor V. Ramraj... [et al.]. – 2nd edn
p.   cm.
Includes index.
ISBN 978-1-107-01467-1 (hardback)
1. Terrorism – Prevention – Government policy.   2. National security – Law and
legislation.   3. War and emergency legislation.   I. Ramraj, Victor Vridar, 1968–   II. Title.
HV6431.G549   2012
363.325′1561–dc23   2011041576

ISBN 978-1-107-01467-1 Hardback

CONTENTS

CONTRIBUTORS

WILLIAM C. BANKS
Director, Institute for National Security and Counterterrorism, Syracuse University

DAPHNE BARAK-EREZ
Professor of Law and the Stewart and Judy Colton Chair for Law and Security, Tel-Aviv University

KEVIN E. DAVIS
Beller Family Professor of Business Law, New York University School of Law

LAURA K. DONOHUE
Associate Professor, Georgetown University Law Centre

MARK FENWICK
Associate Professor, Faculty of Law, Kyushu University

HELEN FENWICK
Professor of Law, University of Durham

COLIN HARVEY
Professor and Head of School, School of Law, Queens University, Belfast

FU HUALING
Professor, Faculty of Law, University of Hong Kong

HIKMAHANTO JUWANA
Professor, Faculty of Law, University of Indonesia

MICHAEL HOR
Professor, Faculty of Law, National University of Singapore

ANDREW LYNCH
Associate Professor, Faculty of Law, University of New South Wales

NICOLA MCGARRITY
Faculty of Law, University of New South Wales

GAVIN PHILLIPSON
Professor of Law, University of Durham

C. H. POWELL
Senior Lecturer, Department of Public Law, University of Cape Town

VICTOR V. RAMRAJ
Associate Professor, Faculty of Law, National University of Singapore

JAVAID REHMAN
Professor, Brunel Law School

KENT ROACH
Professor of Law and Prichard-Wilson Chair in Law and Public Policy, University of Toranto

H. HARRY L. ROQUE, JR.
Associate Professor, College of Law, University of Philippines

EDWARD SANTOW
Faculty of Law, University of New South Wales

UJJWAL KUMAR SINGH
Professor, Department of Political Science, Delhi University

CLIVE WALKER
Professor, School of Law, University of Leeds

GEORGE WILLIAMS
Anthony Mason Professor, Faculty of Law, University of New South Wales

CHRIS OXTOBY
Research Associate, Democratic Governance and Rights Unit, University of Cape Town

LYNN WELCHMAN
Professor, School of Law, SOAS, London

SIMON N. M. YOUNG
Associate Professor, Faculty of Law, University of Hong Kong

ACKNOWLEDGEMENTS

The editors owe a continuing debt of gratitude to Jenna Ng Pei Suin and R. Rueban Balasubramaniam, and especially to Tecla Mapota, Abhinav Bhatt and Elizabeth Chua for their hard work on and dedication to the first edition of this book. Thanks are also due to Keiran Hardy for his research assistance with this second edition, and to Kate Ollerenshaw, our copyeditor, for her keen eye for detail. We are grateful to the Faculties of Law at the University of Toronto, the National University of Singapore and the University of New South Wales and their respective Deans for funding that allowed the editors to work together over a number of years in preparing the previous and current editions of this book and the introduction. We are also extremely grateful to the National University of Singapore and the Australian Research Council for providing the generous grant which made the two editions and the symposia that inspired them possible.

1

Introduction

KENT ROACH, MICHAEL HOR, VICTOR V. RAMRAJ
AND GEORGE WILLIAMS

1. Global anti-terrorism law and policy

The terrorist attacks of 11 September 2001 and subsequent attacks in many other parts of the world have resulted in an increased emphasis on anti-terrorism efforts at all levels of governance. Although many countries had experienced terrorism before 9/11, the prevention of terrorism has since emerged as one of the major tasks of domestic governments and regional and international organisations; as has the need to prevent the abuse of state power in the pursuit of an anti-terrorism agenda. By anti-terrorism law and policy, then, we mean not only efforts to empower governments to prevent and respond to terrorism, but the corresponding need to constrain abuses of those powers. The intensity of the global concern about terrorism is matched by the complexity of devising a proportionate response to it.

The multi-layered nature of anti-terrorism law and policy design makes it especially important for academics to bring their critical and comparative insights to the global development of anti-terrorism law and policy. This is a challenging task because anti-terrorism law crosses boundaries between states and conventional divisions between domestic, regional and international law. Anti-terrorism law and policy also crosses traditional disciplinary boundaries between administrative, constitutional, criminal, financial, immigration, international and military law, as well as the law of war. In addition, insights from a broad range of disciplines including history, international affairs, military studies, philosophy, psychology, religion, sociology and politics are essential in understanding the development of anti-terrorism law and policy. A global view is all the more urgent because what is done in one jurisdiction or international forum has the potential to ripple around the world, one set of decision-makers drawing inspiration from another.

The first edition of this collection was published in 2005, with most chapters having been completed in late 2004. Both terrorism and anti-terrorism are dynamic and much has changed since that time. This new edition represents complete revisions and, in several cases, new chapters with the addition of new authors, new topics and a new co-editor. As before, our aim is to contribute to the growing field of comparative and international studies of anti-terrorism law and policy. The first edition was preceded by a major international research symposium at the National University of Singapore in June 2004. For the second edition, we were fortunate to have a similar meeting in August 2010 at the University of New South Wales in Sydney that brought together leading legal academics from around the world to examine and compare anti-terrorism laws and policies in many major jurisdictions. This meeting allowed the contributors to this volume to revise and refine their chapters in light of our discussions and to provide cross-references to the chapters written by their colleagues.

As with the first edition, a particular feature of this collection is our attempt to compensate for the focus on Anglo-American and European perspectives in much of the existing literature in English. Although those perspectives are very important and well represented in this collection, we also have contributions dealing with anti-terrorism law and policy in Africa, Asia and the Middle East. We also continue to combine jurisdictionally-based chapters that focus on a particular country or region with overarching thematic chapters that take an overtly comparative approach by examining particular aspects of anti-terrorism law and policy, such as criminal or immigration law, in a number of jurisdictions.

The thematically-oriented chapters form the first two parts of the book. The first group of chapters examines some overarching transnational perspectives on terrorism. It includes a chapter that examines the leading role played by the United Nations and in particular its Security Council in responding to 9/11 and shaping anti-terrorism measures, and a chapter which questions whether a truly global anti-terrorism law is possible given the very different ('asymmetric') contexts of various nations. A third chapter considers the problem of 'transplantation' of anti-terrorism regimes both substantively, within a legal system, and geographically, from one state to another. The second set of thematic essays consists of chapters that engage in a comparative study of anti-terrorism measures. They include the criminal law, the legislative process, the effects anti-terrorism efforts have had on fair trial rights, laws against the financing of terrorism, immigration and asylum laws, and policies designed to prevent religious or ideological extremism which have the potential to lead to terrorism.

The next three parts of the book consist of surveys of anti-terrorism law and policy in three groups of states. The chapters in Part III examine anti-terrorism law and policy in the strategically important and theoretically complex region of Asia, looking at the evolution of anti-terrorism law and policy in Singapore, Indonesia, the Philippines, China, Hong Kong, Japan and India. Part IV examines anti-terrorism law and policy in the West with chapters on the United States, United Kingdom and Canada. A final chapter examines both Australia and New Zealand. The last two jurisdictions could have been included in the Asian group, but seem to fit more naturally, in cultural and developmental terms, with the other 'Western' nations. The final Part attempts to complete the world tour with chapters on the important regions of Africa, Israel and the Occupied Territories and a number of countries in the Middle East including Egypt and Tunisia. We are fortunate that the last chapter even examines some of the possible implications of the apparently pro-democracy events of early 2011 on anti-terrorism law and policy in that critically important region.

No doubt other countries should have been included but there are limits to what is already a large volume. We have attempted to be as comprehensive and inclusive as we could given our limits on time and space, but we are well aware that we are only starting to scratch the surface and many other thematic topics, jurisdictions and disciplinary perspectives could usefully have been added to this collection. Although this is a second edition, we see this collection as complementing its earlier edition, the combination of both being a preliminary point of departure for a future generation of scholarship and debate about anti-terrorism law and policy.

2. Transnational anti-terrorism law: the interplay between international and domestic regimes

One of the challenges of the study of global anti-terrorism law and policy is the important interplay between international, regional and domestic sources of law. There have been a number of important conventions on specific forms of terrorism at the international and regional levels, but a universal definition of terrorism has so far proved impossible to achieve. On 28 September 2001, the United Nations Security Council issued Resolution 1373 calling on all member states to criminalise terrorist acts and financing, planning, preparation and support for terrorism. This resolution, however, did not define what was terrorism, leaving that crucial, difficult and, some might argue, impossible task to each national state. Each nation was then to define terrorism according to its own history, objectives and concerns. The end result cannot be fully understood without taking in both the international and the domestic ends of the conversation as well as mediating regional and supra-national forces.

Security Council Resolution 1373 was unprecedented because it set forth in detail an anti-terrorism agenda for all member states. Like Resolution 1267 before it, Resolution 1373 was issued under the mandatory provisions of Chapter VII of the United Nations Charter relating to the maintenance of international peace and security. It created a new Counter-Terrorism Committee and called on all states to report to this Committee no later than ninety days after the resolution was issued. In many countries this facilitated a rush to legislate new anti-terrorism laws, including in jurisdictions such as the United Kingdom which already had tough anti-terrorism laws on the books. The country reports to the Counter-Terrorism Committee provide a unique source of information about how nations are responding to terrorism, though the Committee has recently and for unexplained reasons made the regrettable decision to no longer publicly post new country reports.[1]

Resolution 1373 can be criticised for its relative inattention to international human rights norms and standards[2] and can be contrasted with the 2006 Counter-Terrorism Strategy approved by the General Assembly which features not only measures to combat terrorism, but also the need to respect human rights while countering terrorism and to respond to the conditions conducive to terrorism.[3] Various rapporteurs and other rights protection officers have also often critically evaluated the anti-terrorism activities of both the United Nations and member states as a means of attempting to reconcile the way that various parts of the UN have responded to terrorism.

---

[1] The relevant website simply states: 'No new country reports are being added to the website.' See the Counter-Terrorism Committee's website, available at www.un.org/en/sc/ctc/resources/index.html.

[2] The only reference in the original resolution to human rights standards is found in paragraph 3(f), which calls on states to 'take appropriate measures in conformity with the relevant provisions of national and international law, including international standards of human rights, before granting refugee status, for the purpose of ensuring that the asylum-seeker has not planned, facilitated or participated in the commission of terrorist acts'.

[3] *The United Nations Global Counter-Terrorism Strategy*, UN Doc.A/Res/60/288 (20 September 2006). For a discussion of the role of various parts of the UN with respect to terrorism, see Kent Roach, *The 9/11 Effect: Comparative Counter-Terrorism* (Cambridge University Press, 2011), Chapter 2.

The United Nations has played an important role, but it does not operate in a vacuum. Before the terrorist acts of 11 September 2001, the Security Council had developed a listing and individual sanctions regime under Security Council Resolution 1267 for those associated with the Taliban and al-Qaeda. In recent years, there has been fascinating but often indirect resistance to this listing and individual sanctions regime as a number of courts have ruled that the secret and intergovernmental process of listing violates various international, regional and domestic due process norms. The Security Council has responded with reforms, including in Security Council Resolution 1904 the appointment of an Ombudsperson to consider de-listing requests and in Security Council Resolution 1989 with a restructuring of the al-Qaeda listing committee and processes. Chapter 2 provides an account of these fascinating developments while Chapter 3 raises the broader question of whether truly global anti-terrorism laws as vigorously promoted by the Security Council and its committees are even possible given the very different ('asymmetric') governmental, socio-legal and political contexts into which they are projected. Chapter 4 tackles the problem of transplantation, cautioning against the assumption that legal regimes can be transplanted substantively, from one part of a legal system to another (e.g. from the national security area to the criminal law) or geographically, from one state to another. An important feature of contemporary anti-terrorism law is the way that it emerged from transnational dialogues between international, regional and national institutions.

3.   Defining terrorism

Terrorism is an emotionally charged morally laden and political contentious concept, which has nevertheless emerged as a critical and unavoidable feature of the legal landscape, both internationally and domestically. The United Nation's Security Council in Resolution 1373 required all member states to ensure that terrorism and terrorism financing were treated as serious crimes, but did not provide any guidance to states about how to define terrorism until three years later in Security Council Resolution 1566, after many states had enacted new anti-terrorism laws. As with any attempt to articulate the meaning of a contentious term, the mention of 'terrorism' evokes a range of images. Yet the emergence of terrorism as a crucial legal and political concept has forced the issue, challenging us to articulate a definition that in most cases has profound implications for the way in which individuals, businesses, communities, states and regional and international organisations conduct their affairs.

The first step in defining terrorism consists in distinguishing terrorism from what it is not. Whatever terrorism is in its contemporary legal use, it is conceptually distinct from: (1) legitimate state responses or *counter*-terrorism, (2) national liberation struggles and (3) ordinary criminal offences. And yet, on each of these counts, the attempt to define terrorism is fraught with difficulties. One important problem is that terrorism and counter-terrorism are indistinguishable in as much as they involve violence and fear, seek a broader audience, are purposive and instrumental, and affect noncombatants.[4] Thus, to distinguish *legitimate* state responses from terrorist attacks is more difficult than it might first appear, and might well involve a closer look at what states do and choose not to do – at the range of responses available to states and the ways in which they *refrain* from acting in the face of an act of political violence.

The uncertain distinction between terrorism and counter-terrorism has serious implications for the definition of terrorism under international law. While there is some agreement in international law in defining terrorism for specific purposes (such as stopping the flow of funds to terrorist groups (Chapter 8)), the attempt to formulate a comprehensive definition of terrorism is stymied by long-standing concerns over the legitimate use of political violence by national liberation movements. Given the long-standing political difficulties involved in finding a comprehensive international definition,[5] the task of defining terrorism has fallen on individual states, which have tackled this challenge in distinct ways, with varying degrees of success. Security Council Resolution 1624 calling on all states to enact laws prohibiting the incitement of terrorism also places pressures on the definition of terrorism given that speech in favour of acts in foreign lands may be criminalised under incitement laws.

Once the ordinary criminal law is seen as inadequate for dealing with the perceived threat of terrorism at the domestic level, the tendency of legislators has been to create new super-criminal offences under the banner of terrorism. But this means that the new terrorist offences have to be distinguished from ordinary crimes and the way in which this is done often invites controversy. For example, the UK's influential Terrorism Act 2000 defines terrorism to require proof of religious or political motives. The religious or political motives approach has been followed with some

---

[4] Laura K. Donohue, 'Terrorism and the counter-terrorism discourse', in Victor V. Ramraj, Michael Hor and Kent Roach (eds.), *Global Anti-Terrorism Law and Policy* (Cambridge University Press, 2005), pp. 13 ff.

[5] See C. L. Lim, 'The question of a generic definition of terrorism under general international law', in Ramraj, Hor and Roach, *Global Anti-Terrorism Law and Policy*, pp. 37–64.

variations in other jurisdictions including Australia (Chapter 21), Canada (Chapter 20), Hong Kong (Chapter 15), Israel (Chapter 23), New Zealand (Chapter 21) and South Africa (Chapter 22), but has not been followed in others including the United States (Chapter 18), Singapore (Chapter 11) Indonesia (Chapter 12), the Philippines (Chapter 13) and many countries in the Middle East (Chapter 24), which define terrorism primarily by reference to the nature of the harm caused. In the Middle East, broad definitions of terrorism found for example in both the Egyptian Penal Code and the Arab Convention on Terrorism raise concerns about the use of terrorism laws against dissenters. They also raise concerns about the ambit of 'freedom fighter' exemptions and whether these are a fair application of any such exemption. As this book was going to press, the centrality of these definitional issues has re-emerged as anti-government movements in Tunisia (January 2011), Egypt (February 2011) and Libya (August 2011), which were spreading to the region, brought down authoritarian governments in circumstances that could fall within some definitions of terrorism. Elsewhere in the region, and especially in Syria, similar anti-government movements have been met with force by the state, again in conditions that could fall within some definitions of terrorism that include state actions.

4.   Fairness, emergencies and the rule of law

State concerns about international terrorism have given rise to important questions of practice and principle concerning the emergence in many countries of a new broad anti-terrorism regime or the revitalisation in other countries of older anti-terrorism measures. In Singapore (Chapter 11), Israel (Chapter 23) and many Middle Eastern countries (Chapter 24), few amendments to the anti-terrorism regime were needed in light of pre-existing laws, including those providing for administrative detention and trials before special courts. These countries have not, however, been inactive in responding to new global demands and have enacted new laws. Egypt, for example, enacted constitutional amendments in 2007 to shelter any new anti-terrorism law from much constitutional review and protect the power of the President to refer security cases to special courts including military courts. Recent events at the start of 2011 in Egypt and elsewhere, however, underline the fact that such formal legal developments will not necessarily be the last word and the importance of the continually evolving political and social context. Before he left office, President Hosni Mubarak stated that he was prepared to cancel the 2007 amendments that sheltered terrorism laws from much constitutional review and gave him as President powers to refer security cases to special courts. Subsequent to his resignation, a committee has proposed constitutional changes that also propose to repeal the 2007 amendment relating to security laws and cases. The committee has also proposed that any subsequent Presidential declaration of a state of emergency would have to be approved by the legislature after seven days and by the people in a referendum after six months. These proposals were subsequently approved in a referendum.[6]

The new emphasis that the United Nations, the United States and other powerful actors have placed on the prevention of terrorism also places pressures on new and emerging democracies. In Hong Kong a new Security Bill was introduced in 2002 but withdrawn after protests (Chapter 15), while in China the legacy of 9/11 is complex and in some respects the legalisation of emergency powers may even strengthen a relatively weak rule of law in that country (Chapter 14). Kenya has also resisted attempts to enact a new anti-terrorism law, in part because of concerns about bowing to US pressure and about such laws being used to discriminate against its Muslim minorities (Chapter 22). Concerns have been expressed that US pressure, including extraordinary renditions, played a role in countering reform movements in some states in the Middle East (Chapter 24).

Indonesia is the world's most populous Muslim nation and a newly emerging democracy. It enacted a new anti-terrorism law initially through Presidential decree in response to the 2002 Bali bombings. Parts of this law, particularly those involving the use of intelligence as evidence, have been resisted and other parts, such as the attempt to apply the law retroactively to the first Bali bombings, have been ruled by the courts to be unconstitutional. Chapter 12 examines the evolving Indonesian situation including calls for tougher anti-terrorism laws and a greater role for the military in anti-terrorism efforts. Increased roles and powers for the military in anti-terrorism efforts can be seen in the United States (Chapter 18), Japan (Chapter 16) and in parts of India (Chapter 17) as well as in Israel (Chapter 23) and the Middle East (Chapter 24). This makes the study of military law an increasingly important facet of anti-terrorism law.

In many countries, particularly in the developed West, governments were quick to construct a complex anti-terrorism regime, amending the existing framework of, to name a few examples, criminal law and

---

[6] Other proposed constitutional changes include term limits on the President and Vice President and the restoration of judicial supervision of elections: Reuters 'Factbox: Egypt's Constitution' (10 February 2011); Reuters 'Factbox: proposed changes to Egypt's Constitution' (26 February 2011); 'Constitutional changes pass in Egypt referendum', *New York Times*, 20 March 2011.

procedure, immigration law, administrative law, aviation and maritime law, and financial law in response to the perceived new threat of international terrorism. Money laundering and terrorism financing laws were also enacted in less developed states including in Egypt and Syria (Chapter 24). Although much effort has been invested in expanding the criminal law to cover various acts of preparation and support for terrorism, there has also been interest in less restrained alternatives to the criminal law (Chapter 7) and immigration detention (Chapter 8). Immigration law has often allowed for the use of broader liability rules, secret evidence and lower standards of proof than the criminal law, but its use as anti-terrorism law has been challenged in both the United Kingdom (Chapter 19) and Canada (Chapter 20). In the United States, military detention at Guantánamo and elsewhere has famously been used as an alternative to criminal prosecution. Military detention and military trials, as well as targeted killings, have continued in the United States under President Obama (Chapter 18).

The use of targeted killing increased under the Obama Administration and was defended by the Administration as legitimate acts of self-defence even if committed outside an armed conflict in places such as Yemen and Pakistan and as sanctioned by Congress's Authorization of the Use of Military Force against those responsible for the 9/11 attacks. The most famous targeted killing was the May 2011 killing of Osama bin Laden in Abbottabad, Pakistan by a team of US Navy Seals. President Obama defended the killing as an act of justice, Attorney-General Eric Holder defended it as an 'act of national self-defence' and Harold Koh of the State Department argued it was consistent with the Administration's proportionate use of force.[7] There was much celebration of bin Laden's death, but a few commentators, however, raised questions about the legality of the killing, especially after it was learned that bin Laden was not armed when he was shot in the face and the chest and it was not clear on the facts revealed about the secret raid whether bin Laden, even if otherwise participating in the conflict, had surrendered. Pakistan also raised some concerns about the US operation, but they were muted in comparison to those it raised about earlier US targeted killings in that country. The

---

[7] Thomas Darnstadt, 'Was bin Laden's killing legal', *Der Spiegel*, 3 May 2011; 'US responds to questions about killing's legality', *The Guardian*, 3 May 2011; 'bin Laden killing prompts US–Pakistan War of Words', *The Guardian*, 4 May 2011; 'bin Laden's killing in Pakistan lawful says US', *BBC News*, 4 May 2011; Harold Koh 'The lawfulness of the U.S. operation against bin Laden', available at opiniojuris.org/2011/05/19/the-lawfulness-of-the-us-operation-against-osama-bin-laden/.

killing of bin Laden avoided the need for a trial, but the death penalty is being sought against Khalid sheikh Mohammed and others alleged to have organised the 9/11 attacks. Both the reliance on targeted killing and the use of military commissions as opposed to civil courts underline how the United States had continued to stress a war model towards terrorism a decade after the deadly attacks and despite a change in administration.

The government of the United Kingdom has recently announced plans to reformulate some of its post 9/11 enactments, including the use of control orders and random searches and the reduction of the maximum period of preventive arrests from twenty-eight to fourteen days.[8] The exact nature and effect of these reforms remain to be seen, but they affirm the dynamic nature of anti-terrorism law and policy. India provides an important example of this fluidity: the Prevention of Terrorism Act 2002, enacted after 9/11, was repealed, but has been followed by various amendments of older laws after the 2008 Mumbai terrorist attacks. In India and elsewhere, the changes to the formal law only tell part of the story of how the state has responded to terrorism and the threat of terrorism (Chapter 17).

Despite the retrenchment announced in early 2011, the UK government has affirmed its plans to continue to deport suspected terrorists to a variety of countries on the basis of assurances that the individuals will not be tortured on their return. As outlined in Chapter 9, the UK has concluded agreements and deported terrorist suspects to Algeria and other countries in the Middle East on the basis of assurances that the suspects when returned will not be tortured. Claims of political and other forms of prosecution made by immigrants, and especially asylum seekers who in turn may be suspected as terrorists, take us full circle back to the difficult process of defining what constitutes terrorism, particularly in societies in conflict and failed states. It underlines the transactional complexity and interrelationships that make the study of global anti-terrorism law and policy both challenging and fascinating.

The breadth of many anti-terrorism regimes and the vigour with which they are being enforced give rise to fundamental normative questions about the constitutional order and their implications for the role of the legislative, executive and judicial branches of government. We might question whether fundamental changes to the legal order are needed or justified in the first place. One of the important theoretical questions

---

[8] Her Majesty's Government, *Review of Counter-Terrorism and Security Powers: Review Findings and Recommendations* (Cm 8004, January 2011).

arising from the changing legal landscape is the extent to which the rule of law can and should be preserved. In the first edition, we included a chapter by Oren Gross that defended an extra-legal approach in order to prevent distortions in the constitutional order in an emergency, while at the same time promoting accountability for extra-legal measures taken by public officials by subjecting them to possible *ex post* political or legal checks.[9] This argument provoked a response in the first edition by David Dyzenhaus.[10] Drawing on common law principles of administrative law, Dyzenhaus proposed a 'Legality Model' according to which, in times of emergency, governments adapt to the new circumstances by creating imaginative institutions with the necessary expertise to review national security decisions. While these institutions might not conform strictly to a formal conception of the separation of powers, the right sort of institution would be able to preserve legality while remaining sensitive to the special circumstances of security agencies. The Gross/Dyzenhaus debate was featured in a second collection of essays[11] and is not included in this volume. Nevertheless, it remains an important touchstone in reminding us of the reality of extra-legal conduct in attempts to stop terrorism and the challenges of accommodating terrorism and emergencies within the rule of law without producing permanent states of emergency and exception. The common assumptions of this debate must also be explored. In some countries, especially in the Middle East, Africa and Asia, extra-legal conduct may be more endemic than assumed by either Gross or Dyzenhaus and reflect underlying issues involving culture and capacity.[12]

Whether and to what extent the judiciary should play a role in imposing normative constraints on the executive and legislative branches in times of crisis is an important issue. Either the judiciary or a specialised, independent administrative tribunal may well have a role to play in compelling the other branches of government to justify normatively and publicly any restrictive measure they seek to impose in the name of risk-prevention. But whether the courts are ready in practice to use their

---

[9] Oren Gross, 'Stability and flexibility: a Dicey business', in Ramraj, Hor and Roach, *Global Anti-terrorism Law and Policy* pp. 90–106; see also 'Chaos and rules: should responses to violent crises always be constitutional?' (2003) 112 *Yale Law Journal* 1011.

[10] David Dyzenhaus, 'The state of emergency in legal theory', in Ramraj, Hor and Roach, *Global Anti-terrorism Law and Policy* pp. 65–89.

[11] Victor V. Ramraj (ed.), *Emergencies and the Limits of Legality* (Cambridge University Press, 2008).

[12] See generally, in the Asian context, Victor V. Ramraj and Arun K. Thiruvengadam (eds.), *Emergency Powers in Asia* (Cambridge University Press, 2010).

powers to constrain executive power is, however, another matter. In the United Kingdom (Chapter 19), the United States (Chapter 18), Canada (Chapter 20) and Indonesia (Chapter 12), the highest courts have ruled against major parts of the government's anti-terrorism efforts, including indeterminate detention without trial, the denial of habeas corpus to detainees at Guantánamo, the use of unchallenged secret evidence and the retroactive imposition of anti-terrorism laws. At the same time courts in Australia (Chapter 21), Canada (Chapter 20) and India (Chapter 17) have upheld anti-terrorism laws, including laws that were subsequently repealed or allowed to expire by the legislature. In some countries, such as Egypt (Chapter 24), Singapore (Chapter 11) and the United States (Chapter 18), some anti-terrorism laws and practices may be effectively immune from judicial review. Targeted killings, for example, have been immune from judicial review in the United States but not in Israel.

As with other emergencies, the prospect of terrorist attacks forces us to take a closer look at our assumptions about fundamental values, legality and the role of the branches of government in a crisis. We are forced to consider to what extent we are prepared to subject anti-terrorism measures to judicially imposed, normative side-constraints on state power, even if by doing so we reduce the effectiveness of our anti-terrorism policies. To answer this question, we need to consider whether the anti-terrorism agenda is effective in the first place.

5.   How effective is the anti-terrorism agenda?

Those who study global anti-terrorism law and policy should be concerned not only with normative questions of fairness, but also more empirical questions concerning the effectiveness of anti-terrorism policy. Indeed, normative and positive analysis may complement each other should it prove to be the case that some of the most normatively problematic anti-terrorism strategies – such as the use of torture and other extra-judicial devices or the use of crude stereotypes or profiles based on race, religion or national origins – should also prove to be ineffective in stopping terrorism. Indeed, the hypothesis that violent overreaction to terrorism may spawn more terrorism should be closely examined.

Issues of effectiveness often feature in legal debate. The House of Lords' decision that the indeterminate detention of non-citizens who could not be deported because of torture concerns was a disproportionate response to terrorism[13] was in part premised on the conclusion that a more rational and less discriminatory response to the terrorist threat, including that presented by citizens, could be equally, if not more, effective. The imposition of increased review of detentions at Guantanamo also raises questions about whether a lack of due process produces both false positives, where innocent people are imprisoned, and false negatives, where terrorists are released.

Security Council Resolution 1373 placed much emphasis on laws against the financing of terrorism, and international, regional and domestic jurisdictions have devoted much effort to compiling lists of terrorists who cannot be financially supported and to broad laws against the financing of terrorism (Chapter 8). The effectiveness of these interventions, however, remains an open question. The US 9/11 Commission, for example, found that the cost of mounting those attacks were less than half a million US dollars US, and expressed considerable scepticism about the strategy of stopping terrorists by stopping their financing.[14] This is a particular concern in light of the fact that many informal means of transferring money around the world for legitimate purposes are not easily regulated (Chapter 8). Thus both the effectiveness of terrorism financing (including costs that are often externalised to financial institutions and others with reporting requirements) and the unfairness of listing of terrorists on the basis of secret evidence, should be considered in any evaluation of the almost ubiquitous terrorism financing regimes. Similar concerns could be raised about the use of immigration law as anti-terrorism law and the dangers that such strategies may export terrorism from advantaged to less advantaged states (Chapter 9).

Legislatures often enact criminal laws in response to terrorist acts and threats (Chapter 5). These responses often receive much public and scholarly attention, but it is important not to ignore less visible administrative measures that may be taken to protect sites and substances that can be used for terrorism. The strategies to protect aeroplanes and other vulnerable sites and substances, such as biological, chemical or nuclear substances, often rely on administrative and licensing measures that are softer or less coercive than the use of criminal or immigration law or military force. Technology can play an important role in anti-terrorism law and policy by, for example, increasing the ability to screen material

---

[13] *A* v. *Secretary of State* [2004] UKHL 56.
[14] *The 9/11 Commission Report* (New York: Norton, 2004), [12.3].

on aeroplanes and ships for hazardous substances. At the same time, the use of technology to facilitate surveillance presents serious risks to privacy.

After initially stressing the use of criminal or immigration law as the prime instruments to be used against terrorism, Canada released a new national security policy in 2004 that takes an all-risk approach seeking to address, not only the threats of terrorism, including bio-terrorism and terrorism directed at critical infrastructures, but also diseases such as SARS and the disruptions of essential services by man-made or natural disasters (Chapter 20). The US 9/11 Commission has recommended two other alternative strategies: the softer 'hearts and minds' approach and a more long-term effort to prevent the emergence of failed states as part of its anti-terrorism recommendations.[15] It remains to be seen whether a comprehensive all-risks approach to human security will result in a more rational allocation of resources and restrain some of the excesses and failures that may be associated with interventions that direct their energies to the narrower task of detecting and detaining suspected terrorists.

6. Convergence, divergence and context in anti-terrorism law and policy

It is understandable that the many lawyers that have contributed to this volume should focus on the analysis of law and legal institutions. That should not, however, be allowed to tempt us to underestimate the often decisive political and historical forces that are at play. Exclusive attention to legal and institutional design in anti-terrorism efforts will also fail to capture the fascinating, but troubling, experience of countries like India (Chapter 17) and the Philippines (Chapter 13) where the complicity of governmental elements in acts of terrorism reveal far more basic problems, such as the establishment of a sufficiently orderly and corruption-free government. Here it may be more fruitful to talk about 'rule by law', rather than how the 'rule of law' might constrain governmental excesses in the fight against terrorism. At the same time, terrorism laws may in some countries such as Indonesia (Chapter 12) and in reformed regimes in the Middle East (Chapter 24) be instruments that could advance the

---

[15] *Ibid.*

rule of law and resist traditions of emergency and military rule and human rights abuses.

The widely perceived 'anti-Islamic' flavour of anti-terrorism efforts since 9/11 is a serious problem anywhere, but nowhere does it influence public affairs more strongly than it does in Muslim or Muslim-majority jurisdictions. In Indonesia and the Middle East, there is a popular sentiment that many governments are being pressured by the United States to enact anti-Islamic legislation in the name of anti-terrorism. The results can be both surprising and alarming. Some governments at times appear to 'allow' real terrorists to escape the full force of the law, while at other times they use anti-terrorism legislation against mere political opponents, labelled 'extremist' for this purpose. Anti-terrorism law and policy may frequently be shaped at international and regional levels, but it also often has particular domestic uses that can only be fully understood by those familiar with local context and history.

This volume can only scratch the surface of what is really going on with anti-terrorism law and policy around the globe. In the Philippines, where the lack of institutional capacity to deal with terrorism is the most prominent issue, the alternative of importing US troops to do the work has sparked off an intense political controversy stemming from the historical experience of the Philippines being a US colony, and of the subsequent location of major US military bases there. The 2007 enactment of a new terrorism law in that country should be evaluated in that context. Similarly, India's response to terrorism reflects various geopolitical factors and hot spots as much as the formal law (Chapter 17). Calls for Japan to be more pro-active in the 'war against terrorism' are snagged by the nation's professed total and perpetual renunciation of military solutions in international relations, a legacy of Japan's aggression and subsequent defeat in World War II (Chapter 16). Attempts in Hong Kong to enact a new security law in 2003 foundered both because of human rights concerns and because of a desire not to be dictated to by Mainland China (Chapter 15). In many countries, post-9/11 developments in anti-terrorism policy can only be fully understood in the context of past historical concerns and current geopolitical realities.

In talking about regional and national peculiarities, care ought to be taken not to go to the other extreme of dismissing the common challenges and similarities in anti-terrorism law and policies throughout the world. Indeed, the indefinite detention of suspected terrorists under immigration laws and military orders in countries such as the United Kingdom, the United States and Canada calls into question any thesis that suggests that Western responses to terrorism will necessarily reflect a more individualistic and libertarian culture than those found in the East and the South. This volume would have served its purpose if it gives some insight into the extent to which we can usefully learn from one other, or simply talk to each other, about the challenges presented by terrorism and counter-terrorism, phenomena which, however defined, are common to all.

PART I

Transnational perspectives

2

The United Nations Security Council, terrorism and the rule of law

C. H. POWELL

1. Introduction

The United Nations Security Council is in a unique position amongst interstate bodies. It is entrusted by an institution with almost universal membership – the United Nations – with maintaining international peace and security. To carry out its mandate, the Council enjoys an extraordinary power: if it finds a threat to the peace, a breach of the peace or an act of aggression, the Council is empowered by Chapter VII of the UN Charter to issue mandatory resolutions – resolutions which states are obliged, under the Charter, to implement.[1] An example is the imposition of a mandatory arms embargo against apartheid South Africa in November 1977.[2]

The focus of this chapter will be the extensive anti-terrorism programme which the Security Council has created under Chapter VII of the Charter. In particular, I will be examining two central phenomena: the so-called 'listing' system and the Security Council's creation of global 'legislation'.

2. Listing

A. Description

Originating in Security Council Resolution 1267 of 1999,[3] listing imposes sanctions on individuals and entities connected to the Taliban,

A big thank you to the people who have commented on earlier drafts of this chapter, particularly Chris Michaelsen, Tom Bennett and Chris Oxtoby. Thank you, too, to the participants at the August symposium for their insights. Any remaining errors are my own.

[1] Charter of the United Nations, San Francisco, 26 June 1945, in force 24 October 1945, 1 UNTS XVI (UN Charter), art. 39.
[2] SC Res. 418 (1977), 4 November 1977, UN SCOR, UN Doc. S/RES/418, art. 2.
[3] On the situation in Afghanistan, SC Res. 1267 (1999), 15 October 1999, UN SCOR, UN Doc. S/RES/1267 (1999), art. 4; On the situation in Afghanistan SC Res. 1333 (2000), 19 December 2000, UN SCOR, UN Doc. S/RES/1333 (2000), art. 5.

and through a later resolution, on individuals connected to al-Qaeda.[4] The founding resolution set up a committee, the 'Al-Qaida and Taliban Sanctions Committee' or '1267 Committee',[5] to determine which these entities are[6] and to monitor states' compliance with the sanctions against them.[7]

Once persons or entities have been listed by this Committee, states are obliged under Chapter VII of the UN Charter to implement three types of sanctions against them: freezing of assets, a travel ban and an arms embargo. The freezing of assets applies to all assets within the state's jurisdiction, excluding funds exempted for humanitarian reasons. States must freeze assets controlled by the listed person, as well as those owned or controlled by persons acting on their behalf or at their direction.[8] The travel ban is meant to prevent listed persons from entering or passing through the territory of any state.[9] The arms embargo imposes on states an obligation to prevent listed nationals from selling and supplying military equipment, even if the sales are conducted outside their territories.[10]

Initially, listing provided neither criteria nor avenues for affected parties to challenge listing decisions.[11] While states could assist their listed nationals or residents through normal diplomatic channels, these states also had no access to the information behind listing decisions unless they were on the Security Council. None of the Committee members had to provide reasons for any of their decisions, and the Committee as a whole had no obligation to communicate reasons for its decisions to bodies outside the Committee, whether these were states or listed persons.

Listing has been reformed extensively in recent years, a process that will be analysed further below. Even in its newest form, however, it remains

---

[4] SC Res. 1333, art. 8(c).
[5] The website of the Committee is available at www.un.org/Docs/sc/committees /1267Template.htm.
[6] SC Res. 1267, art. 6(e).   [7] *Ibid.*, arts. 6(a), 6(b), 6(d) and 6(g) and 9.
[8] SC Res. 1452 (2002), 20 December 2002, UN SCOR, UN Doc. S/RES/1452 (2002), art. 1; SC Res. 1267, art. 4(b); SC Res. 1333, art. 8; SC Res. 1390 (2002), 16 January 2002, UN SCOR, UN Doc. S/RES/1390 (2002), art. 2(a); SC Res. 1526 (2004), 30 January 2004, UN SCOR, UN Doc. S/RES/1526 (2004), art. 1(b); SC Res. 1617 (2005), 29 July 2005, UN SCOR, UN Doc. S/RES/1617 (2005), art. 1(a); SC Res. 1735 (2006), 22 December 2006, UN SCOR, UN Doc. S/RES/1735 (2006), art. 1(a); SC Res. 1822 (2008), 30 June 2008, UN SCOR, UN Doc. S/Res/1822 (2008), art. 1(a); SC Res. 1904 (2009), 17 December 2009, UN SCOR, UN Doc. S/Res /1904 (2009), art. 1.
[9] SC Res. 1390, art. 2(b), SC Res. 1526, art. 1(b); SC Res. 1617, art. 1(b); SC Res. 1735, art. 1(b); SC Res. 1822, art. 1(b); and SC Res. 1904, art. 1(b).
[10] SC Res. 1390, art. 2(c); SC Res. 1526, art. 1(c); SC Res. 1617 of 2005, art. 1(c); SC Res. 1735, art. 1(c); SC Res. 1822, art. 1(c); and SC Res. 1904, art. 1(c).
[11] Neither of the two founding resolutions (SC Res. 1267 and SC Res. 1333) nor the resolution which consolidated the two sets of sanctions (SC Res. 1390) provided any criteria.

extremely problematic.[12] There is no advance warning of listing. Criteria have now been provided for it, but they are extremely broad.[13] The delisting procedure, set up in 2002, has provided an Ombudsperson since 2009. This person can communicate with the listed person directly, attempt to acquire information on that person's behalf and advise the Security Council on the delisting request. However, the states on the Security Council remain the sole arbiters of which information can be released, even to the Ombudsperson. It is therefore conceivable that petitioners will have no idea at all of the evidence on which the suspicion against them is based.[14]

The Ombudsperson also has no power to change listing decisions. The 1267 Committee – including the state that suggested the listing of the individual in the first place – therefore retains sole discretion on whether or not to delist. Removal from the list is still possible only with the consent of all 1267 Committee members[15] – and they, in turn, bear no obligation to give reasons for their refusal.

---

[12] *Yassim Abdullah Kadi and Al Barakaat International Foundation* v. *Council of European Union and Commission of the European Communities* (C-402/05 P; C-415/05 P), judgment of 3 September 2008, available at curia.europa.eu/ (*Kadi*); *HM Treasury* v. *Mohammed Jabar Ahmed and others, HM Treasury* v. *Mohammed al-Ghabra, R (on the application of Hani El Sayed Sabaei Youssef)* v. *HM Treasury,* judgment of 27 January 2010 [2010] UKSC (*Ahmed*), 2; P. Gutherie, 'Security Council sanctions and the protection of individual rights' (2004) 60 *NYU Annual Survey of American Law* 491, 503–6; E. de Wet and A. Nollkaemper, 'Review of Security Council decisions by national courts' (2002) 45 *German Yearbook of International Law* 166, 176–7; C. Harlow, 'Global administrative law: the quest for principles and values' (2006) 17 *European Journal of International Law* 187; Christopher Michaelson, 'Kadi and al Barakaat v. Council of the European Union and Commission of the European Communities: the incompatibility of the United Nations Security Council's 1267 sanctions regime with European due process guarantees' (2009) 10 *Melbourne Journal of International Law* 329; Craig Forcese and Kent Roach, 'Limping into the future: the 1267 terrorism listing process at the crossroads' (2010) 42 *George Washington International Law Review* 217.

[13] The term 'associated with' covers:
'(a) participating in the financing, planning, facilitating, preparing, or perpetrating of acts or activities by, in conjunction with, under the name of, on behalf of, or in support of;
(b) supplying, selling or transferring arms and related material to;
(c) recruiting for; or
(d) otherwise supporting acts or activities of;
Al-Qaida, Usama bin Laden or the Taliban, or any cell, affiliate, splinter group or derivative thereof' SC Res. 1822, art. 2.

[14] See Forcese and Roach, 'Limping into the future', for the problem of secret evidence. See also *Abdelrazik* v. *Canada (Foreign Affairs)*, 2009 FC 580 (CanLII), [53] on the requirement that petitioners establish why they 'no *longer*' meet the criteria for listing.

[15] 1267 Committee, *Fact Sheet on Listing* (2008), [11], available at www.un.org/sc/committees/1267/fact_sheet_listing.shtml.

B. Objections

Controversial from the beginning, listing has run into considerable resistance in recent years. In 2005, the 1267 Committee's monitoring body[16] began to note complaints against it[17] from states and non-state actors.[18] It has also faced legal challenges[19] and has been strongly criticised in academic literature and jurisprudence.[20] The European Court of Justice (ECJ) has recently annulled a number of listings, as implemented by the European Union,[21] as did the UK Supreme Court in *Ahmed*.[22]

Objections draw on three main areas of law. First, from a human rights perspective, listing threatens or infringes the right to judicial review, the right to procedural fairness, the right to be heard, the right to a judicial remedy and the right to property.[23] Second, listing has also been strongly criticised, even in its more recent forms, from the perspective of administrative law and the common law of some Anglo-American systems.[24] Finally, listing has been criticised as a threat to the rule of law for the uncontrolled power it confers on the executive arm of government.[25]

3. Legislation

A. Description

It is not unknown for international bodies to influence the creation of international law norms, and the Security Council's authority on some areas of

---

[16] The Security Council established monitoring bodies to assist the 1267 Committee. The 'Monitoring Group' established by SC Res. 1363 (2001), 30 July 2001, UN SCOR, UN Doc. S/RES/1363 (2001), was later replaced by the 'Monitoring Team' set up by SC Res. 1526.

[17] A first reference to the need for humanitarian exemptions was, however, made in the September report of 2002 (S/2002/1050, [42]).

[18] S/2005/83, [54].

[19] By 2006, legal challenges had become an established, detailed section of the Monitoring Team's reports. Examples include the annex to S/2006/154 and annex III to S/2006/750.

[20] See above note 12; Erika De Wet, *Chapter VII Powers of the United Nations Security Council* (Oxford: Hart Publishing, 2004); and Mariam Aziz, 'Implementation as the test case of European Union citizenship' (2009) 15 *Columbia Journal of European Law* 281, 290.

[21] *Kadi* (above note 12). See also *Omar Mohammed Othman v. Council and Commission*, judgment of the Court of First Instance, case number T-318/01, available at curia.europa.eu/.

[22] *Ahmed* (above note 12). This case dealt with the UK's own list of terrorist suspects as well as its implementation of the 1267 Committee's list.

[23] See above note 12 and *Abdelrazik* (above note 14).

[24] Aziz, 'Implementation as the test case of European Union citizenship', 290; *Ahmed* (above note 12).

[25] See *Ahmed* (above note 12), [45]. See also David Dyzenhaus 'The rule of (administrative) law in international law' (2005) 68 *Law and Contemporary Problems* 127; and C. H. Powell,

international law is already well-entrenched,[26] particularly in questions on the legality of the use of force.[27] However, in this chapter, the term 'legislation' refers to a specific type of resolution by which the Council purports unilaterally to create general norms of law binding on all states, irrespective of their consent. Taken in this narrower sense, Security Council 'legislation' must meet four criteria: that the Council be acting unilaterally when it legislates;[28] that it intends its norms to be mandatory (by which the use of Chapter VII of the Charter is generally implied);[29] that the norms in the legislative resolution be general;[30] and that these norms be new.[31]

'The legal authority of the UN Security Council', in Benjamin Goold and Liora Lazarus (eds.) *Security and Human Rights* (Oxford: Hart Publishing, 2007); *Kadi* (above note 12).

[26] J. Alvarez, *International Organisations as Law-Makers* (Oxford University Press, 2005); Powell, 'The legal authority of the UN Security Council'; Rosalyn Higgins, *The Development of International Law through the Political Organs of the United Nations* (Oxford University Press, 1963).

[27] For extensive reliance on the Security Council on questions of the legality of force, see J. Murphy, 'Force and arms', in C. Joyner (ed.), *The United Nations and International Law* (Cambridge: American Society of International Law and Cambridge University Press, 1999), p. 99; Thomas M. Franck, 'Terrorism and the right of self-defense' (2001) 95 *American Journal of International Law*, 839–40, 841, 842; D. J. Harris, *Cases and Materials on International Law* (London: Sweet & Maxwell, 6th edn, 2004), pp. 889, 913, 925, 938, 930, 932, 940 footnotes 71–2, 940, note 1; D. Bowett, 'Reprisals involving recourse to armed force' (1972) 66 *American Journal of International Law* 1.

[28] F. Kirgis, 'The Security Council's first fifty years' (1995) 89 *American Journal of International Law* 506, 520; P. Szasz 'The Security Council starts legislating' (2002) 96 *American Journal of International Law* 901–2; A. Marschik, 'The Security Council as world legislator? Theory, practice and consequences of an expanding world power', IILJ Working Paper 2005/18; S. Talmon, 'The Security Council as world legislature' (2005) 99 *American Journal of International Law* 175, 176–8; M. Happold, 'Security Council Resolution 1373 and the Constitution of the United Nations' (2003) 16 *Leiden Journal of International Law* 539, 596–8; and Masahiko Asada, 'WMD terrorism and Security Council Resolution 1540: conditions for legitimacy in international legislation', IILJ Working Paper 2007/9 (Global Administrative Law Series), pp. 15–19.

[29] Szasz, 'The Security Council starts legislating', 901–2; Marschik, 'The Security Council as world legislator?', 5–6; A. Marschik, 'Legislative powers of the Security Council', in Ronald MacDonald and Douglas Johnston (eds.), *Towards World Constitutionalism* (Leiden: Martinus Nijhoff, 2005), p. 461; Happold, 'Security Council Resolution 1373', 596–8.

[30] Kirgis, 'The Security Council's first fifty years', 520; Szasz, 'The Security Council starts legislating', 901–2; Marschik, 'The Security Council as world legislator?', 5–6; Talmon, 'The Security Council as world legislature', 176–8; Happold, 'Security Council Resolution 1373', 596–8; Asada, 'WMD terrorism and Security Council Resolution 1540', 15–19.

[31] The Security Council must therefore have modified existing norms and introduced new law. Kirgis, 'The Security Council's first fifty years', 520; Szasz, 'The Security Council starts legislating', 901–2; Marschik, 'The Security Council as world legislator?', 5–6; Happold, 'Security Council Resolution 1373', 596–8; Asada, 'WMD terrorism and Security Council Resolution 1540', 15–16. See further C. H. Powell, 'The role and limits of global administrative law in the Security Council's anti-terrorism programme' (2009) *Acta Juridica*.

The criterion of generality requires elaboration, as its meaning changes depending on whether it relates to the subject matter or to the addressees of the resolution. To fulfil the criterion, it is not sufficient that the Security Council issues instructions to all states on particular issues. Otherwise, all sanctions would become legislation because they are 'directed to all member states and sometimes even to nonmembers'.[32] Sanctions, however, constitute specific instructions with respect to specific problems. They are also designed to resolve the specific problem, after which they would fall away. They are therefore limited with respect both to subject matter and to period of application. In Szasz's terms, they are not legislation but 'mere commands relating to a particular situation'.[33]

This interpretation of generality has also been adopted by all commentators writing after 28 September 2001. Thus Marschik requires of 'legislative' norms that they 'do not enforce the peace in a specific political crisis, but regulate rights and obligations of States on a wider issue with long-term or indefinite effect'.[34] Similarly, Happold argues that, because sanctions relate to a specific incident or problem, they are not 'applicable to all persons or particular classes of persons (rather than to specified individuals), in all circumstances or in all situations where particular criteria have been satisfied (rather than to specific situations or conduct)'.[35] This chapter will therefore follow Happold's approach that legislation must consist of 'abstract legal propositions'.

B.   Legislative resolutions

The two resolutions widely accepted[36] as legislation are Security Council Resolution 1373 of 2001,[37] and Security Council Resolution 1540 of

---

[32] Kirgis, 'The Security Council's first fifty years', 520.
[33] Szasz, 'The Security Council starts legislating', 902.
[34] Marschik, 'The Security Council as world legislator?', 5.
[35] Happold, 'Security Council Resolution 1373', 597.
[36] Szasz, 'The Security Council starts legislating'; Talmon, 'The Security Council as world legislature'; R. Lavalle, 'A novel, if awkward, exercise in international law-making: Security Council Resolution 1540 (2004)' (2004) *Netherlands International Law Review* 411; Marschik, 'The Security Council as world legislator?'; E. Rosand, 'The Security Council as "global legislator": *Ultra Vires* or Ultra Innovative?', (2005) 28 *Fordham International Law Journal* 542; Asada, 'WMD terrorism and Security Council Resolution 1540'; M. Koskenniemi, 'International legislation today: limits and possibilities' (2005) 23 *Wisconsin International Law Journal* 61, 74.
[37] Threats to international peace and security caused by terrorist acts, SC Res. 1373 (2001), 28 September 2001, UN SCOR, UN Doc. S/RES/1373 (2001).

2004.[38] The preamble of both resolutions makes it clear that each is aimed at a general and ongoing problem. Resolution 1373 was passed in the wake of the terrorist attacks of 11 September 2001 and refers to them in its pre-amble. However, it states that 'such' attacks, as opposed to 'these' attacks, are threats to international peace and security and notes the concern of the Council about the rise of terrorism globally, thereby focusing on terrorism in general, rather than specific incidents. Reaffirming the duty of all states to refrain from supporting terrorism, it calls on the General Assembly's,[39] and its own, previous resolutions.[40] Resolution 1540 addresses another general problem: the 'proliferation of nuclear, chemical and biological weapons',[41] declaring the proliferation of the weapons and of their means of delivery to be threats to international peace and security. The preamble of Resolution 1540 then focuses specifically on terrorism and the risk pre-sented by non-state actors who gain access to nuclear, chemical and bio-logical weapons. Both resolutions then proceed expressly under Chapter VII of the UN Charter.

Security Council Resolution 1373 contains three sets of general obli-gations for states. The first two are phrased as mandatory ('[The Security Council] decides')[42] and the third in hortatory terms ('[The Security Council] calls upon all States to …').[43] Of the mandatory obligations, one deals entirely with financing, requiring states to criminalise the collection of funds which support terrorism in any form, to freeze resources of per-sons who commit, or attempt to commit, terrorist acts, also freezing the funds of any entities controlled by such persons or acting on their direc-tion, and finally to prevent their nationals and any person on their terri-tory from providing any form of financial or related service to terrorists, attempted terrorists, or any entities under their control or direction.[44] The second mandatory article requires states themselves to refrain from pro-viding any form of support to terrorists, and also to prevent terrorist acts from occurring through a number of steps set out in the article. These steps include suppressing recruitment to terrorist groups,[45] denying safe haven

---

[38] Non-proliferation of weapons of mass destruction, SC Res. 1540 (2004), 28 April 2004, UN SCOR, UN Doc. S/RES/1540 (2004).

[39] Declaration on principles of international law concerning friendly relations and co-operation among states in accordance with the Charter of the United Nations, G A Res. 2625 (XXV), UN GAOR, Supp. No. 28, UN Doc. A/5217 (1970), 121.

[40] SC Res. 1189 (1998), 13 August 1998, UN SCOR, UN Doc. S/RES/1189 (1998).

[41] Preamble, SC Res. 1540, para. 1.

[42] SC Res. 1373, arts. 1–2.   [43] Ibid., art. 3.

[44] Ibid., art. 1.   [45] Ibid., art. 2(a).

to anybody connected to terrorism,[46] prosecuting terrorists and punishing them in a manner that reflects the seriousness of their crimes,[47] and ensuring that their border controls prevent terrorists from moving between states.[48] There is a strong emphasis on international co-operation, as states are required to exchange information in order to provide early warning to one another of planned acts of terrorism,[49] and in order to assist one another in criminal investigations, including the gathering of evidence.[50]

Security Council Resolution 1540 similarly contains a number of binding and hortatory provisions, which together focus on restricting the access of non-state actors to nuclear, chemical or biological weapons. States are instructed not to support non-state actors in their attempt to develop, acquire, transfer or use such weapons,[51] and to adapt their domestic laws in order effectively to block non-state actors from access to such weapons, 'in particular for terrorist purposes'.[52] Article 2 focuses on the criminal law of states, requiring them to deal with attempt, participation, financing and accomplice liability. A final mandatory provision, art. 3, provides other precautions, requiring states physically to protect the weapons,[53] to develop measures to account for and secure the weapons during their production, use, storage and transport,[54] and to devise forms of border control which will detect and deal with illicit trafficking of such items[55] as well as to keep control of their legal export and shipment.[56]

Commenting on the legislative nature of Resolution 1373, Szasz noted that the binding character of the resolution was underscored by the mechanism that Resolution 1373 creates to monitor compliance,[57] that is, the Counter-Terrorism Committee (CTC).[58] The Security Council has subsequently used the committee infrastructure to support the implementation of both binding and non-binding resolutions on terrorism, with the result that a number of committees now promote and oversee the Security Council's anti-terrorism regime as a whole.[59]

Both Resolutions 1373 and 1540 created new obligations for states. In Resolution 1373, these were closely aligned with obligations which had already, to some extent, been adopted by the international community. Resolution 1373 consisted largely of provisions taken from

---

[46] Ibid., art. 2(c).　　[47] Ibid., art. 2(e).　　[48] Ibid., art. 2(g).　　[49] Ibid., art. 2(b).
[50] Ibid., arts. 2(b), (f).　　[51] SC Res. 1540, art. 1.　　[52] Ibid., art. 2.
[53] Ibid., art. 3(b).　　[54] Ibid., art. 3(c).　　[55] Ibid., art. 3(c).　　[56] Ibid., art. 3(d).
[57] Szasz, 'The Security Council starts legislating', 902.
[58] SC Res. 1373, art. 6.
[59] See the website of the Committee, available at www.un.org/en/sc/ctc/.

the International Convention for the Suppression of the Financing of Terrorism,[60] a treaty which had, at the time of the resolution, been annexed to a General Assembly Resolution,[61] but had had insufficient ratifications to come into force.[62] In Resolution 1540, however, the Security Council introduced obligations which had not yet been approved or even considered by the majority of the international community, and part of its very rationale was the closing of gaps in the existing international law against the proliferation of weapons of mass destruction.[63] It pre-empted the consensual treaty process by more than a year.[64]

Furthermore, both resolutions are general in nature. They are aimed at general problems: terrorism and the use of weapons of mass destruction by non-state actors respectively. The measures imposed by both resolutions are general, relating not to a specified situation, state or non-state actor, but to a whole class of persons in all situations where particular criteria have been satisfied.[65] Neither has a time limit, but is phrased such that it may continue indefinitely. Both resolutions can therefore be seen, in Szasz's terms, to 'establish new binding rules of international law – rather than mere commands relating to a particular situation'.[66]

C. *Objections*

Security Council 'legislation' is different from other institutionalised forms of decision-making at the global level. Where treaty bodies allow one group to propose new rules for the membership of the whole, the group in question is a plenary body representing all the states parties to the treaty.[67] Although the consent of the states parties may in some cases be assumed, members of the treaty have the option to opt out either of the

---

[60] International Convention for the Suppression of the Financing of Terrorism, New York, 9 December 1999, entered into force 10 April 2002, 2178 UNTS 229 (Financing Convention). See Szasz, 'The Security Council starts legislating', 902–3; Happold, 'Security Council Resolution 1373', 594–5, 608; Asada, 'WMD terrorism and Security Council Resolution 1540', 17.

[61] Financing Convention; Asada, 'WMD terrorism and Security Council Resolution 1540', 18.

[62] Rosand, 'The Security Council as "global legislator"', 549.

[63] Ibid., 580; Asada, 'WMD terrorism and Security Council Resolution 1540', 19. See also Marschik, 'The Security Council as world legislator?', 18–19.

[64] See the International Convention for the Suppression of Acts of Nuclear Terrorism, New York, 13 April 2005, in force 7 July 2007, 2445 UNTS 89.

[65] See the description of legislation by Happold, 'Security Council Resolution 1373', 597.

[66] Szasz, 'The Security Council starts legislating', 902.

[67] Jutta Brunnée, 'International Legislation', in R. Wolfrum (ed.), *Max Planck Encyclopedia of International Law* (Oxford University Press, 2008).

rule or of the treaty body itself and therefore can ultimately not be bound without their consent. Third, the plenary bodies were created expressly to develop the treaties and propose changes to the law, and the process whereby consent is expressed is also accepted by member states when they join the treaty body.[68]

The Security Council, by contrast, consists of just fifteen states. Combined with the veto power of the five permanent members, this unbalanced structure ensures that the programme followed by the Security Council will never be at odds with the interests of any state holding the veto, and also that it is likely positively to further the interests of these states.[69] Second, the UN Charter does not allow states to opt out of Chapter VII decisions. Third, the current legislative practice by the Security Council was not anticipated when the UN Charter was drawn up, and was unheard of for the first fifty-four years of its existence. Most member states cannot therefore be said to have mandated the Security Council to create new law, or even to have foreseen that it would do so.[70] Two aspects of the programme, in particular, might surprise and disturb: the institutional support for the programme and its serious human rights implications. The anti-terrorism programme enjoys the support of an infrastructure created specially to monitor implementation[71] – one which faced severe criticism for its lack of transparency.[72] That the Council would itself threaten or violate international human rights law was also not foreseeable and has raised serious concerns both for states and for international human rights bodies.[73]

---

[68] The European Union is something of an exception. It does allow for international legislation; that is, it allows its central organs to issue regulations which create rights directly for the citizens of each member state, without the member state's consent. For these particular measures, states do not have the option to 'opt out'. However, this legislative process is provided for by treaty and the legislation drawn up by a number of representative plenary bodies, one of which is directly elected.

[69] M. Matheson, *Council Unbound: The Growth of UN Decision Making on Conflict and Postconflict Issues after the Cold War* (Washington, DC: United States Institute for Peace, 2006), pp. 239–40.

[70] The only possible exceptions in this regard would be states which joined the United Nations after the Security Council began to legislate.

[71] See J. Alvarez, 'Hegemonic international law revisited' (2003) 97 *American Journal of International Law* 874, 875 and Alvarez, *International Organisations as Law-Makers*, pp. 199–217. In the early stages of listing, the committee structure created to implement SC Res. 1373 was strikingly effective: see Rosand, 'The Security Council as "global legislator"', 548–9.

[72] See www.un.org/News/Press/docs/2009/sc9788.doc.htm for an acknowledgement of this problem and some proposed solutions.

[73] See the critics of listing cited above (above note 12); Andrew Hudson, 'Not a great asset: the UN Security Council's counter-terrorism regime: violating human rights' (2007) 25

Finally, legislation by the Security Council has the potential to dictate all areas of law for all states. Unlike treaty bodies, which deal with specific issues, such as trade or environmental protection, or apply only in specific territories, the Security Council has no geographical limits and, depending on its interpretation of art. 39, may have very few subject matter limits as well. Recently, the Council's interpretation of art. 39 has widened considerably. It has used Chapter VII in the absence of obvious threats to the peace[74] or to achieve goals not related to international peace and security. These include providing humanitarian relief,[75] assisting UN personnel on site and promoting democracy.[76]

States have come to see the new capacity which the Security Council has arrogated to itself as an annexation of a function belonging to the international community as a whole. This is apparent from state comments on the two legislative resolutions, and on related debates dealing with the Council's duties towards the wider group of states represented in the General Assembly.

Although initially welcomed, Security Council Resolution 1373 was resisted by states once its legislative character was recognised. The timing of the first General Assembly debates on Security Council Resolution 1373,[77] and the emotional intensity that followed in the wake of 9/11, may have obscured the qualitative distinction between Resolution 1373 and its predecessors. Thus many states praised the Council resolution as

---

Berkeley Journal of International Law 101; and also the report of the United Nations High Commissioner for Human Rights of 2 September 2009 (A/HRC/12/22).

[74] Kirgis, 'The Security Council's first fifty years', 513; Marschik, 'The Security Council as world legislator?', 10.

[75] Humanitarian interventions have increased to such an extent that Österdahl, writing in 2005, described such interventions as 'routine'. See I. Österdahl, 'The exception as the rule: lawmaking on force and human rights by the UN Security Council' (2005) *Journal of Conflict and Security Law* 1, 2.

[76] Examples include: the later 1992 resolutions on Somalia (SC Res. 733, UN SCOR, 47th Sess., Res. & Dec. at 55, UN Doc. S/INF/48 (1992) and SC Res. 794, UN SCOR, 47th Sess., Res. & Dec. at 63, UN Doc. S/INF/48 (1992)); and the interventions in Haiti (see SC Res. 841, UN SCOR, 48th Sess., UN Doc. S/INF/49 (1993), and SC Res. 940, UN SCOR, UN Doc. S/RES/940 (1994)) and Angola (see SC Res. 864 (1993) UN SCOR, UN Doc. S/Res/864 (1993)). Here the civil unrest and conflict had minimal regional impact and intervention was justified partly for the sake of democracy. See also Alvarez, 'Hegemonic international law revisited', 171–3.

[77] The first GA debate, 'Measures to eliminate international terrorism' (the 12th plenary meeting on Monday, 1 October 2001) took place on the morning of the first working day after SC Res. 1373 had been passed. The meeting which passed SC Res. 1373 was held late on Friday night, 28 September 2001. See S/Agenda/4385.

an administrative measure,[78] which would improve the implementation of the anti-terrorism system designed and driven by the larger international community.[79] These early debates proceeded on the assumption that the General Assembly should still draw up a global instrument against terrorism,[80] but praised the Security Council for contributing a 'framework'[81] or 'general direction'[82] to the larger, anti-terrorism project.

However, within a month, the import of the new resolution became evident.[83] In October 2001, the General Assembly debated the annual report of the Security Council. In this debate, the term 'legislation' was used to describe Resolution 1373, and the measure was resisted as an illegitimate extension of Security Council powers.[84] In this and subsequent debates, states suggested requirements for legitimate Security Council legislation: namely, that the Council consult widely before crafting a new norm,[85] keep its workings transparent,[86] remain accountable to the global community[87] (in particular, by explaining its decisions to the broader body of states[88]) and not legislate in its own interests.[89]

In 2004, when the Security Council debated Security Council Resolution 1540, a large number of non-members of the Security Council asked for permission to address the Council. This time there was no doubt as

---

[78] A/56/PV.12: Croatia, p. 25; Belgium, p. 10; Belarus, p. 21. The only reference made by the European Union to SC Res. 1373 is to 'note with interest' that it establishes a monitoring committee, p. 10.

[79] The Algerian representative commented: 'On a different level, that of international law, there is an entire panoply of legal instruments that serve as a normative basis for all efforts to codify or draft a common global anti-terrorism strategy'. (A/56/PV.12, p. 13).

[80] A/56/PV.12: Belarus, p. 22; the President of the General Assembly, p. 2; the Secretary-General, p. 3; Nicaragua, p. 6; Belgium, p. 10; Algeria, p. 13; United Kingdom, p. 18; and Equitorial Guinea, p. 4.

[81] Nicaragua praised SC Res. 1373 as a framework while simultaneously calling for a multilateral Convention on Terrorism (A/56/PV.12, p. 6). See also Egypt (A/56/PV.12, p. 23).

[82] A/56/PV.22: Switzerland, p. 6.

[83] A/56/PV.25: Singapore, p. 10.

[84] A/56/PV.25: Algeria, p. 8; and Singapore, p. 10.

[85] S/PV.4950: Spain, p. 7.

[86] S/PV.4950: Philippines, p. 2; China, p. 6; Romania, p. 14; Russian Federation, p. 16; United States, p. 18; Canada, p. 20; and South Africa, p. 22.

[87] A/56/PV.25: Singapore, p. 13.

[88] A/56/PV.28: Ghana, p. 16.

[89] A/56/PV.25: Colombia, p. 5. In a later debate on a resolution limiting the jurisdiction of the International Criminal Court, delegates emphasised that the Council is meant to act for the international community as a whole. See S/PV.4568: Iran, p. 15; Jordan, p. 16; Mongolia, p. 19; S/PV.4772: Iran, p. 10; Pakistan, p. 21.

to the legislative nature of the resolution,[90] and it was greeted with widespread unease. Proponents of the resolution offered special justifications for bypassing the normal, interstate law-making process. They argued that the problem in question – the possibility that non-state actors might obtain access to weapons of mass destruction – was urgent, leaving no time for the usual channels of multilateral negotiation.[91] They also insisted that it did not interfere with the established treaty regime in any way.[92]

These justifications did not convince many opponents, who found the thought of unilateral law creation by the Council unacceptable. States pointed out that the Security Council should not be imposing its decisions on sovereign states.[93] Thus India refused to 'accept externally prescribed norms or standards, whatever their source, on matters pertaining to domestic jurisdiction of [the Indian] Parliament, including national legislation, regulations or arrangements which are not consistent with its constitutional provisions and procedures which are contrary to its national interests or which infringe on [Indian] sovereignty'.[94] The Indian representative also expressed India's concern that 'the exercise of legislative functions by the Council, combined with recourse to Chapter VII mandates, could disrupt the balance of power between the General Assembly and the Security Council, as enshrined in the Charter'.[95]

Many states also noted that the draft resolution separated two obligations which had hitherto – in the treaty regime – been interlinked; that is, non-proliferation and disarmament. While adding obligations on non-proliferation, the resolution disregarded the disarmament aspect.[96] Noting the one-sidedness of the resolution, Pakistan commented: 'The Security Council, where five States, which retain nuclear weapons, also possess the right veto any action, is not the most appropriate body to be entrusted with the authority for oversight over non-proliferation or nuclear disarmament.'[97]

[90] S/PV.4950. The terms 'legislation', 'legislate' or 'legislative' were used by Angola, p. 10; Pakistan, p. 15; India, p. 23; Singapore, p. 25; Switzerland, p. 28; Indonesia, p. 31; and Iran, p. 32.
[91] S/PV.4950: Philippines, p. 2; Algeria, p. 5; Spain, p. 7; Angola, p. 9; United Kingdom, p. 11; New Zealand, p. 21; India, p. 24; Singapore, p. 25; Sweden, p. 27; Japan, p. 28; Switzerland, p. 28.
[92] S/PV.4950: Philippines, p. 3; United Kingdom, p. 11; Romania, p. 14; United States, p. 18; Germany, p. 18; and New Zealand, p. 21.
[93] S/PV.4950: Brazil, p. 4; Algeria, p. 5; Pakistan, p. 15; Peru, p. 20; Cuba, p. 30; Indonesia, p. 31; and Iran, p. 32.
[94] S/PV.4950, p. 24.   [95] Ibid.
[96] S/PV.4950: Brazil, p. 4; Algeria, p. 5; Peru, p. 20; South Africa, p. 22; India, p. 24; and Cuba, p. 30.
[97] S /PV.4950: Pakistan, p. 15.

Finally, Sweden noted that people whose rights were affected by Resolution 1540 had not been provided with the protection of a judicial process. The Swedish representative suggested that 'an individual who claims that his rights have been violated as a consequence of the implementation of this resolution should be guaranteed access to courts at the national level, and States have a duty to ensure that this happens'.[98] Resisting the notion that the Security Council could unilaterally change the international legal system, Sweden added that states which took measures to implement this resolution remained bound by international law and the United Nations Charter.[99]

The question of the role of the Security Council within the UN as a body, and its duty to the member states, brings to the fore the underlying theme of power and its relationship with law. In these debates, states are aware that a single body is aggregating power to itself, and they are attempting to contain it. They do so partly by insisting on their own autonomy – their national sovereignty – in an attempt to restore the theoretically horizontal structure of the international arena. But they also invoke constitutional features, like democracy, transparency, consultation and justification. Such features come into play when a polity has assumed a hierarchical structure; one in which an institution is exercising governmental functions on behalf of the broader membership.[100]

4. Prognosis: the Security Council and the rule of law

Listing has run into considerable opposition in recent years, forcing the Security Council to reform it. As noted above, the reform is still inadequate, and the ongoing co-operation of states is by no means certain.

Legislation, by contrast, seems not to have been opposed as vocally, and what opposition there has been seems not to have produced any visible results. Admittedly, the Security Council has, for the meanwhile, stopped at two pieces of 'legislation' and not produced a third. However, both existing legislative resolutions are still supported by the Council's committee structure, which monitors states' compliance with them. While not imposing sanctions for non-compliance, committees add to the

---

[98] S /PV.4950: Sweden, p. 27.   [99] Ibid.
[100] Karl Zemanek, 'Was kann die Vergleichung staatlichen öffentlichen Rechts für das Recht der internationalen Organisationen leisten?' (1964) 24 *Zeitschrift für ausländisches öffentliches Recht und Völkerrecht* 454.

pressure on smaller states, in particular, to co-operate with the Council's programme.[101]

In this final section, I investigate what current responses to the Council's anti-terrorism programme, and to listing in particular, suggest for the future of both listing and legislation. The strength of the fight against listing, compared to the tepid discomfort evoked by legislation, might lead us to expect the listing reforms to stay just that: reforms to listing, which have no bearing on the future of legislation. However, my analysis of these reforms suggests they demonstrate a more fundamental change in the global arena. The principles which, I argue, are emerging from listing reform bear out Fuller's theory on the rule of law.[102] My analysis suggests that the Council is slowly being drawn into the constraints which the fundamental principles of law impose on any exercise of power. If my theory is correct, then the rule of law will have an influence on legislation as well. I conclude with a suggestion of what that effect might be.

A.   *The process of listing reform*

As noted above, individuals and listed entities initially had no avenues whatsoever to engage with and challenge listing decisions of the 1267 Committee. Listed persons had no information on either the criteria for listing or the facts to which the criteria were being applied. States attempting to assist listed nationals were similarly handicapped by little or no information, no established appeal procedure and the ability of any one member of the Council to veto delisting without having to explain why.

Security Council Resolution 1390, the resolution which adopted the current three-part sanctions formula for listed persons,[103] also contained a request of the 1267 Committee: that it produce guidelines for inclusion in its list.[104] The guidelines, produced in November 2002, included a procedure for both listing and delisting. The listing procedure focused on clarifying the identity of listed persons and gathering more information on them.[105] The guidelines required of states which proposed a new listing that they provide a statement of the basis for the designation as well

---

[101] See C. Oxtoby and C. H. Powell, Chapter 22, this volume for examples of the 'gentle' coercion which African states experience to co-operate with anti-terrorism measures.

[102] Lon C. Fuller, *The Morality of Law* (New Haven, CT: Yale University Press, revised edn, 1969).

[103] SC Res. 1390, art. 2.   [104] Ibid., art. 5(d).

[105] See note 16 above and the first report of the Monitoring Team (S/2004/679), [37].

as identifying information which the national authorities would need to implement the sanctions.[106]

The early delisting procedure required that persons wishing to be delisted approach their own states of residence or nationality for assistance, after which the state so petitioned should approach the state which initially proposed the listing of the individual (the 'designating state'). Through this process, the petitioned government should obtain additional information relating to the listed individuals. If the petitioned government still wished to have its citizen or resident delisted after reviewing the information, it should seek to persuade the designating government to submit a request for delisting to the 1267 Committee. Once the Committee received a request for delisting from both governments, it decided the delisting request by consensus – a procedure which allowed the chair of the Committee to continue consultations if consensus could not be reached. On the other hand, if the petitioned state could not get the designating state to agree to request delisting, it could submit its own request. However, that request was still decided by the no-objection procedure, which allows a single state to block the delisting request without giving reasons.[107]

On 20 December 2002, Security Council Resolution 1452[108] introduced humanitarian exceptions to the sanctions, allowing states to grant listed persons access to their funds for their daily needs as well as legal costs.[109] The new exemptions procedure established by Resolution 1452 required states to obtain the approval of the 1267 Committee for every exemption granted. The 1267 Committee was, as before, not obliged to offer any reasons for its decisions.

These early reforms of the listing system were precipitated by Sweden's attempt to get its nationals, Adirisak Aden, Abdi Abdulaziz Ali and Ahmed Ali Yusuf, delisted, and to ensure that the freezing of their assets did not threaten their survival.[110] The resolution containing the Security Council's request to the 1267 Committee for guidelines and criteria to

---

[106] Decisions of listing and delisting are guided by the 1267 Committee Guidelines: The Al-Qaida and Taliban Sanctions Committee, UN, *Guidelines of the Committee for the Conduct of Its Work* (2008), available at www.un.org/sc/committees/1267/pdf/1267_guidelines.pdf (Guidelines).

[107] Gutherie, 'Security Council sanctions and the protection of individual rights', 512–13.

[108] SC Res. 1452, art. 1.

[109] Per Cramer, 'Recent Swedish experiences with targeted UN sanctions: the erosion of trust in the Security Council', in E. de Wet and A. Nollkaemper (eds.), *Review of the Security Council by Member States* (Antwerp: Intersentia, 2003), p. 85.

[110] *Adirisak Aden, Abdi Abdulaziz Ali, Ahmed Ali Yusuf and the Al-Barakaat Foundation* v. *Council of the European Union and Commission of the European Communities*, case no. T-306/01, filed on 10 December 2001. See Gutherie, 'Security Council sanctions and

regulate listing and delisting, Security Council Resolution 1390, was passed four days after Sweden lodged its request that the Committee delist its three nationals. The delisting procedure set out in these guidelines reflected the procedure which Sweden had already followed.[111]

In the following years, the Council then tried to ensure that listed persons were informed both of their status and the measures open to them to challenge their listing. Security Council Resolution 1526 of 30 January 2004 'strongly encourage[d]' states to communicate with listed persons, without, however, binding them to do so.[112] This request was finally transformed into an obligation five years later, when Security Council Resolution 1822 obligated states to inform listed persons of their status if possible, and to alert them to both the listing and delisting procedures.[113]

Recognising the difficulty of answering accusations one has not heard, Security Council Resolution 1735 required the 1267 Committee to release a narrative summary of the case against each listed person or entity. However, the evidence on which this case was based could be released only with the consent of the state which provided it. The other weakness which the Council attempted to meet at that time was the individual's lack of access to the delisting procedure. Security Council Resolution 1730[114] established a 'focal point' within the UN Secretariat's Security Council Subsidiary Organs Branch. This focal point, which serves all sanctions committees of the Security Council, was designed to receive delisting requests directly from individuals who were affected by the sanctions regimes.[115] This allowed listed parties to submit their requests even in the absence of their governments' diplomatic protection. However, the focal point simply conveyed petitioners' requests to the states which were to deal with them, without engaging with the merits of the application itself – leading Hovell to describe the mechanism as 'little more than a glorified switchboard operator'.[116]

---

the protection of individual rights', 511 and Cramer, 'Recent Swedish experiences with targeted UN sanctions', for discussions of these cases.

[111] Ibid. All the people represented by Sweden were eventually delisted: see www.un.org/ News/Press/docs/2002/sc7490.doc.htm and www.un.org/News/Press/docs/2006/ sc8815.doc.htm.

[112] SC Res. 1526, art. 18.   [113] SC Res. 1822, art. 17.

[114] SC Res. 1730, UN SCOR, 61st sess, 5599th mtg, UN Doc. S/Res/1730 (19 December 2006).

[115] The 1267 Committee runs one of many targeted sanctions regimes: see www.un.org/sc/ committees/.

[116] Devika Hovell, 'Comment on Kadi', available at www.ejiltalk.org/a-house-of-kadis-recent-challenges-to-the-un-sanctions-regime-and-the-continuing-response-to-the-ecj-decision-in-kadi/#more-1258.

Security Council Resolution 1822 put further pressure on states to provide as much information on their listing proposals as possible, and expressly to indicate which sections of their proposals could be publicised. It directed the 1267 Committee to release the narrative summary behind each listing on its website, asked it to ensure fair and clear procedures and introduced regular reviews of listing decisions, even if those decisions were not appealed.[117]

The latest and most significant reform of the listing process is contained in Security Council Resolution 1904 of 17 December 2009. This resolution once again required review and reform of the listing and exemption procedures to ensure transparency and speed. It also required that the Committee extend the notice period for objections to listing proposals. But by far its most important change was its introduction of an Ombudsperson – an office independent of the Security Council with the mandate to receive listing appeals and promote dialogue between the various parties involved in it, including the individual, listed person.

The process which the Ombudsperson is required to follow differs markedly from that carried out by the 'focal point', which remains in place for other sanctions committees of the Security Council. When receiving a listed person's petition for delisting, the focal point is required merely to 'inform the petitioner on the general procedure for processing that request'. The focal point then passes on the listed person's request, along with the extra information required of such a request, to a closed list of specific governments (the designating government(s) and to the government(s) of citizenship and residence). Any discussion that follows at this stage is restricted to an exchange between the designating state(s) and any state which intends to recommend delisting – an exchange which the designating state can refuse, as it has the option to remain anonymous. From these discussions, any of the states concerned might lodge a recommendation for delisting with the Committee. Without such a recommendation, the listed person's request is considered rejected after a certain period without further discussion. The focal point would then convey the final decision to the listed person. There is no provision that any reasons be given.

The Ombudsperson, on the other hand, must not only 'inform the petitioner on the general procedure for processing [a delisting] request', but also '[a]nswer specific questions from the petitioner about Committee

---

[117] As a preliminary measure, it also required a review of all listing decisions not reviewed in the past three years.

procedures'. The Ombudsperson then communicates the petitioner's request not only to the designating government(s) and the government(s) of citizenship and residence, but also to the Committee itself, the Monitoring Team, 'relevant United Nations bodies, and any other States deemed relevant by the Ombudsperson'. The Ombudsperson is required to go through a three-stage process, set out in detail in the resolution. First, he or she collects a wide range of opinions and information from the bodies who have received the delisting request. During this first stage, the Ombudsperson communicates their requests for further information and clarification back to the petitioner. One of the forms of input required expressly from the Monitoring Team is 'court decisions and proceedings, news reports, and information that States or relevant international organizations have previously shared with the Committee or the Monitoring Team'. The second stage, headed 'Dialogue', provides for a two-month, extendable period, in which the petitioner may be involved. The Ombudsperson then drafts and circulates a report summarising the main arguments for and against delisting. In the third stage, the Ombudsperson presents the report to the Committee and answers its questions. The decision to approve or reject the request lies, once again, exclusively with the Committee, but in this case it must discuss the request whether or not that request is supported by a state. Furthermore, if the request is refused, the Ombudsperson is required to explain the refusal to the extent possible – within the restrictions imposed by the confidentiality of the information – when communicating that refusal to the petitioner.

This last wave of reform was triggered by the *Kadi* case,[118] which presented the Security Council with the possibility that the entire European Union might refuse to co-operate in listing. Security Council Resolution 1617 of 2005, which clarified the listing criteria and referred to the delisting procedure for the first time, was passed on 29 July 2005, while the Court of First Instance was considering its judgments in the *Yusuf* and *Kadi* cases.[119] Security Council Resolution 1822, which attempted to improve the information available to the listed person, was similarly produced during the course of the Grand Chamber proceedings. Security Council Resolution 1904, which introduced the Ombudsperson, was passed in the wake of the Grand Chamber's firm rejection of listing in its

---

[118] *Kadi* (above note 12).

[119] *Yusuf and the Al-Barakaat Foundation* v. *Council and Commission* (above note 110); *Kadi* v. *Council of the European Union and Commission of the European Communities* (Case T-315/01) (2005), printed in [2006] *European Court Reports* II-02139, and also available at eur-lex.europa.eu/LexUriServ/LexUriServ.do?uri=OJ:C:2005:281:0017:0018:EN:PDF.

Kadi decision of 3 September 2008. The reforms suggested by the monitoring bodies, and implemented by the Council, during this period included the introduction of narrative summaries[120] and the establishment of the 'focal point'.[121]

The Security Council has recently acknowledged that listing threatens human rights, and the then chair of the 1267 Committee, Jan Grauls, acknowledged publically that the reforms of Security Council Resolution 1822 had been insufficient to 'ensure that the right individuals and entities were targeted'.[122] The following resolution, Security Council Resolution 1904, 'takes note' of the domestic challenges to listing, 'legal and otherwise', and expresses its intent to 'continue efforts to ensure that procedures are fair and clear'.

I will argue below that these developments demonstrate the slow emergence of rule of law principles. However, this should not be seen as a defence of listing in its present form. Listing still does not comply with rule of law requirements, and this can be confirmed by the most recent *Kadi* developments. After the Grand Chamber of the ECJ invalidated Kadi's listing for its procedural defects, the Commission adapted its procedure to allow Kadi to comment on the 'narrative summary' of the case against him.[123] Having heard Kadi's response, the Commission relisted him. When Kadi challenged his relisting, the Grand Chamber found the latest reforms inadequate:[124]

> The considerations in this respect ... remain fundamentally valid today, even if account is taken of the 'Office of the Ombudsperson'... In essence, the Security Council has still not deemed it appropriate to establish an independent and impartial body responsible for hearing and determining, as regards matters of law and fact, actions against individual decisions taken by the Sanctions Committee. Furthermore, neither the focal point mechanism nor the Office of the Ombudsperson affects the principle that removal of a person from the Sanctions Committee's list requires consensus within the committee. Moreover, the evidence which

---

[120] See S/2005/83, [55].
[121] SC Res. 1730. See also Thomas J. Biersteker and Sue E. Eckert, *Strengthening Targeted Sanctions through Fair and Clear Procedures* (Watson Institute for International Studies, Brown University White Paper, 30 March 2006).
[122] globaladminlaw.blogspot.com/2009/05/kadi-recent-developments.html.
[123] He was not given access to any of the evidence on which the summary was based. For the problems presented by secret evidence, see Forcese and Roach, 'Limping into the future'.
[124] *Kadi* v. *Council of the European Union and Commission of the European Communities* (Case 85/09) [2010], available at curia.europa.eu/.

may be disclosed to the person concerned continues to be a matter entirely at the discretion of the State which proposed that he be included on the Sanctions Committee's list and there is no mechanism to ensure that sufficient information be made available to the person concerned in order to allow him to defend himself effectively ... For those reasons at least, the creation of the focal point and the Office of the Ombudsperson cannot be equated with the provision of an effective judicial procedure for review of decisions of the Sanctions Committee.

I am not, therefore, arguing that the listing process complies with the rule of law. Instead, I am merely identifying the direction that the reforms are taking. They may never go far enough to validate listing[125] but, by introducing the principles I discuss below, they may perform the fundamental function of subjecting the Council to law.

B. *The march of the rule of law*

To find the rule of law aspects of this process, we must note that Fuller saw the rule of law as a set of principles, but also as an activity – a process whereby the law is established and maintained. His vision of the rule of law can be summarised as a requirement of publicised, non-retroactive, understandable and internally consistent rules, which do not demand the impossible and are administered congruently with how they are announced.[126] On their content, these requirements overlap closely with those of other rule-of-law theorists; that is, that there be predictable, reliable rules and equality and consistency in their application.[127] However,

---

[125] See the prognosis of Forcese and Roach, 'Limping into the future'.

[126] Fuller's eight specific requirements of the rule of law were that there be (1) rules, which are (2) publicised, (3) understandable, (4) not retroactive and (5) internally consistent (that is, not contradictory). The rules must also be (6) relatively consistent over time; that is, they may not change so frequently that the legal subjects can no longer orient their conduct in compliance with the rules. In addition, (7) compliance must not be physically impossible; that is, law cannot demand that legal subjects act beyond their powers. Finally, (8) the administration of law must reflect the rules as announced: Fuller, *The Morality of Law*, p. 39.

[127] Judith Shklar, 'Political theory and the rule of law', in Allan C. Hutcheson and Patrick Monahan (eds.), *The Rule of Law: Ideal or Ideology* (Toronto: Carswell, 1987), p. 1; Jeremy Waldron, 'Is the rule of law an essentially contested concept (in Florida)?' (2002) 21 *Law and Philosophy* 137; Lon L. Fuller, *The Morality of Law*, p. 39; A. V. Dicey, *Introduction to the Study of the Law of the Constitution* (London: Macmillan, 1961), pp. 188 and 193; F. A. Hayek, *The Road to Serfdom* (London: Routledge, 1944), p. 54; Joseph Raz, 'The rule of law and its virtue', reprinted in *The Authority of Law* (Oxford: Clarendon, 1979), pp. 214–18; John Rawls, *A Theory of Justice* (Oxford University Press, 1971); Colleen Murphy, 'Lon Fuller and the moral value of the rule of law' (2005) 24 *Law and Philosophy* 239, 241.

whereas many theorists see this list as a wish list – which law as a system may or may not fulfill – Fuller saw them as essential for legality, that is, the quality of being law.[128]

Beyond being a set of prerequisites, however, Fuller's eight elements were also meant to show how law works. For Fuller, law was not a top-down process whereby the body in power imposed rules on the subjects of the legal system, but a reciprocal process in which the power-wielder and subject remain in dialogue while fashioning a system to which all participants can bind themselves. His eight rule-of-law requirements therefore give expression to the underlying principles of reciprocity, congruency and agency.[129] The reciprocity of the law-making process relies on and encourages the agency of the subjects, who are, in turn, able to hold the power-wielders to a congruent application of the laws they have accepted as their own. Together, these three principles are the elements through which system remains – or even becomes – a legal system.

The reform of the listing system provides an effective example of the rule of law at work in Fuller's conception, because the 'fit' between the reforms and his underlying requirements is strong. The programme in its current form has been shaped through interaction with the subjects of the legal system, as their assertion of their agency has forced the Council to soften the managerial[130] character of the initial listing system. Second, as set out in Security Council Resolution 1904, listing is designed to encourage and respond to further interaction. The wide range of bodies from whom the independent arbiter may gather facts, opinions and case law relevant to a delisting request factors the views of states and other international actors into the analysis from the very outset.

But perhaps the most significant development has been the (tentative) embrace of legality by the Council. The Council, the Monitoring Team and 1267 Committee representatives have increasingly depicted law as a facilitator of, rather than a hindrance to, the listing process. Thus Grauls, on admitting the shortcomings of Security Council Resolution 1822, asserted that respect for fair and clear procedures would increase the effectiveness of the sanctions regimes.[131] Similarly, the Monitoring

---

[128] Fuller, *Morality of Law*; cf. Raz, 'The rule of law and its virtue', pp. 219–25.

[129] Jutta Brunnée and Stephen Toope, *Legitimacy and Legality in International Law* (Cambridge University Press, 2010), pp. 21–6.

[130] See Lon L. Fuller, 'A reply to critics' in Fuller, *The Morality of Law*, pp. 209–10 for the central distinction between law and a managerial system.

[131] globaladminlaw.blogspot.com/2009/05/kadi-recent-developments.html.

Team described the Council's reforms as steps to create a 'more legal character',[132] noting that '[w]eak listings undermine the credibility of the sanctions regime, whether or not they are subject to legal challenge'.[133] Indeed, such is the glamour of legality that the Monitoring Team has even claimed that domestic review of listing decisions should be seen as a strength of the 1267 Committee's system.[134]

C.   Legislation under the rule of law

The Security Council has long been seen as a primarily political body. Because of its expertise and powers, some commentators have argued that it must work outside of the law in order to respond to pressing emergencies which only it can recognise and counter.

Listing has shown the dangers of such thinking, and the response to listing has helped to demonstrate law's proper place in the Council. The growing legal paradigm suggests two main limits to Security Council powers. The first limitation emerges in the public law discourse, which now treats as self-evident that the Security Council is situated not only within a flat structure of sovereign states but also at the apex of a hierarchy of states and individuals. These vertical power relationships require public law principles, including constitutional, administrative and human rights law, to protect the persons at the lower levels of the hierarchy.[135]

But second, it emerges in the very idea that persons affected by the exercise of power must be able to shape the form it takes. In this sense, it is law pure – in Fuller's conception – that is limiting the Council. Listing reforms demonstrate the Council's return to law as it attempts to make listing acceptable to law's subjects. These reforms, while unsatisfactory, are evidence of a slow nudging towards Fuller's underlying principles of reciprocity, congruency and agency. Thus listed persons have gradually obtained the ability to engage in some form with decisions of the 1267 Committee. Through the Ombudsperson, the 1267 Committee can be drawn into an interaction with listed persons, as each is given the opportunity to raise issues with the other. The Ombudsperson's report,

---

[132] See S/2009/502, [40]. The Monitoring Team thus praises the addition of 'associated with' criteria, the introduction of narrative summaries of reasons for listing and the review mechanisms contained in SC Res. 1822.

[133] S/2009/502, [40].

[134] S/2009/245, [18]. See also [23], [27]–[30], [35], [37].

[135] Zemanek, 'Was Kann die Vergleichung staatlichen öffentlichen Rechts für das Recht der internationalen Organisationen leisten?'.

drawing on case law, academic comment and the views of states, also encourages the Committee to engage with and respond to the legal convictions of the subjects of international law. Whether the listing system ever attains the status of law will depend on the extent to which the Ombudsperson manages to attain genuine accountability on the part of the Committee. Should the Ombudsperson manage this, it is not impossible that the Committee might one day justify its decisions adequately, engage meaningfully with objections and act in congruence both with its own criteria and the existing framework of international law – including fundamental rights. At this point, listing may have attained enough congruency and reciprocity that it accommodates the agency of states and individuals and may claim to be law.

If law limits the Security Council's exercise of power, it remains to consider how law will limit the Council's legislative capacity. On the global level, the subjects of law include states and non-state bodies.[136] The Council's limited membership and the imbalance of power within that membership discourage it from creating rules through interaction with the subjects of the legal system. Without widespread consultation by the Council, it will generally be incapable of producing rules that satisfy the minimum requirements of the rule of law.

This is not to exclude the possibility that the international community may accept the Council's rules and confer on them the status of law. But it does suggest that the Council needs to be in an ongoing process of engagement and justification with the broader community.[137] The level of justification the Council has hitherto offered for its legislation has been negligible.[138] It has relied instead on a largely unstated premise that any action it takes in the name of anti-terrorism is automatically legitimate.

This premise no longer holds. And as it cracks, legal requirements are emerging which limit the Council's power to carry out large portions of its anti-terrorism programme. Thus, while listing continues to be critiqued for its violation of particular individual's rights, other voices have begun to question the institutional competence of the Council to impose

---

[136] Although states bear full legal personality in international law, individuals, organisations and even corporations have attained limited personality through the conferment of rights and duties by international law.

[137] On justification and the rule of law, see David Dyzenhaus, 'Law as justification: Etienne Mureinik's conception of legal culture' (1998) 14 *South African Journal on Human Rights* 11; Etienne Mureinik, 'A bridge to where?' (1994) 10 *South African Journal on Human Rights* 10.

[138] See the complaints of states listed in section 3 above, and Marschik, 'The Security Council as world legislator?', 22.

either its individual decisions or its general norms on the global community. Thus Martin Scheinin, the Special Rapporteur on the promotion and protection of human rights and fundamental freedoms while countering terrorism, recently questioned the Security Council's use of Chapter VII to enact its anti-terrorism programme, arguing that the prerequisites for the use of Chapter VII had not been met. His report emphasises the need for accountability in international organisations and insists that the anti-terrorism treaty regime has precedence over the Council's programme.[139] This argument echoes the protests of states when the Council claimed unilaterally to override the existing processes of international law-making.[140] As noted above, the protesting states also set conditions for the valid use of such a power: wide consultation,[141] transparency,[142] accountability,[143] and the ongoing justification of exercises of power to the broader community.[144]

These conditions rephrase Fuller's essential prerequisites of reciprocity, congruency and respect for the agency of law's subjects. If it does not fulfill them, the Council will not produce law.

---

[139] www.un.org/News/briefings/docs/2010/101026_Scheinin.doc.htm and www.un.org/News/Press/docs/2010/gashc3988.doc.htm.
[140] S/PV.4950, p. 24.   [141] S/PV.4950: Spain, p. 7.
[142] S/PV.4950: Philippines, p. 2; China, p. 6; Romania, p. 14; Russian Federation, p. 16; United States, p. 18; Canada, p. 20; and South Africa, p. 22.
[143] A/56/PV.25: Singapore, p. 13.   [144] A/56/PV.28: Ghana, p. 16.

3

The impossibility of global anti-terrorism law?

VICTOR V. RAMRAJ

1. Introduction

The unfolding of legal developments around the world post-9/11 is a familiar story. In the days following the attacks, the US Congress and the Bush Administration sprang into action, laying the legal foundation for a decade-long domestic and international response by the US government as part of a 'global war on terrorism'. Declaring that the rest of the world was either 'with us or ... with the terrorists',[1] the Bush Administration went to the UN Security Council and obtained a novel legal instrument, Resolution 1373,[2] opening the door to a co-ordinated legislative response by states to international terrorism, and centralised monitoring of that response by the Counter-Terrorism Committee. In capital after capital, new anti-terrorism laws were enacted in response to US political pressure, the Security

This chapter was originally presented at the Anti-Terrorism Symposium at the University of New South Wales, Sydney, 5–6 August 2010; a revised version was presented at the Transnational Law Colloquium, Center for Transnational Legal Studies (CTLS), London, 3 September 2010. The title of this chapter echoes the title of Pierre Legrand's article, 'The Impossibility of "Legal Transplants"' (1997) 4 *Maastricht Journal of European and Comparative Law* 111–24. Although I do not engage directly with Legrand's arguments in this chapter, I share some of his concerns about legal transplants, though, as will become clear, I am more optimistic than Legrand is about the ability of law to transcend borders, provided it is sufficiently sensitive to local contexts and differences. I am grateful to Sandy Meadow, Kent Roach, Ben Saul and my students and colleagues at CTLS for their comments on earlier versions of this chapter.

[1] George W. Bush, Address to a Joint Session of Congress and the American People (20 September 2001).

[2] S/RES/1373(2001). Invoking mandatory language, the Security Council 'decided' 'that all States shall ... [c]riminalize the wilful provision or collection, by any means, directly or indirectly, of funds by their nationals or in their territories with the intention that the funds should be used, or in the knowledge that they are to be used, in order to carry out terrorist acts' and '[e]nsure that ... the financing, planning, preparation or perpetration of terrorist acts ... are established as serious criminal offences in domestic laws and regulations and that the punishment duly reflects the seriousness of such terrorist acts'.

Council's call to action and a general trend of revisiting anti-terrorism laws. In one fell swoop, the Security Council assumed the role of an international legislative body, and assumed the power to monitor domestic legislative compliance. In her chapter in this volume, Powell discusses the Security Council's role in the formation of an international anti-terrorism regime.[3] But the 'globalisation' of anti-terrorism norms did not end with the United Nations. Roach, for instance, has described how the UK's anti-terrorism laws have served as templates that have migrated around the world.[4] At the level of enforcement, national security agencies around the world are collecting and sharing intelligence more than ever before,[5] sometimes with tragic consequences.[6] And although it took some time to catch up, human rights law too has been revisited with a view to articulating afresh the principles according to which states might legitimately pursue an anti-terrorism agenda,[7] principles that are, however, only gradually seeping back into the work of the Counter-Terrorism Committee.[8]

In light of these legal developments, it might therefore be assumed that there is something we can coherently describe as 'global anti-terrorism law'. Indeed, the evidence seems compelling. Resolution 1373 and its successors have created a legal legislative template that has been widely followed by states;[9] model anti-terrorism laws have proliferated around the globe; and

[3] C. H. Powell, Chapter 2, this volume.

[4] Kent Roach 'The post-9/11 migration of Britain's Terrorism Act 2000', in Sujit Choudhry (ed.), *The Migration of Constitutional Ideas* (Cambridge University Press, 2006), pp. 347–402.

[5] Simon Chesterman, *One Nation Under Surveillance: A New Social Contract to Defend Freedom Without Sacrificing Liberty* (Oxford University Press, 2011).

[6] Commission of Inquiry into the Actions of Canadian Officials in Relation to Maher Arar, *Report of the Events Relating to Maher Arar* (Ottawa: Government of Canada, 2006). The report is available on the Canadian Security Intelligence Review Committee's website: www.sirc-csars.gc.ca/opbapb/opbapb-eng.html.

[7] See, for example, 'The Ottawa principles on anti-terrorism and human rights' in Nicole LaViolette and Craig Forcese (eds.), *The Human Rights of Anti-terrorism* (Toronto: Irwin Law, 2008).

[8] According to the Counter-Terrorism Committee's website, with 'the establishment of the Counter-Terrorism Committee Executive Directorate (CTED) by Security Council Resolution 1535 (2004), the Committee began moving to a more pro-active policy on human rights. CTED was mandated to liaise with the Office of the UN High Commissioner on Human Rights (OHCHR) and other human rights organizations in matters related to counter-terrorism (S/2004/124), and a human rights expert was appointed to the CTED staff' (see www.un.org/en/sc/ctc/rights.html).

[9] Other examples in the anti-terrorism financing area include the UN Office on Drugs and Crime's model legislation on money laundering and terrorism financing (www.unodc. org/unodc/en/money-laundering/Model-Legislation.html) and the work of the Financial Action Taskforce (FATF).

there is widespread co-ordination among governments on the implementation of these laws and legal norms. These developments suggest, in turn, three assumptions: that a coherent legal regime governing anti-terrorism measures is starting to emerge; that we can theorise about global anti-terrorism law in a way that makes sense broadly or universally; and that, normatively speaking, it succeeds or fails as a whole, however we might define success or failure.

Against the view that a global anti-terrorism regime with these practical and theoretical consequences is starting to emerge, this chapter argues that when we look beyond legal forms, it becomes clear that neither the positing of a global anti-terrorism regime nor the three assumptions about its consequences is warranted. It is argued instead that the actual experience of anti-terrorism laws around the world suggests diversity rather than uniformity, and that we have to rethink our approach to anti-terrorism laws, particularly in light of recent and uneven changes in the modern state, to make these laws – as well as the constraints imposed on them – more effective. The next part of this chapter (Section 2) explains in more detail the three assumptions about global anti-terrorism law: its emergence, normative implications and theoretical dimensions. Section 3 explains why these assumptions are problematic, highlighting the disparate and asymmetrical impact of formally equivalent legal norms. It also explains why our normative assessment of anti-terrorism and emergency legislation must differ according to the context and urges that the complexity of anti-terrorism law and policy be taken into account in formulating anti-terrorism theories and policies. Finally, Section 4 situates this discussion of the complexity of anti-terrorism law in the broader frame of law and globalisation, arguing that anti-terrorism policy remains a moving target precisely because the status of legal norms and of the modern state itself are in flux and thus our approach to empowering and constraining governments and transnational legal entities in their anti-terrorism policies must be equally malleable.

2.   Global anti-terrorism law

It is not surprising that in the weeks, months and years after the 2001 attacks on the United States, law became a key instrument both in the 'war on terror' and in attempts to moderate and constrain that 'war'. Although much of the rhetoric of the Bush Administration seemed almost contemptuous of legal norms and constraints, preferring instead sheer force, an enormous amount of energy was spent, domestically and internationally,

both to justify legally what was being done and to establish a legal framework for international co-operation and co-ordination. The 'torture
memos'[10] serve as a notorious example of the former tendency; Resolution
1373 provides an example of the latter. At the same time, those concerned
about abuses of power in the 'war on terror' also turned to law for support, drawing on international human rights norms and domestic constitutional protections (often themselves drawing on constitutional norms
in other jurisdictions) to limit those abuses. It is not unreasonable, then,
to assume that over the span of almost a decade, a coherent 'global anti-
terrorism law' might have begun to emerge, the conceptual dimensions of
which might be explained theoretically, and the normative implications
of which might generally be assessed. This part of the chapter examines
the basis for this assumption.

A.   The emergence of global anti-terrorism law

In his contribution to this volume, Banks argues that a decade after 9/11,
the United States 'is now creating more durable structures, processes
and institutions to undertake and control efforts to counter terrorism' and that 'a longer term realignment of the relative importance of
security among our government's objectives may be taking place'.[11] He
argues that the scrutiny of counter-terrorism measures by the courts
and Congress has resulted in new arrangements that 'represent the
emergence of a new counter-terrorism paradigm, the shape and dimensions of which are slowly beginning to appear'.[12] Could the same process
be taking place internationally? Might we be witnessing a convergence
of norms and an evolving global consensus on both the importance of
national security and the limits of counter-terrorism powers? Does it
make sense, even in a cautious way, to speak – as some scholars do –
of 'the international standardisation of national security law' and 'the
emerging international law of terrorism'?[13] There are two broad reasons
to think so.

---

[10] See Karen L. Greenberg and Joshua L. Dratel (eds.), *The Torture Papers: The Road to Abu Ghraib* (New York: Cambridge University Press, 2005).

[11] William C. Banks, Chapter 18, this volume, p. 450.

[12] Ibid.

[13] See Kim Lane Scheppele, 'The international standardization of national security law' (2010) 4 *Journal of National Security Law and Policy* 437 and Ben Saul, 'The emerging international law of terrorism' (2009) *Indian Yearbook of International Law and Policy* 163–92.

First, through Security Council Resolution 1373, the Security Council has been said to have assumed the role of a global legislator,[14] claiming the authority under Chapter VII of the UN Charter to legislate counter-terrorism norms at the international level ('to restore international peace and security'[15]) and requiring states to implement those norms through domestic legislation. Resolution 1373 has now been institutionalised through the work of the Counter-Terrorism Committee, which monitors compliance with the resolution and provides technical assistance to states in implementing it.[16] In terms of compliance with the reporting requirements under the Resolution 1373 regime, the statistics show that states have taken their obligations seriously: 'All 192 U.N. member states filed at least one report with the Security Council's Counter-Terrorism Committee (CTC)... By August 2007, 107 countries had filed four reports and 42 had filed five. The reports show that there was extraordinary uptake of the new anti-terrorism framework.'[17] In terms of formal law, while some international anti-terrorism norms are still developing, there does appear to be 'a genuinely new international law of terrorist financing' with a powerful bureaucracy in the shape of the Financial Action Taskforce, an inter-governmental body established at the G-7 Summit in Paris in 1989, which 'has had a powerful influence on both norm creation and norm enforcement in the area of global terrorist financing'.[18]

Second, convergence is also occurring horizontally, in the sense that many states have looked to other states in drafting and implementing anti-terrorism laws and in adjudicating anti-terrorism cases. As Roach has argued, the UK's anti-terrorism legislation, especially the Terrorism Act 2000, has served as a model for defining terrorism in other jurisdictions, albeit with local variations.[19] Roach does not go so far as to suggest a uniformity in the definition of terrorism or in anti-terrorism legislation,

[14] E. Rosand 'The Security Council as "global legislator": *ultra vires* or ultra innovative?' (2005) 28 *Fordham International Law Journal* 542.

[15] UN Charter, art. 51.

[16] See C. H. Powell, 'The role and limits of global administrative law in the Security Council's anti-terrorism programme', in Hugh Corder (ed.), *Global Administrative Law* (Cape Town: Juta/*Acta Juridica*, 2009), pp. 32–67.

[17] Scheppele, 'The international standardization of national security law', 442.

[18] Saul, 'The emerging international law of terrorism', 184, 174–5. See also Kevin E. Davis, Chapter 8, this volume. Not surprisingly, the FATF's recommendations have been taken seriously by major financial centres, such as Hong Kong, who are among its members: see Simon N. M. Young, Chapter 15, this volume.

[19] Roach, 'The post-9/11 migration'.

but he argues that the UK's terrorism laws (unlike US legislation) have had a significant influence on other legislation because the Terrorism Act 2000 happened to be 'at hand when other countries started their hurried drafting of new anti-terrorism laws in [response] to 9/11 and Security Council Resolution 1373'.[20] Much as it did in colonial times, in India and much of the Commonwealth,[21] UK security laws continue to have a significant impact on much of the English-speaking world and beyond.[22] Similarly, international agencies, such as the United Nations Office on Drugs and Crime, facilitate the transmission and harmonisation of anti-terrorism laws through, for instance, their model legislation on anti-terrorism financing.[23]

Some degree of convergence can also been seen in the judicial realm, particularly in liberal democracies. While the jurisprudence has by no means been consistent, recent analyses of the case law indicate, after a slow start, a growing trend on the part of the courts to moderate at least some of the excesses of anti-terrorism powers, with courts in Canada, Germany, Israel, the United Kingdom and the United States limiting the anti-terrorism powers claimed by their respective governments.[24] For example, McGarrity and Santow show how the principle of proportionality 'both as a legal principle to be applied by the courts and a generally

---

[20] Ibid., p. 376.
[21] Anil Kalhan, Gerald P. Conroy, Mamta Kaushai, Sam Scott Miller and Jed S. Rakoff 'Colonial continuities: human rights, terrorism, and security laws in India' (2006) 20 *Columbia Journal of Asian Law* 93.
[22] In his analysis of legislation in Australia, Canada, New Zealand, the United Kingdom and the United States, Lynch argues that despite the differences 'regarding governance and their likely priority as a terrorist target, clear trends in the creation of anti-terrorism laws both as to form and process are discernible', Andrew Lynch, Chapter 7, this volume.
[23] See above note 9.
[24] See, for example, E. Benvenisti, 'United we stand: national courts reviewing counter-terrorism measures' in A. Bianchi and A. Keller (eds.), *Counterterrorism: Democracy's Challenge* (Oxford: Hart Publishing, 2008), pp. 251–76. Among the cases regularly cited as part of this trend are: *Charkaoui* v. *Canada (Citizenship and Immigration)*, 2007 SCC 9; *Air-transport Security Act* case, Bundesverfessungsgericht (VerfG – Federal Constitutional Court), 59 *Neue Juristische Wochenschrift* 751 (2006); *Public Committee against Torture in Israel* v. *Government of Israel* (HCJ 769/02) (available in English at elyon1.court.gov.il/Files_ENG/02/690/007/A34/02007690.A34.HTM); *A* v. *Secretary of State for the Home Department* [2004] UKHL 56; and the line of cases in the United States Supreme Court leading up to and including *Beaumediene* v. *Bush*, 128 S Ct 2229 (2008). The US Supreme Court's decision in *Holder* v. *Humanitarian Law Project*, 130 S. Ct. 2705 (2010), upholding the constitutional validity of a material-support statute against a constitutional challenge, might be seen as going against this trend.

influential idea'[25] is increasingly used by courts not only in Europe (where it originated) and Canada (where it was judicially adopted in *R* v. *Oakes*[26]), but even in Australia, in security cases.[27]

Moreover, the practice of anti-terrorism also shows an increasing co-ordination among governments and, in particular, intelligence agencies, on matters of national security.[28] Co-ordination in such matters is not entirely unusual, but was mandated by the Security Council in Resolution 1373, which called upon states to assist one another by exchanging information and 'to co-operate on administrative and judicial matters to prevent the commission of terrorist acts'.[29] International regulatory co-ordination is now widely regarded as an essential aspect of an effective counter-terrorism framework, which has prompted co-ordination through intergovernmental networks in a variety of sectors such as aviation security, policing, immigration, financial regulation and intelligence.[30]

Global anti-terrorism law might refer, then, to two phenomena: the vertical dimension of the anti-terrorism regime, which seeks to articulate international legal norms and standards which, in turn, are adopted and applied by states; and the horizontal dimension of global anti-terrorism law, which posits a convergence of principles and practices through borrowing and co-ordination between or among states. These two phenomena are not always distinct and may well be mutually reinforcing. It may be, then, that we have reason to believe that a grand narrative of global anti-terrorism law is possible, one that shows how the events of 9/11 have triggered a global dialogue that, in fits and starts, is generating a coherent set of principles and practices to be followed by states in their counter-terrorism efforts.

---

[25] Nicola McGarrity and Edward Santow, Chapter 6, this volume.
[26] [1986] 1 SCR 103.
[27] Nicola McGarrity and Edward Santow Chapter 6, this volme referring to *Gypsy Jokers Motorcycle Club Inc* v. *Commissioner of Police* (2007) 33 WAR 245, para. 57, in support of this claim.
[28] Chesterman, *One Nation Under Surveillance*.
[29] Paragraph 3(b); see also Powell, 'The role and limits of global administrative law', p. 25.
[30] The dark side of such co-operation can be seen in cases such as that of Maher Arar, who was subjected to extraordinary rendition and tortured as a consequence of erroneous intelligence-sharing agencies in Canada and the United States. Arar was later vindicated (in Canada) and compensated (in the amount of Can $10.5 million) by the Canadian government following the publication of the report of the Commission (above note 6).

B. Theorising global anti-terrorism law

A grand narrative of this sort, highlighting an increasingly coherent global anti-terrorism regime, opens the door to a particular kind of theoretical inquiry and modelling, at a high degree of generality. We could ask, for instance, whether anti-terrorism law, in its international or domestic dimensions, is part of ordinary law or something extraordinary or exceptional that stands apart from it.[31] Global anti-terrorism law could be seen, ideally, as an articulation of the circumstances in which states are justified, either alone or collectively, in limiting the rights of individuals in the interests of national or international security. Contemporary theories of anti-terrorism and emergency powers are often framed in this way, as having something important to say about these powers generally and their relationship to legality,[32] although sometimes with the caveat that they are concerned primarily with liberal democracies.[33]

The importance of understanding the relationship between emergency powers and legality in the West is particularly acute in light of the experience of emergency powers in Weimar Germany,[34] which suggests that the 'exception' contains within it the seeds of destruction of the modern liberal state. It is not surprising then that contemporary theorists are particularly concerned with the threat emergency powers pose to legality, with some seeking to ensure that such powers are subject to legality in the sense of judicial supervision,[35] or to formal legislative oversight,[36] and others seeking to insulate the legal system from emergency powers

---

[31] For a survey of recent theories of emergency powers, see Victor V. Ramraj (ed.), *Emergencies and the Limits of Legality* (Cambridge University Press, 2008).

[32] See Oren Gross, 'Chaos and rules: should responses to violent crises always be constitutional?' (2003) 112 *Yale Law Journal* 1011.

[33] Ferejohn and Pasquino concede that the countries spoken of in their analysis 'are very stable and entrenched democracies that have little need to invoke extreme constitutional measures to protect their regimes': John Ferejohn and Pasquale Pasquino, 'The law of the exception: a typology of emergency powers' (2004) 2 *International Journal of Constitutional Law* 210, 216.

[34] Kim Lane Scheppele, 'Law in a time of exception' (2004) *University of Pennsylvania Journal of Constitutional Law* 1001, 1009.

[35] See, for instance, David Dyzenhaus, 'The state of emergency in legal theory' in Victor V. Ramraj, Michael Hor and Kent Roach (eds.), *Global Anti-Terrorism Law and Policy* (Cambridge University Press, 2005), Chapter 4; David Dyzenhaus, 'The compulsion of legality' in Ramraj, *Emergencies and the Limits of Legality*, 33–59.

[36] Bruce Ackerman, 'The emergency constitution' (2004) 113 *Yale Law Journal* 1029; William E. Scheuerman, 'Presidentialism and emergency government' in Ramraj, *Emergencies and the Limits of Legality*, pp. 258–86.

by locating these powers outside the legal system and subjecting them largely to formal and informal political checks.[37] Although sometimes qualified to apply to only a certain class of countries (or countries that are 'worth saving'[38]) these theories often purport to say something general about the relationship between emergency powers and legality, and about the nature of law in the modern state. Gross, for example, insists that his essay on the extra-legal measures model of emergency powers is 'not an "American" study, nor is it a post-September 11th one' and should be 'treated as generally applicable to constitutional democratic regimes faced with the need to respond to extreme violent crises.'[39] And in his response to Gross in the first edition of this volume, Dyzenhaus defends a theoretical argument that extends to 'well-ordered societies' that do more than 'pay mere lip service to the rule of law'.[40] Legal theory, it often seems, remains committed to the idea that we can articulate a general approach to law that is widely or universally applicable – an idea that is extended to the conceptualisation of emergency powers and anti-terrorism law.

C.   Evaluating global anti-terrorism law

The desire to provide a normative assessment of legal developments suggests another reason why a grand narrative of anti-terrorism law might be considered important. As the events of 9/11 powerfully demonstrated, political violence was not exempted from the increase in what Sklair calls 'transnational practices' and sees as the defining characteristic of globalisation:

> Globalization, therefore, is defined as a particular way of organizing social life across existing state borders. Research on small communities, global cities, border regions, groups of states, and virtual and mobile communities of various types provides strong evidence that existing territorial boundaries are becoming less important and that transnational practices are becoming more important. The balance of power between state and non-state actors and agencies is changing.[41]

---

[37] Gross, 'Chaos and rules'.
[38] Gross, 'Stability and flexibility: a Dicey business' in Ramraj, Hor and Roach, *Global Anti-Terrorism Law and Policy*, p. 90.
[39] Gross 'Chaos and rules', 1027.
[40] Dyzenhaus 'The state of emergency in legal theory', p. 88.
[41] Leslie Sklair, *Globalization: Capitalism and its Alternatives* (Oxford University Press, 3rd edn, 2002), p. 8.

If, as the evidence seems to suggest, territorial boundaries are also becoming less important to agents of political violence, it is not surprising that states, and legislatures, judges, bureaucrats and agencies within states, would look beyond national borders to coordinate, harmonise and set limits on their counter-terrorism activities.

It is entirely reasonable that we would want to map these activities, understand legally their scope and limits, and set them within a theoretical context that we can subject to critical scrutiny and, especially, to normative evaluation. For instance, it might be argued that global anti-terrorism law is inconsistent with rule-of-law principles to the extent that it permits states to designate individuals and groups as 'terrorists' without an adequate judicial process.[42] Or it might be argued that global anti-terrorism law is insufficiently attuned to human rights standards or that the rise of global anti-terrorism law has led to the decline of constitutionalism. For instance, Scheppele has argued that the 'anti-terrorism campaign' has taken 'a toll on constitutional governance' in both weak and strong constitutional states.[43] Similarly, NGOs, such as the International Commission of Jurists, expressed a concern in 2004 about the 'cumulative impact of emerging counter-terrorism measures, and the risk of unraveling the international human rights standards that have been painstakingly developed over the second half of the last century', and commissioned a panel of 'eminent jurists' to study the impact of anti-terrorism laws around the world.[44] The articulation of a grand narrative account of global anti-terrorism laws, it seems, can help us better to understand, evaluate and address the structural changes that have taken place in the relationship between state and citizen post-9/11.

3.   Challenges to the grand narrative

Whatever the merits of articulating a grand narrative account of global anti-terrorism law, and there are many, this kind of account is problematic.

---

[42] See generally Powell 'The role and limits of global administrative law'.

[43] Kim Lane Scheppele 'The migration of anti-constitutional ideas: the post-9/11 globalization of public law and the international state of emergency' in Choudhry, *The Migration of Constitutional Ideas*, p. 372.

[44] Eminent Jurists Panel (Arthur Chaskalson, Chair), *Assessing Damage, Urging Action* (Geneva: International Commission of Jurists, 2008), p. 5. The report details the erosion of human rights in many jurisdictions and warns in its conclusion against the 'enduring long term harm' that practices such as 'torture and cruel, inhuman, and degrading treatment, secret detentions, abductions, illegal transfers, *refoulement*, arbitrary, prolonged, and *incommunicado* detention, unfair trials, and enforced disappearances' might have.

For one thing, a formal account of international and domestic anti-terrorism powers is unlikely to provide a full picture to the extent that it disregards the practical consequences of these powers and the disparate informal social and political constraints on them. Consequently, any attempt to provide a theoretical account of global anti-terrorism law is likely to be incomplete. Similarly, any normative assessment of the global anti-terrorism regime will be a limited one if it ignores the unobvious but important ways in which a global anti-terrorism regime might interact with legality beyond the liberal democracies of the West, in some cases possibly even strengthening constitutionalism.

A. The limits of formal legality

The gap between law on the books and law in action is nothing new, but it is particularly important to bear it in mind in the context of international legal regimes because of the profoundly asymmetrical way in which legal norms are realised, or not, in different parts of the world. It might be assumed that in many of the liberal democracies of the West and in other rule-oriented societies, domestic anti-terrorism laws, including laws imposing limits on executive power, have a significant impact on official conduct because that conduct is subject to judicial review or because the legal norms have been internalised by public officials. However, it is not clear that formal laws always have quite the same hold on officials in others parts of the world. The reasons for this may have to do with the inability or unwillingness of officials to abide by formal laws, the relative unimportance of law in those societies, or the political illegitimacy of those laws (e.g. if they are seen as externally imposed). These problems are not unique to global anti-terrorism law, but they are perhaps particularly acute in light of the geopolitical dimensions, inasmuch as the global anti-terrorism regime is regarded as furthering a US or Western agenda.[45]

Consider the problem of capacity. In a recent report on Resolution 1373, the Security Council's Counter-Terrorism Committee has highlighted the difficulties many countries face in implementing the resolution,[46] and the mandate of the Committee itself appears to be shifting from one

[45] Hikmahanto Juwana, 'Indonesia's anti-terrorism law' in Ramraj, Hor and Roach, *Global Anti-Terrorism Law and Policy*, pp. 295–306; see also Hikmahanto Juwana, Chapter 12, this volume.

[46] Counter-Terrorism Committee, 'Survey of the Implementation of Security Council Resolution 1373 (2001) by Member States' (3 December 2009), S/2009/620.

of primarily monitoring to also providing technical assistance.[47] This makes sense if, as the statistics cited earlier suggest, most states take their Resolution 1373 obligations seriously – with every country having filed at least one report. But statistics can be misleading. For instance, Scheppele draws on the following 2009 CTC survey of compliance with the resolution to conclude that there has been 'widespread compliance':

> Most States in the Western Europe and other States [sic], Eastern Europe, and Central Asia and the Caucasus regions have introduced comprehensive counter-terrorism legislation. More than half of the States in South Eastern Europe and almost half of the States in South America have comprehensive counter-terrorism legislation. In Africa, Western Asia, Southeast Asia, Central America and the Caribbean, many States do not have comprehensive counter-terrorism legislation in place, although most do have some elements in place.[48]

But consider this passage again. We can credibly, on the same information, conclude that in Africa, Western Asia, Southeast Asia, Central America and the Caribbean, most states do not have a comprehensive counter-terrorism legislative framework and fewer than half of the states in South America do. The CTC's technical assistance office clearly has its hands full.

However much success technical assistance programmes might have in helping states to adopt model counter-terrorism legislation, the superficial penetration of international legal norms into particular legal systems might also be a matter of the relative unimportance of formal law in particular societies. While it is sometimes assumed that the failure to implement formal legal norms and formally ratified international agreements is largely a matter of underdevelopment or lack of capacity (to which technical assistance is the answer), comparative law scholars remind us that there are profound societal differences in the relative importance that is accorded to formal law itself. Here, Mattei's tripartite classification of legal systems into those that privilege 'rule of professional

---

[47] The Counter-Terrorism Committee is now producing 'technical guides' for implementing Resolution 1373 and describes part of its role as capacity-building, including facilitating 'the provision of technical assistance to Member States by disseminating best practices; identifying existing technical, financial, regulatory and legislative assistance programmes; promoting synergies between the assistance programmes of international, regional and subregional organizations; and, through its Executive Directorate (CTED), serving as an intermediary for contacts between potential donors and recipients and maintaining an on-line directory of assistance providers, all within the framework of resolution 1373 (2001)' (see www.un.org/sc/ctc/capacity.html).

[48] Scheppele, 'The international standardization of national security law', 442–3.

law', 'rule of political law' and 'rule of traditional law' is helpful.[49] Mattei explains that while the Western legal tradition is relatively homogenous in as much as 'the legal arena is clearly distinguishable from the political arena' and 'the legal process is largely secularized',[50] outside of the West, politics and traditional social structures are likely to have greater normative force than formal law. And in these societies, it is unlikely that formal global anti-terrorism laws would have the same impact on actual practices as they would in Western legal systems, where the 'rule of professional law' prevails. For example, in the anti-terrorist financing context, changes in formal banking laws might not be capable of controlling ancient, informal means of transferring funds such as '*hawala*'-type systems – informal systems of money transfer that have been used for centuries in China, India, Southeast Asia and the Middle East to facilitate trade over vast distances;[51] so 'even if authorities make it prohibitively risky for terrorists to transfer funds from Egypt to the United States by way of wire transfer, they may not be able to prevent them from transferring funds through a *hawaladar* from Egypt to an accomplice in Malaysia and then by ordinary wire transfer to the United States via Singapore'.[52] On the other hand, attempting to regulate the informal banking sector risks increasing the cost of these services to poorer households that rely on overseas remittances 'as a means to escape poverty'.[53]

Finally, it may be that the resistance to global anti-terrorism laws is not primarily a matter of lack of capacity or of the lower status of formal law. Rather, it may be that the resistance to adopting or implementing the law is largely political or ideological. In his contribution to the first edition of this volume, Juwana describes the resentment that many Indonesians felt in the wake of the Bali bombings at the external pressure to reform their anti-terrorism laws, sometimes at the expense of human rights protections.[54] In the face of this pressure, the Indonesian Constitutional Court

---

[49] Ugo Mattei, 'Three Patterns of Law: Taxonomy and Change in the World's Legal Systems' (1997) 45 *American Journal of Comparative Law* 5.

[50] Ibid., 23.

[51] Mohammed El Qorchi, Samuel Munzele Maimbo and John F. Wilson *Informal Funds Transfer Systems: An Analysis of the Informal Hawala System* (Washington, DC: International Monetary Fund, 2003), p. 10.

[52] Kevin E. Davis, Chapter 8, this volume, p. 206.

[53] El Qorchi *et al.*, *Informal Funds Transfer*, p. 3. See also, Kevin E. Davis, Chapter 8, this volume.

[54] Ramraj, Hor and Roach, *Global Anti-Terrorism Law and Policy*, Chapter 14. The external pressure on Indonesia might be contrasted with the absence of such pressure in the Japanese context: see Mark Fenwick, Chapter 16, this volume.

held that the imposition of the death penalty on the bombers was unconstitutional, but its ruling would not apply retroactively,[55] so three of the
'Bali bombers' were eventually executed by firing squad in November
2008. Despite the concerns of many Indonesians about the executions,
many remain concerned about terrorism; in fact, since 2001, Indonesia
has experienced numerous terrorists attacks, including several devastating attacks in Bali and Jakarta.[56]

The challenge, then, is to address the threat of terrorism within a
framework that is fair and reasonable, but equally sensitive to religious
and political sentiments. Indonesia has tried, with mixed success, to
employ rehabilitation techniques that involve religious counselling of
militants (through its controversial elite policing unit, Detachment
88[57]), so as to treat them as 'good men gone astray' and engage them on
their distorted and often simplistic views of Islam.[58] At the same time,
Indonesia has sought to reassure a suspicious public that it is not blindly
following an 'anti-Islamic' Western agenda or abusing its citizens at the
behest of Western countries.[59] It may be that in a country with complex
ethnic and religious sensitivities such as Indonesia, where the automatic
association of 'terrorism' with 'Islam' is deeply resented, some forms
of religious counselling may represent a more effective and culturally
appropriate response to terrorism than formal criminal prosecution.
As Hor argues in the context of Singapore, the authorities seem to be
aware that national security detentions must be 'handled in a "discreet
and carefully measured" manner' to prevent feelings of victimisation
within (in Singapore) the Muslim minority.[60] So the official approach

---

[55] Hikmahanto Juwana, Chapter 12, this volume, pp. 295–6.

[56] Recent terrorist attacks include attacks in Bali (Kuta, 12 October 2002; Kuta, 1 October
2005) and Jakarta (JW Marriot Hotel, 5 August 2003; Australian Embassy, 9 September
2004; JW Mariott Hotel and Ritz-Carlton Hotel, 17 July 2009).

[57] Hikmahanto Juwana, Chapter 12, this volume.

[58] Hannah Beech, 'What Indonesia can teach the world about counterterrorism' *Time*,
7 June 2010, available at www.time.com/time/magazine/article/0,9171,1992246,00.html.

[59] Hikmahanto Juwana, Chapter 12, this volume. Indonesian resistance to externally-im-
posed legal reforms is not limited to anti-terrorism legislation. In the wake of the 1997
financial crisis, international financial institutions such as the World Bank insisted on
reforms to its bankruptcy laws. While the government formally complied with these
requests and the World Bank was able to report success, traditional methods for dealing with financially distressed companies continued unabated: Terence C. Halliday and
Bruce G. Carruthers, 'Foiling the financial hegemons: limits of globalisation of corporate
insolvency regimes in Indonesia, Korea and China' in Christoph Antons and Volkmar
Gessner, (eds.), *Globalisation and Resistance: Law Reform in Asia since the Crisis* (Oxford
and Portland, OR: Hart Publishing, 2007), pp. 255–301.

[60] Michael Hor, Chapter 11, this volume, p. 282.

in Singapore seems to be that detainees are treated not 'as criminals – i.e., bad people who chose to do evil – but as misguided individuals who could be salvaged by right teaching. The philosophy was a therapeutic, and not a retributive or deterrent, one.'[61] These sorts of methods are, of course, open to abuse and need to be carefully monitored, but it is less than obvious that the prospects of abuse are always significantly less in a system that formally authorises 'enhanced interrogation techniques' and military tribunals.

B.   *The assumptions of legal theory*

As we have seen, theoretical accounts of anti-terrorism and emergency powers are important in helping us to understand the tension between the modern state's aspirations of legality on the one hand, and the idea of a state of emergency that allows the state to ignore or suspend ordinary law in the face of an acute threat to the state on the other. Some theories of emergency powers, though, make one or more assumptions about the state that limit their explanatory power. Some of these assumptions are contentious within contemporary legal theory, such as debates about the normativity of law and the relative importance of the political; others, however, are particularly important when it comes to the global aspirations of anti-terrorism law, such as assumptions about the liberal–democratic and unified nature of the state.

Some Anglo-American theories assume that they are dealing primarily with liberal democracies, and often with liberal democracies in the common law tradition. There are, of course, important differences between the common law and civil law traditions, differences which can easily be overlooked in studies of counter-terrorism policy.[62] But even if we are justified in assuming some common ground within the 'Western' constitutional tradition, some caution is needed in assuming a particular role for the courts or the legislature within the scope of one's theory when

---

[61] Ibid.

[62] There are, of course, important differences within Anglo-American traditions as well. For example, the human rights culture in Australia may not be as strong as in, say, Canada or the United Kingdom. But even accepting these differences, there remains a significant difference between societies where, however important human rights might be, law is regarded as central to the ordering or private and public affairs and those where it is not – as Mattei's tripartite distinction, discussed earlier, suggests. I am grateful to Patrick Emerton for his observation at the symposium in Sydney that Australia is probably more of a populist democracy than a liberal democracy.

extending it further afield.[63] This brings us back to Mattei's point. What is often taken for granted in the construction of a grand narrative is the presence of a legal tradition that firmly embraces the rule of professional law. It may be, however, that thinking theoretically about anti-terrorism law in a way that makes sense globally requires a heightened sensitivity to the social significance of formal law in a given society; we cannot assume that a transplanted legal text or constitutional framework will always (if at all[64]) have the same meaning in different legal systems. So faced with pressure to adopt model anti-terrorism laws, some states may amend their legislation whatever their capacity to implement it; others might amend their laws to satisfy one (say, external) constituency while interpreting those laws to justify existing practices or ignoring them altogether.[65]

Indeed, the Counter-Terrorism Committee's recommendations in its survey of the implementation around the world of Resolution 1373 tend to gloss over the deeper sociological obstacles to anti-terrorism law reform. While it recommends – in the context of Southeast Asia, for instance – encouraging 'states to accelerate the development of comprehensive and coherent counter-terrorism legal frameworks in compliance with the international counter-terrorism instruments and to enhance their criminal justice systems in order to bring terrorists to justice while upholding international human rights obligations',[66] it assumes an important social and political role for law in the first place, both in empowering governments to anticipate and respond to political violence and in constraining its ability to do so. Yet these sorts of assumptions, which in turn inform many Western theories of law, are problematic in other contexts, whether in Thailand with its ongoing political and constitutional instability, or in East Timor, with its nascent institutions and sometimes still volatile internal politics.[67] Even in societies more oriented to

---

[63] See Werner Menski, 'Beyond Europe' in Esin Örücü and David Nelken (eds.), *Comparative Law: A Handbook* (Oxford and Portland, OR: Hart Publishing, 2007), pp. 189–216, on the need for caution in seeking to extend formal, 'Western' legal principles to Asia and Africa.

[64] See Legrand 'The impossibility of "legal transplants"'. See also Laura Donohue, Chapter 4, this volume.

[65] Chris Oxtoby and C. H. Powell demonstrate, Chapter 22, this volume on East and South Africa, how similar anti-terrorism legislation can have dramatically different consequences in the practice of different states.

[66] Counter-Terrorism Committee 'Survey of the Implementation of Security Council Resolution 1373', p. 28.

[67] Victor V. Ramraj, 'The emergency powers paradox' in Victor V. Ramraj and Arun K. Thiruvengadam (eds.), *Emergency Powers in Asia* (Cambridge University Press, 2010), pp. 21–55.

the rule of professional law, they ignore the gap between a state's formal legislative response to Resolution 1373, as in Singapore's United Nations (Anti-Terrorism) Regulations 2001, and the reality of legal practice, demonstrated by Singapore's continued use of the Internal Security Act as its primary counter-terrorism instrument to detain terrorist suspects without trial.[68] A focus on formal theories of law and legal institutions also obscures informal efforts, such as the Singapore government's efforts, following the arrest of suspected Jemaah Islamiyah terrorists in the months after 9/11, to promote dialogue and trust across religious and ethnic communities through 'Inter-Racial and Religious Confidence Circles' and 'soft' constitutional law measures such as the adoption, following government-initiated inter-faith dialogue and a collaborative drafting process, of a Declaration on Religious Harmony.[69]

Finally, when theorising about anti-terrorism law and emergency powers we need to be especially cautious in our assumptions about the nature of the modern state. Slaughter's thesis that the modern state is 'disaggregating',[70] such that different parts of that state (the courts, legislators, government agencies) are interacting as part of complex government networks with their counterparts in other states in ways that are often inconsistent and contradictory, suggests that the modern state is far from unified in anti-terrorism matters. Although the disaggregation of the modern state is not itself antithetical to a global anti-terrorism regime, it does suggest a higher degree of complexity in understanding the relationship between legal norms at the state, regional and international levels, particularly when the different networks produce inconsistent rules

---

[68] Michael Hor, 'Terrorism and the criminal law: Singapore's solution' [2002] *Singapore Journal of Legal Studies* 30.

[69] See Kent Roach, 'Multiculturalism and Muslim minorities' [2006] *Singapore Journal of Legal Studies* 417; Thio Li-ann, 'Constitutional "soft" law and the management of religious liberty and order: the 2003 Declaration on Religious Harmony' [2004] *Singapore Journal of Legal Studies* 414. See also Victor V. Ramraj 'Beyond the Ottawa principles: social and institutional strategies and counter-terrorism' in Nicole LaViolette and Craig Forcese (eds.), *The Human Rights of Anti-Terrorism* (Toronto: Irwin Law, 2008), pp. 371–84. These sorts of approaches have been tried elsewhere, including in Western liberal democracies (see Clive Walker and Javaid Rehman, Chapter 10, this volume), but are often overshadowed by formal legal responses and remain politically contentious; in early February 2011, UK Prime Minister David Cameron declared his dissatisfaction with the failure of mutliculturalism, throwing into question, at least at the level of political rhetoric, the UK government's commitment to 'soft' responses and strategies and its efforts to co-operate with minority communities to contain 'extremists': see 'Bagehot: muscle v multiculturalism', *The Economist*, 12 February 2011, 38.

[70] Anne-Marie Slaughter, *A New World Order* (Princeton University Press, 2004).

or policies, the legal and legal–systemic consequences of which are not immediately clear.[71] Our accounts of anti-terrorism law need to acknowledge not the demise of the modern state, which is far from imminent, but the complexity of the relationships between the domestic, regional and international legal orders, and the asymmetrical and uneven patterns of relationships, particularly in light of the disaggregation (in some states more than others) of the modern state.

C.   Emergency powers and constitutionalism

A third problem with grand narrative accounts of global anti-terrorism law and, particularly, attempts to provide a normative assessment of it, is the tendency of such accounts to overlook some important ways in which a global anti-terrorism regime might interact with legality and aspirations of legality beyond the liberal West. Consider, for instance, the view that one important legal consequence of the global anti-terrorism regime post-9/11 has been the demise of constitutionalism around the world.[72] This is, on its face, a plausible claim, particularly in light of the Security Council's preliminary attempts to impose a uniform legal response to terrorism without (at least initially) formal consideration of the human rights implications of anti-terrorism law. But there is also reason to think that in some contexts, effective domestic anti-terrorism laws, in the form of an emergency powers regime, might even strengthen constitutionalism and the rule of law, at least in the longer term. Consider two examples: China and East Timor.

In his study of China's recent reforms to its emergency laws, deLisle argues that the introduction of these laws, while in some respects legitimating the state's use of coercive powers, also has the potential to strengthen the regime's commitment to the rule of law. Criticisms of China's emergency power laws, deLisle argues, 'overlook the prospect that Chinese emergency power law could have state-limiting and rights-protecting

---

[71] For instance, it may be that the executive branch of government, working through horizontal (other governments) and vertical (the UN Security Council) networks produces lists, not formally susceptible to judicial review, of individuals and entities suspected to be associated with Osama bin Laden, whose assets must be frozen, while a European court finds the listing procedure to be inconsistent with human rights norms and thus orders the assets unfrozen, thus throwing into question the relationship among different legal orders. See *Kadi and Al Barakaat International Foundation* v. *Council of the European Union and Commission of the European Communities* (2008) 3 CMLR 41 (Grand Chamber, European Court of Justice).

[72] See above notes 43 and 44, and accompanying text.

features analogous to those asserted by some analysts for liberal constitutional democracies'.[73] For a regime that 'operates in a permanent, but
almost never declared, state of emergency',[74] but one that is increasingly
rule-of-law oriented, the step of delimiting the powers that accrue to the
state in times of crisis and the precise conditions that trigger them, and
holding itself accountable to those powers under the increasingly watchful
eyes of increasingly demanding citizens, is a remarkable one. While the
enumeration of such powers might, in other contexts, be power-expand-
ing, in the context of China's already-powerful executive government, the
enumeration of the very same powers may well be power-constraining.

Along similar lines, it may be that in nascent, post-conflict states,
emergency powers of the sort that might be of concern in stable states
play an important role in establishing 'the basic conditions of relative stability in which a legal structure and culture of accountability can take
hold'.[75] East Timor provides a textbook example of how, in a post-conflict
context, emergency powers can be invoked for the limited purpose of
restoring political stability and quickly rolled back as soon as conditions
permit. Thus on 11 February 2008, following an assassination attempt on
the President and Prime Minister by a rebel group, a nation-wide state of
emergency was imposed for forty-eight hours with restrictions on assemblies and demonstrations, and a curfew was imposed.[76] The nation-wide
state of emergency was renewed on 13 February and again, on 22 February,
as a nation-wide 'state of siege' under Article 25 of the Constitution.[77] As
the rebel group was contained by government forces, the state of siege
was renewed again in March, but only in seven districts, and again in
April, but only in the district of Ermera.[78] Although the presence in East
Timor of UN and international NGOs meant very close scrutiny of how

---

[73] Jacques deLisle 'State of exception in an exceptional state' in Ramraj and Thiruvengadam,
    Emergency Powers in Asia, pp. 342–90, 344.
[74] Ibid., p. 342.
[75] Victor V. Ramraj, 'The emergency powers paradox', pp. 21–55, 23.
[76] Ibid., p. 32.
[77] Article 25, para. 1 of the Constitution of the Democratic Republic of East Timor provides
    that '[s]uspension of the exercise of fundamental rights, freedoms and guarantees shall
    only take place if a state of siege or state of emergency has been declared as provided by
    the Constitution'. The other paragraphs of art. 25 set out the circumstances in which a
    state of siege or state of emergency may be declared (para. 2), the obligation to specify
    limits on rights, freedoms, and guarantees (para. 3), the maximum duration of 30 days
    and possibility of renewal (para. 4), the non-derogability of particular rights, freedoms,
    and guarantees (para. 5), and the obligation to restore constitutional normality as soon
    as possible (para. 6).
[78] Ramraj, 'The emergency powers paradox', p. 32.

this emergency unfolded, the relatively successful execution of exceptional powers by a nascent democracy sent precisely the right signal to the Timorese – that emergency powers could be invoked (notably, in a post-9/11 context) in a manner consistent with the liberal–democratic aspirations of a young nation.

These are but two examples, and there is much more that could be said about each of them. But they demonstrate an important point – that however much emergency powers under the banner of 'anti-terrorism' laws might contribute to the erosion of constitutionalism in the United States and many of its closest allies, there are other stories that could be told about the emergence of constitutionalism even in the face of novel emergency-powers regimes. Indeed, it would not be absurd to claim that the creation and invocation of emergency powers in China and East Timor might even contribute to the strengthening of constitutionalism in the longer term.

4. The complexity of transnational legality

Global anti-terrorism law is therefore much more complex than the grand narrative might suggest. And this complexity itself can be seen as part of the rise of transnational legality, consisting of both the increasingly tangled web of international, regional and domestic legal norms and the emergence of legal norms and practices that cross borders but do not fall squarely within our traditional conception of inter-state law. This legal complexity makes a sophisticated and comprehensive account of global anti-terrorism law and policy a moving target precisely because the status of legal norms and of the modern state itself are in flux. But it makes it all the more imperative that we seek to understand it as fully as possible so that our approach to empowering and constraining national governments, international bodies and complex networks of transnational bodies in their anti-terrorism activities are equally malleable and adaptable.

What, then, are the elements of a sophisticated and comprehensive account of global anti-terrorism law and, crucially, policy? First, the account would acknowledge the disaggregation of the state;[79] it would attempt to map formal legal norms at the international, regional and domestic (including sub-state) levels; and it would articulate the multiple, complex relationships between and among these levels. The account

---

[79] Slaughter, *A New World Order.*

would acknowledge both the pluralism of legal norms and the asymmetry of those norms in different parts of the world. The pluralism of anti-terrorism norms is increasingly evident, and as Roach observes, 'one of the fascinating features of comparative anti-terrorism law is its complex blend of international, regional, and domestic sources of law'.[80] An ambitious account of this aspect of anti-terrorism law might also engage with debates about transnational law and consider whether an emerging regime of global anti-terrorism law is part of a regime of transnational law that is '*neither* national nor international nor public [nor] private at the same time as being *both* national and international, as well as public and private'.[81] But the asymmetric nature of anti-terrorism laws is also critical.[82] To take one important example, as *Kadi*[83] shows, the European Union is in a much stronger position to resist (formally) the imposition of international legal norms than are other countries, although there are also informal ways of resisting international pressure while appearing formally to comply.[84]

Second, a sophisticated and comprehensive account would acknowledge both in theory and in practical application the gap between law and society in many countries and thus of the disparate impact of formal legal norms on state and non-state actors and practices. This will, of course, make policy development and implementation more challenging; it borders on the absurd to think we could develop global 'legislation' for 195 or so countries that is sensitive both to their capacity to implement those laws and, more importantly, to the social significance of law such that the substantive objectives of 'global' law can be translated into formal and informal norms appropriate to that society and, in many cases, to particular sub-regions within a particular state. Our accounts of global anti-terrorism law and policy, then, must be comfortable with the idea that there are different concepts of the state and different ways of governing,

---

[80] Roach 'The post-9/11 migration', p. 402.
[81] Craig Scott, ' "Transnational law" as proto-concept: three conceptions' (2009) 10 *German Law Journal* 859–76, 873.
[82] I am exploring the asymmetrical nature of law in other work: e.g. 'Asymmetric transnationalism: the multiple roles of law in a complex world', presented at the annual Center for Transnational Legal Studies Conference, which in May 2010 was held at the Faculty of Law at the University of Torino.
[83] See above note 71.
[84] Halliday and Carruthers, 'Foiling the financial hegemons', pp. 255–301, 263–73, referring to the Indonesian experience following the 1997 financial crisis.

and that law might have a distinct place and social significance in different societies.

Third, and closely linked to the previous point, a sophisticated and comprehensive account of global anti-terrorism law and policy would acknowledge the importance of a multidisciplinary approach to the prevention of political violence and the limiting of state and other forms of 'public' power intended to prevent such violence. Here I have in mind not only the increasingly trite observation that it is necessary to address the root causes of 'terrorism' but also that non-legal means of constraining the state might also be important. A viable account of global anti-terrorism law and policy must be capable of encompassing two distinct kinds of observations. On the one hand, it must be able to make sense of Tushnet's observation that whatever the shortcomings of the post-9/11 military commissions in Guantánamo Bay, sociological context was critically important; the professional training of military lawyers and the sense of military honour and reciprocity were such that legal shortcomings would have been compensated, in part, by a legal culture that was 'increasingly comfortable as procedural formality increases'.[85] The erosion of legal rights in the United States post-9/11 may well have been resisted, at least in part, by a socially embedded political culture in which procedural fairness is central. At the same time, a viable account must also be sensitive to the observation that, in a country as vast and diverse as Indonesia, without a deeply embedded culture of legal formality, locally sensitive policing techniques and softer strategies, if carefully monitored and infused with a professional ethos, might be more important and effective (in that particular context, at that particular time) than high-level law reform in preventing political violence.

The kind of account of global anti-terrorism law and policy envisioned here is a rather tall order, and the idea of a comprehensive account is more of an aspiration than a realistic goal. But even in less-than-comprehensive accounts, it is worthwhile to be mindful of the limits of positing a one-size-fits-all global anti-terrorism law regime, whether aimed at enabling or constraining the state, and the dangers of assuming that anti-terrorism laws, policies and strategies can easily be transplanted from one society to another.

---

[85] Mark Tushnet 'The political constitution of emergency powers: some conceptual issues' in Ramraj, *Emergencies and the Limits of Legality*, pp. 145–55.

5. Conclusion

It is not the argument of this chapter that global perspectives are unhelp-ful; rather, approaching law from a global perspective enriches our under-standing of law and is imperative in the formulation of sophisticated and effective policies. The argument advanced here is that thinking about glo-bal anti-terrorism law requires a nuanced and sophisticated approach, one that is mindful of local differences and particularities that transform the way legal norms are understood, articulated, implemented and resisted in different parts of the world. The introduction to the first edition of this volume observed that 'students of anti-terrorism law and policy will have to be attentive to the complex interplay between international, regional, and domestic laws and structures'.[86] What has become clear in the dec-ade since that terrible September morning is that anti-terrorism law, like many areas of law from environmental law to international commercial law, is increasingly and unavoidably *transnational*. This in itself presents a host of challenges for how we think about law and society and, in par-ticular, about co-ordinated responses to problems that extend across bor-ders and vastly different societies. Despite the globalisation of popular culture, business transactions, telecommunications, travel and, for that matter, political violence, the legal world is as complex as it has ever been. It is worth bearing this reality in mind as we reflect on the current state of anti-terrorism law and policy.

[86] Victor V. Ramraj, Michael Hor and Kent Roach 'Introduction in Ramraj, Hor and Roach, *Global Anti-terrorism Law and Policy*, p. 5.

4

Transplantation

LAURA K. DONOHUE

1. Introduction

In the first edition of this volume, I suggested that in liberal–democratic states, it is a spiral, not a pendulum, that best describes the evolution of counter-terrorist law.[1] Introduced in the wake of the latest attack, new measures seek to expand executive authority. Legislators tend to capitulate to the executive's demands, often under expedited circumstances and without careful analysis of how the attack occurred. The most onerous provisions may be subject to sunset clauses, but thereafter repeal becomes extremely difficult. To allow such measures to lapse, legislators must demonstrate that the threat no longer exists, that by repealing the provisions violence will not ensue or that some level of violence is acceptable. The first two are impossible to prove and the third politically untenable. Such provisions thus not only remain, but then become a baseline on which further authorities are built, expanding the power of the executive and restricting rights.[2]

In this edition, I would like to raise concerns about an intersecting phenomenon: transplantation. It contributes to the evolution of the counter-terrorist spiral by both driving the introduction of new measures and ensuring, in the transfer of rules to other areas, the entrenchment of counter-terrorist law.

I divide transplantation into two categories. By substantive transplantation I mean the method by which counter-terrorist measures are applied

---

Special thanks to Greg Klass, David Luban and Victor Ramraj for their comments on this chapter.

[1] Laura K. Donohue, 'Terrorism and the counter-terrorist discourse', in Victor V. Ramraj, Michael Hor and Kent Roach (eds.), *Global Anti-Terrorism Law and Policy* (Cambridge University Press, 2005). For further development of the theory and further exposition of many of the examples used in this chapter, see Laura K. Donohue, *The Cost of Counterterrorism: Power, Politics, and Liberty* (Cambridge University Press, 2008).

[2] See Donohue, 'Terrorism and the counter-terrorist discourse', pp. 2–4, 14–20.

to other areas of the law and, in turn, provisions developed in other substantive realms, such as military, criminal or civil law, are applied to counter-terrorism. Geographic transplantation, in turn, deals with the regional transfer of legal rules, which occurs either through parallel adoption of provisions, or through directed implementation from international organisations.[3] While transplantation may be consistent with the arguments from analogy that permeate legal analysis, in a world of counter-terrorism, where the types of threats faced by the state may be *sui generis*, the powers thereby introduced may be substantial and the movement of parallel provisions may result in a broad range of unintended effects, such transfers carry considerable costs.

The transplantation from counter-terrorism to criminal law, for instance, embeds counter-terrorist authorities in the broader legal code. Three effects follow: first, the ratcheting effect identified in the counter-terrorist spiral, above, expands beyond counter-terrorism. Once such measures proliferate, their repeal becomes extremely difficult, and they thus become a baseline on which further measures are built. Second, the effect is felt in the further transfer of powers to the executive realm, raising questions about power distribution between the legislative, judicial and executive functions of government. Third, the effect is felt in the further restriction of rights within the state, shifting the relationship between the individual and the government. What makes this remarkable is that the reason counter-terrorist measures are often allowed in the first place is precisely because of the level of threat faced by the state. But on what grounds are the erosion of ordinary protections – such as probable cause as an antecedent for arrest, the presumption of innocence and the right to fair trial – lifted, when the extraordinary challenge is absent?

This chapter begins with a typology of transplantation. It then turns to examples of how transplantation can go wrong. The chapter considers

---

[3] For a narrower conception of transplantation, as 'the moving of a rule…from one country to another, or from one people to another', see Alan Watson, *Legal Transplants: An Approach to Comparative Law* (Georgia University Press, 2nd edn, 1993), p. 21. I use the term in a broader sense, incorporating both substantive transfer between areas of the law, as well as geographic transfer through borrowing and design. I am sympathetic to Legrand's critique of Watson's effort to isolate the rules from their social and cultural context; indeed, part of the problem in the counter-terrorist realm is the shifting meaning of such rules when geographically transplanted into different jurisdictions. See Pierre Legrand, 'The impossibility of "legal transplants"' (1997) 4 *Maastricht Journal of European and Comparative Law* 111.

substantive transfer between criminal law and counter-terrorism, with particular emphasis on the use of financial mechanisms. It next turns to transplantation within national security, highlighting the unique situation of speech restrictions in the nuclear realm and comparing it to similar efforts to restrict microbiologists in an effort to counter the threat posed by biological weapons. The chapter concludes with thoughts about ways in which some of the negative effects of transplantation could be mitigated through *ex ante* considerations.

2. Typology of transplantation

Two modes of transplantation mark the counter-terrorist realm. Substantive transplantation centres on the movement of legal mechanisms between different areas of the law – e.g. from counter-terrorism to criminal or civil law, and from other legal regimes to counter-terrorism. It is aided by (1) normalisation, (2) a lack of specificity in the original instruments, (3) the manner of implementation and (4) the occurrence of reverse transplantation. Geographic transplantation, in turn, focuses on the international or domestic transfer of provisions between legal regimes. Four mechanisms appear to be at work: (1) transplantation between culturally, legally or linguistically related countries or regions, (2) transplantation between developed and developing regions, (3) a mirroring of, or piggybacking on, other regional initiatives, and (4) transplantation as a result of concerted efforts by multinational organisations to standardise rules.

A.   *Substantive transplantation*

Transplantation from counter-terrorist law to criminal or civil law occurs by way of four mechanisms.[4] The first I refer to as normalisation, which operates in a straightforward way: initially, legislation may try to limit the new authorities to fighting terrorism. The idea is that such measures are so extraordinary, that they can only be justified by the unique kind of threat presented by the extremist organisations that the state is facing. Once such measures enter into the law, however, they are no longer extraordinary. They become accepted and, indeed, part of the ordinary legal code.

---

[4] For a discussion of transfer between criminal law and counter-terrorist law, see Laura K. Donohue, 'The perilous dialogue' (2009) 97 *California Law Review* 357, 373–9.

Myriad examples – from search and seizure authorities to property forfeiture – present themselves.[5] Consider, for instance, the House of Lords' 2005 effort to counter the adoption of control orders. In the end, the Lords' capitulation turned on the guarantee that the issue would return for debate the following year. But by the time the debate was to be held, the urgency and exceptionalism represented by the introduction of the provisions no longer applied. The debate never transpired. Such patterns are common: in the United Kingdom from 1973 to 2000, the intense scrutiny applied to new authorities repeatedly fell away upon renewal considerations, with often not more than a handful of legislators even bothering to show up at subsequent debates.[6]

Normalisation may be considerably aided by the apparent effectiveness of such measures. Counter-terrorist provisions often lack the same level of protection that marks other areas of the law. By relaxing restrictions that might otherwise apply, officials may pursue their ends with greater latitude.

Once the idea of using such powers is no longer exceptional, subsequent statutes may isolate and drop counter-terrorist provisions into different areas of the law. The Flags and Emblems (Display) Act (Northen Ireland) 1954, for instance, drew directly from statutory instruments introduced under the 1922–43 Civil Authorities (Special Powers) Acts.[7] Juryless trial in Northern Ireland, implemented despite considerable objection in 1973, later became applied to complex fraud and organised crime cases throughout the United Kingdom.[8] Even the control orders – which earned such enmity from the House of Lords – were swiftly echoed in proposals to restrict those suspected of involvement in drug-related activity, despite any conviction for criminal offences. In the United States, as I discuss below, further examples could be found in anti-terrorist finance measures.

The second way in which counter-terrorist provisions transfer to other areas of the law – and criminal law, in particular – stems from a lack of

---

[5] Ibid., 374–7.
[6] See Laura K. Donohue, *Counter-Terrorist Law and Emergency Powers in the United Kingdom 1922–2000* (Dublin: Irish Academic Press, 2008).
[7] Flags and Emblems (Display) Act (Northern Ireland) 1954 (UK), repealed under Direct Rule by Public Order (Northern Ireland) Order 1987.
[8] Northern Ireland (Emergency Provisions) Act, 1973, c. 53 and Criminal Justice Act, 2003, c. 44, s. 43(2), (5). For discussion of the evolution of the Diplock courts, see Laura K. Donohue, 'Terrorism and trial by jury: the vices and virtues of British and American criminal law' (2007) 59 *Stanford Law Review* 1321.

specificity in the initial statutory authorities.[9] It can be difficult, if not impossible, to limit the scope of provisions seeking to prevent terrorism – a term itself amorphous and subject to scores of definitions.[10] To address this concern, legislators often craft statutes to apply to a series of criminal acts, which may – or may not – be carried out by individuals committed to political violence. At other times, the wording of the statute is broad, thus allowing the new authorities to be applied to both terrorist and non-terrorist crimes. The emphasis here is on the implementation of the statute, although the absence of controls in the primary legal instrument is equally important.

In the United Kingdom, for instance, the first counter-terrorist statute to be introduced by Westminster following the proroguement of the Northern Ireland Parliament created the juryless courts mentioned above. The legislation included a schedule of offences, the prosecution of which would automatically be assigned to the single-judge courts. The scheduled offences included murder, manslaughter, arson, riot, offences under the Malicious Damage Act of 1861, violations of the Offences against the Person Act 1861, violations of the Firearms Act 1969, offences under the Theft Act (Northern Ireland) 1969, offences against the Protection of the Person and Property Act (Northern Ireland) 1969 and a range of inchoate and related offences.[11] Despite subsequent efforts to certify out non-terrorist-related cases, by the mid-1980s, some 40 per cent of the cases coming before the juryless trials had nothing to do with terrorism.[12]

The United Kingdom is not alone in this regard. The habeas corpus provisions of the US Antiterrorism and Effective Death Penalty Act 1996 now figure largely in criminal law. Government reports have, in turn, repeatedly found the Patriot Act powers applied to non-terrorist crimes.[13] Perhaps the most egregious example is the use of National Security Letters (NSLs). The Patriot Act, enacted to respond to the terrorist attacks of 9/11, 2001, eliminated the requirement that the record information obtained

---

[9] Donohue, 'The perilous dialogue', 377–8.

[10] See, e.g., Alex Schmid and A. J. Jongman, *Political Terrorism* (New Brunswick, NJ: Transaction, 1988) and Walter Laqueur, 'Terrorism: A Brief History' (2007), pp. 20–3 available at www.america.gov/st/peacesec-english/2007/May/20080522172730SrenoD0. 6634027.html.

[11] Northern Ireland (Emergency Provisions) Act 1973, c. 53, Sch. 4.

[12] Dermot Walsh, *Ten Years on in Northern Ireland* (Belfast: Cobden Trust Study, 1980).

[13] See, e.g., US Department of Justice Office of the Inspector General, *A Review of the FBI's Use of National Security Letters: Assessment of Corrective Actions and Examination of NSL Usage in 2006* (March 2006), p. 110; Eric Lichtblau, 'US uses terror law to pursue crimes from drugs to swindling', *New York Times*, 28 September 2003, A1.

in an NSL itself be pertinent to a foreign power or an agent of a foreign power.[14] Instead, it need only be relevant to an investigation to protect against international terrorism or foreign spying (along with the caveat that where US citizens were involved, such investigation could not be predicated solely on the basis of First Amendment protected activities).[15] The FBI's use of the measures dramatically increased, expanding from 8,500 requests in 2000 to 47,000 by 2005.[16] A subsequent report by the US Department of Justice Office of the Inspector General found that the bureau did not keep adequate records linking the NSLs to ongoing counter-terrorism or counter-espionage investigations, that NSLs had been issued without the appropriate authorisation and that they had become a routine tool in preliminary investigations.

The manner in which counter-terrorist provisions are implemented provides yet a third way in which counter-terrorist authorities are transplanted. Secondary and tertiary instruments may be implemented in a manner that departs from the original intent. In 2002, for instance, as part of its counter-terrorist regime, the FBI issued guidelines allowing it to monitor Internet sites, libraries and religious institutions – with no requirement that evidence exist of potential criminal activity, much less terrorism.[17] Even where an effort is made at the administrative level to limit the broad use of powers to counter-terrorism – but not, as a statutory matter, specifically restricted to terrorist cases – memoranda and guidelines appear unable to stem the flow.[18]

---

[14] USA PATRIOT Act, §505, amending the Electronic Communications Privacy Act (18 USC 2709), the Right to Financial Privacy Act (12 USC 3414(a)(5)), and the Fair Credit Reporting Act (15 USC 1681u).

[15] Ibid.

[16] Office of the Inspector General, *A Review of the FBI's Use of National Security Letters*, p. 120. But note that, according to the OIG, because of the failure of the FBI to adequately record and report the use of NSLs, the total number is estimated to be approximately 22 per cent higher: ibid.

[17] See The Attorney General's Guidelines on General Crimes, Racketeering Enterprise and Terrorism Enterprise Investigations, 30 May 2002, available at www.usdoj.gov/olp/generalcrimes2.pdf; The Attorney General's Guidelines on Federal Bureau of Investigation Undercover Operations, 30 May 2002, available at www.usdoj.gov/olp/fbiundercover. pdf; The Attorney General's Guidelines Regarding the Use of Confidential Informants, 30 May 2002, available at www.usdoj.gov/olp/dojguidelines.pdf; and Memorandum for the Heads and Inspectors General of Executive Departments and Agencies, From the Attorney General, 30 May 2002, Regarding Procedures for Lawful, Warrantless Monitoring of Verbal Communications, available at www.usdoj.gov/olp/lawful.pdf.

[18] See, e.g., Memorandum from General Counsel, National Security Law Unit, Federal Bureau of Investigation, to All Field Offices National Security Letter Matters, Ref: 66F-HQ-A1255972 Serial 15, 28 November 2001, available at sccounty01.co.santa-cruz.ca.us/ bds/govstream/BDSvData/non_legacy/Minutes/2003/20030429/PDF/084.pdf.

While the above examples focus on the transplantation from counter-terrorist law to criminal law, such transfers mark civil law as well. Anti-terrorist finance provisions in the United Kingdom, for instance, quickly became applied to civil forfeiture in regard to money laundering.[19]

Transplantation, moreover, does not just take place in the transfer of counter-terrorism to criminal or civil law. And here we have the fourth manner in which transplantation takes place. The reverse also occurs, whereby measures employed in a different context are simply picked up and dropped into a terrorism context. This raises significant concerns about efficacy and appropriateness.

In the criminal law realm, the assumption is that what may useful for countering crime, presents a sort of minimum – such that its application to counter-terrorism is unquestioned. The problem is that the terrorist threat may be entirely different from criminal enterprise. This is not to say that it is always the case that the two represent separate phenomena. Terrorist organisations may engage in a significant amount of criminal activity. But before simply assuming that criminal devices should be used, prior thinking that takes values in other spheres and compels careful consideration is necessary.

In the national security realm, a similar assumption applies: i.e., that the type of threat for which the initial provisions were appropriate are commensurate with the terrorist threat – and that such provisions will be appropriate for counter-terrorism. Such assumptions, however, may be both inaccurate and dangerous in their failure to consider the unique challenges posed by the threat. Section 3 of this chapter provides further examples of substantive transplantation and the attendant negative effects, in the case of the counter-terrorism–criminal law transfer, on both areas, as well as, in the national security domain, the unintended consequences that may ensue.

B. Geographic transplantation

In addition to substantive transplantation, a growing body of law suggests greater movement towards geographic transplantation of counter-terrorist measures. Much of the focus has been across country borders; however, such transfer works at both an international and a domestic level.[20]

---

[19] See Donohue, 'Terrorism and the counter-terrorist discourse'.

[20] See Laura K. Donohue and Juliette Kayyem, 'Federalism and the battle over counter-terrorist law: state sovereignty, criminal law enforcement, and national security' (2002) 25 *Studies in Conflict and Terrorism* 1 (discussing the various state measures introduced in the United States prior to 9/11).

Traditionally, international comparative law has focused on three devices at work in regard to both statutory and constitutional transplantation: the tendency of related countries to adopt similar measures, the influence of countries with more sophisticated legal systems on developing countries and the tendency of some countries to simply mirror, in their own legal code, laws observed in other states.[21] Transplantation via each of these devices occurs with some regularity in counter-terrorist law.

For example, as Roach notes elsewhere, the UK's Terrorism Act 2000 influenced the evolution of anti-terrorism legislation in Australia, Canada, Hong Kong, Indonesia, South Africa and elsewhere.[22] The Commonwealth countries that altered their legal regimes to reflect Britain's legislation share a common history, language and, in many respects, legal structure. Other initiatives reflect the device framed by legal sophistication: the UK's national security strategy addresses this directly, proposing, as a means of countering terrorism, developing laws in fragile states, as a form of early engagement.[23] The US Department of State similarly has convened numerous international conferences to encourage newly developing states to adopt stronger counter-terrorist regimes. Yet further instances of states mirroring other country's initiatives abound.

The concerns raised such by convergences are significant. As Ramraj points out, such legal norms are realised in profoundly asymmetrical ways.[24] The exercise of Russian counter-terrorist law in Chechnya provides a salient example. New legislation introduced in the wake of 9/11,

---

[21] See Kim Lane Scheppele, 'The international standardization of national security law' (2010) 4(2) *Journal of National Security Law and Policy* 438, citing Alan Watson, *Legal Transplants*; Michele Graziadei, 'Comparative law as the study of transplants and receptions', in Mathias Reimann and Reinhard Zimmermann (eds.) *Oxford Handbook of Comparative Law* (Oxford University Press, 2006), p. 441; 'Symposium: Constitutional Borrowing' (2003) 1(2) *International Journal of Constitutional Law* 177; Sujit Choudhry (ed.), *The Migration of Constitutional Ideas* (Cambridge University Press, 2006). For a sceptical view of 'the reality of "legal transplants"' see Legrand, 'The impossibility of "legal transplants"', 113, 116 (writing, 'there could only occur a meaningful "legal transplant" when both the propositional statement as such and its invested meaning – which jointly constitute the rule are transported from one culture to another. Given that the meaning invested into the rule is itself culture-specific, it is difficult to conceive, however, how this could ever happen.')

[22] Kent Roach, 'The post-9/11 migration of Britain's Terrorism Act 2000', in Choudhry, *The Migration of Constitutional Ideas*, p. 374.

[23] United Kingdom Government, *The National Security Strategy of the United Kingdom: Security in an Interdependent World* (Cm 7291, March 2008), pp. 2, 7, available at interactive.cabinetoffice.gov.uk/documents/security/national_security_strategy.pdf.

[24] Victor V. Ramraj, Chapter 3, this volume.

On Countering Extremist Activities, was soon followed by a Federal Law, On Counteraction to Terrorism. These measures legalised the application of armed force for counter-terrorism operations in the North Caucasus and suspended a broad range of individual rights – which quickly earned for Russia the enmity of human rights organisations.[25] Although the counter-terrorism campaign ended in 2009, following further terrorist attacks, Russian President Dmitry Medvedev announced in 2010 that additional counter-terrorist laws were needed. The Russian Foreign Minister quickly linked the recent attacks to a global counter-terrorist threat, while the chairman of the G8 foreign ministers, Canadian Foreign Minister Lawrence Cannon, vowed in solidarity that the G8 'would continue to collaborate to thwart and constrain terrorists'.[26] He reiterated the G8 foreign ministers' 'commitment to further enhance the central role of the United Nations and to adhere to its Global Counter-terrorism Strategy and relevant United Nations Security Council resolutions'.[27]

Cannon's remarks point to a fourth device by which geographic transplantation occurs and which has received less notice: the (increasingly) coercive role of international organisations in *requiring* countries to adopt certain types of provisions. Scheppele highlights this shift specifically in regard to the UN Security Council Resolution 1373.[28] This measure, discussed also in detail by Powell requires states to address terrorist finance by creating new anti-terrorist finance criminal provisions, freezing the assets of individuals or entities engaged in terrorism and preventing contributions to terrorist organisations.[29] States themselves must refrain from supporting terrorism and take affirmative steps to prosecute any individuals suspected of terrorism found within domestic bounds.[30]

---

[25] See, e.g., Human Rights First, 'Russia's new direction', available at www.humanrightsfirst.org/wp-content/uploads/pdf/06622-hrd-russia-update-web.pdf; Mariya Y. Omelicheva, 'Russia's counterterrorism policy: variations on an imperial theme' (2009) 3(1) *Perspectives on Terrorism* 3.

[26] 'Suppression of terrorism in Russia will continue – Medvedev', *RT*, 30 March 2010, available at rt.com/news/moscow-blast-emergency-meeting/; 'G8 stands with Russia in fight against terrorism', *The Economic Times*, 30 March 2010, available at economictimes.indiatimes.com/news/politics/nation/G8-stands-with-Russia-in-fight-against-terrorism/articleshow/5741325.cms.

[27] 'G8 Stands with Russia in fight Against Terrorism'.

[28] S/RES/1373(2001); Scheppele, 'The international standardization of national security law', 439–43; Powell, Chapter 2, this volume. See also Victor V. Ramraj, Chapter 3, this volume.

[29] C. H. Powell, Chapter 2, this volume. See also Victor V. Ramraj, Chapter 3, this volume. UN Security Council Resolution 1373, art. 1.

[30] SCR 1373, art. 2.

The United Nations is not the only body to engage in coercive action to ensure geographic transplantation of counter-terrorist law. The Financial Action Task Force (FATF), for instance, is 'an inter-governmental body whose purpose is the development and promotion of national and international policies to combat money laundering and terrorist financing.'[31] Established in 1989 by the G7 Summit, the mission of the organisation is to monitor members' progress in implementing necessary measures and to promote the adoption of anti-terrorist finance measures globally.[32] Thirty-four countries and two regional organisations, representing most major financial centers in the world, are members.[33]

The FATF has adopted specific standards to address money laundering and terrorist finance. For the latter, the organisation recommends (and monitors), the ratification and implementation of UN instruments, criminalising the financing of terrorism, freezing and confiscating terrorist assets, reporting suspicious transactions related to terrorism, engaging in international co-operation, restricting alternative remittance systems, monitoring wire transfers, scrutinising non-profit organisations and placing restrictions on cash couriers. The organisation creates obligations on member states to comply with the recommendations.[34] FATF Special Recommendation III, for instance, on the freezing and confiscation of terrorist assets, 'requires jurisdictions to implement measures that will freeze or, if appropriate, seize terrorist-related funds or other assets without delay in accordance with relevant United Nations Resolutions'.[35]

As Ramraj discusses, despite strong coercive mechanisms, the result of such devices is far from coherent. Part of the difficulty derives from formal distinctions between legal systems, part from the unique histories and cultural and socio-economic conditions of each region, and part

[31] FATF-GAFI, available at www.fatf-gafi.org/pages/0,3417,en_32250379_32236836_1_1_1_1_1,00.html.

[32] Ibid.

[33] Membership includes: Argentina, Australia, Austria, Belgium, Brazil, Canada, China, Denmark, the European Commission, Finland, France, Germany, Greece, the Gulf Co-operation Council, Hong Kong (China), Iceland, India, Ireland, Italy, Japan, the Netherlands, Luxembourg, Mexico, New Zealand, Norway, Portugal, South Korea, Russia, Singapore, South Africa, Spain, Sweden, Switzerland, Turkey, the United Kingdom and the United States: ibid.

[34] For detailed discussion of FATF recommendations, see Kevin E. Davis, Chapter 8, this volume.

[35] Interpretative Note to Special Recommendation III: Freezing and Confiscating Terrorist Assets, Financial Action Task Force, available at www.fatf-gafi.org/document/44/0,3746, en_32250379_32236920_43751788_1_1_1_1,00.html.

from the vagueness inherent in the concept of terrorism.[36] The types of devices adopted, moreover, may be ripe for abuse. Here, Powell's discussion of the 1267 Committee, and the problems with listing, is particularly valuable.[37]

This particular type of geographic transplantation – i.e. that promoted by coercive international organisations – raises concerns about exactly what is being forced on other countries in the first place. There is significant evidence to suggest that many of the measures driven through international organisations by the United States and the United Kingdom in particular carry enormous costs and themselves have a checkered history in terms of their domestic use prior to their entry on the international stage.[38]

In light of the careful consideration given to UN Security Council Resolutions 1373 and 1540 by Powell, as well as the careful analysis of Resolution 1373 by Ramraj, I focus in the next section on examples of substantive domestic transplantation, both between counter-terrorist law and criminal law, and within the national security realm, as a way of illustrating the considerable difficulties that accompany the transplantation of such authorities.

3. Substantive transplantation: between criminal law and counter-terrorism

Anti-terrorist finance in the United States and the United Kingdom provides a good example of how transplantation between counter-terrorist, criminal and civil law proves concerning.[39] I will here focus more narrowly on the United States and the interplay between the counter-terrorist and criminal law realms, where a considerable amount of activity has occurred.

Executive Order 13224, for instance, introduced by President Bush just after 9/11, established a Specially Designated Global Terrorists list, blocking 'all property and interests in property' of those providing material support to terrorism. Any business that interacts with targets can itself

---

[36] Victory V. Ramraj, Chapter 3, this volume.
[37] C. H. Powell, Chapter 2, this volume.
[38] See generally Donohue, 'Terrorism and the counter-terrorist discourse'.
[39] The following discussion draws heavily from Donohue, *The Cost of Counterterrorism*, Chapter 6. See also Kent Roach, Chapter 5, this volume (discussing the use of criminal law in the counter-terrorism realm and over-broad definitions of terrorism that expand counter-terrorism into the criminal law realm).

be listed and have its assets frozen. Under the Patriot Act, assets can be blocked pending an investigation – allowing the Treasury to indefinitely freeze the assets of those not yet listed but under review.

The state can also pursue criminal conviction through the courts for providing material support to terrorism.[40] The Secretary of State designates groups considered Foreign Terrorist Organizations (FTOs), thereby blocking financial institutions from handling any of their assets.[41] The number of designated foreign terrorist organisations has nearly doubled since 9/11 – there are currently nearly four dozen FTOs, and scores of terrorism cases post-9/11 have included charges related to the provision of material support.[42]

To identify potential targets, the state relies on both private sector information and intelligence. As a result, the law has expanded in two areas: reporting requirements and surveillance authorities. Title III of the Patriot Act, for instance, expanded the number of institutions required to file suspicious activity reports (SARs). It also significantly broadened due diligence provisions, which had previously been *rejected* for the criminal realm, requiring that a broader range of financial institutions collect more customer information, quite independent of whether the concern was criminal or terrorist in nature.

Surveillance authorities embedded in the Patriot Act were soon broadly applied to the financial industry, further blurring the distinction between anti-terrorist finance and anti-money laundering investigations. Just after 9/11, for instance, the Administration served a National Security Letter on a Belgian banking co-operative called Swift, which routes approximately $6 trillion per day between thousands of financial institutions worldwide. The programme collected information on international transactions, including those entering and leaving the United States.

Looked at solely in regard to counter-terrorism, it could be argued that the use of criminal measures in the counter-terrorism realm carried a number of advantages. The aim was to tighten the regulated sector, to make it more difficult to move terrorist money through conventional

---

[40] 18 USC §2339.

[41] 18 USC §2339B(a)(1); see also 8 USC §1189 and Immigration and Nationality Act, §219 (as amended).

[42] Foreign Terrorist Organizations, Office of the Coordinator for Counterterrorism, 24 November 2010, available at www.state.gov/s/ct/rls/other/des/123085.htm. See also 'Supreme Court upholds PATRIOT Act's "material support" provision', *Examiner.com*, 21 June 2010, (stating approximately 150 prosecutions under the material support provisions of the Patriot Act since 2001).

means. There is some evidence that this occurred. The approach also discouraged contributions to suspect individuals, charities and regions. It was international in reach – and terrorist organisations operate in the global environment. And it adapted existing institutions, suggesting less of a start-up cost to go after terrorist funds. At the same time, it could be argued that the due diligence requirements and the loosened controls on surveillance went some way towards bolstering the state's ability to identify criminal activity more broadly.

However, the transplantation of financial measures carried substantial drawbacks. Significant constitutional and legal concerns presented themselves, such as the weak standard of judicial review under the Administrative Procedure Act, equal protection claims, procedural due process violations and the possibility that some of the measures (e.g. in regard to the IEEPA and Executive Order 13224) were *ultra vires* the governing law. Perhaps most concerning, however, was the extent to which important policy goals were undermined by the wholesale transplantation of criminal provisions: i.e. anti-money laundering devices, in many ways, prove particularly ill-suited to anti-terrorist finance.

There are important structural differences between the underlying behaviour of each.[43] As discussed in *The Cost of Counterterrorism*, money laundering depends upon an underlying crime.[44] Terrorist finance does not. Put somewhat crudely, the former takes dirty money and tries to make it clean, whereas the latter often takes clean money (e.g. a contribution to a charitable organisation) and tries to make it dirty – that is, use it to fund violent attacks. This means that victims who otherwise might alert law enforcement to criminal activity are unlikely to come forward. They may not know where their money is going, or they may know and be afraid of the terrorists – or of the state prosecuting them.

There are no good algorithms to determine who is a terrorist. Unlike those involved in organised crime, terrorists tend not to have previous criminal convictions. They avoid living conspicuous lifestyles, and identifying terrorists through transaction patterns proves extremely difficult: thus New York Clearinghouse, an organisation of the largest money-centre banks, concluded, after a post-9/11 two-year study, that it cannot be done.[45] The Financial Actions Task Force, despite significant efforts to develop an appropriate typology, reached a similar conclusion.[46]

---

[43] See Donohue, 'Terrorism and the counter-terrorist discourse'.
[44] The following discussion comes directly from *The Cost of Counterterrorism*, Chapter 6.
[45] Staff Report, 9/11 Commission; Donohue, *The Cost of Counterterrorism*, Chapter 6.
[46] 2003 Financial Action Task Force Report, p. 4, [10]. See also Financial Action Task Force on Money Laundering, *Report on Money Laundering Typologies: 2001–2002* (2002), p. 6.

As for the volume of money involved, the International Monetary Fund puts the total money laundered globally each year at around US $600 billion. In contrast, terrorists require significantly less money – suggesting that devices aimed at intercepting major transfers will miss the movement of terrorist funds.

Stopping money from flowing through the regulated sector by freezing it or by introducing sweeping regulations, moreover, undermines an important national security aim: obtaining information about the threat. Indeed, because of post-9/11 measures, while the initial aim of tightening the regulated sector may have succeeded, unintended consequences followed. Terrorist networks began turning to alternative remittance systems, such as *hawaladars* and couriers, as well as harder-to-trace commodities, to move their wealth.[47] These avenues made it harder for the government to trace funds and find those responsible for terrorist violence.

Even the manner in which success is determined radically differs between the different emphases. Despite the fundamental difference in the nature of the threat, accounting measures in the anti-terrorist finance realm rely on traditional money-laundering metrics to gauge success, such as the number of states with blocking orders in force, the number of entities with seized assets and the value of money frozen. These standards, though, are out of synch with what may be the most effective indicators of success for counter-terrorism – e.g. the conviction rate of those responsible for supplying money, the level within the terrorist network of those apprehended or the number of operations thereby aborted.

Structural differences also play out in bureaucratic gridlock. Consider SARs – a standard anti-money laundering device now used for anti-terrorist finance. SARs did not discover – nor should they have discovered, nor would they now discover – any of the financial activity in which the 9/11 hijackers engaged.[48] Title III of the Patriot Act, however, as

---

[47] See, e.g., *Underground Finance Mechanisms: Hearing Before the Subcommittee on Banking, Housing and Urban Affairs, Subcommittee on International Trade and Finance of the Subcommittee on Banking, Housing and Urban Affairs*, 107th Congress 1. See also 'Moving Target', *The Economist* (US), 14 September 2002; 'Still Flush', *The Economist*, 7 September 2002.

[48] Donohue, *The Cost of Counterterrorism*, Chapter 6. Al-Qaeda moved the money to fund the 9/11 attacks in three ways: US $130,000 was wired to hijackers in the United States from the United Arab Emirates and Germany; members physically carried cash/traveller's cheques to the United States; and some established overseas accounts, which they drew on via ATM or credit cards in the United States. When they arrived in the United States, they opened bank accounts under their real names in both large national banks and smaller regional ones. While they lived in the United States, they made wire transfers

previously mentioned, expanded the number of organisations required to file SARs, increasing the number of annual filing in the United States from approximately 163,000 in 2000 to nearly 920,000 by 2005. This made it difficult not just to find terrorists, but to go after ordinary money launderers. Accordingly, across the Atlantic, where the same pattern played out, an independent audit of SARs by KPMG International raised concern about the low signal-to-noise ratio and the tendency of entities to over-report.[49]

The filing of SARs, moreover, appeared to be tied to the political environment. States, which are privy to classified intelligence material, are more likely than banks to know the identity of terrorist suspects. Without this information, and lacking a reliable algorithm, financial institutions began reverting to racial profiling.

A final, and important, point to make in respect to the application of money laundering devices to anti-terrorist finance is that, as a result of the new regulatory environment and its associated costs, we have seen a drying up of remittances – money flowing from charities and expat communities – to Islamic regions. The United States, however, has a strong interest in ensuring that many of these regions remain economically viable and tied to US influence as a way to prevent the creation of a vacuum into which extremist movements can move.

While this example demonstrates the difficulties that characterise domestic substantive transplantation, it is worth noting that it is precisely the domestic measures considered above that form the framework for US efforts to drive global provisions through international organisations. UN Security Council Resolution 1373 sought to make many of the anti-terrorist finance measures universal. This simply adds another layer of complexity – and concern – to the issues that accompany the geographic transplantation of counter-terrorist law.

---

of between US $5,000 and US $70,000, making the transactions virtually invisible in comparison to the billions of dollars moving daily through the international financial system. Their banking pattern – depositing a significant amount of money and then making smaller withdrawals – fit their student profiles. They did not use false social security numbers and their grasp of the US banking system was not particularly sophisticated. Staff Report, 9/11 Commission, p. 53. See also Michael Peel and John Willman, 'The dirty money that is hardest to clean up: financial institutions are keen to eradicate money-laundering by terrorists and to freeze assets', *Financial Times*, (London), 20 November 2001, p. 16. See also discussion in Donohue, 'Terrorism and the counter-terrorist discourse'.

[49] Privy Counsellor Review Committee, *Anti-Terrorism, Crime and Security Act 2001 Review: Report Presented to Parliament Pursuant to s. 122(5) of the Anti-terrorism, Crime and Security Act 2002* (18 December 2003), HC 100.

4. Substantive transplantation: from nuclear
to biological security

It could be argued that one of the reasons criminal law measures prove so ill-fitting in the counter-terrorist realm is because the threat posed by terrorism is closer to national security than to criminal law. This argument is not without its opponents – particularly in regard to extended detention or coercive interrogation. But let us consider a stronger and even narrower parallel: the potential terrorist use of weapons of mass destruction. The threats posed by nuclear or biological terrorism may be seen as similar. Both clearly fall within a national security realm, both depend upon constantly evolving technologies, both have been sought by terrorist organisations and use of either could result in the massive loss of human life. Yet even here, the tranplantation of specific devices proves concerning.

Speech restrictions serve to illustrate the point. In the United States, the Atomic Energy Act of 1946 controls nuclear information. Under this legislation, all atomic discoveries, even if funded and discovered by private citizens – without any government funding or information – are classified from birth. Restricted data includes all information concerning the design, manufacture or utilisation of atomic weapons, the production of nuclear material, or the use of nuclear material in the production of energy.[50]

Efforts to transplant similar restrictions to microbiology have begun. The pressure to do so derives from the threat perceived in relation to biological weapons. Since the end of the Cold War, concern has increased about the potential for materials and knowledge to proliferate beyond industrialised states' control, and for 'rogue states' or non-state actors to acquire and use biological weapons.[51] The broad concern about

---

[50] Atomic Energy Act of 1954, §11(y).

[51] See, e.g., The National Security Strategy of the United States of America (September 2002), available at www.whitehouse.gov/nsc/nss.pdf (stating, 'With the collapse of the Soviet Union and the end of the Cold War, our security environment has undergone profound transformation. [...] [N]ew deadly challenges have emerged from rogue states and terrorists. ... [T]he nature and motivations of these new adversaries, their determination to obtain destructive powers hitherto available only to the world's strongest states, and the greater likelihood that they will use weapons of mass destruction against us, make today's security environment more complex and dangerous.') Accordingly, in 1993 Senators Samuel Nunn (D-GA), Richard Lugar (R-IN), and Pete Dominici (R-NM) expanded the Cooperative Threat Reduction Program to assist the former Soviet republics in securing not just fissile material, but biological agents and weapons knowledge.

the biological weapons threat has been punctuated by actual terrorist acquisition and use of non-conventional weapons.[52]

From previously a dozen or so investigations per year, in 1997 the FBI opened seventy-four investigations relating to the possible acquisition and use of chemical, biological, radiologic and nuclear materials; and in 1998, 181. Eighty per cent of the cases turned out to be hoaxes, but a significant number were unsuccessful attacks.[53] By 31 January 1999, Monterey Institute for International Studies had compiled an open-source database of 415 incidents – most of which occurred towards the end of the twentieth century – where terrorists had sought to acquire or use weapons of mass destruction. These developments pre-dated the attacks of 9/11 and al Qaeda's stated intent to use biological weapons in the future, backed by actual efforts to obtain biological agents.[54] The anthrax attacks in autumn 2001 further underscored the threat, killing five people and infecting eighteen others.[55]

In the midst of growing concern about biological weapons, attention was drawn to an experiment conducted in Australia and published in the United States – and the question arose as to whether the censorship

The Defense Against Weapons of Mass Destruction Act gave the Pentagon lead agency responsibility for biological matters: Title XIV, National Defense Authorization Act for FY 1997.

[52] E.g., in 1994 Aum Shinrikyo released sarin gas in Nagano and, in 1995, on the Tokyo subway, killing twelve people and causing an estimated 6,000 people to seek medical attention. When the police raided the cult's shrines, they found that the cult also cultured and experimented with botulinum toxin, anthrax, cholera and Q fever: Jonathan B. Tucker, 'Historical trends related to bio-terrorism: an empirical analysis', *Emerging Infectious Diseases*, available at www.cdc.gov/ncidod/eid/vol5no4/tucker.htm. See also Mark Fenwick, Chapter 16, this volume. In February 1998, Larry Wayne Harris boasted to an informant that he had enough military-grade anthrax to wipe out Las Vegas. Eight bags marked 'biological' had been found in the back of a car he had been driving: Tucker, 'Historical trends related to bio-terrorism', Table 1.

[53] J. Parker-Tursman, 'FBI briefed on district's terror curbs', *Pittsburgh Post-Gazette*, 5 May 1999; and 'Weiner T. Reno says U.S. may stockpile medicine for terrorist attacks', *New York Times*, 23 April 1998, A:12.

[54] Remarks by Homeland Security Secretary Michael Chertoff at the Stanford Constitutional Law Center's Germ Warfare, Contagious Disease, and the constitution Conference, Washington, DC, 11 April 2008, available at www.dhs.gov/xnews/speeches/sp_1208283625146.shtm (stating 'We know, for example, in the late 1990s, al-Qaeda became focused on developing a biological weapons program. After the invasion of Afghanistan, we determined that there was a low-tech facility in Kandahar, which was actually aimed at producing anthrax and the purpose obviously was to create a weapon.'

[55] American Association for the Advancement of Science, 'Science and security in the post-9/11 environment: bioterrorism', available at www.aaas.org/spp/post911/agents/.

laws surrounding nuclear material should be transplanted to a biological realm.

The Australian case stemmed from a non-terrorist, indeed, an economic concern: on a cyclical basis, Australia suffers from a rodent infestation, which devastates the crops and takes a considerable toll on the gross domestic product of the country. In 1998 some Australian scientists decided to try to engineer a biological disease – they did not want to kill the rodents, because this would have created a problem with disease. Instead, they chose Mousepox, a highly virulent disease, and attached a secondary disease to make it impossible for the rodents to reproduce. After extensive experiments, the scientists found, much to their surprise, that in making the disease effective even against rats with immune systems that rejected Mousepox, they ended up with a disease that was 100 per cent virulent – and fatal. What made their findings particularly salient in the counter-terrorism realm is that Mousepox is closely linked to Smallpox – one of the most devastating diseases in the history of humankind, responsible for killing some 500 million people in the twentieth century alone.[56]

The researchers were faced with a difficult decision: publish the information and risk transferring potentially deadly information to individuals bent on destruction, or keep the information private and risk not finding a way to respond to the vulnerability. The researchers initially decided to bring the risk to the attention of the authorities privately. After the Australian military dragged its heels, however, the researchers published a paper in the *Journal of Virology*, an American journal of the American Society for Microbiology (ASM).[57] Initially the publication attracted little attention, but following the anthrax mailings in autumn 2001, the incident attracted the attention of the President and members of Congress. The fact that the experiment, which had achieved a devastating lethality, required just three feet of countertop and basic knowledge of microbiology to perform heightened concern about terrorist acquisition of scientific information.

In the face of increasing pressure, Dr Ronald Atlas, the President of the American Society of Microbiology, contacted the Chair of the ASM publishing board and reported that the Bush Administration was concerned

---

[56] 147 *Congressional Record*, S. 12378 (statement of Senator Joseph Lieberman regarding S. 1764).

[57] Ronald J. Jackson *et al.*, 'Expression of a Mouse Interleukin-4 by a Recombinant Ectromelia Virus Suppresses Cytolytic Lymphocyte Responses and Overcomes Genetic Resistance to Mousepox' (2001) 75 *Journal of Virology* 1205.

about ASM's decision to publish the Mousepox article. ASM convened a meeting of its publishing board and changed its internal review policies to focus on the national security implications of future articles. While ASM's decision headed off any formal legislation, there may be little, as a constitutional matter, to prevent Congress from passing stringent laws limiting microbiologists from being able to publish information that would be particularly helpful to terrorists.[58]

As a policy matter, however, the decision to transplant such restrictions from the nuclear realm to the biological realm would be fraught with danger. Microbiology is not a field amenable to compartmentalisation. Incremental discoveries, which require public airing, may yield a series of unintended insights into a wide range of threats to public health. Extremely valuable information, moreover, might be obtained from studying particularly virulent diseases – and then allowing such discoveries to be subjected to broader scrutiny. Many of the diseases that have been weaponised by state biological weapons programmes stem from natural sources – suggesting that (with the exception of Smallpox), their occurrence in nature may present an equally grave threat. By restricting research in microbiology, the government may end up damaging its ability to respond to naturally occurring outbreaks of disease.

Efforts to isolate the 'purpose of research' as a trigger for speech restrictions, moreover, would prove difficult. Information that finds how a disease works could be used to find a treatment – or cure – for a disease. Similarly, efforts to narrow restrictions to the 'type of research' engaged in fails: how can it be ascertained at the outset of a scientific experiment which approach is more or less likely to yield bad results? It may be, for instance, that genetic manipulation may be unlikely to occur naturally; however, preventing scientists from engaging in research in this area because of national security considerations may prevent a government from being able to ensure the general health of the population.

Initiatives restricting speech, moreover, may negate other efforts to improve national security. If it is in the country's best interests to encourage microbiologists to look at the threats posed by disease, acting to classify such discoveries immediately upon recognition discourages such research. Further, such restrictions may force scientists out of the country and encourage them to go to regions where fewer restrictions will be placed on their ability to perform basic science. In sum, the costs could be

---

[58] See Donohue, 'Terrorism and the counter-terrorist discourse'.

considerable, with a significantly different impact than the introduction of similar measures in the nuclear realm.

5. Conclusion

In both substantive and geographic transplantation, prudence dictates not that such transplantation never occur, but that such measures be considered in their original constitutional, legal, political and instrumental context and, equally carefully, in the context of the particular realm to which they are being transferred. I thus conclude by suggesting a tripartite *ex ante* inspection, based on the concerns raised above (in both the typology and the examples provided), as a way to identify potential pitfalls. The aim is to take account of the values and the impact of the provisions in the realm whence the provisions derive as well as the area to which they are transplanted.

The first step would be to consider the values applied in the parallel sphere. The inquiry here takes three forms: what is the underlying rationale of the previous regime? If the aim, for instance, is to ensure due process of law while preventing the use of funds for nefarious means – or, to the contrary – to relax due process to allow for greater flexibility, then such a value needs to be identified. The question then becomes, what distortion may result to the pre-existing legal regime to which such measures are being transferred? The purpose of such an inquiry is to head off the potential weakening of values that may occur. Next, one could consider how the terrorist threat itself may have altered the underlying values. By directly addressing this question, the tendency to put off such considerations, prevalent in the counter-terrorist spiral identified at the outset of this piece – e.g. through the imposition of temporary provisions – may be avoided. This discussion would force a difficult conversation to the fore. Such an audit may help to preserve the values of the systems themselves – for instance, by identifying points of discrepancy and considering how the new measures fit in to the overall values of the legal regime, as well as what shifts may be occurring.

The second step would be to employ a sort of Kantian condition of publicity.[59] This step takes account of the tendency of counter-terrorist

---

[59] Immanuel Kant, *Perpetual Peace: A Philosopical Essay* (1795), Translated with Introduction and Notes by M. Campbell Smith (London: Swan Sonnenschein & Co, 1903) p. 381; David Luban, 'The principle of publicity', in Robert E. Goodin (ed.), *The Theory of Institutional Design*, (Cambridge University Press, 1996), p. 155 ('All actions relating to the right of other human beings are wrong if their maxim is incompatible with publicity').

law to have a direct impact on individual rights. In the transplantation of the measures, is their use and implementation sufficiently transparent to ensure accountability? This proves equally important for measures developed within counter-terrorist law and transferred to other areas and vice versa, as well as for geographic transplantation. It recognises the disparate implementation of measures that cross international borders – either through the first three devices considered above (common ancestry, sophisticated to developing legal systems and mirroring), as well as through the coercive international instruments that are increasingly marking this realm. What makes this condition particularly important is the isolation of rules from their original context. The constitutional, judicial and legislative constraints that might be at play in the original context may shift. Absent the transplantation of the legal culture, distortions occur.

The third inquiry would turn on the effectiveness of the new measures. This divides into three concerns: do the measures themselves actually do any good against the threat towards which they are directed? With the concerns posed by the anti-terrorist finance example in mind, does using them in the new realm interfere with the state's effectiveness in the previous regime? And does their application in the new context have detrimental effects well beyond any of the two spheres considered? Posing such questions *ex ante* may go some way towards illuminating the potential concerns that accompany the transplantation of counter-terrorist law.

PART II

Cross-cutting themes

5

The criminal law and its less restrained alternatives

KENT ROACH

1. Introduction

Many societies instinctively and quickly reach for the criminal law as a response to terrorism. The first part of this chapter will explore the many dangers of relying on new and re-enforced criminal laws as the main response to terrorism. In the aftermath of 9/11, UN Security Council Resolution 1373 (2001) encouraged nations to enact new laws against terrorism without offering any guidance about how terrorism should be defined. The result was extremely broad definitions of terrorism that attempt to respond to the many vulnerabilities of modern society, but also blur the boundaries between terrorism and illegal, but non-violent, forms of dissent. These dangers have been aggravated by Security Council Resolution 1624 (2005), which calls on states to prohibit speech that incites terrorism. Terrorism offences that require only acts of material support, financing, membership, participation or association in listed or broadly defined terrorist groups strain traditional criminal law understandings of the need to prove criminal acts and fault beyond a reasonable doubt before applying society's strongest sanction. Terrorist trials, featuring multiple counts and multiple accused, evidence relating to the politics and religion of the accused, frequent applications to close courts and to order non-disclosure of secret intelligence and the use of anonymous witnesses produce a danger of wrongful convictions. In short, there are many risks in using the criminal law to respond to terrorism.

The post-9/11 experience, however, underlines that there are even greater risks in using less restrained alternatives to the criminal law to confine and punish suspected terrorists. The less restrained alternatives include indefinite military or administrative/immigration detention or

I thank all those who attended and organised a preliminary conference at the University of New South Wales and in particular Miiko Kumar for valuable comments on an earlier draft.

control orders on the basis of secret evidence, and targeted killings of suspected terrorists. These less restrained alternatives to the criminal law are inspired by the idea that we can no longer afford to rely on the costly, slow and public process of establishing guilt beyond a reasonable doubt in order to incapacitate, punish or deter terrorists. The United States led the way with post-9/11 departures from criminal law with its use of indeterminate detention and military commissions at Guantánamo Bay, Cuba, but many other countries followed suit. The many less restrained alternatives to the criminal law underline the many virtues of the criminal law in insisting on proof of guilt beyond a reasonable doubt through the use of reliable evidence in a public forum. One of the greatest dangers of using the criminal law to respond to terrorism is that the innocent will be wrongfully convicted, as occurred in a number of Irish terrorism cases in Britain in the 1970s. Nevertheless, less restrained alternatives to the criminal law are even more dangerous because they accept false positives and collateral damage as a necessary part of the state's anti-terrorism efforts.

The third part of this chapter will outline how a proper use of the criminal law could fit into more comprehensive strategies to combat terrorism. Criminal law should be used to denounce and punish terrorist violence even if it does not deter. The focus of anti-terrorism laws should, following the general definition of terrorism in the 1999 Convention on the Suppression of Terrorism Financing, be on violence against civilians outside of armed conflict. The state should have to prove a high degree of subjective fault especially as the criminal law legitimately expands to include relatively remote acts of preparation for terrorism. States should not be able to rely on administrative lists of terrorist groups in terrorism prosecutions and instead should have to prove the existence of a particular terrorist group beyond a reasonable doubt. The criminal law can justifiably expand to deal with the harms of terrorism, but states should be careful not to allow a pre-emptive and risk-averse intelligence mindset to distort the criminal law by creating status crimes or crimes based solely on a person's associations. Secret evidence should not be allowed in terrorist trials, but the state should have an opportunity to establish to a judge that non-disclosure or selective redaction of unused but sensitive material is justified and can be reconciled with the accused's right to a fair trial. Although one of the virtues of the criminal law is its ability to conduct a fair and public trial that can convince a sceptical public of the reality of a terrorist threat and its commitment to punish only the guilty, the state should also be able to demonstrate the need to close parts of criminal trials as a proportionate restriction on freedom of expression. The sentence provided for terrorist crimes should not be disproportionate to the accused's actual actions and intent and mandatory sentences may not be appropriate given the breadth of many terrorism offences.

The criminal law can play a unique role in exposing, denouncing and punishing terrorism, but it should only be one element in a comprehensive anti-terrorism strategy. States should also pursue various target-hardening strategies that will feature administrative regulation of sites and substances likely to be used by terrorists. They should also collect intelligence about potential security threats and when necessary engage in intense forms of surveillance, including electronic surveillance. Indeed one key to avoiding the distortion of the criminal law is to understand that some security risks are so ambiguous and remote that they should be subject to surveillance, but not criminalisation. States should also address the causes of extremism and terrorism and also provide for emergency preparedness in order to place terrorism in the context of other threats to human security and to speed recovery from acts of terrorism.

The potential of a public, fair and denunciatory criminal law to de-legitimise terrorism is especially important with respect to home-grown terrorism. That said, there is a danger that the expansion of the criminal law in an attempt to prevent terrorism, as well as innovations in the criminal trial process, may sap the criminal law of its unique and important role in justly stigmatising and punishing those who are intent on committing acts of terrorist violence.

2.   The dangers of distorting the criminal law to respond to terrorism

There is a long history of new criminal laws being enacted as a direct response to horrific acts of terrorism.[1] One danger of reactive legislation is that there may often be inadequate time for debate either in the legislature or in civil society about the proposed measures. The dangers to civil liberties and general principles of criminal law and legality are particularly great when new anti-terrorism laws are enacted as a direct and immediate response to terrible acts of terrorism. New criminal laws may serve

---

[1] Andrew Lynch, Chapter 7 this volume. Philip Thomas, 'Emergency terrorist legislation' (1998) *Journal of Civil Liberties* 240; Philip Thomas, 'September 11 and good governance' (2002) 53 *Northern Ireland Law Quarterly* 366.

what Ackerman has defended as a necessary 'reassurance'[2] function in the wake of traumatic terrorist attacks, but the reassurance may be false if laws are enacted without a full understanding of why the terrorists succeeded and if the laws themselves are politically or legally controversial because they have been developed with inadequate deliberation.

A. Security Council Resolution 1373 and the problematic focus on terrorism financing

On 28 September 2001 and with less than five minutes of public debate, the UN Security Council enacted Resolution 1373 under the mandatory provisions of Chapter VII of the UN Charter relating to the maintenance of international peace and security. In what has aptly been characterised as global legislation,[3] the Security Council required all states to ensure that terrorist acts, including the financing of terrorism, 'are established as serious criminal offences in domestic laws and regulations and that the punishment duly reflects the seriousness of such terrorist acts'.[4] Much of Resolution 1373 contemplated criminalisation and punishment as the primary response to terrorism. This process suggests that the perils of 'governing through crime'[5] and enacting new criminal laws as 'retaliatory measures' designed to 'to respond with immediate effect to public outrage'[6] are not limited to the domestic arena. Although it called on all states to establish 'terrorist acts' as serious criminal offences, Resolution 1373 offered no guidance on the proper definition of terrorism. As will be seen, many states opted for over-broad definitions of terrorism.

The global rush to enact new anti-terrorism laws in response to 9/11 manifests many of the flaws of reactive legislation enacted in response to previous acts of terrorism. Resolution 1373 confirmed the UN's focus on terrorism financing both in the 1999 Convention on Terrorism Financing and the 1267 Committee imposing assets freezes and travel bans on al-Qaeda and the Taliban despite the failure of such measures to prevent 9/11, perhaps the most expensive act of terrorism to date. Terrorism financing laws were

---

[2] Bruce Ackerman, *Before the Next Attack* (New Haven, CT: Yale University Press, 2005), pp. 44–7.
[3] See C.H. Powell, Chapter 2, this volume.
[4] UN Security Council Resolution 1373. See Kim Lane Scheppele, 'Other people's Patriot Acts' (2004) 50 *Loyola Law Review* 89, 91–3.
[5] Jonathan Simon, *Governing Through Crime* (New York: Oxford University Press, 2007).
[6] David Garland, *The Culture of Control: Crime and Social Order in Contemporary Society* (University of Chicago Press, 2001), pp. 11, 133–4.

often based on a money laundering model even though terrorism, unlike organised crime, could be funded by relatively small amounts of money from legitimate sources. The Security Council did not have full information about the causes of 9/11 when it stressed the need for all countries to enact criminal laws including those prohibiting the financing of terrorism. Three years later, however, the 9/11 Commission revealed that what happened that terrible day was not a failure of the criminal law[7] but rather a failure of intelligence co-ordination and distribution. The Commission also concluded that 'trying to starve the terrorists of money is like trying to catch one fish by draining the ocean'.[8]

The objects of terrorist financing laws are not so much terrorists or even their ideological supporters but third parties such as bankers and landlords.[9] Duties were placed on financial institutions and others to report dealings to the authorities. These new laws represented both an expansion of the traditional scope of anti-terrorism laws and the impact of security strategies that relied less on state imposition of punishment and more on risk management strategies throughout society. New laws against the financing of terrorism combine punitiveness on behalf of the state with newer security strategies that deputise third parties, including the private sector, to fight crime.

A problematic feature of terrorism financing laws is that their enforcement by third parties depends on the circulation of lists of terrorists. The UN Security Council had in 1999 established a committee under Security Council Resolution 1267 that compiled lists of individuals associated with the Taliban and al-Qaeda. This list was expanded after 9/11 often at the request of the United States, but many concerns have been raised about the fairness of an intergovernmental process which involves secret intelligence and no due process for individuals. Reliance on lists of terrorists can have a distorting effect on criminal law. Proscription can act as a bill of attainder that can substitute an executive decision taken on the basis of secret evidence for proof beyond a reasonable doubt in a criminal trial.[10] A person or group listed as a terrorist becomes a virtual

---

[7] The conviction of the so-called twentieth hijacker, Zaccarias Moussaoui, for conspiracy to commit murder underlines the ability of pre-9/11 criminal law to punish terrorist plots: *United States* v. *Moussaoui* 591 F 3d 263 (4th Cir. 2010).

[8] The National Commission on Terrorist Attacks upon the United States, *The 9/11 Report* (2004), [12.3].

[9] See Kevin E. Davis, Chapter 8, this volume.

[10] David Paciocco, 'Constitutional casualties of September 11' (2002) 16 *Supreme Court Law Review* (2d) 199.

outlaw. The European Court of Justice in *Kadi* v. *Council of the Europe Union and Commission of the European Communities*[11] found that regulations implementing the Security Council financing regime violated fundamental rights and should be annulled. It noted that there was no effective judicial review at the UN level and that the delisting process remained an intergovernmental one which did not provide the affected individual with a judicial remedy. Similar decisions criticising the listing process have been made by the new UK Supreme Court and by the Federal Court of Canada.[12] The United Nations has attempted several times to reform its listing process, but problems persist given that the Security Council is not likely to abandon control over listing and countries are not likely to consent to disclosing the intelligence behind the listing.[13]

Listing will remain legally problematic, but the disruption and diffusion of al-Qaeda makes it less likely that the United Nations or states can rely on the shortcut of proscription. It is not possible for the executive to proscribe random groups of individuals who may be motivated by al-Qaeda ideology, but have no definite connections to that or other listed terrorist groups. Recent prosecutions of 'home grown' terrorism in many parts of the world have not relied on proscribed groups of terrorists, but instead had to establish that those charged in fact functioned as a terrorist group.

B.   Domestic criminal law responses to 9/11

Resolution 1373 facilitated a pattern of reactive domestic law reform by calling for countries to report back to the Counter-Terrorism Committee within ninety days on the steps taken to comply with the resolution. Some countries took the ninety-day reporting requirement as a virtual deadline for enacting new anti-terrorism laws. Domestic criminal law reform was shaped and speeded up by the Security Council.

The quickest domestic response to 9/11 not surprisingly came from the United States. The Patriot Act was introduced into Congress on 23 October 2001. It was approved by the House of Representatives by a vote of 357–66

---

[11] Joined cases C-402/05 P and C-415/05 P, [2009] AC 1225.

[12] *Abdelrazik* v. *Canada* 2009 FC 580; *Treasury* v. *Ahmed* 2010 UKSC 2.

[13] Christopher Michaelson, 'The Security Council AQ and Taliban sanctions regime: "essential tool" or increasing liability in the UN's counterterrorism efforts?' (2010) 33 *Studies in Conflict and Terrorism* 448; Craig Forcese and Kent Roach, 'Limping into the future: the UN 1267 terrorist listing process at the crossroads' (2010) 42 *George Washington International Law Review* 217.

and by the Senate in a 98–1 vote. It was signed into law by President Bush on 26 October 2001.[14] The Patriot Act responded to Resolution 1373 with a new criminal offence that punished with imprisonment of up to 10 years 'whoever harbors or conceals any person who he knows, or has reasonable grounds to believe, has committed or is about to commit' a long list of offences associated with terrorism. By its use of negligence liability, this offence created the possibility of an accidental terrorist, surely a contradiction in terms.

The Patriot Act demonstrated a faith that broadening and toughening the criminal law will help stop terrorism. The crime of providing material support for terrorism, which was first created in 1996 in the wake of the first World Trade Centre and Oklahoma City bombings, was broadened to include the provision of monetary instruments and 'expert advice and assistance' to terrorists groups. The maximum penalty for this offence was increased from ten to fifteen years with the possibility of life imprisonment if death results.[15] The US Supreme Court upheld this provision in 2010 even while accepting that it could apply to those who provided advice about international law to listed terrorist groups. A majority of the Court concluded that it was impossible to separate support for the violent and non-violent activities of terrorist groups.[16] Most anti-terrorism laws assert universal jurisdiction and this, along with executive proscription of groups, means that financial support and even advocacy for groups in foreign lands may often be a domestic crime. Courts have not shown much attraction to 'freedom fighter' arguments even when terrorism is directed against repressive regimes.[17]

The phenomena of enacting new criminal laws as a response to acts of terrorism was not limited to the West.[18] One study of reports to the

---

[14] John Whitehead and Steven Aden, 'Forfeiting "enduring freedom" for "homeland security"' (2002) 51 *American University Law Review* 1087, 26 ff.

[15] USA PATRIOT Act, ss. 803, 805, 810.

[16] *Holder* v. *Humanitarian Law Project* 561 US_ (2010).

[17] *R* v. *F* [2007] EWCA Crim 243, [31].

[18] Other countries such as Singapore and Malaysia enacted new laws, but relied on the existing Internal Security Act. See Michael Hor, Chapter 11, this volume. Egypt, Syria and Israel all relied on existing laws, but also enacted new terrorism financing and money laundering laws to comply with Resolution 1373. See Lynn Welchman, Chapter 24, this volume; See Daphne Barek-Erez, Chapter 23, this volume. See also Kent Roach *The 9/11 Effect: Comparative Counter-Terrorism* (Cambridge University Press, 2011), Chapter 3 for a discussion of states that relied on old laws to respond to 9/11. Still other states including some African states enacted new laws, but lacked the capacity or the will to enforce the laws. See Chris Oxtoby and C. H. Powell, Chapter 22, this volume. For a discussion of the many different contexts and starting points of various nations in responding to 9/11 and Resolution 1373, see Victor V. Ramraj, Chapter 3, this volume.

Counter-Terrorism Committee concludes that ninety-four states have defined terrorism as a crime since 9/11.[19] A new anti-terrorism law was proposed in Indonesia shortly after 9/11, but met significant resistance in civil society. After the Bali bombings killed over 200 people on 12 October 2002, however, a new anti-terrorism regulation was enacted by presidential decree as an emergency measure on 18 October 2002. Unlike the Patriot Act, the new law was made effective with retroactive force. In July 2004, the Indonesian Constitutional Court held in a 5:4 decision that the law making the new terrorism law retroactive to the Bali bombings violated the prohibition against retroactive punishment in the 1999 Constitution. Indonesia is currently debating new amendments to the law in response to continued terrorism in that country.[20] As was the case with *Moussaoui*,[21] however, the existing criminal law was used to convict the Bali bombers, some of whom were executed. Both Indonesia and the United States turned to instant criminal law reform in the wake of terrible terrorist attacks and relied on broader and tougher criminal law to prevent acts of terrorism.

C. Over-broad definitions of terrorism and the focus on religious and political motives

The failure of Security Council Resolution 1373 to provide any guidance about the proper definition of terrorism reflected the absence of an international consensus. Nevertheless, it is regrettable that the Security Council did not call the attention of states to a generic definition of terrorism contained in the 1999 Convention for the Suppression of Terrorism Financing that stressed the essence of terrorism as the intentional killing of those not involved in armed conflict. Some guidance was finally provided in October 2004 in Resolution 1566, but by that time most new anti-terrorism laws had already been enacted with much broader and more controversial definitions of terrorism.[22]

In the absence of international guidance, many countries looked to the broad definition of terrorist acts in s. 1 of the UK Terrorism Act

---

[19] James Fry, 'The swindle of fragmented criminalization: continuing piecemeal responses to international terrorism and al Qaeda' (2009) 43 *New England Law Review* 424.
[20] See Hikmanto Jurawa, Chapter 12, this volume.
[21] *United States* v. *Moussaoui* 591 F 3d 263 (4th Cir. 2010).
[22] Ben Saul, *Defining Terrorism in International Law* (Oxford University Press, 2006), p. 248.

CRIMINAL LAW AND LESS RESTRAINED ALTERNATIVES   99

2000 as the starting point for their own definitions of terrorism.[23] The UK definition was broader than previous definitions in UK law and defined terrorism to include property damage and interferences with electronic systems. This definition, and in particular the inclusion of damage to electronic systems, recognised the many vulnerabilities of modern society. The British reference to the protection of electronic systems was expanded in Canadian legislation to include interference with all essential public or private services and in Australia by listing many examples of electronic systems. Both Australia and Canada, however, departed from the British example by providing protections for at least some forms of advocacy, strikes and protests. One of the broadest definitions of terrorism was ironically enacted in South Africa where anti-terrorism laws had been used against the African National Congress. In response to this particular history, the South African legislation was named the 2004 Protection of Constitutional Democracy Act and included a broad 'freedom fighter' exemption. Nevertheless, the South African law defined terrorist activities very broadly to include politically motivated acts that seriously disrupt essential public or private services, cause major economic harm or create a serious public emergency situation in order to compel governments to act or to intimidate the public with regard to its security, including its economic security.[24] Such broad definitions recognise the many vulnerabilities of modern society, but they extend the ambit of terrorism laws so that they could apply to illegal but non-violent protest. Broad terrorism offences are often verbally convoluted and thus difficult to explain to the juries or police officers that enforce them.

The danger that anti-terrorism laws could target dissenters was also related to the frequent use of religious and political motive as a feature to distinguish terrorism from other crimes. Although religious and political objectives sociologically motivate most acts of terrorism, the criminal law has traditionally not required proof of motive and took the position that no motive could justify or excuse crime. In Australia, failure to prove religious or political motive has led to acquittals for terrorism offences of

---

[23] Kent Roach, 'The migration of Britain's Terrorism Act, 2000', in Sujit Choudhry (ed.), *The Migration of Constitutional Ideas* (Cambridge University Press, 2006).

[24] Protection of Constitutional Democracy Act No. 33 of 2004, s. 1 (xxv) (South Africa). See Chris Oxtoby and C. H. Powell, Chapter 22, in this volume and Kent Roach 'A comparison of South African and Canadian anti-terrorism legislation' (2005) 18 *South African Journal of Criminal Justice* 127.

those who possessed guns and bombs, but may have been acting for personal as opposed to political reasons.[25]

The requirement for proof of religious or political motive requires police to collect information about a suspect's politics or religion in order to obtain a conviction, even though they might not be adequately trained in distinguishing extremist religious and political views from terrorist intentions. In the case of Maher Arar, the Canadian police wrongly characterised Mr Arar and his wife as 'Islamic extremists' associated with al-Qaeda and then passed on such inflammatory statements to US officials. In its emphasis on the motives of the accused, the accused's past and present associations and training, and remote and non-specific possibilities of harm, much modern anti-terrorism law has incorporated an intelligence mindset.[26] In doing so, there is a danger that terrorism laws will abandon the criminal law's traditional insistence on harm and fault as a basis for just punishment.

Some countries were uneasy with the emphasis on religious and political motives in many new anti-terrorism laws. The Indonesian law enacted after the Bali bombings rejected a previous draft that had defined terrorism as a crime with a political motive and stressed that terrorism should not be considered a political crime and that it should not be applied in a manner that discriminated against any particular religion.[27] Singapore borrowed heavily from the UK definition of terrorism in its post-9/11 terrorism laws, but perhaps in recognition of the religious sensitivities of its significant Muslim minority, it did not duplicate the religious and political motive requirement in new terrorism laws.[28] Perhaps because of concerns about a First Amendment challenge, terrorism was not defined in the Patriot Act by reference to religious or political motive. The US Supreme Court upheld a broad pre-9/11 offence prohibiting material support, but only on

---

[25] Zeky Mallah was acquitted of doing an act in preparation of a terrorist act in relation to his possession of a rifle and ammunition and video threatening to kill ASIO members and John Amundsen had terrorism charges withdrawn after it was discovered that he planned to use home-made bombs for personal reasons related to an ex-girlfriend: Nicola McGarrity, '"Testing our counter-terrorism laws": the prosecution of individuals for terrorism offences in Australia' (2010) 34 *Criminal Law Journal* 95, 104.

[26] On the different values embraced by intelligence about security risks as opposed to evidence about crimes, see Kent Roach 'The eroding distinction between intelligence and evidence in terrorism investigations', in Nicola McGarrity, Andrew Lynch and George Williams (eds.), *Counter-Terrorism and Beyond* (London: Routledge, 2010).

[27] Indonesian Anti-Terrorism Law, arts. 2, 5.

[28] Terrorism (Suppression of Financing) Act 2003, s. 2; Terrorism (Suppression of Bombing) Act 2007, s. 2.

the basis that it did not criminalise membership in a terrorist group or political advocacy independent of the terrorist group.[29] In Canada, an interpretative clause was added to a new Anti-terrorism Act after concerns were raised that the religious and political motive requirement would assist the police in targeting certain minorities. It provided that the expression of religious or political thought in itself would not constitute a terrorist activity.[30] Nevertheless, the trial judge in Canada's first trial under the new provision struck the reference to religious and political motive down as a disproportionate and unnecessary restriction on freedom of religion and speech, but this decision was overturned on appeal.[31]

D.   The expansion of criminal liability: intelligence mindsets and the precautionary principle

The breadth of the definition of terrorism in many post-9/11 laws was enhanced by the broad definition of crimes designed to criminalise even remote acts of preparation for terrorism and broad forms of association with terrorist groups. Laws such as the US offence of material support for terrorism, the Australian offences of possessing things connected with a terrorist act,[32] the UK offence of preparation or training for terrorism[33] and the Canadian offence of participating in a terrorist group or facilitating a terrorist act[34] pushed the boundaries of inchoate and accomplice liability. The potential breadth of the broad Australian offence of associating with a terrorist group is underlined by the need that the drafters felt to exempt interactions with family members, public religious worship and the provision of legal assistance or humanitarian aid.[35] The British offence of withholding information has been applied to convict close family members of terrorists.[36] The breadth of new terrorism offences incorporated both a precautionary principle that sought to criminalise even remote risks before they were actualised and an intelligence mindset that focused on a person's capabilities, motives and associations and did not wait for threats to become imminent.

---

[29] *Holder* v. *Humanitarian Law Project* 561 US_ (2010).
[30] Criminal Code, s. 83.01 (1.1) (Can).
[31] *R* v. *Khawaja* (2006) 214 C C C (3d) 399 (Ont.Sup.Ct.J.) rev'd 2010 ONCA 862 as discussed in Kent Roach, Chapter 20, this volume.
[32] Criminal Code (Aus), s.101.4.   [33] Terrorism Act 2006 (UK), ss. 5–6.
[34] Criminal Code (Can), s.83.18–83.19.   [35] Criminal Code (Aus), s.102.8 (4).
[36] Clive Walker, 'Conscripting the public in terrorism policing' [2010] *Criminal Law Review* 445.

Some terrorism offences are defined in such a broad manner that they resemble both status offences and guilt by association. The most frequently used terrorism offence in the UK is possession of 'an article in circumstances which give rise to a reasonable suspicion that his possession is for a purpose connected with the commission, preparation or instigation of an act of terrorism'.[37] Clive Walker has argued the courts have had 'to slam on the judicial brakes'[38] to prevent this serious offence, punishable by up to fifteen years imprisonment, being applied to possession of innocuous items. Tadros has concluded that such 'flexible laws ... create a high risk of unjust convictions, as well as unjust police intrusion and unjust prosecution'. Even if they make marginal contributions to the prevention of terrorism, they constitute 'an erosion of security from these forms of injustice, especially the security of young Muslim men'.[39] The expansion of post-9/11 terrorism offences also creates a risk of sentences that the public consider too lenient given the emotive terrorist label, or alternatively, sentences that are not lenient but are disproportionate to the actual severity of what the accused did.

Drafters of post-9/11 anti-terrorism laws employed a precautionary principle that went well beyond criminalising violence and often spelled out that a person could be guilty even if he or she did not know the specifics of any particular terrorist activity. In some cases, the new laws invaded on the traditional domain of the judiciary by deeming certain evidence to be admissible and by trying to preclude any attempt by the courts to adopt anything but a broad reading of the offence. One tactic commonly used was to take actions that could normally be evidence of a conspiracy or an attempt and make those actions independent crimes. Such an expansion of the criminal law runs the risk of distortion, especially if the offence also does not require proof of a high degree of fault or if it places onuses on the accused to provide an innocent explanation for ambiguous conduct. To be sure, the drafting of many post-9/11 anti-terrorism laws reflected the reality of what was known about the cell structure of terrorist groups such as al-Qaeda and the fact that a cell might not know the specifics of an attack or of the existence of co-ordinated attacks. Nevertheless, the end result was to create a mass of overlapping crimes targeting preparation

---

[37] Terrorism Act 2000, s. 57; Home Office, *Statistics on Terrorism Arrests and Outcomes in Great Britain* (May 2009), p. 3.

[38] Clive Walker, 'Prosecuting terrorism: the Old Bailey versus Belmarsh' (2009) 79 *Amicus Curiae* 23. On the complexity and breadth of the criminal offences, see Clive Walker, *The Anti-Terrorism Legislation* (Oxford University Press, 2009), Chapter 6.

[39] Victor Tadros, 'Crimes and security' (2008) 71 *Modern Law Review* 969.

and association in a way that strained the criminal law's traditional insistence on proof of harm and fault.

E.   *The difficulties and dangers of the new terrorism trial*

There is a danger that new terrorism offences and new police powers of preventive and investigative arrest will be used as a pretext to disrupt suspected terrorist cells with little or no expectation of subsequent prosecution. From 9/11 to 31 March 2010, 1,834 terrorist arrests were made in Great Britain, but only 35 per cent of those arrests resulted in charges, with 279 being charged with terrorism-related crimes and 143 being charged with non-terrorism-related crimes such as forgery and theft. One thousand people were released without charge.[40] These figures suggest that terrorist arrests may have been used for disruption, destabilisation and intelligence gathering, including the collection of intelligence regarding the religious and political motives and beliefs of detainees and their associates. It also suggests that the US is not alone in using a so-called 'Al Capone strategy'[41] where those suspected of involvement in terrorism are prosecuted for non-terrorist crimes. The low rates of prosecutions also underline that reliance cannot be placed on the criminal courts to provide accountability for the state's intensified national security activities.[42]

When terrorist arrests do result in charges, there appears to be high conviction rates. Europol reported an 83 per cent conviction rate in terrorism trials in 2009, including a 92 per cent conviction rate in France and an 81 per cent conviction rate in the United Kingdom.[43] In the United Kingdom, however, the Home Office estimates a lower conviction rate of about 59 per cent from 2001 to 2010. Interestingly, the conviction rate under terrorism legislation is only 49 per cent while it is 77 per cent under non-terrorism legislation which may suggest some resistance by juries to the attempt in new terrorism legislation to criminalise ambiguous

---

[40] Home Office, *Operation of Police Powers under the Terrorism Act 2000 and Subsequent Legislation* (28 October 2010), [2]–[6] and Table 1.2, p. 15.

[41] On some of the dangers of pretextual 'Al Capone' prosecutions where a person suspected of a serious crime is prosecuted and convicted of a less serious crime, see Daniel Richmond and William Stuntz, 'Al Capone's revenge: an essay on the political economy of pretextual prosecutions' (2005) 105 *Columbia Law Review* 583.

[42] Commission of Inquiry into the Activities of Canadian Officials in Relation to Maher Arar, *A New Review Mechanism for the RCMP's National Security Activities* (Ottawa: Public Works, 2006).

[43] EURPOL, *EU Terrorism Situation and Trend Report* (2010), p. 17 (Figure 6).

conduct that may be very remote from any act of violence.[44] In the United States, an 88 per cent conviction rate has been estimated for 593 completed terrorism prosecutions. As in the United Kingdom, many of these prosecutions were not under terrorism-specific statutes. Unlike in the United Kingdom, however, the average sentence for convictions of non-terrorist offences is much lower: 1.2 years, as opposed to the average sentence of sixteen years for a person convicted of a terrorism offence.[45] This result can perhaps be explained by a greater willingness of US officials to use even minor criminal offences as an Al Capone-type strategy to disrupt suspected terrorists.

The challenges of terrorism prosecutions should not be underestimated. In Canada, a trial in the 1985 Air India bombing case took 217 trial days; involved over 1.5 million pages of disclosure; cost over Can $57 million and resulted in acquittals in 2005 of the two men charged.[46] In Australia, a number of accused have been acquitted of terrorism offences and convicted of less serious offences, in part because of concerns that prosecutors could not establish political or religious motive. In addition, two prosecutions floundered when the judge found statements taken in Australia and in Pakistan were involuntary.[47] In the latter case, the quashing of Jack Thomas's conviction was met less than two weeks later with the issuance of a control order. In this way an administrative measure based on a lower balance of probabilities standard was substituted for the use of the criminal law.[48] Control orders have also been ordered in the United Kingdom against those acquitted of terrorism offences.[49] The

[44] Home Office, *Operation of Police Powers*, [20], [22].

[45] 362 of the 593 resolved prosecutions were for non-terrorism-related offences and these prosecutions were brought under 130 different statutes such as conspiracy, mailing injurious substances, extortion, fraud, false statements, immigration and child pornography: New York University Centre on Law and Security, *Terrorist Trial Report Card* (January 2010), pp. 8–12.

[46] *R v. Malik and Bagri* 2005 BCSC 350; *Report of the Air India Commission* Vol. 3 (2010), pp. 267–79. The cost included Can $21 million in defence funding and Can $22 million for prosecution services including Can $1.7 million for victim services.

[47] *R v. Ul-Haque* (2007) 177 A Crim R 348; *DPP v. Thomas* (2006) 163 A Crim R 567.

[48] Nicola McGarrity, "'Testing our counter-terrorism laws'", 102; Andrew Lynch, 'Australia's "war on terror" reaches the High Court' (2008) 32 *Melbourne University Law Review* 1187–8. In the *Mohammed Haneef* case, his visa was cancelled after he was granted bail. This decision was eventually set aside, but he had already left Australia. The constitutionality of the control order on Thomas was later upheld in a divided High Court decision with the majority stressing that it was within the judicial power to make predictive judgments on the basis of intelligence: *Thomas v. Mowbray* (2007) 233 CLR 307.

[49] *Secretary of State v. AY* [2009] EWCA 3053 (Admin), [196]

threat of less restrained administrative and immigration measures may hang over criminal proceedings if the criminal proceedings do not produce the result desired by the state.

Terrorism trials place greater emphasis on secrecy than other criminal trials. They often feature publication bans and redactions of judgments. Witnesses in terrorism trials have given evidence anonymously and from remote locations. Defence lawyers who delve into matters affecting broadly defined security interests may find themselves in proceedings from which they are excluded and threatened with punishment if they disclose information that the government claims should be secret.[50] Judges who have presided in terrorism trials have expressed frustration about how the hearing of secrecy claims in the absence of the jury and the accused may adversely affect both the fairness and the efficiency of the criminal trial.[51] Public interest immunity applications where the state seeks non-disclosure to the accused of unused but potentially relevant intelligence are a feature of terrorist trials and in most democracies the trial judge has to weigh the competing interests in disclosure or non-disclosure to the accused.[52] In Australia judges are specifically instructed to 'give greatest weight' to 'the risk of prejudice to national security' over the adverse effect of non-disclosure to the accused's fair trial. The Australian approach represents a conscious decision to increase the risk of wrongful convictions by erring on the side of not disclosing intelligence to the accused that may well assist the accused in their defence.[53] States have always had the choice to prioritise their interest in secrecy over their interest in prosecutions,[54]

---

[50] Phillip Boulten, 'Preserving national security in the courtroom: the new battleground' in Andrew Lynch, Edwina Macdonald and George Williams (eds.), *Law and Liberty in the War on Terror* (Sydney: Federation Press, 2007), p. 100.

[51] A. G. Whealy, 'Difficulty in obtaining a fair trial in terrorism cases' (2007) 81 *Australian Law Journal* 743.

[52] For an examination of the role of public interest immunity applications in terrorism trials in Canada, the United States, the United Kingdom and Australia, see Kent Roach, *The Unique Challenges of Terrorism Prosecutions* (Ottawa: Public Works, 2010).

[53] *Lodhi* v. *The Queen* (2007) 179 A Crim R 470, upholding s. 31(8) of the National Security Information (Criminal and Civil Proceedings) Act 2004 (Aus). A retired judge of the Australian High Court has written that the Australian legislation 'does not direct the court to make the order the Attorney-General wants. But it goes as close to it as it thinks it can' and 'in a practical sense directs the outcome of the closed hearing'. Hon Michael McHugh, 'Terrorism legislation and the Constitution' (2006) 28 *Australian Bar Review* 117.

[54] The United States did this when it refused to allow intelligence to be disclosed in a German trial where the conviction of a man for being an accessory to the 9/11 murders was eventually overturned. Helen Duffy, *The 'War' on Terror and the Framework of International Law* (Cambridge University Press, 2005), p. 119.

but the non-disclosure of relevant intelligence to the accused can in some cases result in unfair trials and wrongful convictions.

The risk of wrongful convictions may always be present in terrorism cases. In the United Kingdom, a series of wrongful convictions occurred with respect to IRA bombings. Suspects were identified in part because of their nationality and political sympathies. They were mistreated in custody, made false confessions and did not have adequate disclosure that may have helped cast doubt on the faulty forensic evidence used against them and the false confessions they made.[55] Although there is always a risk of wrongful convictions even under the ordinary criminal law, some features of new anti-terrorism laws produce even greater risks. In other words, many of the predisposing circumstances of wrongful convictions – horrific crimes or threats thereof, prejudice against the suspect, non-disclosure of relevant information, intense pressure on police, prosecutors, judges and juries – will be present in most terrorism prosecutions.[56] Dworkin has eloquently warned of the dangers of concluding that 'the requirements of fairness are fully satisfied, in the case of suspected terrorists, by laxer standards of criminal justice which run an increased risk of convicting innocent people'.[57]

It is important that criminal law not lose sight of its foundational principles such as the presumption of innocence and the necessity of proof of individual fault beyond a reasonable doubt. These demanding standards, however, create another risk, namely that states will find the crime model to be too constraining and weak.[58] When the state goes beyond the criminal law, however, the restraining rules become much less clear and demanding. Indeed, at times, there appear to be no rules at all.

3.   Less restrained alternatives to the criminal law

Although there are many dangers in using the criminal law to combat terrorism, the focus on individual responsibility and deserved punishment

---

[55] Kent Roach and Gary Trotter, 'Miscarriages of justice in the war against terror' (2005) 109 *Penn State Law Review* 976–81.

[56] Ibid.

[57] Ronald Dworkin, 'The threat to patriotism', *New York Review of Books*, 28 February 2002.

[58] For arguments that the crime model is not sufficient to deal with terrorism and new rules are required, see Bruce Ackerman, 'The emergency constitution' (2004) 113 *Yale Law Journal* 1029. For arguments against Ackerman's proposed regime, including its use of preventive detention, see David Cole, 'The priority of morality: the emergency constitution's blind spot' (2004) 113 *Yale Law Journal* 1753.

in the criminal law has many virtues, especially when compared to some of the other techniques that have been used against terrorism. Since 9/11, many countries have chosen to use other instruments that, like the criminal law, rely on coercive force and detention, but do so without most of the safeguards and restraints associated with the criminal law. These less restrained alternatives to the criminal law have included wars in Afghanistan and Iraq, targeted killings,[59] extraordinary rendition to countries with poor human rights records, detention and trial by military commission at Guantánamo Bay, administrative detention and the use of executive measures such as control orders. All of these measures starkly reveal the virtues of the criminal law and the dangers of opting out of, or losing confidence in, the crime model.

In his 2004 State of Union address, President George W. Bush made clear that the United States would not rely on the criminal law in its war against terrorism. He stated:

> I know that some people question if America is really in a war at all. They view terrorism more as a crime, a problem to be solved mainly with law enforcement and indictments. After the World Trade Center was first attacked in 1993, some of the guilty were indicted and tried and convicted, and sent to prison. But the matter was not settled. The terrorists were still training and plotting in other nations, and drawing up more ambitious plans. After the chaos and carnage of September the 11th, it is not enough to serve our enemies with legal papers. The terrorists and their supporters declared war on the United States, and war is what they got.[60]

The idea that it is not 'enough to serve our enemies with legal papers' ran throughout much of the Bush Administration's and subsequently Congress's attempts to preclude habeas corpus review of the Guantánamo detentions. This approach is not as popular as it once was, but impatience and a lack of confidence in the criminal law can still be seen in hostile and successful reactions to the Obama Administration's plans to try terrorists in criminal courts and its continued use of both military commissions and indeterminate detention without trial at Guantánamo as well as targeted killing, including the widely celebrated killing of bin Laden.

---

[59] Plans by both Presidents Clinton and Bush to capture and preferably kill bin Laden before the 9/11 attacks are discussed in *The 9/11 Report*, Chapters 3 and 4. Justice Thomas has expressed concerns in *Hamdi* v. *Rumsfeld* 542 US 507 (2004) that some due process might be required before the US engages in targeted killings abroad (per Thomas J in dissent). But see *Al-Aulaqi* v. *Obama* 2010 US Dist Ct Lexis 129601 dismissing an attempt to judicially review a targeted killing on standing and political questions grounds.

[60] State of the Union Address, 20 January 2004.

A.   Military courts and detention

The US Supreme Court responded negatively to Bush's attempt to create a law-free zone in Guantánamo, first in its decision holding that detainees at Guantánamo could seek habeas corpus in 2004 and eventually in 2008 by holding that the test for suspending habeas corpus had not been satisfied.[61] The Court also held in 2006 that the rules used to review detentions at Guantánamo did not meet the fairness standards required under the Uniform Code of Military Justice or Common Article 3 of the Geneva Conventions, in part because they allowed the use of secret evidence. Although these decisions rejected the extreme claims made by the Bush Administration and the US government eventually released the majority of those held at Guantánamo, they did not insist on the application of criminal law standards to the Guantánamo detainees. A plurality of the Court even approved of robust departures from criminal law standards, such as a rebuttable onus in favour of the government's evidence and trial before a military tribunal. Only Justices Scalia and Stevens, in an interesting alliance between the conservative and liberal wings of the Court, defended the criminal law for American citizens and criticised their colleagues for approving 'an unheard-of system in which the citizen rather than the Government bears the burden of proof, testimony is by hearsay rather than live witnesses, and the presiding officer may well be a "neutral" military officer rather than a judge and jury'.[62]

Although many expected him to abandon military commissions, President Obama has attempted to legitimise them through 2009 enhancements of the 2006 Military Commission Act. The sustained bipartisan desire of the US executive and Congress to depart from reliance on the criminal law is striking in light of the very high conviction rates for terrorism prosecutions in ordinary courts and the ability of the United States to securely imprison over 2 million people. There is a large element of symbolic rejection of criminal justice norms in successful opposition to the attempts to try Khalid Sheik Mohammed (KSM), the alleged mastermind of 9/11, in the ordinary courts in New York and proposals to deprive terrorist suspects of Miranda rights. Other more substantive objections to the use of the criminal law involve concerns about the disclosure of intelligence, but even here there are strong provisions in

---

[61] *Rasul* v. *Bush* 542 US 466 (2004); *Boumediene* v. *Bush* 553 US 723 (2008).
[62] *Hamdi* v. *Rumsfeld* 542 US 507 (2004).

US law that allow for non-disclosure and selective redaction of sensitive material. A more pernicious reason for avoiding the criminal law is that some terrorist suspects, such as KSM [63] and Ahmed Ghailani were tortured when interrogated by the CIA in a manner that might make prosecution in the regular courts difficult and embarrassing.[64] The FBI was excluded from extreme interrogation for intelligence purposes and the torture that was used may have irrevocably severed links with the ordinary criminal courts. Even here, Ghailani's subsequent conviction on one of 280 terrorism counts and his life imprisonment sentence underline the power of criminal prosecutions in the ordinary courts.[65]

The US example of departing from the criminal law has not been lost to the rest of the world. In 2007, Egypt amended its Constitution to ensure that its President would have an explicit constitutional power to refer terrorism cases to military courts or special state security courts. This amendment was criticised on the basis that it could make emergency rule and reliance on special courts in Egypt permanent.[66] Israel has expanded its use of administrative detention since 9/11 relying on the notion that such detention is preventive and is necessary because of the dangers of disclosing intelligence.[67] Singapore and Malaysia have also used the post-9/11 environment to claim legitimacy for detention without trial under their Internal Security Acts.[68] One interesting feature of Singapore's approach, however, is that detainees are released once the authorities have been

---

[63] Jane Mayer, *The Dark Side* (New York: Anchor Books, 2008), pp. 273–9
[64] The judge excluded testimony from a key witness in the *Ghailani* trial because the witness was discovered through harsh interrogation techniques. The jury subsequently acquitted Ghailaini of 280 charges while convicting him of one charge in the 1998 African embassy bombings: 'Terror verdict tests Obama's strategy on trials', *New York Times*, 18 November 2010.
[65] Clyde Haberman 'A verdict replies to terrorists and critics', *New York Times*, 28 January, 2011.
[66] Sideq Reza, 'Endless emergency: the case of Egypt' (2007) 10 *New Law Review* 532. See also Lynn Welchman, Chapter 24, this volume.
[67] See Daphne Barek-Erez, Chapter 23, this volume
[68] See Michael Hor, Chapter 11, this volume. Singapore, in its second report to the Counterterrorism Committee, justified its use of the Internal Security Act as preventive detention without trial on the basis that 'the character of terrorist activities, in particular the planning and preparation of terrorist acts, makes disclosure of intelligence collected as evidence in open court a threat to the sources of information': Singapore Report (S/2002/690), p. 2. Section 10 of Singapore's recent Hostage Taking Act Act 19 of 2010 also recognises the need to protect informers, but unlike the Internal Security Act contemplates that the identity of informers may have to be disclosed if they have made false statements and to ensure that justice is done.

convinced that they have been rehabilitated through the use of religious counselling and after-care.[69] Preventive detention may have its own instrumental, therapeutic and restorative logic at least as practised in Singapore. In Guantánamo, however, it seems to have been implemented in a punitive and haphazard manner that resulted in both the detention of the innocent and the release of others who subsequently engaged in terrorism.

B.   Targeted killings

The Israeli High Court considered targeted killings in a decision rendered in late 2005. The Court rejected the government's arguments that terrorists should be treated as unlawful combatants and affirmed that terrorists were civilians for the purposes of the law of war. At the same time, however, the Court accepted that civilians who directly participated in hostilities could be targeted and defined direct participation broadly to include those who acted as human shields or played an important role in the terrorist organisation.[70] Although criticised,[71] this approach is consistent with the breadth of most criminal laws against terrorism. What is not consistent with any criminal law, however, was the Court's acceptance that collateral damage to innocent civilians would be justified so long as it was proportionate to the military advantage of the killings in protecting civilians and soldiers.[72] The degree of collateral damage is striking with the Court candidly noting that 300 members of terrorist organisations had been killed, but so too had 150 civilians in those attacks.[73] Although the decision attempts to impose legal and institutional restrictions on targeted killings, it is undeniable that it accepts a degree of collateral damage to the innocent that would never be acceptable under the criminal law. The US approach to targeted killing is even more aggressive with the Obama Administration both accelerating the use of targeted killing and successfully resisting attempts to judicially

---

[69] A recent Rand study has reported that 40 out of 60 terrorist detainees have been released under Singapore's sophisticated rehabilitation programme with only one subsequent arrest. Angel Rabasa, Stacie C. Pettyjohn, Jeremy J. Cihez and Christopher Boucek, *Deradicalizing Islamic Extremists* (Santa Monica, CA: Rand Corporation, 2010), p. 104. See also Michael Hor, Chapter 11, this volume for a partial defence of the use of preventive detention in the unique Singaporean context and in relation to concerns that public trials might create hostility to Singapore's Muslim minority.

[70] *Public Committee Against Torture* v. *Israel* (Israel High Court, 11 December 2005), [36]–[37], available at elyon1.court.gov.il/Files_ENG/02/690/007/a34/02007690.a34.htm.

[71] Note 'On target? The Israeli Supreme Court and the expansion of targeted killings' 116 *Yale Law Journal* 1873 (2007). See also Daphne Barak-Erez, Chapter 23, this volume for a detailed description of the proportionality requirements imposed by the Israeli Court.

[72] *Public Committee Against Torture* v. *Israel*, [45].   [73] Ibid., [3].

review targeted killings. The Obama Administration claims the right to engage in targeted killing of terrorists outside as well in situations of armed conflict and without having to demonstrate that capture and prosecution are not possible as less drastic alternatives.[74]

C. Administrative and immigration law detention and control orders

Immigration law, particularly in Western countries, has frequently been used to counter international terrorism since 9/11. It routinely employs what in criminal law would be seen as problematic status-based offences and standards of proof well below the criminal law standard of proof beyond a reasonable doubt. Although it is not a crime to be a member of a terrorist group in either the United States or Canada, it is a ground for apprehension and removal under both countries' immigration laws. Immigration law is also more accepting of preventive, investigative and indefinite detention and the use of secret evidence than the criminal law.

The United Kingdom relied on immigration law as anti-terrorism law in the immediate aftermath of 9/11, but in response to a court decision holding that its approach was both disproportionate and discriminatory, it repealed this provision and enacted control orders. Control orders, like immigration laws, are administrative measures that are imposed on a standard significantly less than proof of guilt beyond a reasonable doubt. They also use secret evidence not disclosed to the detainee even though they may impose strict conditions of house arrest. The courts have forced the state to disclose more information and as of the end of 2010, there were only eight control orders remaining.[75] A 2011 review stressed that control orders, and in particular onerous conditions restricting any use of mobile phones or computers, hindered criminal investigations.[76] Control orders

---

[74] See William C. Banks, Chapter 18, this volume. For arguments that current US approaches to targeted killing, as well as the apparent continuation of extraordinary renditions, demonstrate American attraction to extra-legal measures, see Roach *The 9/11 Effect*, Chapter 4. Unlike under Gross's proposals, these extra-legal measures are conducted secretly and are not apparently restrained by credible threats of sanctions for the extra-legal conduct. See Oren Gross 'Chaos and Rules' (2003) 112 *Yale Law Journal* 1011. But for arguments that US officials were restrained by worries about prosecutions in connection with the torture memos, see Jack Goldsmith *The Terror Presidency* (New York: Norton, 2007), Chapter 5.

[75] Helen Fenwick and Gavin Phillipson, Chapter 19 this volume.

[76] 'The evidence obtained by the Review has plainly demonstrated that the present control order regime acts as an impediment to prosecution', Lord Macdonald *Review of Counter-Terrorism and Security Powers*, (Cm 8003, January 2011), p. 9 para. 2.

will now be replaced by a less onerous regime with a greater emphasis on surveillance and evidence gathering with the aim of preparing for criminal charges and prosecutions.[77] This can be seen as a healthy correction in favour of the criminal law, if not necessarily liberty. In contrast, the United Kingdom continues to use immigration law as anti-terrorism law by deporting terrorist suspects on the basis of assurances that they will not be tortured when returned.[78] This approach, as opposed to one based on domestic criminal law investigations and prosecutions, runs both the risk of torture and of exporting terrorism.

In the past, terrorism-inspired innovations in the criminal law context such as limits on the right to silence have spread to the rest of the criminal law.[79] This danger still exists, but, in the post-9/11 environment, the more immediate danger seems to be that terrorism-inspired innovations such as secret evidence and special advocates may spread from administrative law to the criminal law. In addition, terrorist innovations in the criminal law may also draw on dramatic expansions of the criminal law in other areas. For example, in Canada much of the basic structure of post-9/11 terrorism offences was taken from previously enacted organised crime offences. In the UK, control orders had precedents both in pre-World War II emergency measures but also in more contemporary measures like Anti-Social Behavioral Orders.[80] The UK's controversial Terrorism Act 2006 not only criminalised indirect encouragement of terrorism through its glorification but also allows police officers to serve notices to require unlawful terrorist related material to be removed from the Internet. The Act thus blurs criminal law and less restrained administrative measures.

D. Summary

The criminal law faces challenges as many continue to argue that terrorism is too dangerous and sensitive a matter to be left to the demands of proving guilt beyond a reasonable doubt on the basis of public evidence.

---

[77] *Review of Counter-Terrorism and Security Powers & Review Findings and Recommendations*, (Cm 8004, January 2011) pp. 40–3.

[78] See *RB (Algeria)* v. *Secretary of State* [2009] UKHL 10 applying a deferential standard of judicial review to hold that terrorist suspects could be deported to Jordan and Algeria with assurances that they would not be tortured. See Colin Harvey, Chapter 9 this volume.

[79] Oren Gross and Fionnuala Ni Aolian, *Law in Times of Crisis* (Cambridge University Press, 2006), pp. 214–20.

[80] Lucia Zedner, 'Preventive justice or pre-punishment? The case of control orders' (2007) 60 *Current Legal Problems* 174–203.

The persistence of military commissions, administrative detention without trial and targeted killings under the Obama Administration suggests that the challenges to the criminal law are deep and fundamental.

At the same time as it faces external threats, the criminal law will face internal challenges in dealing with terrorism. There is a danger that, in an attempt to preserve its role in combating terrorism, the criminal law may be distorted beyond recognition. Procedural distortions will occur if terrorist trials are frequently closed to the public and the accused is denied access to full disclosure or full confrontation. Substantive distortions will occur if offences are so broadly and vaguely worded that they do not provide meaningful act or fault requirements and are incomprehensible for juries. In addition, the use of membership and association offences combined with an emphasis on religious and political motives create the risk that terrorism crimes will be perceived as political and religious crimes. Such distortions will undermine the rights of the accused and deprive the criminal law of its unique and principled role in preventing and denouncing terrorism.

4. The role of an ideal criminal law in a broader anti-terrorism strategy

Much of this chapter has been pessimistic in warning about the dangers of distorting the criminal law and the even greater dangers of using less restrained alternatives to the criminal law. In this section, I will take a more positive approach by briefly outlining the optimal use of the criminal law in a broader counter-terrorism strategy.

A. An ideal criminal law to combat terrorism

One threshold question is whether countries should enact terrorism laws or rely on existing laws targeting crimes such as murder and bombings. The answer depends in large part on the nature of inchoate offences within the particular country.[81] It may not be necessary to enact laws against the incitement of terrorism as called for in Security Council Resolution 1624 if existing laws against the incitement of violence are adequate. The 2002 terrorism law in Indonesia responded to a very restrictive law of

---

[81] For a discussion of these issues, see s. 2.1.2 of the Ottawa Principles on Anti-Terrorism and Human Rights in Nicola LaViolette and Craig Forcese (eds.), *The Human Rights of Anti-Terrorism* (Toronto: Irwin Law, 2008), pp. 22–9.

attempts and the absence of general conspiracy offences in that country and could be justified on that basis. The trend in many countries is for terrorism-specific laws that target remote acts of preparation and planning that would not be caught by general offences of attempts, conspiracy or incitement. Terrorism-specific laws may be a better alternative to wholesale expansion of the criminal law, but only if terrorism is defined in a restrained and determinate fashion.

One possible definition of terrorism taken from the 1999 Terrorism Financing Convention would target intentional killing or harming of those not engaged in armed conflict in order to intimidate a population or compel a government or international organisation to act. To be sure, such a definition errs on the side of under-inclusion. It also relegates difficult issues of state terrorism and liberation struggles– issues that have prevented international agreement on a definition of terrorism– to the evolving laws of war. Nevertheless, it is an improvement on many overbroad definitions of terrorism, especially those that require proof of religious and political motive. It should not be forgotten that acts omitted from a definition of terrorism, for example property damage and blockades, may still often be illegal under ordinary criminal laws.

The expansion of criminal law to include remote acts of preparation and planning for terrorism can be justified as a response to the devastating harm of terrorism, but only if the state can establish a high level of subjective fault or intent to commit a terrorist act. In other words, the criminal law should be able to punish a person who is only starting to plan a terrorist act provided that it is clear that the person is intent on committing terrorist violence. Similarly, departures from narrow approaches to conspiracy law can be justified in order to ensure that a person can be convicted even if they have not selected a specific target for their terrorist plot. At the same time, it should be accepted that the broadening of the criminal law may in some cases result in sentences that may at first glance seem too lenient for the terrorist label. It should also be accepted that the remoteness of the preparation for terrorism may in some cases raise a reasonable doubt about whether the accused had the necessary intent.

In general, the state should avoid procedural shortcuts in terrorism law both to minimise the possibility of conviction of the innocent and to demonstrate the state's commitment to fairness. The criminal law's concerns about only punishing the guilty distinguishes it as the moral superior to the willingness of terrorists to punish the innocent. The high standard of proof of guilt beyond a reasonable doubt has been defended in the Canadian *Air India* case as 'the essence of the Rule of Law' and one that 'cannot be applied any less vigourously in cases of horrific crimes'.[82] The use of reverse onuses should generally be avoided in terrorism laws given the dangers of convicting someone in the face of a reasonable doubt about guilt. The state should also not be able to rely on administrative or international lists of terrorist groups in cases where part of the criminal offence is proof that a terrorist group existed. An administrative listing on the basis of secret evidence should not be substituted for proof beyond a reasonable doubt on the basis of public evidence that the accused can challenge. The accused should be able to make the same due process claims that are allowed in other criminal trials including claims that he or she has been entrapped into committing crimes by state agents. Proactive investigation is acceptable in terrorism investigations but it should not result in discriminatory forms of virtue testing in the absence of individualised suspicion and it should not induce the commission of terrorism crimes.[83]

Criminal trials should never use secret evidence against the accused. At the same time, however, public interest immunity procedures should allow the state to demonstrate that non-disclosure, summarisation or selective redaction of unused material is justified given the dangers of disclosure compared to the use that the accused could make of such material. The trial judge should make non-disclosure decisions and retain the right to re-open them and if necessary stay proceedings should non-disclosure of such material result in an unfair trial.[84] The state should also have an opportunity to justify the use of closed courts and even anonymous witnesses subject to the overriding concern that the accused still have a fair trial. The state may have legitimate reasons relating to witness and source protection, ongoing investigations and future trials to close parts of terrorist trials, but it should also be sensitive to the value of publicity in demonstrating to a sceptical public that terrorist suspects were willing to harm innocent civilians. Fair and public criminal trials can be an important part of a 'heart and minds' approach that exposes and denounces terrorism and may even help convince those with extremist views to stop short of violence. Courts should be careful when admitting evidence about the accused's political

---

[82] *R v. Malik and Bagri* 2005 BCSC 350, [662], [1254].
[83] Kent Roach 'Entrapment and equality in terrorism prosecutions: a comparative examination of North American and European approaches' (2011) 80 *Mississippi Law Journal* 1455.
[84] *R v. Ahmed* (2011) SCC 6 stressing importance of stays to prevent unfair trails; Roach, *The Unique Challenges of Terrorism Prosecutions*.

and religious views to ensure that the probative value of such evidence does not exceed its prejudicial effects. Terrorism prosecutions should not become or appear to become political or religious trials.

The issue of sentencing is more difficult than might be imagined. There has been a trend towards heavy sentences that stress the need to denounce, deter and incapacitate terrorists. At the same time, rehabilitation should not be discarded especially in cases where accused have pled guilty and genuinely renounced violence. Some have argued that US terrorism sentences have been 'soft', but Chesney has shown that this critique pays inadequate attention to the specific offences charged including the use of preventive 'Al Capone'-type prosecutions.[85] The UK courts have stressed the need for higher sentences than before 9/11 on the basis that 'IRA terrorists were not prepared to blow themselves up for their cause. It is this fanaticism that makes it appropriate to impose indeterminate sentences on today's terrorists, because it will often be impossible to say when, if ever, such terrorists will cease to pose a danger'.[86] The Canadian courts have also imposed higher sentences on al-Qaeda inspired terrorism including sentences of life, twenty and eighteen years imprisonment in cases where eighteen- to twenty-year-old offenders without prior records pled guilty and expressed remorse for their deadly plots.[87] The Australian courts have also handed out high sentences, but the Victorian Court of Appeal has wisely warned that attention must be paid to the breadth of new crimes of terrorism, differences among terrorist organisations and terrorists plots and the dangers of double punishment for overlapping crimes.[88]

---

[85] Robert Chesney, 'Federal prosecutions of terrorism-related offences' (2007) 11 *Lewis and Clark Law Review* 851, 885. (The median sentence for material support of designated foreign terrorist group is ten years.)

[86] *R* v. *Barot* [2007] EWCA Crim 1119 (54). See also *R* v. *DaCosta* [2009] EWCA Crim 482 (30) on the need for higher post-9/11 sentences for illegal speech associated with terrorism.

[87] *R* v. *Amara* 2010 ONCA 858 (life imprisonment for twenty-year-old mastermind of truck bomb plot who pled guilty and expressed remorse) *R* v. *Khalid* 2010 ONCA 861 (twenty-year sentence for a nineteen-year-old first offender who was willfully blind but not fully aware of the details of the truck bomb plot and who had renounced violence); *R* v. *Gaya* 2010 ONCA 860 (eighteen-year sentence for an eighteen-year-old first offender who was willfully blind but not fully aware of the details of the truck bomb plot and who was genuinely remorseful). In *R* v. *Khawaja* 2010 ONCA 862, a life imprisonment sentence was justified in part because the offender had not renounced violence. The Court of Appeal also stressed that the trial judge had erred in applying a totality principle to five separate terrorism offences because of a statutory direction that sentences for terrorist offences be served consecutively.

[88] *Benbrika and Ors v. The Queen* [2010] VSCA 281 (555) (fifteen-year sentence for a ringleader who had not renounced violence).

Western democracies with traditions of separating religion from state may find the rehabilitation of Islamic (or other religious) terrorists awkward. There is a danger that they will simply abandon any attempt to rehabilitate even though terrorists may be convinced of the errors of religious beliefs that encourage violence. Although Singapore's intense rehabilitation model may not be appropriate for Western democracies,[89] the lack of concern with rehabilitation in the West may also ignore the possibility of prison radicalisation of convicted terrorists who may eventually be released.

Regardless of their approach to rehabilitation, courts should limit terrorism sentences on the basis of the seriousness of the accused's actions and intent. Many new terrorism offences expand the criminal act to remote forms of preparation and support and qualify the fault element to not require that the accused intend a specific terrorist act. These qualifications may be justified to allow earlier prosecution of terrorists, but they also affect the seriousness of the offence for sentencing purposes. The courts should not allow the terrorist label of an offence to be an excuse for sentences that are excessive in relation to what the accused actually did or intended.

B.   *The place of the criminal law in a comprehensive strategy*

Although criminal law reform often figures prominently in public discourse and in country reports concerning compliance with Resolution 1373, most governments are taking a whole of government approach to terrorism which goes well beyond police, prosecutors and courts and includes various security intelligence agencies, immigration and customs officials, aviation and transport security, the regulation of financial institutions, emergency preparedness and foreign policy.

The full development of a comprehensive anti-terrorism policy is obviously beyond the scope of this chapter, but the project can be advanced by selective incorporation of regulatory strategies from outside the field of terrorism or crime. A promising construct for situating the criminal law in broader anti-terrorism policy can be taken from the field of public health.[90] In order to assess a variety of counter-measures that could reduce death and injury from traffic accidents, epidemiologist William

---

[89] Rabasa *et al.*, *Deradicalizing Islamic Extremists*, p. 104.
[90] National Research Council, *Making the Nation Safer: The Role of Science and Technology in Countering Terrorism* (Washington, DC: National Academy Press, 2002).

Haddon constructed a matrix evaluating counter-measures that could be taken to minimise harm before, during and after the accident. Haddon argued that too many resources had been devoted to changing the behaviour of the direct agent and that harm could be reduced by greater regulation of third parties and the environment. I have argued elsewhere that the Haddon Matrix can be modified to apply to terrorism.[91] Following Haddon, we should assume that at least some terrorist activity cannot be deterred and spend more resources on regulating the environment before, during and after acts of terrorism so as to minimise the harms of terrorism. Before the act of terrorism, this means better regulation of sites and substances that are attractive to terrorists. It is particularly important to prevent potential terrorists from obtaining access to lethal substances such as toxins, nuclear material, large amounts of explosive substances and aeroplanes. Much of this type of environmental regulation may be achieved by administrative laws that may present less of a threat to values such as liberty, due process and equality than the criminal law. Some of these preventive measures may also have the advantage of making us safer from accidents involving nuclear material and toxins.

The Haddon Matrix approach should make policymakers think about what can be done to minimise harm during and after an act of terrorism. Although this will be dismissed as defeatist damage control by some, it remains crucial to minimising the harms of terrorism. Without evacuation strategies introduced after the 1993 attacks, the death toll at the World Trade Centre might have been in the tens of thousands.[92] Both Canada and the United Kingdom have stressed preparation for a wide range of emergencies as part of their post-9/11 terrorist strategies, but US strategies changed only after the failure to respond to Hurricane Katrina. It will be interesting to see if the extensive damage and loss of life caused by forest fires in Israel in December 2010 will inspire that country to put a greater emphasis on an all-risk emergency preparedness approach to national security.

---

[91] William Haddon, 'A logical framework for categorizing highway safety phenomena and activity' (1972) 12 *Journal of Trauma* 193. For an application of the Haddon Matrix for preventing and reducing injury to the field of terrorism, see Kent Roach, *September 11: Consequences for Canada* (Montreal: McGill Queens University Press, 2003), pp. 168–74.
[92] It took four hours to evacuate the World Trade Centre in 1993 whereas all but 2,152 of the 16,400 to 18,800 civilians in the towers were evacuated in less than one hour in 2001: *The 9/11 Report*, [9.4].

Another instrumental concept that could inform a comprehensive anti-terrorism policy is the idea of responsive regulation advocated by Braithwaite. The central idea of responsive regulation is a regulatory pyramid which allows for the escalation of the state's response when regulation fails. Braithwaite stresses that the behaviour of potential wrongdoers can often be best controlled by third parties who have greater influence over the target of regulation than the state. Attempts at persuasion, negotiation, dissuasion from extremism and peaceful problem-solving lie at the base of the pyramid with escalation to deterrent threats of punishment and finally to incapacitation of irrational actors.[93] Some argue that persuasion, problem solving and even deterrence should quickly be ruled out when applied to groups like al-Qaeda that seem bent on death and destruction.[94] Nevertheless, the 9/11 Commission recognised that failed and repressive states, desperation and lack of education are contributing factors to terrorism that should be addressed. For example, Egypt's traditional repression of the Muslim Brotherhood played a role in inspiring some in al-Qaeda.[95] The subsequent development of home-grown terrorism underlines the importance of providing alternative avenues for the expression of grievances and not relying on criminal law to prosecute praise of terrorism. One of the dangers of a focus on criminal law or its less restrained alternatives is that softer strategies that address the causes of terrorism will be ignored.

There is a need to think carefully about the proper relation between the criminal law and the collection of intelligence to warn governments about possible terrorist attacks. The creation of many new terrorist crimes of preparation and association has blurred the distinction between intelligence about security threats and evidence of crime. In many cases, there will be overlapping terrorism investigations by police and intelligence agencies. Intelligence agencies are slowly learning to comply with evidential standards and this is a necessary part of an effective anti-terrorism strategy that will allow the criminal law to be used to punish those who plan terrorist violence. At the same time, however, we must be aware that

---

[93] John Braithwaite, *Restorative Justice and Responsive Regulation* (Oxford University Press, 2002), pp. 31–2.

[94] Although he recognises the potential for democratic outlets for grievances in Spain, Canada and Northern Ireland, Michael Ignatieff has argued that the 'apocalyptic nihilists' of al-Qaeda 'cannot be engaged politically and must instead be defeated militarily': Michael Ignatieff, *The Lesser Evil Political Ethics in an Age of Terror* (Toronto: Penguin, 2004), p. 99.

[95] *The 9/11 Report*, [12.2]–[12.3]. See also Lawrence Wright, *The Looming Tower* (London: Allen Lane, 2006).

too much merging of intelligence and criminal law paradigms can undermine the moral force of the criminal law and its claim to impose just punishment for clear wrongdoing. The use of the criminal law to respond to remote and speculative risks or to the status of the accused, for example as a person who in the past received terrorist training, can undermine the unique denunciatory force of the criminal law.

A refusal to use the criminal law to respond to particularly remote or ambiguous risks does not mean that society has no defence against such risks. One layer of defence is the use of intelligence to engage in surveillance of potential security threats; another layer of defence is administrative regulation to harden targets and control dangerous substances and likely sites for terrorist activities. Yet another is outreach and co-operation with communities that may be best able to detect potential terrorists in their midst.

There is a need to be aware of the limits of the criminal law in responding to extremist speech. In some cases, it may be better to keep those who engage in extremist speech under surveillance than to prosecute them. Although the criminal law is society's strongest tool of disapproval and denunciation, it is not its only tool. Sometimes exposure and criticism of extremist speech may be enough to stop it from spreading. At the same time, it is possible to defend extremist speech and hate speech prosecutions as an attempt to regulate the ideological environment and prevent radicalisation. Much will depend on the respective values that particular societies place on freedom of expression and social harmony. Care should, however, be taken in transplanting European concepts of militant democracy and abuse of rights to countries without real democratic freedoms or traditions or in using the militant democracy concept within democracies to crush Islamic and other forms of legal pluralism.[96] It should also be recognised that speech, including extreme speech, will often be an important alternative to violence in expressing various grievances at home and abroad that may motivate terrorism.

The core of the criminal law – the idea that intentional violence is not justified regardless of its motives and the grievances that may motivate the violence – should send a powerful message to all those who may contemplate terrorism that violence is out of bounds. To be sure, the denunciation

---

[96] Kent Roach, 'Anti-terrorism and militant democracy: some Western and Eastern responses', in Andras Sajo (ed.), *Militant Democracy* (Amsterdam: Eleven Publishing, 2004); Patrick Macklem 'Militant democracy. Legal pluralism and the paradox of self-determination' (2006) *International Journal of Constitutional Law* 488.

provided by the core of the criminal law will not eliminate terrorism any more than it has eliminated murder. It will, however, help marginalise and stigmatise terrorism in a way that less restrained alternatives to the criminal law are unable to do because they do not have the same rigorous commitment to public proof of wrongdoing as does the criminal law.

5. Conclusion

To paraphrase Winston Churchill about democracy, the criminal law appears to be the worst way to respond to terrorism – except for all the others that have been tried. The criminal law has been distorted and mis-used since 9/11 as the Security Council called on all states to enact criminal laws against terrorism and terrorism financing without offering guidance about how terrorism should be defined. The dangers of over-broad defini-tions of terrorism have only been aggravated by subsequent calls by the Security Council to criminalise incitement of terrorism. Criminal laws against terrorism that are over-broad, duplicative and complex have pre-sented fundamental challenges for terrorism trials, as have attempts to keep intelligence and witnesses secret within those trials.

Although the criminal law has been stretched and strained by the demands of prevention of terrorism, there are signs that democracies are being drawn back to the criminal law as the best way to denounce, incap-acitate and punish terrorists. Less restrained alternatives to the criminal law including the use of secret evidence and indeterminate detention without trial have proven to be both legally and politically controversial. The criminal law represents important values of individual responsibility, legally authorised detention, deserved punishment and due process that should not be lightly discarded. Although the terrorist threat can prod-uce distorted and unjust criminal laws and trials, the greater danger since 9/11 is that states will abandon the criminal law in favour of much less restrained and less discriminating anti-terrorist measures including war, targeted killing and the imposition of military or administrative deten-tion on the basis of secret evidence.

6

Anti-terrorism laws: balancing national security and a fair hearing

NICOLA MCGARRITY AND EDWARD SANTOW

1. Introduction

Increasingly since 9/11, national security questions have arisen in civil litigation, in areas as diverse as immigration, family law and contractual disputes. This chapter considers the situation where security-sensitive information is withheld from a party or the public. The denial of access to such information, in circumstances where it would ordinarily be available, can impact deleteriously on a party's right to a fair hearing and the principle of open justice.

Taking a comparative approach involving Australia, Canada and the United Kingdom, this chapter assesses the extent to which these jurisdictions accommodate the right to a fair hearing where national security is at stake. While our focus is on civil proceedings, with particular reference to proceedings dealing with immigration and so-called 'control orders', the chapter also addresses some forms of criminal proceeding. We do not suggest that a robust response to the threat of terrorism inevitably corrodes the enjoyment of human rights and undermines democratic government. Nor do we believe that *any* encroachment on human rights generally, or the right to a fair hearing specifically, no matter how trivial the encroachment or how pressing the counter-terrorism imperative, is necessarily illegitimate. Instead, we argue that the proportionality principle should be applied more rigorously in this area, because we believe that this would better calibrate the law to take account of the nature and scope of the threat of terrorism while paying due regard to the protection of civil liberties.

The authors would like to thank the editors and the participants at the 2010 symposium for their comments on this chapter, and Keiran Hardy, Qi Jiang and Jesse Galdston for their research assistance. The authors would also like to thank Andrew Lynch and Tessa Meyrick for their research on an earlier version of this chapter.

Section 2 of this chapter outlines the competing demands of a fair hearing and a nation's counter-terrorism response. Focusing on the constraints that national security places on open justice and procedural fairness, we propose that proportionality should be the guiding principle to accommodate these conflicting demands. Section 3 assesses the common law doctrine of public interest immunity, which has been the conventional means of preventing security-sensitive information from being adduced as evidence. Section 4 considers more recent statutory attempts, including by way of 'special advocates', to deal with such information in civil litigation.

2. The counter-terrorism imperative and the right to a fair hearing

A state that values 'open justice' must operate its courts and tribunals transparently and openly. As reflected in international law, a system of open justice requires at least the following two features. First, the machinery of justice must be subject to independent scrutiny by people who can verify whether the rule of law is being applied by the three arms of government. Second, procedural fairness must be accorded to all parties, such that they are aware of the evidence against them and given the opportunity to rebut such evidence. The denial of procedural fairness is anathema to the right to a fair hearing. In such a situation, individual parties to a dispute can be subjected to a Kafka-esque nightmare in which their ignorance of crucial material leaves them unable to argue their case effectively.

The right to a fair and public hearing by an independent and impartial tribunal – proclaimed in the Universal Declaration of Human Rights (UDHR),[1] the International Covenant on Civil and Political Rights (ICCPR)[2] and other more specific international instruments[3] – directly mandates a system of open justice. This system of open justice is applicable to civil and criminal proceedings, although its requirements are generally

---

[1] GA Res. 217A (III), UN GAOR, 3rd sess, 183rd plen mtg, UN Doc. A/Res/217A (10 December 1948), art. 10.

[2] New York, 16 December 1966, in force 23 March 1976, 999 UNTS 171, art. 14(1).

[3] See, e.g., Convention on the Rights of the Child, New York, 20 November 1989, in force 2 September 1990, 1577 UNTS 3, art. 40; International Convention on the Elimination of All Forms of Racial Discrimination, New York, 7 March 1966, in force 4 January 1969, 660 UNTS 195, art. 5(a); Convention on the Rights of Persons with Disabilities, New York, 30 March 2007, in force 3 May 2008, 189 UNTS 137, art. 13.

(but not always) more onerous in relation to criminal proceedings.[4] In addition, the recognition of many other rights is itself contingent on open legal proceedings. After all, how can one be confident that a jurisdiction respects the right to 'equal protection of the law'[5] unless its justice system transparently shows this to be the case? Moreover, where proceedings are held *in camera*, there is a greater likelihood that dissident or unpopular people will be denied a fair resolution of their dispute.[6]

Generally, modern liberal democracies understand the value of open justice and construct their dispute resolution systems in a way that preserves its fundamental tenets. However, under international law, open justice is not an absolute principle, and democracies routinely permit derogation from complete transparency in appropriate circumstances. Clearly, the need to protect national security generally, and to counter the threat of terrorism specifically, is felt keenly by all states, and especially those that have suffered terrorist attacks. International law requires states to take appropriate steps to counter the threat of terrorism,[7] but as the United Nations Security Council made clear, such steps must be in accordance with 'international human rights law, refugee law and humanitarian law'.[8]

There is an obvious tension between withholding security-sensitive information (which may obviously be damaging to national security if disclosed to a terrorism suspect or the public at large) and the right to a fair hearing. At one level, this is simply a manifestation of the dichotomy between liberty and security.[9] However, the search for an effective and principled basis to reconcile these competing imperatives must involve an understanding of the basis in law and policy for each of these competing demands, and the application of a well-reasoned formula for achieving reconciliation. The remainder of this section of the chapter addresses those issues.

---

[4] See, e.g., *Secretary of State for the Home Department* v. *MB and AF* [2008] 1 AC 440, [17] (Lord Bingham).
[5] See, e.g., UDHR, art. 7; ICCPR, art. 26.
[6] Sangeeta Shah, 'Administration of justice', in Daniel Moeckli, Sangeeta Shah and Sandesh Sivakumaran (eds.), *International Human Rights Law* (Oxford University Press, 2010), p. 323.
[7] See, e.g., United Nations Security Council, SC Res. 1373 (28 September 2001); United Nations Security Council, SC Res. 1566 (8 October 2004).
[8] United Nations Security Council, SC Res. 1624 (14 September 2005).
[9] See generally: Daniel Farber (ed.), *Security* v. *Liberty: Conflicts Between Civil Liberties and National Security in American History* (New York: Russell Sage, 2008); Martin Scheinin, 'Terrorism', in Moeckli, Shah and Sivakumaran, *International Human Rights Law*, p. 583.

A.   Procedural fairness

The principle of procedural fairness – known also as natural justice and due process – has two main elements: the decision-maker should not exhibit bias and a person affected by a decision should be given a fair hearing in relation to the substance of the matter. It is the second of these requirements that is of central relevance for our purposes, because it is the source of the duty to disclose relevant information to an affected party, at least where that information is adverse to the party's interests.[10]

Procedural fairness is an important element of any system founded on the English common law, which has long protected the right to a fair hearing.[11] This is further reinforced by legislation. In the UK, the passing of the Human Rights Act has strengthened the legal foundations of procedural fairness, helping it to move beyond its common law roots and broadening its application.[12]

In Canada and Australia, procedural fairness is also protected by a combination of the common law, statute and the Constitution. For example, s. 7 of the Canadian Charter of Rights and Freedoms, which provides that '[e]veryone has the right to life, liberty and security of the person and the right not to be deprived thereof except in accordance with the principles of fundamental justice', has been held to guarantee procedural fairness in legal proceedings.[13] In Australia, s. 75(v) of the Australian Constitution has been held to require anyone exercising the powers and duties of the federal government to accord procedural fairness to those affected by their actions.[14] This, in turn, requires that a decision-maker should give a person with standing to commence judicial review proceedings the opportunity to comment on adverse information that is 'credible, relevant and significant'.[15]

Such constitutional protections are neither absolute nor comprehensive in their coverage. For instance, the constitutional protection in Australia only applies to legal proceedings arising from disputes involving action

---

[10]   On the centrality of the duty of disclosure, see, e.g., the Privy Council decision in *Kandu* v. *Government of Malaya* [1962] AC 322, 337 (Lord Denning).

[11]   See, e.g., *R* v. *University of Cambridge* (1723) 1 Str 557.

[12]   H. W. R. Wade and C. F. Forsyth, *Administrative Law* (Oxford University Press, 10th edn, 2009), 405. (This edition of the text was published after the death of Sir William Wade).

[13]   *R* v. *Lyons* [1987] 2 SCR 309, 361 (per La Forest J for the majority).

[14]   See *Plaintiff S157/2002* v. *Commonwealth* (2003) 211 CLR 476.

[15]   See *Kioa* v. *West* (1985) 159 CLR 550, 638 (Brennan J); *Applicant VEAL of 2002* v. *Minister for Immigration and Multicultural Affairs* (2005) 225 CLR 88, 95–6 (Gleeson CJ, Gummow, Kirby, Hayne and Heydon JJ).

carried out by the federal government (and not by the state governments). Nor do such protections prescribe in precise detail what procedural fairness requires in the myriad circumstances that might arise. This, in turn, creates room for disagreement as to the precise scope of the protection that should be accorded where national security is at stake.

B.   From deference to proportionality

Where the measures taken by a government to protect national security impinge on procedural fairness, thereby bringing collective security and individual liberty into conflict, there is inevitable debate as to where the balance should lie. Traditionally, the common law has prioritised national security considerations. The *GCHQ case* perhaps represents a high-water mark of judicial deference on questions of national security.[16] This case involved a judicial review challenge to the responsible Minister's decision to prevent employees of 'Government Communications Headquarters', which played an important espionage role for the UK in the Cold War, from joining a trade union. Here, national security was invoked as a justification for failing to afford affected employees procedural fairness in the Minister's decision. In accepting this argument, Lord Diplock said:

> National security is the responsibility of the executive arm of government; what action is needed to protect its interests is ... a matter upon which those upon whom the responsibility rests, and not upon the courts of justice, must have the last word. It is *par excellence* a non-justiciable question. The judicial process is totally inept to deal with the sort of problems which it involves.[17]

In Canada, in the specific context of security-sensitive information, Roach has observed that during the Cold War such information tended to be collected for the dominant purpose of being 'distributed within government to those with appropriate security clearances', and was rarely intended to be used in legal proceedings.[18] As a result, '[u]ntil 1982, Ministers were able to assert an essentially unreviewable discretion to prevent the disclosure of intelligence on ground of harms to national security'. However, with such information becoming an increasingly significant component

---

[16] *Council of Civil Service Unions* v. *Minister for Civil Service* [1985] AC 374.

[17] Ibid., 391–2.

[18] Kent Roach, 'When secret intelligence becomes evidence: some implications of *Khadr* and *Charkaoui II*' (2009) 47 *Supreme Court Law Review* 147, 156.

of the evidence in legal proceedings, Roach went on to say that there has been a shift:

> In the post-September 11 environment, there are signs of change, including an increased skepticism to claims that the non-disclosure of intelligence is justified by concerns about the mosaic effect in which the disclosure of even innocuous intelligence can assist the enemy.[19]

We believe that the traditional approach, involving a high level of judicial deference to the executive on national security issues, ought properly to be discarded. Instead, we applaud and encourage what we see to be a new, emerging consensus in which the concept of proportionality helps to guide how far national security concerns can justify incursions into procedural fairness and the right to a fair hearing. As explained below, total judicial deference to the executive is inimical to a proportionality approach, and we urge that this approach become more explicit, more widespread and more sophisticated in its application.

'Proportionality' – both as a legal principle to be applied by the courts and a generally influential idea – is especially important in helping to reconcile the needs of national security with the right to a fair hearing. The concept of proportionality denotes the balancing of competing rights and interests, as well as the necessity of achieving legitimate public aims (here, to combat terrorism) in a manner that imposes the minimum deleterious impact necessary on human rights (viz., the right to a fair hearing). The origins of the proportionality principle are in European law,[20] and it has been enshrined by the European Convention on Human Rights jurisprudence. The Convention does not itself use the term 'proportionality', but the principle has been crucial in the operation of its limitation provisions. For example, the general right in art. 6(1) to 'a fair and public hearing' in both the civil and criminal contexts is limited as follows:

> Judgment shall be pronounced publicly but the press and public may be excluded from all or part of the trial in the interest of morals, public order or *national security in a democratic society*, … or to the extent strictly necessary in the opinion of the court in special circumstances where publicity would prejudice the interests of justice.[21]

---

[19] Ibid., 152.
[20] Ultimately, it can be traced back to Prussian law: see Jürgen Schwarze, *European Administrative Law* (London: Sweet & Maxwell, 1992), Chapter 5.
[21] European Convention on Human Rights, art. 6(1) (emphasis added).

Such limitations are the foundation for proportionality being applied by the European Court of Human Rights and the courts of some state parties to the Convention, including the UK. This leads to two important tests. First, a *balancing test* considers whether the means adopted to achieve the relevant objective disproportionately impinges on protected human rights. Second, a *necessity test* asks whether the objective could be achieved using an alternative means to that adopted by the government, and whether this alternative means is less harmful to the enjoyment of the protected rights.

Especially since the incorporation of the European Convention on Human Rights in the Human Rights Act, UK courts now require that, to the extent that the executive or legislative branches of government adopt national security measures that impinge on rights that are expressed in non-absolute terms, such impingement must not be disproportionate to the government's legitimate national security objective.[22] Article 6 of the Convention has been held to require that any measure that impinges on a fair and public hearing in civil proceedings must be subjected to a proportionality analysis.[23] The same approach applies to art. 14(1) of the ICCPR, which protects the right to a fair hearing in similar terms to the European Convention.[24]

The Canadian Charter imports the principle of proportionality in a way that also resembles the European Convention on Human Rights. That is, s. 1 provides that the Charter 'guarantees the rights and freedoms set out in it subject only to such reasonable limits prescribed by law as can be demonstrably justified in a free and democratic society'. In *R* v. *Oakes*, the Supreme Court of Canada held that this required a proportionality analysis in respect of government limitations on protected rights.[25]

The necessity test noted above encourages the adoption of national security measures that involve any incursion on the right to a fair hearing to be the minimum necessary to achieve the competing legislative objective. In applying this test, a court can consider the approach taken in other jurisdictions to the same or a similar issue. As discussed later in this chapter, this is precisely what happened in *Chahal*, where the European Court of Human Rights compared the differing approaches taken in the

---

[22] *Secretary of State for the Department* v. *Rehman* [2001] 3 WLR 877.
[23] *Secretary of State for the Home Department* v. *MB and AF* [2008] 1 AC 440, [32] (Lord Bingham); *Jasper* v. *United Kingdom* (2000) 30 EHRR 441, [52].
[24] Shah, 'Administration of Justice', p. 323.
[25] *R* v. *Oakes* [1986] 1 SCR 103. See generally P. W. Hogg, 'Interpreting the charter of rights' (1990) 28 *Osgoode Hall Law Journal* 817.

UK and Canada in respect of withholding information for national security reasons, concluding that the Canadian approach struck a far superior
balance.[26]

Technically, the influence of the proportionality principle should
be only very slight in Australia. Australia's Constitution lacks a Bill of
Rights; nor indeed is there a statutory Human Rights Act (akin to the UK
Act) operating at the federal level,[27] and so there has been little perceived
need to develop principles to determine the validity or effect of legislation said to infringe human rights. As Gleeson CJ, then Chief Justice of
Australia, pointed out in the context of the Australian Constitution, only
jurisdictions with human rights laws require 'both a rational connection
between a constitutionally valid objective and the limitation in question,
and also minimum impairment to the guaranteed right'.[28]

In practice, however, the Australian courts seem to be engaging in an
increasingly similar analysis to jurisdictions that expressly require a proportionality approach. In the celebrated UK text, *Administrative Law*, the
authors suggest that the demands of art. 6 of the European Convention on
Human Rights (which protects procedural fairness) 'often mirror those of
the common law'. However, they note that the Convention's 'uncomprom-
ising terms have encouraged the courts to enforce [procedural fairness]
in many cases where the more tolerant common law would have allowed
exceptions or qualifications'.[29] Martin CJ of the Western Australian Court
of Appeal seems to support the belief that the traditional common law
approach does not differ markedly from a human rights approach involving the proportionality principle. He observes that whether or not a jurisdiction has some kind of bill of rights has been a relatively minor factor in
determining the approach taken by the jurisdiction's courts regarding the
withholding of security-sensitive information.[30]

Two practices in particular allow Australian courts to use the common
law to protect the right to a fair hearing in a manner similar to courts in
jurisdictions that have a human rights statute. First, Australian judges
routinely refer to human rights in the process of statutory interpretation,

---

[26] *Chahal* v. *United Kingdom* (1996) 23 EHRR 413, [131].

[27] However, it is worth noting that two of Australia's provincial legislatures have enacted
statutory Human Rights Acts: Human Rights Act 2004 (ACT); Charter of Human Rights
and Responsibilities Act 2006 (Vic).

[28] *Roach* v. *Electoral Commission* (2007) 233 CLR 162, 178.

[29] Wade and Forsyth, *Administrative Law*, pp. 147–8. To similar effect, see *Attorney-General*
v. *Guardian Newspapers (No. 2)* [1990] 1 AC 109, 283 (Lord Goff).

[30] *Gypsy Jokers Motorcycle Club Inc* v. *Commissioner of Police* (2007) 33 WAR 245, [57].

applying the presumption that the courts will 'not impute to the legislature an intention to interfere with fundamental rights. Such an intention must be clearly manifested by unmistakable and unambiguous language.'[31] Related to this is the common law presumption that courts should interpret ambiguous legislation in conformity with Australia's international law obligations.[32]

Second, there is a recognition that the precise contours of the procedural fairness requirement will depend on the circumstances of the case, and that the principle must wax and wane depending on other competing demands, such as national security.[33] This allows courts to seek the kind of pragmatic compromise between human rights and other interests which a proportionality approach facilitates. An example is a case involving a confidential letter provided to the Australian government which revealed information highly prejudicial to an asylum seeker's application for refugee status.[34] The High Court held that procedural fairness did not here require that the letter itself, or the identity of its author, be disclosed to the asylum seeker (as this could put the author at risk, and damage the state by discouraging others from providing useful information to the government for fear of reprisals when that information is revealed). Instead, the Court unanimously held that the government was required to protect its interests in a manner that was less harmful to the asylum seeker's right to a fair hearing, and that it ought to have informed the asylum seeker at least of the gist or 'substance' of the allegations made in the letter and given him the opportunity to respond to those allegations.[35]

In sum, restrictions on a fair hearing are already being subjected to a proportionality analysis, or something resembling that analysis. We endorse this development, and argue that it should be codified and regularised by way of further legislative guidance in relation to those mechanisms for withholding information in civil proceedings discussed in Sections 3 and 4 below.

---

[31] *Coco* v. *The Queen* (1994) 179 CLR 427, 437 (Mason CJ, Brennan, Gaudron and McHugh JJ).

[32] See, e.g., *Chu Kheng Lim* v. *Minister for Immigration, Local Government and Ethnic Affairs* (1992) 176 CLR 1, 38 (Brennan, Deane and Dawson JJ).

[33] See, e.g., *Russell* v. *Duke of Norfolk* [1949] 1 All ER 109, 118; Wade and Forsyth, *Administrative Law*, pp. 420–1; Mark Aronson, Bruce Dyer and Matthew Groves, *Judicial Review of Administrative Action* (Sydney: Thomson Reuters, 4th edn, 2009), pp. 519–24.

[34] *Applicant VEAL of 2002* v. *Minister for Immigration and Multicultural Affairs* (2005) 225 CLR 88.

[35] Ibid., 100 (Gleeson CJ, Gummow, Kirby, Hayne and Heydon JJ). A similar approach is taken by courts in the UK: see, e.g., *R (Roberts)* v. *Parole Board* [2005] UKHL 45.

3.   Common law public interest immunity

This section considers the principle of public interest immunity (PII), particularly as it applies at common law in the UK and Australia. The reason for focusing on these two jurisdictions is because, in each, the common law rules relating to PII remain largely intact. In Canada, by contrast, the Evidence Act 1985 (Can) has modified these rules in a number of significant respects. Before continuing to a discussion of the substance of PII in the UK and Australia, two important points must be noted about the latter jurisdiction. First, PII exists both at common law and in statute in Australia. The common law rules have been incorporated into the Evidence Act 1995 (Aus) with minor amendment.[36] Second, the National Security Information (Criminal and Civil Proceedings) Act 2004 (Aus) (NSIA) now provides a parallel regime for dealing with national security information in court proceedings. The extent to which the NSIA and the Evidence Act 1985 (Can) deviate from the common law rules relating to PII, and address the problems that arise from PII claims, will be considered in Section 4 of this chapter.

A.   *Rules of public interest immunity*

PII – known also as 'state interest immunity' and (misleadingly) as 'crown privilege' – has long been an effective means of preventing certain information, the revelation of which would be contrary to the public interest, from being adduced as evidence in legal proceedings. Where PII applies, it operates bluntly and completely to exclude certain evidence from being adduced. In this way, it differs from other methods of dealing with security-sensitive information, where the information might be considered by the court but withheld only from a particular party, or provided only to a party's legal representative, or where some of the information is obscured.[37]

National security represents an archetypal situation for the application of PII.[38] Traditionally, the courts, especially in the UK, were almost

---

[36] For the differences between the statutory and common law positions, see Australian Law Reform Commission, *Keeping Secrets: The Protection of Classified and Security Sensitive Information* (ALRC Report No. 98, 2004), [8.165]–[8.166]. The most significant difference is that the Evidence Act does not apply to pre-trial proceedings, and so common law PII covers this in Australia.

[37] These methods are discussed in Section 4 below.

[38] Australian Law Reform Commission, *Keeping Secrets*, [8.192], [8.210].

entirely deferential to the executive government's claims of PII in the national security context, accepting ministerial certificates as conclusive evidence that it would be contrary to the public interest to reveal certain national security-related information.[39] Now, in the UK and Australia, ministerial certification is no longer an authoritative means of determining the public interest.[40] This position has even been accepted publicly by the UK's domestic intelligence and security agency, MI5.[41] If a party wishes to exclude information on PII grounds, then that party bears the onus of proving that the public interest lies in withholding the information.[42] However, where security sensitive information is at stake, a person seeking to withhold the information starts from an advantage, as courts accept as a general rule that it would be prejudicial to national security to reveal security intelligence.[43]

While conclusive ministerial certification has been abolished in the UK and Australia, the courts in those jurisdictions nevertheless attach considerable weight to the claim by a Minister or senior government officer that a PII order should be made on the ground of national security.[44] Given the still relatively deferential approach taken by the courts in relation to the views of the executive government in this context, it remains difficult for a party to repel a PII claim. However, the misuse of PII is especially pernicious because it could operate to prevent a party (government or otherwise) in civil proceedings from establishing their claim or defence.[45]

At common law, PII now operates as follows in civil proceedings:[46]

(1) At any point in the proceedings, but often at the interlocutory stage before the substantive hearing, any person may make a claim for the immunity.

---

[39] *Duncan* v. *Cammell, Laird & Co* [1942] AC 264, discussed in Jill Hunter, Camille Cameron and Terese Henning, *Litigation I: Civil Procedure* (Sydney: LexisNexis Butterworths, 7th edn., 2005), [8.103].

[40] In the UK, see, e.g., *Conway* v. *Rimmer* [1968] AC 910; *R (on the application of Mohamed)* v. *Secretary of State for Foreign and Commonwealth Affairs* [2010] EWCA Civ 65. In Australia, see: *Sankey* v. *Whitlam* (1978) 142 CLR 1, 57 (Stephen J); *Alister* v. *R* (1984) 154 CLR 404, 435–6, (Wilson and Dawson JJ).

[41] MI5, *Evidence and Disclosure* (2009), available at www.mi5.gov.uk/output/evidence-and-disclosure.html. This fact was noted in Roach, 'When secret intelligence becomes evidence' 165.

[42] Australian Law Reform Commission, *Keeping Secrets*, [8.161].

[43] In Australia, see *Church of Scientology* v. *Woodward* (1982) 154 CLR 25, 59 (Mason J).

[44] J. D. Heydon, *Cross on Evidence* (Sydney: LexisNexis Butterworths, 7th edn, 2004), [27,065].

[45] Ibid., [27,015].

[46] See Australian Law Reform Commission, *Keeping Secrets*, [8.174]–[8.179].

(2) This claim is usually supported by affidavit evidence, often sworn by the responsible Minister or a senior public servant. Cross-examination and presentation of counter-evidence is generally not permitted lest the objective of the application thereby be defeated.

(3) The court will balance the competing public interests in favour and against disclosure.

(4) If the court believes that the affidavit evidence does not support the claim, it may seek further information, or in exceptional cases may examine the documents *in camera*. Ultimately, the court will rule on the claim.

B.   Problems identified in the operation of public interest immunity

The deficiencies with PII (under both the common law and statute) as a means of protecting national security information from disclosure are demonstrated by the trial of Simon Lappas in Australia.[47] While this was a criminal prosecution, and so technically falls outside the scope of this chapter, it is nevertheless instructive given that courts are even *more* disposed towards accepting PII claims in civil proceedings.[48]

Lappas was charged in 2000 with four offences, including the offence of communicating to another person, for a purpose intended to be prejudicial to the safety or defence of Australia, two documents that were intended to be directly or indirectly useful to a foreign power.[49] The government opposed disclosure of these documents on national security grounds.

The first problem revealed by *Lappas* was that the potential PII issue was not raised as soon as possible – that is, before the committal proceedings. The PII claim was made on behalf of a Minister, and not the prosecuting authority, only when the defence sought to tender the two documents at trial.[50] In particular, there is no requirement at either common law or

---

[47] *R* v. *Lappas & Dowling* [2001] ACTSC 115. Comments to this effect were made by the then Australian Attorney-General and the Australian Law Reform Commission: Commonwealth, *Parliamentary Debates*, House of Representatives, 27 May 2004, 29307 (Philip Ruddock); Australian Law Reform Commission, *Keeping Secrets*, [8.194].

[48] In Australia, see *Alister* v. *R* (1983) 154 CLR 404. In the UK, see *Conway* v. *Rimmer* [1960] AC 910, 942 (Lord Reid). However, note the more nuanced approach developing in the UK and European jurisprudence: see, e.g., *Secretary of State for the Home Department* v. *MB and AF* [2008] 1 AC 440, [17] (Lord Bingham).

[49] *Lappas* [2001] ACTSC 115, [1]. The offence provision was: *Crimes Act 1914* (Aus), s. 78(1)(b).

[50] *Lappas* [2001] ACTSC 115, [4].

under the Evidence Act 1995 (Aus) for a party who becomes aware of the potential disclosure of national security information to notify the other parties to the proceedings, the government or the court; closed hearings are not mandatory for determining claims for public interest immunity; and national security information is not protected from disclosure prior to the making of a court order.

In this case, Gray J exercised the discretion to order a closed hearing to determine the Minister's PII claim. At this hearing, the Minister provided Gray J with a general summary of the documents in question and then, later, the documents themselves 'with much of the contents blacked out'.[51] Affidavits were also filed in support. Gray J upheld the Minister's claim for PII, noting:

> I think that I must accept that any further disclosure of the contents other than what has been so far proposed will give rise to the apprehensions deposed to. If that is the view taken by the appropriate government representative, I have no reason to go behind it.[52]

However, the Minister's victory on the PII claim created problems for the prosecution. The prosecution case depended on inferences drawn from the content of the two documents. In the absence of being able to tender the full documents, the prosecution proposed to put 'empty shells' of the documents before the jury (that is, photocopies of the documents with only the headings 'Top Secret' and 'Not to be Copied' remaining) and to adduce evidence from a witness who would say that a certain construction could be placed on the text of the documents. However, Gray J held that upholding the PII claim rendered the evidence in question inadmissible, and on this basis stayed the prosecution in relation to the offence of communicating the two documents to a foreign power.[53] He further held that even if the evidence *were* admissible, it would violate the defendant's right to a fair trial for the prosecution to be able to adduce the evidence in the manner proposed:

> Presumably there could be no cross-examination on whether the interpretation accurately reflected the contents for that would expose their contents. Nor could a person seeking to challenge the interpretation give their own oral evidence of the contents for that would also expose those contents. The whole process is redolent with unfairness.[54]

---

[51] Ibid., [8]–[9].   [52] Ibid., [26].
[53] Ibid., [15]. He referred to Evidence Act 1995 (Cth), s. 134.
[54] *Lappas* [2001] ACTSC 115, [14].

The government strongly criticised the court's inability in *Lappas* to permit summaries or stipulations to be adduced in place of information covered by PII. A successful PII claim may result in a case being 'unable to proceed due to a lack of admissible evidence or because withholding information from a defendant may prevent them from mounting a full defence and receiving a fair trial'.[55] On the other hand, the government also noted that significant problems arose where a claim for PII is *rejected*. In such a case, the government

> may face the unpalatable decision of whether to risk disclosing sensitive information relating to national security or to protect this information by abandoning a prosecution, even where the alleged crimes could themselves have grave consequences for our national security.[56]

C.   Does the principle strike the right balance?

There are perhaps two central criticisms of the PII principle. First, PII operates as a blunt instrument, in that it applies either to exclude or include evidence entirely. For this reason, PII cannot be deployed to achieve the sorts of compromises, in which information can be revealed in limited or partial ways, which are possible via the mechanisms discussed in the later sections of this chapter. This problem might be difficult to overcome, as this feature of PII has traditionally been viewed as inherent to its operation.

The second central criticism is that PII tilts the balance inordinately in favour of the government party seeking to withhold the evidence in question. As the UK law reform non-government organisation, JUSTICE, observed in 2009:

> By its very nature, the process of one party applying to withhold material on public interest grounds from the other party would require at least some *ex parte* submissions, and it would inevitably fall to the judge sitting alone *in camera* to determine the balance between the public interest in disclosure as against the public interest in nondisclosure.[57]

One might respond by pointing to cases such as *Lappas*, where the government party enjoyed only a Pyrrhic victory, given that the decision to

---

[55] Australian Government, Attorney-General's Department, National Security Information (Criminal and Civil Proceedings) Act 2004: Practitioners' Guide (June 2008), p. 6.

[56] Commonwealth, *Parliamentary Debates*, House of Representatives, 27 May 2004, 29307 (Philip Ruddock).

[57] JUSTICE, *Secret Evidence* (2009), 129.

withhold the information in question led to a stay in the prosecution of at least some of the offences with which the defendant had been charged. However, this does not adequately address the criticism. As Mason J of the High Court of Australia noted, there will be many cases, involving the suppression of material that would otherwise be adducible as evidence, which will simply go ahead regardless:

> The fact that a successful claim to [PII] handicaps one of the parties to litigation is not a reason for saying that the court cannot or will not exercise its ordinary jurisdiction; it merely means that the court will arrive at the decision on something less than the entirety of the relevant materials.[58]

On the other hand, in applying the PII principle in the UK and Canada, the balancing of competing public interests has been altered, at least to a small degree, by the advent of human rights legislation, which expressly requires consideration of human rights, including the right to a fair hearing. The proportionality analysis mandated by the Human Rights Act and Canadian Charter provides something of a counter-balance to the often apparently overwhelming public interest in national security. This is a welcome development.

Given that PII turns on the weighing of competing public interests, the principle is well suited to the express application of a proportionality analysis. However, at present, the courts are not given any statutory guidance in how they should review the executive's assessment of the danger to national security if the information in question were adduced as evidence. Instead, courts should be provided with guidance that assists them in accommodating a fair hearing while protecting national security. In addition, there are no express evidentiary requirements governing how to prove that revealing the information in question would cause intolerable harm to national security. Given that the traditional disposition of courts is to be highly deferential on national security matters, the executive governments of the UK, Canada and Australia have probably been content with this state of affairs. However, faced with a judiciary that is starting to question such claims more closely, the absence of such evidentiary standards might lead to the courts unilaterally setting their own standards. This, in turn, could disadvantage the executive, where a court sets too high the bar for proving a risk to national security.

---

[58] *Church of Scientology v. Woodward* (1982) 154 CLR 25, 61.

To the extent that PII continues to operate at common law, such problems are probably unavoidable, but it is worth noting that these problems also have not been addressed in relation to statutory PII. We believe that PII would operate more effectively and fairly if it were codified in a statute that sets out more precisely how it should operate. In particular, legislation should specifically mandate factors that should be taken into account in the weighing of the competing public interests; it should establish workable evidentiary standards for the court to be satisfied of an intolerable risk to national security, and rules governing how each party might be able to test public interest claims (including by the use of special advocates); and it should set out clear triggers for a court or a party to disclose to the executive government that a PII issue might arise. To some extent, this has been attempted in the UK, Canada and Australia. In Section 4, we assess whether these attempts strike the right balance. That is, we ask: where national security is invoked to justify impinging on the right to a fair hearing, does the system guarantee that the impingement is no greater than is proportionate in the circumstances?

4. Statutory alternatives to common law public interest immunity

This section examines some of the statutory procedures enacted in the UK, Canada and Australia which apply where security-sensitive information might be adduced in civil proceedings. These include the Canadian Evidence Act 1985 and the Australian NSIA, which establish comprehensive regimes for dealing with national security information in court proceedings, as well as the appointment of special advocates to represent individuals where they are excluded from closed hearings in the United Kingdom and Canada.[59] Part of the rationale of these procedures was to address the problems arising from the application of PII, especially at common law, and they aim to strike a more appropriate balance between the public interests for and against disclosure of national security information. However, whether this aim has been achieved is questionable.

In this section, we consider three aspects of the statutory procedures. First, to what extent are the courts (rather than the executive) able to

---

[59] See Helen Fenwick and Gavin Phillipson, Chapter 19 this volume, for a detailed discussion of the UK case law relating to the use of special advocates in control order proceedings. See also Kent Roach, Chapter 20 this volume, who discusses how special advocates were able to exclude evidence from the Canadian Federal Court that was likely obtained through torture.

classify information as open or closed? That is, to what extent are they able to decide whether information that the Crown wishes to rely upon should be disclosed to the parties (open information), or should be restricted to the Crown and the court (closed information)? Second, is there an irreducible minimum (or 'core') of information that must be provided to the parties in civil proceedings? And, finally, how effective are special advocates in protecting the right to a fair hearing?

A.   Classification of information

The ability of the courts to classify information as open or closed is essential to ensuring that an appropriate balance is struck between the need to protect national security and the right to a fair hearing. This is because there is an understandable inclination on the part of members of the executive, in whose hands the responsibility for protecting the security of the nation rests, to over-classify information as closed. In *Secretary of State for the Home Department* v. *MB and AF*,[60] Baroness Hale stated that there was 'ample evidence … of a tendency to overclaim the need for secrecy in terrorism cases'.[61]

The Canadian Evidence Act 1985 and the NSIA deal with the general problem that arose in *Lappas*, namely, that the potential disclosure of national security information was not dealt with at the earliest possible stage, by requiring the parties to identify such issues and notify them to the Attorney-General (being the relevant government Minister in Australia and Canada) as soon as possible. The Attorney-General may thereafter make an application to the court for an order that the information should not be disclosed or should be disclosed in a particular form. The types of orders that the courts may make are dealt with in more detail below.

As under the common law of PII, it is ultimately for the Canadian and Australian courts to classify information as open or closed and to decide whether to order disclosure. However, there is one major difference between these statutory regimes and common law PII: in deciding whether to uphold a PII claim, the court decides at common law what weight should be given to the public interest for and against disclosure; that is, the individual's right to a fair hearing is weighed against the apparently conflicting need to protect national security. By contrast, the statutory regimes in Canada and Australia now appear to have weighted the

---

[60] [2008] 1 AC 440 (*MB and AF*).   [61] Ibid., [66].

scales heavily *against* disclosure of national security information. This is particularly significant because of the broad definition of 'national security' in both jurisdictions. In Australia, for example, this term is defined to mean 'Australia's defence, security, international relations or law enforcement interests'.[62] In turn, 'international relations' means 'political, military and economic relations with foreign governments and international organisations'[63] and 'security' has the same meaning as in the Australian Security Intelligence Organisation Act 1979 (Cth) (ASIO Act),[64] which includes the protection of Australians from 'politically motivated violence' or the 'promotion of communal violence'.[65]

The NSIA requires Australian courts to 'give greatest weight' to 'the risk of prejudice to national security' by the disclosure of the information in deciding what orders to make. Any 'substantial adverse effect on the defendant's right to receive a fair trial, including in particular on the conduct of his or her defence' is a subsidiary consideration.[66] While the constitutionality of this provision has been upheld by the New South Wales Court of Criminal Appeal,[67] former justice of the High Court, the Hon Michael McHugh AC QC, has condemned it as 'a legislative attempt to usurp the judicial power of the Commonwealth'. He went on:

> It is no doubt true that in theory the *National Security Information (Criminal and Civil Proceedings) Act 2004* does not direct the court to make the order which the Attorney-General wants. But it goes as close to it as it thinks it can. It weights the exercise of the discretion in favour of the Attorney-General and in a practical sense directs the outcome of the closed hearing. How can a court make an order in favour of a fair trial when in exercising its discretion, it must give the issue of fair trial less weight than the Attorney-General's certificate. Imagine the appellate fate of a custody order where the trial judge has said I give custody to the father although his claim has less weight than that of the mother.[68]

---

[62] National Security Information (Civil and Criminal Proceedings) Act 2004 (Cth), s. 8. The Bill originally included 'national interests' in the definition of 'national security' but this was subsequently deleted.

[63] Ibid., s. 10.

[64] Ibid., s. 9.

[65] Australian Security Intelligence Organisation Act 1979 (Cth), s. 4.

[66] National Security Information (Criminal and Civil Proceedings) Act 2004 (Cth), s. 31(8).

[67] *Lodhi* v. *The Queen* (2007) 179 A Crim R 470. See also George Williams, Chapter 21 this volume.

[68] Michael McHugh, 'Terrorism legislation and the Constitution' (2006) 28 *Australian Bar Review* 117. See also Anthony Gray, 'Alert and alarmed: the *National Security Information Act* (Cth) (2004)' (2005) 24(2) *University of Tasmania Law Review* 1.

The Australian Law Reform Commission also expressed concern about this aspect of the Bill, noting that its alternative scheme, being the adoption of a balancing exercise such as that which applies to PII claims, 'acknowledges that possible prejudice to national security ought to be given great weight, but formally would leave the court with more discretion to ensure that the interests of justice are served in the case before it'.[69]

The Anti-Terrorism Act 2001 (Can) (ATA) amended two parallel regimes in the Evidence Act 1985 (Can), making it significantly easier for the Crown to prevent the disclosure of information in court proceedings on the basis that disclosure could injure international relations, national defence or national security.[70]

First, under s. 37(1) of the Canadian Evidence Act, the Attorney General may apply to the Court for an order preventing the disclosure of information. While the Court is ostensibly required to weigh the public interests for and against disclosure,[71] in reality, the scales are heavily weighted against disclosure. In Singh (JB) v. Canada (Attorney General),[72] the Federal Court noted that 'the public interest served by maintaining security in the national security context is weighty. In the balancing of public interests here at play, that interest would only be outweighed in a clear and compelling case for disclosure'.[73] More generally, in Canada v. Ribic,[74] it was held that the Attorney General's submissions 'should be given considerable weight' and '[i]f his assessment … is reasonable, the judge should accept it'.[75]

Second, even if the court makes an order for the disclosure of information, the Attorney-General may issue a certificate under s. 38.13 that prohibits such disclosure for the purpose of protecting, among other things, national defence or national security. As originally enacted, there was no opportunity for a party to appeal against the issue of a prohibition certificate. The regime has since been modified to provide for a right to appeal to a single judge of the Federal Court, who may confirm, vary or cancel the certificate.[76] However, two aspects of the regime remain of particular

---

[69] Australian Law Reform Commission, Keeping Secrets, p. 41. See also John von Doussa, 'Reconciling human rights and counter-terrorism: a crucial challenge' (2006) 13 James Cook University Law Review 104, 119.

[70] See Peter Rosenthal, 'Disclosure to the defence after September 11: sections 37 and 38 of the Canada Evidence Act' (2003) 48 Criminal Law Quarterly 186, 190.

[71] See Evidence Act 1985, RSC 1985, c. 5, ss. 37(1.1),(2).   [72] 2000 FCJ No. 1007.

[73] Ibid., [32].   [74] 2003 FCA 246.   [75] Ibid., [19].

[76] Evidence Act 1985, RSC 1985, c. 5, ss. 38.13 and 38.131.

concern.[77] First, a certificate operates for fifteen years and may be reissued.[78] Second, when considering a prohibition certificate, the Federal Court is not required to balance the public interests for and against disclosure. Instead, an appellant is required to establish that the information does not 'relate to' national defence or national security.[79] This means that the Attorney-General would only be required to establish a minor (and possibly innocuous) connection between the information and national defence or national security to sustain the certificate.

Unquestionably, it is important that national security should be given great weight in court proceedings. However, as John von Doussa, former President of the Australian Human Rights and Equal Opportunity Commission, notes, 'it is also important that courts retain a flexible discretion to consider the circumstances of each particular case'.[80] Such discretion is undermined by the principles set out in the Canadian and Australian legislation discussed above. The proportionality principle requires any measures adopted to be 'strictly required' by the exigencies of the situation. Where the scales are weighted against disclosure, as they are in the Canadian and Australian legislation, the courts are clearly less able to restrict the orders they make to what is necessary to protect national security.

B.   A minimum core of information?

The common law rules of evidence are based on the general (but not absolute) rule that any information upon which one party seeks to rely must be provided to all other parties. Thus, if the Crown successfully objects to the disclosure of information on the ground of PII, it will no longer be permitted to rely upon that information. Statutory procedures introduced in the UK, Canada and Australia aim to remedy the rigidity of this 'all or nothing' approach. They establish mechanisms whereby, for example, the Crown may rely upon the whole of a document but only disclose to other parties such part as would not injure national security.

The key advantage of this approach lies in its flexibility. However, with flexibility comes the potential for confusion and for the individual's right

---

[77] These two concerns are discussed in more detail in: Senate of Canada, Special Senate Committee on the Anti-Terrorism Act, *Fundamental Justice in Extraordinary Times: Main Report of the Special Senate Committee on the Anti-Terrorism Act* (2007), pp. 64–8.

[78] Evidence Act 1985, RSC 1985, c. 5, ss. 38.13(9).

[79] Evidence Act 1985, RSC 1985, c. 5, s. 38.131.

[80] von Doussa, 'Reconciling human rights and counter-terrorism', 118–19.

to a fair hearing to be whittled down. The latter is particularly concerning when the new hybrid civil/criminal proceedings developed in response to 9/11 are considered. For example, in both the UK and Australia, 'control orders' may now be issued against persons deemed to present an unacceptable threat of terrorism.[81] Whilst the court proceedings relating to such orders are ostensibly civil in nature, the consequences for the subject of a control order may be as severe as those attaching to a finding of criminal guilt. These include: restrictions on movement, limits on the ability to contact other persons, curfews and even house arrest. As the Canadian Supreme Court has stated, the content of the right to a fair hearing 'does not turn on a formal distinction between the different areas of law. Rather, it depends on the severity of the consequences of the state's actions for the individual's fundamental interests of liberty and security and, in some cases, the right to life'.[82] The severe consequences stemming from the issue of a control order reinforce the necessity that the right to a fair hearing be protected.

In Canada and Australia, the relevant statutory regimes spell out the minimum level of disclosure permitted if the Crown is to rely upon information. The Evidence Act 1985 (Can) and the NSIA both provide that the courts may authorise disclosure of all the information, a part or summary of the information or a written statement of facts relating to the information.[83] There are no equivalent statutory provisions in the UK. The question whether there is an irreducible minimum (or 'core') of information that must be provided to the parties is left entirely to the UK courts to determine. Even in Canada and Australia, there is little detail contained in the statutory regimes and it remains necessary for the courts in these countries to ask similar questions to those in the UK. What is meant by a 'summary' or a 'statement of facts'? Is there a core of information that must be contained in these documents in order for a party to receive a fair hearing?

The most thorough discussion of the question whether there is a core of information that must be provided to the parties emerges from UK control order cases. In *Secretary of State for the Home Department* v. *AF*,[84] the

---

[81] See George Williams, Chapter 21, this volume and Helen Fenwick and Gavin Phillipson, Chapter 19, this volume, for a discussion of the control order regimes and its interpretation in each jurisidction.

[82] *Charkaoui* v. *Canada (Citizenship and Immigration)* [2008] 2 SCR 326, [53].

[83] Evidence Act 1985, RSC 1985, c. 5, s. 38.06(2); National Security Information (Criminal and Civil Proceedings) Act 2004 (Cth), s. 38L.

[84] [2009] UKHL 28 (*AF*).

House of Lords concluded that a person seeking review of a control order 'must be given sufficient information about the allegations against him to enable him to give effective instructions in relation to these allegations'.[85] It will not be necessary for him to be given details of the evidence forming the basis of the allegations or the sources of that evidence. However, if 'the open material consists purely of general assertions and the case against the controllee is based solely or to a decisive degree on closed materials the requirements of a fair trial will not be satisfied, however cogent the case based on the closed materials may be'.[86] This was where the balance was struck by the European Court earlier in 2009 in *A v. United Kingdom*,[87] and the House of Lords (with considerable regret expressed by Lord Hoffman)[88] felt bound to follow. The European Court recognised that a person involved in civil proceedings could not always be given all the information concerning them. Furthermore, the person's legal representative could not always be given all the information concerning their client. Extenuating circumstances, such as where disclosure posed a risk to national security, may prevent this. However, the proportionality principle requires that any limitation on the right to a fair hearing must be sufficiently counter-balanced by the procedures followed by the judicial authorities.

C.   *Special advocates*

Lord Hoffmann was not the only member of the House of Lords to change his approach in *AF*. Just two years earlier in *MB and AF*, a majority of the House of Lords found that the right to a fair hearing did not mandate that a party be provided with a minimum level of information. In making this finding, the House of Lords placed its faith in the UK's special advocates regime. In the words of Baroness Hale:

> I do not think we can be confident that Strasbourg would hold that *every* control order hearing in which the special advocate procedure had been used ... would be sufficient to comply with Article 6. However, with strenuous efforts from all, difficult and time consuming through it will

---

[85]   Ibid., [59].   [86]   Ibid.

[87]   *Application 3455/05* [2009] ECHR 301 (19 February 2009).

[88]   Lord Hoffmann would have preferred to ask 'whether in all the circumstances it would really be unfair not to tell the applicant or accused' rather than adopting the rigid rule espoused by the European Court. His Lordship stated: 'I think that the decision of the ECtHR was wrong and ... it may well destroy the system of control orders which is a significant part of this country's defence against terrorism': [2009] UKHL 28, [70], [72].

be, it should usually be possible to accord the controlled person 'a substantial measure of procedural justice'.[89]

Two years later, however, Baroness Hale stated: 'I was far too sanguine about the possibilities of conducting a fair hearing under the special advocate procedure'.[90] Similarly, Lord Hope (who had reached the same conclusion in *MB and AF*) stated that 'this was an optimistic assessment. It assumed that the disadvantages that the use of closed material gives rise to could be overcome by looking at the proceedings in the round'.[91] The main reason for this change in attitude (apart, of course, from the decision of the European Court in *A*) appears to have been the increasing recognition by the House of Lords of the deficiencies in the system of special advocates. In particular, they recognised the system's inability to compensate for the failure to provide information to a party.

i.   The introduction of special advocates in the UK

The special advocates regime in the UK was enacted partly in response to the decision of the European Court of Human Rights in *Chahal* v. *United Kingdom*.[92] The European Court held that the issuing of a deportation certificate for Karamjit Singh Chahal, an Indian national residing in the UK, by the Secretary of State for Home Affairs on the ground of national security violated the European Convention on Human Rights. This was because the review panel, colloquially known as the 'Three Wise Men', was not a 'court': Chahal was not entitled to legal representation before the panel, he was only given an outline of the grounds forming the basis for the certificate on the ground of PII, and the panel's advice to the Home Secretary was not binding.[93] The European Court concluded:

> The Court recognises that the use of confidential material may be unavoidable where national security is at stake. This does not mean, however, that the national authorities can be free from effective control by the domestic courts whenever they choose to assert that national security and terrorism are involved.[94]

In response to the European Court's decision, the Special Immigration Appeals Commission Act 1997 (UK) (SIAC Act) was enacted. This replaced the 'Three Wise Men' with an independent quasi-judicial tribunal (SIAC) before which foreign nationals could appeal against a deportation order made by the Secretary of State. SIAC's jurisdiction

---

[89] *Secretary of State for the Home Department* v. *MB and AF* [2008] 1 AC 440, [66].
[90] [2009] UKHL 28, [101].   [91] Ibid., [79].   [92] (1996) 23 EHRR 413.
[93] Ibid., [130]–[133].   [94] Ibid., [131].

was later expanded to include appeals against revocation of citizen-ship[95] and, under the Anti-Terrorism Crime and Security Act 2001, to review the detention of foreign nationals who had been designated by the Secretary of State as 'suspected international terrorists'.[96] This 2001 Act was repealed in 2005.[97]

In finding that the pre-1997 UK regime violated the European Convention on Human Rights, the European Court emphasised that there were alternative mechanisms that were less intrusive in their impact on the right to a fair hearing. The Court noted in particular the use of special advocates before the Canadian Security Intelligence Review Committee (SIRC) under the now-repealed Immigration Act 1976 (Can).[98] In large part, the SIRC system of special advocates was incorporated into the SIAC Act. In contrast to the usual approach to procedural fairness whereby a person is entitled to all the information against him or her, SIAC is permitted to withhold material from the appellant and the appellant's legal representative and to hold closed proceedings in the absence of the appellant and the appellant's legal representative. In these circumstances, a special advocate may be – but, in practice, always is – appointed by SIAC to represent the interests of the appellant. The special advocate's role is to challenge the Secretary of State's designation of material as closed (the disclosure function),[99] and to appear before SIAC on the appeal if closed material continues to be relied on (the substantive function).[100]

ii.   Restrictions on communication

There is one critical difference between the SIRC and SIAC systems. Ip notes that SIRC special advocates were allowed to communicate with

---

[95] Nationality, Immigration and Asylum Act 2002 (UK).

[96] Anti-Terrorism, Crime and Security Act 2001 (UK), s. 23.

[97] The Act was repealed after the decision of the House of Lords in the *Belmarsh Detainees* case: [2005] 2 AC 68. The House of Lords held that the Act was incompatible with the Human Rights Act 1998 (UK) because the detention provision was disproportionate (in the sense that it was not strictly required by the emergency) and discriminatory.

[98] Ibid. The functions of special advocates before SIRC are discussed in *Charkaoui v. Canada (Citizenship and Immigration)* [2007] 1 SCR 350, [71]–[76].

[99] For a discussion of the similarities and differences between the disclosure function of special advocates and the approach devised by the courts to deal with PII, see: House of Commons Constitutional Affairs Committee, *The Operation of the Special Immigration Appeals Commission (SIAC) and the Use of Special Advocates (Volume 1)*, Seventh Report of Session 2004–5, HC 323–1, p. 24.

[100] Joint Committee on Human Rights, United Kingdom Parliament, *Counter-Terrorism Policy and Human Rights: 28 days, Intercept and Post Charge Questioning*, Nineteenth Report of Session 2006–7, HL Paper 157, HC 394, 50.

the affected person even after they had viewed the closed material.[101] By contrast, under the SIAC Act, special advocates are generally only permitted to communicate with an appellant *before* they have viewed the closed material.[102] The rationale for this is that, after viewing the closed material, the special advocate may inadvertently reveal the content of that material to the appellant.[103]

While there are some exceptions to this prohibition on communication, these are extremely limited and do little to mitigate the unfairness caused to the appellant. First, an appellant is allowed, on his or her own initiative, to contact the special advocate.[104] Any information provided by an appellant is likely to be of limited assistance to the special advocate given that, in many instances, the nature of the case against the appellant is only revealed by the closed material. Second, with the permission of the Secretary of State, SIAC may grant the special advocate permission to ask specific questions of the appellant.[105] However, it has been noted by special advocates that such a system is rarely (if ever) used.[106] This is because there is a belief among special advocates that the Secretary of State is unlikely to grant permission, and also because it may reveal to the Secretary of State a strategy that the special advocate intends to adopt.[107]

The prohibition on communication places considerable hurdles in the way of a fair trial, as it makes it virtually impossible for the appellant to give effective instructions regarding the conduct of his or her case. Lord Bingham, in *Roberts* v. *Parole Board*,[108] said that a special advocate deprived of effective instructions is inevitably 'taking blind shots at a hidden target'.[109] Even Lord Carlile, the UK Independent Reviewer of Terrorism Legislation and a well-known supporter of the special advocates regime, has noted that 'there should be available to special advocates an easier and closer relationship with the individuals whose interests they represent'.[110]

---

[101] John Ip, 'The rise and spread of the special advocate' [2008] *Public Law* 717, 720.
[102] Ibid., 721; Special Immigration Appeals Commission (Procedure) Rules 2003, rule 26(2).
[103] This rationale simply does not wash when it is considered that government lawyers and agency members with knowledge of the closed material are permitted to communicate with the appellant.
[104] Special Immigration Appeals Commission (Procedure) Rules 2003, rule 36(6).
[105] Special Immigration Appeals Commission (Procedure) Rules 2003, rules 36(4)–(5).
[106] Joint Committee on Human Rights, Nineteenth Report of Session 2006–2007, [201].
[107] Lani Inverarity, 'Immigration Bill 2007: special advocates and the right to be heard' (2009) 40 *Victoria University of Wellington Law Review* 471, 481.
[108] [2005] 2 AC 738 (*Roberts*).   [109] Ibid., [18] (in dissent).
[110] Lord Carlile of Berriew QC, *Anti-Terrorism, Crime and Security Act 2001: Part IV Section 28 – Review 2004* (2004), [78].

Options that may go some way towards achieving this could involve the establishment of detailed protocols regarding communications between special advocates and appellants to minimise the possibility of inadvertent disclosure, or the presence of a person from the Special Advocates Support Office during any such communications.[111] While either of these options would obviously fall short of the freedom generally attaching to the lawyer–client relationship, they would come much closer to striking a balance between the interests of national security and the appellant's right to a fair hearing.

The special advocate regime has subsequently been adopted in Canada for PII issues following the Supreme Court decision in *Charkaoui v. Minister of Citizenship and Immigration*.[112] Unfortunately, instead of following the SIRC procedure with its more permissive approach to communication between the special advocate and his or her client, the Canadian Parliament chose to adopt the UK approach.[113] Notably, the Canadian Senate Special Committee has since supported allowing more communication, suggesting that the special advocate 'might communicate with the client in the company of another person, likewise sworn to secrecy, so that there can be close monitoring of what is discussed and inadvertent errors of disclosure prevented'.[114]

iii.   Function creep

In *Chahal*, the European Court noted that the SIRC system of special advocates 'accommodate[s] legitimate security concerns about the nature and sources of intelligence information and yet accord[s] the individual a substantial measure of procedural fairness'.[115] However, this conclusion has been strongly criticised. In *Roberts*, Lord Steyn said that the 'special advocate procedure strikes at the root of the prisoner's fundamental right to a basically fair procedure':[116]

> It is important not to pussyfoot around such a fundamental matter: the special advocate procedure undermines the very essence of elementary justice. It involves a phantom hearing only.[117]

[111]   Joint Committee on Human Rights, Nineteenth Report of Session 2006–7, pp. 53–4.
[112]   [2007] 1 SCR 350. For a detailed discussion of this case, see Roach, 'When secret intelligence becomes evidence', 147.
[113]   An Act to amend the Immigration and Refugee Protection Act, SC 2008, c. 3.
[114]   Special Senate Committee on the Anti-Terrorism Act, *Fundamental Justice in Extraordinary Times*, p. 36.
[115]   Ibid.   [116]   *Roberts* v. *Parole Board* [2005] UKHL 45, [93].
[117]   Ibid., [88].

In this chapter, we have only addressed one of the concerns in relation to the ability of special advocates to represent the interests of their clients. Others include: the small pool of special advocates; inability of clients to choose their own special advocate from a list; lack of resources and assistance for special advocates; reliance upon the government to disclose all relevant material; inability to call expert witnesses; and, most significantly, the fact that a special advocate is required to 'represent the interests' of his or her client but is not 'responsible' to him or her.[118] Despite these deficiencies, most commentators, special advocates and judges seem to accept that the special advocates regime represents an important safeguard of the individual's right to a fair hearing in the face of a need to protect the security of the nation and its citizens. In *M* v. *Secretary of State for the Home Department*,[119] the UK Court of Appeal stated:

> Individuals who appeal to SIAC are undoubtedly under a grave disadvantage. So far as it is possible this disadvantage should be avoided or, if it cannot be avoided, minimised. However, the unfairness involved can be necessary because of the interests of national security. The involvement of a special advocate is intended to reduce (it cannot wholly eliminate) the unfairness which follows from the fact that an appellant will be unaware at least as to part of the case against him.[120]

Similarly, Roach stated:

> [S]pecial advocates constitute one example of an approach that is a more proportionate response to reconciling the need to keep some information secret and the need to ensure as much fairness and adversarial challenge as possible.[121]

We agree that there is an important role to be played by special advocates in proceedings such as those before SIAC and control order proceedings. However, as noted by the House of Lords in *AF*, the special advocates system is not of itself sufficient to protect the individual's right to a fair hearing. The doctrine of proportionality requires that measures restricting fundamental rights be the least intrusive available. The current special advocates regime does not satisfy this test. It is only when combined with other protections that any special advocates regime can strike an

---

[118] For a discussion of the various problems relating to the use of special advocates, see House of Commons Constitutional Affairs Committee, Seventh Report of Session 2004–5, pp. 30–9.

[119] [2004] EWCA Civ 324.   [120] Ibid., [13].

[121] Kent Roach, 'Ten ways to improve Canadian anti-terrorism law' (2006) 51 *Criminal Law Quarterly* 102, 120.

appropriate balance between national security and the right to a fair trial. As *AF* sets out, one of these protections is a requirement that individuals be provided with sufficient details of the allegations against them to provide effective instructions. This should be complemented by an amendment of the regulatory arrangements to enable special advocates to communicate with their clients even after they have viewed the closed information. In these circumstances, special advocates assist in ensuring 'that the judge has been exposed to the whole factual picture'[122] rather than simply the picture that the Crown wishes to present.

The starting point in all proceedings – civil and criminal – must be that the Crown is required to disclose all information it relies upon to the person affected. This includes not only the allegations made against that person, but also the evidence upon which those allegations are based and the sources of that evidence. The alternative system, as epitomised by the proceedings before SIAC, is not and should not be allowed to become the norm. It is only in cases where there are exceptional grounds for so doing that information may be withheld, and the appointment of a special advocate will be both proportionate and necessary. It is therefore concerning that the use of special advocates, in the UK in particular, has spread far beyond the counter-terrorism context.[123] While it is beyond the scope of this chapter to assess the appropriateness of appointing a special advocate in each of these cases, we would adopt the test set out by Lord Bingham in *R* v. *H and C*.[124] In the context of discussing whether it was appropriate to appoint a special advocate for a criminal defendant, Lord Bingham stated:

> Such an appointment will always be exceptional, never automatic, a course of last and never first resort. It should not be ordered unless and until the trial judge is satisfied that no other course will adequately meet the overriding requirement of fairness to the defendant.[125]

5. Conclusion

In combating terrorism, we have started from the position that the right to a fair hearing must cede, at least to a certain degree, to legitimate national

---

[122] *Charkaoui* v. *Canada (Citizenship and Immigration)* [2007] 1 SCR 350, [51].
[123] See House of Commons Constitutional Affairs Committee, Seventh Report of Session 2004–5, pp. 21–2. The spread of special advocates in the UK and across jurisdictions is also discussed in Ip, 'The rise and spread of the special advocate'.
[124] [2004] UKHL 3.   [125] Ibid., [22].

security concerns. However, we argue for a more sophisticated approach to the withholding of security-sensitive information in civil litigation. We applaud the approach of courts in the UK to be less deferential to the assertion of national security exigencies by the executive arm of government. However, courts in Canada, and particularly in Australia, have been less successful in this regard. We argue for these courts to assume a more significant role in testing such executive claims.

We argue that the concept of proportionality should become more overtly the guiding principle in determining how far national security concerns can justify incursions into procedural fairness and the right to a fair hearing. In particular, we believe that the PII principle should be codified in legislation in a manner that better permits the courts to accommodate the right to a fair hearing while responding to the demands of national security. The articulation of clearer duties on parties, and the court, in testing claims for PII would better allow the court to carry out its duty of weighing the competing public interests.

Significant progress has been made by the UK, Canadian and Australian parliaments to deal with the challenges posed by the potential disclosure of national security information in civil proceedings. However, a failure on the part of these legislatures to give adequate consideration to the proportionality principle has resulted in legislation that does not properly accommodate the fundamental right to a fair hearing. Some of these deficiencies have been rectified by the courts; for example, with the UK House of Lords (now Supreme Court) recognising that a person must always be provided with sufficient information so they can provide effective instructions to the special advocate acting on their behalf. Nevertheless, there is still considerable room for improvement. But that improvement requires the legislature to provide the appropriate tools to the judiciary, so that in individual cases in which security sensitive information is at issue, any impingement on the right to a fair hearing will be no more than is absolutely necessary.

7

Legislating anti-terrorism: observations on form and process

ANDREW LYNCH

1. Introduction

The likely conduct of the three arms of government in responding to threats to national security – and the strengths and weaknesses possessed by each in doing so – has been the subject of a considerable amount of academic debate in the years since the terrorist attacks on the United States in 2001. Although the question of how democracies can defeat an enemy while still maintaining essential checks and balances on government is far from a new one, it has certainly received sustained attention, frequently enriched through use of comparative perspectives and experiences, in the first decade of this century.

In the immediate aftermath of World War II, Rossiter concluded that 'it is always the executive branch in the government which possesses and wields the extraordinary powers of self-preservation of any democratic, constitutional state' and that the other arms of government should facilitate, rather than obstruct it from doing so.[1] Drawing parallels between the use of strictly limited dictatorships by the Roman Republic and the behaviour of the US and UK governments during the then recently concluded hostilities, Rossiter's advocacy of virtually unchecked executive power in times of crisis – a 'constitutional dictatorship' – was underpinned by his appreciation of the capacity of the other arms of government to reclaim their status and functions once the danger had passed.[2] The ability of the

I gratefully acknowledge the excellent research assistance of Keiran Hardy in preparation of this chapter and the comments and suggestions of participants at the 2010 Anti-Terrorism Law Symposium and Dr Dominique Dalla-Pozza on an earlier version of this work. I thank the editors for their invitation to contribute to the symposium and this collection. Any errors are, of course, mine alone.

[1] Clinton L. Rossiter, *Constitutional Dictatorship* (Princeton University Press, 1948), p. 12.
[2] Ibid., pp. 8–25. The use of dictators by the Roman Republic is something of an ubiquitous entry point to modern discussion of emergency constitutionalism: see particularly John

polity to revert swiftly to its more familiar constitutional contours must surely depend on the strength of its democratic culture and institutions.[3] But such a reversion is also greatly assisted by the clear identification of a point when victory or safety has been secured. The subsequent experience of decades of Cold War and, of course, the contemporary realisation that however else we might seek to describe the present security environment, a 'war on terror' it simply is not, has exposed the limitations of Rossiter's study. The embrace of executive unilateralism by the White House Administration of President George W. Bush after 9/11 has, in turn, served to amply demonstrate the dangers of such an approach outside the parameters of total war.[4]

Other than those few voices whose support of essentially unchecked presidential war powers was relied on by the Bush White House to furnish it with legal justification for the many extraordinary methods it employed against foreign nationals and its own citizens in the name of national security,[5] the bulk of recent literature overwhelmingly favours the retention of some limits upon executive power, even in times of emergency or danger to the polity. But across this broad consensus there is an internal divide as to whether the judiciary or legislature is best equipped to effectively counter or control the likely excesses of the executive. Although the arguments are numerous and set out at length

E. Finn, *Constitutions in Crisis: Political Violence and the Rule of Law* (Oxford University Press, 1991), pp. 15–16; Oren Gross, 'The concept of "crisis": what can we learn from the two dictatorships of L. Quinctius Cincinnatus' (Paper presented at the Centro Nazionale di Prevenzione e Difesa Sociale XVII International Conference, 'Civil and economic rights in times of crisis', Stresa, Italy, 13–14 May 2005); Oren Gross and Fionnuala Ní Aoláin, *Law in Times of Crisis: Emergency Powers in Theory and Practice* (Cambridge University Press, 2006), pp. 17–26.

[3] Samuel Issacharoff, 'Political safeguards in times of war' (2009) 29 *Oxford Journal of Legal Studies* 189, 206. See also Finn, *Constitutions in Crisis*, p. 149; and Rossiter, *Constitutional Dictatorship*, p. 71.

[4] See Jack Goldsmith, *The Terror Presidency* (New York: W.W. Norton, 2007); Kim Lane Scheppele, 'Law in a time of emergency: states of exception and the temptations of 9/11' (2004) 6 *University of Pennsylvania Journal of Constitutional Law* 1001.

[5] See Karen J. Greenberg and Joshua L. Dratel (eds), *The Torture Papers: The Road to Abu Ghraib* (New York: Cambridge University Press, 2005); Eric Posner and Adrian Vermeule, *Terror in the Balance: Security, Liberty and the Courts* (New York: Oxford University Press, 2008); John Yoo, 'Executive power, civil liberties, and security: constitutional trade-offs in fighting global terrorism' in Stuart Gottlieb (ed.), *Debating Terrorism and Counterterrorism: Conflicting Perspectives on Causes, Contexts, and Responses* (Washington, DC: CQ Press, 2010), pp. 339–52 (cf. Goldsmith, *The Terror Presidency*); Stephen Holmes, *The Matador's Cape: America's Reckless Response to Terror* (New York: Cambridge University Press, 2007), pp. 286–302.

by many elsewhere,[6] basically the perceived strength of the judiciary as a safeguard hinges on its independence when contrasted with the constraining effects of populism and party discipline on the legislature. Conversely, judges rarely have the access to information or experience to make determinations on the reasonableness of security measures.[7] The judicial arm of government is also the most reactive, with its power of intervention dependent upon individuals to seek legal redress. Considerable time may elapse before the hearing of specific claims results in the courts placing a clear curb on political power, if at all.[8] The judiciary's historical record of affording individuals meaningful protection in times of national emergency is far from stellar. While some might point to key cases in the last few years in both the United States and the United Kingdom[9] as proof that the judiciary has overcome its traditional deference so as to take a stand against rights abuses by their respective governments in responding to terrorism (particularly in the United Kingdom by virtue of the courts' use of the Human Rights Act 1998),[10] others strongly argue that this favourable assessment of judicial performance is contestable when one examines the actual impact the decisions made have had both on the rights of the individuals in question, and more broadly.[11]

My own position on this debate is that it starts from an artificial premise. While separate evaluation of the capacity and performance of the legislature and judiciary is worthwhile in promoting a better

---

[6] Though for an especially succinct and balanced presentation of both points of view, see Fiona de Londras and Fergal Davis, 'Controlling the executive in times of terrorism: competing perspectives on effective oversight mechanisms' (2010) 30 *Oxford Journal of Legal Studies* 19.

[7] Mark Tushnet, 'Controlling executive power in the war on terrorism' (2005) 118 *Harvard Law Review* 2673, 2679.

[8] Consider the cumulative effect of the decisions of the United States Supreme Court in *Rasul v. Bush*, 542 US 466 (2004); *Hamdi v. Rumsfeld*, 542 US 507 (2004); *Hamdan v. Rumsfeld*, 548 US 557 (2006); *Boumediene v. Bush*, 553 US 723 (2008).

[9] Namely *Boumediene v. Bush*, 553 US 723 (2008) and *A v. Secretary of State for the Home Department* [2005] 2 AC 68 (*Belmarsh* case).

[10] See David Bonner, *Executive Measures, Terrorism and National Security: Have the Rules of the Game Changed?* (Aldershot: Ashgate, 2007); de Londras in de Londras and Davis, 'Controlling the executive in times of terrorism', 41–3; Colm O'Cinneide, 'Strapped to the mast: the siren song of dreadful necessity, the United Kingdom Human Rights Act and the terrorist threat' in Miriam Gani and Penelope Mathew (eds.), *Fresh Perspectives on the 'War on Terror'* (Canberra: ANU E Press, 2008), p. 327.

[11] Davis in de Londras and Davis, 'Controlling the executive in times of terrorism', 28–9; Keith Ewing and Joo-Cheong Tham, 'The continuing futility of the Human Rights Act' [2008] *Public Law* 668.

understanding of how each may act as a safeguard against an overreaching executive in times of existential crisis, to the question, 'which of them is best placed to check the power of the executive?' I would simply answer 'both'.[12] Apart from the fact that this shared responsibility accords with constitutional arrangements generally in many countries (making the championing of one arm of government over the other in times of emergency, most usually as an expression of judicial review scepticism,[13] a fairly curious exercise), there is much to be said for the view that the legislature and judiciary together contribute to ensuring the accountability of the executive. Although they obviously act in distinctive ways and at different stages, they may often complement each other's efforts. The weight of contemporary experience since 9/11 increasingly supports this stance. De Londras and Davis, after offering a dialectic examination of the most effective means of checking executive power in responding to terrorism, and while maintaining their individual emphasis on judicial and political controls respectively, ultimately conclude that 'it seems likely that … the most effective form of oversight will be through a legislative–judicial dialogue focused on achieving a sustainable, proportionate balance between the exigencies of a security crisis and the fundamentality of rights'.[14] 'Dialogue' might best describe the optimal interaction between the non-executive arms of government in such circumstances, but there seems little cogent reason why the judiciary should not act simply as 'a back-up' for when political controls fail.[15] Tushnet's argument that the danger of this is that the political branches of government will discharge their own responsibilities with less care than they ought to exercise,[16] is difficult to verify. The judiciary in the United Kingdom enjoyed a far less significant role in the review of legislation prior to the arrival of the Human Rights Act and yet this did not appear to influence parliamentary scrutiny for the better – consider, for example, the manifestly draconian laws hurriedly enacted in response to the declaration of war in

---

[12] Andrew Lynch, 'Exceptionalism, politics and liberty: a response to Professor Tushnet from the antipodes' (2008) 3 *International Journal of Law in Context* 305.

[13] Mark Tushnet, 'The political constitution of emergency powers: some lessons from Hamdan' (2007) 91 *Minnesota Law Review* 1451. Ewing and Tham are further motivated by scepticism over the effectiveness of the UK statutory Human Rights Act in protecting individual freedoms: Ewing and Tham, 'The continuing futility of the Human Rights Act'.

[14] de Londras and Davis, 'Controlling the executive in times of terrorism', 46.

[15] Issacaharoff, 'Political safeguards in times of war'.

[16] Tushnet, 'Controlling executive power in the war on terrorism', 2680; shared by Davis in de Londras and Davis, 'Controlling the executive in times of terrorism, 32, 45.

1939 and the threat of Irish terrorist activity.[17] In any case, while I am sympathetic to the view that legislators are frequently not as mindful of the constitutionality of the bills they enact as they should be and instead appear to be content to await judicial decision on such questions,[18] the prospect of the latter can hardly be used to let parliamentarians off the hook. Apart from anything else, the judiciary may be expected to defer to elected representatives when questions of national security arise. Far better to appreciate the value of judicial scrutiny, while at the same time seeking to enhance that of law-makers, than to dispense with the former and risk no improvement in the latter.

The performance of legislatures, then, has clearly been central to consideration as to how best to restrain executive excess in responding to terrorism – but too often this has been in the service of debates over its effectiveness relative to that of the judiciary. If we abandon attempts to place the legislature and judiciary on opposing sides of the ledger whereby the weakness of one strengthens the appeal of the other, then the focus becomes less on competition than on the quality of each in its own right. The purpose of this chapter is to explore some of the recurrent themes in the enactment of anti-terrorism laws by national legislatures since 9/11. This provides essential context for the substantive analysis of many of these laws in the other chapters of this book.[19] A study of the law-making process in this area necessarily involves making generalised observations, given the range of different jurisdictions which are included in the discussion and also the significant number of enactments made by some of those. But it is important to state at the outset that the arguments made here about the general adequacy of pre-enactment scrutiny and deliberation of anti-terrorism laws in legislative chambers are not consciously presented as part of a case for judicial review. As stated above, I am of the view that, quite independently of the performance of the legislative arm, the courts should play a meaningful role, within their traditional capacities, in the restraint of executive abuse of power in times of emergency. The legislature should be

---

[17] Respectively the Emergency Powers (Defence) Act 1939, the Prevention of Violence Act (Temporary Provisions) 1939 and the Prevention of Terrorism (Temporary Powers) Act 1974.

[18] Andrew Lynch and Tessa Meyrick, 'The Constitution and legislative responsibility' (2007) 18 *Public Law Review* 158.

[19] See especially George Williams, Chapter 21, this volume (Australia and New Zealand); Kent Roach, Chapter 20, this volume (Canada); William C. Banks, Chapter 18, this volume (United States); Helen Fenwick and Gavin Phillipson, Chapter 19, this volume (United Kingdom).

appraised on its own terms and where strengthening is required, then that should be through its own practices and culture – and not by simply passing the ball to judges.

2.   Anti-terrorism laws: form and process

For the purposes of discussion, this Section first examines some common trends in the form of the bills which have been brought by governments to their legislatures for enactment, before then considering the process by which the latter has typically occurred. Admittedly this is somewhat artificial since of course the members of legislative bodies cannot readily isolate form and process from each other. Nor should those observing the pattern of legislative enactment since all too frequently the two operate in tandem to give rise to objections. The dense complexity of draft anti-terrorism legislation is itself not necessarily a legitimate ground for complaint, especially given the gravity of the harm it is seeking to forestall, until one also considers the timeframe within which the government has pushed parliamentarians to act. Essentially, a holistic examination of legislating anti-terrorism laws is required in order to appreciate how the discrete features of that experience have worked in combination to affect the strength of the legislature's oversight of counter-terrorism initiatives of the executive.

Before commencing to look for themes in the way in which jurisdictions have responded legislatively to the terrorist threat in the wake of 9/11, it is perhaps worth indicating that this discussion focuses mainly upon Australia, Canada, New Zealand, the United Kingdom and United States as nations offering particularly fruitful avenues of comparison. That said, even amongst these common law countries there are significant distinctions which should be kept in mind at all stages. Government in the United States does not, of course, adhere to the Westminster doctrine of responsible government by which the executive governs through rather than separately from parliament. The dominance of the executive in the lower house of the parliaments of the four other nations (and, in Australia, occasional control of the upper house as well) clearly impacts upon the capacity of those institutions to resist government legislative demands and act as a truly independent check at all times. Another clear distinction is the level of formal human rights protection against which legislation is made. The United States alone enjoys constitutionally entrenched strong judicial review, while Canada, the United Kingdom and New Zealand all possess less conclusive forms of judicial involvement in the protection of rights.[20] In Canada the Charter of Rights and Freedoms 1982 is a constitutional document but the Parliament may enact laws notwithstanding its protections – either in the first instance or by way of re-enactment following invalidation by the Supreme Court of the initial Act as in breach of the Charter. In the United Kingdom, the courts do not possess the power to strike out laws and can merely issue a declaration when they find one to be incompatible with the freedoms recognised by the Human Rights Act 1998. The Parliament need not repeal or amend the law in response. Initially, the New Zealand Bill of Rights Act 1990 conferred upon the courts an interpretative power only so that laws were to be read consistently with its protections, but a power to issue declarations of incompatibility was claimed by the judiciary in 2000.[21] As in the United Kingdom, a declaration of incompatibility does not invalidate the relevant legislation. Lastly, Australia has no formal instrument of rights protection whatsoever at the national level, though a handful of constitutional provisions limit the powers of either or both the Commonwealth and States to impair some specific rights of individuals.

However, the main point of difference between these five jurisdictions must, in the context of this volume, be their distinctive security challenges and the level of the terrorist threat. Including the atrocities of 9/11, of the five, only the United States and the United Kingdom have suffered a major terrorist attack in the last decade. Australian and Canadian authorities have each foiled plans for a major strike involving a sizeable number of individuals apparently motivated by Islamic fundamentalism, many of whom have since been convicted of terrorist offences.[22] In 2007, New Zealand's terrorism laws were used by police to arrest seventeen indigenous and environmentalist activists, but the Solicitor-General declined to prosecute for these offences. Lastly, Australia and the United Kingdom were participants in the US-led 'coalition of the willing' which invaded Iraq in 2003, while Canada and New Zealand were not. All five countries have participated to some extent in the military operations in Afghanistan since October 2001.

It is noteworthy that, despite these differences between the countries regarding governance and their likely priority as a terrorist target, clear

---

[20] Stephen Gardbaum, 'The new Commonwealth model of constitutionalism' (2001) 49 *American Journal of Comparative Law* 707, 719–39.

[21] *Moonen* v. *Film and Literature Board of Review* [2000] 2 NZLR 9.

[22] For a comprehensive account of Australian terrorism trials, see Nicola McGarrity, '"Testing" our counter-terrorism laws: the prosecution of individuals for terrorism offences in Australia' (2010) 34 *Criminal Law Journal* 92.

trends in the creation of anti-terrorism laws both as to form and process are discernible. With direct reliance on the records of parliamentary and congressional debates themselves, it is to a consideration of these that we now turn.

A. Form

The most striking similarity between the laws enacted in the first flush of legislative activity in the aftermath of 9/11 was their sheer scale. The current British Prime Minister, then sitting on the opposition benches, listed size as the first of his objections to the Blair government's Anti-Terrorism, Crime and Security Bill 2001 (ATCSB), adding pithily that 'we do not have to read it, as we can simply weigh it'.[23] Given that the Westminster Parliament had enacted what aspired to be comprehensive and permanent anti-terrorism law in just the preceding year, David Cameron's incredulity at the density of the ATCSB was understandable. The ATCSB not only amended existing provisions of the Terrorism Act 2000 but provided for, amongst other things, the freezing of terrorist assets, the disclosure of information for law enforcement purposes and the indefinite detention of terrorist suspects (later held by the House of Lords to be incompatible with the UK Human Rights Act).[24] In other jurisdictions, hefty legislation was perhaps to be expected. Australia, for instance, had no national laws generally criminalising terrorist activity or providing special powers to the authorities to investigate and prevent it. And while others had at least some legislative experience in anti-terrorism, they had certainly not revisited the area as recently as the British.[25]

Size alone was clearly not the problem, but merely reflected the deeper difficulty that these were 'omnibus bills' – a single enactment of diverse and discrete parts amending a range of existing laws and creating new ones.[26] Although the various components might be grouped as complementary paths to the overall goal of enhanced security, the bills were

---

[23] *Hansard*, HC, vol. 375, col. 101, 19 November 2001 (David Cameron).

[24] *A v. Secretary of State for the Home Department* [2005] 2 AC 68.

[25] Roach has highlighted how this had the effect of many nations seizing on the Terrorism Act 2000 (UK) as a template – particularly as regards the definition of terrorist acts: Kent Roach, 'The post-9/11 migration of Britain's Terrorism Act 2000' in Sujit Choudhry (ed.), *The Migration of Constitutional Ideas* (New York: Cambridge University Press, 2006), pp. 374–402.

[26] This is not a new phenomenon in respect of such laws: Laura K. Donohue, *The Cost of Counterterrorism: Power, Politics, and Liberty* (New York: Cambridge University Press, 2008), p. 12 (discussing the Civil Authorities (Special Powers) Act 1922 (UK)).

unquestionably difficult to debate and put to a simple vote. In this, the US Patriot Act set the tone admirably. Director Michael Moore, in his 2004 film *Fahrenheit 9/11*, famously lampooned the fact that apparently very few legislators (by the admission of some) had even read the whole Bill before enacting it. Writing the year after, Vervaele conjectured that as the 'Patriot Act document numbers approximately 350 pages and in ten titles amends over 15 existing federal laws...the complexity of the Act is doubtless the reason why not a single book has yet been published in the US analysing it in-depth and in its entirety'.[27] Although it enjoyed enormous congressional support in the wake of the 9/11 attacks, Senator Russ Feingold, the only Senator to vote against the Bill (and one of those who apparently *did* read it), lamented that its breadth required him to oppose enactment despite finding that 'many of its provisions are entirely reasonable, and I hope they will help law enforcement more effectively counter the threat of terrorism'.[28]

The Canadian Parliament confronted a similar problem with Bill C-36, enacted as the Anti-Terrorism Act 2001. Making substantial amendments to the Canadian Criminal Code, the Official Secrets Act the Canada Evidence Act, and the Proceeds of Crime (Money Laundering) Act and lesser changes to many other laws, the Bill provoked this reaction from one legislator:

> Let us talk about Bill C-36. It is 175 pages. I am not a lawyer, thankfully. However there are a number of lawyers in the House and elsewhere who will help us wade through the legislation. It is 175 pages and it affects 28 acts. I have never seen such an omnibus bill. In my experience ... I have not seen a bill of this nature come before the House. We must tread carefully and softly with it.[29]

This quote is indicative of others made by non-lawyer members occasionally expressing the view that they were out of their depth.[30] Commentators

---

[27] John A. E. Vervaele, 'The anti-terrorist legislation in the US: *inter arma silent leges?*' (2005) 13(2) *European Journal of Crime, Criminal Law and Criminal Justice* 207, 213.

[28] United States of America, *Congressional Record*, Senate, 107th Congress, 25 October 2001, S11021 (Russ Feingold).

[29] Canada, *Parliamentary Debates*, House of Commons, 18 October 2001, 1100 (Rick Borotsik). Stuart described Bill C-36 as 'a complex melange of tortuous legalistic sections and exceptions which can only serve to encourage expensive litigation': Don Stuart, 'The anti-terrorism bill C-36: an unnecessary law and order quick fix that permanently stains the Canadian criminal justice system' (2002) 14 *National Journal of Constitutional Law* 153, 163.

[30] Ibid.; Canada, *Parliamentary Debates*, House of Commons, 16 October 2001, 1530 (Reg Alcock).

have highlighted that too much of the deliberation over the Bill became concentrated on the question of whether it was 'Charter-proof', that is, able to withstand successful legal challenge under Canada's Charter of Rights and Freedoms. That had two negative effects. First, it risked rendering the debate a highly exclusive one in which participants required a level of legal expertise that many parliamentarians and, more broadly, the public did not possess.[31] Second, in narrowing discussion of the Bill in this way, the broader issues about the necessity, effectiveness and possible application in practice by police and other agencies of various components of the Bill were arguably neglected.[32] In the United Kingdom's case, Fenwick similarly has argued that the government, after entering a derogation under the European Convention on Human Rights, proceeded to use the purported compatibility with the Convention rights 'to cast a legitimising cloak over legislation which was clearly rights-abridging'.[33]

The size and complexity of many of the first wave of anti-terrorism bills was directly due to the frequent inclusion of material that, while perhaps justifiable as elements in a broad and comprehensive strategy of combating terrorism,[34] could hardly be said to be immediately and urgently necessary. At the same time, governments also used the bills as vehicles for making changes to the general regulation of police powers and community behaviour in areas that were clearly beyond the terrorist threat itself. For example, the United Kingdom's ATSCB was objected to on the basis that:

> Part 5 deals with incitement to religious hatred, which is a very important issue, but it has nothing to do with terrorism; part 10 on police powers, ditto; part 1 on retention of communications data, ditto; part 12 on bribery and corruption, ditto; part 13 on implementation of the European Union third pillar, ditto. All those matters are important, but they are certainly not about terrorism, and yet we are subjecting them to a very tight timetable.[35]

---

[31] Roach notes the democratic objections to government defence of its Bill as Charter-proof, but concluded that, commendably, many 'were not overawed by the idea that the legislation was "Charter-proof"': Kent Roach, 'Did September 11 change everything? Struggling to preserve Canadian values in the face of terrorism' (2001–2) 47 *McGill Law Journal* 893, 943.

[32] Ibid.; Wesley Pue, 'The war on terror: constitutional governance in a state of permanent warfare' (2003) 41 *Osgoode Hall Law Journal* 267, 287.

[33] Helen Fenwick, 'The Anti-Terrorism, Crime and Security Act 2001: a proportionate response to 11 September?' (2002) 65(5) *Modern Law Review* 727–8.

[34] *Hansard*, HC, vol. 374, col. 989, 15 November 2001 (Robin Cook).

[35] *Hansard*, HC, vol. 375, col. 94, 19 November 2001 (Douglas Hogg).

The frustration of UK legislators that the Bill dealt 'not only with national and international terrorism but with many other matters', was one echoed in other jurisdictions.[36] In the United States, one congressman claimed that the Patriot Act 'could have been passed 3 or 4 weeks ago without much discussion', had it been limited to terrorism and not a 'general search warrant and wiretap law'.[37] As a New Zealand legislator succinctly exposed the strategy in play, many amendments 'have been sneaked into the bill because the Government knows that if a counter-terrorism label is put on amendments, members will be more reluctant to oppose them'.[38] The extended scope of the contents of 'emergency legislation' is reflective of such laws as an opportunity for government to secure changes to the law which it has previously been unable to pull off. The Patriot Act, for instance, contained several controversial provisions affecting criminal law and procedure that Congress had previously rejected.[39] In the United Kingdom, there was strong suspicion that 'the Home Office's back lobby … has a lot of stuff that it wants to put before Parliament, and it has attached it to this Bill'.[40] The New Zealand government's Terrorism (Bombings and Financing) Bill had been endorsed by the Parliament's Foreign Affairs, Defence and Trade Committee just prior to 9/11, but it was substantially revised and broadened and then presented for swift enactment as the rebadged Terrorism Suppression Bill.[41] In his analysis of Canada's C-36, Whitaker wrote:

> The opportunity offered by 9/11 was alertly seized by the Canadian security and intelligence community, which has ended up with much more than it would likely have achieved had 9/11 not happened. But most of these ideas were already in the pipeline in Ottawa, sometimes for years,

---

[36] Ibid., col. 56 (Simon Hughes).

[37] United States of America, *Congressional Record*, House of Representatives, 107th Congress, 23 October 2001, 7200 (Scott).

[38] New Zealand, *Parliamentary Debates*, House of Representatives, 1 April 2003, 4629–30 (Keith Locke). See Alex Conte, 'Crime and terror: New Zealand's criminal law reform since 9/11' (2005) *New Zealand Universities Law Review* 635, 636.

[39] Regina Germain, 'Rushing to judgment: the unintended consequences of the USA PATRIOT Act for *bona fide* refugees' (2001–2) 16 *Georgetown Immigration Law Journal* 505; Michael P. O'Connor and Celia M. Rumann, 'Into the fire: how to avoid getting burned by the same mistakes made fighting terrorism in Northern Ireland' (2003) 24 *Cardozo Law Review* 1657, 1707.

[40] *Hansard*, HC, vol. 375, col. 94, 19 November 2001 (Douglas Hogg); see also *Hansard*, HC, vol. 375, col. 56, 19 November 2001 (Simon Hughes); *Hansard*, HL, vol. 629, col. 212, 27 November 2001 (Lord Beaumont).

[41] New Zealand, *Parliamentary Debates*, House of Representatives, 8 October 2002 (Keith Locke).

awaiting the political push that would bring them to the front of the policy agenda.[42]

It is not simply that the legislation's status as anti-terrorism law provides
cover for the passage of these measures – though, as is discussed in the next
section, this is indeed significant when the government of the day is willing
to portray any who express concern about the Bill as terrorist sympathisers. But additionally, the sheer size and diversity of the Bill's contents will
mean there is a good chance that all but the most objectionably draconian
elements will, even allowing for committee scrutiny, escape parliamentary
attention due to a shortage of time and limited access to information and
expertise. It is also highly conceivable, though of course difficult to verify,
that the executive loads its Bill up with material some of which it is quite
prepared to give ground on in order that its main goals are met. In other
words, 'concessions are built into the legislative process'.[43]

The speed with which governments have been able to draft large, complex bills in the aftermath of a terrorist attack (whether at home or abroad)
further suggests that much of this legislation is prepared in advance.
Indeed, there appears to be a tradition of this – the Home Secretary of the
United Kingdom having admitted that his government's anti-terrorism
legislation of 1974 was drafted 'long before' it was rushed before Parliament
in response to the Birmingham bombings of that year.[44] Thomas has
described the basic process, and its consequences, as follows:

> Emergency legislation passed as a consequence of national catastro-
> phe associated with terrorism has a predictable pattern. It involves an
> unseemly scramble between the Executive and legislature so that they are
> seen by the public and the media to be doing 'something'. A previously
> prepared emergency Bill is dusted down and hastily pushed through the
> legislature. Policy and law are thereby tightened, with scant recourse to
> reasoned chamber debate or recognition of standard procedures, in order
> to respond to the media and public outcry. Thus, the politicians' anxiety
> to be viewed as resolving the crisis overrides both established process and
> rational action.[45]

---

[42] Reg Whitaker, 'Keeping up with the neighbours? Canadian responses to 9/11 in histor-
      ical and comparative context' (2003) 41 *Osgoode Hall Law Journal* 263.
[43] Mark Shepherd, 'Parliamentary scrutiny and oversight of the British "war on terror":
      from accretion of executive power and evasion of scrutiny to embarrassment and conces-
      sions' (2009) 15 *Journal of Legislative Studies* 191, 211.
[44] Owen G. Lomas, 'The executive and the anti-terrorist legislation of 1939' [1980] *Public
      Law* 16, 18.
[45] Philip A. Thomas, 'Emergency and anti-terrorist powers: 9/11 – USA and UK' (2002–3)
      26 *Fordham International Law Journal* 1193, 1196.

Under these circumstances, what was previously unpassable can quickly ripen for enactment. The Indian experience is instructive in this respect. The national government in that country failed to gain support for its Prevention of Terrorism Bill 2000, five years after the Terrorist and Disruptive Activities (Prevention) Act 1987 had been allowed to expire. Just over a year later, after not only the events of 9/11 but also an attack on the Indian Parliament itself on 13 December 2001 which resulted in the death of fourteen innocents, the Bill was passed in essentially its initial form.[46] Even then, in order to ensure passage of the Bill the government controversially arranged for a joint sitting of both houses of Parliament to deliver a simple majority in its favour.[47] Following a change of government in 2004, the Prevention of Terrorism Act 2002 (POTA 2002) was prospectively repealed – however, several key provisions were simply re-enacted as amendments to the Unlawful Activities (Prevention) Act 1967 (UAPA).[48] India was rocked by a major terrorist strike on Mumbai on 11 July 2006, but the government did not reintroduce the POTA 2002 legislation; it instead sought to upgrade the investigative and intelligence capacities of its agencies. Although observers at the time saw in this an apparent recognition that 'special antiterrorism laws have not proven particularly effective in combating terrorism',[49] this ignored the strength of the provisions added to UAPA when POTA 2002 was repealed. After 'India's 9/11' – three days of bombings and shootings in key locations around Mumbai in November 2008 – further amendments (including 180 days pre-charge detention) were made to the UAPA 'that further harmonized it with previously retracted anti-terror legislation'.[50]

---

[46] Manas Mohapatra, 'Learning lessons from India: the recent history of antiterrorist legislation on the subcontinent' (2004) 95 *Journal of Criminal Law and Criminology* 315, 332–3. In the intervening weeks, a major attack had also been made by suicide bombers on the Kashmir state assembly: ibid., 323.

[47] Jayanth K Krishnan, 'India's "Patriot Act": POTA and the impact on civil liberties in the world's largest democracy' (2004) 22 *Law and Inequality* 265, 272.

[48] Ted Svennson, 'Fixing the elusive: India and the foreignness of terror' in Asaf Siniver (ed.), *International Terrorism Post-9/11: Comparative Dynamics and Responses* (Oxford: Routledge, 2010), pp. 168, 170. For a more positive assessment of the differences between the POTA and UAPA provisions, see Oliver Mendelsohn, 'Law, terror and the Indian legal order' in Christoph Antons and Volkmar Gessner (eds.), *Globalisation and Resistance: Law Reform in Asia since the Crisis* (Oxford: Hart, 2007), pp. 174–5. See also Ujjwal Kumar Singh, Chapter 17, this volume.

[49] Anil Kalhan, Gerald P. Conray, Mamta Kaushal, Sam Scott Miller and Jed S. Rakoff 'Colonial continuities: human rights, terrorism, and security laws in India' (2006–7) 20(1) *Columbia Journal of Asian Law* 96, 100.

[50] Svensson, 'Fixing the elusive', pp. 170–1.

The strongly reactive nature of anti-terrorism law-making[51] has also been evident in those jurisdictions that, while avoiding any successful terrorist strike over the relevant period, have nevertheless not been immune from 'a global convergence of policy prescriptions and widespread calls for greater harmonization of legislative responses'.[52] Indeed, in Australia, where over forty separate pieces of anti-terrorism law have been enacted since 9/11, a peculiarly heightened and vicarious reactivity has been the dominant driver in the construction of the new national security legislative framework, with the government regularly responding in domestic law to many of the attacks occurring overseas.[53] To cite a particularly prominent example, in the wake of the bombing of the London transport system in July 2005, the Howard government in Australia unveiled one of its more sweeping and ambitious bills, enacted not long after as the Anti-Terrorism Act (No 2) 2005 (Cth), providing for control orders, preventative detention orders, fresh sedition offences, the power to proscribe terrorist organisations on the basis of 'advocacy' and expanded police powers to issue notices to produce. The sheer range of the topics piled into the Bill was suggestive both of government opportunism and also extensive forethought.

Government responses to acts of political violence which occur elsewhere in the world are not necessarily confined to those countries bound by historical and cultural ties and joined in an explicit alliance against terrorist organisations such as al-Qaeda. The overarching globalisation of the terrorist threat in recent years has seen attacks on Western nations used by both the Russian and Chinese governments to relabel and re-energise existing campaigns, including through the introduction of harsh legislative measures, against separatist groups or ethnic minorities within their borders.[54] Russia's President Putin has used international

---

[51] Donohue, *The Cost of Counterterrorism*, p. 11; see also Ben Golder and George Williams, 'Balancing national security and human rights: assessing the legal response of common law nations to the threat of terrorism' (2006) 8 *Journal of Comparative Policy Analysis* 43, 45.

[52] Andrew Goldsmith, 'The governance of terror: precautionary logic and counterterrorist law reform after September 11' (2008) 30 *Law & Policy* 141, 144.

[53] Anthony Reilly, 'The processes and consequences of counter-terrorism law reform in Australia 2001–2005' (2007) 10 *Flinders Journal of Law Reform* 81, 84–90.

[54] Regarding the Russian Federation, see Svante E. Cornell, 'The war against terrorism and the conflict in Chechnya: a case for distinction' (2003) 27(2) *Fletcher Forum of World Affairs* 167. Of course, the Chechnyan conflict has inflicted significant domestic attacks on civilians upon the Russian population over the last fifteen years, which have also provided the basis for ever-stronger anti-terrorism measures quite independently of

terrorism generally so as to acquire remarkable powers for security agencies to 'eliminate' terrorist threats located outside the Federation[55] and also to further facilitate a broader legislative agenda of centralised executive power 'aimed at strengthening the unity of the country' (for example, by replacing the election of regional governors with a system of presidential appointment).[56]

Lastly on form, some mention should be made of the planned duration of the laws in question. As is discussed in the next section, governments have frequently introduced many of these laws to legislatures with an invocation of the labels of 'emergency' or 'exception', yet they have done so without any temporal limit on their operation.[57] However, legislators have generally displayed a keen awareness of the capacity of emergency measures to become permanent features of the legal landscape.[58] One of the easiest things for them to insist upon as a safeguard when being pressured to enact laws quickly is the inclusion of a sunset clause stipulating a date on which the law will expire and require re-enactment. In turn, agreeing to limit the duration of controversial laws or hold a later review has been something which governments have been far more willing to do than back down on the scope of new terrorism offences or the process by which novel powers are regulated.[59] With this in mind, Canada's Senator Fraser opined that 'sunset clauses have the serious potential to be

---

developments in the West: see Cerwyn Moore and David Barnard-Wills, 'Russia and counter-terrorism' in Asaf Siniver (ed.), *International Terrorism Post-9/11*, pp. 144–67. For that reason, an arguably more pronounced use of 9/11 to justify aggressive new laws and other acts of oppression was that which accompanied the Chinese government's crackdown on the Muslim Uighur population in the west of that country: see Amnesty International, *People's Republic of China: China's Anti-Terrorism Legislation and Repression in the Xinjiang Uighur Autonomous Region* (2002), available at www.amnesty. org/en/library/info/ASA17/010/2002/en.

55 Seth T. Bridge, 'Russia's new counteracting terrorism law: the legal implications of pursuing terrorists beyond the borders of the Russian Federation' (2009) 3 *Columbia Journal of East European Law* 1.

56 Thomas F. Remington, 'Putin, parliament, and presidential exploitation of the terrorist threat' (2009) 15 *Journal of Legislative Studies* 219, 231.

57 Maureen Webb, 'Essential liberty or a little temporary safety? The review of the Canadian Anti-terrorism Act' (2005–6) 51 *Criminal Law Quarterly* 53, 54.

58 This was a particularly dominant feature of United Kingdom and Indian anti-terrorism laws in the twentieth century: see Donohue, *The Cost of Counterterrorism*, pp. 14–15; and Kahlan *et al.*, 'Colonial continuities, 125–55.

59 Consider the nature of all three of the 'important concessions' which Ewing identifies as secured by the UK Parliament during enactment of the ATCSB 2001: Keith Ewing, 'The political constitution of emergency powers: a comment' (2008) 3 *International Journal of Law in Context* 313, 314–15.

pernicious in their effect' – as a concession legislators may secure in order to ease their misgivings over the contents of a bill.[60]

The extent to which sunset clauses elicit a fresh appraisal of the necessity or wisdom of the legislation upon expiration is open to question. Various key components, if not the entirety, of the terrorism laws in many of the jurisdictions discussed in this chapter were made subject to sunset clauses as a result of parliamentary deliberation – but the vast majority of them have been renewed over generally far less objection than the original enactment, despite the passage of time since the precipitating terrorist event. An exception has been the failure of the Canadian government to renew controversial provisions in the Anti-Terrorism Act 2001 allowing for special investigative hearings and recognisance with conditions, despite several attempts both just before and in each year since their expiry in 2007. The minority government's insistence that Parliament should, at the eleventh hour, simply renew the original provisions rather than deliberate possible enhancements, including those flagged by a Commons Committee Review,[61] led the opposition parties to block the move. While on one hand this did demonstrate that security measures will not simply be extended as a matter of course, Roach's detailed account of the episode makes it clear that the result owed far more to 'partisan maneuvering in a minority Parliament than with issues of principle'.[62] Not only was the renewal debate brought on so late as to be a race against the clock for expiration, but it was deeply 'partisan and largely uninformed'.[63] Ultimately, the non-renewal of these sunsetted components of the 2001 Canadian Act does not amount to much of an endorsement of the mechanism since it was not the result of 'a sustained debate about either the merits or the dangers of those provisions'.[64]

B. Process

Given the typical characteristics of much anti-terrorism law enacted in recent years, there should be little wonder that so many have expressed concern over the process by which it has regularly been enacted. The bills have all too often been presented by governments to legislatures

---

[60] Canada, *Parliamentary Debates*, Senate, 13 December 2001, 1620 (Joan Fraser).

[61] See House of Commons Standing Committee on Public Safety and National Security, *Review of the Anti-Terrorism Act Investigative Hearings and Recognizance with Conditions – Interim Report* (2006) 2.

[62] Kent Roach, 'The role and capacities of courts and legislatures in reviewing Canada's anti-terrorism law' (2008) 24 *Windsor Review of Legal and Social Issues* 20, 54.

[63] Ibid., 25.   [64] Ibid., 28.

accompanied by assertions of urgency and with the expectation that accordingly they will be enacted in a very quick timeframe. There can be no better example of this than the call by US Attorney-General John Ashcroft on Congress, six days after the 9/11 attacks, to pass the Bush Administration's (as yet unseen and incomplete) Patriot Act proposal 'this week'.[65] Both Houses of Congress passed legislation barely three weeks after the White House unveiled its Bill and just six weeks after the attacks themselves.[66]

The sense of urgency that pervaded the legislative process of the Patriot Act in the United States was hardly surprising. But the same theme dominated legislative responses in many other nations. In the United Kingdom, to which several of the 9/11 hijackers had links, the ATCSB 2001 was introduced to the House of Commons on 12 November 2001 and given its second reading one week later on 19 November. The Committee consideration occurred between 21 and 26 November, with this stage concluding at 11:57 pm on the last of those days and being immediately followed by the third reading of the Bill before midnight. By Thomas's calculations, the Bill's passage through the House of Commons took sixteen hours and debate over whether the Act should be permitted to derogate from Article 5 of the ECHR took a total of ninety minutes.[67] The House of Lords took rather more time and insisted on making several amendments, but the Act received Royal Assent on 14 December. The statement by one member of the Commons that 'with every day that goes by, we are risking our safety' was perhaps symptomatic of the parliamentary mood.[68]

Interestingly, similar invocations of the need for urgent action to preserve community safety were heard in parliaments that could not have been further removed from the immediate events of 9/11. In introducing the Security Legislation Amendment (Terrorism) Bill 2002 and the other four Bills which comprised the so-called 'SLAT package' to the House of Representatives on 12 March 2002, the Australian Attorney-General, Daryl Williams, said:

> Since September 11 there has been a profound shift in the international security environment. This has meant that Australia's profile as a terrorist target has risen and our interests abroad face a higher level of threat … We must

---

[65] Beryl A. Howell, 'Seven weeks: the making of the USA PATRIOT Act' (2003–4) 72 *George Washington Law Review* 1145, 1152.

[66] The process involved competing versions of the Bill which were eventually reconciled into one legislative enactment passed by the House on 24 October and by the Senate the next day.

[67] Thomas, 'Emergency and anti-terrorist powers', 1216–18.

[68] *Hansard*, HC, vol. 375, col. 93, 19 November 2001 (Caroline Flint).

direct all available resources ... at protecting our community and ensuring
that those responsible for threatening our security are brought to justice.
And we must do so as swiftly as possible ... We cannot afford to become
complacent. And we should never forget the devastation of September 11.[69]

All five bills in the package were passed by the lower chamber just twenty-
four hours later. Quite aside from domestic political pressures on governments to 'do
something' in response to the world-wide shock at the events of 9/11,[70] UN
Security Council Resolution 1373 issued on 28 September 2001 required
governments to report back within just ninety days on their progress in
taking the various counter-terrorism measures stipulated. Roach says
that 'this short reporting deadline was taken as a virtual deadline for the
enactment of new anti-terrorism laws' in a number of countries,[71] and
the effect of Security Council Resolution 1373 more generally has been
viewed as promoting the rapid globalisation of security law at the direct
expense of human rights law.[72] The novelty of the Security Council effectively 'legislating' to compel responses to 9/11 from all member nations has
been identified as an unprecedented development in international law.[73]
It unquestionably added a substantial layer of justification to the insistence by governments that action was required and quickly, particularly in
nations where the threat level might have been seen as not necessitating
a response of that order. Additional motivating factors in the decision to
legislate were undoubtedly the extent to which certain jurisdictions were
allied with the United States in the prosecution of the 'war on terror' more
broadly,[74] and also the significance of trading relationships.[75]

---

[69] Commonwealth, *Parliamentary Debates*, House of Representatives, 12 March 2002,
1040–3 (Daryl Williams).

[70] 'Circumstances and public opinion demanded urgent and appropriate action after the 11
September attacks': *Hansard*, HC, vol. 375, col. 22, 19 November 2001 (David Blunkett).

[71] Kent Roach, 'Sources and trends in post-9/11 anti-terrorism laws' in Benjamin Goold and
Liora Lazarus (eds.), *Security and Human Rights* (Oxford: Hart, 2007), pp. 227, 231.

[72] Kim Lane Scheppele, 'The migration of anti-constitutional ideas', in Choudhry, *The
Migration of Constitutional Ideas*, 347, 350.

[73] Ibid.; Craig Forcese, 'Hegemonic federalism: the democratic implications of the UN
Security Council's "legislative" phase' (2007) 38 *Victoria University of Wellington Law
Review* 175–98. See also C. H. Powell, Chapter 2, this volume.

[74] John E. Owens and Riccardo Pelizzo, 'The impact of the "war on terror" on executive–
legislative relations: a global perspective' (2008) 15 *Journal of Legislative Studies* 119, 135.

[75] This was very direct in respect of implications for the movement of people and goods
across the shared border between Canada and the United States, exemplified by the statement during debate on Bill C-36 that: 'Our economy, our trade, our way of life, depends

The presence of urgency as a contextual factor in augmentations to the initial raft of laws is even more interesting given the lack of such a direct international impetus on those later occasions. Despite the lapse of time, governments continued to employ the events of 9/11 as the justification, not merely for more laws, but their urgent necessity. This sense pervaded US Congressional debates on the Homeland Security Bill which was deliberated over an approximately five-month period before being enacted in November 2002.[76] The Bill's main function was to establish a Department of Homeland Security, headed by a Secretary of Homeland Security appointed by the President. In so doing, it amounted to the 'largest re-structuring of the US federal government since the passage of the National Security Act 1947'.[77] In this sense the Bill's contents were arguably much more complex than those of the earlier Patriot Act. Although the enactment process took months rather than weeks, there were complaints from some legislators as to being rushed in their consideration of a vast bill containing many significant amendments only tangentially linked to the topic of 'homeland security'.[78] North of the border, the Canadian government's tactics in scheduling time for the parliamentary debate of its second major legislative response, the Public Safety Act 2002, was another illustration of the continued and selective invocation of urgency at some remove from the events of 9/11.[79]

---

on ready access to the US, and Canada must give assurance to the US that future terrorists will not be spawned inside Canada.': Canada, *Parliamentary Debates*, Senate, 13 December 2001, 1610 (Douglas Roche). See further, Kent Roach, *September 11: Consequences for Canada* (Montreal: McGill-Queen's University Press, 2003), pp. 134–6. Interestingly, trading implications have also been raised in parliamentary debate over New Zealand's anti-terrorism laws: New Zealand, *Parliamentary Debates*, House of Representatives, 8 October 2002 (Ken Shirley) and New Zealand, *Parliamentary Debates*, 29 March 2007, 8514–5 (Shane Jones).

[76] See, e.g., United States of America, *Congressional Record*, House of Representatives, 107th Congress, 25 July 2002, H5634 (Mr Richard Armey); United States of America, *Congressional Record*, Senate, 107th Congress, 4 September 2002, S8156 (Senator Lieberman). See generally Rena Steinzor, '"Democracies die behind closed doors": The Homeland Security Act and corporate accountability' (2002/3) 12 *Kansas Journal of Law and Public Policy* 642.

[77] Kym Thorne and Alexander Kouzmin, 'The USA PATRIOT Acts (et al): collective amnesia, paranoia and convergent, oligarchic legislation in the "politics of fear"' (2007/8) 10 *Flinders Journal of Law Reform* 554, 554.

[78] United States of America, *Congressional Record*, Senate, 107th Congress, 19 September 2002, S8881 (Senator Thompson); United States of America, *Congressional Record*, Senate, 107th Congress, 19 November 2002, S11358 (Senator Byrd).

[79] Canada, *Parliamentary Debates*, House of Commons, 7 October 2003, 1150 (John Herron); 1350 (Bev Desjarlais).

Two particularly pronounced, and indeed linked, examples of this phenomenon occurred in respect of the control orders legislation passed by
both the United Kingdom and Australia in 2005.[80] After the December
2004 decision of the House of Lords in the *Belmarsh* case, the UK's Blair
government set upon the creation of a control order regime for terrorism suspects to replace the indefinite detention of foreign suspects under
Part 4 of the Anti-Terrorism, Crime and Security Act. The latter scheme
had been declared incompatible with the ECHR by their Lordships and
was due to lapse on 14 March 2005. Having committed to not renewing
the scheme, the government used this date as a deadline for the enactment
of its replacement, eventually the Prevention of Terrorism Act (POTA),
which it introduced to Parliament in late February. Although commentators have praised the quality of parliamentary scrutiny – namely that
offered by the Joint Committee on Human Rights in its report on the bill
and the concessions won by the House of Lords[81] – the spectacle of the Bill
being 'ping-ponged' between the latter and the House of Commons in a
single parliamentary sitting day of record-breaking length (thirty hours)
before being finally passed on 10 March was testament to the constraints
imposed upon deliberation by a manipulated sense of urgency.

As already mentioned, following the London bombings in July 2005,
the Australian Commonwealth government under Prime Minister
John Howard released an extensive list of counter-terrorism proposals
a fortnight in advance of its meeting with State and Territory leaders at
the Council of Australian Governments in late September of that year.
Agreement to those far-reaching measures was secured at that meeting after less than two hours' discussion, even though draft legislation
was not made available to the participants until 7 October.[82] The draft

---

[80] A detailed comparative study of the passage of the enactments in question is available at
   Joo-Cheong Tham, 'Parliamentary deliberation and the national security executive: the
   case of control orders' [2010] *Public Law* 79. The substance of the control order schemes
   in both countries and their judicial consideration are discussed by Helen Fenwick and
   Gavin Phillipson, Chapter 19, this volume (UK) and George Williams, Chapter 21, this
   volume (Australia).
[81] Tham, 'Parliamentary deliberation and the national security executive' 92; Janet L.
   Hiebert, 'Parliamentary Review of Terrorism Measures' [2005] *Modern Law Review* 676.
[82] The necessity for the Commonwealth to seek co-operation from the other Australian
   governments and a detailed critique of this process is discussed in Greg Carne, 'Prevent,
   detain, control and order?: Legislative process and executive outcomes in enacting the
   Anti-Terrorism Act (No 2) 2005 (Cth)' (2007) 10 *Flinders Journal of Law Reform* 17,
   26–32. See more generally on COAG's role in national security matters: Phil Larkin and
   John Uhr, 'Bipartisanship and bicameralism in Australia's "war on terror": forcing limits
   on the extension of executive power' (2009) 15 *Journal of Legislative Studies* 239, 242–4.

Bill was subsequently leaked via the Internet by the Chief Minister of the Australian Capital Territory which enabled rather more public examination and debate of the government's law than it had planned. Initially, the Commonwealth proposed bringing the Bill forward on Tuesday 1 November, the day of the Melbourne Cup horse-race, an event of national distraction, and allowing only that day for debate in the House of Representatives followed by a Senate Committee inquiry also of just one day's duration.[83] It is important to appreciate that from July of that year, the government had gained control of the Senate as well as the House of Representatives – a very rare turn of events in the Australian political system.[84] This strongly increased the capacity of the Howard government to evade serious parliamentary scrutiny of its Bill.[85]

However, as it transpired, Melbourne Cup week saw a fairly minor, but arguably very significant, amendment contained in the Bill broken off and rushed with breakneck speed through the national parliament (including a recalled Senate) as a standalone enactment in order to equip law enforcement agencies with the capacity to thwart a 'potential terrorist threat' on which the government publicly stated it had received a specific intelligence briefing.[86] By 3 November, and against the backdrop of these dramatic developments, the remaining bulk of the initial draft bill, reflecting the government's suite of controversial new measures was introduced to the Parliament as Anti-Terrorism Bill (No 2). It was immediately referred to a Senate Committee inquiry which was to report on 28 November. Although Tham, contrasting this result favourably against the government's original plan, says that the inquiry took place 'over 25 days',[87] Carne highlights the strictness of even this extended timeframe by pointing out that only six days separated the call for submissions on this complex bill and the closing date for their receipt, as well as the need for the Committee to expend massive effort in order to finalise its report in time.[88] This month-long legislative process was punctuated by major arrests by Commonwealth and State police on 8 November of groups of

---

[83] Tham, 'Parliamentary deliberation and the national security executive', 91.

[84] John Halligan, Robin Miller and John Power, *Parliament in the Twenty-First Century: Institutional Reform and Emerging Roles* (Melbourne University Press, 2007), p. 255.

[85] Larkin and Uhr, 'Bipartisanship and bicameralism in Australia's "war on terror"', 250–1.

[86] This episode is analysed in Andrew Lynch, 'Legislating with urgency: the enactment of the Anti-Terrorism Act [No 1] 2005' (2006) 30 *Melbourne University Law Review* 747.

[87] Tham, 'Parliamentary deliberation and the national security executive', 92.

[88] Greg Carne, 'Hasten slowly: urgency, discretion and review – a counter-terrorism legislative agenda and legacy' (2008) 13 *Deakin Law Review* 49, 66–7.

men in Sydney and Melbourne charged respectively with doing acts in preparation of a terrorist act and membership of a terrorist organisation.[89] The government maintained throughout that it was necessary for the entire Bill to be passed before the Christmas holidays – echoing its insistence three years earlier that the opposition should support controversial new questioning and detention powers for the Australian Security Intelligence Organisation (ASIO) because of the necessity to 'clothe our intelligence agencies with this additional authority over the summer months'.[90]

On that earlier occasion, the government did not have control of both legislative chambers and the passage of its Australian Security Intelligence Organisation Legislation Amendment (Terrorism) Bill 2002 (ASIO Bill) was greatly protracted. That episode, involving no fewer than three committee inquiries into the Bill, is often viewed as an example of thorough scrutiny and deliberation over many months resulting in some important changes to the law – namely clearer procedures by which ASIO's new powers were to be used and the scrapping of the initial plan to make them applicable to children over the age of ten. But ultimately, it demonstrated the ability of government to simply wear down its parliamentary opposition.[91] The Bill's most controversial feature – its conferral upon an intelligence agency of the power to detain non-suspects for up to seven days for questioning – remained in the final enactment. While the dynamics of the Australian political landscape at the time meant that the legislation was certainly not rushed, assertions of urgent necessity clearly still have an impact beyond mere speed. They have a damaging effect on the quality of the debate itself and the capacity of political parties in opposition, reluctant to be tagged as 'soft on terror', to offer sustained resistance.[92] In this regard, it is instructive that the performance of the unelected House of Lords in the United Kingdom has been favourably contrasted with that of the popularly elected opposition in the Commons[93] – though, as we saw

---

[89] See McGarrity, '"Testing" our counter-terrorism laws'.
[90] Prime Minister John Howard on 13 December 2002, quoted in Jenny Hocking, *Terror Laws: ASIO, Counter-Terrorism and the Threat to Democracy* (Sydney: University of New South Wales Press, 2004), p. 198.
[91] For a thorough analysis see Dominique Dalla-Pozza, 'The Australian approach to enacting counter-terrorism laws', PhD Thesis, University of New South Wales (2010), pp. 271–362.
[92] Larkin and Uhr, 'Bipartisanship and bicameralism in Australia's "war on terror"', 252; Hocking, *Terror Laws*, pp. 218–20.
[93] Shepherd, 'Parliamentary scrutiny and oversight of the British "war on terror"', 194–5.

in respect of the POTA, even their Lordships are not immune from the pressure of urgency.

Consideration of these experiences inevitably prompts reflection on the role played by parliamentary committees in the enactment of anti-terrorism laws. Have committees generally served to enhance that process? To this the answer must certainly be positive. Apart from anything else, the referral of a bill to a committee for scrutiny, even when the inquiry is set to a brief timetable, interposes an additional step before enactment that creates space for political and community debate that might not otherwise be afforded. A parliamentary committee inquiry also obviously creates a focused setting in which civil society, as well as non-government parties and even occasionally government back-benchers who are perturbed by the contents of a bill, can voice their objections and propose alterations.[94] The receiving of submissions and oral evidence in public hearings undoubtedly assists legislators in their ability to scrutinise and challenge aspects of a bill. Debate on the floor of a parliamentary chamber is a markedly inefficient way to deliberate the merits and deficiencies of modern legislation and develop specific amendments to complex omnibus bills, and the constructive capacity of committees in the creation of law is well noted.[95]

Of course, the ability of committees to fill this role is far from assured. There appears to be a recognition on behalf of government that anti-terrorism laws are of such importance that providing opportunity for public input via a committee inquiry cannot be bypassed: the Australian experience of the Anti-Terrorism Act (No 2) 2005 illustrates that even when a government controls both legislative chambers it will be reluctant to be so heavy-handed as to flout any committee scrutiny.[96] But that said, all too frequently governments have done their best to inhibit the opportunity of committees to give detailed consideration to these bills.

[94] Roach, *September 11: Consequences for Canada*, pp. 67–8. For an empirical study of this in respect of parliamentary committee inquiries examining Australian anti-terrorism bills, see Dominique Dalla-Pozza, 'Promoting deliberative debate? The submissions and oral evidence provided to Australian parliamentary committees in the creation of counter-terrorism laws' (2008) *Australasian Parliamentary Review* 39.

[95] Lawrence D. Longley and Roger H. Davidson, 'Parliamentary committees: changing perspectives on changing institutions' in Lawrence D. Longley and Roger H. Davidson (eds.), *The New Roles of Parliamentary Committees* (London: Frank Cass & Co., 1998) pp. 1, 5.

[96] 'As for legislative appraisal, the referral of bills has become standard in the Senate, and it is unimaginable that this would be substantially curtailed': Halligan, Miller and Power, *Parliament in the Twenty-First Century*, p. 258.

If they cannot do so by mere force of numbers, then the familiar assertions of urgent necessity and accusations that the delay caused by political opponents endangers the community will still prove powerful. The Blair government's enactment of the POTA is an excellent example of the latter technique.

The railroading of pre-enactment scrutiny by committees often results in expressions of frustration from those bodies or their individual members. These should not be lost sight of when reporting positively on the role played by committees in parliamentary deliberation. For example, the United Kingdom's parliamentary Joint Committee on Human Rights was explicit in its criticism of the legislative timetable for the POTA and also in underscoring the effect of this upon its own contribution:

> We regret that the rapid progress of the Bill through Parliament has made it impossible for us to scrutinise the bill comprehensively for human rights compatibility in time to inform debate in Parliament.[97]

Nor was the Committee impressed when, in the following year, the Home Secretary exercised his power to renew the control order legislation in such a way as to curtail any meaningful deliberation of the merits of the scheme on that occasion also:

> In view of the very considerable human rights implications of the control orders regime and the very limited opportunity for proper scrutiny during passage of the 2005 Act, we regret this .... We also regret the limited time which has been made available for us and any other interested committees to report to Parliament. Laying the renewal order ... on 2 February and scheduling the renewal debate in both Houses for 15 February severely restricts the possibility for committees such as ours to discharge our responsibility to scrutinise and report in a fully considered way to both Houses.[98]

Any ultimate evaluation of a committee's contribution must depend substantially upon what changes, if any, it was able to promote to the final form of the legislation enacted by the parliament. Given the various conditions under which anti-terrorism bills are typically brought forward by the government of the day, not least simply their size, it is appropriate to be realistic about just how many alterations a committee is going to be able

---

[97] Joint Committee on Human Rights, Parliament of United Kingdom, *Prevention of Terrorism Bill: Tenth Report of Session 2004–5* (2005), p. 3.

[98] Joint Committee on Human Rights, Parliament of United Kingdom, *Counter-Terrorism Policy and Human Rights: Draft Prevention of Terrorism Act 2005 (Continuance in Force of Sections 1 to 9) Order 2006* (2006), p. 9.

to recommend and how likely it is that a percentage of these will translate into amendments agreed to by the government. It seems reasonable to expect that limited, rather than substantial, amendments will be made – if only because the government, having made such a big deal about the need for the law to be passed quickly, will be reluctant to tarry. As Carne pointed out in the case of Australia's Anti-Terrorism Act (No 2) 2005, 'the deliberate assertion of executive authority to enact the law according to a pre-determined timetable' signalled an unwillingness to consider making major amendments including even those which might actually strengthen the law.[99] For this reason, the insertion of sunset clauses or provisions for formal review of the law's operation tend, as observed earlier, to be prominent among those demands to which the government is more prepared to accede than others.

Assessing the impact of committee recommendations is nevertheless far from straightforward. To consider the extent to which the Australian Senate Legal and Constitutional Legislation Committee's inquiry resulted in changes to the Anti-Terrorism Act (No 2) 2005 as an example, it is true that the government amended the Bill to reflect the Committee's recommendations that confirmation of interim control orders should be by an *inter partes* hearing and that hearsay evidence should be inadmissible on that occasion.[100] But the most significant change to the government's Bill, indeed a precondition for those successfully moved by the Committee, occurred between the draft version which was publicly leaked and that which was eventually put before Parliament. Specifically, the government surrendered the power to issue the orders to the federal judiciary. It is impossible to know whether the government would have gone ahead with executive-issued control orders in the Bill it took to Parliament had it not had to weather three weeks of unanticipated political and public opposition on this matter. That portion of the debate over the proposed law, while highly effective in some respects, was hardly to be expected and was essentially a bonus brought about by the most unlikely of political manoeuvres. If the Bill presented to Parliament had been essentially the same as the draft which had been circulated to State and Territory leaders, we can only speculate whether the Committee itself would have been successful in recommending a move to court-issued control orders.

---

[99] Carne, 'Hasten slowly: urgency, discretion and review', 69. See further John Uhr, 'Terra infirma? Parliament's uncertain role in the "war on terror"' (2004) 27 *University of New South Wales Law Journal* 339, 341.

[100] Tham, 'Parliamentary deliberation and the national security executive', 94–5.

In contrast to any impact one might credit the Senate Committee with having on the control order scheme of Anti-Terrorism Act (No 2) 2005 was the failure of any of its recommendations concerning the sedition offences in Schedule 7 of the Bill to be picked up by the government. This aspect of the Bill excited more widespread distrust in the community than any other and was targeted by influential backbenchers in the government as something which should be dispensed with, at least for the present. The bipartisan Committee was unanimous on this point and recommended that Schedule 7 be scrapped and the matter of reform of seditious offences referred to the Australian Law Reform Commission (ALRC). Failing that, the Committee made specific recommendations to improve the Schedule if the government persisted with it.[101] The government did not accept either course and instead took the quite extraordinary step of retaining the Schedule in the Bill and, once enacted, immediately referring the relevant provisions to the independent ALRC for review. As Carne identifies in his recounting of these events, the Attorney-General's position was explicitly justified by the urgent necessity of having the new laws in place – regardless of what the ALRC's review might later find in respect of them.[102] The ALRC delivered a substantial and constructive report, largely echoing the views of the Senate Committee, to the government in July 2006.[103] The government made no move to implement its recommendations and amend the relevant legislation. The Labor government which won office in 2007 did substantially incorporate aspects of the ALRC report into amendments contained in the National Security Legislation Amendment Bill 2010, but the Parliament was dissolved for a general election before that Bill was passed (ironically demonstrating the dangers of legislating with an insufficient sense of urgency).[104]

In conclusion, the value of pre-enactment scrutiny of anti-terrorism laws by parliamentary committee must always be better than not having such a step in the legislative process. It clearly provides opportunities for independent experts and civil society lobby groups to engage with legislators and promotes greater and more constructive deliberation about the measures in question amongst parliamentarians. But the role of

---

[101] Carne, 'Hasten slowly: urgency, discretion and review', 70.   [102] Ibid., 71.

[103] Australian Law Reform Commission, *Fighting Words – A Review of Sedition Laws in Australia* (ALRC Report 104, 2006).

[104] The Bill was subsequently reintroduced to the Commonwealth Parliament by the Labor government, which now holds office as a minority government since the election produced a hung parliament. It was enacted in December 2010.

committees should not be overstated. In the context of 'emergency' omnibus bills in the politically sensitive area of national security, about which government has the distinct advantage of access to secret intelligence,[105] committees cannot be expected to mitigate, let alone overcome, the pressures upon the quality of parliamentary deliberation more generally.[106]

3. Consequences

The consequences of the sort of legislative processes that have just been examined are far better appreciated through the detailed analysis of the anti-terrorism laws of specific jurisdictions provided by the many other chapters of this volume. It is, however, possible to make some general observations in this regard.

It should not be surprising that laws made against a constant background noise of assertions that they are urgently necessary in order to prevent heightened risk of a terrorist attack being made upon the community tend to be imprudently drafted. United Kingdom legislators, with their long experience of anti-terrorism measures devised in response to political violence over the Northern Ireland situation, expressed a particular awareness of the fact that 'a Bill rushed through with such speed will before long be found to be deficient in some way'.[107] If this seems like something of an ambit claim, consider the widespread dissatisfaction with many of the domestic definitions of 'terrorism' itself. Many studies of domestic anti-terrorism legislation grapple with the breadth and vagueness of the way in which this central concept has been defined. While finding a perfect definition of this activity, upon which a nation's entire anti-terrorism legal edifice is built and against which it is designed to guard, is destined to be highly challenging, it is striking how many subtle variations exist between definitions in like jurisdictions, even those which drew upon that provided by the UK's Terrorism Act 2000.[108] Often worse than the definition are the offences that flow from it, which are

---

[105] See Goldsmith, 'The governance of terror', 153.

[106] Tham identifies the 'tyranny of the national security executive' and its aggressive pursuit of secrecy, its own pre-eminence and the principle of pre-emption as crucial impediments to better parliamentary debate: see Tham, 'Parliamentary deliberation and the national security executive', 102–8.

[107] *Hansard*, HC, vol. 375, col. 73, 19 November 2001 (Andrew Hunter). See also col. 24 (Mark Fisher); col. 56 (Simon Hughes); *Hansard*, HL, vol. 629, col. 212, 27 November 2001 (Lord Beaumont).

[108] See generally Ben Golder and George Williams, 'What is "terrorism"? Problems of legal definition' (2004) 27 *University of New South Wales Law Journal* 270.

frequently cast in terms of such ambiguous width as to create a worry-ingly broad scope for the operation of executive discretion in respect of their application. This inevitably leads to operational failures where the lack of guidance provided by the law means it fails to restrain authorities from pursuing misguided investigations at the expense of individuals' privacy and even occasionally their freedom.[109]

These same features are also prevalent amongst the more novel and insidious legal tools designed to restrict the liberty of individuals with the aim of protecting the public: control orders, proscription of organisations and limitations on speech, such as the UK's offence of indirectly encour-aging terrorism through statements that glorify such acts 'whether in the past, in the future or generally'.[110] As O'Cinneide explains, 'the crim-inal law as developed over time attempts to provide clarity, certainty and proportionate responses: counter-terrorism laws frequently cut through this careful organic growth, and establish parallel systems of control and repression that can contradict the values of the "mainstream" legal code'.[111] However, the overarching preventative justification of counter-terrorism laws does more than shape such measures themselves in 'contradic-tion' of the orthodox principles of criminal justice. Instead, as we know from history and as more recent experience has begun to show, so-called 'exceptional' legal powers and prohibitions have a strong tendency to seep into what O'Cinneide calls 'the "mainstream" legal code'.[112] In short, the reactive enactment of anti-terrorism laws as a matter of urgency regularly produces bad laws – both the security measures as immediately passed and then by extension as those laws influence others outside the anti-terrorism paradigm over time. As discussed earlier, attempts to contain these 'exceptional' measures through the use of sunset clauses or the pro-vision of post-enactment review mechanisms are rarely successful.

Not unrelated to the problem of legislative quality and consistency is the deleterious phenomenon of legislative inflation. In a specific sense, this is rather more observable in some jurisdictions over others – particularly the United Kingdom and Australia, as the anti-terrorism legislation burgeons

---

[109] The arrest, detention and deportation of Dr Mohamed Haneef by the Australian Federal Police is an excellent case in point: see The Hon. John Clarke QC, *Report of the Clarke Inquiry into the Case of Dr Mohamed Haneef* (November, 2008).

[110] Terrorism Act 2006 (UK), s. 1.

[111] O'Cinneide, 'Strapped to the mast', p. 349.

[112] See generally, Nicola McGarrity, Andrew Lynch and George Williams, *Counter-Terrorism and Beyond: The Culture of Law and Justice After 9/11* (Oxford: Routledge, 2010).

unabated due to ever-renewed executive demands. The Australian legislative cycle in the area of national security may, without any exaggeration, be described as having been in constant motion for roughly the first five years after 9/11. The UK Parliament enacted fewer laws numerically but they were each fairly substantial and had an ever-increasing impact on the powers of the state at the expense of individuals' liberty. In both cases, the legislative process was not seen as finite or limited to the creation of any one particular law. Instead, each bill was just the latest round in an ongoing tussle between the executive and a brow-beaten legislature. Dalla-Pozza points out that just months after the exhausting and protracted parliamentary process by which the Australian government's 2002 ASIO Bill was enacted, government began agitating for changes to be made to the national intelligence agency's newly conferred questioning and detention powers, with the Attorney-General describing the legislation passed just five months earlier as 'possibly ... third or fourth best'.[113] A similar mindset appeared to grip the Blair/Brown government in the UK as it repeatedly sought parliamentary approval of ever increased extensions to the length of pre-charge detention of terrorism suspects.[114] The unwillingness of executives to accept the outcome of the legislative process as a final determination, even for just the short to intermediate term, has meant that anti-terrorism laws have accreted with inexorable predictability.

But even in jurisdictions which have managed to avoid this wearying cycle, such as Canada, New Zealand and the United States, it is wrong to think that there is no legislative inflation whatsoever as a by-product of recent anti-terrorism law-making. For one thing, the magnitude of the bills means that just a few enactments add significantly to the statutory powers of government agencies and the regulation of the community. It is not as if many of these laws are filling a vacuum, despite what the political rhetoric might say. They are placed alongside existing powers, criminal offences and other forms of regulation which might be just as applicable in any given situation of planned or executed political violence. This is not to revisit the claims heard from some quarters when the first wave of anti-terrorism laws was created after 9/11 that they were wholly unnecessary because the existing criminal law provided everything needed to address

---

[113] Dalla-Pozza, 'The Australian approach to enacting counter-terrorism laws', p. 364.

[114] Shepherd, 'Parliamentary scrutiny and oversight of the British "war on terror"', 211. Although the House of Commons endorsed an extension to forty-two days, due to the resistance of the House of Lords pre-charge detention remains capped at twenty-eight days.

the threat. But it is to acknowledge that there is indeed a substantial corpus of law already in place to which these new laws are a sizeable addition, creating quite a stockpile of emergency laws.[115]

The fact that substantial portions of these acts are then not actually used in combating terrorism not only belies the fact that they were 'urgently necessary' but is also worrying since they simply lie around for possible application in other situations. The experience in New Zealand, a country which has been comparatively restrained in the quantity of anti-terrorism bills enacted since 9/11, provides a perfect example of this aspect of the dangers of legislative inflation. The New Zealand Parliament passed the Terrorism Suppression Act in 2002 but no part of it had been used when the Foreign Affairs, Defence and Trade Committee reviewed it three years later.[116] The only occasion in which its provisions have been brought to bear was by police in making a number of arrests in 2007 of indigenous and environmental activists. While those charges did not proceed to trial, the inappropriate use of the law as a factor in police actions is itself deeply embarrassing and highlights the potential latent in measures that depend so heavily upon executive discretion. Even when laws are not used at all they may exert an influence. The existence of laws regulating speech, such as sedition offences or censorship of materials 'advocating' or 'praising' terrorism, may well have a dampening effect on public discourse,[117] while the presence in the statute books of exceptional measures such as Australia's preventative detention orders may act as a template for similar devices in other contexts where they may be used.[118]

4.   Conclusion – an end to reactive anti-terrorism laws?

Despite the manifest deficiencies of legislating with urgency as a response to terrorist activity, it is hard to imagine that this will not continue to occur in future. Although the reaction of the Spanish government to both 9/11 and then the Madrid train bombings of 2004, which killed 191 of its own citizens and injured over 2,000 more, involved no legislative dimension, this is clearly quite exceptional. Spain already had a number of strict laws directed towards terrorism, of which it has had considerable

---

[115] Webb, 'Essential liberty or a little temporary safety?', 98.
[116] Foreign Affairs, Defence and Trade Committee, Parliament of New Zealand, *Review of the Terrorism Suppression Act 2002* (2005), pp. 4–5.
[117] David Hume and George Williams, 'Australian censorship policy and the advocacy of terrorism' (2009) 31 *Sydney Law Review* 381.
[118] Criminal Code Act 1995 (Cth), div. 105.

experience at the hands of the Basque separatist organisation ETA, and it was content not to supplement or replace these laws with new ones. Instead, the country's defining response to the 2004 bombings was the withdrawal by its newly elected government of all troops from the conflict in Iraq. At the time, one commentator criticised Spain's failure to 'provide the law enforcement community with special powers' as not 'consistent with a developing global response to Islamic terrorism'.[119] Even setting aside the three countries against which this unfavourable comparison was made – the United States, Russia and Israel, all of which have employed a 'proactive and aggressive'[120] legislative response to international terrorism – the criticism itself seems an odd one. It appears to assume that anti-terrorism laws need to be specifically tailored to different sources of political violence, though it is hard to imagine what this would look like in practice and how even greater attempts at the specification of terrorist motivation in determining the application of anti-terrorism laws would assist in protecting the community. It also assumes that legislative responses are more significant in preventing terrorism than, say, a repositioning of national foreign policy – despite the high likelihood that the converse is true.[121]

It may be that as we move beyond the first decade after the events of 9/11, the propensity for knee-jerk legislative responses in many countries will diminish. But history gives little cause for optimism on this score. Governments seem all too vulnerable to the pressure to react to terrorist violence with legislation and they will ensure that the legislature is given as little opportunity as possible to impede the swiftness of that response. The fact that legislators are at a distinct disadvantage in this scenario from the outset due to their very limited access to current security intelligence assessments means that deliberation over a government's measures hardly occurs on an even playing field. Parliamentary committees provide a forum in which an array of views and perspectives may be gleaned so as to inform and deepen debate of the bills, but even when these bodies

---

[119] Amos N. Guiora, 'Legislative and policy responses to terrorism: a global perspective' (2005) 7 *San Diego International Law Journal* 154, 165.

[120] Ibid.

[121] In addition to the Spanish experience, the recent testimony to the UK's Iraq Inquiry of Dame Eliza Manningham-Buller, the former director of M15, supports the view that while the Blair government was busy drafting legislation designed to prevent terrorism, its decision to go to war in Iraq served to dramatically increase the likelihood of domestic terrorist attack: Richard Norton-Taylor, 'Iraq Inquiry: Eliza Manningham-Buller's devastating testimony', available at www.guardian.co.uk/uk/2010/jul/20/iraq-inquiry-eliza-manningham-buller.

work effectively so as to offer constructive and clear criticism, their influence is inevitably circumscribed by a range of political and institutional factors beyond their control. Walker has suggested that the existence of ongoing independent review, such as that provided by the office of the Independent Reviewer in the United Kingdom, is another way in which to 'ensure rational policy-making and not panic legislation' since it provides a more immediate form of scrutiny as to the effectiveness and impact of anti-terrorism laws than the judicial arm can offer.[122] Certainly post-enactment review is intrinsically valuable, but it may prove difficult to structure and empower the office of review in such a way that it has a cautionary effect upon governments at times of actual or perceived crisis.

Reference to the post-enactment review of anti-terrorism laws passed in haste or otherwise aggressively pushed through legislatures prompts one final observation. There is a very discernible contrast between the way in which these laws have been created and the distinct lack of enthusiasm that governments (even subsequent to a different political party winning office) have shown for their sober appraisal afterward, let alone the amendment or excision of those aspects which are demonstrably problematic in terms of providing effective security and/or respecting human rights. The focus is almost entirely upon the making of new laws or the extension of existing ones – rarely on refinement or repair. Perhaps the latter course is seen as riskily amounting to an admission of executive fallibility? In the area of national security, the politics of avoiding that perception exerts a most powerful influence on a government's legislative agenda.

---

[122] Clive Walker, 'Clamping down on terrorism in the United Kingdom' (2006) 4 *Journal of International Criminal Justice* 1137, 1144.

8

The financial war on terrorism

KEVIN E. DAVIS

1. Introduction

In the aftermath of the attacks of 9/11 many facets of counter-terrorism legislation came under intensive scrutiny. Provisions granting state officials enhanced investigative powers, greater authority to withhold information from the public and broader powers to detain people without trial were all hotly debated around the world. In contrast, relatively little attention was paid to the provisions aimed at the financing of terrorism. Surprisingly though, in the decade following the 9/11 attacks it is the instruments aimed at countering the financing of terrorism which have become the flashpoints for some of the most profound debates about the legitimacy and effectiveness of counter-terrorism legislation.

This chapter provides an overview of those legal instruments and the concerns they raise. Section 2 describes three main types of legal provisions designed to combat the financing of terrorism (prohibitions, provisions authorising deprivations of property and monitoring provisions), different approaches that have been taken to the design of those provisions and the advantages and disadvantages of each approach. The central objective of this Section, which represents the bulk of the chapter, is to discuss the range of actors and transactions that are likely to be affected by the various legal initiatives, with particular attention to how legislators have responded to the need to capture illegitimate terrorist activity while protecting legitimate activities on the part of terrorist organisations and those who might wish to deal with them. Courts have made little effort to second-guess the balance that international organisations and other branches of government have struck between combating terrorist

Beller Family Professor of Business Law, New York University School of Law. I am grateful to GuyLaine Charles, Alan Tan Khee, Victor Ramraj, Samuel Rascoff, Mary Wong and participants in the Symposium on Comparative Anti-Terrorism Law & Policy for helpful comments upon an earlier version as well as to Maxwell Kardon and Kevin Lees for excellent research assistance.

financing and safeguarding legitimate commercial activity. On the other hand, courts have become increasingly willing to insist that basic norms of procedural fairness be observed when the more punitive aspects of the regime are applied to particular individuals or organisations.

Section 3 suggests several reasons why the fog of uncertainty that surrounds counter-terrorism policy and officials' circumscribed political incentives might distort the implementation and enforcement of provisions aimed at combating financing of terrorism. Officials subject to imperfect scrutiny and partial accountability are prone to emphasise measures that are observable and favoured by powerful actors, and to de-emphasise measures that are unobservable or which disproportionately burden disempowered groups. These concerns underscore the importance of identifying legal mechanisms capable of checking abuse of discretion on the part of law enforcement officials.

Section 4 provides a reminder that even if reasonably well implemented and enforced, there are reasons to doubt these provisions will be effective in combating the financing of terrorism. The amounts of money at issue may be too small and the means of financing terrorism may be too numerous and variable to justify hopes of victory in the financial war on terrorism. Not surprisingly, the chapter concludes with a call for continuous evaluation of whether the benefits of the regime warrant its costs.

2.   The scope of legislation concerned with financing of terrorism

A.   Background

Much of the recent interest in counter-terrorism legislation in general, and legislation concerned with financing of terrorism in particular, dates to the terrorist attacks of 9/11. Even before that date, countries such as the United States and the United Kingdom had adopted legislation that prohibited the most significant forms of financing of terrorism.[1] Moreover, much of the conduct governed by provisions focused on the financing of terrorism could have been prosecuted under pre-existing legislation imposing liability upon those who aid, abet or conspire in the commission of activities such as murder, arson, hijacking or bombing. However,

---

[1] For a brief discussion of the initiatives prior to 2001 see Michael Levi, 'Combating the financing of terrorism: a history and assessment of the control of "threat finance"' (2010) 50 *British Journal of Criminology* 650.

prior to September 2001, the international community as a whole does not appear to have been fully committed to legislating against the financing of terrorism, as evidenced by the fact that the United Nations Convention for the Suppression of Terrorist Financing (Financing of Terrorism Convention) was only opened for signature in January 2000 and prior to 9/11 had been ratified by only four countries. Strikingly, the Financing of Terrorism Convention has now been ratified by 173 countries.[2]

Since 2001 there has, naturally, been significantly more international interest in the development of legal instruments designed to combat the financing of terrorism. In the immediate aftermath of the attacks, the United Nations Security Council passed Resolution 1373 which, among other things, bound all of the UN's member states to 'Prevent and suppress the financing of terrorist acts…', to implement the Financing of Terrorism Convention, and to co-operate with other countries in this regard.[3] Resolution 1373 also created specific obligations for states to criminalise the financing of terrorism and to freeze the assets of entities implicated in terrorism. This Resolution builds upon a series of previous Security Council resolutions binding states to freeze the assets of individuals or entities related to al-Qaeda and the Taliban, including those designated upon a list maintained by the Security Council Committee established pursuant to Resolution 1267 concerning al-Qaeda, the Taliban and associ-ated individuals and entities (the 1267 Committee).[4] Resolution 1373 was also complemented by the efforts of other influential international organi-sations. For example, on 31 October 2001 the Financial Action Task Force (FATF) released a list of eight recommendations – a ninth was added in 2004 – concerning terrorist financing. In addition to the matters referred to in Resolution 1373, the FATF recommendations also provide for moni-toring of transfers of funds and reporting of suspicious transactions.[5]

The legislative provisions that have emerged from or coincided with this wave of international initiatives can be grouped into three categor-ies: prohibitions upon various types of dealings with terrorists and their property; provisions permitting terrorists to be deprived of their property; and measures designed to make it easier for the government to monitor

---

[2] UN Doc. A/RES/54/109 (1999), 39 ILM 270, entered into force 1 April, 2002. See, treaties. un.org/Home.aspx?lang=en.

[3] UN Doc. S/RES/1373 (2001).

[4] See S/RES/1526 (2004), S/RES/1455 (2003), S/RES/1452 (2002), S/RES/1390 (2002), S/RES/1388 (2002), S/RES/1363 (2001), S/RES/1333 (2000), S/RES/1267 (1999).

[5] Financial Action Task Force, *Special Recommendations on Terrorist Financing*, 22 October 2004.

dealings with terrorists or their property, often by imposing obligations on third parties to collect and report information. Each of these categories of provisions is discussed in turn below. The final section discusses the procedural norms that govern the application of these provisions.

B. Prohibitions

i. Overview and objectives

The legislation most obviously concerned with countering the financing of terrorism is generally designed to prohibit, upon pain of criminal sanction, activities that in some way allow resources – a general term that I will use to refer to both property and services – to be directed toward terrorism. These provisions appear to be designed both to punish and prevent dealings with terrorists. The purely punitive objective reflects the fact that in many cases knowingly financing terrorist activity seems just as blameworthy as more direct forms of participation. As for the preventative function, there are two points to consider. The first is that, to the extent that these provisions discourage various actors from providing property or services to terrorists, they cut off terrorists' access to resources that they may need to carry out terrorist activities. The second and perhaps less obvious point stems from the fact that, typically, provisions ostensibly concerned with the financing of terrorism actually cover a broad range of dealings with terrorists. As a result, they affect actors who have had even relatively innocuous dealings with terrorists and, in many cases, expose them to risk of criminal liability. This in turn gives law enforcement officials a great deal of leverage over those actors (i.e. those that technically may be guilty of dealing with terrorists). Officials might be able to use that leverage to persuade those actors to assist in efforts to apprehend the actual terrorists.

The extent to which the prohibitions upon financing terrorism achieve these objectives depends upon the physical and mental elements of the conduct that they capture. In other words, they depend upon which sorts of activities are considered to be 'financing', what sorts of activities constitute the 'terrorism' whose financing is prohibited and what mental state must accompany the physical acts that amount to financing of terrorism in order to attract liability.

ii. What activities are covered?

There is a strong international consensus on the core of the definition of 'financing' of terrorism. That consensus is embodied in the Financing of

Terrorism Convention. The Convention's main operative articles provide that criminal liability should be imposed upon not only individuals or entities that engage in financing of terrorism but also their accomplices, leaders and co-conspirators.[6] The Convention effectively defines 'financing' to mean providing or collecting funds (defined to mean assets of all kinds) with the intention or knowledge that they will be used, in whole or in part, to carry out terrorist activity.[7] Terrorist activity is defined both by reference to a list of specific criminal acts that are commonly committed by terrorists as well as a broad principled definition that essentially captures politically motivated violence, that is to say, violence whose purpose 'is to intimidate a population, or to compel a government or an international organization to do or to abstain from doing any act'.[8] It is worth noting that the term 'provides' seems to capture not only the donation of property for use in connection with terrorism, but also the sale or lease of property for use in connection with terrorism on commercially reasonable terms.[9]

Many jurisdictions depart from the terms of the Financing of Terrorism Convention by employing relatively broad definitions of the concept of 'financing'. For instance, Canada and the United Kingdom explicitly proscribe the solicitation of funds for the purposes of terrorism.[10] Furthermore, in Canada and the United Kingdom it is an offence merely to 'use' or 'possess' property with the intention or knowledge that it will be used for terrorist purposes.[11] This language suggests that virtually nothing in the way of an overt act need be committed in order to trigger liability, raising concerns that people may be punished simply for having bad thoughts.[12] In addition, many countries explicitly prohibit the provision of certain services as well as property. For instance, the US legislation, whose operative provision is a broad prohibition on providing 'material support or resources', expressly proscribes the provision of financial services, lodging, training and transportation.[13]

---

[6] Financing of Terrorism Convention, art 2(5).
[7] Ibid., art 2(1).   [8] Ibid., art 1(b).
[9] This point is made explicit in the UK's Terrorism Act 2000 s. 15(4) ('In this section a reference to the provision of money or other property is a reference to its being given, lent or otherwise made available, *whether or not for consideration*' (emphasis added)).
[10] See Criminal Code, s. 83.03 and Terrorism Act 2000, s. 15(1) (referring to a person who 'invites a person to provide' financing).
[11] Criminal Code, s. 83.04(b); Terrorism Act 2000, s. 16(2).
[12] Ibid.
[13] US Code, s. 2339A ('In this section, the term 'material support or resources' 'means currency or other financial securities, financial services, lodging, training, expert advice

For the purposes of prohibiting financing of terrorism some countries also define 'terrorist activity' in ways that go beyond the terms of the Financing of Terrorism Convention. For instance, in the United States there are three separate criminal prohibitions on financing of terrorism. One, the offence of 'providing material support to terrorists', is formulated as the provision of support or resources for use in preparation for, or in carrying out, violations of specified provisions of the US Code.[14] Meanwhile, a second prohibition against 'financing of terrorism' is defined as providing funds to carry out, essentially, the set of terrorist activities referred to in the Financing of Terrorism Convention.[15] Other jurisdictions also employ general definitions of terrorist activity but have modified the definition used in the Financing of Terrorism Convention. The Convention's definition essentially equates terrorism with politically motivated violence but it is not uncommon for law-makers to limit the types of political motivations that qualify as terrorist motivations or to expand the set of acts that qualify as terrorist forms of violence.

Perhaps the most significant type of departure from and expansion of the prohibition set out in the Financing of Terrorism Convention is the fact that many instruments prohibit the financing of terrorists as well as the financing of terrorist activities. (This is one respect in which dedicated counter-terrorism legislation clearly goes beyond more general prohibitions on conspiracy or aiding and abetting – those prohibitions do not sanction activities based simply on their connections to terrorists as opposed to terrorist activities.[16]) The most prominent examples of the organisational approach to prohibition of terrorist financing involve prohibitions upon dealings with individuals or organisations that have been placed upon some sort of official list.[17] The best-known list of this sort is the Consolidated List of Individuals and Entities associated with al-Qaeda,

---

or assistance, safehouses, false documentation or identification, communications equipment, facilities, weapons, lethal substances, explosives, personnel, transportation, and other physical assets, except medicine or religious materials'). The Canadian legislation separately proscribes making available 'financial or other related services' and 'participating in or contributing to an activity of a terrorist group' (a term that is defined to include providing training, skill or an expertise). See Criminal Code, ss. 83.03 and 83.18.

[14] US Code, Title 18, s. 2339A.   [15] US Code, Title 18, s. 2339C.

[16] Also, although this goes somewhat beyond the scope of the matters discussed to this point in this chapter, it is not clear that the pre-existing framework granted law enforcement agencies equally effective investigative powers and procedural flexibility, or contemplated the imposition of penalties as severe as those contained in the recently enacted legislation.

[17] US Code s. 2339B; Executive Order 13224, s. 1.

Osama bin Laden and the Taliban maintained by the 1267 Committee,[18] but many countries maintain their own lists as well. So for example, the third US prohibition on financing of terrorism makes it an offence to provide material support to 'designated foreign terrorist organizations' that appear on a list maintained by the Secretary of State.[19]

Prohibitions upon financing of terrorists are not always limited to prohibitions upon dealings with organisations that have been placed on official lists, nor are they always limited to foreigners. For example, under Canadian law it is an offence to finance a 'terrorist group', defined as an 'entity', regardless of its nationality, that has *either* been placed on an official list *or* 'has as one of its purposes or activities facilitating or carrying out any terrorist activity'. Significantly, this definition appears to include even an individual who has expressed an intention to support terrorist activity.[20] As a result, the Canadian provisions apply to dealings with home-grown terrorists who have not been placed on any official list.

There are several advantages to legislating against terrorists as opposed to terrorist activities. First, this approach makes it possible to target individuals who provide 'blank cheque' to terrorists by providing financing for terrorist organisations' general purposes as opposed to specific activities. Second, dispensing with the need for proof that financing is connected to specific terrorist activities may, by reducing the burden on law enforcement agencies, make it easier for those agencies either to secure convictions or to recruit informers.[21]

The principal disadvantage of the organisational approach to legislating against financing of terrorism is the danger of proscribing legitimate as well as illegitimate dealings with terrorists. This problem arises in a variety of contexts but perhaps most frequently in connection with organisations with mixed purposes and activities. For example, it is not uncommon for organisations suspected of sponsoring terrorist acts to have official purposes that encompass poverty relief and peaceful political engagement. It may be difficult to establish that either the purpose or the

---

[18] UN Doc. S/RES/1333 (2000), art. 8(c).

[19] US Code s. 2339B ; Immigration and Nationality Act, s. 219(1)(a).

[20] Criminal Code, ss. 83.03, 83.08. The conclusion that a single natural person can qualify as a terrorist group follows from the fact that the term 'entity' as it is used in s. 83.01 is defined to include a 'person'. By contrast, the US legislation refers to 'foreign terrorist organizations' and the term organisation is defined to include 'a group of persons' but not simply a 'person.' See US Code, Title 18, ss. 2339B and 1101.

[21] *Legislation Against Terrorism: A Consultation Paper*, Cm 4178 (London: Stationery Office, 1998), Chapter 6.

effect of financing such an organisation will be to support terrorist activity. Under these circumstances, subjecting either the organisation or its supporters – whose interests in freedom of speech and association are in play – to the harsh sanctions contemplated by counter-terrorism legislation may be a disproportionate response to the threat they pose.

At the same time, it may be difficult to rule out the possibility that funding an organisation with mixed purposes will indirectly support both legitimate and illegitimate activities. This is more than simply an evidentiary challenge. Funding used entirely to support legitimate activities may free up resources for illegitimate activities. Moreover, in principle, any resources that enable an organisation to survive, or serve to buttress its legitimacy, will enhance the organisation's ability to engage in future terrorist activity. In *Holder* v. *Humanitarian Law Project* a majority of the US Supreme Court accepted these arguments, deferring to what they considered to be the considered expert judgment of the executive and the legislative branches that any kind of support to a terrorist organisation would support its terrorist activities.[22]

Prohibitions upon financing of terrorists rather than terrorist activity also risk capturing transactions that are legitimate in the sense that they enable terrorists and the people who wish to deal with them to exercise their human rights.[23] For example, access to legal services is guaranteed to some extent under virtually all human rights instruments. However, an unqualified ban on dealings with terrorists seems to render lawyers potentially liable for providing services to terrorists. Similarly, provisions that proscribe the provision of 'training' or 'advice' can easily infringe upon the freedom of expression and freedom of association of terrorists' interlocutors. The larger the number of proscribed types of dealings and the broader the set of terrorists with whom those dealings are proscribed, the more significant will be these concerns. For example, the language of Security Council Resolution 1373, which is reflected in the domestic legislation of countries such as Canada, contains a sweeping ban upon dealings with terrorists. It is difficult to see how such legislation, if applied to its fullest extent, can be compatible with human rights norms.[24] By

---

[22] *Holder* v. *Humanitarian Law Project*, 130 S Ct 2705 (2010).

[23] The US legislation does, however, exclude the provision of medicine or religious materials. See US Code, Title18, s. 2339A.

[24] Security Council Resolution 1452 permits the 1267 Committee to create exceptions from the sanctions overseen by that Committee in respect of funds required to meet targeted individuals' 'basic expenses,' such as expenditures upon food and medical care. However, as Jose Alvarez has pointed out, the Committee has the discretion to refuse to authorise

comparison, UK law, which covers only the provision of property and 'financial or related services' and in certain circumstances allows parties to seek a licence to engage in prohibited transactions, is less suspect.[25]

These concerns about the organisational approach to prohibition of terrorist financing were canvassed in *Holder v. Humanitarian Law Project*, in which the US Supreme Court held that the US ban on providing material support to designated foreign terrorist organisations did not impermissibly violate the plaintiffs' freedom of speech or freedom of association. The plaintiffs' proposed forms of support included 'training [members of the organisation] on how to use humanitarian and international law to peacefully resolve disputes', 'political advocacy', and 'teaching [members of the organisation] how to petition various representative bodies such as the United Nations for relief'. It is difficult to imagine a more innocuous set of activities for a terrorist organisation. Two factors seemed to drive the majority's decision that it was constitutionally permissible to ban support for such activities. First, as we have already discussed, they accepted the argument that abandoning the organisational approach would necessarily permit terrorist organisations to receive material support for their terrorist activities. Second, the majority believed that the prohibition at issue had limited impact on protected speech because it did not bar independent advocacy in support of a terrorist organisation (that is to say, advocacy not under the direction of or in co-ordination with the organisation).

Prohibitions upon the financing of terrorists can also threaten legitimate economic activity when individuals or organisations have ambiguous purposes. This sort of ambiguity threatens to create two types of problems. First, wholly legitimate entities may be shunned by third parties concerned about violating the prohibitions. Second, some parties may be prosecuted for unwittingly supporting terrorists. The most obvious way to mitigate these concerns is by limiting the scope of organisational prohibitions to entities that have been placed upon an official list and granting entities that have been or are about to be listed an opportunity to challenge the decision. However, publicly proscribing the financing of

---

member states to use this exception. See José E. Alvarez, 'Hegemonic international law revisited' (2003) 97 *American Journal of International Law* 873, 877 note 26.

[25] The Canadian Criminal Code contains a provision that allows the Solicitor General to authorise transactions with a terrorist group. Unfortunately, however, the provision only seems to permit the Solicitor General to provide an exemption from liability arising under one of several provisions that prohibit the financing of terrorists. See Criminal Code s. 83.09.

only listed terrorists as opposed to all terrorists is only an effective tactic when law-makers have solid prior information about both the existence of terrorist groups and their *nommes de guerre* at any given point in time. This seems unrealistic, especially with respect to relatively new terrorist organisations that do not have any links with notorious listed groups.

iii.   Mental elements

In addition to the physical elements described so far, the criminal laws concerned with financing of terrorism also include some sort of mental element, typically either intention or knowledge. Unfortunately, the meanings of these concepts are not wholly self-evident. For instance, does a person who provides financing to an organisation possess the requisite mental element if he or she is unaware that the organisation has been placed upon some sort of official list and unaware of the organisation's specific terrorist activities, but is aware in a general way that it engages in terrorist activities? Suppose the financier lacks even the most general sort of knowledge about the terrorist activities? Or, what if the financier is aware of some of the terrorist activities but honestly believes that their resources will be channelled toward non-terrorist activities?

The legislation in some jurisdictions provides guidance on some of these issues. For example, the Canadian provision that makes it an offence to participate in or contribute to the activity of a terrorist group states that the offence may be committed 'whether or not...the accused knows the specific nature of any terrorist activity that may be facilitated or carried out by a terrorist group'.[26] In the United States, the provision making it an offence to provide material support to a foreign terrorist organisation initially left these issues open but was amended in 2004 to require awareness of either the organisation's designation as a foreign terrorist organisation or its terrorist activities.[27]

The manner in which these mental states are defined will be an important determinant of the range and effectiveness of the corresponding prohibitions upon financing of terrorism. In many circumstances, the approach taken to defining the mental elements of these offences will be at least as important in determining the practical effects of the offences as will the approach taken to defining the physical elements. This point is particularly important to keep in mind in assessing the significance of prohibiting financing of terrorists as opposed to financing of terrorist

---

[26] Criminal Code, s. 83.18(2)(c).
[27] Intelligence Reform and Terrorism Prevention Act 2004, 118 Stat. 3638, s. 6603(c) (amending USC § 2339B(1)).

activity. Suppose that financing a terrorist group with knowledge of its general purposes is taken to qualify as proof of an intention to finance terrorist activity. Now suppose that this determination is made in the context of a prosecution for conspiring to finance terrorist activity. This possibility suggests that a broad definition of the concepts of intention or knowledge can allow legislation that appears to capture only financing of terrorist activity to effectively capture financing of terrorists. Of course the reverse is also true. If a person is not considered to have knowingly financed a terrorist group unless he has specific knowledge of the activities that support the conclusion that the group is a terrorist one, then provisions that ostensibly take an organisational approach to legislating against the financing of terrorism will be essentially vitiated.

C.   Deprivation of property

i.   Overview and objectives

Lawmakers concerned with financing of terrorism have not limited themselves to pursuing the individuals who participate in channelling resources to terrorists or terrorist activity. They have also crafted laws that, where physically possible, permit resources connected to terrorists or terrorist activity to be removed from the control of terrorists, whether by freezing, seizing or confiscating the property, often without securing a criminal conviction.

When a government freezes property, it prohibits transfer, conversion, disposition or movement of assets, although other legal rights over the property remain intact. Seizure of property has similar effects to a freeze but in addition the government typically takes control of the property. Freezes and seizures of property are often designed to be temporary measures.[28] By contrast, forfeiture or confiscation permanently transfers legal rights over the property to the government and extinguishes the rights

---

[28] In the United Kingdom, assets can be seized for just forty-eight hours. Terrorism Act 2000, s. 25(4). However, authorities can obtain an order for further detention for no more than three months from the time of the initial seizure, ss. 26(1) and 26(2). It is possible to have more than one order, but the assets cannot be seized for more than two years from the time of the first order, s. 26(4). In Canada, a report is required within seven days identifying the property seized and the location of the property. Criminal Code, s. 462.32(4). Property may be detained for up to six months, s. 462.35(1). Property can be detained even longer if forfeiture proceedings have been instituted, s. 462.35(2). The period can be extended from six months upon a judge's satisfaction, s. 462.35(3). In the United States, however, the broad language of the International Emergency Economic Powers Act appears to permit assets to be seized or blocked so long as the unusual and extraordinary threat exists or the US remains in armed hostilities

of some or all other parties. Regardless of the nature of the deprivation contemplated, however, legislation providing for deprivation of property associated with terrorism typically has two main components: a definition of the types of property that can be targeted, and a description of the procedural steps that must be followed in order to accomplish various forms of deprivation.

To a certain extent, these provisions are designed to complement the prohibitions upon financing of terrorism discussed in the previous section by ensuring that significant economic consequences flow from violating those prohibitions. This is consistent with a global trend towards ensuring that legal mechanisms exist to deprive offenders of property that represents the instruments or proceeds of crime.[29] However, as will be shown below, not all of the provisions that permit deprivation of property are triggered by violations of the prohibitions upon financing of terrorism. Consequently, the deprivation provisions can be used in circumstances where it is inconvenient or impossible to link assets that are discovered to be under the control of terrorists to transactions with specific actors. This may be particularly helpful in combating terrorist organisations that rely heavily upon resources generated by business enterprises – either legitimate or illegitimate – operated by full-blown members of the organisation.

It is also worth noting that measures which have the effect of depriving terrorists of their property can, unless they are carefully drafted, also affect the interests of other actors, such as people who unwittingly violate freezing orders or those with interests in the affected property. These issues are particularly salient when the measures are applied against charitable organisations. There is substantial evidence that measures aimed at US Islamic charities have had a chilling effect on prospective donors in the Muslim community.[30]

ii. Which property?

Perhaps the most interesting conceptual issue that arises in defining the types of property that can be removed from the control of terrorists is whether it is appropriate to include only property associated with terrorist

---

[29] See generally, Guy Stessens, *Money Laundering: A New International Law Enforcement Model* (New York: Cambridge University Press, 2000) pp. 4–5; R. T. Naylor, 'Washout: A critique of follow-the-money methods in crime control policy' (1999) 32 *Crime, Law and Social Change*1.

[30] American Civil Liberties Union, *Blocking Faith, Freezing Charity: Chilling Muslim Charitable Giving in the 'War on Terrorism Financing'* (New York: American Civil Liberties Union, June 2009).

activity, or whether it is important to include any and all property associated with terrorists.[31] As far as freezing property is concerned, the issue is
settled by Resolution 1373. That resolution calls upon states to freeze the
property of 'persons who commit, or attempt to commit, terrorist acts
or participate in or facilitate the commission of terrorist acts; of entities
owned or controlled directly or indirectly by such persons; and of persons
and entities acting on behalf of, or at the direction of such persons and
entities...'[32]

Resolution 1373 is silent on the question of what sort of property ought
to be subject to forfeiture as opposed to a freeze. Here the Financing of
Terrorism Convention adopts a narrow approach, instructing states to
take appropriate measures for the forfeiture of only those funds 'used or
allocated for the purposes of committing terrorist offenses and the proceeds derived from such offenses'.[33] However, some states adopt a broader
approach in their domestic legislation. For example, Canadian law allows
the Attorney-General to apply for an order of forfeiture not only for property that 'has been or will be used, in whole or in part, to facilitate or carry
out a terrorist activity',[34] but also for 'property owned or controlled by or
on behalf of a terrorist group'.[35] Meanwhile, the Patriot Act extends the
possibility of forfeiture not just to all instruments and proceeds and all
property belonging to terrorist groups or entities, but to all assets affording any person a 'source of influence' over terrorist entities.[36] Furthermore,
additional Patriot Act provisions amending the International Emergency
Economic Powers Act (IEEPA) allow for confiscation of *any* property
of any foreign person, foreign organisation, or foreign country that the
President or his officials have determined has 'planned, authorized, aided,
or engaged' in an attack on the United States.[37]

The advantages and disadvantages of targeting property of terrorists
as opposed to simply property associated with specific terrorist acts parallel the advantages and disadvantages of targeting actors who are linked
to specific terrorist activities as opposed to terrorist groups. On the one

---

[31] Another important issue is to what extent should the interests of third parties be affected
by measures designed to deprive terrorists of property? For a general discussion of the
issue of the effects of forfeiture on third parties see Kevin E. Davis, 'The effects of forfeiture on third parties' (2003) 48 *McGill Law Journal* 183.

[32] Resolution 1373, art. 1(c).   [33] Financing of Terrorism Convention, art. 8(2).

[34] Criminal Code, s. 83.14, as am ended by S.C. 2001, c. 41, s. 4.   [35] Ibid., s 83.14(1).

[36] 18 USC 981(G) [as amended by Patriot Act, s. 806]. This language is derived from the
Racketeer Influenced Corrupt Organizations (RICO) implying that the draftsperson of
the Patriot Act equated terrorist groups with 'criminal enterprises'.

[37] 50 USC 1702(a)(1)(C) [as amended by Patriot Act, s. 806].

hand, the organisational approach makes it possible to deprive terrorists of property that has not been allocated to specific activities but is none-theless available for their general purposes. This approach also relieves law enforcement agents of the burden of linking property to specific ter-rorist activities. On the other hand, depriving actors of property that is not linked to any particular terrorist activity may be inappropriate in cases involving organisations with ambiguous or mixed purposes.

D. Monitoring provisions

i. Overview and objectives

The prohibitions upon financing of terrorism may be the most vis-ible components of the financial war against terrorism. Less visible but equally important are a raft of initiatives designed to make it difficult for terrorists and their affiliates to hold or transfer property anonymously and thereby facilitate detection of terrorists' activities.[38] Naturally, these provisions can also aid in enforcing prohibitions upon dealings with ter-rorists and in depriving terrorists of their property.

ii. Reporting obligations

The least remarkable sorts of monitoring provisions are those that impose obligations upon financial institutions to report to the authorities when they have information about dealings with or the property of terror-ists.[39] The Financing of Terrorism Convention and FATF recommend the imposition of such reporting obligations[40] and they can be found in all of the jurisdictions that have been mentioned so far in this chapter.[41] Canada also imposes a blanket obligation for people to report when prop-erty in their possession or control is owned or controlled by a terrorist group[42] and the United Kingdom requires individuals to report instances

---

[38] For an in-depth analysis of the relevant US provisions, see Mariano-Florentino Cuéllar, 'The tenuous relationship between the fight against money laundering and the disrup-tion of criminal finance' (2003) 92 *Journal of Criminal Law and Criminolody* 311.

[39] These provisions sometimes also encourage sharing of information between financial institutions. See, for example, Patriot Act 2001, s. 314(b).

[40] Financing of Terrorism Convention, art. 18(1)(b); FATF, *Special Recommendations on Terrorist Financing*, Recommendation IV.

[41] Criminal Code, ss. 83.1, 83.11; Proceeds of Crime (Money Laundering) and Terrorist Financing Act, ss. 5–11 (in Canada); 31 CFR 103 (in the US); Terrorism Act 2000, s. 19, Proceeds of Crime Act 2002, ss. 330–2 (in the UK);

[42] Criminal Code, s. 83.1.

of financing of terrorism.[43] Future debates surrounding these provisions are likely to revolve around which actors are subject to the disclosure obligation, what circumstances should trigger a duty to report and the extent to which those who file reports are entitled to indemnification for or exemption from any resulting liability.

The net value of these reporting obligations is difficult to assess. Some of the benefits may only appear over time as financial institutions and law enforcement agencies develop expertise in analysing reported information. Meanwhile, calculating the costs of these reporting requirements involves aggregating the potentially negligible costs – in terms of both financial impact and intrusions upon privacy – of large numbers of individual transactions. It is also important to bear in mind that the costs of these provisions may not be equally distributed across members of society, particularly if racial or ethnic stereotypes are used to determine when reporting is warranted.[44]

iii. Other monitoring provisions

Other monitoring provisions are more remarkable, and costly, because they impose new obligations upon actors dealing with the general population in the ordinary course of business rather than just those dealing with suspected terrorists or involved in inherently suspicious transactions. For example, the Patriot Act includes a provision requiring financial institutions to verify the identity of any person opening an account and to maintain records of the information used to verify the person's identity with a view to enabling a determination of whether the person appears on any list of known or suspected terrorists or terrorist organisations.[45] For these purposes the term 'financial institution' is defined extremely broadly.[46]

Most obligations of this sort are initially formulated at the international level through the FATF. For instance, the Special Recommendations on Terrorist Financing include recommendations that information about both originators and recipients of wire transfers be included in the wire transfers and remain with it throughout the payment chain[47] and that all persons or entities who engage in the transmission of money or value be

---

[43] Terrorism Act 2000, s. 19.
[44] Cheryl R. Lee, 'Constitutional cash: are banks guilty of racial profiling in implementing the United States Patriot Act?' (2006) 11 *Michigan Journal of Race and the Law* 557.
[45] 31 USC s. 5318, [as amended by Patriot Act, s. 326].
[46] See, 31 USC 5312.
[47] FATF, *Special Recommendations on Terrorist Financing*, Recommendation VII.

subjected to licensing and registration requirements and required to comply with FATF's recommended anti-money laundering obligations.[48]

The requirements aimed at formalising and monitoring cross-border transfers are aimed at so-called alternative remittance systems such as *hawala*.[49] They were motivated by the belief that al-Qaeda and its associated groups placed great reliance upon such systems to transfer money.[50] However, alternative remittance systems are also important – and less costly – methods of transferring funds for legitimate purposes, particularly for migrants or refugees attempting to remit money to family members in rural areas not served by banks. The social costs of restricting legitimate actors' access to these alternative remittance systems appear to be substantial, while the effects on terrorist financing remain unclear.[51]

It is worth noting that monitoring provisions need not be targeted simply at either highly suspicious transactions or the entire universe of ordinary business transactions. Between those polar alternatives it is possible to design intermediate measures that target only a narrow range of transactions that are unusually amenable to the purposes of terrorists. For example, charities are widely believed to have played a significant role in channelling funds to al-Qaeda, and associated individuals and organisations, especially in Southeast Asia.[52] In response the FATF Special Recommendation VIII sets out a number of measures designed to facilitate the monitoring of non-profit organisations, including record-keeping requirements and 'know your beneficiaries and associate non-profit organisations' rules.[53]

The costs of these monitoring provisions include not only the direct costs imposed on the actors who must comply with them, but also the 'cost' of infringing upon the privacy of the people being monitored. These

---

[48]   Ibid., Recommendation VI.
[49]   31 USC 5330; Tim Golden, '5 months after sanctions against Somali company, scant proof of Qaeda tie', *NY Times*, 13 April 2002, A10 (reporting that after the 9/11 attacks, the United States rapidly shut down al Barakat, Somalia's main *hawala* network).
[50]   See, e.g., Second Report of the 1363 Monitoring Group, para. 85
[51]   Nikos Passas and Samuel Munzele Maimbo, 'The design, development, and implementation of regulatory and supervisory frameworks for informal funds transfer systems', in Thomas J. Biersteker and Sue E. Eckert (eds.), *Countering the Financing of Terrorism* (New York: Routledge, 2008), p. 174.
[52]   Second Report of the 1363 Monitoring Group, paras. 57–8; Jeroen Gunning, 'Terrorism, charities and diasporas: contrasting the fundraising practices of Hamas and al Qaeda among Muslims in Europe', in Biersteker and Eckert *Countering the Financing of Terrorism*, p. 93.
[53]   FATF, *Special Recommendations on Terrorist Financing*, Recommendation VIII.

concerns have animated the EU's efforts to restrict sharing of data on bank transfers between the EU and the US.[54]

E. Procedural norms

Application of the regime designed to counter financing of terrorism can produce harsh results. For one thing, individuals subject to these provisions are liable to receive long prison sentences. In addition, individuals deprived of access to their own property and resources from employers, family or friends are 'effectively prisoners of the state'.[55] Moreover, their spouses and family members may also suffer. In one case the wife of a man subject to freezing orders under the UK regime was required to report to the Treasury on every item of household expenditure, however small.[56] Finally, intrusive monitoring regimes impinge significantly upon privacy interests.

The potential severity of the consequences of applying the various elements of the regime designed to counter financing terrorism has focused attention on the processes that states and international organisations follow before applying those provisions. One set of issues concerns the evidentiary burden the government must meet. A second set of issues revolves around the question of which institutions ought to be involved in deciding whether to apply the provisions: should that authority be vested exclusively in the UN Security Council together with the executive branches of the relevant national governments? Should there be opportunities for review, either before or after determinations are made, by some sort of Ombudsperson within the United Nations system? What about judicial review and the right to be heard? Should legislatures have the final word on which approach is taken? A third set of issues relate to the amount of transparency that accompanies the decision-making process. On each of these issues demands for procedural fairness have to be weighed against the interest in permitting states to impose sanctions rapidly on the basis of limited information, particularly in cases where delay or prior notice might give the targets of sanctions time to transfer funds to safety. Meanwhile, the benefits of transparency have to be weighed against interests in protecting confidential sources.

---

[54] James Kanter 'Europe resumes sharing bank data with U.S.', *NY Times*, 8 July 2010.
[55] *A and others* v. *HM Treasury* [2008] EWCA Civ 1187; [2009] 3 WLR 25, para. 125, per Sedley LJ.
[56] *R(M)* v. *HM Treasury* [2008] 2 All ER 1097 (HL).

The law in this area has evolved significantly since 2001. Most notably, the Security Council has progressively added safeguards to the process of constructing its Consolidated List. Those safeguards include: requiring designating states to provide greater information about the basis for listing requests; providing a narrative summary of reasons for listing at the time a name is added to the list; publishing information on reasons for listing (unless the designating state requests otherwise); creating an Ombudsperson and a Monitoring Team to assist in gathering information pertaining to requests for delisting; and requiring an annual review of all names on the list that have not been reviewed in three or more years in order to update the list and confirm that listing remains appropriate.[57] However, there is still no provision for judicial review of the 1267 Committee's decisions within the UN system.

Some of the Security Council's reforms were prompted by judicial decisions or other commentary complaining about the limited procedural fairness of the regimes put in place immediately after 9/11. The relevant judicial decisions were handed down in proceedings in which individuals have challenged 1267 Committee listing decisions and their domestic implementation before national or supranational courts. The most notable decision is *Kadi & Al Barakaat Int'l Found. v. Council of the European Union and Commission of the European Communities* in which the European Court of Justice annulled a European Community regulation designed to implement Security Council resolutions pertaining to al-Qaeda and the Taliban because that regulation contravened the rights to be heard and the principle of effective judicial protection.[58] That decision appeared to prompt the most far-reaching reforms to date of the 1267 Committee's procedures.[59] However, those reforms have not satisfied all the critics. Just over one month after the Security Council adopted its reforms the UK Supreme Court struck down a set of Orders-in-Council designed to implement the Security Council resolutions on the grounds that the scheme they contained should have been approved by Parliament rather than just the executive.[60] In their reasons the judges referred to the draconian nature of the regime, the low burden of proof it imposed on the state and the absence of any provision for an effective judicial remedy.[61] A few months later the European General Court struck down a regulation affirming the listing of Kadi on the basis that the new procedure did not

---

[57] UN Doc., S/RES/1735 (2006), S/RES/1822 (2008), S/RES/1904 (2009).
[58] 3 CMLR 41 (2008).   [59] UN Doc., S/RES/1904 (2009).
[60] *A and others* v. *HM Treasury* [2008] EWCA Civ 1187, [2009] 3 WLR 25.
[61] Ibid., paras. 58–61, 78–82, per Lord Hope.

provide him with effective notice of the basis of the listing or an opportunity to seek a judicial remedy for a wrongful listing.[62] Domestic regimes have typically displayed more regard for procedural fairness than the Security Council, and the trend has been toward increased procedural fairness. For example, in the United Kingdom, provisions for judicial review of orders made by the UK Treasury were created under Part 6 of the Counter-Terrorism Act 2008.[63] Canadian law has not changed but increasingly onerous procedural requirements must be satisfied in order to freeze, seize and confiscate property. Specifically, assets can be frozen by the merely administrative act of designating an organisation as a terrorist organisation (with opportunities for subsequent judicial review), whereas seizure requires satisfying a judge that there are 'reasonable grounds' for suspicion that the property is related to terrorist activities,[64] and forfeiture requires satisfying a judge on a 'balance of probabilities'.[65]

For the most part this is broadly consistent with the approach typically taken in US federal law, especially since 2004 when the procedure for designation of foreign terrorist organisations was amended to allow an organisation to petition for revocation of a designation and to require a review of an existing designation after five years if no petitions for review have been made.[66] A notable exception to the generally increasing regard for procedural fairness is the IEEPA. As amended by the Patriot Act, the IEEPA gives the Treasury Department nearly *carte blanche* to freeze, indefinitely, a person's assets without the evidentiary and due process protections normally afforded through federal forfeiture law.[67] Provisions of the IEEPA that permit property to be frozen indefinitely pending completion of an investigation, without opportunity for judicial review, have been challenged successfully – in at least one case – as violations of constitutional protections against warrantless seizures and guarantees of due process.[68]

---

[62] *Kadi v. Commission of the European Union and Council of the European Communities*, 30 September, 2010.
[63] Counter-Terrorism Act 2008, s. 63.   [64] Criminal Code, s. 83.13(1).
[65] Criminal Code, s. 83.14(5).
[66] Intelligence Reform and Terrorism Prevention Act 2004, Pub.L. 108–458, 118 Stat. 3638, Titles VI (subtitles B, D, G) and VII (subtitle A), amending 8 USC § 1189.
[67] US Code, Title 50, s. 1702 [as amended by Patriot Act, s. 106]. As already mentioned, the trigger is an attack upon the United States by foreign nationals and the President's determination that the group or entity planned, authorised, aided or engaged in the attacks.
[68] *KindHearts for Charitable Humanitarian Development, Inc. v. Geithner*, 647 F Supp 2d 857 (ND, Ohio 2009). Cf. *Islamic Am. Relief Agency v. Unidentified FBI Agents*, 394 F Supp 2d 34, 47–8 (DDC 2005); *Holy Land Foundation for Relief and Development v. Ashcroft*, 219 F Supp 2d 57, 79 (DDC 2002).

3.   Implementation and enforcement

The sweeping criminal prohibitions and proprietary measures aimed at combating terrorist financing provide law enforcement officials with considerable discretion. There have been numerous complaints about that discretion being abused, especially in relation to immigrants and Muslims in Western countries.[69]

There is reason to believe that these complaints are symptomatic of fundamental problems with officials' incentives to enforce measures against financing of terrorism. Cuéllar has recently advanced a sophisticated argument in support of the idea that law enforcement officials cannot be expected to exercise their discretion to enforce prohibitions upon financing of terrorism wisely.[70] He adopts a model of law enforcement officials' behaviour premised on the idea that they are generally motivated by a desire to please voters. He then assumes that voters have imperfect information about the steps that law enforcement agencies have taken to combat the financing of terrorism and their likely efficacy. Cuéllar posits that in this context voters will typically reward officials who take highly visible steps to prosecute financiers of terrorism, regardless of the actual efficacy of those steps and regardless of whether the officials have taken more efficacious but less visible steps to counter terrorism.

Using this model, Cuéllar predicts that law enforcement officials typically will not exercise their discretion in a manner that is designed to minimise the threat of terrorism. Rather officials are likely to be biased against such a strategy in at least three different ways. First, they are likely to be unduly interested in cases that are relatively easy to detect because investments in detecting other types of cases are not particularly observable to voters. Second, officials are likely to prefer to bring cases against actors who are already stigmatised by voters because it will be relatively easy to persuade voters that such cases are effective means of countering terrorism. Third, officials will be inclined to bring cases against actors that they personally disfavour if voters cannot readily distinguish those actors from others who pose a greater threat.

One weakness in Cuéllar's model is its assumption that voters reward officials based solely upon their perceptions of the *efforts* that the officials

---

[69]   See, e.g., American Civil Liberties Union, *Blocking Faith, Freezing Charity.*
[70]   Mariano Florentino Cuéllar, 'The mismatch between state capacity and state power in the global attack on criminal finance' (2003) 22 *Berkeley Journal of International Law* 15.

are making to counter terrorism. It seems equally plausible to assume that voters judge officials at least in part upon the *results* of their actions and accordingly officials who fail to prevent terrorist attacks can expect to be punished by voters. In countries that are highly likely to be the targets of attacks this incentive may be sufficient to ensure that officials are properly motivated to minimise the threat of terrorism. On the other hand, Cuéllar's model may have greater application in countries that are not targets of terrorism but face pressure from targeted countries to undertake counter-terrorism activities. In those countries the government may behave in the ways that Cúellar suggests in order to please imperfectly informed foreign actors (rather than imperfectly informed voters).[71]

Even if we leave aside Cuéllar's concerns about voters' imperfect information and assume that officials are motivated to minimise the threat of terrorism, there remain grounds for concern about the manner in which they are likely to go about this task. In an ideal world officials would arguably strive not only to minimise the costs of terrorism, but also to minimise the costs that counter-terrorist initiatives impose upon innocent actors. However, as Cuéllar observes, public officials may not be equally sensitive to the interests of all actors. For instance, they may not be particularly sensitive to the interests of minority groups who cannot attract the sympathies of members of more powerful groups. Similarly, the officials in any given jurisdiction will often be relatively insensitive to the interests of inhabitants of foreign jurisdictions. Consequently, it seems reasonable to fear that public officials will systematically tend to impose undue costs upon members of certain minority groups and inhabitants of foreign jurisdictions in the course of their counter-terrorism activities. This is consistent with minority groups' complaints about enforcement of counter-terrorism measures. It also implies that countries that are targets of terrorism will favour global adoption of monitoring provisions that are likely to be viewed as excessively costly from the perspective of countries that are not targets of terrorism.

An important challenge for the future will be to devise legal tactics capable of responding to concerns about abuse of discretion. For instance, the constitutionality of the US prohibition on providing material support to designated foreign terrorist organisations has been challenged on the

---

[71] For anecdotal evidence supporting this conjecture see Salman Masood, 'Path out of poverty is cut short by antiterror snare', *NY Times*, 10 May 2004 (Quoting a Macedonian government official claiming that a previous administration had killed seven economic migrants as part of an attempt to '… present themselves as participants in the war against terrorism and demonstrate Macedonia's commitment to the war on terrorism').

grounds of overbreadth and vagueness. As we have already discussed, the argument that the provision represented an overly broad infringement of freedom of expression and association was rejected by the majority in *Holder* v. *Humanitarian Law Project*. The plaintiffs in that case also argued that the definition of material support was so vague as to deprive them of fair notice of whether their proposed conduct was prohibited. The US Supreme Court unanimously rejected that argument, largely because the definition was clearly broad enough to cover virtually all of the plaintiffs' proposed activities. This ruling is, however, limited in scope because the Court only considered whether the statute was unconstitutional as applied to the particular activities the plaintiffs expressed an interest in engaging in. Although it acknowledged the desirability of permitting people to avoid running the risk of a criminal prosecution in order to test the constitutionality of a statute, the Court was reluctant to speculate about the statute's validity in relation to hypothetical circumstances. So for instance, the Court avoided the issue of whether the prohibition on providing a 'service' to a foreign terrorist organisation set clear bounds on advocacy performed in co-ordination with or at the direction of a foreign terrorist organisation.[72]

Even in the US the decision in *Humanitarian Law Project* leaves open several alternative legal mechanisms for checking potential abuse of discretion. For instance, the plaintiffs in that case did not argue that the provision in question violated due process requirements by encouraging arbitrary or discriminatory enforcement. They also made no reference to prohibitions on racial or ethnic discrimination.[73] Moreover, the decision only deals with one of the many provisions that make up the US regime designed to counter terrorist financing.

4. Effectiveness

Patterns in terrorist financing are, naturally, difficult to observe, and any data that has been collected is not available to the public. Perhaps as a consequence, there do not appear to have been any systematic evaluations of the effectiveness of the current regime.[74] In the absence of such analysis there is disagreement about how effective those efforts have been. There

---

[72] *Holder* v. *Humanitarian Law Project*, 130 SCT 2705 (2010).
[73] See generally, Laura K. Donohue, 'Constitutional and legal challenges to the anti-terrorist finance regime' (2008) 43 *Wake Forest Law Review* 643.
[74] Levi, 'Combating the financing of terrorism'.

is some indication that terrorist groups' funding has been disrupted – though not cut off – and that financial information gained through monitoring has been of assistance in understanding and disrupting their networks and operations.[75]

The idea that the elaborate regime designed to counter financing of terrorism is largely ineffective is plausible because legal efforts to reduce terrorist financing face two significant obstacles. First, terrorists' economic activities are often inherently difficult to detect because, at least for terrorist operations aimed at 'soft' targets, they often involve property of relatively little value. It has been estimated that the attacks of 9/11 were carried out on a budget of between US $400,000 and US $500,000, with approximately US $300,000 flowing through the US banking system.[76] Even if it is able to monitor a significant proportion of the enormous number of transactions involving such small amounts of money, it will be difficult for any law enforcement agency to use the resulting data effectively to identify illegitimate transactions.

A second challenge is the possibility of substitution between various forms of terrorist financing. Even if recent legal reforms have enhanced law enforcement authorities' ability to detect and punish certain types of dealings with terrorists, they almost certainly have not allowed them to disrupt all of the alternative channels through which terrorists may obtain resources. For example, it is now believed that al-Qaeda finances itself through a combination of external funding from state actors, external funding from private individuals or organisations such as Islamic charities, funds generated internally through illicit activity such as drug trafficking and fraud, and funds generated internally through legitimate business activities such as trading in honey and tanzanite, and ownership of shipping.[77] Recent legislative initiatives and diplomatic pressure aim to deprive terrorist organisations of certain forms of external funding. But even if those efforts are completely successful, they may simply encourage organisations like al-Qaeda to substitute internal funding for external

---

[75] See generally, Arabinda Acharya, *Targeting Terrorist Financing* (New York: Routledge, 2009), pp. 117–19; Biersteker and Eckert, *Countering the Financing of Terrorism*; Levi, 'Combating the financing of terrorism'.

[76] John Roth, Douglas Greenburg and Serena Wille, *Monograph on Terrorist Financing*, (National Commission on Terrorist Attack Upon the United States, 2004), Appendix A.

[77] Second Report of the 1364 Monitoring Group, para. 31; Judith Miller and Jeff Girth, 'Honey trade said to provide funds and cover to bin Laden', *NY Times*, A1 11 October 2001; Robert Block and Daniel Pearl, 'Underground trade: much-smuggled gem called tanzanite helps bin Laden supporters', *Wall Street Journal*, A1, 16 November 2001; 'Peril on the sea', *The Economist*, 4 October 2003.

funding. For instance, funding for the Madrid attacks may have all been obtained internally.[78]

Alternatively, law enforcement activities may cut off access to certain forms of external funding in certain jurisdictions while allowing terrorists to use alternative channels and/or jurisdictions. For example, even if authorities make it prohibitively risky for terrorists to transfer funds from Egypt to the United States by way of wire transfer, they may not be able to prevent them from transferring funds through a *hawaladar* from Egypt to an accomplice in Malaysia and then by ordinary wire transfer to the United States via Singapore.

Section 2 of this chapter has shown that the regime designed to counter the financing of terrorism threatens to impose significant costs upon legitimate economic activities. It is also important to bear in mind that the people who bear those costs may be alienated by measures aimed at countering financing of terrorism and may become less willing to support broader efforts to counter terrorism. All of these costs ought to be kept in mind when assessing the merits of proposals to retain or amend the current legal framework, particularly if the offsetting benefits are small.

5. Conclusion

This chapter has outlined the legislative provisions that provide the legal underpinnings of the financial war against terrorism as well as some of the concerns they have generated. Some of the most substantial concerns revolve around the question of whether the legislation captures an overly broad range of conduct. Many have suggested that the legislation permits costs – financial or otherwise – to be imposed upon actors engaged in wholly legitimate activities. For example, prohibitions upon donating funds to charities with ambiguous or mixed purposes may serve to discourage donations to a broad range of charitable organisations that find it too costly to generate detailed documentation of their activities.[79] The costs of such regulations are ultimately borne by the prospective beneficiaries of the charities. Similarly, the procedures governing the opening of bank accounts and wire transfers have imposed enormous costs upon

---

[78] Elaine Sciolino, 'Complex web of Madrid plot still entangled', *NY Times*, A1, 12 April 2004.

[79] Stephanie Strom, 'Small charities abroad feel pinch of U.S. war on terror', *NY Times*, 5 August 2003, A8. See also *Humanitarian Law Project* v. *United States DOJ*, 130 SCT 2705 (2010).

financial institutions and their customers, including both the financial costs of compliance and the less tangible but arguably just as significant costs represented by loss of privacy. Imposing costs upon innocent actors in this way not only seems unjust but also may serve to deter socially valuable activities and foster dangerous levels of resentment in affected communities.

A second and related concern about the new regime is that it will be enforced irrationally or arbitrarily. At the domestic level, the concern is that it will be used against some of the most vulnerable members of society such as members of racial or ethnic minorities. At the international level, there are analogous grounds for concern that enforcement of the new regime may cause the weakest members of the international community to bear disproportionate costs. In addition, in both contexts some reason exists to believe that law enforcement agents might focus upon only the most easily detected threats and ignore targets that pose threats that are just as serious, if not more.

A third and final concern is that the financial war against terrorism is doomed to failure in light of the inherent difficulty of combating some methods of terrorist financing. The chain of domestic and international legal provisions that has been forged to combat financing of terrorism may turn out to be only as strong as its weakest link. Under these circumstances it may be difficult to justify the tremendous costs that have been incurred to create the regime.

In light of these concerns it is clear that the legal tools being deployed in the financial war on terrorism warrant regular and systematic examination.

9

Our responsibility to respect the rights of others: legality and humanity

1. Introduction

A. Challenge and continuity

States tend to be concerned about self-definition, and immigration law arose as one attempt to mark out territory by establishing a regulatory system which defined who could enter, remain and be removed (with nationality and citizenship laws addressing membership). The risk with migration law, however, is the governmental temptation to nurture a continuing form of communal insecurity by constructing 'others' as a threat.[1] Governments have given into this urge all too often, and the application of migration law often says as much about national communities as it does about those seeking to enter or remain

Migration brings with it many benefits, but from the governmental perspective it also carries potential risks. Immigration law has historically been used to limit these risks at the entry stage, and also its enforcement provisions have been applied against those considered a danger to public order or national security. This has included, for example, internment during times of war,[2] mass and individualised deportations[3] or the expulsion of those who had simply outstayed their original welcome. It is a well-established area of legal regulation that vests formidable powers with the executive, and has done so for some time and in many states.

---

[1] Jef Huysmans, *The Politics of Insecurity: Fear, Migration and Asylum in the EU* (Oxford: Routledge, 2006), p. 47: 'migration and asylum become a factor in a constitutive political dialectic in which securing unity and identity of a community depends on making this very community insecure.'

[2] See David Cole, *Enemy Aliens: Double Standards and Constitutional Freedoms in the War on Terror* (New York: The New Press, 2003).

[3] *R v. Secretary of State for the Home Department, ex parte Cheblak* [1991] 2 All ER 319 (deportation of Iraqis and Palestinians following the outbreak of the Gulf War in 1991).

Refugees and asylum seekers generally require an effective form of international protection, as they are fleeing human rights abuses in their state of origin where national forms of protection have broken down. They may even be fleeing conflicts that they themselves were participants in or became the targets of. If they do secure a form of international protection, they may become politically active (perhaps renewing earlier commitments) or develop support for political movements overseas. Although they may be victims and survivors of conflict, that does not render refugees and asylum seekers empty of all the complex political and social human associations, allegiances and commitments that everyone can become party to. It is when this activity begins to slide into the counter-terrorism frame or the person concerned is simply a member of a 'suspect community'[4] that enhanced problems can arise. In three broad areas the impact can become marked: first, in the attempts to exclude terrorists from refugee status (as envisaged in the 1951 Convention relating to the Status of Refugees, art. 1F); second, in the deployment by states of repressive internal measures to deal with established and emerging 'suspect communities' (which may include refugees and those seeking asylum);[5] and third in attempts (ever more elaborate) to secure the removal of asylum seekers who pose a threat to national security. Although serious concern continues about the use of exclusion clauses, it is in the last two categories where matters have raised stark and ongoing human rights problems. States like the United Kingdom are increasingly uneasy about the risks they face from transnational terrorist networks, and the scale and extent of the proactive and preventative responses (which did not, however, involve repeal of the Human Rights Act 1998) demonstrate this clearly. The starting point now is frequently framed in rights-based terms, for example, the positive obligation on the state to protect the right to life of all within its jurisdiction confronts the absolute rights established under art. 3 of the European Convention.

B.   Using migration law?

The events of 11 September 2001 (US), 11 March 2004 (Spain) and 7 July 2005 (UK) prompted an intense focus on the effectiveness of existing counter-terrorism law and policy, and the rapid international promotion

---

[4] Paddy Hillyard, *Suspect Community: People's Experience of the Prevention of Terrorism Acts in Britain* (London: Pluto Press, 1993).

[5] Ibid.

of new and more proactive approaches. As part of this general mood of anxiety and fear, asylum, immigration and nationality law have been put to use in the 'global war against terror'.[6] The ease with which this body of law could be deployed (as well as amended and enhanced) highlights the flexibility embedded in pre-existing law and policy; a point further underlined when laws are selected precisely because they lack the procedural and other protections that are present in, for example, the criminal law.[7] Immigration and asylum law appeared to permit just the right level of room required by states to achieve some counter-terrorist aims (these existing powers could always be extended), but also contained enough constraints to generate significant and vocal governmental frustration. A reason for this is, of course, that a connection between the national security obligations of states and their migration laws and policies is already present.[8] Aspects of immigration and asylum law at the national level were put in place precisely because of security fears resulting from migration flows. To those engaged with immigration and asylum law (in all its long-established normality in public law terms), the new discourse of radical departures seemed odd and over-egged. States had been thinking proactively and preventatively in a migration context for some time. Had public lawyers not noticed?

Claims to novelty by those who suggest that the position changed the rules should therefore be treated with caution for three reasons. First, refugee and asylum law in particular was designed precisely to address the supposedly 'exceptional situation' of forced migration, where instability and insecurity are at the core of the human dilemma.[9] The law emerged in the aftermath of massive global conflict and huge population movements when war crimes, crimes against humanity and serious criminality were firmly in view. It was designed with these problems in mind and is reflective of a world where conflict and complexity are ever present. It is a regime that recognises that people may be involved in legitimate political struggle in their societies and this might be the reason why they are seeking

---

[6] Kent Roach, Chapter 20 in this volume; Howard Adelman 'Refugees and border security post-September 11' (2002) 20 *Refuge* 5; Kate Martin 'Preventive detention of immigrants and non-citizens in the United States since September 11th' (2002) 20 *Refuge* 23.

[7] See Stephen Legomsky 'The new path of immigration law: asymmetric incorporation of criminal justice norms' (2007) 64 *Washington and Lee Law Review* 469.

[8] Daniel Moeckli, 'Immigration law enforcement after 9/11 and human rights', in Alice Edwards and Carla Ferstman (eds.), *Human Security and Non-Citizens: Law, Policy and International Affairs* (Cambridge University Press, 2010), Chapter 13.

[9] Adelman, 'Refugees and border security', 11 ('there is virtually no evidence linking *global* terrorism with refugees…').

asylum elsewhere. The dilemma may arise when this political struggle takes violent form and falls under a counter-terrorism framework.

Second, the 'security discourse' being constructed around the treatment of forced migration was evident for some time and well before 9/11.[10] The construction of the institution of asylum as a potential security threat has a history, with the last decade witnessing a further escalation. This is not to deny that potential security threats posed by global migration can be real and credible; terrorists make use of our interdependent world too. It is to suggest that the responses can be viewed as part of a historical pattern.[11] Arguably, the pressures exerted in the national security context are simply more intense versions of the strain the overall asylum system is under.[12] The 1951 Convention relating to the Status of Refugees contains such express recognition of the security concerns of states that at times it appears to privilege these over asylum, particularly when viewed within a European human rights context. The final point is, as noted, that the models were already in place in existing law. New measures were actively promoted and adopted, but much of this worked off established legal settings rather than signifying appalling breaks with the past.

In the United Kingdom, the government has woven migration policy into the narrative of providing generalised security for all citizens, as well as into debates on national self-definition; a trend also evident internationally in the actions of other states. Concern about asylum, and the implications for counter-terrorism policy, reached the highest political levels and extended beyond national contexts. The UN Security Council, for example, made clear after 9/11 that there should be no safe havens for terrorists and that refugee status should not be 'abused' by 'perpetrators, organizers or facilitators of terrorist acts'.[13] This position was underlined further after 7 July 2005, when the-then British Prime Minister, Tony Blair, stressed that the 'rules of the game were changing'.[14] It should also be noted that this international discourse is aligned with an expressed commitment to enduring respect for international law, including refugee

[10] See Huysmans, *The Politics of Insecurity.*
[11] See Prakash Shah, 'Taking the "political" out of asylum: the legal containment of refugees' political activism', in Frances Nicholson and Patrick Twomey (eds.), *Refugee Rights and Realities: Evolving International Concepts and Regimes* (Cambridge University Press, 1999), pp. 119–35.
[12] See Reg Whitaker, 'Refugee policy after September 11: not much new' (2002) 20 *Refuge* 29.
[13] UN SC Res. 1373 (28 September 2001) and 1377 (12 November 2001). See generally C. H. Powell, Chapter 2, this volume.
[14] UN SC Res. 1624 (16 September 2005); Tony Blair, Speech, *The Guardian*, 5 August 2005.

law and human rights law. In other words, this period did not witness the rhetorical abandonment of rights, in fact something of a rights resurgence took place as governments sought to justify their actions in precisely these terms. This confirms that the principle of legality continues to matter, and the practical impact of counter-terrorism policy on the treatment of refugees and asylum seekers is evidence that constant vigilance is required. This prompts the suggestion that the values which give life to the principle need not be tied to any one institutional context and must become embedded in the wider (globalised) public sphere if the abuse of human rights is to be effectively confronted. There are few more challenging contexts than the collision of counter-terrorism, globalised conflict and migration, but there is evidence of a globalised public sphere rising to meet it.

C.   The rules remain the same

In this overall context, what is the argument here? This chapter seeks to argue for the significance of the principle of legality, and what it should imply in this and other contexts, using evidence available from the United Kingdom primarily.[15] It is a contribution framed by scepticism about the melodramatic deployment of discourses of novelty. Although perhaps not 'eternal recurrence',[16] or first as tragedy and then as farce,[17] the story of human history is underpinned by enough constancy to suggest other factors are at work when we are told that the 'rules of the game' have changed,[18] or that we are facing singular, unique or unprecedented threats in the face of which innovation and flexibility are required.[19] These are discourses that in their obsessive use of existential angst (and decisionist rhetoric) oddly and eerily mirror the appalling aesthetic of the terrorist attack, and carry within them the seeds of essentially anti-democratic and anti-rule of law tendencies. The differences are clearly there, but both seek symbolic and material breaks with the past for particular political, social and economic purposes. Both wish to side-step the constant and often messy demands and constraints of democratic life – with the hard work of democratic dialogue and persuasion avoided. The careful nurturing

---

[15] Appellate Committee of the House of Lords, and now the UK Supreme Court in particular.
[16] Friedrich Nietzsche, *The Gay Science* (New York: Random House, 1991).
[17] Karl Marx, 'The eighteenth brumaire of Louis Napoleon', in Lawrence H. Simon (ed.), *Selected Writings* (Indiana Polis, IN: Hackett Publishing Company Ltd, 1994), p. 187.
[18] Tony Blair, *The Guardian*.   [19] Ibid.

of insecurity, anxiety, fear and doubt can be contrasted with the values which stand over constitutional democracies, and which march under the banner of the political ideal of the rule of law. To gain life, however, these values must flow through and from institutions and people (and find concrete expression in precise and detailed laws, policies and practices). Those who defend conceptions of legality are rightly criticised for disappearing into a common law constitutionalist haze of vague principles.[20] If it is a shared project to be aspired to, and worked towards, the steps need to be clear and we should know what the destination might look like.

2. Does the political ideal of legality matter?

The conceptual debates in UK public law remain polarised between those who are sceptical of the judicial role (and troubled by what has happened to Parliament) and those who believe that judges do not go far enough in defence of individual rights (who are also worried about what has happened to Parliament). Both share a belief that executive domination is something to curb, but disagree on what the precise remedy might be. It is a tired and old debate given fresh life by a recent resurgence in liberal constitutionalism. Those sceptical of the judicial role place their trust in the potential of Parliament (in a richer and wider democratic context) to deliver more effective protection of rights. They believe that Parliament is not only best placed but has the democratic legitimacy and power required to keep the executive in check (to become a genuine obstacle to bad practice). Those who view the majoritarian nature of parliamentary democracy with suspicion look to the law and the courts to provide necessary restraints. Viewed pragmatically (from the perspective of the effective protection of refugees and asylum seekers) overreliance on parliaments that are dominated by their executives is troubling. Just as judges can provide a cloak of legality to otherwise questionable practices, so Parliament can offer a veneer of democracy that masks a rather more decisionistic reality. Individuals and groups with a marginal democratic voice have good reason to fear executive-dominated legislatures (as well as executives dominated by the Prime Minister), particularly at times of profound local and global insecurity. That is why the values which animate the notion of legality should also inform the work of Parliament. The courts have, of course, a key and central role, and a construction of the judicial role must

---

[20] See Thomas Poole, 'Constitutional exceptionalism and the common law' (2009) 7 *International Journal of Constitutional Law* 247.

form part of any analysis of public law which has not abandoned adjudication as a form of decision making. Even under a thoroughly democratic and republican reading of public law, we need to know what the courts should do and what principles should guide their approach (and this is evident in the recent work of, for example, Tomkins).[21] This debate has significant practical implications in the field of immigration law where legislatures and executives can be unresponsive.

One practical problem is that the UK government is steadily narrowing the scope for individuals to challenge asylum decisions. If there is a theme of the last decade, it is the crushing pressure on the asylum regime to deliver speedier results, as well as the creative ways of ensuring people never reach the United Kingdom to make a claim (for example, visa requirements on refugee-producing countries, combined with carrier sanctions and safe third country rules, and much else). From the mid-1990s, the introduction of accelerated procedures in combination with a barrage of other measures, including the giving and then the restriction of rights of appeal, resulted in an 'abused system' which continues to display a suspicion of challenge.[22] This was particularly evident in the failed attempts to oust judicial review entirely.[23] Similar objectives can, however, be achieved through a variety of other more nuanced legal and policy mechanisms – which perhaps do not attract a similarly robust response from the wider legal community. Whatever view is taken of the judicial role, it must confront a legal system that is making it increasingly difficult to contest asylum decisions, or for many to receive effective scrutiny of their claims. The rule of law is not only undermined through direct attempts to exclude judicial review. It may also be eroded by a creative legal and policy framework which seeks to immunise itself from scrutiny. This is also why advocates of the 'rule of law project' (to use Dyzenhaus' term) must spread over a range of institutions and societal contexts. The 'rule of law project' needs to move beyond judges, lawyers, public administrators

---

[21] See, for example, Adam Tomkins, 'The role of the courts in the political constitution' (2010) 60 *University of Toronto Law Journal* 1–22 and Adam Tomkins, 'National security and the role of the courts: a changed landscape?' (2010) 126 *Law Quarterly Review* 543. Tomkins argues that the *Belmarsh* decision looks rather more like a 'one-off' than a 'landmark', and in practice the lower courts (Administrative Court, SIAC, and the Proscribed Organisations Appeal Commission) are being consistently more robust in the intensity of review.

[22] This is not unique; such generalised critiques are evident in many areas of legal regulation where quick results are desired but legal processes appear to stand in the way.

[23] A. W. Bradley, 'Judicial independence under attack' [2003] *Public Law* 397.

and politicians and work with a richer understanding of what it means in practical terms.

An approach is needed to public law in the United Kingdom which recognises both the importance of parliamentary democracy, properly understood in a democratically diverse setting (devolution), and the robust parliamentary, judicial and societal protection of the rights of all persons, with particular emphasis on vulnerable and marginalised individuals and groups (objectively determined).[24] This will not be found in excessive deference to executives, even in matters of immigration and asylum, and particularly when national security concerns are raised. It is not to be discovered either in attempts to place too much strain on the judicial role. Courts cannot be expected to become permanent surrogates for the institutional failings of democratic, parliamentary and civic life (as pragmatically understandable as it is to pursue this route when all other avenues are blocked). The establishment of 'hybrid' mechanisms, such as the Special Immigration Appeals Commission (SIAC), raise intriguing questions around attempts to reconcile the competing demands, and further complicate an already complex debate.[25] The alternative has been sketched out well by others. A start might be made by switching attention from the institutional question of 'who decides' to what the content of the political ideal of the rule of law is. Here, however, the danger is of a drift into vagueness, uncertainty and rights-based abstraction. What does Dyzenhaus' 'rule of law project' commit us to in contexts where there is every reason to question the dire common law record? In my view, the stress on the priority of legality is not a political argument for a resurgent common law constitutionalism, it is a defence of starting the constitutional conversation on the basis of principles, values and arguments rather than simply circling around institutions, or promoting a subservient notion of deference to

---

[24] Rabinder Singh, 'Equality: the neglected virtue' [2004] *European Human Rights Law Review* 141.

[25] SIAC was established as a direct result of *Chahal* v. *UK* (1996) 23 EHRR 413. The Court held that the old advisory committee system in the United Kingdom violated arts. 5(4) and 13 of the European Convention. See also David Dyzenhaus, *The Constitution of Law: Legality in a Time of Emergency* (Cambridge University Press, 2006), p. 205: while recognising the problems with the SIAC model he does also see positive elements, '... it goes much further than the United Kingdom had gone before in trying to ensure that a rule-by-law response to a perceived emergency is coupled with the rule of law'. He talks about the creation of grey (rather than black) holes, which if put to use can assist in reducing 'official arbitrariness' but offer nothing substantive. In defending the 'rule of law project' throughout this book, Dyzenhaus also has in mind judges who uphold rule by law rather than the rule of law.

hierarchies (judicial, political or any other). When national security concerns are prominent, the existing normative framework – and the principles which give it tangible meaning and life – must be interpreted and applied appropriately and convincingly. This process need not be exclusively undertaken by the judiciary, although we should expect judges to demonstrate an understanding of the principled constitutional context within which they function. In the United Kingdom, parliamentary committees, MPs, devolved administrations, human rights and equality bodies, the legal profession and NGOs all have a responsibility to argue for the values which underpin legal order. This could be pressed further: everyone has a responsibility to uphold and respect human rights. Vibrant networks have emerged to challenge human rights abuses, and they often draw inspiration from the political ideal of legality. Approaches which therefore aim to hold onto a substantive understanding of the rule of law remain persuasive in this context. All these participants seem to assume that adherence to the notion of legality has a distinctive ethical and political component. As Dyzenhaus has consistently argued, the rule of law is a political ideal which should draw attention to the substance of legal argumentation and ultimately assist in promoting a general political and legal culture of justification.[26] The aim should be to highlight the arguable and dynamic nature of law as well as its basis in distinct values.[27] It means something, in substantive political terms, to be committed to legal order (rule of law rather than rule by law). The rule of law is essential to the construction of a democratic culture in which people are treated equally, but the preferred approach should shift attention towards reasons, arguments and justifications as opposed to a rigid focus on the institutions or the decision-maker. 'Who decides' does matter (particularly where experience and expertise is demonstrably there), but the rationale for decisions matters more. When national security is raised in the asylum context, judges should operate consistently in the application of principle and thus bring it fully under legal order; others must do so too.

The weakness in such an approach is that it can appear naive and unrealistic, and miss the highly strategic orientation of participants in legal and political arenas. In such contexts, precise rules are often being

[26] David Dyzenhaus, 'The permanence of the temporary', in Ronald J. Daniels, Patrick Macklem and Kent Roach (eds.), *The Security of Freedom: Essays on Canada's Anti-Terrorism Bill* (University of Toronto Press, 2001), pp. 21–37.

[27] David Dyzenhaus, 'Recrafting the rule of law', in David Dyzenhaus (ed.), *Recrafting the Rule of Law* (Oxford: Hart Publishing, 1999), pp. 1–12; Neil MacCormick, 'Rhetoric and the rule of law' in Dyzenhaus, *Recrafting the Rule of Law*, pp. 163–77.

used in context-sensitive, pragmatic and strategic ways to achieve specific outcomes. The strength of the approach rests on the respect for the individual it generates, and respect for the basic principles of fairness which it implies. These are logical outcomes of a basic point: the evasion of legality should not be condoned, especially by those charged with being its guardians. Legality as a convenient mask should also be challenged, as a potentially even more insidious erosion of standards. For example, what might we do if the whole edifice of an area of legal regulation is just a sophisticated cloak for injustice which we perpetuate by condoning its more positive elements?

We should move beyond the idea (evident in debates in some national contexts) that the respect flowing from legality is owed primarily to citizens. It is still too often the case that non-national status is used unreflectively in local contexts to justify separate and unjust treatment, thus neglecting and eroding the rights of non-nationals. In asylum law, where extensive pressures are often placed on government and public administration by opposition parties, hostile media and sections of the electorate, insistence on the importance of respect for each individual is significant. A commitment to legalism thus still has an overriding ethical dimension.[28] This does not, however, mean exclusive support for a particular institutional belief that the courtroom is the only forum for its vindication (we do need to know what it is we think judges should do), or that our morality is exhausted in the legal framework, and it is not a plea for an inappropriate revival of ineffective common law constitutionalism.

3. Refugees, asylum seekers and counter-terrorism in the United Kingdom

A.   A culture of suspicion, hostility and fear

Asylum law in the United Kingdom has developed (within the wider body of immigration law) rapidly in the last two decades as a highly specialised area of public law (and now must also be viewed in the context of EU law and policy). Legal regulation has responded to the twin objectives of recognising the humanitarian institution of asylum, anchored around the 1951 Refugee Convention (and other human rights commitments), and seeking to manage an inherently selective process within which tragic choices will often be made. The challenge in this area of public law is

---

[28] Ibid.

to maintain the principled imperatives of the rule of law (as this applies
to each human person) in the face of other formidable pressures and
demands on the system. The tensions are built into the regulatory regime,
with decision-makers, adjudicators and courts tasked with making an
essentially selective system function, all in a profoundly unjust global setting of human rights abuse and severe inequality. It is an area of public
law where the substantive understanding of legality is consistently tested,
even without national security concerns arising.

The policy premise in the United Kingdom often reflects an embedded official view that the current system is being widely abused by those
who are not in genuine need of international protection. This has also
become the official narrative of Western democracies, who evidently view
the humanitarian institution of asylum as a doorway into their states for
those they would generally rather exclude (these states can often have
quite generous entry rules for selected and desirable migrants). A 'culture
of suspicion' remains evident, and the events of 9/11 and 7/7, and what
has followed, simply intensified an existing process of national deterrence
and restriction. An overriding focus on the reduction in the number of
applicants in general remains, combined with the criminalisation and
securitisation of the entire migration debate.[29] Nevertheless, it is worth
observing that the UK Government did not repeal its refugee and human
rights law commitments, despite moments of evident irritation and frustration with particular judicial outcomes, a trend which is generalisable
beyond the United Kingdom. The arguments were intense at times, and
remain so, but thus far they have largely been conducted within the terms
of the human rights and refugee law regimes.

The refugee regime should primarily be concerned with the provision of protection to asylum seekers from return to another state where
there is a real risk of sufficiently serious human rights abuse. Asylum is a
humanitarian institution designed to offer surrogate protection to those
in genuine need of it; a terrorist facing lawful and legitimate prosecution
is therefore not someone who necessarily has a well-founded fear of being
persecuted. Even that seemingly simple statement is, however, problematic. A terrorist may well have faced torture or other forms of mistreatment as part of the prosecution process in another state and may have a
well-founded expectation of similar treatment if returned.

Permanent settlement in the UK may be the result of a grant of refugee
status, however, the principal official purpose of the legal regime is to offer

---

[29] See Huysmans, *The Politics of Insecurity.*

international protection as long as it is needed (international refugee law also includes the notion of cessation of status). Decision making in asylum cases is particularly challenging because it involves judgments about future risk based on the individual's testimony, and available objective evidence about the applicant's state of origin; the outcome can have serious implications for each individual. The risks involved in getting this future-oriented assessment wrong are substantial, as are the challenges involved in getting it right.

Legal provision is now extensive, intricate and complex. An expansive statutory framework, and a substantial body of case law dealing with immigration and asylum, has evolved.[30] Counter-terrorism legislation has also progressed further over the last decade and has had an impact on nationals and non-nationals (the adverse impact on particular minority ethnic communities, refugees, asylum seekers and migrants remains marked).[31] The restrictive legal developments progressed alongside moves to further embed a culture of human rights in the United Kingdom. The Human Rights Act 1998 changed the human rights context by permitting localised access to European Convention rights in domestic law. The creation of human rights commissions (Northern Ireland Human Rights Commission, Scottish Human Rights Commission, Equality and Human Rights Commission), the establishment of a Joint Parliamentary Committee on Human Rights and the creation of a new UK Supreme Court are all notable trends on the positive side of the balance sheet. Restrictive and repressive trends have therefore not gone unchallenged

---

[30] The Immigration Act 1971 remains the governing legislation for entry and removal generally and sets the overall legal framework. It includes, for example, in s. 2A the power to deprive a person of the right of abode in the United Kingdom, if the Home Secretary thinks it would be conducive to the public good for the person to be excluded or removed (a power subject to human rights and refugee convention obligations). The British Nationality Act 1981 is the principal legislation dealing with nationality and includes, for example, a power to deprive a person of British citizenship if the Home Secretary thinks it would be conducive to the public good, s. 40. The following list gives an indication of the legislative activity since the early 1990s: Borders, Citizenship and Immigration Act 2009; Criminal Justice and Immigration Act 2008; UK Borders Act 2007; Immigration, Asylum and Nationality Act 2006; Asylum and Immigration (Treatment of Claimants, Etc.) Act 2004; Nationality, Immigration and Asylum Act 2002; Immigration and Asylum Act 1999; Special Immigration Appeals Commission Act 1997; Asylum and Immigration Act 1996; Asylum and Immigration Appeals Act 1993. More detail is provided in the Immigration Rules (made by the Home Secretary under the Immigration Act 1971 s. 3(2) and, for example, the Asylum Policy Instructions.

[31] For example, Counter-Terrorism Act 2008; Terrorism Act 2006; Terrorism (Northern Ireland) Act 2006; Prevention of Terrorism Act 2005.

on the basis of existing law, inside and outside of Parliament and by the courts, but there remains a sense that what was given in human rights terms was constantly undermined by an increasingly authoritarian approach and ever more elaborate attempts to evade accountability. The asylum debate became ominously and routinely entangled with a broader governmental anxiety about British national identity, and the old narrative of defining 'self' against the terrifying other re-emerged.

National security *may* become relevant to the asylum process at different stages, but there is no necessary or intrinsic connection between the asylum system and national security. A link may emerge if asylum seekers, like other individuals, engage in specified actions in the asylum state or before entry. Counter-terrorism law can be applied, and deportation for reasons of public order (with recognised and appropriate limitations and protections) is a well-established concept in immigration law. No state could afford to permit its asylum system to become a domestic vehicle of internal attack, and no one concerned with the rule of law or human rights would suggest that this should be the case. Some asylum seekers and refugees will have been politically active in their state of origin – and that can be precisely why they are seeking refuge. That need not mean that they are terrorists, or pose a threat to national security. Such a formal, official and highly regulated route of entry does not seem an obvious choice for the determined terrorist.

National security concerns may arise when the exclusion clauses are being considered during the status determination process. National security is not intended to be the primary concern at this stage, as the focus will ultimately be on the risk if returned, but the exclusion clauses do need to be considered and applied. At this initial stage it can be assessed. If a person is still awaiting determination of their claim, or is recognised as a refugee, their actions in the asylum state may trigger concern about a possible security risk. At this point their removal may be sought with reference to national security considerations, and again, immigration law has historically provided for deportation for reasons of public order and national security. Removal in this context presents particular challenges where the individual faces a real risk of serious ill-treatment upon return – as there are clear prohibitions under the European Convention on Human Rights. But there are also no necessary impediments to prosecution under anti-terrorism or criminal laws. The re-emergence of more proactive and ultimately preventative counter-terrorism strategies is where problems may arise, mainly because offences may not have been committed, as yet. However, it is important to stress that the existing legal framework in the

United Kingdom includes provision for dealing with asylum seekers and refugees who are suspected of being involved in terrorism, lawfully and appropriately (and provides human rights safeguards against abuse). This has not, however, prevented the emergence of specialised regimes and the creation of a new and special immigration status in the United Kingdom.

B. Exclusion from refugee status

The institution of asylum and the law of refugee status both contain express provision for excluding certain persons from protection while containing no direct references to terrorism.[32] The exclusion clauses are not optional, but an intrinsic part of refugee law. The clauses are now (inevitably) viewed in the context of counter-terrorism policy and attempts internationally to challenge impunity (particularly as this relates to those responsible for war crimes and crimes against humanity[33] but also in the context of globalised counter-terrorism policies). There is a determined global effort to ensure there are no safe havens for terrorists.

The United Nations High Commissioner for Refugees (UNHCR) provides guidance on their interpretation and application.[34] It suggests that the primary purpose of these clauses 'is to deprive those guilty of heinous acts, and serious common crimes, of international refugee protection and to ensure that such persons do not abuse the institution of asylum to avoid

---

[32] Universal Declaration of Human Rights 1948, art. 14(2); Convention relating to the Status of Refugees 1951, art. 1F. See Immigration Act 1971, s. 3(5) and the relevant Immigration Rules made under s. 3(2); Asylum and Immigration Appeals Act 1993, ss. 1 and 2; Nationality, Immigration and Asylum Act 2002; Immigration, Asylum and Nationality Act 2006. See also arts. 32 and 33 of the 1951 Convention. In the UK, see UKBA Asylum Policy Instructions 'Exclusion – articles 1F and 33(2) of the refugee convention'; 'Humanitarian Protection'; 'Discretionary leave'. See also, IND Asylum Policy Unit Notice 1/2003 'Humanitarian Protection and Discretionary Leave'; UKBA, Asylum Policy Unit Notice, 'Exceptional leave to remain: suspected war criminals and perpetrators of crimes against humanity and genocide'.

[33] For a comparative analysis of Australia, Canada, New Zealand, the United Kingdom and United States, see Joseph Rikhof, 'War criminals now welcome; how common law countries approach the phenomenon of international crimes in the immigration and refugee context' (2009) 21 *International Journal of Refugee Law* 453. After a detailed examination of law and practice he concludes that all the states identified take war crimes very seriously.

[34] UNHCR, *Guidelines on International Protection: Application of the Exclusion Clauses – Article 1F of the 1951 Convention relating to the Status of Refugees*, 4 September 2003, UN Doc. HCR/GIP/03/05. See also Volker Türk, 'Forced migration and security' (2003) 15 *International Journal of Refugee Law* 113; Geoff Gilbert 'Editorial' (2004) 16 *International Journal of Refugee Law* 1. See also, Federal Administrative Court (German), 10 C48.07, 14 October 2008, reported in (2009) 21 *International Journal of Refugee Law* 592.

being held legally accountable for their acts'.[35] The guidelines also address the issue of terrorism:

> Despite the lack of an … agreed definition of **terrorism**, acts commonly considered to be terrorist in nature are likely to fall within the exclusion clauses even though Art. 1F is not to be equated with a simple anti-terrorism provision. Consideration of the exclusion clauses is, however, often unnecessary as suspected terrorists may not be eligible for refugee status in the first place, their fear being of legitimate prosecution as opposed to persecution for Convention reasons.[36]

The UNHCR's view is that each case requires individual consideration, and the fact that someone may be on a list of terrorist suspects might trigger assessment under the exclusion clauses but should not in itself justify exclusion.[37] In addition, it suggests that the exclusion decision should in principle be addressed within the regular status determination process.[38]

In the 1990s, the Law Lords addressed exclusion in *T* v. *Home Secretary*.[39] The appellant, an Algerian citizen whose claim for asylum in the UK was rejected, was involved in a bomb attack on Algiers airport (ten people were killed) and a raid on an army barracks (another person was killed). The special adjudicator concluded that this brought him within the exclusion clause in art. 1F(b) because, as provided in that provision, 'there were serious reasons for considering' that he had committed serious non-political crimes.[40] The House of Lords dismissed his appeal. The ruling contains extensive consideration of the meaning of 'serious non-political crime' within the context of refugee law, and provides a test to define a 'political crime' with two conditions:

> (1) it is committed for a political purpose, i.e. with the object of overthrowing or subverting or changing the government of a state or inducing it to change its policy; and (2) there is a sufficiently close and direct link between the crime and the alleged political purpose.

---

[35] UNHCR, *Guidelines on International Protection*, [2].

[36] Ibid., [25].   [37] Ibid., [26].   [38] Ibid., [31].

[39] [1996] AC 742 (HL). In the UK see, *R (JS)* v. *Secretary of State for the Home Department* [2010] UKSC 15; *MH (Syria), DS (Afghanistan)* v. *Secretary of State for the Home Department* [2009] EWCA Civ 226. See also *Canada* v. *Ward* [1993] 2 SCR 689; *Pushpanathan* v. *Canada* [1998] 1 SCR 982; *Zrig* v. *Minister of Citizenship and Immigration* (2003) FCA 178; and, in the United States, see *INS* v. *Aguirre-Aguirre* (1999) 526 US 415.

[40] Article 1F provides: 'The provisions of this Convention shall not apply to a person with respect to whom there are serious reasons for considering that: … (b) he has committed a serious non-political crime outside the country of refuge prior to his admission to that country as a refugee.'

In determining (2), the majority stated that the means used should be examined, as well as the nature of the targets (governmental or civilian), and whether indiscriminate killing of members of the public was involved. It was held in this case that (2) had not been satisfied and the decision to exclude him was upheld.

The position on the exclusion clauses has been further clarified (and expanded in the counter-terrorism context) in domestic law, with provision made for a new immigration status. The new legislation followed the events of 7 July 2005 in London and the-then Prime Minister's twelve-point plan for tackling terrorism[41] – a plan which focused heavily on foreign nationals even though, as Walker has emphasised, the bombings were carried out by British citizens.[42]

The Immigration, Asylum and Nationality Act 2006, s. 54 specifically provides for an interpretation of art. 1F(c) of the 1951 Convention which links the assessment of whether something is 'contrary to the purposes and principles of the UN' to acts of committing, preparing or instigating terrorism, and acts of encouraging or inducing others to commit, prepare or instigate terrorism.[43] The domestic statutory provision therefore connects the exclusion clause directly to terrorism and is widely drawn.

This statutory theme is mapped onto the appeal process through a system of certification whereby the Tribunal, or Special Immigration Appeals Commission (SIAC), must begin substantive consideration of the appeal on the basis of the Secretary of State's certification that the individual is not entitled to art. 33(1) protection because art. 1F or art. 33(2) applies. In other words, exclusion is to be considered as a preliminary issue, and application of the clause arguably widened. Other matters addressed in the Act include, for example, the removal of British citizenship if this would be 'conducive to the public good', and this again has been meshed with the national security context.[44] At EU level, the Qualification Directive art. 12 addresses exclusion.[45] It follows the language of the 1951 Convention

[41] See Tony Blair, *The Guardian*, 5 August 2005. This plan included a commitment to refuse asylum automatically to anyone who had participated in terrorism anywhere.

[42] Clive Walker, 'The treatment of foreign terror suspects' (2007) 70 *Modern Law Review* 427, 428.

[43] See also Terrorism Act 2000, s. 1. For a recent application of art. 1F(c) see *SS* v. *Secretary of State of the Home Department*, 30 July 2010, SC/56/2009 (SIAC).

[44] Sections 56–7. The twelve-point plan included a commitment to stripping citizens of citizenship. See also, *Secretary of State for the Home Department* v. *David Hicks* [2006] EWCA Civ 400.

[45] EU Qualification Directive, 29 April 2004, OJ L 304, p. 12. For comment see, Hugo Storey, 'EU Refugee Qualification Directive: a brave new world?' (2008) 20 *International Journal*

with some notable additions. For example, particularly cruel actions – even if committed with an alleged political objective – may be classed as 'non-political'. The Directive also makes clear that the exclusion clauses apply to those who instigate or otherwise participate in the commission of crimes or other relevant acts.

R (JS) v. *Secretary of State for the Home Department* involved the correct interpretation of art. 1F(a) of the 1951 Convention.[46] The question here essentially hinged on membership of an organisation (that had corporately been involved in war crimes) and what more than simple membership was required to determine personal responsibility and thus exclude a person from refugee status. The respondent in the case was a Tamil and member of the LTTE (an organisation that the court acknowledged was not exclusively terrorist in nature), and held a variety of roles and positions. His application for asylum and humanitarian protection was refused by the Home Secretary expressly on art. 1F(a) grounds.[47]

In the Supreme Court, Lord Brown stated:

> Put simply, I would hold an accused disqualified under article 1F if there are serious reasons for considering him voluntarily to have contributed in a significant way to the organisation's ability to pursue its purpose of committing war crimes, aware that his assistance will in fact further that purpose.[48]

of Refugee Law 1. This also means that the European Court of Justice has recently been involved in providing clarification of the meaning of a number of aspects of EU law and policy relating to refugee status. See also art. 14 of the Directive, which provides for revocation, ending or refusal to renew refugee status in cases of refugees who are a danger to the security and/or the community of a member state.

[46] *R (JS)* v. *Secretary of State for the Home Department* [2010] UKSC 15. For Canadian practice, see James C. Simeon, 'Exclusion under article 1F(a) of the 1951 Convention in Canada' (2009) 21 *International Journal of Refugee Law* 193, which concludes that the post-9/11 fears about enhanced use of the exclusion clauses has not come to pass in Canada.

[47] Following the Court of Appeal judgment in *KJ* v. *Secretary of State for the Home Department* [2009] EWCA Civ 292, the application of art. 1F(c) (purposes and principles of the UN) to cases from Sri Lanka involving the LTTE had become less straightforward.

[48] *R (JS)* v. *Secretary of State for the Home Department* [2010] UKSC 15, [38]. Lord Hope stated: 'Lord Brown puts the test for complicity very simply at the end of para 38 of his judgment. I would respectfully endorse that approach. The words "serious reasons of considering" are, of course, taken from article 1F itself. The words "in a significant way" and "will in fact further that purpose" provide the key to the exercise. Those are the essential elements that must be satisfied to fix the applicant with personal responsibility. The words "made a substantial contribution" were used by the German Administrative Court, and they are to the same effect. The focus is on the facts of each case and not on any presumption that may be invited by mere membership.'

The judgment attempts to shift the exclusive focus away from the nature of the organisation[49] and any attempt to carve out sub-categories amongst organisations engaged in terrorism[50] (and in this Lord Brown was critical of the influential Immigration Appeal Tribunal decision in *Gurung*)[51] and presumptions of individual liability, towards an assessment of the war crimes and crimes against humanity alleged to have been committed. It also reflected a concern not to narrow notions of responsibility in an excessively restrictive way (there is some criticism in the judgment of the Court of Appeal in this respect). In its approach the Supreme Court drew heavily on the Rome Statute of the International Criminal Court, as well as guidance from UNHCR,[52] and the EU Qualification Directive.[53] In revisiting the decision, the Secretary of State was directed explicitly to the Supreme Court's reasoning and guidance, which now forms the basis for considering Article 1F(a) in the United Kingdom.

C.   A well-founded fear of prosecution?

What should be done about those who are seeking asylum from persecution arising from anti-terrorism operations in other states? While a state may seek to arrest and prosecute terrorists, there is ample evidence of human rights being abused in the process of counter-terrorist operations locally and globally. In *R (Sivakumar)* v. *Secretary of State for the Home Department*, the claimant was a Tamil from Sri Lanka whose claim for asylum was rejected by the Home Secretary.[54] Article 1F was not raised. On appeal the adjudicator accepted he had been detained and tortured, but this was due to the suspicion held that he was involved in terrorism and not to his political opinions. In the House of Lords, Lord Steyn stated that 'not all means of investigating suspected terrorist acts fall outside the protection of the Convention'.[55] By suggesting that being investigated for involvement in terrorist acts took a person outside the protection of the 1951 Convention, the Special Adjudicator had got it wrong. He also noted

---

[49] Lord Brown at [32]: 'War crimes are war crimes however benevolent and estimable may be the long-term aims of those involved. And actions which would not otherwise constitute war crimes do not become so merely because they are taken pursuant to policies abhorrent to western liberal democracies.'

[50] Lord Brown did, however, provide a seven-point guide to assessing complicity with reference to membership (at [30]).

[51] *Gurung* v. *Secretary of State for the Home Department* [2008] Imm AR 115.

[52] For example, UNHCR *Addressing Security Concerns without Undermining Refugee Protection: UNHCR's Perspective* (November 2001).

[53] (2004/83/EC).   [54] [2003] UKHL 14.   [55] Ibid., [17].

the clear evidence of torture, and concluded that the Special Adjudicator had not approached the matter correctly. At the time of the decision the applicant had a well-founded fear of persecution, but four years had passed since then and the case was remitted to the Immigration Appeal Tribunal to reconsider in the light of the Law Lords' judgment. For Lord Hutton, the proper conclusion was that the acts of torture were inflicted not solely to obtain information to tackle terrorism, but also 'by reason of the torturers' deep antagonism towards him because he was a Tamil'.[56]

D. Due deference?

Past cases reveal that when national security, immigration and asylum collide, judges are likely to defer to the executive. The leading recent example of this approach is *Secretary of State for the Home Department* v. *Rehman*.[57] The issue here was whether the Home Secretary could make a deportation order under the Immigration Act 1971 on the grounds that the appellant's deportation was conducive to the public good for national security reasons. The appellant, a Pakistani national, arrived in the UK in February 1993 after being given entry clearance to work as a minister of religion in Oldham. Both his parents were British citizens. The Home Secretary refused his application for indefinite leave to remain, citing information connecting him to a terrorist organisation; he appealed to SIAC.[58]

The Home Secretary stated that the appellant had directly supported terrorism in the Indian subcontinent and was therefore a threat to national security. But SIAC held, to the contrary, that the term 'national security' should be narrowly defined:

> we adopt the position that a person may be said to offend against national security if he engages in, promotes, or encourages violent activity which is targeted at the United Kingdom, its system of government or its people. This includes activities directed against the overthrow or destabilisation of a foreign government if that foreign government is likely to take reprisals against the United Kingdom which affect the security of the United Kingdom or of its nationals. National security extends also to situations where United Kingdom citizens are targeted, wherever they may be.[59]

---

[56] Ibid., [29].   [57] [2001] UKHL 47.

[58] SIAC was created in 1997 in response to the judgment of the European Court of Human Rights in *Chahal* v. *UK* (1996) 23 EHRR 413. See Special Immigration Appeals Commission Act 1997.

[59] [2003] UKHL 14, [2].

SIAC concluded that it had not been established to a high civil balance of probabilities that the appellant was likely to be a threat to national security. The Home Secretary appealed successfully to the Court of Appeal.[60]

On further appeal to the House of Lords, Lord Slynn acknowledged that the term 'in the interests of national security' could not be used to justify any reason the Home Secretary had for seeking the deportation of an individual.[61] However, he did not accept the narrow interpretation suggested by the appellant.

> I accept that there must be a real possibility of an adverse affect on the United Kingdom for what is done by the individual under inquiry but I do not accept that it has to be direct or immediate. Whether there is a real possibility is a matter which has to be weighed up by the Secretary of State and balanced against the possible injustice to that individual if a deportation order is made.[62]

Lord Slynn stressed the need for SIAC to give due weight to the assessment and conclusions of the Home Secretary in the light of his responsibilities.[63] Lord Steyn agreed, adding that 'even democracies are entitled to protect themselves, *and* the executive is the best judge of the need for international co-operation to combat terrorism and counter-terrorist strategies'.[64] He concluded by acknowledging the well-established position that issues of national security do not fall beyond the competence of the courts. But it was 'self-evidently right that national courts must give great weight to the views of the executive on matters of national security'.[65]

Lord Hoffmann continued this theme, stating that SIAC had failed to acknowledge the inherent limitations of the judicial function which flowed from the doctrine of the separation of powers and the need 'in matters of judgment and evaluation of evidence, to show proper deference to the primary decision-maker'.[66] This restraint did not limit the appellate jurisdiction of SIAC and the need for it 'flows from a common-sense recognition of the nature of the issue and the differences in the decision-making processes and responsibilities of the Home Secretary and [SIAC]'.[67] In a postscript Lord Hoffmann stated:

> I wrote this speech some three months before the recent events in New York and Washington. They are a reminder that in matters of national security, the cost of failure can be high. This seems to me to underline

---

[60] [2000] 3 WLR 1240 (CA).   [61] [2003] UKHL 14, [15].   [62] Ibid., [16].
[63] Ibid., [26].   [64] Ibid., [28].   [65] Ibid., [31].   [66] Ibid., [49].   [67] Ibid., [58].

the need for the judicial arm of government to respect the decisions of ministers of the Crown on the question of whether support for terrorist activities in a foreign country constitutes a threat to national security … If the people are to accept the consequences of such decisions, they must be made by persons whom the people have elected and whom they can remove.[68]

The notion that the executive must be deferred to because of its democratic legitimacy and expertise in times of crisis is one that is often advanced. Lord Hoffmann's comments suggest that the executive can step outside the normal application of the rule of law in times of public emergency by making its own decision about what the law is. This is the essence of what is being said here on the question of legal interpretation. As Allan suggests, the focus is probably better placed on the quality of the reasons advanced about the meaning of the law, rather than on who should make the decision.[69] The main question should be whether the legal reasoning is worthy of support in the individual case, and if a convincing account is provided of what the law is, even when national security is raised. Criticism can therefore be made of the ruling, on the basis that the Law Lords acted reasonably in interpreting national security more broadly than SIAC, but erred in placing great reliance on the concept of judicial deference. If the focus should remain on the reasons for the substantive decision, rather than who made it, this view is a compelling one. To defer mainly because it is an executive decision based on assessments of the national security threat is problematic (even when factual information may be held by the executive). In the national security context, the rule of law is tested, both in the sense of protecting individual rights and ensuring that an effective regulatory framework exists. By according decisive weight to the views of the executive, judges are not discharging their responsibility to take a view on the meaning of law. If the courts do this they risk abandoning one of the values of the rule of law: the defence of the person against arbitrary power through an established legal framework properly interpreted and applied.

---

[68] Ibid., [62]. Cf. *R v. BBC, ex parte Pro Life Alliance* [2003] UKHL 23, [74] ff; *R v. Secretary of State for the Home Department, ex parte Simms and O'Brien* [2000] 2 AC 115, Lord Hoffmann at 131 on the principle of legality; and see *A and others v. Secretary of State for the Home Department* [2004] UKHL 56.

[69] Trevor Allan, 'Common law reason and the limits of judicial deference' in David Dyzenhaus (ed.), *The Unity of Public Law* (Oxford: Hart, 2004), pp. 289–306.

E.   The prohibition on return to torture, human rights and national security

These debates were played out in cases such as *A and others* v. *Secretary of State for the Home Department*,[70] which was concerned with the detention of a number of individuals suspected of international terrorism under the Anti-Terrorism, Crime and Security Act 2001 (Part IV now repealed). What should be done with those who could not be deported for human rights reasons, but who the government believed constituted a continuing threat to national security? The Act and the Human Rights Act 1998 (Designated Derogation) Order 2001 were introduced after the terrorist attacks of 9/11. The Act empowered the Home Secretary to issue a certificate if he reasonably believed that an individual's continuing presence in the United Kingdom was a risk to national security and suspected that the person was a terrorist. A suspected international terrorist could therefore be detained indefinitely. There was a right of appeal to SIAC.[71] A challenge was brought against the provisions of the 2001 Act. SIAC held that the measures were discriminatory and contrary to arts. 5 and 14 of the European Convention on Human Rights, as they did not apply equally to British nationals.

On appeal against the SIAC decision the Court of Appeal reached a different conclusion. Following an approach with echoes of *Rehman*, Lord Woolf stated:

> Decisions as to what is required in the interest of national security are self-evidently within the category of decisions in relation to which the court is required to show considerable deference to the Secretary of State because he is better qualified to make an assessment as to what action is called for.[72]

British nationals were not in the same position as foreign nationals in this context. According to Lord Woolf, the non-nationals involved in this case no longer had a right to remain, only a right not to be removed.[73] This distinguished their plight from that of nationals. He also stressed the distinction in international law between the treatment of nationals and non-nationals. Parliament was entitled to limit the measures to foreign

---

[70] [2004] UKHL 56. See Court of Appeal judgment at [2002] EWCA Civ 1502.
[71] For criticism of SIAC from a former member, see Sir Brian Barder 'The Special Immigration Appeals Commission' (18 March 2004) 26(6) *London Review of Books*.
[72] [2003] UKHL 14, [39].   [73] Ibid., [47].

nationals on the basis that art. 15 of the European Convention permitted measures that derogate only 'to the extent strictly required by the exigencies of the situation'. The tension between arts. 14 and 15 had, Lord Woolf argued, an important impact. The Secretary of State was obliged to derogate only to the extent necessary and widening the powers of indefinite detention would conflict with this objective.

The case subsequently progressed to the House of Lords,[74] and the issues were also tested eventually before the Grand Chamber of the European Court of Human Rights.[75] In one of the leading judgments under the Human Rights Act, the majority of the Law Lords concluded that there was a public emergency threatening the life of the nation (art. 15(1)) but (unlike the Court of Appeal) were willing to quash the derogation order and declare s. 23 of the 2001 Act incompatible with art. 5(1) and art. 14 on the basis of proportionality and that it allowed discriminatory detention of suspected international terrorists who were non-nationals. The judgments are filled with profound concern about the notion of executive detention, with Lord Hoffmann scathing in his comments about the 2001 Act, Lord Nicholls expressing his concern about indefinite detention and Lord Bingham making pointed comments about the nature of judicial decision-making in these cases. In striking a blow for constitutional principle in the face of executive detention the case did not herald the end of deference. As is clear in the judgment of Lord Bingham, it underlines the idea of degrees of deference, and in confirming the role of the Home Secretary in determining when there was a public emergency endorsed the concept of variable institutional competencies (some people are better placed to make certain judgments than others).

The judgment of the European Court largely followed the conclusions reached by the House of Lords; however, in the operation of the SIAC process (on the issue of reliance on closed material and the lack of disclosure of sufficient information) the Court found a breach of art. 5(4).

The procedures used by SIAC were also questioned in the other *A* case to reach the House of Lords.[76] This case addressed the matter of the admissibility of evidence by SIAC, which may have been procured by torture

---

[74] [2004] UKHL 56. See David Feldman, 'Proportionality and discrimination in anti-terrorism legislation' (2005) 64 *Cambridge Law Journal* 271. See also, David Campbell, 'The threat of terrorism and the plausibility of positivism' [2009] *Public Law* 501. Cf. J. Finnis, 'Nationality, alienage and constitutional principle' (2007) 123 *Law Quarterly Review* 417.

[75] (2009) 49 EHRR 29. See also *Charkaoui v. Canada* [2007] SCC 9.

[76] *A v. Secretary of State for the Home Department* (No. 2) [2005] UKHL 71.

inflicted by officials of other states without the complicity of the British authorities. Here the value and importance of the rule of law was underlined (with Lord Bingham stressing the constitutional principles at stake), as the Court concluded that evidence obtained in this way should not be admissible (the majority disagreed with Lord Bingham on the burden of proof). The two *A* cases (while by no means perfect in human rights terms) therefore demonstrated the role that courts might have in setting out a principled vision of what the rule of law is, even when national security is raised.

Following the *A* judgment, a new regime was put in place under the Prevention of Terrorism Act 2005,[77] providing for the much criticised control order system in the United Kingdom. One form of executive detention was therefore replaced by a more carefully engineered method of executive control and restraint. The Act established an elaborate system of individualised monitoring and control of those suspected of terrorist activity who were assessed as a risk to the UK. The new regime quite explicitly applies to British nationals and non-nationals alike. The system has attracted considerable judicial scrutiny, where the terms of particular control orders have been assessed with reference to Convention obligations,[78] as well as the procedure for making and challenging them.[79] In these cases the Law Lords, and now the Supreme Court, have given careful, close and anxious scrutiny to the regime in place, with human rights concerns noted (taking into account developments in the Strasbourg jurisprudence) on the nature of the repressive restrictions imposed (holding that they have in specific contexts amounted to a deprivation of liberty) and on aspects of the procedure (the disclosure of information, the use of special advocates and the need – stressed by the Grand Chamber of the European Court of Human Rights – for the provision of sufficient

---

[77] The long title states: 'to provide for the making against individuals involved in terrorism related activity of orders imposing obligations on them for purposes connected with preventing or restricting their further involvement in such activity'. However, see the recommendation that a new regime be established: HM Government, *Review of Counter-Terrorism and Security Powers: Review Findings and Recommendations* (Cm 8004, 2011) and compare *A Report by Lord MacDonald: Review of Counter-Terrorism and Security Powers* (Cm 8003, 2011).

[78] *Secretary of State for the Home Department* v. *AP* [2010] UKSC 24; *Secretary of State for the Home Department* v. *JJ* [2007] UKHL 45; *Secretary of State for the Home Department* v. *E* [2007] UKHL 47. See generally Helen Fenwick and Gavin Phillipson, Chapter 19 this volume.

[79] Cf. *Secretary of State for the Home Department* v. *AF* [2009] UKHL 28 and *Secretary of State for the Home Department* v. *MB* [2007] UKHL 46.

information to a 'controllee' to permit effective instruction to his or her special advocate). The case law emerging suggests a determined executive placing ever more 'sophisticated', complex and oppressive processes in place with judges attempting to ensure the correct level of scrutiny and careful assessment is applied, and ultimately challenging their severity through the use of human rights standards.

Despite the best efforts of the British government, the Grand Chamber of the European Court of Human Rights, in *Saadi* v. *Italy*, has confirmed the absolute nature of the prohibition against return in art. 3. The UK government has sought, for some considerable time, to argue that there should be a balancing element injected into art. 3 assessments (the risk of return balanced against the national security threat similar to the approach adopted by the Canadian Supreme Court in *Suresh*[80]). The European Court has consistently held to its established jurisprudence, much to the evident frustration of the UK government.[81] No balancing is involved or permitted,[82] and the 'conduct of the person concerned, however undesirable or dangerous, cannot be taken into account'.[83] The sole focus will remain on whether the well-established standard in art. 3 has been met. This continues to cause the executive in the United Kingdom much anxiety, and was the subject of several negative comments by the former Prime Minister, Tony Blair, during his time in office. This linked with his general view that the 'rules of the game were changing' and his clear frustration with the implications of his own human rights legislation.[84]

The Criminal Justice and Immigration Act 2008 provides for a special immigration status to attach to designated foreign nationals who have committed terrorism or other serious criminal offences but who cannot be removed for Human Rights Act reasons.[85] The impact is that a person so

---

[80] *Suresh* v. *Canada (Minister of Citizenship and Immigration)* [2002] 1 SCR 77.

[81] See the governmental response to the Afghan hi-jackers case: *S and others* v. *Secretary of State for the Home Department* [2006] EWCA Civ 1157, see [50]: 'We commend the judge for an impeccable judgment...Judges and adjudicators have to apply the law as they find it, and not as they wish it to be.' The-then Prime Minister, Tony Blair, described the first instance judgment of Mr Justice Sullivan as 'an abuse of common sense', see BBC News, 10 May 2006. See also, Lord Carlile of Berriew QC, *Sixth Report of the Independent Reviewer Pursuant to Section 14(3) of the Prevention of Terrorism Act 2005* (3 February 2011), [79]: 'The effect is to make the UK a safe haven for some individuals whose determination is to damage the UK and its citizens, hardly a satisfactory situation save for the purist.'

[82] *Saadi* v. *Italy* [2008] ECHR 37201/06. See also Rene Bruin and Kees Wouters, 'Terrorism and the non-derogability of *non-refoulement*' (2003) 15 *International Journal of Refugee Law* 5, [139].

[83] Ibid., [138].   [84] Tony Blair, *The Guardian*.   [85] Part 10.

designated does not have leave to enter or remain in the United Kingdom,[86] and a range of conditions may be imposed on residence, employment, reporting and monitoring (in relation to the police, the Secretary of State or an immigration officer)[87] and particular arrangements have been put in place to limit existing support.[88] This new regime was a reaction to a variety of challenges to the previous system, and intended to grapple with a governmental concern about those believed to be a terrorist threat who could not be returned for art. 3 European Convention reasons.

F. Challenging the regime: legality in action?

Suspected international terrorists have used the courts to challenge other aspects of their detention.[89] In *Secretary of State for the Home Department v. M*, SIAC allowed an appeal against an order deporting a Libyan national.[90] M failed in his asylum application, but he was not removed, and it came to be accepted that he could not be returned. He was certified in November 2002 as a suspected international terrorist, his deportation was sought and he was subsequently detained. M's argument was that he feared persecution on return to Libya as a result of his opposition to the Gaddafi regime. However, the Home Secretary believed that he had links to al-Qaeda. The judgment of the-then Chief Justice, Lord Woolf, contained strong comment on the value of SIAC, which can perhaps be viewed in the light of the public criticism of this body.[91] Lord Woolf stressed the critical nature of the value judgment which SIAC had to make:

> While the need for society to protect itself against acts of terrorism today is self evident, it remains of the greatest importance that, in a society which upholds the rule of law, if a person is detained, as 'M' was detained, that individual should have access to an independent tribunal or court which can adjudicate upon the question of whether the detention is lawful or not. If it is not lawful, then he has to be released.[92]

This was the first time SIAC had allowed an appeal under the 2001 Act, and thus also the first time that the Home Secretary had reason to challenge the decision. It also followed the resignation of Sir Brian Barder from SIAC. He was a lay member of SIAC who resigned in January 2004, and his reasoning remains revealing in his critique of the Court of Appeal and House of Lords in *Rehman*, and the way that legal imperatives handed

---

[86] Section 132.   [87] Section 133.   [88] Section 134.
[89] See *R (A) v. Secretary of State for the Home Department*, [2004] HRLR 12 (Admin).
[90] [2004] EWCA Civ 324.   [91] [2003] UKHL 14.   [92] Ibid., [34] (iii).

down by the higher courts were hobbling the work of SIAC. His well-founded worry was that the government could use SIAC's existence to offer a cloak of legality to highly disturbing practices.[93] Despite evidence that SIAC has been robust in its approach, there remains a constant concern for those who fear the concept of legality becomes drained of substance in such contexts.

Another case of interest is *G* v. *Secretary of State for the Home Department*.[94] The case again involved an individual who had been certified as a suspected international terrorist. He applied to SIAC for a grant of bail, claiming that his mental and physical health had deteriorated rapidly as a result of detention. SIAC held that once certain conditions were met he should as a matter of principle be granted bail. The Home Secretary appealed against this decision. The Court of Appeal held that it had no jurisdiction to hear the appeal, since bail was not a final determination of an appeal for the purposes of the legislation. The Home Secretary reacted badly to the decision,[95] and the government's response was to introduce an amendment to the Asylum Bill then going through Parliament.[96] *A, B, C and others* v. *Secretary of State for the Home Department* involved an appeal against SIAC decisions not to cancel certificates issued by the Home Secretary.[97] The Court of Appeal held that SIAC had not erred in its approach, but the issue which provoked considerable comment was the admissibility of evidence which may have been gathered through the use of torture by other states – and this would eventually be considered by the House of Lords (as noted above).

G.   Securing assurances?

In addition to further promoting a harsh internal regime through legislative and other mechanisms (e.g., the 2006 and 2008 Acts), the British government has also worked hard to secure deportation assurances from other states to facilitate the process of removal. This is additional evidence of a government determined to achieve its counter-terrorism objectives; again, however, conducting the engagement within the framework of legal argumentation and often in human rights terms. It has achieved more

---

[93] [2004] UKHL 56.   [94] [2004] EWCA Civ 265.
[95] 'Blunkett may change law over suspect's bail', *The Guardian*, 23 April 2004.
[96] Mr Browne, *Hansard*, HC, vol. 421, col. 778w, 17 May 2004. See Asylum and Immigration (Treatment of Claimants, Etc.) Act 2004, s. 32.
[97] [2004] EWCA Civ 1123.

success in agreeing diplomatic assurances[98] than it has in persuading the European Court of Human Rights to abandon its decision in *Chahal*.[99] Diplomatic assurances have been secured with a number of North African and Middle Eastern states.[100]

What has been the response when the counter-terrorism measure adopted is deportation to another state from which assurances have been received? The protection of refugee law can be limited, as the 1951 Convention provides for the concept of permissible return, as well as exclusion from status. The focus will therefore often be on the European Convention on Human Rights – which contains a strong and clear prohibition on return, a position consistently confirmed and upheld by the European Court of Human Rights. The hard questions will often arise around how effective these assurances are. Seeking them in the first place is an open acknowledgement of risk, but can there be certainty around their application in practice? Detailed tests have been developed to determine compliance with human rights obligations, but the government has no absolute guarantee that it will be upheld.

In the cases of *RB (Algeria) and another* v. *Secretary of State for the Home Department* and *OO (Jordan)* v. *Secretary of State for the Home Department* precisely that question arose.[101] The absolute prohibition under art. 3 of the European Convention on Human Rights remains clear, but the European Court of Human Rights has established that assurances may provide a basis for safe return, with the adequacy of the assurance determined on a case-by-case basis.[102] The result has been the development by SIAC of a set of tests to determine if reliance on the assurances is permitted. The Law Lords held unanimously in both cases that SIAC reached the correct conclusion on the facts, that the assurances given by Jordan and Algeria contained appropriate levels of protection. The

---

[98] There are currently agreements with five states: Algeria, Jordan, Ethiopia, Libya and Lebanon.

[99] 'The Court notes first of all that States face immense difficulties in modern times in protecting their communities from terrorist violence. It cannot therefore underestimate the scale of the danger of terrorism today and the threat it presents to the community. That must not, however, call into question the absolute nature of Article 3.' *Saadi* v. *Italy* [2008] ECHR 37201/06, [137].

[100] [2004] EWCA Civ 1123.

[101] [2009] UKHL 10. See Jennifer Tooze, 'Deportation with assurances: the approach of the UK Courts' [2010] *Public Law* 362, who examines the approach taken by domestic courts in the UK to deportation with assurances (DWA); Clive Walker, 'The treatment of foreign terror suspects', 441–50.

[102] *Saadi* v. *Italy* [2008] ECHR 37201/06.

judgment therefore confirmed the potential of deportation with diplomatic assurances as one tool in counter-terrorism policy which includes
removal from the UK.[103]

The approach has been considered as part of the UK's Counter-
Terrorism Review with recommendations made for further development.[104] The Review rejected the argument that deportation with
assurances provided insufficient protection or that it undermined the
absolute prohibition on torture.[105] The recommendations included the
view that generic agreements should be preferred, but assurances for
specific individuals should not be ruled out if 'viable assurances' could
be obtained.[106] In addition, the Review recommended a range of possible
improvements, including commissioning an annual independent review
of the system and better engagement with other countries, international
organisations and NGOs to increase understanding of the objectives of
the policy.[107]

H.   Dealing with dissent?

Individuals are not only removed from the United Kingdom, but can also
be refused admission on national security and public order grounds.[108]
In the intriguing case of R (Farrakhan) v. Secretary of State for the Home
Department the claimant was an African–American refused entry on
public order grounds (the concern of the Home Secretary that disorder
might result from his visit).[109] A question here was whether art. 10 of the
European Convention was engaged in this pre-emptive decision to refuse
admission on the basis of a future risk. The Court of Appeal held that art.
10 was engaged (he was being excluded precisely to prevent him exercising his right to free expression in the United Kingdom), but concluded
that the decision of the Home Secretary could be justified as it was for a
legitimate aim under art. 10(2). The Court of Appeal held that the Home
Secretary had provided sufficient explanation for the decision (although
no convincing evidence was offered in this respect), which was based

---

[103] See, for example, XX v. Secretary of State for the Home Department, 10 September 2010,
SC/61/2007 (SIAC), assurance regime between the United Kingdom and Ethiopia held
to provide sufficient safeguards to permit Convention compliant return.
[104] HM Government Review of Counter-Terrorism and Security Powers, pp. 33–5.
[105] Ibid.   [106] Ibid., p. 35.
[107] Ibid. The pending judgment of the European Court of Human Rights in the Abu Qatada
case in 2011 should prove instructive.
[108] Immigration Act 1971, s. 3.   [109] [2002] 3 WLR 481 (CA).

around an alleged risk to community relations between Muslims and Jews in Britain. There have been several recent high profile examples of the use of this power, and it continues to attract considerable debate on the balance to be struck between freedom of speech and public order in the United Kingdom.[110]

The case of Abu Hamza is also of interest in this context.[111] He is a prominent Muslim cleric, currently in prison in the United Kingdom serving a seven-year sentence for inciting murder and racial hatred, and challenging through the European Court of Human Rights attempts to extradite him to the United States. He has expressed open and vocal support for terrorism, and is the subject of considerable official interest (going back some time). His case was complicated for the UK authorities by the fact that he held British citizenship. In 2003, the Home Secretary opted to attempt to deprive him of his British citizenship, a decision which was successfully appealed to SIAC in November 2010, on the basis that it would render him 'stateless'.[112]

Following *Hicks*, and the events of 7 July 2005, the British Nationality Act 1981 was amended in 2006 in order to further enhance the powers available on 'citizenship stripping'. David Hicks (who was detained at Guantanamo Bay) sought to register as a British citizen (his mother was born in the UK). The Home Secretary acceded to the request but also, at the same time, made a deprivation order. The case revolved around whether the Home Secretary could rely on conduct prior to the acquisition of citizenship. In concluding that the respondent could not have been 'disaffected' within the meaning of the 1981 Act, the Court of Appeal sided with the first instance judgment. The provisions relating to deprivation of citizenship in the 2006 Act (which align it more closely with other 'conductive to the public good' mechanisms) can be viewed in the context of, and in reaction to, *Hicks*.

These two cases (one dealing with admission, the other with British nationality law) provide useful examples of the approaches adopted by

---

[110] See also *Naik* v. *Secretary of State for the Home Department* [2010] EWHC 2825 (Admin). N is a leading Muslim writer and public speaker whose views were alleged by the Home Secretary to have influenced those who instigated terrorist attacks. He was excluded from admission to the United Kingdom and his entry clearance visa revoked. The Court ruled that art. 10 was engaged (as a consequence of the right of others to receive information and the potential audience in the United Kingdom) but that the interference with the right was lawful and proportionate. See also, for example, 'US preacher banned from speaking in Milton Keynes', *BBC News*, 20 January 2011.

[111] See *Abu Hamza*, 5 November 2010, SC/23/2005.

[112] The Home Secretary has no such power: see British Nationality Act 1981, s. 40(4).

the Home Secretary to deal with those (citizens and non-citizens) perceived to be a threat (primarily through the expression of their radical
views) to public order and/or national security.

I. What should judges do?

The question in all these cases is not whether judges should have a role,
but what should judges do with the law that currently exists. Beyond the
national security context, the views of the Home Secretary, and the governmental perspective, are accorded significant weight, but they are not
generally regarded as decisive. While one can understand a certain judicial unease in addressing national security matters, excessive deference to
the executive is inappropriate if there is a principled commitment to the
consistent interpretation and application of the law.[113] Evidence suggests
that this is precisely the time when the values which underpin the rule
of law need to be upheld, and there are examples to prove that the courts
in the UK have responded to the challenge and have the experience and
expertise to do so.[114]

While the Home Secretary will have access to detailed factual information, and is the person who will face democratic accountability through
Parliament (and ultimately to the electorate) for the decision, judges
should not automatically defer to his or her understanding of the substantive content of what the law means. On this matter the Home Secretary is
in no better position than a judge – he or she can have a view, but it will
not necessarily be the definitive one. This is reinforced when one considers
that human rights standards are now a relatively secure part of domestic
law, in the form of the Human Rights Act 1998. Judges have a responsibility to ensure that the law, properly understood, is applied to all on an
equal basis. The risk is that exceptional treatment of particular groups
and individuals will lead to further erosion of existing guarantees and
ultimately undermine the principle of legality as it applies to everyone.

The overall picture is too complex and varied to offer one definitive
judgment on performance, and much remains context sensitive. The normative argument advanced about legality is, however, clear. The focus

---

[113] See Tomkins, 'National security and the role of the courts', 545, who states on the evidence of the lower courts: '… judicial scrutiny of government actions and decisions taken
in the interests of national security appears never to have been more intense than it is
now'. He places particular emphasis on *Al Jedda*, 7 April 2009, SIAC. See also, *Secretary
of State for the Home Department* v. *Al Saadi* [2009] EWHC 3390 (Admin).

[114] Cf. Tomkins, 'National security and the role of the courts'.

must remain on the substance of legal argumentation across particular cases. The judicial role should not be exaggerated, or too great a burden placed upon it. But it is clear that it is the role of the courts to give voice to what the current law is. So much of the debate is now conducted within the terms of legal argumentation, for example: that 'we did X but the legal advice told us it was not torture', 'we invaded Y but the legal advice said that this was in accordance with international law', 'we do not believe the control order regime constitutes a deprivation of liberty' or 'yes, we deported A (and he was tortured), but the diplomatic assurances had all the relevant safeguards'. The courts have a secure constitutional role in focusing on what the law is, rather than 'who decides'. If any express democratic reassurance is needed, in the United Kingdom this is located within the Human Rights Act 1998 and its enactment by Parliament. In some instances judges have displayed admirable courage by insisting on the application of a convincing account of what the law requires. In other cases judges have been too ready to step aside in the face of a determined and creative executive operating in the midst of a public mood of anxiety, insecurity and fear – fuelled by credible terrorist threats and attacks.

3. Conclusion

Asylum law is a significant site of continuing skirmishes between the executive, judiciary, and occasionally the legislature, in many common law jurisdictions. It often raises in stark terms the tensions between a normative commitment to respect for human dignity, with the attempts of states to create bounded communities of belonging. All the rigid legal or political doctrines in the world can never wash away the strains and tensions of dealing humanely with the physical presence of the suffering other who is in need. Asylum is a humanitarian route to entry that has not been closed down (it remains a home for humanity within legality), but which is approached by many governments with profound suspicion and unease. One of the early reactions to 9/11 was to identify refugee status determination systems as possible safe havens, and in the United Kingdom the events of 7/7 prompted a renewed focus on the deportation of foreign nationals (even though the attacks were carried out by British nationals). The argument is still made that human rights protections create safe havens for terrorists, with a renewed focus on the work of the European Court of Human Rights.

It is an area where the commitment to *human* rights is tested, asylum seekers cannot rely on national status as a basis of entitlement (intriguingly in a counter-terrorism context even nationals from certain minority ethnic communities cannot depend on the rights and entitlements of citizenship in such contexts[115]). The basis for protection often rests on legal provisions which owe their allegiance to notions of personhood and which seek legal acknowledgement of a common humanity.[116] These are areas of law and policy where the moral commitment to respect for humanity as the basis of entitlement finds a fragile home.

The global resurgence in counter-terrorism policies and strategies intensified the pressure on an already contested arena of constitutional law and politics. The story can be portrayed simply: in the face of rising security threats, and terrorist attacks, a determined executive sought to advance authoritarian measures in the context of existing constitutional and human rights constraints (within which it generally sought to operate rather than abandon). It was always likely to lead to constitutional conflict, and so it did. Despite a change of government in 2010, and attempts at reform, the challenges will remain, and for now the Human Rights Act and the protections of the European Convention on Human Rights survive.[117]

The traditional values associated with the principle of legality are of particular significance for refugees and asylum seekers. The protection against the exercise of arbitrary power and the commitment to basic principles of fairness, which should be securely embedded within any proper understanding of legal order, remain vital for vulnerable and marginalised groups. There is a duty to uphold the rule of law in the face of public criticism and in times of insecurity and fear. While founded on an enabling and humanitarian basis, asylum law and policy in the UK has largely followed a restrictive path, made worse by counter-terrorism policies, and is now marked by measures (accelerated procedures, reduced appeal rights) which limit in practice the ability of individuals to challenge asylum decisions. While not as blatant as the deliberate exclusion of judicial review, the practical impact can be similar. The rule of law may be undermined by a slow and deliberate accumulation of laws and policies which

---

[115] See Daniel Moeckli, *Human Rights and Non-Discrimination in the 'War on Terror'* (Oxford University Press, 2008).

[116] On the complex relationship between personhood and citizenship see Linda Bosniak, 'Persons and citizens in constitutional thought' (2010) 8 *International Journal of Constitutional Law* 9. She notes that personhood brings with it a challenge function in almost any context it is deployed, but also stresses just how complicated a notion it is.

[117] See Colin Harvey, 'Taking the next step? Achieving another bill of rights' [2011] *European Human Rights Law Review* 24.

make it difficult to contest the legality of administrative decision-making in a rigorous and thorough way. This is a pattern that is not confined to the United Kingdom.

Under a substantive concept of legality, adherence to the rule of law should bring with it respect for the inherent dignity of the human person. While its application is associated with judges, they are not the only ones responsible for ensuring widespread and lasting respect for the principle. When national security is raised, in the asylum context and in related areas, there is an ever-present danger of excessive deference undermining a thorough examination of the substantive legal issues, and practical risks to the individual. Those who are vulnerable in normal times are even more so when there is an intimidating climate of hostility and fear which circles menacingly around particular individuals and particular 'suspect communities'. They will depend on people and institutions prepared to uphold the values which underpin legal order, in the good times and bad. All those institutions and actors in the public sphere who have the current capacity to give practical life to the principle of legality must do so. They must unearth and probe the strength of the arguments, reasons and justifications advanced when judged against the fabric of a constitutional democracy that all would wish to protect and promote. The responsibility to defend a culture of human rights falls unevenly on those who must not remain silent in the face of oppression, from whatever source it emanates. When the state insists on enthusiastically embracing the positive obligation to protect the right to life of everyone, this endorsement of a robust human rights culture should be welcomed and put to use by all of us. The real risk at the present time is of a retreat into national protectionism combined with the anxious construction of external (and internal) threats. Terrorism must be confronted, effectively, lawfully and directly, but to surrender hard-won values, and allow terrorism to erode respect for our common humanity is a mistake. States like the United Kingdom depend on all those who recognise the responsibility to protect the rights of others and who will continue to remain insistent and firm, even in these hard times.

10

'Prevent' responses to jihadi extremism

CLIVE WALKER AND JAVAID REHMAN

1. Introduction

Changes in the nature of jihadi terrorism,[1] its likely proponents, and its potential temporal and geographical extent have tipped counter-terrorism more towards holistic and preventative stances than hitherto. Examples can be found at an international level in the United Nations Global Counter Terrorism Strategy,[2] at a regional level in the European Union Counter Terrorism Strategy of 2005,[3] at a national level in the United States National Strategy for Combating Terrorism[4] and also in the UK's Countering International Terrorism (CONTEST) strategy.[5] Given the intellectual commonality between these statements, this chapter will select for fuller exploration only the UK version as perhaps the most fully articulated and implemented. In assessing official efforts, this chapter will canvass three themes.

The first theme is that the changing features of terrorism have encouraged greater official emphasis on addressing the causes of terrorism. It will be asked why there is this impetus to understand terrorists and not

---

[1] In this chapter, the term 'Jihad' reflects commonly received meaning, whether heretical or not. 'Terrorism' bears the meaning ascribed at a national level by the Terrorism Act 2000 (UK), s. 1, and at an international level under instruments such as the United Nations International Convention for the Suppression of the Financing of Terrorism 1999, New York, 9 December 1999, in force 10 April 2002, 2178 UNTS 229.

[2] UN GA Res. 60/288, 20 September 2006.

[3] Strasbourg, 14469/4/05 (2005), p. 2. The Strategy is divided into the four pillars: Prevent, Protect, Pursue and Respond – a taxonomy very redolent of the UK version.

[4] Washington, DC (September 2006), p. 8. The original version was published in 2003.

[5] Home Office, *Countering International Terrorism* (London: Cm 6888, 2006); *Pursue, Prevent, Protect, Prepare: The United Kingdom's Strategy for Countering International Terrorism* (London: Cm 7547, 2009); *The United Kingdom's Strategy for Countering International Terrorism Annual Report 2010* (London: Cm 7833, 2010). See House of Commons Home Affairs Committee, *Project CONTEST: The Government's Counter-Terrorism Strategy* (2008–09 HC 212) and *Government Reply* (London: Cm 7703, 2009).

just to condemn and eradicate. What explanations have been attributed to terrorism?

The second theme of this chapter is that state authorities have been impelled to conceive their counter-terrorism responses on a wider social scale than hitherto. Counter-terrorism is no longer confined to security personnel, powers or hardware, albeit that those aspects still represent the most powerful and expensive aspect of the official agenda. Rather, the trend is towards softer engagement with local entities. These community-based approaches are not an entirely new departure, for it has long been recognised by UK policy-makers that counter-terrorism involves the need to 'win the battle of hearts and minds', an idea which can be traced to theatres of conflict as long ago as Malaya.[6] However, the prominence of the current policy diverges from the era of Irish terrorism, when, so far as Britain was concerned, the 'Ulsterisation' of the terrorist problem was preferred.[7] Even in Northern Ireland, counter-terrorism was the business of the 'securitocracy', and local communities were not mobilised as allies.[8] There is also a contrast with the period from 2001 until 2005, when international terrorism was depicted as primarily the work of foreigners. Consequently, once again, local communities were not viewed as relevant to its suppression.

The third theme is a shifting disposition within policing. Secretive and specialised 'high' policing[9] must adjust in organisation and style to match counter-terrorism work embedded in communities. Two results have flowed. One is that there is the genesis of an effort by security bodies to engage in a variant of community policing in response to terrorism. This strand does not wholly displace the more secretive non-consensual policing which remains the paradigm stance,[10] but it does form an important adjunct. The other result is a widening of what counts as 'policing',

---

[6] General Templer stated in 1952: 'The answer lies not in pouring more troops into the jungle, but in the hearts and minds of the Malayan People.' See R. Sunderland, *Winning the Hearts and Minds of the People: Malaya 1948–1960* (Santa Monica, CA: Rand, 1964); F. Kitson, *Low-Intensity Operations* (London: Faber & Faber, 1971); R. Stubbs, *Hearts and Minds in Guerrilla Warfare* (Singapore: Oxford University Press, 1989); P. Dixon, '"Hearts and minds"? British counter-insurgency from Malaya to Iraq' (2009) 32 *Journal of Strategic Studies* 353.

[7] See Clive Walker, *The Prevention of Terrorism in British Law* (Manchester University Press, 2nd edn, 1992).

[8] See Dixon, '"Hearts and minds"?' 445.

[9] See Jean-Paul Brodeur, 'High and low policing in post-9/11 times' (2007) 1 *Policing* 25.

[10] See Clive Walker, 'Intelligence and anti-terrorism legislation in the United Kingdom' (2006) 44 *Crime, Law and Social Change* 387.

with the melding of various policy strands not only within the Home Office but also in the Communities and Education ministries.

2.   Determining the causes of jihadi activity

The bombings in London on 7 July 2005 rightly gave pause for official reflection upon counter-terrorism measures. In contrast to many prior crises, there was no panic response. After all, already forearmed with most conceivable varieties of measures under the Terrorism Act 2000, the Anti-Terrorism, Crime and Security Act 2001 and the Prevention of Terrorism Act 2005, an increasingly 'militant democracy'[11] had already emerged with no manifest legal gaps. Nevertheless, the then Prime Minister, Tony Blair, issued a warning on 5 August 2005 of future amendments: 'Let no one be in any doubt, the rules of the game are changing'.[12] The measures then announced included the promise to inaugurate extra anti-terror legislation, not least a new offence of condoning or glorifying terrorism and extra powers for the police to detain after arrest for ninety days.

One might question the relevance of this reform agenda, which empha-sised the diminution of individual rights rather than any examination of intelligence and administrative failings going beyond the production of a 'narrative'.[13] All the same, the ensuing months witnessed some startling adjustments through the Terrorism Act 2006, which delivered the new offences and the banning of groups which engaged in extreme speech, though the ninety-day detention proposal was reduced by Parliamentary opposition to twenty-eight days.[14]

One further aspect of the 'game' being played with terrorism con-cerned the treatment of foreign terrorist suspects.[15] There was a con-certed effort in the summer of 2005 to round them up and deport them, though its accomplishment proved difficult because of the risk of torture in the receiving states contrary to art. 3 of the European Convention on

---

[11]   See A. Sajó (ed.), *Militant Democracy* (Amsterdam: Eleven International, 2004); M. Thiel (ed.), *The 'Militant Democracy' Principle in Modern Democracies* (Aldershot: Ashgate, 2009).

[12]   Prime Minister's Press Conference, 5 August 2005, available at www.number10.gov.uk/ archive/2005/08/pm-s-press-conference-5-august-2005–8041.

[13]   See also Intelligence and Security Committee, *Report on the London Terrorist Attacks on 7 July 2005* (London: Cm 6785, 2005).

[14]   For fuller details, see Clive Walker, *Terrorism and the Law* (Oxford University Press, 2011), Chapters 4 and 8.

[15]   For fuller details, see Clive Walker, 'The treatment of foreign terror suspects' (2007) 70 *Modern Law Review* 427.

Human Rights.[16] The government therefore sought to smooth the path to the exit door by new restrictions on entry, asylum and citizenship in the Immigration, Asylum and Nationality Act 2006 and also via the device of diplomatic assurances.[17] In these ways, the London attacks of July 2005 have triggered a political epiphany in the form of a fundamental revaluation of the dangers of jihadism at home and a decisive policy switch away from 'Londonistan' – the stance of tolerance of political dissidents.[18] The era of toleration of the apparent provocations of Abu Hamza,[19] Abu Qatada,[20] and Omar Bakri Muhammed[21] is at an end. The official intolerance of offensive speech contrasts with earlier times, illustrated by the divergent official reactions to the publication of the Danish cartoons of the Prophet Mohammed first appearing in the Danish newspaper *Jyllands-Posten* in 2006[22] and Salman Rushdie's book, *The Satanic Verses*, in 1989.[23]

While the foreign bogeymen have not entirely vanished, there emerged after 7/7 a much sharper official focus on home-grown jihadis. At first, the official reaction was denial. For example, it is perfectly correct at one

---

[16] *Chahal* v. *United Kingdom*, App. no. 22414/93, 1996-V. For a discussion of the *Chahal* case in relation to the UK special advocates regime, see Nicola McGarrity and Edward Santow, Chapter 6, this volume.

[17] *AS and another (Libya)* v. *Secretary of State for the Home Department* [2008] EWCA Civ 289; *RB* v. *Secretary of State for the Home Department; OO* v. *Secretary of State for the Home Department* [2009] UKHL 10; *Saadi* v. *Italy*, App. no. 37201/06, 28 February 2008; J. Tooze, 'Deportation with assurances' [2010] *Public Law* 362.

[18] See M. Phillips, *Londonistan: How Britain is Creating a Terror State from Within* (London: Gibson Square, 2006).

[19] His citizenship was withdrawn under the Nationality, Immigration and Asylum Act 2002, s. 4, he was convicted of soliciting murder (*R* v. *Abu Hamza* [2006] EWCA Crim 2918), and he has been ordered to be extradited to the United States (*Mustafa* v. *United States* [2008] EWHC 1357 (Admin)) but European Convention proceedings are pending (*Mustafa* v. *United Kingdom*, App. no. 36742/08).

[20] See *OO* v. *Secretary of State for the Home Department* [2009] UKHL 10. His removal is under consideration by the European Court of Human Rights: *Othman* v. *United Kingdom*, App. no. 8139/09.

[21] He departed for Lebanon after being threatened with deportation: *The Times*, 9 August 2005, 1.

[22] The Foreign Secretary encouraged British media outlets not to reproduce them: *The Times*, 4 February 2006, 1.

[23] The Foreign Office expressed concern at protests and halted diplomatic relations with Iran (*The Times*, 15 February 1989; 27 February 1989). The then Prime Minister Thatcher stated that: 'Freedom of speech and expression is subject only to the laws of this land, in particular libel and blasphemy, and will remain subject to the rule of law. It is absolutely fundamental to everything in which we believe and cannot be interfered with by any outside force': *Hansard*, HC, vol. 148, col. 157, 28 February 1989.

level to label as 'rubbish'[24] the 'grievances' of Mohammed Sidique Khan, one of the four 7/7 bombers who spoke as follows on video released after his death: 'Until you stop the bombing, gassing, imprisonment and torture of my people we will not stop this fight … We are at war and I am a soldier. Now you too will taste the reality of this situation.'[25] But it is evident that the sentiments were felt deeply, and that there was too limited analysis of this 'new reality'.[26] Whatever the explanation, it gradually dawned that what was so remarkable about those London bombings was that they were perpetrated by British citizens (so-called 'neighbour terrorists').[27] They were Yorkshiremen, whose mundane backgrounds set at nought several of the tactics of the security forces on the hunt for cells of foreigners.[28] It later emerged that they were not all entirely divorced from foreign links and support,[29] but their operation seems to have been in the main locally devised and executed. The attempted bombings in London on 21 July 2005 were likewise perpetrated by long-term residents.[30] The same is true of most major terrorist conspiracies since that time.

On further reflection, the July 2005 'neighbour' bombers were not isolated or novel aberrations. Prior examples include Richard Reid, who attempted to explode a shoe bomb on a trans-Atlantic flight in 2001,[31] and the suicide bombings in Tel Aviv in 2003 by Asif Mohammed Hanif and Omar Khan Sharif.[32] There followed successive warnings about the growing number of local extremists. In March 2005, the former Metropolitan Police Commissioner, Sir John Stevens, estimated there were 200 fanatics.[33] The head of MI5, Dame Eliza Manningham-Buller, revealed in November 2006 that there were 1,600 in the ranks of the

---

[24] House of Commons Liaison Committee, Oral Evidence given by Rt. Hon. Tony Blair MP (2005–6, HC 709) p. 126.

[25] See news.bbc.co.uk/1/hi/uk/4206800.stm.

[26] Sir Ian Blair, Dimbleby Lecture 2005, available at news.bbc.co.uk/1/hi/uk/4443386.stm.

[27] See further Clive Walker, '"Know thine enemy as thyself": discerning friend from foe under anti-terrorism laws' (2008) 32 *Melbourne University Law Review* 275; Clive Walker, 'Neighbor terrorism and the all-risks policing of terrorism' (2009) 3 *Journal of National Security Law and Policy* 121.

[28] See Intelligence and Security Committee, *Report on the London Terrorist Attacks on 7 July 2005* (London: Cm 6785, 2005); Home Office, *Report of the Official Account of the Bombings in London on 7 July 2005* (2005–6 HC 1087).

[29] See Intelligence and Security Committee, *Could 7/7 have been Prevented?* (London: Cm 7617, 2009); B. Hoffman, 'Radicalization and subversion' (2009) 32 *Studies in Conflict and Terrorism* 1100.

[30] See *The Times*, 10 July 2007, 1.   [31] *The Washington Post*, 31 January 2003, A01.

[32] See *Daily Telegraph*, 20 May 2003, 2.   [33] *News of the World*, 6 March 2005.

'enemy within'.[34] Speaking in late 2007, Jonathan Evans said the service was aware of more than 2,000 people who posed a direct threat to national security plus as many again yet to be identified.[35] The switch of attention from aliens to 'neighbours' was also proclaimed in 2007 by Peter Clarke, Deputy Assistant Metropolitan Police Commissioner, when he revealed that this realisation began to dawn in 2003.[36]

In light of this information, no longer can it be claimed that the enemy in war is 'in a particularly intense way, existentially something different and alien' and 'the negation of our existence, the destruction of our way of life'.[37] The main terrorist threat is no longer from archetypal outsider embodied by the convenient figure of the now deceased Osama bin Laden – depicted as an alien, uncivilised cave-dweller who imports terrorism from foreign lands.[38] Rather, the embedded nature of the terrorist risk seems to demand the treatment of one's neighbour as potentially friend and foe since the 2005 attacks confirmed the intimate, local and indigenous nature of terrorism. One consequence is mounting attention to the causes of extremism amongst some British Muslims, so as to manage and reduce the risk of terrorism. This trend encounters two severe problems, one definitional and one substantive.

The definitional problem concerns the meanings of, and boundaries between, terms such as 'radicalisation', 'extremism', and 'terrorism'. As for 'radicalisation' and 'extremism', a Home Office paper offers definitions as follows:[39]

> Radicalisation is often a social process, involving interaction with others.
>
> ...
>
> Radicalisers may be propagandists, ideologues or terrorists and may be in face-to-face contact with the subject or in dialogue over the internet.
>
> ...
>
> Radicalisers use a particular interpretation of history, politics and religion to convince individuals of the necessity for indiscriminate violence.

[34] *The Times*, 10 November 2006, 1.   [35] *Manchester Evening News*, 5 November 2007.
[36] Cramphorn Memorial Lecture (London: Metropolitan Police Service, 2007).
[37] C. Schmitt, *The Concept of the Political*, G. Schwab transl. (New Brunswick, NJ: Rutgers University Press, 1976), p. 26.
[38] President Bush referred in 2001 to bin Laden as 'a guy who, three months ago, was in control of a country. Now he's maybe in control of a cave': see georgewbush-whitehouse. archives.gov/news/releases/2001/12/20011228–1.html.
[39] Home Office, *The Prevent Strategy: A Guide for Local Partners* (London: 2008), Annex 1, p. 69. See further *Delivering the Prevent Strategy: An Updated Guide for Local Partners* (London: 2009).

Extremist material – Books, pamphlets and audio/visual material (including websites) reflecting the extremist narrative, and often including images of violence that could be portrayed as representing an ideological or religious conflict, can influence people towards supporting violent extremism.

The evident chronic imprecision is reflected further in the tasking missions of policing organisations,[40] with consequent dangers for legitimate (but radical) political activity.[41] The substantive identification of the triggers for these afflictions is just as inexact.[42] Early official explanations included the ludicrous comments in 2006 of John Reid, then Home Secretary, in which he urged Muslim families to 'watch for signs of brainwashing in their children by radicals grooming them to kill themselves in order to murder others. ... Look for the tell-tale signs now and talk to them before their hatred grows and you risk losing them for ever.'[43] Yet, the complex picture of 'neighbour' terrorism arising within the United Kingdom cannot simplistically be depicted as psychotic behaviour or the religious fervour of Muslims, even in the extreme case of suicide attacks.[44] Fortunately, the government began to recognise a range of possible factors: attendance at a mosque linked to extremists; the influence of an extreme spiritual leader; the Internet; the role of personal mentors and then bonding with a group of fellow extremists.[45] This greater subtlety became reflected in more sophisticated counter-measures, as shall be described later.

[40] See the remit of the UK National Extremism Tactical Coordination Unit, available at www.netcu.org.uk/de/default.jsp, and of Europol: *EU Terrorism Situation and Trend Report* (The Hague, 2008), p. 7.

[41] See A. Kundani, *Spooked! How Not to Prevent Violent Extremism* (London: Institute of Race Relations, 2009).

[42] See J. Horgan, *The Psychology of Terrorism* (Abingdon: Routledge, 2005); T. Abbas (ed.), *Islamic Political Radicalism: A European Perspective* (Edinburgh University Press, 2007); J. M. Post, *The Mind of the Terrorist* (London: Palgrave MacMillan, 2008); T. Bjørgo and J. Horgan (eds.), *Leaving Terrorism Behind* (Abingdon: Routledge, 2009); J. Horgan, *Walking Away from Terrorism* (Abingdon: Routledge, 2009).

[43] *The Times*, 21 September 2006, 6.

[44] See A. Pedahzur, 'Toward an analytical model of suicide terrorism – a comment' (2004) 16 *Terrorism and Political Violence* 841; D. K. Gupta and K. Mundra, 'Suicide bombing as a strategic weapon: an empirical investigation of Hamas and Islamic Jihad' (2005) 17 *Terrorism and Political Violence* 573; P. Pape, *Dying to Win* (New York: Random House, 2005); A. Silke, 'The role of suicide in politics, conflict, and terrorism' (2006) 18 *Terrorism and Political Violence* 35.

[45] Home Office, *Report of the Official Account of the Bombings in London on 7th July*, Annex B. Cf. Commission of the European Communities, *Communication to the Commission Concerning Terrorist Recruitment: Addressing the Factors Contributing to Violent Radicalisation*, COM(2005) 313 Final, p. 14.

By contrast, the Blair premiership remained reluctant to admit the negative consequences of foreign policies, such as the invasion of Iraq, even though the explanations given by both Mohammad Sidique Khan and Shehzad Tanweer, two of the 7/7 London bombers, in video testaments released after their deaths, emphasise as grievances Western military interventions in Afghanistan and Iraq and Western abandonment of Palestinians.[46] It was left to the House of Commons Foreign Affairs Committee to point out that 'the situation in Iraq has provided both a powerful source of propaganda for Islamist extremists and also a crucial training ground for international terrorists associated with al Qaeda'.[47] The days of denial faded after the resignation of Blair, and a more comprehensive official analysis of jihadism in 2008 still pointed to 'ideologues' and vulnerable young people, but also included ideology, communities which are ill-equipped to challenge extremism, plus grievances which may be domestic and foreign.[48] Another iteration in 2008 included radicalisers, extremist material, group identity, personal or identity crisis and change, under-employment, links to criminality, social exclusion, real or perceived grievances, and lack of trust in political structures and civil society.[49]

By degrees, a more reflective and realistic analysis has been outlined. The espousal of extremist causes is perhaps suggestive of theories of social anomie,[50] with some young Muslim men caught between the conservative and unreplicable culture of their parents and the unappealing culture of the West, both to be rejected in favour of a pure, simple and strong identity based on Islamism.[51] The modal setting of the small group of action-oriented friends certainly makes life more difficult for security authorities who cannot follow formal chains of hierarchical command but must try to distinguish social from operational bonding and group affinity from radical rejection.[52] Unfortunately, the indicia of jihadism

---

[46] *The Times*, 2 September 2005, 2; *The Times*, 7 July 2006, 4.
[47] *Foreign Policy Aspects of the War Against Terrorism* (2005–6 HC 573), [21]. See further M. Rai, *7/7: The London Bombings, Islam and the Iraq War* (London: Pluto Press, 2006).
[48] Home Secretary Jacqui Smith, 'Our shared values – a shared responsibility' (International Centre for the Study of Radicalisation and Political Violence, First International Conference, 2008).
[49] Home Office, *The Prevent Strategy*, Annex I.
[50] E. Hussein, *The Islamist* (London: Penguin, 2007), p. 69.
[51] See V. J. Siedler, *Urban Fears and Global Terrors* (Abingdon: Routledge, 2007), p. 98.
[52] See J. M. Post, 'The socio-cultural underpinnings of terrorist psychology' in T. Bjørgo (ed.), *Root Causes of Terrorism* (Abingdon: Routledge, 2005); O. Nasiri, *Inside the Global Jihad* (London: Hurst & Co, 2006); M. Sageman, *Leaderless Jihad* (University of Pennsylvania Press, 2007).

may not be palpable or, according to a leaked Security Service memorandum in 2008, prey upon any remarkable personal characteristics.[53] Finally, there should be assumed no linear relationship from radicalism through extremism to violence. Radicalisation is a normal experience for many young people, and violence may not emerge from radicalism but from group loyalty. Too often, policy-makers fail to distinguish adequately between 'radical' and 'extreme',[54] with dangerous consequences for expression in locations such as universities, as shall be illustrated later.

Whatever causes are in play, the presence of jihadis in neighbourhoods rather than foreign fields inevitably impels the state to refocus on the communities. This change is fundamental to the treatment not only of communities but also of policing. The need arises to understand not only the mechanisms and impacts of terrorism but also its social causes. A wider range of official modes of intervention will thereby be triggered. The changing nature of responses, first social and then security-based, will next be analysed.

3.   Social 'prevent' responses

A.   Strategy

A more social strategic scope has been signalled by the Home Office's Countering International Terrorism (CONTEST) documentation, formulated during 2003 but not published or implemented with vigour until 2006.[55] As well as the traditional security-oriented 'Pursue' of terrorists, such as through arrest and prosecution, there is an important 'Prevent' element which points toward a social agenda. It is overseen by a national Prevent Board headed by the Home Secretary.[56] The programme contains elements of challenging extremism, disruption, supporting those at risk, increasing community resilience, and addressing social grievances.[57] Therefore, 'Prevent' is now a high priority which is addressed at many levels. This chapter will now consider its impact on a sectoral basis.

---

[53]   *The Guardian*, 21 August 2008, 1.
[54]   See J. Bartlett and J. Birdwell, *The Edge of Violence* (London: Demos, 2010), p. 38.
[55]   See above note 5; R. Briggs, C. Fieschi and L. Lownsbrough, *Bringing It Home: Community-Based Approaches to Counterterrorism* (London: Demos, 2006).
[56]   Home Office, *Delivering the Prevent Strategy*, [3.2], [3.3].
[57]   See Home Office, *The Prevent Strategy*; *Preventing Violent Extremism: A Strategy for Delivery* (London, 2008).

B. Local communities

The most important element of 'Prevent' concerns its applications to local communities defined by geography and ethnic or religious clustering. The aim is to reduce extremism by making community engagement a cornerstone of counter-terrorism strategy. The proposition that community involvement might prevent terrorism assumes that terrorism has resonance with Muslim communities and therefore that community-based partners can strive to reduce that appeal, can identify sources of disaffection, can aid those at risk and can bolster police legitimacy.[58] These assumptions incorporate the untested views that Muslim communities can be identified, have resilience against extremism, can exercise social control and can be motivated to do so.[59]

There immediately arises uncertainty over what constitutes a target 'community' for these purposes. British Muslims are not monolithic, either in religious tenets or in ethnicity. The 2001 UK census estimated a figure of 1.6 million Muslims, (2.7 per cent of the total resident population of the United Kingdom).[60] However, this quantification of religious affiliation embodies tremendous diversity in ethnicity, with different mixtures of Pakistani, Bangladeshi and Indian origin residents in urban areas such as London, the Midlands and West Yorkshire. This problem of targeting became even more delicate when in 2009 the government announced the application of some 'Prevent' initiatives to 'white enclaves' at risk of racist extremism,[61] though these were subject to cuts in June 2010.

The initial 'Prevent' programme for local community safety against terrorism was entitled, 'Preventing Extremism Together'.[62] It was announced in August 2005 and consisted of seven working groups: Engaging with

---

[58] See Department for Communities and Local Government, *Preventing Violent Extremism: Next Steps For Communities* (London: 2008), [14]–[15]; R. Briggs, 'Community engagement for counterterrorism: lessons from the United Kingdom' (2010) 86 *International Affairs* 971, 972.

[59] A survey from 2003–5 found resilience but that 'signal crimes' did not include terrorism: M. Innes, C. Roberts, T. Lowe and L. Abbott, *Hearts and Minds and Eyes and Ears* (Cardiff University Press, 2007).

[60] www.statistics.gov.uk/statbase/expodata/spreadsheets/d6891.xls. See also J. Rehman, 'Islam, "War on Terror" and the future of Muslim minorities in the United Kingdom' (2007) 29 *Human Rights Quarterly* 831, 846.

[61] *The Independent*, 15 October 2009, 16.

[62] Home Office *Preventing Extremism Together Working Groups Aug-Oct 2005* (London, 2005). See D. McGhee, *The End of Multiculturalism* (Maidenhead: Open University Press, 2008), Chapter 3.

Young People; Education; Engaging with Muslim Women; Supporting Regional and Local Initiatives and Community Actions; Imams Training and Accreditation and the Role of Mosques as a Resource for the Whole Community: Working; Community Security – Including Addressing Islamophobia,[63] Increasing Confidence in Policing and Tackling Extremism; and Tackling Extremism and Radicalisation. A number of proposals emerged from this work, and the Department for Communities and Local Government eventually rationalised its responses around four approaches: promoting shared values; supporting local solutions; building civic capacity and leadership; and strengthening faith institutions and leadership.[64]

These policy strands, promoting shared values, interacted with even broader debates about citizenship rights and responsibilities,[65] attempting to distil attractive rallying points for the potentially disaffected and emphasising that Britishness is no enemy of Muslims. The drawback with this exercise is that British identity remains highly contested and even divisive. National pride to some appears to be a celebration of racist imperialism to others. Resolutions to this divergence of views often take refuge in bland universal, rather than national, values such as liberty, responsibility and fairness.[66] Thus, it has proven very problematic to promulgate a cohesive 'good' cultural identity as a rallying point against 'bad' jihadi stances.[67]

Despite these pitfalls, the distillation of Britishness has been pursued for some years and even prior to July 2005. For example, citizenship was added in 2000 to the National Curriculum for schools,[68] while a 'Life in

---

[63] See C. Allen and J. Neilsen, *Report on Islamophobia in the EU after 9/11* (Vienna: European Monitoring Centre for Racism and Xenophobia, 2002); Commission on British Muslims and Islamophobia, *Islamophobia: Issues, Challenges and Action* (London: Runnymede, 2004); T. Abbas (ed.), *Muslim Britain* (London: Zed Books, 2005), part II.

[64] Department for Communities and Local Government, *Preventing Violent Extremism* (London, 2007), [10]. See further Department for Communities and Local Government, *Preventing Violent Extremism: Next Steps For Communities.*

[65] See Home Office, *Strength in Diversity* (London, 2004), Chapter 2; Commission for Racial Equality, *Britishness* (London, 2005); Lord Goldsmith, *Citizenship: Our Common Bond* (London: Ministry of Justice, 2008).

[66] Gordon Brown, 'Liberty and the role of the state' (Chatham House, 13 December 2005), available at www.guardian.co.uk/politics/2005/dec/13/labour.uk.

[67] See Commission for Racial Equality, *Britishness*; S. Brighton, 'British Muslims, multiculturalism and UK foreign policy' (2007) 83 *International Affairs* 1.

[68] curriculum.qcda.gov.uk/key-stages-1-and-2/subjects/citizenship/index.aspx. See further the Final Report of the Advisory Group, *Education for Citizenship and the Teaching of Democracy in Schools* (London: Qualifications and Curriculum Authority, 1998).

the UK' test was set in 2005 for would-be citizens.[69] After the events of July 2005, added attention was paid to the promotion of citizenship education in supplementary schools and *madrassas*.[70] Prime Minister designate, Gordon Brown, called in 2006 for celebrations of patriotism,[71] with the celebration of Veterans Day (now Armed Forces Day) as a tangible outcome.[72]

During 2006, the 'Prevent' work in local communities was largely transferred from the Home Office to the Department of Communities and Local Government, itself a signal of policy span. An early initiative was the Commission on Integration and Cohesion[73] which, in its 2007 report, *Our Shared Future*, examined issues of diversity, the forging of cohesive and resilient communities, segregation and the dissemination of extremist ideologies. It called for integration and cohesion (not assimilation) and so did not clearly signal an end to the policy of multiculturalism.[74] However, that tenet has weakened.[75] The accusation that multiculturalism encourages de facto segregation[76] and thereby provides a space for extremist rhetoric has gathered traction and has resulted in the rejection of segregated Islamic jurisdictions[77] and criticism (but not banning) of the *burqa* and *niqab*.

Moving to the next strand of policy, support for local solutions, one notable initiative was the Preventing Violent Extremism Pathfinder Fund,

---

[69] See www.lifeintheuktest.gov.uk.

[70] *Hansard*, HC, vol. 440, col. 67, 15 December 2005 (Charles Clarke); Department for Communities and Local Government, *Preventing Violent Extremism*, [12]; Department for Communities and Local Government, *Preventing Violent Extremism: Next Steps For Communities*, [56].

[71] See T. Nairn, *Gordon Brown: Bard of Britishness* (Cardiff: Institute of Welsh Affairs, 2006); McGhee, *The End of Multiculturalism*, Chapter 4.

[72] See www.armedforcesday.org.uk/.

[73] www.communities.gov.uk/archived/general-content/communities/commission integration.

[74] See T. Modood, *Multiculturalism: A Civic Idea* (Cambridge: Polity, 2007); Brighton, 'British Muslims, multiculturalism and UK foreign policy'.

[75] See C. Joppke, 'The retreat of multiculturalism in the liberal state' (2004) 55 *British Journal of Sociology* 237.

[76] Trevor Phillips, the chairman of the Commission for Racial Equality, warned of 'sleepwalking towards segregation': *Sunday Times*, 18 September 2005, 1. See further T. Modood, A. Triandafyllidou and R. Zapata-Barrero (eds.), *Multiculturalism, Muslims and Citizenship* (Abingdon: Routledge, 2005).

[77] See 'Civil and Religious Law in England' (2008), available at www.archbishopofcanterbury.org/1575. Lord Chief Justice Phillips supported the use of Sharia law as a basis for mediation: *The Guardian*, 4 July 2008, 4. The controversy resurfaced in Scotland with the reporting of 'secret talks' with the Muslim Arbitration Tribunal: *The Scotsman*, 9 October 2008, 1.

launched in 2006 to support priority local authorities to develop projects with local partners against extremism.[78]

Under the strand of building civic capacity and leadership, the Preventing Violent Extremism Community Leadership Fund[79] has been used for capacity-building of groups and projects and support for faith leaders as well as Local Forums against Extremism and Islamophobia.[80] Various initiatives have been taken, including: developing opportunities for young British Muslims to be leaders and active citizens; and a national campaign and coalition to empower Muslim women, including through a Muslim Women's Advisory group.[81]

The final strand, strengthening faith institutions and leadership, was arguably the prime driver at the beginning of the Preventing Extremism Together initiative. There are around 1,400 mosques, plus 130 Islamic schools, in the United Kingdom. Often their management is not systematic or clearly delineated. The government pointed to a number of notorious cases, such as the North London Central Mosque, where extremists were able to gain prominence.[82]

The most extreme reaction was contained in the Home Office paper, *Preventing Extremism Together: Places of Worship.*[83] It floated the creation of a legal process whereby those controlling a place of worship could be required by court order 'to take steps to stop certain extremist behaviour occurring in a place of worship ("a requirement order")'.[84] A failure to comply with the order would be an offence, and if the activity persisted, a further order could restrict the use of the place of worship ('a restriction of use order') which could include temporary closure.[85] In the event, the policy was not enacted. There were concerns in principle about the state regulation of religion, as well as practical difficulties over defining 'worship' and 'places of worship'.[86] However, the Charity Commission has set

---

[78] Department for Communities and Local Government, *Preventing Violent Extremism: Pathfinder Fund* (London, 2007). See K. Kellard, R. Mitchell and D. Godfrey, *Preventing Violent Extremism Pathfinder Fund: Mapping of Project Activities 2007/2008* (London: Department for Communities and Local Government, 2008).

[79] Department for Communities and Local Government, *Preventing Violent Extremism: Community Leadership Fund* (London, 2007).

[80] See also Home Office, *Countering International Terrorism* (London: Cm 6888, 2006), [58]; Department for Communities and Local Government, *Preventing Violent Extremism: Next Steps For Communities*, [28].

[81] Ibid., [44].   [82] Ibid., [7].   [83] London, 2005.

[84] Ibid., [17]–[18].   [85] Ibid., [21].

[86] See *Hansard*, HC, vol. 440, col. 167, 15 December 2005 (Charles Clarke); Lord Carlile, *Proposals by HMG for Changes to the Laws against Terrorism* (London: Home Office, 2005), [109].

up a Faith and Social Cohesion Unit to encourage registration as a charity so as to improve governance and oversight.[87]

Other, less radical, ideas were acted upon in relation to faith institutions. One was to be the establishment of a National Advisory Council of Imams and Mosques. In the event, the Mosques and Imams National Advisory Board (MINAB) was launched in 2006 with the backing of groups such as the Muslim Council of Britain. Guidelines have been issued, including basic standards of English, about the accreditation of foreign imams which can also be used in entry and visa decisions.[88] As well as MINAB, the Department for Communities and Local Government has also floated the idea of a board of academics and scholars based in the Universities of Oxford and Cambridge to ensure that any false ideology is corrected.[89]

Next, the Home Office launched in September 2005 a £5 million Faith Communities Capacity Building Fund to support all faith communities to play an active role in building a cohesive society by engaging with communities and government.[90] This initiative closed in 2008. Another project, the 'Preventing Extremism Together' (PET) Scholars' Roadshows, involves government funding for the promotion of religious scholars who can offer alternatives to extremist doctrines.[91]

The 'Prevent' work in local communities became a requirement for all local authorities in 2008, when the Home Office and Department of Communities and Local Government issued a National Indicator, *Self Assessing Local Performance Against NI 35: Building Resilience to Violent Extremism*.[92] It offers a checklist of issues and processes (based around understanding and engagement of Muslim communities, the development of an action plan and effective oversight) rather than levels of outcomes to be secured. Measurement of achievement remains highly problematic. The Department for Communities and Local Government's own 'Rapid Evidence Assessment' could proffer no evidence as to which interventions worked best, other than the general observation that outreach and peripatetic work was preferable to hierarchical reliance on leaders.[93]

---

[87] Department for Communities and Local Government, *Preventing Violent Extremism*, [21].

[88] Ibid., [20].

[89] Department for Communities and Local Government, *Preventing Violent Extremism: Next Steps For Communities*, [65].

[90] *Improving Opportunities, Strengthening Society* (London: 2005), [4.18].

[91] Home Office, *Countering International Terrorism* (London: Cm. 6888, 2006), [58].

[92] www.opm.co.uk/resources/565/download.

[93] *Preventing Support for Violent Extremism through Community Interventions: A Review of the Evidence* (London: 2010).

Localities with predominant Muslim populations are not the only type of 'community' to become the focus of 'Prevent' work. Attention will next be turned to prison and educational communities.

C. Prison communities

There has been a growing appreciation of the dangers presented by extremist groups in prisons. There are now around 110 imprisoned jihadis who are in a position, both through their characters as celebrity prisoners and through their commitment to their cause, to subvert other Muslim prisoners.[94] Such allegations have been levelled against Dhiren Barot, who was convicted in 2006 for bomb plots.[95] Another example is Whitemoor Prison, where the presence of eight out of 120 Muslim inmates, skewed staff perceptions of dangerousness and produced a regime which most of those prisoners viewed as unsafe.[96] The Directorate of Security has highlighted the problems not only of extremism but also the difficulties of staff in understanding and handling cultures which they do not share.[97] The main concentration of terrorist remand prisoners is in Belmarsh Prison,[98] and violence with white inmates has occurred as well as radicalisation.[99]

The Prison Service recognises the problem of violent extremism but also the complexity of distinguishing threats to security and demands for religious autonomy.[100] Responses have included training for HM Prison Service (HMPS) Imams.[101] A Prison Service Extremism Unit was instituted in 2007 within the high security estate to deal with these problems and the interplay between political extremists and gang cultures.[102]

The HM Chief Inspector of Prisons' thematic review, *Muslim Prisoners' Experiences*, in 2010 found that Muslim terrorist prisoners form under 1

---

[94] See Home Office, *The United Kingdom's Strategy for Countering International Terrorism Annual Report 2010* (London: Cm. 7833, 2010), [3.07]; D. A. Pluchinsky, 'Global jihadist recidivism' (2008) 31 *Studies in Conflict and Terrorism* 182; M. S. Hamm, 'Prison Islam in the age of sacred terror' (2009) 49 *British Journal of Criminology* 667.

[95] *The Observer*, 10 February 2008, 4.

[96] HM Chief Inspector of Prisons, *Report on an Unannounced Full Follow-up Inspection of HMP Whitemoor* (London, 2008), [3.79].

[97] *The Guardian*, 26 May 2008, 11.

[98] HM Chief Inspector of Prisons, *Report on a Full Announced Inspection of HMP Belmarsh 8–12 October 2007* (London, 2008).

[99] See *The Observer*, 10 February 2008, 4; *The Times*, 15 April 2008, 22.

[100] See Prison Service, *Race Equality Scheme Annual Report 2006–2007* (London, 2007), [3.13].

[101] See Home Office, *Countering International Terrorism*, [51].

[102] *Hansard*, HL, vol. 714, col. 229, 12 November 2009 (Lord Bach).

per cent of the 10,300 Muslim prisoners in England and Wales but that they had an undue impact on shaping the perceptions of prison staff toward the non-terrorist Muslim inmates, leading to undue feelings of distrust and lack of safety. She called for a national strategy for Muslim prisoners, with better monitoring of treatment of religious needs and instances of religious conversion, better opportunities for education and discussion about religion, more staff training, enhanced dialogue and better links with external community and faith groups.

D. Educational communities

The susceptibility to extremism of higher educational communities may be a problem because of the supposed impressionable nature of the student population.[103] Some view the situation as dire.[104] However, the evidence for any linear connection between the undoubted availability of radical materials and the engendering of violence is more ambiguous. The leading case of *R* v. *Zafar*[105] centred upon Bradford University students who were accused of planning to travel and train in Pakistan, as well as fight in Afghanistan. However, the prosecution revealed evidence of curiosity, immaturity and incredulity but could not sustain evidence of a formed intent as to the commission of violence.

The more realistic assessment of the government is that there is evidence of a 'serious threat' of extremism but that higher education is not 'awash' with jihadis[106] and the value of free expression remains of countervailing importance. Indeed, it is a legal duty for universities to promote free speech for outside speakers under the Education (No. 2) Act 1986, s. 43.[107] The advice in *Promoting Good Campus Relations* is didactic rather than directive – giving examples and encouraging attention. It also adopts a narrow focus on 'Violent Extremism in the Name of Islam'[108]

---

[103] E. Hussein, *The Islamist* (London: Penguin, 2007), Chapters 6–7. For a wider perspective, see E. Gerstmann and M. J. Streb (eds.), *Academic Freedom at the Dawn of a New Century* (Stanford University Press, 2006); Network for Education and Academic Rights (www.nearinternational.org/).

[104] A. Glees and C. Pope, *When Students Turn to Terror* (London: Social Affairs Unit, 2005).

[105] [2008] EWCA Crim 184.

[106] B. Rammell, Speech on Academic Freedom, University of Leeds, 17 June 2008.

[107] Department for Education and Skills, *Promoting Good Campus Relations; Working with Staff and Students to Build Community Cohesion and Tackle Violent Extremism in the name of Islam at Universities and Colleges* (London, 2006), [1.2]–[1.3].

[108] Ibid., Chapters. 2–3.

which caused criticism of the demonisation of Muslims. A later edition in 2008 avoided this error, though it is al-Qaeda which alone merits an Appendix.[109] More comprehensive and precise guidance is given in the Universities UK document, *Promoting Good Campus Relations*.[110]

The highlighting of the threat of extremism has left some university authorities in a state of nervous agitation. Their concerns have been heightened by offences of the direct and indirect encouragement of terrorism under ss. 1 and 2 of the Terrorism Act 2006.[111] However, it is a defence under s. 2(9) to show that the published statement neither expressed the accused's views nor had his endorsement and that it was clear, in all the circumstances of the statement's publication, that it did not express his views and did not have his endorsement. Nevertheless, when an academic officer suspects or believes that a student intends to use the available materials for terrorist purposes rather than scholastic endeavour, she should 'as a good citizen' report the matter to the security authorities.[112] This injunction was taken to heart by the University of Nottingham when a student, Rizwaan Sabir, was arrested in 2008 for the downloading of materials in connection with his postgraduate research, together with his friend and ex-student, Hicham Yezza, to whom he had passed the materials.[113] The offending materials were the al-Qaeda training manual seized in Manchester and published in redacted form since 2005 on the US Department of Justice website.[114] Both were later released without charge. The Vice Chancellor, Sir Colin Campbell, warned that it is illegitimate in his university to study the operational or tactical aspects of terrorism, as opposed to its political dimensions.[115] The official reviewer of terrorism legislation, Lord Carlile, had cautioned against the danger that academic research into terrorism might be 'turned into samizdat activity'.[116]

While one former Secretary of State for Education, Ruth Kelly, called for universities to adopt a policing role over 'unacceptable behaviour',[117]

---

[109] Department for Innovation, Universities and Skills, *Promoting Good Campus Relations, Fostering Shared Values and Preventing Violent Extremism in Universities and Higher Education Colleges* (London, 2008).
[110] (London, 2005).
[111] See Walker, *Terrorism and the Law*, Chapter 8.
[112] *Hansard*, HL, vol. 676, col. 629, 7 December 2005 (Baroness Scotland).
[113] See *The Guardian*, 24 May 2008, 8; freehicham.co.uk.
[114] www.usdoj.gov/ag/manualpart1_1.pdf, 2005.
[115] *Times Higher Educational Supplement*, 24 July 2008.
[116] Lord Carlile, *Proposals by Her Majesty's Government for Changes to the Laws against Terrorism*, [28].
[117] *The Times*, 16 September 2005, 8.

McCarthyite purges of staff and students have been avoided. However, more insidious threats remain to academic freedom, including the practices of surveillance which are routinely undertaken within campuses, such as of computer usage,[118] and also the threat of blacklisting and greylisting based on expressed opinions.[119] There was also the Voluntary Vetting Scheme of potential applicants to around thirty higher education institutes within the United Kingdom. Those institutes were advised of concerns about proliferation and technology transfer whenever the student applicant came from one of ten target countries and was interested in one of twenty-one disciplines.[120] That scheme was replaced in 2007 by the more comprehensive Academic Technology Approval Scheme (ATAS), covering forty-one disciplines and potentially all countries.[121] Finally, leading scientific journals have agreed to the evaluation (and rejection) of papers on grounds of usefulness to terrorists.[122]

These measures have not allayed all concerns, and two further incidents have kept the pressure on universities to monitor and restrict. First, Operation Pathway in 2009 involved several foreign students arrested in Manchester and Liverpool for plotting terrorism. There were no convictions, but some were subsequently ordered to be deported.[123] The allegation was that they had obtained student visas for admission to 'bogus' colleges as a cover for their terrorism activities. However, no substantial evidence of terrorism links to any 'bogus' college was uncovered in this or other cases.[124] The second case involved Umar Farouk Abdulmutallab who attempted to detonate a bomb on an aircraft bound for Detroit on 25 December 2009. A review panel rejected the proposition that radicalisation had occurred because of his studies at University College London.[125]

---

[118] See Data Retention (EC Directive) Regulations 2009 SI 2009/859.

[119] See www.stoptheboycott.org.

[120] See House of Commons Science and Technology Committee, *The Scientific Response to Terrorism* (2003–4 HC 415), [200].

[121] www.fco.gov.uk/en/about-us/what-we-do/services-we-deliver/atas.

[122] See M. S. Lindes, 'Censuring science', in Gerstmann and Streb, *Academic Freedom at the Dawn of a New Century*, p. 90.

[123] See Lord Carlile, *Operation Pathway* (London: Home Office, 2009); *XC* v. *Secretary of State for the Home Department* (SC 02, SC 77–82, 2009). Deportations were halted in 2010 because of risk of torture.

[124] House of Commons Home Affairs Committee, *Bogus Colleges* (2008–9 HC 595), [15]–[16].

[125] *Umar Farouk Abdulmutallab: Report to UCL Council of Independent Inquiry Panel* (London, 2010). Cf. *Radicalisation on British University Campuses* (London: Quilliam 2010).

Apprehension about extremism in educational establishments has even extended to school children. Following consultation through a youth panel and head-teachers' forum,[126] the Department for Children, Schools and Families has launched a toolkit, *Learning Together to be Safe*.[127] It sensibly accepts that there is no 'typical profile' of extremists but encourages matters of political and social controversy to be tackled though understanding of extremist narratives, preventing harm (especially through Internet filters) and supporting the vulnerable while 'affirming the multiple dynamic identities we all have' alongside values such as rights and equality.[128] The encouragement to engage with radical ideas is welcome, but the document is stronger on warning than on elaborating any positive alternative narratives.

E.   Foreign communities

The engagement with Muslim communities in the United Kingdom has been extended into foreign policy on the basis that problems affecting diaspora within the United Kingdom may be aggravated by malign influences elsewhere. It has been claimed that 75 per cent of terrorist plots in Britain bear some link to Pakistan.[129] The Foreign and Commonwealth Office has therefore engaged in 'Prevent'.

Some work is undertaken by an Islamic Media Team (established in 2002 as the Islamic Media Unit to explain and discuss British government policies to the Islamic world and to brief Ministers and officials) and then by an Engaging with the Islamic World Group (established in 2004 and offering assistance and advice to different country sections and staging seminars and colloquia abroad as well as arranging for scholars to tour Britain such as under the 'Radical Middle Way' banner).[130] Other programmes include[131] the Global Opportunities Fund to support the development of effective, accountable and democratic institutions and the promotion of human rights. The Global Opportunities Fund later merged with the Islamic World Programme to form a new combined Countering Terrorism and Radicalisation Programme.[132]

---

[126] Department for Children, Schools and Families, *The Children's Plan* (London: Cm. 7280, 2007), [6.64].
[127] (London, 2008).   [128] Ibid., pp. 21, 31.
[129] *Daily Telegraph*, 14 January 2009, 14.   [130] www.radicalmiddleway.co.uk.
[131] See Home Office, *Countering International Terrorism* [49].
[132] Home Office, *The United Kingdom's Strategy for Countering International Terrorism Annual Report 2010* (London: Cm. 7833, 2010), [3.14].

Turning to initiatives abroad, a major focus has been the activities of religious schools, *madrassas*, especially those in Pakistan, the ancestral home to 43 per cent of British Muslims[133] who continue to send 'home' their teenage sons for cultural reasons. The sometimes malign impact of *madrassas* was highlighted by investigations into the backgrounds of the July 2005 London bombers. The ringleader, Mohammad Sidique Khan, had visited Pakistani *madrassas* during 2003 and 2004.[134] A response was the announcement in 2006 by the Foreign and Commonwealth Office of financial aid to Pakistan to help them regulate the schools.[135] However, *madrassas* continue to retain significant political force, and Pakistani state regulatory impacts have been at best uncertain or at worst 'a shambles'.[136] It is most unlikely that current Foreign and Commonwealth Office initiatives will prove decisive.

4. Security 'Prevent' responses

The policing of terrorism in the United Kingdom has long shaped policing organisational change. Within the Metropolitan Police, a Special Branch was formed in 1883 to respond to the then Irish bombing campaign. The sector is also normally marked by features such as secrecy and unaccountability. The relevant agencies refuse for operational reasons to engage with local communities, inform them what is going on or account to them afterwards. There is also limited accountability to the courts.

These traditional features within the tactic of 'Pursue' sit uncomfortably with a 'Prevent' strategy and so there is pressure for change. What was appropriate for countering isolated foreign extremists, when there was no referent local community, is less salient now that the government and the police must rely on communities for support in counter-terrorism. Thus, the pressures of counter-terrorism have sparked changes in organisational formations and styles which recognise the need to apply neighbourhood policing and a multi-agency approach to counter-terrorism.[137]

---

[133] Rehman, 'Islam, "War on Terror" and the Future of Muslim Minorities in the United Kingdom', 846.
[134] See Intelligence and Security Committee, *Report into the London Terrorist Attacks on 7 July 2005* (London: Cm. 6785, 2006), pp. 17–18; see also Home Office, *Report of the Official Account of the Bombings in London on 7 July 2005*, p. 15.
[135] *The Independent on Sunday*, 19 November 2006, 46.
[136] International Crisis Group, *Pakistan: Karachi's Madrasas and Violent Extremism* (Brussels: Asia Report no.130, 2007), p. i.
[137] Home Office, *From the Neighbourhood to the National* (London: Cm. 7448, 2008), [1.49]–[1.51]. Given this local emphasis, proposals for police force mergers have not been implemented: see HM Inspectorate of Constabulary, *Closing the Gap* (London, 2005).

The new institutional formations are as follows. First, local police Special Branches began to be reformed into regional clusters in 2003, and a parallel process is the regional co-ordination of ports policing.[138] Next, in 2006, the Metropolitan Police formed the Counter Terrorism Command (SO15) which has merged its Special Branch with the more operational Anti-Terrorist Branch, which had begun in the 1970s in response to Irish terrorism. The new unit links intelligence analysis and development with investigations and operational support activity. It has 1,500 staff and is headed by a National Co-ordinator of Counter-Terrorism Investigations who will normally take charge of major terrorist investigations anywhere in the country. Corresponding Counter-Terrorism Units (CTUs) have been formed in four regions, including West Yorkshire.[139] Another national appointment is the National Co-ordinator for Community Engagement who works on activities to combat radicalisation, to promote community confidence and to reassure communities that are most affected. Outside the Counter-Terrorism Units, other areas have developed sixteen Regional Intelligence Cells (RICs). The CTUs are larger than the RICs, the difference being mainly the possibility of action as well as intelligence gathering. But regionalisation does not equate with remoteness.

As for the Security Service (MI5), it opened for the first time ever in Britain a number of regional offices in order to gather intelligence more easily from the regions potentially affected by jihadi activities: West Yorkshire, the West Midlands and Greater Manchester. Furthermore, the Security Service has become more open in its advice work through a network of Counter-Terrorism Security Advisers, most of whom are Special Branch officers, who are located within the Centre for the Protection of National Infrastructure,[140] which is within the Security Service and also incorporates the National Infrastructure Security Co-ordination Centre and MI5's National Security Advice Centre.

Overlain upon this structure are several institutions which oversee the work of 'Prevent'. The National Prevent Delivery Unit in the Association of Chief Police Officers' (Terrorism and Allied Matters) structure handles national strategy, and delivery is handled by a national Police Prevent Board and Regional Police Prevent Co-ordinators.[141]

---

[138] See HM Inspectorate of Constabulary, *A Need to Know: HMIC's Thematic Inspection of Special Branch and Ports Policing* (London, 2003).

[139] See S. Bebbington, 'The good fight' (2008) 116 *Police Review* 34.

[140] www.cpni.gov.uk.   [141] Home Office, *Delivering the Prevent Strategy*, [3.2]–[3.3].

As for operational changes, equally radical developments have occurred. The National Policing Plan 2005–8 required the police to build and increase trust and confidence within minority faith communities as part of their counter-terrorist strategy.[142] The police emphasise that terrorism policing must involve local police units and local community partners. For instance, the bomb manufacturing activity by the 7/7 bombers caused leaves to fall from the trees outside their flat because of chemical fumes. Why did no one report this, ask the police?[143] As a result, new counter-terrorism initiatives should reflect this wider network. A prime example is Project Channel whereby in twelve police force areas responsible citizens in Muslim communities will provide an early warning system for the identification of extremists.[144] Social intervention in the forms of counselling and engagement in approved activities are then applied. Though this non-security label is put upon the project, there arise attendant dangers of loose labelling and net-widening: 'Which self-appointed busybodies will use what yardstick to define a "radical", an "extremist" or "a Wahhabi"?'[145]

Added to Project Channel, the Preventing Violent Extremism Community Leadership Fund has been diverted to mentoring and related community work.[146] However, there is as yet no de-radicalisation programme,[147] though the idea has been proposed for prisoners.[148]

[142] (London: Home Office, 2004) [3.60].

[143] Speech by Andrew Staniforth, Conference on Crime and Disorder Act 1998 (Centre for Criminal Justice Studies, University of Leeds, 2008).

[144] See Home Office, *Channel: Supporting Individuals Vulnerable to Recruitment by Violent Extremists* (London, 2010).

[145] H. Siddiqui, 'Muslim-bashing dilutes our democratic values', *Toranto Star* 11 June 2006, p. A17.

[146] See Home Office, *The Prevent Strategy: A Guide for Local Partners*, p. 27; Department for Communities and Local Government, *Preventing Violent Extremism: Next Steps For Communities*, [51].

[147] Cf. Counter-Terrorism Implementation Task Force, *First Report of the Working Group on Radicalisation and Extremism that Lead to Terrorism: Inventory of State Programs* (Rome: United Nations Interregional Crime and Justice Research Institute, 2008); G. Audenaert, 'De-radicalisation and the role of police forces', in R. Coolsaet (ed.), *Jihadi terrorism and the Radicalisation Challenge in Europe* (Aldershot: Ashgate, 2008); O. Ashour, *The De-Radicalization of Jihadists* (Abingdon: Routledge, 2009); Bjørgo and Horgan (eds.), *Leaving Terrorism Behind*, chaps. 10–13; Horgan, *Walking Away from Terrorism*; J. Horgan, and K. Braddock, 'Rehabilitating the Terrorists?' (2010) 22 *Terrorism and Political Violence* 267.

[148] See J. Brandon, *Unlocking Al Qaeda* (London: Quilliam 2009); P. R. Neumann (ed.), *Prisons and Terrorism* (International Centre for the Study of Radicalisation and Political Violence, London, 2010).

These policies of community policing of terrorism have limits. The Counter-terrorism Commands do not yet regularly attend local neighborhood forums to explain their actions, though they recognise the future value in doing so. Their liaison with communities tends to be *ex post facto* – to explain operations and hear representations. They are also seeking to increase their community interface through recruitment from ethnic Asian localities. Targets have been issued for the recruitment of ethnic minorities into the police since 1999, but they have generally not been met.[149]

Another limitation is the assessment of the impact of counter-terrorism policing. The relevant Public Service Agreement 26, one of thirty such documents which describe how governmental targets will be achieved and how performance against these targets will be measured, does not contain, because of national security, any published indications as to targets, accountability or governance.[150]

5. Conclusion

The emergence of 'neighbour' terrorism has prompted a welcome reappraisal of counter-terrorism strategy and has placed a radically strong emphasis on 'Prevent'. The results have been impressive in terms of the amount and breadth of activity.[151] This redesign of counter-terrorism strategy has been significant[152] and has occurred despite the apparent paradox between the perceived globalising nature of terrorism represented by al-Qaeda and the growing localism of its proponents. While the strategic thrust is correct, policy delivery can be criticised on five grounds.

The first point of criticism concerns the apparently slow and uncertain rate of achievement. It is perhaps a consequence of greater reliance upon localism that uniformity becomes more difficult to secure. The approach has been one of 'civil association' in which multi-agency players are afforded discretion within a broad framework rather than an 'enterprise association' with imposed requirements to achieve specified

---

[149] Cf. Home Office, *Staff Targets for the Home Office, the Prison, the Police, the Fire and the Probations Services* (London: 1999); J. Riley, D. Cassidy and J. Becker, *Statistics on Race and the Criminal Justice System 2007/8* (London: Ministry of Justice, 2009), p. 185.

[150] HM Treasury, *PSA Delivery Agreement 26: Reducing the Risk to the UK and its Interests Overseas from International Terrorism*, available at www.hm-treasury.gov.uk/pbr_csr07_psaindex, [1.3].

[151] See further Home Office, *Pursue, Prevent, Protect, Prepare*, [9.09].

[152] Compare the absence of holistic policy during the Northern Ireland campaign: *Operation Banner* (London: Army Code 71842, 2006).

goals.[153] The result has often been an emphasis on general community engagement with limited connection to extremism.[154] This inherent drawback of reliance on localism is not assisted by the fact that no special mechanisms of audit have yet to be put in place.[155]

Second, concerns have been raised about the direction and emphasis of 'Prevent' policies. In particular, the authorities selected at the outset what appeared to be the easy target of mosques, whereas the problem of extremism does not lie in mosques in general (leaving aside the isolated cases of foreign rabble-rousers who have been now largely silenced), but in deeper social problems. This misfire has in part been recognised by the government,[156] though the focus on mosques still persists to some degree.[157] Furthermore, once the obvious target is discarded, it becomes a more complex and diffuse task to respond since 'evidence suggests that extremists are increasingly moving away from mosques to conduct their activities in sports centres, paintball centres or activity camps, private homes or other premises to avoid detection'.[158]

The third criticism is that the official analysis of radicalisation took too long to reach an acceptable level of sophistication. Early attempts too often emphasised external agency, such as foreign Imams or Internet sites. However, the evidence from the bombings and plots of 2005 and later suggests that there are deeper-lying causes within diaspora communities, which relate to social and political conditions and generational changes in identities. Further work should also be undertaken on the non-linear relationship between radicalisation and violence.[159]

The fourth criticism is that inherent in the new policy initiatives towards communities is the net-widening of policing. The point is of course shared with critiques of non-terrorism community policing initiatives in recent decades.[160] The 'Prevent' work can become perceived as a mode of embedding political policing within local services so as to allow

---

[153] M. Oakeshott, *On Human Conduct* (Oxford: Clarendon Press, 1975), pp. 279–311.
[154] See Kellard *et al.*, *Preventing Violent Extremism Pathfinder Fund*, p. 64.
[155] Intelligence and Security Committee, *Could 7/7 have been Prevented?*, [180].
[156] Home Office *Preventing Extremism Together: Places of Worship* (London, 2005), [10].
[157] House of Commons Communities and Local Government Committee, *Preventing Violent Extremism* (2009–10 HC 65), [83].
[158] *Report of the Official Account of the Bombings in London on 7th July 2005*, Annex B, [2].
[159] See L. Richardson, *What Terrorists Want* (London: John Murray, 2006); Directorate of General Judicial Strategy, *Policy Memorandum on Radicalism and Radicalisation* (The Hague: Ministry of Justice, 2005); National Coordinator for Counterterrorism, *Radicalisation in Broader Perspective* (The Hague: Ministry of Justice, 2007).
[160] See A. Crawford, *The Local Governance of Crime* (Oxford University Press, 1997).

intelligence-gathering and intrusion which generates a lack of trust in the programme.[161] To this charge might be added the state control of religion and the censorship of radical discourse. One response might be an organisational division in 'Prevent' activities with those concentrating on community cohesion falling within the remit of local authorities and those dealing with individuals or organisations at risk assigned to the police.[162]

The fifth point concerns the dissonance between the community approaches and other aspects of government policy. Leaving aside the negative impacts of foreign policy such as the invasion of Iraq, there may be costs to the construction of social capital even within other aspects of counter-terrorism. The sacrifice of rights to expression caused by the Terrorism Act 2006 has been mentioned. The government champions this policy as closing down channels to the encouragement of terrorism, but it correspondingly delimits comprehension and dialogue. There are also costs in terms of community support from the policing aspects of security measures such as stop and searches. Its negative outcomes were recorded by the House of Commons Home Affairs Committee[163] which found 'a clear perception among all our Muslim witnesses that Muslims are being stigmatised by the operation of the Terrorism Act: this is extremely harmful to community relations'. Another instance of clashing strands of CONTEST concerned the installation in 2010 of surveillance cameras in Washwood Heath and Smallwood, areas of Birmingham with large Muslim populations. On the one hand, the cameras were presented by the Safer Birmingham Partnership as combating anti-social behaviour and crime. On the other hand, the communities were not told that the cameras were financed by a grant from the Association of Chief Police Officers (Terrorism and Allied Matters) and included covert cameras with automatic number plate recognition technology. After protests, those covert cameras were removed.[164]

---

[161] Kundani, *Spooked! How not to Prevent Violent Extremism*; House of Commons Communities and Local Government Committee, *Preventing Violent Extremism*, [40].

[162] See House of Commons Communities and Local Government Committee, *Preventing Violent Extremism*, [148], [169], [172], [173]; Bartlett *et al.*, *The Edge of Violence*, p. 41; Briggs, 'Community engagement for counterterrorism', 972.

[163] Home Affairs Committee, *Terrorism and Community Relations* (2005–6 HC 165-I), [153]. See also G. Mythen, S. Walklate and F. Khan, '"I'm a Muslim, but I'm not a terrorist"' (2009) 49 *British Journal of Criminology* 736, 744; Defence Science and Technology Laboratory, *What Perceptions do the UK Public Have Concerning the Impact of Counter-Terrorism Legislation Implemented since 2000?* (London: Home Office Occasional Paper 88, 2010).

[164] See S. Thornton, *Project Champion* (Kidlington: Thames Valley Police, 2010).

The impact of excessive policing may not necessarily translate into the generation of new terrorists. The jihadi cause is not the same as Northern Ireland Republicanism, where the aggressive imposition of security policies within tightly drawn communities was a prime aggravating factor.[165] Nevertheless, insensitive interventions will create social tensions which deter communities from being forthcoming with information and assistance.[166]

The official assessment remains that 'the UK faces a serious and sustained threat from terrorism', as a result of which the security level was increased to 'severe' in January 2010.[167] Within this heightened sense of public vulnerability, an emphasis on community safety will have mounting cogency to police and politicians, and so further 'Prevent' measures can be anticipated. Their attractiveness is driven especially by the emergence of 'neighbour' terrorism and by the impetus towards responses to the anticipatory risk of attack rather than perpetrated crime. But with risk-based responses comes uncertainty, giving rise to the inevitability that innocent persons and communities will be unfairly affected and that the discomfort of state intervention will not easily be confined to exceptional situations bounded by temporal, spatial or communal divisions.[168] Even with that price being paid, and even with communities onside, one can be certain that not every catastrophe will be averted. The dismal prospect is that, no matter how much the state strives to 'Prevent', the current emanations of violent extremism will take many decades to assuage.[169]

---

[165] Cf. S. Greer, 'Human rights and the struggle against terrorism in the United Kingdom' [2008] *European Human Rights Law Review* 163; C. Pantazis and S. Pemberton, "From the "Old" to the "New" Suspected Community' (2009) 49 *British Journal of Criminology* 646.

[166] See T. M. McDonnell, 'Targeting the foreign born by race and nationality' (2004) 16 *Pace International Law Review* 19.

[167] Cabinet Office, *National Risk Register of Civil Emergencies 2010 Edition* (London, 2010), [2.77].

[168] O. Gross, 'Chaos and rules' (2003) 112 *Yale Law Journal* 1011, 1073–89.

[169] House of Commons Defence Select Committee, *UK National Security and Resilience* (2007–8 HC 718), 21 October 2008, p. 63 (Lord West).

Postscript: Restatements of prevent policies appeared in 2011 after the completion of this chapter. For the United Kingdom, see: Home Office, *Prevent Strategy* (London: Cm 809b, 2011). For the United States, see President of the United States, *Empowering Local Partners to Prevent Violent Extremism* (Washington DC, 2011).

PART III

Anti-terrorism law and policy in Asia

11

Singapore's anti-terrorism laws: reality and rhetoric

MICHAEL HOR

1. Introduction

This chapter discusses the incipient debate over the power of detention without trial that appears to have been brewing over the last decade. The apparently uncontroversial use of such powers against militant Islamic networks stands in contrast to the emergence of detainees of past operations contesting the official story that their detentions were justified. This chapter also looks at terrorism-related legislation in Singapore and observes the strange phenomenon that prosecutions under those laws inevitably involve non-terrorists, and sounds a caution against 'hysterical' sentencing of non-terrorists.

Singapore's current concern about terrorism began just three months after the events of 9/11 in the United States. In December 2001, a group of thirteen people suspected of associating with the Jemaah Islamiyah (JI), an extremist Islamic network, were detained without trial[1] under the Internal Security Act (ISA) – a piece of legislation dating from the immediate post-World War II context of militant communism.[2] A string of similar detentions were to follow in the next decade; the latest, at the time of writing, was announced on 6 July 2010.[3] The power of detention without trial has been at the forefront of these operations, and its use appears to have generated fresh justification, at least from the official viewpoint, for its continued existence after more than sixty years. Curiously, the last

---

[1] Ministry of Home Affairs, Press Releases, 5 January 2002, available at www.mha.gov.sg/index.aspx. Information about Operation JI is most conveniently culled from this website. Although they contain specific URLs, these occasionally change and the parent website is provided here instead, from which the specific press release (and all press releases and ministerial statements in subsequent references) may be easily searched.
[2] See my chapter in the first edition of this work, 'Law and terror: Singapore stories and Malaysian dilemmas', in Victor V. Ramraj, Michael Hor, and Kent Roach (eds.), *Global Anti-Terrorism Law and Policy* (Cambridge University Press, 2005), Chapter 13. The legislation itself, and all other current legislation, is available at statutes.agc.gov.sg/.
[3] Ministry of Home Affairs, Press Release, 6 July 2010.

decade has also witnessed the emergence of alternative accounts of opera-tions past, primarily of former detainees, which argue that the power of detention without trial had been wrongly used. These other voices urge either the abolition or the severe curtailment of the power of detention. This chapter explores the core questions of whether such a power ought to exist, and if so, what would amount to a legitimate use of it.

Although the focus of real anti-terrorism measures has been detention without trial – i.e. a method which short circuits the normal criminal law and process – there has also been a flurry of legislative anti-terrorism activity. New terrorism-related offences have been created and rules gov-erning terrorist-related situations have been laid down. Curiously, when these terrorism-inspired offences started to come before the courts, the context of these prosecutions has almost invariably been unrelated to actual terrorism. Yet we see prosecutors pressing for extra-deterrent sen-tences on the basis that the laws were enacted principally to deal with terrorism. This chapter also looks at this phenomenon and asks if these new offences were really needed in the first place, and now that they are in place, whether they create a real potential to distort proportionate senten-cing when they are used in non-terrorism contexts.

There is of course much more that has been done, and that has happened,[4] in Singapore than can be recounted in a discussion of this nature. It is necessarily selective, but hopefully not in a way which materi-ally affects that which is indeed discussed.

2.   My ISA, right or wrong

The last decade has witnessed a fascinating tension between the apparent proof of the necessity for the power of detention without trial as evidenced

---

[4] For example, perhaps the most politically significant event has been the escape of the head of the Singapore branch of the JI, Mas Selamat, from detention. In a manner worthy of the best action movies, he made his getaway from a toilet window, over a wall and across the Johor Straits, drifting on some flotation device: Parliamentary Debates, Committee of Inquiry on Mas Selamat Kastari's Escape, 21 April 2008, available at www.parliament. gov.sg/parlweb/hansard_search_latest.jsp. He was eventually arrested in Malaysia and remains in detention there at the time of writing: Joint Press Conference by Prime Minister Lee Hsien Loong and Prime Minister Dato' Sri Mohd Najib bin Tun Haji Abdul Razak, 22 May 2009, available at www.pmo.gov.sg/News/Speeches/Prime+Minister/Join t+press+conference+transcript.htm. Unfortunately, there appeared to have been little in this fascinating turn of events which is relevant to the present discussion, except perhaps the observation that the unexpected freedom of Mas Selamat did not actually lead to any immediate harm to anyone, or to any apparent long-term prejudice to national security which the enforcement authorities could not handle.

by its intensive use against the JI,[5] and a growing alternative view that the power of detention has been used in the past in circumstances which fall short of those which might reasonably have been perceived as threats to national security. It is likely that the years to come will see a heightening of debate on the two central questions which must dog any regime of detention without trial: should such a power exist at all, and if so, under what circumstances ought it to be exercised?

The lynchpin of official justifications of the power of detention without trial is the claim of a sterling track record of its sparing and correct use.[6] In short, the power has only ever been used when it was necessary to prevent intolerable harm to society, and in circumstances in which the regular criminal law and processes would have been in some manner unsatisfactory. The rise of alternative stories – which tell essentially of zealous people detained, but who were bent on anything but unlawful violence to subvert law and order – ought surely to lead to a re-examination of the official discourse. It is not the intent of this chapter to adjudicate between the contrasting accounts. Its purpose is the more modest one of describing the phenomenon.

Operation Coldstore in 1963 was perhaps the largest single exercise in detention without trial: more than 100 persons were detained, and a few were to remain in detention for over twenty years. The story is an exciting one of a young Lee Kuan Yew, then in the Opposition, successfully defending the editors of a publication called *Fajar* against sedition charges. The lawyer and his clients appeared to join forces for a while, but they split over merger with Malaysia. The rift culminated in Lee Kuan Yew, who became Prime Minister after the 1959 elections, effecting a massive detention exercise against some his former clients whom he had helped acquit, ahead of the merger with Malaysia. The official account was that the detentions were necessary as the detainees were Communists bent on subverting the existing democratic order by any means, foul or fair. Lee Kuan Yew had ridden the Communist tiger and managed to cage it just in time to prevent unlawful subversion of the political system.[7]

---

[5] A handful of detainees were involved with the similar but apparently unrelated network called the Moro Islamic Liberation Front (MILF), which appears to specialise in the liberation of Islamic Mindanao in the Philippines.

[6] Home Affairs Minister Wong Kan Seng declared that 'we do not invoke such powers lightly': Ministerial Statement, 14 January 2004.

[7] Perhaps the most sophisticated and accessible account is found in Mark Ravinder Frost and Yu-Mei Balasingam Chow, *Singapore: A Biography* (Singapore: National Museum of Singapore, Editions Didier Millet and Hong Kong University Press, 2009). See also the almost equally interesting 'blog behind the book', available at www.singaporebiography.com/.

In 2001, a Coldstore detainee of seventeen years, Said Zahari, editor of a Malay daily when he was detained, published a book called *Dark Clouds at Dawn: A Political Memoir*, which he was to follow up in 2007 with *The Long Nightmare: My 17 Years as a Political Prisoner*.[8] The thrust of these publications was clear: although the Coldstore detainees had a different vision of Singapore, perhaps a more socialistic one, they were no more intent on achieving their aims through unlawful means than their captors were. They were a legitimate and lawful political opposition in a democratic political system, so the alternative story goes, and their only sin was to oppose the ruling party. Film-maker Martyn See was to shoot a video of Said Zahari being interviewed on the subject matter of the books. Curiously the film was banned by the government but not the books.[9] Martyn See was later to film another Coldstore alumnus: Lim Hock Siew who was detained for almost twenty years and spoke on the video to similar effect. This too was to be banned in 2010.[10] Yet one cannot help but be struck by the tokenism of these prohibitions. For better or for worse, the Internet has made it intolerably costly to prevent Singaporeans from access to these materials effectively. The government didn't even try to ban the Said Zahari books, or another publication to like effect by several Coldstore alumni – *The Fajar Generation: The University Socialist Club and the Politics of Postwar Malaya and Singapore*.[11] Of course, the banned videos which had to be taken down from the Internet by See himself were at once loaded onto other websites by others.[12]

Operation Spectrum in 1987 was perhaps the second largest exercise until the recent JI-related detentions. Twenty-two essentially Catholic social activists were detained initially. The government's account was that they were members of a Marxist conspiracy inspired by liberation theology and the 'People Power' movement in the Philippines, prepared to use any means, including violence and bloodshed, to achieve their ends.[13]

---

[8] Respectively (Kuala Lumpur: Institute of Social Analysis, 2001) and (Kuala Lumpur: Utusan Publications and Distributors Sdn Bhd, 2007).

[9] See the account in Martyn See's blog, available at singaporerebel.blogspot.com/2007/04/zaharis-17-years-rated-pg-by-censors.html.

[10] See singaporerebel.blogspot.com/2010/07/here-we-go-again-govt-bans-another.html.

[11] Poh Soo Kai, Tan Jing Quee and Koh Kay Yew (Malaysia: Strategic Information and Research Development Center, 2010).

[12] See www.youtube.com/watch?v=aaLaeDN4t2U; www.youtube.com/watch?v=Aia_lZ7ccdI.

[13] The barrage of governmental statements following the arrests are conveniently collected in theonlinecitizen.com/2009/05/straits-times-of-may-87-four-days-of-government-statements-on-marxist-conspiracy/.

A few other detentions followed, notably that of former Solicitor-General Francis Seow, who was dramatically detained while he was waiting to interview one of the original detainees whom he represented as counsel. His detention was on the grounds of colluding with a US embassy official in fomenting opposition politics in Singapore.[14] Many of the detainees were to appear on television in recorded interviews in which they appeared to admit to the government's allegations. Most were released thereafter, but eight were re-detained when they issued a statement after their initial release repudiating the apparent confessions, saying that they were practically coerced into submitting to the televised interviews. Most were released a second time after they signed a fresh statement reinstating their televised confessions, on severe conditions that they were not to speak to the Press about their detentions.[15]

In 1994, Seow, who had left Singapore, published his account of the detention in a book called *To Catch a Tartar: A Dissident in Lee Kuan Yew's Prison*, essentially refuting the allegation that he ever was engaged with the Americans to interfere with Singapore politics.[16] The book was never officially banned, but bookshops were reportedly advised by the government not to sell it.[17] Activist Seelan Palay,[18] in the footsteps of See, recently filmed an interview with Seow; the video has been submitted to the government for approval and a decision has yet to be made on the application.[19] Alternative accounts by alleged conspirators themselves were to trickle out,[20] culminating in the publication of a book called *Beyond the Blue Gate: Recollections of a Political Prisoner* in 2010 by Teo Soh Lung,[21] one of the initial detainees. It paints a picture of sustained coercion under detention to admit to governmental allegations. Again, the thrust of these alternative stories is that the alleged conspirators were really Catholic social activists working towards a fairer social order within the existing

---

[14] Governmental justifications were exhaustively aired in Parliament: Parliamentary Debates, beginning 25 May 1988, vol. 51, col. 68.

[15] The events are succinctly related in the Court of Appeal judgment in *Chng Suan Tze v. Minister of Home Affairs* [1989] SGCA 16.

[16] Yale University South-East Asia Studies, 1994.

[17] It has been remarkably difficult to locate official confirmation of this. See the anecdotal account of Martyn See at singaporerebel.blogspot.com/2006_01_01_archive.html.

[18] See Sue-Ann Chia, 'Film-makers on the fringe', *Straits Times*, 7 September 2008, available at www.asiaone.com/News/Latest%2BNews/Showbiz/Story/A1Story20080906–86237.html.

[19] See the entry in Seelan Palay's blog, available at seelanpalay.blogspot.com/2009/09/seelan-palay-submits-francis-seow-video.html.

[20] See, e.g., Fong Hoe Fang (ed.), *That We May Dream Again* (Singapore: Ethos, 2009).

[21] (Malaysia: Strategic Information Research and Development Center, 2010).

democratic political order, not demented revolutionaries who would not
bat an eye if their activities resulted in violence and bloodshed. The book
remains, at the time of writing, on the shelves. Nor has Teo Soh Lung been
re-detained yet again, or prosecuted for making false declarations to the
government.[22] This was quickly followed by similar revelations from the
alleged 'mastermind' of the conspiracy – Vincent Cheng – who publicly
denounced his detention in a recorded speech.[23]

Perhaps the deepest cut of all came not from an ex-detainee, but with
the disclosure in 2009 by former Prime Minister Goh Chok Tong in a
book called *Men in White: The Untold Story of Singapore's Ruling Political
Party* where it was revealed for the first time that a prominent government
Minister, S. Dhanabalan, had left the Cabinet because he 'was not fully
comfortable with' the detention of the alleged Marxist conspirators.[24] The
discomfort must have been intense enough for that very well regarded
Minister to give up office. This naturally raises the question of whether
there were others in the government who felt the same way but who did
not act upon it.

What seems to have happened in the last decade is a gradual, but dramatic by Singapore standards, build-up of a case against the power of
detention without trial, or at least against some prominent instances in
which it has been used. Equally striking is the apparently tolerant official
attitude towards this movement. It is not yet clear whether this is borne
out of an implied agreement with the alternative accounts,[25] increasingly
mature governance, or simply of resignation to a cyberworld inimical to
censorship without intolerable cost. Once again, the task of adjudicating between the official and alternative stories would require much more
evidence than is now publicly available. Nonetheless, this intensifying
challenge to the official story might well become in time the germ of significant public concern about the power of detention without trial.

---

[22] Apparently to secure their release, the re-detainees had to execute statutory declarations
that their press release alleging ill treatment and coercion (during the initial detention)
was untrue.

[23] See www.youtube.com/watch?v=D8ohOwc79Sc and www.youtube.com/watch?v=37pv4
rRWD7o&feature=related.

[24] Sonny Yap, Richard Lim and Weng Kam Leong (Singapore: Marshall Cavendish, 2010),
pp. 467–8.

[25] This, of course, is officially denied. When the Lim Hock Siew video was banned on 14
July 2010, that former detainee was charged with making 'baseless accusations against
the authorities' and giving 'a false portrayal' of his 'previous activities' in order to excul-
pate himself and to undermine public confidence in the Government: Ministry of Home
Affairs Press Release, 12 July 2010.

As if to counterbalance this development, there appears to have been little public, or even international, controversy over the most recent 'operation' – one which is on-going at the time of writing and which bore no snappy title as was the practice before. I take the liberty of naming it Operation JI because almost all of the detainees were alleged to have had links or at least sympathies with Jemaah Islamiyah (JI), a kind of South-East Asian version of al-Qaeda intent on murder and mayhem to further a holy war against perceived enemies of Islam – essentially the United States and its allies. Operation JI commenced very soon after the 9/11 attacks in the United States. In the first round, fifteen persons were arrested and thirteen detained for varying degrees of involvement in plans to attack certain sites in Singapore associated with the United States and/or its allies.[26] Several other rounds were to follow, and the latest at the time of writing was announced as recently as 6 July 2010.[27] The operation is on-going and it seems that it will be so indefinitely.[28]

What is striking is that, just as the alternative and potentially damaging accounts of previous operations were beginning to stir, the negative reaction to the JI detentions, both domestic and international, has been muted at best – involving only a token protest or two by the usual human rights organisations and journalists.[29] Perhaps it was because the Western world could now understand and feel Singapore's fear. Nonetheless, we need to ask if indeed detention without trial was the only satisfactory way of dealing with this threat. What was it about the regular criminal law and its processes that made that avenue unsuitable? This official attempt was made in 2007 in response to a letter published in the local press:[30]

> Such special power is especially important in terrorism-related cases. These cannot afford to follow the standard processes and rules of evidence of normal criminal cases. Terrorists plan and carry out their acts with great stealth and secrecy and often in conspiracy with foreign operatives. The priority must be to act swiftly to prevent an attack, and not to

[26] Ministry of Home Affairs Press Release, 30 May 2002, probably contains the most detailed account.

[27] Ministry of Home Affairs Press Release, 6 July 2010.

[28] The most recent disclosure of the total still being detained was in a Ministerial Statement in Parliament, Parliamentary Debates, 9 April 2007, vol. 83, where it was revealed that of the thirty-nine people then currently in detention, at least ten were from the initial JI arrests. Presumably the rest were made up of those detained for JI activity subsequently, and for other non-terrorist reasons, namely espionage.

[29] For example, Amnesty International issued a protest, and the government rebuttal is found in a press release on 4 June 2004.

[30] Ministry of Home Affairs Press Release, 17 June 2007.

wait for the terrorists to kill large numbers of innocent people and only
arrest, charge and convict them after the event.

Again, it is probably dangerous to make any assessments only from what
is publicly available, but here it is the turn of the academic observer to
be in a position where there is no better alternative. At the risk of over-
simplification, it is convenient to group the detainees into a few broad
categories.

First is the core group of those who were detained very early on, and
those whom the authorities wanted to detain from the start but had fled
the country.[31] They were complicit in rather advanced plans to blow up several targets of symbolic significance – for example, the UK and Australian
High Commissions, Changi Airport and train stations which US navy
personnel and their families were likely to use. They had either master-
minded, helped plan or carried out reconnaissance, surveillance and other
preparatory operations. In all probability their plans would have come to
fruition, just as the 9/11 attacks did, had the authorities not uncovered the
plot. The official justification was that 'the standard processes and rules
of evidence of normal criminal cases' would have been deficient. It is difficult to understand why. 'Great stealth and secrecy' is not the exclusive
preserve of religiously motivated terrorists. Indeed, there was evidence
aplenty presented before the ISA Advisory Boards: witnesses, confessions
made before a judge, video-recordings taken as part of the planning.[32]
There appears to be no reason why most of it would have been inadmissible. That what they have committed was a crime cannot be in serious
doubt: it would have clearly fulfilled the elements of a conspiracy to commit any number of crimes ranging from murder to mischief, the cumulative punishment for which must be considerable. The priority is indeed
to prevent the plans from being carried out, but the normal criminal law
does not expect the police to wait until 'large numbers of innocent people'
are killed. The concepts of abetment, by instigation, intentional aiding or
conspiracy, and of attempt are well established in the normal criminal law
to capture this very kind of situation.[33]

---

[31] Most of those in the two largest rounds of arrest – December 2001 and August 2002 –
were probably in this category: Ministry of Home Affairs Press Release, 19 September
2002.

[32] Ministry of Home Affairs Press Release, 30 May 2002.

[33] Abetment by either instigation, intentional aiding or conspiracy is punishable under the
Penal Code, ss. 107 and 109. Attempts to commit a crime are generally punishable under
s. 511 of the Penal Code.

The second category consists of detainees who had not been involved in actual terrorist operations. They were members of the JI or the MNLF or sympathisers and had undergone some sort of general military or terrorist training in preparation for future operations.[34] Most of them were not detained at the early stages of Operation JI but on subsequent investigation. Whether or not what each of them did would amount to an attempt to commit terrorism-related crimes, or an abetment thereof, would depend very much on exactly what they have done. One might have thought that a decision to undergo terrorist training would be very strong evidence of a settled intention to commit terrorist crimes, or at least a firm intention to join in the conspiracy thereof. But the normal criminal law asks the very questions that someone in security services would be expected to: have they reached a point where it can be said that they have become a real danger to those whom they have decided to harm? That is where, essentially, the normal criminal law draws the line between what is a crime and what is not.[35] Similarly, it does not appear that there is likely to be unusual evidential problems. I would place into this category some other detainees whose primary role was to 'educate' and persuade others of the righteousness of waging a holy war by terrorist means.[36] These too will pose no unusual problems for the normal criminal law: they are potentially liable for abetment by instigation of violent crimes. That the contemplated terrorist activities are outside of Singapore is also not a problem: the Penal Code has always criminalised abetment of a crime to be committed outside of Singapore.[37]

The third category is more penumbral. This is the territory of the 'self-radicalised' detainee. The distinguishing feature amongst these detainees is that they desired, but failed, to make contact with established terrorist organisations in order to join their activities. Most prominently, in 2007 a lawyer who practised and taught at an educational institution had been self-radicalised through the Internet. He went to a Middle Eastern country to learn Arabic and purchased an air ticket to Pakistan to try to make contact with a militant group to join

---

[34] See, e.g., the 'Karachi Cell' detentions: Ministry of Home Affairs Press Release, 18 December 2003.

[35] In the law of abetment and attempt, much care is taken to ascertain that there was a settled intention to commit or to abet the crime. In the law of attempt, the 'substantial step' test is just such a calculus.

[36] See e.g., Mahfuh bin Haji Halmi, Ministry of Home Affairs Press Release, 15 September 2004.

[37] Section 108A.

them. But he was apprehended and returned to Singapore.[38] The most recent publicly known detention, announced in July 2010, is that of a twenty-year-old who was self-radicalised online. He established online contact with a suspected al-Qaeda recruiter who encouraged him to fight in Afghanistan. He searched online for information about bomb-making and produced and posted online a video 'glorifying martyrdom and justifying suicide bombing'. He is probably the first detainee to be held on purely online activity.[39] Again, it is difficult to understand why the criminal law would have been unsuitable. What the lawyer did is classically the domain of the law of attempt: has he gone far enough to warrant the intervention of the state? Our twenty-year-old would-be bomber has probably not gone far enough to attract the law of attempt, but posting the video might well amount to abetment by instigation of unlawful bombing. There does not seem to be a convincing case that these situations are so exceptional that the criminal law cannot deal with them.

There is another category – not of detainees but those on whom Restriction Orders have been placed.[40] They are not incarcerated but are subject to curfew, reporting and non-association conditions. It is clear that they posed no real danger and understandably the criminal law would probably not have been a suitable recourse. It is more in the nature of a slap on the wrist, and one wonders if in a small and efficient country like Singapore, Restriction Orders are needed at all. There are very few cases indeed where persons under Restriction Orders have 'relapsed' – and in the one situation that I could uncover, someone who was under such an order but continued to associate with and provided assistance to MILF members and sympathisers was subsequently detained.[41] But it is difficult to believe that his continued involvement would not have been detected without the Restriction Order.

So what could the real reason have been? I suggest that the key lies in a 2004 Ministerial Statement to this effect:

---

[38] Ministry of Home Affairs Press Release, 8 June 2007, available at www.mha.gov.sg/index. aspx. See also the case of Muhammad Zamri bin Abdullah, Press Release, 24 January 2008, available at www.mha.gov.sg/index.aspx.
[39] Ministry of Home Affairs Press Release, 6 July 2010.
[40] For example, the twelve who were issued 'ROs', Ministry of Home Affairs Press Release, 14 January 2004.
[41] Mohd Agus bin Ahmad Selani, Ministry of Home Affairs Press Release, 24 January 2008.

On a Measured Approach to Protect Inter-Racial Harmony

The security investigation since Aug 2002 has in fact dealt with about 130 persons.

One of the key operational challenges of this investigation is how to move without causing undue public alarm and traumatizing communal relations.

Wherever practicable, the approach taken, therefore, has been a discreet and carefully measured one.[42]

This, I think, is the true rationale for Operation JI and the manner in which it has been conducted. The 'communal' or racial context is this: each and every target of Operation JI was Muslim and almost all were Malay. Singapore has a majority, 75 per cent, Chinese population and a significant minority, 13 per cent, Malay population who are almost invariably Muslim.[43] The history of race relations in Singapore has in the not-too-distant past been a rocky one, especially in the framework of Malaysia (of which Singapore was once a part), its much larger neighbour whose racial demographics are roughly reversed,[44] and in Southeast Asia where the Indonesian giant is even more overwhelmingly Malay and Muslim.[45] Both Malaysia and Indonesia have a history of delicate racial and religious interactions.[46] The need to preserve the peace between the racial components of Singaporean society is never far from official thinking. It was not so much that the criminal process could not deal with the JI, but the calculation must have been that the cost of doing so – the publicity and potential contentiousness of so many trials against accused persons of a particular race and religion – outweighed the cost of using the power of

---

[42] Ministry of Home Affairs Press Release, 14 January 2004.

[43] Statistical tables from 2009 Yearbook, Singapore Department of Statistics, available at www.singstat.gov.sg/stats/themes/people/demo.html.

[44] CIA World Factbook, www.cia.gov/library/publications/the-world-factbook/geos/my.html (50 per cent Malay, 24 per cent Chinese in 2004).

[45] CIA World Factbook, www.cia.gov/library/publications/the-world-factbook/geos/id.html (86 per cent Muslim – almost all of whom would be Malay/Indonesian). The intricacies of anti-terrorism efforts in an overwhelmingly Muslim *majority* jurisdiction is described in Hikmahanto Juwana, Chapter 12, this volume.

[46] The merger with Malaysia in 1963–5 is generally seen to have been potentially disastrous for race relations. Indonesia was for a time in a 'Confrontation' with Singapore and Malaysia, and had championed a greater Malay world comprising Malaysia, the Philippines and Indonesia. Internally, the incident referred to even now is that of Maria Hertogh in 1950, where a court decision to award custody of Maria to her biological and Christian parents, although she had grown up during World War II, apart from them, as a Muslim. Race riots ensued. See generally Frost and Chow, *Singapore: A Biography*. It is interesting that the Internal Security Act (or more correctly, its predecessor) was totally powerless to defuse this.

detention without trial, where the information can be carefully controlled for content and tone. Indeed, it had to be handled in a 'discreet and carefully measured' manner – in order to prevent or at least contain minority feelings of being victimised, and majority prejudices against the minority. The distinct impression one gets is that the government did not want to treat the detainees as criminals – i.e. bad people who chose to do evil – but as misguided individuals who could be salvaged by right teaching. The philosophy was a therapeutic, and not a retributive or deterrent, one. In short, and somewhat surprisingly, the power of detention without trial was used as a more merciful alternative than the criminal law.[47]

Perhaps the Singaporean public, majority and minority, could sense this compassionate motivation behind the use of the Internal Security Act in the JI context; protest from either side has been very muted, if any. Indeed, even the proponents of alternative stories in connection with previous operations have not in express terms condemned the use of the power against the suspected JI operatives. Could it be the case that there are situations in which detention without trial is preferable to a criminal prosecution? If so, this is the crucial divide and the key question is whether the government has good reasons why it needs to proceed under the Internal Security Act as opposed to the normal criminal process. The government is keen to impress on all who care to listen that there is 'due process' under the Internal Security Act and that there are significant checks and balances.[48] But thus far, this has been taken to

---

[47] This reason for using the power of detention without trial might well appear to be counterintuitive for someone approaching the matter from a strong tradition of 'due process'. Surely, it might be observed, the use of the criminal process is more likely to quell communal suspicions and dissatisfaction: the government would then be seen to be doing everything properly and above board. The peculiarity about Singapore is the high degree of trust its population confers on governmental decisions. In the eyes of a vast majority of Singaporeans, the government can be trusted to correctly identify terrorists without the stamp of approval of a criminal trial. A very recent revelation by the Minister of Home Affairs, Singapore Parliamentary Debates, 22 November 2011, disclosed that the family of the brother of escaped detainee Mas Selamat (see above note 4) had been prosecuted for harbouring a 'prisoner of State' (Penal Code, s. 130) and sentenced to varying terms of imprisonment *in camera*. It is yet unclear if this signals a change towards a greater reliance on the regular criminal process, or if resort to the criminal law was here seen as the more compassionate alternative given the relatively less serious charges which they faced. They were sentenced to serve terms of imprisonment of between three and eighteen months.

[48] See, e.g., Ministry of Home Affairs Press Release, 17 June 2007, where it was asserted that '[in] all cases of detention without trial under the Internal Security Act (ISA), the due process of the law is observed'. I explored the differences between regular and ISA due process in 'Terrorism and the criminal law: Singapore's solution' [2002] *Singapore Journal of Legal Studies* 43–4.

mean primarily that the government has to satisfy the President and the Advisory Committee that the detainees were indeed a threat to national security. However, the fact that a particular individual may be a threat to national security does not in itself justify the use of detention without trial – for it is at least conceivable that the normal criminal law can also deal with the situation. The important question is whether there are convincing reasons why the person concerned ought not to be tried in court as opposed to being detained without trial. That should be the focus of all endeavours to put in place safeguards against the abuse of the power. The legislation should direct the mind of the government to this issue, and the Advisory Committee ought to demand strict justification of the use of the power in preference to a criminal charge. I would also argue that the exemption clause hastily put in place in heat of the skirmish with the 'Marxist conspirators' in 1989[49] should be repealed and the power of judicial review reinstated, perhaps even in the stronger form of a supervisory jurisdiction akin to the judicial function in the context of professional misconduct proceedings. If we have no choice but to recognise that there can be legitimate exceptions to the right to a trial, then due process – i.e. process which is due and not just that which is now prescribed – ought to be rethought along these lines.[50] Perhaps this is the only satisfactory way of preserving the power in the context of what appears to be increasing misgivings about its use in the past.

3. The importance of being terrorist legislation

One might have thought that with the formidable array of terrorist-related legislation holding over from Singapore's tumultuous pre-Independence

---

[49] See the discussion in Hor, 'Law and terror: Singapore stories and Malaysian dilemmas'.

[50] This chapter does not permit a full-blown discussion on how 'due process' can be improved. A very important factor is the existence of alternative investigative mechanisms: it is often the case that supervisory bodies have no choice, practically, than to accept the case as constructed and presented to them by the security services. Without an independent investigative machinery, it is unlikely that wrongful use of the power of detention can ever be detected. Another innovation that ought to be considered is the use of 'special advocates' (to represent the detainee). These advocates have security clearance to look at sensitive material and can be relied upon not to disclose it to the detainee. Although one can imagine the difficulties of conducting a 'defence' whilst labouring under a duty not to disclose critical evidence to the detainee, it is nonetheless better than an advocate who cannot even see the evidence: see the account of Sir Nicholas Blake, Judge of the High Court, 'The UK experience of special advocates', available at jura.ku.dk/cec/nyheder/blake/specadvoc.pdf/. See also Nicola McGarrity and Edward Santow, Chapter 6 this volume.

days, there would have been little need to introduce fresh provisions to deal with terrorism. Yet there has been a degree of legislative activity on this front. It is not the intent of this chapter to be comprehensive. What follows is admittedly selective.

First off is an odd set of what appears to be purely symbolic amendments to the existing law. A new 'illustration' was added to the Penal Code in 2007 to make it explicit that, in terrorist type situations, the defence of necessity is available to naval personnel who have to sacrifice six innocent people in order to save 100 from an imminent terrorist attack.[51] One might have thought that this hardly needs clarification. Similarly, another illustration was inserted into the defence of reasonable mistake: a police officer is absolved from liability if he or she acts to counter a mistakenly but reasonably perceived terrorist threat. Yet again, technically, this hardly needs to be spelt out. In the same category is the addition of a fresh provision in the Criminal Procedure Code permitting police officers to use lethal force to prevent a terrorist attack.[52] A 'terrorist act' is defined in such a manner – involving 'serious violence' and the like – that it is highly unlikely that, even without the new provision, the police would not have been able to kill if that was the only way to prevent the harm from occurring. Perhaps more controversial is the inclusion of 'serious damage to any building or structure'. It surely cannot be the intent that lethal force can be used to prevent a 'terrorist' from destroying a small tent in circumstances where there would be no danger to anyone. It is likely that some condition of proportionality and reasonableness prevails even under the new provision. In short, these measures are legally futile: the law has not, in my view, changed; nor have they made things any clearer. At worst they might give our law enforcers a false sense of security if they are somehow under the impression that the usual requirements of reasonableness and

---

[51] Illustrations (b), (c) and (d) to s. 79 and illustration (c) to s. 81. I have been made aware of the German Constitutional Court decision of 15 February 2006 (1 BvR 357/05) which held that it was an unconstitutional violation of the right to life and human dignity for security forces to sacrifice even one innocent life in order to save many others. There has been no significant judicial elucidation of the defence of necessity in Singapore, but I entertain considerable doubt if the constitutional right to life in pragmatic Singapore will ever be interpreted in like manner, and predict that if the illustration is ever called into question, the court is likely to approve it. See the lucid discussion (in the context of Australia) in Simon Bronitt, 'The limits of necessity: part IIIAAA, *Defence Act 1903* (Cth)', available at law.anu.edu.au/ACMLJ/Bronitt-Navy.pdf. I share his sentiment, on p. 2, that if United Airlines Flight 93, which was apparently blown up from within during the 9/11 incidents, had been shot down instead by security forces, 'it would not have created significant moral or political controversy'.

[52] Criminal Procedure Code Act 2010, ss. 63(2),(3).

proportionality are lifted for terrorist cases. The legislative motive was good – it was to encourage law enforcers not to be too timid – but I hope that law enforcers do not come away thinking that the law in terrorist situations is somehow special and more permissive than in other dangerous circumstances.

Then there is the more familiar phenomenon of the creation of overlapping crimes, often with increased penalties. Typically, there are already in existence criminal provisions which prohibit a certain kind of activity generally, whether there is an element of terrorism or not. But the legislature creates a special offence to deal with terrorist situations, often accompanied by a significant increase in penalties. A good example is the creation of a terrorist bomb hoax offence under Regulation 8 of the United Nations (Anti-Terrorism Measures) Regulations 2001 which carries a maximum penalty of five years' imprisonment.[53] This is notwithstanding an old Penal Code prohibition (s. 182) against giving false information to a public servant, which is punishable by up to a year's imprisonment. A third layer is the more recent offence of sending a false message through a telecommunications system under the Telecommunications Act (s. 45) – which is punishable by up to three years' imprisonment, or seven years if it concerns an explosive. Another example is the offence of terrorist bombing under the Terrorism (Suppression of Bombings) Act (s. 3), where the punishment is a mandatory death penalty if death or serious injury was intended, or otherwise a mandatory life imprisonment. Apart from an array of obvious offences under the Penal Code (murder, for example), there is in addition the Explosive Substances Act which contains offences punishable with ten years' imprisonment and caning.[54] One wonders why this complex multi-layering of similar offences is thought to be desirable for one and the same criminal activity. They bear an ominous potential of being used as bargaining chips: plead guilty to the lesser charge or we shall proceed with the greater one. No doubt the Terrorism (Suppression of Bombings) Act does contain useful provisions on extraterritoriality,

[53] Itself a piece of subsidiary legislation under the United Nations Act. I have elsewhere pointed out that there might be a problem with the legality of the creation of a bomb hoax offence by means of such a device. Security Council Resolutions 1373 of 2001 and 1390 of 2002, which the regulations purport to give effect to, make no mention of hoaxes. It appears that the perceived need for multiple overlapping offences has become an global phenomenon: see, e.g., the Philippine experience in H. Harry L. Roque Jr., Chapter 13 this volume.
[54] All primary legislation in Singapore is available without cost online at statutes.agc.gov. sg/, but unfortunately this source does not include subsidiary legislation.

mutual assistance and extradition, but again the multi-layering does give rise to potential problems of coercive plea bargaining.

Strangely enough, notwithstanding these and other legislative innovations prompted by terrorism, I have not been able to detect a single instance in which a real (suspected) terrorist has been charged under any of them in the past decade. Instead, as we have seen, the government has chosen to employ the extra-criminal route of detention without trial. It may be that, in the future, prosecutions will be used instead, but in the context of the most important and perhaps only terrorist threat now and in the foreseeable future – the JI network – that is unlikely. Yet this has not prevented the prosecution from using terrorist-related legislation against non-terrorists and in the course of doing so pressing for extra-deterrent sentences because the provisions were anti-terrorism inspired.

There has been a striking proliferation of bomb hoax cases in the past decade. The recent decision of *Public Prosecutor* v. *Wong Shan Shan* contains a convenient list of cases that have come before the court.[55] We see a very similar pattern of moderately to seriously mentally-imbalanced accused persons falsely making or reporting bomb threats in different contexts. The disturbing thing is the huge discrepancy in sentencing: a case in 2004 (*PP* v. *Sim Gim Tiong*),[56] for example, resulted in a cumulative punishment of sixty months' imprisonment for what was essentially a single episode of four repeated bomb hoax phone calls over the course of slightly over one hour. Other cases in this category resulted in sentences like forty-four months' imprisonment (*PP* v. *Nanda Sudhir Kumar*)[57] and thirty months' imprisonment (*PP* v. *Neo Khoon Sing*).[58] On the other hand there have also been a line of cases like *Wong Shan Shan* itself where probation, fines and very short terms of imprisonment were ordered. Granted there were aggravating circumstances in the cases more severely dealt with – the number of people involved, inconvenience to law enforcers and the like – but can any of this ever justify the difference between probation and a five-year jail term (the sentence in *Sim Gim Tiong*)? No doubt creating a bomb hoax ought to be an offence and suitably deterred, but it must be remembered that the accused persons here are not terrorists and are almost invariably mentally imbalanced. Perhaps the apparent inconsistency is because of judicial hesitation about the appropriate weight to be given to anti-terrorism rhetoric in sentencing non-terrorist but terrorism-related offenders.

---

[55] [2010] SGDC 193.   [56] [2004] SGDC 273.
[57] [2008] SGDC 54.   [58] [2008] SGDC 225.

It appears to have become the practice of prosecutors to press for extra-deterrent[59] sentences on the grounds of anti-terrorism, or for judges to take note of the context of terrorism, for a whole range of crimes – from immigration offences,[60] to credit card fraud,[61] to money-laundering-related offences, to illegal arms sales,[62] to the importation of toy guns.[63] We cannot be certain about the real impact this has had on actual sentencing,[64] but the difference between a tempered and a hysterical response to anti-terrorism rhetoric can perhaps be illustrated by the currency infringement case of *Luyono Lam* v. *PP*.[65] Section 48C of the Corruption, Drug Trafficking and Other Serious Crimes (Confiscation of Benefits) Act prohibits taking into or out of Singapore more than SG$30,000 without the permission of the authorities. Luyono, a legitimate money-changer in Jakarta, had brought more than that sum into Singapore on a few occasions, without permission. He had known of the requirement but thought that a breach of the rule would be considered to be 'technical' – so he decided to take the convenient path of not reporting. All the money was accounted for as part of his legitimate money-changing activities. At the trial, the District Judge sentenced him to a cumulative term of eight months' imprisonment, drawing attention in the judgment to Ministerial statements made in conjunction with the passing of the provision that:

> there is an urgent need to address the increasingly complex challenges posed by the abuse of our financial systems by terrorists and money launderers. The devastating 9/11 attacks underscore the urgent need for governments around the world to implement measures to suppress terrorist financing as part of the global effort to combat terrorism

---

[59] All punishments are deterrent to a degree, but it has become the practice of Singapore courts to label as 'deterrent' a sentence which has been increased or enhanced in order to deter a particularly urgent or pressing antisocial activity – i.e. a sentence which presumably goes beyond what is proportionate to the wrongdoing.

[60] *Luong Thi Trang Kathleen* v. *PP* [2009] SGHC 250, where on appeal a High Court judge reduced the sentence considerably because the accused was patently not flouting passport regulations for terrorist purposes. See also *PP* v. *Ong Chin Huat* [2008] SGDC 76 and *PP* v. *Md Mahbubul Hoque Md Sirajul Hoque* [2009] SGDC 317.

[61] *PP* v. *Marius Neagoe* [2010] SGDC 125.

[62] *PP* v. *B R Chaandran* [2006] SGDC 301. It was possible that the arms here did go to terrorists, but there was no evidence of that.

[63] *PP* v. *Wong Ser Kuen* [2007] SGDC 330.

[64] Because of the inherent uncertainties in determining the 'going rate' for certain offences.

[65] [2010] SGHC 158.

It took a very senior Judge on an appeal to the High Court to point out that the real targets of the legislation were those involved with money laundering and terrorist activities, which the accused was not. The actual coverage of the prohibition was over-inclusive, although understandably so. The sentences were reduced to a fine of SG$24,000. The prosecution had pressed for a 'deterrent sentence' at trial and apparently sought to defend the sentence on appeal. This particular story had a happy ending, but wonders about other such offenders who for some reason or other did not appeal against their sentences.

We see a curious phenomenon of anti-terrorism inspired laws which have been used on anything but real terrorists. A significant risk then arises of non-terrorist offenders caught by 'over-inclusive' legislation and then subject to deterrent sentences because their offences happen to have the flavour of terrorism. The spectre of terrorism distorting sentencing proportionality exists even for non-terrorism related crimes. The incident which caught the attention of the Singapore public in June 2010 was the discovery that two persons had broken into an MRT (the city underground) installation and spray-painted a carriage with graffiti. One of them was apprehended and sentenced to five months in jail and three strokes of the cane. The other fled the jurisdiction. One only hopes that the anti-terrorism rhetoric that appears to have surrounded this case has not led to an increase in the sentencing tariff, because they certainly were not terrorists.[66]

4. Conclusion: the two towers

One tower is the Internal Security Act with its potent power of detention without trial. The other is the regular criminal law, increasingly peppered with anti-terrorism provisions. It is likely that for the foreseeable future the power of preventive detention is the measure that will be used on real terrorists, or at least when there is also a danger of prejudice to race or religious relations. The breadth of the power of detention is likely to come

---

[66] www.bloomberg.com/news/2010-07-02/swiss-executive-fricker-appeals-singapore-vandalism-caning-jail-sentence.html. The caning sentence is mandated by the Vandalism Act which the accused was charged under – but that is another story: see Michael Hor, 'Singapore criminal law: examining the etiology of exception' (2009) 1 *City University of Hong Kong Law Review* 1. Since the writing of the chapter, the sentence was increased on appeal (*Fricker Oliver* v. *PP* [2010] SGHC 239) to seven months' imprisonment and the mandatory three strokes of the cane. Although the spectre of terrorism may have been implicitly recognised, there was, thankfully, no explicit mention of it in the judgments.

under increasing scrutiny as alternative accounts of previous operations grow. It is not yet possible to foresee if this will result in any moderation of the present system of detention, or of an increased role for the judiciary in supervising the use of the power – but the pressure will certainly be in that direction. It is also likely that more and more anti-terrorism-related offences will enter the normal criminal law, but curiously they will be used much more often against non-terrorists who will then stand in danger of collateral damage in the form of deterrent sentencing if judicial and prosecutorial authorities are not sufficiently vigilant.

12

Anti-terrorism efforts in Indonesia

HIKMAHANTO JUWANA

1. Introduction

Since the Bali Bombing of 12 October 2002[1] the Indonesian government has taken various measures to eradicate terrorism. The government promulgated the Anti-terrorism Law in 2002, which categorised a terrorist act as an extraordinary crime. Subsequently, the three persons most responsible – Imam Samudra, Amrozi and Mukhlas – were brought to justice, convicted and sentenced to death. On 9 November 2008, the three were executed by firing squad.

In spite of its earnestness to prevent terrorism, the government has not succeeded in substantially diminishing the incidence of terrorism in Indonesia. Several terrorist attacks in Jakarta and Bali attracted international attention. On 5 August 2003 the J W Marriott Hotel in Jakarta was attacked. One year after, on 9 September 2004, the Australian Embassy, also in Jakarta, was targeted. Subsequently, on 1 October 2005, Bali was attacked a second time. The most recent attacks occurred in Jakarta on 17 July 2009, when the J W Marriott was bombed again, this time simultaneously with the Ritz Carlton Hotel.

Nevertheless the government, from time to time, has succeeded in overcoming some of the most wanted and influential terrorists in Indonesia. Dr Azahari bin Husin, a Malaysian national, was shot dead on 9 November 2005 in a police raid in Malang, East Java. Noordin M. Top, another Malaysian national who has been suspected of masterminding the bomb attacks in Bali and Jakarta, was shot dead by the police on 17 September 2009 in Solo, Central Java. In the most recent incident, Dulmatin, an influential terrorist, was killed in crossfire with the police on 9 March 2010 in Pamulang, Banten.

This chapter will attempt to analyse the reasons behind the intricacies of anti-terrorism efforts in Indonesia. This chapter argues that the

---

[1] This resulted in the death of 202 Indonesians and foreign nationals.

successful experience of some other countries in eradicating terrorism may not be applicable to Indonesia. Indonesia has peculiar problems which require anti-terrorism efforts to be sufficiently sensitive to the local context.

2. The Anti-Terrorism Law

The Indonesian Anti-Terrorism Law began with the issuance of Government Regulation in Lieu of Law (GRL)[2] No. 1 of 2002 concerning the Eradication of Criminal Acts of Terrorism on 18 October 2002 (Anti-Terrorism Law).[3] On the same day, the government issued GRL No. 2 of 2002, which made GRL No. 1 retroactively applicable to the Bali bombings.[4] In 2003, the Anti-Terrorism Law and GRL No. 2 became law after being confirmed by the legislature. Since its promulgation in 2002 there has been no amendment or revision to the Anti-Terrorism Law.

The Anti-Terrorism Law provides four reasons for its promulgation. First, terrorism had 'claimed human lives intolerably and raised widespread fear among the community and caused loss of freedom and damage of property'. Second, terrorism had maintained extensive networks, posing a threat to national and international peace and security. Third, national legislation was required to implement international conventions relating to terrorism. Lastly, the Anti-Terrorism Law was a matter of urgency because existing legislation in Indonesia was inadequate and failed to deal comprehensively with combating criminal acts of terrorism.[5]

The Anti-Terrorism Law applies to any person (including a corporation[6]) who commits or intends to commit a criminal act of terrorism in Indonesia and/or another nation that has jurisdiction and expresses an intention to prosecute that person.[7] It also applies to criminal acts of terrorism which are committed:

(a) against the citizens of Indonesia outside the territory of Indonesia;

---

[2] GRL is a form of legislation enacted by the President in emergency circumstances. In the hierarchy of Indonesian law, a GRL (or 'Perpu') is one rank below a law or act ('Undang-undang'). Under the Constitution it is required for the Perpu to be brought before Parliament for approval.

[3] For an English translation, see www.law.unimelb.edu.au/alc/indonesia/perpu_1.html.

[4] For an English translation, see www.law.unimelb.edu.au/alc/indonesia/perpu_2.html.

[5] GRL No. 1 of 2002, considerations (b)–(e).

[6] Anti-Terrorism Law, art. 17.

[7] Ibid., art. 3(1).

(b) against the state facilities of Indonesia overseas, including the premises
    of the diplomatic officials and consuls of the Republic of Indonesia;
(c) with violence or threats of violence to force the Government of
    Indonesia to take or not to take an action;
(d) to force any international organization in Indonesia to take or not
    take an action;
(e) on board a vessel sailing under the flag of Indonesia or an aircraft
    registered under the laws of Indonesia at the time when the crime is
    committed;
(f) by any stateless person who resides in Indonesia.[8]

Terrorism is defined generally under the Anti-Terrorism Law as the
intentional use of 'violence or the threat of violence to create a widespread
atmosphere of terror or fear in public or to create mass casualties, by forcibly taking the freedom, life or property of others or to cause damage or
destruction to vital strategic installations or the environment or public
facilities or international facilities'.[9] Those who commit this kind of act
of terrorism can be sentenced to death, life imprisonment or a minimum
sentence of four years and a maximum of twenty years.[10] Those who have
the *intention to commit* an act of terrorism can be sentenced to a maximum of life imprisonment.[11]

Specific acts of terrorism defined under the Anti-Terrorism Law
include a range of specific offences relating to various aspects of aviation
security,[12] explosives, firearms and ammunition,[13] and the use of chemical,
biological and other weapons to 'create an atmosphere of terror or fear in
the general population, causing danger and destruction to vital strategic
installations or the environment or public facilities or international facilities'.[14] Penalties for these offences range from life imprisonment or death
to incarceration for a period of between three and twenty years. It should
be noted, however, that the Anti-Terrorism Law provides that the various acts of terrorism will not be applicable to 'political criminal acts or
criminal acts relating to criminal crimes nor criminal acts with political
motives nor criminal acts with the political objective of obstructing an
extradition process'.[15]

Those who intentionally provide or collect funds[16] or assets[17] with the
'objective that they be used or if there is a reasonable likelihood that the
funds will be used partly or wholly' for criminal acts of terrorism will

---

[8] Ibid., art. 4.   [9] Ibid., art. 6.   [10] Ibid.   [11] Ibid., art. 7.   [12] Ibid., art. 8.
[13] Ibid., art. 9.   [14] Ibid., art. 10.   [15] Ibid., art. 5.   [16] Ibid., art. 11.   [17] Ibid., art. 12.

bear criminal responsibility under the Anti-Terrorism Law and can be sentenced to a minimum of three years or a maximum of fifteen years' imprisonment.[18]

A person also commits an act of terrorism if such person intentionally provides or collects assets with the objective, or if there is a reasonable likelihood, that the assets will be used partly or wholly for:

(a) committing any unlawful act of receiving, possessing, using, delivering, modifying or discarding nuclear materials, chemical weapons, biological weapons, radiology, microorganisms, radioactivity or its components that causes death or serious injuries or causes damage to assets;

(b) stealing or seizing nuclear materials, chemical weapons, biological weapons, radiology, microorganisms, radioactivity or its components;

(c) embezzling or acquiring illegally nuclear materials, chemical weapons, biological weapons, radiology, microorganisms, radioactivity or its components;

(d) requesting nuclear materials, chemical weapons, biological weapons, radiology, microorganisms, radioactivity or its components;

(e) threatening to:

(1) use such nuclear materials, chemical, biological weapons, radiology, microorganisms, radioactivity or its components to cause death or injuries or damage to property; or

(2) commit criminal acts as stipulated in (b) with the intention to force another person, an international organization, or another country to take or not to take an action;

(f) attempting to commit any criminal act as stipulated in (a), (b) or (c); and (g) participating in committing any criminal act as stipulated in (a) to (f).

The sentence for those found guilty is imprisonment with a minimum sentence of three years and a maximum of fifteen years.[19]

Any person found guilty of intentionally providing assistance to any perpetrator by: 'providing or lending money or goods or other assets to any perpetrator of criminal acts of terrorism; harbouring any perpetrator of any criminal act of terrorism; or hiding any information on any criminal act of terrorism' is liable to imprisonment for a minimum term of three years and a maximum of fifteen years.[20] Planning or inciting

---

[18] Ibid., arts. 11–12.   [19] Ibid., art. 12.   [20] Ibid., art. 13.

another person to commit any criminal act of terrorism can result in the death sentence or life imprisonment.[21]

The act expands the scope of criminal liability by providing that anyone who 'conducts any plot, attempt, or assistance to commit any criminal act of terrorism' will be sentenced the same as those who are committing such an act of terrorism.[22] One interesting point to note is that the Anti-Terrorism Law can also be applied to those who provide any assistance, facilities, means or information for any criminal acts of terrorism committed extraterritorially. The sentence is the same as for committing the act of terrorism itself.[23]

Indonesia is obliged to co-operate with other nations in the areas of 'intelligence, policing and other technical cooperation connected with anti-terrorism measures in accordance with the applicable legislative provisions'.[24]

The Anti-Terrorism Law introduces a novel procedure from that of ordinary criminal procedure, namely that an investigator may use any intelligence report as preliminary evidence.[25] However, the Anti-Terrorism Law provides that the adequacy of the preliminary evidence obtained must be determined through an inquiry process by the Head or Deputy Head of the District Court. The inquiry process is conducted in closed session within a maximum period of three working days.[26]

Various extraordinary powers are conferred on investigators, public prosecutors or judges. Investigators may detain any person strongly suspected of committing a criminal act of terrorism based on adequate preliminary evidence for a maximum period of a week.[27] Investigators, public prosecutors or judges are authorised to order banks and other financial institutions to freeze the assets of any individual whose assets are known or reasonably suspected to be the proceeds of any criminal act connected to terrorism.[28] In addition, for the purpose of investigation, the investigators, public prosecutors or judges are authorised 'to request information from banks and other financial institutions regarding the assets of any person who is known or strongly suspected of having committed a criminal act of terrorism'.[29]

In addition, investigators are authorised: 'to open, examine and confiscate mail and packages by post or other means of delivery' and 'to intercept any conversation by telephone or other means of communication

---

[21] Ibid., art. 14.   [22] Ibid., art. 15.   [23] Ibid., art. 16.   [24] Ibid., art. 43.
[25] Ibid., art. 26(1).   [26] Ibid., art. 26.   [27] Ibid., art. 28.   [28] Ibid., art. 29(1).
[29] Ibid., art. 30(1).

suspected of being used to prepare, plan and commit a criminal act of terrorism'.[30] However, investigators may only intercept based on an order of the Head of the District Court for a maximum period of one year.[31]

The Anti-Terrorism Law stipulates other criminal offences related to acts of terrorism. For example, any person who uses violence or the threat of violence or who intimidates detectives, investigators, public prosecutors, solicitors and/or judges who are handling any criminal act of terrorism, so as to hamper the judicial process, is guilty of an offence subject to a minimum sentence of three years and a maximum of fifteen years. A person who provides false testimony, submits false material evidence, or unlawfully influences a witness during a court session or attacks a witness, including the officials in the trial of a criminal act of terrorism, is also guilty of an offence subject to a minimum sentence of three years and a maximum of fifteen years. Witnesses, investigators, judges and their families are entitled to protection by the state before, during and after the investigation process.[32]

The Anti-Terrorism Law also imposes an obligation on the state to pay compensation and restitution to victims and families of victims of terrorist acts.[33] In addition, any individual is entitled to rehabilitation if he or she is discharged of all legal charges of terrorism by the court.[34]

3. Judicial review

In November 2003 the application of Anti-Terrorism Law to the Bali bombing was challenged in the Constitutional Court by Masjkur Abdul Kadir, who was sentenced to fifteen years' imprisonment for his involvement in the deadly attack in Bali. The basis for the challenge was that the retroactive application of the Anti-Terrorism Law contradicted the Constitution, which states that a person has the right not to be tried under a law with retroactive effect.[35]

On 23 July 2004 the Constitutional Court gave its decision that the retroactive application of the Anti-Terrorism Law violated the Constitution. Five out of nine judges agreed while the other four were against. The

---

[30] Ibid., art. 30.   [31] Ibid., arts. 31(1)(a)–(b).   [32] Ibid., art. 33.
[33] Ibid., art. 36.   [34] Ibid., art. 37.
[35] The Indonesian Constitution, art. 28(I)(1) provides as follows: 'The rights to life, freedom from torture, freedom of thought and conscience, freedom of religion, freedom from enslavement, recognition as a person before the law, and the right not to be tried under a law with retroactive effect are all human rights that cannot be limited under any circumstances.'

Constitutional Court argued that, since acts of terrorism do not constitute international crimes, or 'gross violation of human rights', the law may not be applied retroactively, but the Court's decision itself applied only prospectively. The decision raised controversy among Indonesians. Some were concerned that the ruling could lead to the acquittals of those convicted of the Bali bombing. But others felt that the Constitutional Court decided correctly.

The Anti-Terrorism Law has also been challenged in the Constitutional Court for allowing execution by firing squad. This challenge was made by Amrozi, Mukhlas and Imam Samudra, but the Court upheld the constitutionality of that provision.

4. Proposed amendments to the Anti-Terrorism Law

The Ministry of Law and Human Rights is in the process of formulating a draft amendment to the Anti-Terrorism Law.[36] The draft provides for two categories of revisions.

The first category concerns the substance of what is meant by an act of terrorism. New offences have been proposed. These include the selling of materials that have the potential to be used to manufacture explosives or other substances which endanger life or damage the environment. The punishment is to be increased if a terrorist attack using such substances does in fact take place. Another new offence is for someone who has information about a terrorist attack but fails to make a report to the authorities. Once again, an increased punishment is to be applied where a terrorist attack does in fact occur. Furthermore, a person who caused another person or persons to engage in a terrorist attack will also be subject to criminal sanction. The provision is directed at those who preach in a way that encourages other people to be involved in terrorist attack. The proposed amendment also extends the law to legal entities such as corporations.

The second category deals with procedural issues. Under the revision, the police, when investigating a suspect for a terrorist act, may arrest and detain a person for up to thirty days based on initial evidence. Once enough evidence is gathered, the police may detain a suspect for up to 120 days for further investigation. If the case is brought to the prosecutor's

---

[36] The Bahasa Indonesia text is available on the Ministry's website at www.djpp.info/kegiatan-bulan-ini/icalrepeat.detail/2010/10/14/205// YmViMDFkN2I0MjcxNjI5OTc4ZWU5YzgzZDc2ODlZjQ=/ruu-tentang-pemberantasan-tindak-pidana-terorisme.html.

office, the prosecutor may extend the detention for another sixty days. Lastly, if the case is brought to court, the court may extend the detention to sixty days. The detention by the prosecutor and the court may each be further extended for a cumulative maximum of sixty days.

Another set of amendments liberalise the use of evidence not normally permitted under the Criminal Procedure Code. These include intelligence reports, oral communication which is heard or recorded and any data which is recorded. The police will also be permitted to open mail or tap telephone conversations with the permission of a judge. A witness may testify remotely through teleconference facilities. These revisions are still under discussion and they have not yet been considered by the Parliament.

5.   Indonesia's circumstances

Indonesia is a victim of terrorism, but at the same time, is seen as a safe haven for terrorists. Indonesia is also a country which is relatively new in practising democracy. Western-style democracy was introduced in Indonesia after the fall of Soeharto as President in May 1998. Since then Indonesia has experienced a spectacular transition to democracy. The President and Vice-President are elected through a direct vote. Press freedom is guaranteed and the Press enjoys more freedom than it ever has in the past. No draconian law prevents the establishment of political parties and non-governmental organisations.

Indonesia is often said to be the country with the greatest Muslim population in the world. The Muslim population is not, however, homogeneous in its devotion to the practice of Islam: there are those who are religious zealots as there are those who are Muslim only in name. Nonetheless, in recent times, the Muslim population has been increasingly devoted to the practice of Islam. For example, it has become common for Muslim women to wear a headscarf or *hijab*.

There are also strong Islamic political parties. The Partai Keadilan Sejahtera (Prosperous Justice Party) is one of them. In the 2009 General Election it came in fourth. Some successful gubernatorial and mayoral candidates were supported by Partai Keadilan Sejahtera. Some of them have subsequently issued *syariah*-based local regulations. In addition, fundamentalist Islamic groups that are not political parties, which were previously suppressed, have gone public.

The Indonesian government has enjoyed close relations with Western countries, such as the United States, Australia and a number of European countries. Due to its close ties with them the Indonesian government has received assistance from these governments, including assistance in its efforts to eradicate terrorism. Nonetheless, the government from time to time has been critical of the actions of Western governments. The Megawati Administration questioned the legality of the US attack against Afghanistan and Iraq.[37] The Administration insisted that any attack against an independent state should be under the direction of the United Nations.

Another key development has been the rise of human rights. The human rights movement has gained enough momentum to be respected by the government. After the fall of the Soeharto Administration, the government has shown its commitment to human rights by promulgating laws and regulations which advance human rights. In addition, the government has ratified numerous international agreements relating to human rights. That said, there are still problems in enforcing human rights in Indonesia.[38] In recent years, due to the lack of enforcement by the authorities, there have been horizontal conflicts among groups within society. The sources of these conflicts are varied, from ethnic sentiment to clashes between supporters of opposing candidates in gubernatorial and mayoral elections. This has resulted in violations of human rights by the people themselves.

The last feature is that Indonesia still holds a significant number of poor people. According to the 2009 Central Statistics Agency (Badan Pusat Statistik) the proportion of poor people is 14.15 per cent.[39]

6.   Anti-terrorism and the majority Muslim population

Eradicating terrorism in a majority Muslim population has its peculiar challenges. Although official policy has been consistent in its anti-terrorism stance, there has been debate amongst the public at large as to whether these terrorist acts should be condoned.

---

[37] At the 13th APEC Conference in 2001 it was reported that Megawati condemned the act of aggression by the United States against Afghanistan: see 'AS Menyerukan Pembentukan Koalisi Antiterorisme' ('The US urges the formation of a coalition of anti-terrorism'), *Berita Liputan 6 SCTV*, 21 October 2001 available at berita.liputan6.com/luarnegeri/200110/22165/AS.Menyerukan.Pembentukan.Koalisi.Antiterorisme.

[38] For further reading, see Hikmahanto Juwana, 'Human rights in Indonesia', in Randall Peerenboom, Carole Petersen and Hongyi Chen (eds.), *Human Rights in Asia* (New York: Routledge, 2006), pp. 364–83.

[39] See www.bps.go.id/tab_sub/view.php?tabel=1&daftar=1&id_subyek=23&notab=3.

According to those who sympathise with the terrorist cause, victims are but collateral damage for a greater purpose. When the most wanted terrorists – Imam Samudra, Amrozi and Mukhlas – were convicted in court as terrorists, there were those who considered them as heroes. Similarly, when Dulmatin was buried, it was reported that the crowd which gathered was saying that the cloud was forming the Arabic word 'Allah'.[40] The crowd of mourners of more than 2,000 chanted '*Allahu Akbar*' or 'God is greater' as they bid farewell to their 'hero'.[41] This situation prompted Dulmatin's eldest brother, Azam Ba'afut, to claim that his deceased brother was a good man.[42] Another relative, Sahid Ahmad Sungkar, said that Dulmatin is not a terrorist but a holy warrior and his death is the will of Allah.[43]

The government has to be very sensitive in its anti-terrorism efforts. Sometimes an apparently good policy may be perceived negatively by the public. The government has sometimes failed in gathering support from the various Islamic organisations in its effort to eradicate terrorism. Also, if anti-terrorism policy is not communicated well to the public, public uproar and anger might be triggered. In turn, this will provoke anti-government action. Some Islamic groups will support the terrorists instead of the government, if they think that the official anti-terrorism policy is anti-Islam.

Terrorists may take advantage of Indonesia's majority Muslim population, especially in the provinces where Islam is practiced with greater fervour. An atmosphere favourable to terrorists is easily created when terrorists use Islam to bolster their legitimacy. The Nanggroe Aceh Darussalam (NAD) province, which practises a strict Islamic *syariah* culture, was recently chosen as a base camp and hide-out by terrorists.[44] In addition, NAD is considered a perfect choice as there was a concurrent

[40] 'Pelayat Dulmatin Heboh Lihat Lafal Allah di Langit' ('Dulmatin's procession excited by the sighting of the words of Allah in the sky'), *detik.com*, 12 March 2010, available at www.detiknews.com/read/2010/03/12/110408/1316950/10/pelayat-dulmatin-heboh-lihat-lafal-allah-di-langit.

[41] 'Ribuan Orang Padati Pemakaman Dulmatin' ('Thousand attend Dulmatin's burial'), *Kompas.com*, 12 March 2010, available at regional.kompas.com/read/2010/03/12/11072596/Ribuan.Orang.Padati.Pemakaman.Dulmatin.

[42] '2,000 at Dulmatin's burial,' *Straits Times*, 12 March 2010, www.straitstimes.com/BreakingNews/SEAsia/Story/STIStory_501250.html.

[43] Ibid.

[44] 'Ada Upaya Jadikan Aceh seperti Mindanao' ('There are attempts to make Aceh like Mindanao'), *Jawa Pos*, 8 March 2010, available at www.jawapos.co.id/halaman/index.php?act=detail&nid=121239.

problem of separatism. The terrorists calculate that the government or police will be reluctant to use force and clamp down on them, which could rupture the peace agreement between the Indonesian government and the Gerakan Aceh Merdeka or the Free Aceh Movement. Furthermore, the mix of religion and separatism is fertile ground for terrorist recruitment.

7. New awareness of human rights

The public's new-found awareness of human rights has placed anti-terrorism efforts under close scrutiny. The public is often furious when police shoot dead terrorist suspects instead of arresting them alive.[45] The police have killed at least thirteen terrorist suspects during raids from February to June 2010.[46] In its defence, the police said it had to protect itself and also the public. The police argued that the terrorist suspects resisted arrest, and that the police are not willing to take the risk of officers being killed in an attempt to take them alive.

On the other hand, human rights groups and security analysts have questioned this police 'shoot-on-sight' policy. The police have been asked to focus more on judicial accountability so that suspects' rights can be upheld according to law. This is because some of the suspects were unarmed and were not committing any harmful acts at the time of the raids. Rights activists have claimed that disproportionate force, beyond what was necessary for an arrest, had been used. If so, it would be a violation of the right to life as enshrined in Human Rights Law of 1999 and the International Covenant on Civil and Political Rights, which Indonesia has ratified.

The National Commission on Human Rights (Komnas HAM) has gone as far as to say that most anti-terrorism raids by the police have violated human rights. A Commissioner of Komnas HAM, Stanley Adi Prasetyo, issued a reminder that terrorists also have the right to live.[47] He also pointed out the Commission's finding that abusive interrogation

---

[45] 'Anti-terror "shoot-on-sight policy" only fuels cries for vengeance, former jihadist claims', *The Jakarta Globe*, 16 May 2010, available at www.thejakartaglobe.com/home/anti-terror-shoot-on-sight-policy-only-fuels-cries-for-vengeance-former-jihadist-claims/375314.

[46] 'Indonesian terrorist sweeps raise concern over police tactics', *VOANews.com*, 24 June 2010, available at www1.voanews.com/english/news/Indonesian-Terrorist-Sweeps-Raise-Concern-About-Police-Tactics-97068794.html.

[47] 'Teroris pun Punya Hak Hidup' ('Terrorists also have the right to live'), *tempointeraktif.com*, 24 June 2010, available at www.tempointeraktif.com/hg/hukum/2010/06/24/brk,20100624-258156,id.html.

techniques against suspected terrorists have been practised, and this has been in the face of Indonesia's ratification of the UN Anti-Torture Convention. Komnas HAM chief, Ifdhal Kasim, has said that neither the government nor the police have responded to reports of possible abusive methods in the investigation of terrorist activity. Some activists, such as Noor Huda Ismail, have asked for an open investigation of police practices. The suspicion is that the police may be purposely targeting some terrorist suspects and killing them on the excuse of resisting arrest, rather than to 'risk' relying on a legal system that the police think is too lenient.[48]

The police have also come under criticism for the manner in which they have treated suspects and offenders in detention. For example, the terrorist suspect from NAD who turned himself in to the police, Abu Rimba, did not get enough legal assistance from the lawyers. In addition, his family was not given enough visitation rights. According to his elder brother, Yusri, the family was not given enough time to visit prior to his transfer from NAD to his detention in Greater Jakarta. Yusri has voiced concern that if Abu Rimba were convicted, the family cannot afford to pay for the expenses of visiting him if he is imprisoned outside Aceh.[49]

Issues related to burial are another area impacted by human rights awareness issue which the government has to cope with. The families of dead terrorist suspects have also criticised the police. They have complained about the red tape involved in claiming the bodies for burial. There are some complex problems with respect to the burial of terrorist suspects. First, it is not easy for the family to bury their relatives in accordance with Islamic tradition. Second, villagers in the hometowns of some terrorist suspects have forbidden the burial of the suspects. Ahmad Maulana and Urwah, the two terrorist suspects shot dead, experienced this. In the case of Maulana, the village community did not want their village to be known as a terrorist's village, even though Maulana was never convicted or even tried as a terrorist. The burial issue is considered as not respecting human rights according to Shabbirin Syakur, the spokesperson of Majelis Mujahidin (MM). According to MM, the denial of burial issue may prompt horizontal conflict in the society. This situation has prompted Soeparno Zainal Abidin of Sragen Central Java to allocate his

---

[48] 'Indonesian terrorist sweeps raise concern over police tactics', *VoANews.com*, 24 June 2010, available at www.voanews.com/english/news/asia/Indonesian-Terrorist-Sweeps-Raise-Concern-About-Police-Tactics-97068794.html.

[49] 'Tersangka Terorisme Minim Bantuang Hukum' ('Terrorism suspects lack legal aid'), *Kompas.com*, 16 May 2010, available at regional.kompas.com/read/2010/05/16/17323359/Tersangka.Terorisme.Minim.Bantuan.Hukum.

land for a cemetery, especially for terrorist suspects who are denied burial in their hometowns. He gave 400 square metres of his land in 1999 for this special cemetery.

Another hotly debated issue concerns the right of convicted terrorists to be released for good behaviour before their full term of imprisonment has been served. Those who are in favour of early release say that terrorists ought to enjoy the same right of early release as any other prisoner, as this is provided for under the law. In 2006, the government amended the Government Regulation on the Rights of Prisoners (GR). Based on this GR, a terrorist prisoner has the right to serve a shorter term due to good behaviour after undergoing a third of the sentence. This is different from ordinary crimes, where inmates may be entitled to early release after serving six months of their sentence.

Those who are against the early release of convicted terrorists argue that terrorist suspects have committed extraordinary crimes. They claim that terrorists should serve the full term and not be given any reduction in time due to good behaviour.

The government's decision to allow a reduction in the sentence for good behaviour seemed to have backfired when Urwah, a convicted terrorist, was released earlier than he should have been. After his release in 2007, Urwah was involved in the 2009 J W Marriott and Ritz Carlton Hotel terrorist attacks.[50] Recently, Abdullah Sunata was taken into custody again after his early release in April 2009, as he was found to be planning to attack on the Danish Embassy. Sunata was earlier sentenced to prison for hiding suspected terrorist Noordin M. Top.[51] Because of these events, the Minister of Law and Human Rights, Patrialis Akbar, has made a statement that a convicted terrorist should be given careful consideration before being released early for good behaviour.[52]

An other human rights issue surrounds the families of terrorist suspects. These families cannot enjoy privacy as they are constantly disturbed by media coverage. The children are ashamed to go to school because they

---

[50] 'Jakarta hotel bomb terror suspect believed dead after Indonesian police raid', *The Jakarta Globe*, 17 September 2009, available at thejakartaglobe.com/home/jakarta-hotel-bomb-terror-suspect-believed-dead-after-indonesian-police-raid/330395.

[51] 'Abdullah Sunata, Indonesia's most wanted man arrested', *Digital Journal*, 24 June 2010, available at www.digitaljournal.com/article/293784.

[52] 'Patrialis Minta Proses Pembebasan Narapidana Teroris Lebih Hati-hati' ('Patrialis calls for a more careful process before convicted terrorists are released'), *detik.com*, 17 May 2010, available at www.detiknews.com/read/2010/05/17/171046/1358669/10/patrialis-minta-proses-pembebasan-narapida-teroris-lebih-hati-hati.

are worried that their friends will distance them because their parents are terrorist suspects.

Child protection activist Seto Mulyadi has warned of the danger of labelling these children as the children of suspect terrorists. The children were not in fault and they should not be discriminated against. The children are victims of terrorism as well. If these children are not handled delicately, they may become terrorists and take revenge. Like the burial issue, the matter of publicity seems not to implicate either the police or the government. This suggests a lack of awareness of human rights issues in which the children of terrorist suspects are implicated. The government seems not to be taking any measures on this issue.

In sum, rising human rights awareness in Indonesia has changed the perception that security must always take priority over human rights.

8.   Lack of a rehabilitation programme for released terrorist prisoners

Another problematic issue in eradicating terrorism is the lack of a rehabilitation programme for released prisoners. Currently, about 200 convicted terrorists have been released. The issue concerns the question of whether a prison term is enough to prevent a convicted terrorist from re-immersion in jihad once they have regained their freedom. Do released terrorists regret what they have done, and will their communities accept them again?

Programmes to reintegrate released terrorists back into society are lacking. Some rejoin their former terrorist groups. For example, some of the terrorists arrested in NAD were released from imprisonment for involvement in prior acts of terrorism. According to Noor Huda, the reason is that the government has failed to de-radicalise them. The public has also been blamed because the majority cannot accept the presence of convicted terrorists when they are released. This has prompted some ex-prisoners, such as Urwah,[53] to return to their terrorist groups.

In order to solve this issue, Noor Huda has established a foundation named 'Prasasti Perdamaian', which concentrates on rehabilitating former convicted terrorists.[54] These former terrorists are given opportunities to

---

[53] 'Menelusuri Jejak dan Peran Bagus Budi Pranoto Alias Urwah' ('Tracing the steps and exploring the character of Bagus Budi Pranoto alias Urwah'), *detik.com*, 21 August 2010, available at www.detiknews.com/read/2009/08/21/143505/1187222/10/menelusuri-jejak-dan-peran-bagus-budi-pranoto-alias-urwah.

[54] The website of Prasasti Perdamaian is available at www.prasastiperdamaian.com.

engage in social activities in order for them to be reintegrated into society. Former head of the National Intelligence Agency, A. M. Hendropriyono, has suggested that convicted terrorists, once released, could be recruited as security guards in hotels or other important places.[55] This is because their knowledge of terrorism can be used to prevent similar acts of terrorism. Recently, the Ministry of Law and Human Rights in co-operation with the Ministry of Religious Affairs has designed a programme for convicted terrorists.[56] The Ministry of Law and Human Rights is in the process of erecting a new specialised prison for terrorists so that their special needs may be catered for.[57] However, the biggest obstacle has been the funds to run these programmes. According to one high ranking police officer, Petrus Golose, not very much has been done to de-radicalise convicted terrorists.[58]

9. The problem of 'euphoric' democracy

Anti-terrorism measures in Indonesia have also had to contend with the euphoria of a new-found democracy, where even justifiable and necessary restrictions to civil liberties are viewed with apprehension. This has led some to coin the word 'democrazy' to describe this situation.

Take, for example, the freedom of the press. Although the media has been used for countering terrorism by sending messages of its negative consequences, it has nonetheless also had a negative impact on anti-terrorism measures.

---

[55] 'Hendropriyono: Mantan Teroris Harus Dipekerjakan' ('Hendropriyono: former terrorists ought to be given employment'), *detik.com*, 24 July 2009, available at www.detiknews.com/read/2009/07/24/215818/1171189/10/hendropriyono-mantan-teroris-harus-dipekerjakan.

[56] 'Jadi Sumber Terorisme, Kemiskinan Terus Coba Diturunkan' ('We must continue to try to reduce the incidence of poverty, a cause of terrorism'), *detik.com*, 14 March 2010, available at www.detiknews.com/read/2010/03/14/115113/1317862/10/jadi-sumber-terorisme-kemiskinan-terus-coba-diturunkan.

[57] 'Menteri Hukum Usulkan Program Khusus Napi Terorisme' ('Minister of Justice proposes a special programme for imprisoned terrorists'), *VHR Media.com*, 19 May 2010, available at www.vhrmedia.com/Menteri-Hukum-Usulkan-Program-Khusus-Napi-Terorisme-berita4235.html.

[58] 'Petrus Golose: Program Deradikalisasi Teroris Baru Secuil Dilakukan' (Petrus Golose: the new programme for the de-redacalistion of terrorists is not being carried out in earnest'), *detik.com*, 20 August 2009, available at www.detiknews.com/read/2009/08/20/1314 57/1186299/10/petrus-golose-program-deradikalisasi-teroris-baru-secuil-dilakukan.

The first problem is the unrestrained and indiscriminate coverage of operations to apprehend suspected terrorists while they are still in progress.[59] TV and web-based media run on-site and live broadcasts, minute by minute.[60] There are even reporters who are 'embedded' in the police force. The public can watch the work of the police live on television, including the removal of the dead body of a suspected terrorist. This completely unrestrained reporting has sometimes caused the perpetration of falsehoods.[61]

The second problem is that terrorists may monitor the strategies of the police by watching them in operation through live broadcasts. This enables terrorist suspects to take anticipatory action to prevent arrest. It may also warn other terrorist suspects and their networks, and they may retaliate or try to do something to help the suspected terrorist under siege.

The third problem is that the media may be unknowingly helping to promote terrorist ideology, or to cast terrorists in a sympathetic light. The terrorists, suspected and convicted, are often interviewed for their opinions. Terrorist suspects under siege who are the subject of live coverage can be perceived by viewers to be underdogs who should be supported. In addition, coverage of the funeral of terrorists might give the impression that the persons being buried are heroes.

The fourth problem of live television coverage is that it is considered to be too vulgar for young viewers. The Head of Children Protection, Seto Mulyadi, claimed that this might influence a child's psychology and create a sense of fear in children, as if Indonesia is not a safe place.

The fifth problem is that the media's efforts to develop a story might lead them to locate and question the family of suspects, and this in turn might interfere with police investigations.

The other issue concerns the regulation of associations and organisations. Should the government ban religious organisations that are suspected of non-violently supporting terrorist causes? The government has been reluctant to do so, fearing that it will be accused of violating the freedom of association and therefore democracy.

---

[59] This occurred on 8 August 2009 when police were involved in a shoot out with Ibrahim, a terrorist suspect of the J W Marriott and Ritz Carlton Hotel attacks.

[60] The national television, TV One and Metro TV, run live broadcasts the whole day as 'Breaking News', with commentators giving their assessment.

[61] It was initially reported that the alleged terrorist was Noordin M. Top, but later the police announced it was Ibrahim: see 'Noordin M. Top believed killed in police raid In Temanggung', *Antara News*, 8 August 2009, available at www.antaranews.com/en/news/1249705820/noordin-m-top-believed-killed-in-police-raid-in-temanggung.

10.   Alignment with the Western world

The war on terror has relieved external pressure on the Indonesian government to respect human rights. Foreign countries are ready to overlook Indonesia's human rights abuses so long as the government is co-operative in the war against terror. The United States, which had in the past expressed concerns about the condition of human rights in Indonesia, has not been exerting such pressure because the United States needs Indonesia's support in its war on terror.

The public in Indonesia has resented the silence of international NGOs about human rights abuses of Indonesian nationals abroad who are suspected of terrorism. There is a perception of unfair double standards when NGOs fiercely criticise Indonesia for human rights abuse but are silent about the abuse of the human rights of Indonesians by other countries. The negative impact of the war on terror on human rights has caused the public in Indonesia to question whether human rights are only an instrument to weaken Indonesia as a country, including its government and military.

The war on terror has led Western countries traditionally seen as 'defenders of human rights' to encourage and expect abuses of human rights to recur in Indonesia. Human rights protection and promotion in Indonesia can be undermined if powerful states condone or encourage such a state of affairs. This leads to the conclusion that foreign governments do not have a sincere intention of upholding human rights in Indonesia. They rather have used human rights issues as a political instrument against Indonesia. Since the launch of the war against terror, Indonesia's human rights cause has become one of its casualties through the revival of legislation legitimising human rights abuses from what was thought to be a bygone era.

The public perception in Indonesia is that anti-terrorism measures have been unduly influenced by the Western world. These measures are seen to be an extension of the policies of the West.[62] The public perceives the fight against terrorism not as a fight against terrorists, but as a fight against Islamic groups. Anti-terrorism policies are seen to be anti-Islam.

---

[62] Azyumardi Azra said that terrorism has grown due to influence of foreign policy: see 'Penyebab Terorisme Kompleks Tak Hanya Kemiskinan' ('The sources of terrorism are complex and poverty is not the only reason)', *beritabaru.com*, 4 September 2009, available at www.beritabaru.com/index.php?option=com_content&view=article&id=2908:penye bab-terorisme-kompleks-tak-hanya-kemiskinan&catid=62:nasional&Itemid=54.

The government has been criticised because the Indonesian counter-terrorism squad, called the Special Detachment 88 (Detasemen Khusus 88, or 'Densus 88'), is believed to be funded and equipped by Western countries, such as the United States. Many believe that the unit is being trained by the CIA, FBI, US Secret Service and ex-US Special Forces personnel. In addition, Densus 88 has received assistance in the form of forensic expertise, such as DNA analysis and communications monitoring from foreign agencies, including the Australian Federal Police.

The public has also been very suspicious of government and police action against alleged terrorists ahead of visits by Western dignitaries. The recent operation against suspected terrorists in NAD was believed to have been due to President Barrack Obama's visit to Indonesia.

11.   The debate on military involvement

The only organisation which has been at the forefront of anti-terrorism operations has been the police. While the military has the capacity to play a much larger role, it has been idle in the context of terrorism. There was a time when the government was willing to invite the military to take part in eradicating terrorism. Members of Parliament concurred with the government on military involvement. Under the TNI (Tentera National Indonesia or Indonesian National Army) Law, military involvement in anti-terrorism was sanctioned in principle.[63]

The potential involvement of the military prompted a public debate.[64] Those who were in favour argued that the military has the capacity to combat terrorism and terrorism is a threat to national interest. Under the Bush Administration the Indonesian military was seen as important factor in cracking down on Southeast Asian terrorist networks. For this reason the Bush Administration wanted to see the resumption of full military-to-military relations. This would have allowed the Indonesian military to be trained by the US military.

[63] 'Pelibatan TNI Tangani Terorisme Punya Payung Hukum' ('The involvement of TNI in anti-terrorism efforts has a legal basis'), *Antara News*, 31 August 2009, available at www.antaranews.com/berita/1251697931/pelibatan-tni-tangani-terorisme-punya-payung-hukum.

[64] 'Pelibatan TNI Tidak Boleh secara Lisan' ('The involvement of TNI should not only be with words'), *Kompas.com*, 24 August 2009, available at nasional.kompas.com/read/2009/08/24/20163397/Pelibatan.TNI.Tidak.Boleh.secara.Lisan.

Those who do not agree are afraid that this would become a new entry point for the military to re-enter the civilian sphere.[65] This fear is understandable in the context of Indonesia's recent history of the military interfering undesirably in civilian government. Human rights activists warned that the involvement of the military is unjustified, as terrorism is a civilian, and not a military, act. Thus, the appropriate agency to deal with it is the police. The Indonesian government, to its credit, sees terrorism as a law enforcement problem to be handled by the police, and not an insurgency to be addressed by the military.

12.   Poverty as fuel for terrorism

Poverty has made it easier for terrorists to recruit followers from amongst the unemployed and the young. For example, the suicide bomber of the J W Marriott Hotel, Dani Dwi Permana, was an eighteen-year-old graduate of a private senior high school in Bogor who was not employed. For this reason, President Susilo Bambang Yudhoyono has instructed the Governors that eradicating poverty would lead to the eradication of terrorism. The former Head of Muhammadiyah (the second largest Islamic organisation in Indonesia), Ahmad Syafii Maarif, similarly believes that the eradication of poverty should be prioritised, and justice upheld before terrorism can be effectively dealt with.[66]

Nevertheless, this view has not gone unchallenged. They argue that convicted terrorists and terrorist suspects do not typically come from poor families. Some are highly educated and some have degrees in engineering. The former Head of Densus 88, Surya Dharma, dismissed poverty as the source of terrorism.[67] He believes that the spread of terrorist ideology, especially to young people, has been the main cause of terrorism. Azyumardi Azra, an Islamic scholar from the Islamic Public University Hidayatullah, has the same view. He maintains that poverty and unemployment have nothing to do with the roots of terrorism.[68]

---

[65] 'Pengaktifan Koter TNI Bukan Jalan Keluar Cegah Teror' ('Reviving the territorial command of TNI is not a solution to prevent terrorism'), *Suara Merdeka*, 7 October 2005, available at www.suaramerdeka.com/harian/0510/07/nas13.htm.

[66] 'Syafii: Kemiskinan Penyebab Munculnya Terorisme' ('Syafii: poverty is the source for the emergence of terrorism'), *detik.com*, 5 July 2010, available at www.detiknews.com/read/2006/10/05/143311/689775/10/syafii-kemiskinan-penyebab-munculnya-terorisme.

[67] 'Kemiskinan Tak Picu Terorisme' ('Poverty Does Not Trigger Terrorism'), *Inilah.com*, 16 August 2009, available at www.inilah.com/berita_print.php?id=142627.

[68] 'Azyumardi Azra: Tak ada Hubungan antara Terorisme dengan Kemiskinan' ('Azyumardi Azra: no connection between terrorism and poverty'), *Primaironline*, 24

13. Conclusion

The enactment of the Anti-Terrorism Law has not prevented Indonesia from being a target of national and international terrorist attacks. Implementation and enforcement of the Anti-Terrorism Law has not been an easy task. The fact that combating terrorism is led by Western countries has caused the Indonesian public to be suspicious. Debate has shifted from fighting terrorist acts to concerns that Western countries are undermining Indonesia's sovereignty.

The Anti-Terrorism Law gives legitimacy to law enforcement agencies that use legal measures different from those available for other criminal offences. Moreover, it imposes severe sanctions on those who commit acts of terrorism. Yet the Anti-Terrorism Law has not been effective in eradicating terrorist acts in Indonesia. The threat of severe sanctions including the death penalty will not deter those who believe they are fighting a jihad that will reward them with a place in heaven. Those with such beliefs will go anywhere in Indonesia or elsewhere for the opportunity to die in a holy war.

The solution to the problem of terrorism in Indonesia runs deeper than merely promulgating a law to combat terrorism. Terrorism for Indonesia is a complex and multifaceted issue. The government has taken firm actions supported by the majority of the people. Nevertheless, these actions have yet to satisfy countries whose nationals are threatened, such as the United States and Australia. Facing the Indonesian condition and context it would be relatively difficult for any government in Indonesia to combat terrorism. It should be understood that Indonesia's challenge in combating terrorism is different from that faced by the United States or Australia.

Efforts to eradicate terrorism in Indonesia continue to face many challenges. Even though there have been some success stories, acts of terrorism keep on occurring. As discussed in this chapter, there are various causes that may hinder efforts to eradicate terrorism. Put simply, eradicating terrorism in Indonesia is not as straightforward as it is in many other jurisdictions. Anti-terrorism policies must recognise the peculiar Indonesian context and background.

July 2010, available at www.primaironline.com/berita/detail.php?catid=Sosial&artid=-azyumardi-azra-tak-ada-hubungan-kemiskinan-dengan-terorisme#.

13

The Human Security Act and the IHL Law of the Philippines: of security and insecurity

H. HARRY L. ROQUE, JR.

'Ignorance of the constitutional Bill of Rights by the erring officials is no justification. It only aggravates the situation. It shows unpardonable derelic- tion of duty and recklessness of responsible high authorities' *Lino* v. *Fugoso*, 77 Phil. 983 (1947), Justice Perfecto, concurring.

1. Introduction

The Philippine government has adopted two major pieces of legislation that the country hopes will become powerful weapons to combat terror- ism. The first is the Human Security Act (HSA) of 2007.[1] This law was filed as a bill in the House of Representatives as early as July 2004.[2] This and a handful of proposed anti-terror bills in the House of Representatives[3] were consolidated into House Bill No. 4839, authored by Representative Imee Marcos, the daughter of the former President Ferdinand Marcos. Around the same time, the Senate drafted its own version, Senate Bill No. 2137, authored by Senator Juan Ponce Enrile, a former Defense Minister during the Marcos and Aquino eras. The HSA mirrors prevailing counter- terrorist doctrine as it goes by the premise that terrorists are overwhelm- ingly effective because they have an unfair advantage over law-abiding

---

[1] Republic Act No. 9372 (HSA) effective on 15 July 2007, available at www.senate.gov.ph/ republic_acts/ra%209372.pdf.
[2] Representative Robert Ace Barbers authored House Bill No. 1925, which is one among the many anti-terror bills filed in the Philippine House of Representatives.
[3] The other anti-terror bills filed were: House Bill No. 2639, authored by Representative Marcelino Libanan; House Bill No. 3032, authored by Representative Robert Vincent Jude Jaworski; House Bill No. 3103, authored by Representative Douglas R. A. Cagas; House Bill No. 309, authored by Representative Imee Marcos; House Bill No. 948, authored by Representative Judy Syjuco; House Bill No. 3767, authored by Representative Conrado Estrella III; House Bill No. 3800, authored by Representative Eduardo Gullas.

governments. However, glaring questions of legality are raised when the HSA attempts to redress the imbalance.

The second is Republic Act No. 9851[4] of 2009, entitled 'An Act Defining and Penalizing Crimes Against International Humanitarian Law, Genocide and other Crimes Against Humanity, Organizing Jurisdiction, Designing Special Courts, and for Related Purposes' (IHL Law). This legislation was in discharge of treaty obligations under the 1949 Geneva Conventions to enact domestic laws criminalising grave breaches and serious violations of the Conventions.[5] In addition, the law also penalises the international crimes of genocide and crimes against humanity. Insofar as terrorism may constitute violations of international humanitarian law, this second law thus also provides the Philippines with a potent tool against modern-day terrorism.

This chapter will critically examine the provisions of the HSA to determine its compatibility with international human rights standards. It will also address its relationship with the recently enacted IHL Law.

2.   Salient provisions of the HSA

The HSA was prepared by its authors purportedly to help law enforcement agencies and the government to deal with the emerging threat of terrorism to national security.[6] It does so by providing a definition for terrorism,[7] authorising surveillance of suspects and intervention of communication,[8] providing for the procedure to declare groups and organisations as terrorist organisations,[9] providing for detention without judicial warrant of arrest,[10] granting the power to examine bank accounts and deposits,[11] and creating an anti-terrorism council with the mandate to properly implement the act.[12]

A common feature behind each of the extraordinary powers granted to the state is that resort to these must be sanctioned by the court. Hence, the Council must first apply for a judicial warrant prior to surveillance and interception of communication[13] and to the examination of bank accounts and deposits.[14] Likewise, a declaration that an organisation is a terrorist organisation must be sanctioned by a court with notice to the

---

[4] Republic Act No. 9851 (IHL Law), available at senate.gov.ph/republic_acts/ra%209851.pdf.
[5] Articles 49, 50, 129 and 146 of the four Geneva Conventions of 1949.
[6] Senate Proceedings, 22 May 2006, p. 157.
[7] HSA, s. 3.   [8] Ibid., s. 7.   [9] Ibid., s. 17.   [10] Ibid., s. 18.
[11] Ibid., s. 28.   [12] Ibid., s. 53.   [13] Ibid., ss. 7–8.   [14] Ibid., s. 27.

group sought to be declared as such.[15] Even pre-trial detention, where it exceeds three days, must have the imprimatur of a municipal, city, provincial or regional official of a Human Rights Commission or a judge of the municipal or regional trial court, the Sandiganbayan,[16] or a justice of the Court of Appeals.[17] The law, to safeguard abuses, regulates the manner in which both intercepted communication[18] and information derived from the examination of bank accounts[19] may be used. It reiterates the prohibition on torture[20] and also provides for penalties in case law enforcement agencies wrongfully apply for any of the extraordinary measures authorised by the law,[21] and vests the Commission on Human Rights with prosecutorial powers in these cases.[22]

A.   Presumption of constitutionality does not apply to the Human Security Act

While the principles of statutory construction normally provide that statutes are presumed constitutional, this presumption will not apply if, on its face, the terms of the legislation violate constitutionally-protected fundamental rights like the right to free speech, the right to freely associate, and the right to privacy. In *Social Weather Station, Inc* v. *COMELEC*,[23] the Philippine Supreme Court held that due to the preferred status of the constitutional rights of speech, expression and the press, a law that imposes a prior restraint on their exercise is vitiated by a weighty presumption of *invalidity*.[24]

The Supreme Court has even held in *Ople* v. *Torres*[25] that, when the integrity of a fundamental right is at stake, it will give the challenged law a stricter scrutiny, and that, in case of doubt, the Court will lean

---

[15] Ibid., s. 17.
[16] The Sandiganbayan is a court which is created by Presidential Decree No. 1606 according to art. XIII, s. 5 of the defunct 1973 Constitution, and is in existence due to art. XI, s. 4 of the present Constitution. Its jurisdiction covers those offences committed by public officers under s. 4 of Republic Act No. 8249 as amended. Republic Act No. 8249 is available at: www.doj.gov.ph/files/1606.pdf.
[17] HSA, s. 19.   [18] Ibid., ss. 13–15.   [19] Ibid., ss. 33–5.   [20] Ibid., s. 24.
[21] Ibid., ss. 16, 20, 25, 36, 38, 42, 44, 46–7.
[22] Ibid., s. 55.   [23] G.R. No. 147571, 5 May 2001.
[24] Ibid.: '[B]ecause of the preferred status of the constitutional rights of speech, expression, and the press, such a measure is vitiated by a weighty presumption of invalidity. Indeed, any system of prior restraints of expression comes to this Court bearing a heavy presumption against its constitutional validity … The Government thus carries a heavy burden of showing justification for the enforcement of such restraint. There is thus a reversal of the normal presumption of validity that inheres in every legislation' (emphasis added).
[25] G.R. No. 127685, 23 July 1998.

towards a stance that will not put in danger the rights protected by the Constitution.[26]

Also, the Supreme Court has stated as far back as *Ermita-Malate Hotel and Motel Operators Association, Inc* v. *City Mayor*[27] that the standard for the validity of governmental acts is '*much more rigorous*' if the liberty involved the freedom of the mind or the person.

Certain provisions of the HSA appear in fact to infringe these basic freedoms. For instance, while the 1987 Constitution provides that a warrant of arrest may only be issued by 'a judge', the law, while requiring that pre-trail detentions should be authorised, among others, by a lower court judge, also gives a regional director of the Commission on Human Rights the power to authorise such detentions.[28] Worse, while the Constitution requires that a warrant of arrest may issue only upon the existence of 'probable cause', pre-trial detention, even for an indefinite period, may be issued upon 'mere suspicion of terrorism'.

The law on its face also appears to infringe the freedom of speech and expression. Under existing jurisprudence,[29] words, owing to the constitutional commitment to the freedom of expression and a free press, must actually lead to a clear and present danger before they could be repressed by the state. This apparently has been statutorily modified in that ordinary utterances, whether or not they are in fact acted upon, can be classified as 'terrorist' in nature. Under the HSA, words are now actionable as long as they 'create terror or panic in the mind of the public'.

Additionally, the new law may have a chilling effect on a free press. This was made painfully clear by the then Secretary of Justice who illustrated in clear terms how it may be applied to journalists as suspected terrorists:

> If you are a journalist, you are free from wiretapping because the law says that journalists and their sources of information cannot be subjected to

---

[26] Ibid: '*[A]nd we now hold that when the integrity of a fundamental right is at stake, this court will give the challenged law, administrative order, rule or regulation a stricter scrutiny ... This approach is demanded by the 1987 Constitution whose entire matrix is* designed to protect human rights and to prevent authoritarianism. *In case of doubt, the least we can do is to lean towards the stance that will not put in danger the rights protected by the Constitution.*'

[27] G.R. No. L-24693, 31 July 1967: 'What may be stressed sufficiently is that if the liberty involved were freedom of the mind or the person, the standard for the validity of governmental acts is much more rigorous and exacting, but where the liberty curtailed affects at the most rights of property, the permissible scope of regulatory measure is wider.'

[28] See HSA, s. 19.

[29] One recent is *Integrated Bar of the Philippines* v. *Honorable Manila Mayor Jose 'Lito' Atienza*, G.R. No. 175241, 24 February 2010.

wiretapping. The fact that your source is a terrorist does not make you a terrorist per se. But if the journalist is now a suspect, then he can be wiretapped... Nobody is immune to the possibility of wiretapping but it must be predicated on the fact that he is a suspect[.][30]

Likewise, the right to privacy appears to be imperiled because the law allows interception and surveillance of personal communication. Even religious confessions do not appear to be exempt from this invasion, prompting a priest to challenge the constitutionality of the law on this ground.[31]

B. Defining terrorism: a legal 'Nessie'[32]

One of the foremost problems in international law is the fact that the term 'terrorism', while widely used in contemporary culture, is very difficult to define and often any definition chosen is subject to abuse. It must be stressed that terrorism is not an end in itself, but a means to an end; hence any definition of terror is likely to be coloured by the purpose which is to be achieved. However, the mere use of terror is not how terrorism is usually defined, since the use of violence for the achievement of political ends is common to both state and non-state groups.[33] Any attempt to come up with a comprehensive definition only serves to highlight the difficulty of defining terrorism. For example, the distinction between legitimate independence movements and actual terror groups is often not embodied.

The Supreme Court in *Estrada* v. *Sandiganbayan*,[34] citing *People* v. *Nazario*, stated that:

> A statute or act may be said to be vague when it lacks comprehensible standards that men of common intelligence must necessarily guess at its meaning and differ in its application. In such instance, the statute is

---

[30] Leila Salaverria and Jerome Aning, 'Media may be bugged', *Inquirer.net*, 5 July 2007, available at newsinfo.inquirer.net/breakingnews/nation/view/20070705-74884/ Media_may_be_bugged.

[31] *Father Joe Dizon* v. *Executive Secretary*, SP No. Q-07-60778, filed with the Quezon City Regional Trial Court Branch 92.

[32] Nessie is the term of endearment for the still mythical Loch Ness Monster.

[33] Terrorism expert Laqueur in 1999 also has counted over 100 definitions and concludes that the 'only general characteristic generally agreed upon is that terrorism involves violence and the threat of violence': Walter Laqueur, *The New Terrorism: Fanaticism and the Arms of Mass Destruction* (Oxford University Press, 1999), p. 5.

[34] G.R. No. 148560, 19 November 2001.

repugnant to the Constitution in two respects – it violates due process for failure to accord persons, especially the parties targeted by it, fair notice of what conduct to avoid; and, it leaves law enforcers unbridled discretion in carrying out its provisions and becomes an arbitrary flexing of the Government muscle.[35]

The Supreme Court noted in *David* v. *Macapagal-Arroyo*[36] that the phrase 'acts of terrorism' is still an amorphous and vague concept. The extent of this vagueness can be gleaned from the comment in the same decision, which deserves to be quoted in full:

In fact, this 'definitional predicament' or the 'absence of an agreed definition of terrorism' confronts not only our country, but the international community as well. The following observations are quite apropos:

In the actual unipolar context of international relations, the 'fight against terrorism' has become one of the basic slogans when it comes to the justification of the use of force against certain states and against groups operating internationally. Lists of States 'sponsoring terrorism' and of terrorist organizations are set up and constantly being updated according to criteria that are not always known to the public, but are clearly determined by strategic interests.

The basic problem underlying all these military actions – or threats of the use of force as the most recent by the United States against Iraq – consists in the absence of an agreed definition of terrorism.

Remarkable confusion persists in regard to the legal categorization of acts of violence either by states, by armed groups such as liberation movements, or by individuals.

The dilemma can by summarized in the saying 'One country's terrorist is another country's freedom fighter.' The apparent contradiction or lack of consistency in the use of the term *terrorism* may further be demonstrated by the historical fact that leaders of national liberation movements such as Nelson Mandela in South Africa, Habib Bourgouiba in Tunisia, or Ahmed Ben Bella in Algeria, to mention only a few, were originally labeled as terrorists by those who controlled the territory at the time, but later became internationally respected statesmen.

What, then, is the defining criterion for terrorist acts – the *differentia specifica* distinguishing those acts from eventually legitimate acts of national resistance or self-defense?

Since the times of the Cold War the United Nations Organization has been trying in vain to reach a consensus on the basic issue of definition. The organization has intensified its efforts recently, but has been unable to bridge the gap between those who associate 'terrorism' with any violent act by non-State groups against civilians, state functionaries or infrastructure or military installations, and those who believe in the concept

---

[35] Ibid.   [36] G.R. No. 171396, 3 May 2006.

of the legitimate use of force when resistance against foreign occupation or against systematic oppression of ethnic and/or religious groups within a state is concerned.

The dilemma facing the international community can best be illustrated by reference to the contradicting categorization of organizations and movements such as Palestine Liberation Organization (PLO) – which is a terrorist group for Israel and a liberation movement for Arabs and Muslims – the Kashmiri resistance groups – who are terrorists in the perception of India, liberation fighters in that of Pakistan – the earlier Contras in Nicaragua – freedom fighters for the United States, terrorists for the Socialist camp – or, most drastically, the Afghani Mujahedeen (later to become the Taliban movement): during the Cold War period they were a group of freedom fighters for the West, nurtured by the United States, and a terrorist gang for the Soviet Union. One could go on and on in enumerating examples of conflicting categorizations that cannot be reconciled in any way – because of opposing political interests that are at the roots of those perceptions.

How, then, can those contradicting definitions and conflicting perceptions and evaluations of one and the same group and its actions be explained? In our analysis, the basic reason for these striking inconsistencies lies in the divergent interest of states. Depending on whether a state is in the position of an occupying power or in that of a rival, or adversary, of an occupying power in a given territory, the definition of terrorism will 'fluctuate' accordingly. A state may eventually see itself as protector of the rights of a certain ethnic group outside its territory and will therefore speak of a 'liberation struggle', not of 'terrorism' when acts of violence by this group are concerned, and vice-versa.

The United Nations Organization has been unable to reach a decision on the definition of terrorism exactly because of these conflicting interests of sovereign states that determine in each and every instance how a particular armed movement (i.e. a non-state actor) is labeled in regard to the terrorists–freedom fighter dichotomy. A 'policy of double standards' on this vital issue of international affairs has been the unavoidable consequence.[37]

While the HSA was intended to provide a statutory definition of 'terrorism', the definition under s. 3 is still utterly vague since it does not provide comprehensible standards to guide the authorities and the suspect as to what acts constitutes 'terrorism'. The definition enumerated acts already punishable under the Revised Penal Code or special penal laws, and then added the phrase '*thereby sowing and creating a condition of widespread and extraordinary fear and panic among the populace, in order to coerce the government to give in to an unlawful demand*'. The vagueness of the

[37] Ibid.

definition of *terrorism* stems from the use of words and phrases such as 'widespread', 'extraordinary', 'fear', 'panic', and *'unlawful demand'*. This qualifying phrase does not really qualify at all. It is quite obvious that the creation of a condition of widespread and extraordinary fear and panic among the populace depends on how a crime is sensationalised, either by the state, or by the mass media, or by anyone who wants a certain criminal conduct to be characterised as 'terrorist'.

The core criticism against the HSA is that it does not satisfactorily define what is being prohibited. This places an additional burden for the prosecution to prove yet another element in addition to the elements of the predicate crimes enumerated by which terrorism may be committed. This also requires law enforcers and the public to perform the difficult exercise of classifying criminal acts as terrorism.

The test of a sufficiently defined crime under Philippine law is:

> That the terms of a penal statute creating a new offense must be sufficiently explicit to inform those who are subject to it what conduct on their part will render them liable to its penalties is a well recognized requirement, consonant alike with ordinary notions of fair play and the settled rules of law, and *a statute which either forbids or requires the doing of an act in terms so vague that men of common intelligence must necessarily guess at its meaning and differ as to its application violates the first essential of due process of law.*[38]

The more important aspect of the vagueness doctrine is not actual notice, but the other principal element of the doctrine: the requirements that legislatures place reasonably clear guidelines for law enforcement officials and triers of fact in order to prevent arbitrary and discriminatory enforcement.[39] To the extent that the law is vague, it might have an *in terrorem* effect and deter persons from engaging in protected activities.[40] An unclear law, a law that does not draw bright lines, might regulate, or appear to regulate, more than is necessary, and thus deter or chill persons from engaging in protected activities.[41]

Applying the foregoing test to the HSA, at least one highly respected academic has opined that the law fails the test:

---

[38] *Connally v. General Construction Co.* 269 US 385 (1926) cited in *Romualdez v. Sandiganbayan*, G.R. No. 152259, 29 July 2004 (emphasis added).
[39] See *Kolender v. Lawson* 461 US 352 (1983).
[40] *Bates v. State Bar of Arizona*, 97 S. Ct. 2691, 2707 (1977).
[41] John E. Nowak and Ronald Rotunda, *Constitutional Law* (St Paul, MN: West Group, 6th edn, 2000), p. 1071.

Does the Bill cover even premeditated use of force or violence with the intention of creating danger or fear to just one solitary soul? Does it include threatening the use of force or violence, with intent of creating fear of God in their hearts, against a group of kidnappers, thieves or robbers? What about miners, loggers, fishermen, and other workers who, by means of the tools of their trade, intentionally destroy the environment, creating a state of fear or danger to a group of environmentalists?[42]

To date, the Philippine authorities have charged only one person with violation of the HSA. In *People* v. *Edgar De La Cruz Candule*,[43] the Information read:

> That on or about the 21st day of March 2008 in Sitio Alamac, Brgy Carael, Municipality of Bololan, Province of Zambales, Philippines, and within the jurisdiction of this court, the said accused, did then and there willfully, unlawfully, and feloniously commit acts of terrorism by openly professing himself to be a member of the New People's Army, a terrorist organization, and by advocating the overthrow of the legitimate government by force of arms and by inciting others to commit the acts of sedition.[44]

The Supreme Court in *David* v. *Arroyo*, in holding that the portion of General Order No. 5 of then President Arroyo calling out the Armed Forces of the Philippines to suppress acts of terrorism was invalid for violating the due process clause, observed as follows:

> So far, the word 'terrorism' appears only once in our criminal laws, i.e., in P.D. No. 1835 dated January 16, 1981 enacted by President Marcos during the Martial Law regime. This decree is entitled 'Codifying The Various Laws on Anti-Subversion and Increasing The Penalties for Membership in Subversive Organizations'. The word 'terrorism' is mentioned in the following provision: 'That one who conspires with any other person for the purpose of overthrowing the Government of the Philippines ... by force, violence, terrorism, ... shall be punished by *reclusion temporal*[.]
>
> P.D. No. 1835 was repealed by E.O. No. 167 (which outlaws the Communist Party of the Philippines) enacted by President Corazon Aquino on May 5, 1985. These two (2) laws, however, do not define 'acts of terrorism'. Since there is no law defining 'acts of terrorism', it is President Arroyo alone, under G.O. No. 5, who has the discretion to determine

---

[42] See Dean Pacifico Agabin, 'A Comment on the constitutionality of the proposed bill entitled "an act defining terrorism, establishing institutional mechanisms to prevent and suppress its commission, providing penalties therefor and for other purposes"', available at www.prolife.org.ph/forum/general-discussion/anti-terrorism-act-torpedoed-by-constitutional-expert/.

[43] Criminal Case No. RTC-5175-I, Regional Trial Court Branch 69 (Iba Zambales).

[44] Ibid.

what acts constitute terrorism. Her judgment on this aspect is absolute, without restrictions. Consequently, there can be indiscriminate arrest without warrants, breaking into offices and residences, taking over the media enterprises, prohibition and dispersal of all assemblies and gatherings unfriendly to the administration ... These acts go far beyond the calling-out power of the President.[45]

Candule, a member of an indigenous community, has been charged with terrorism on the grounds of belonging to and fighting for the New People's Army (NPA). He therefore appears to have been charged for, substantially, what President Corazon Aquino had decriminalised – that is, membership in the Communist Party of the Philippines and its armed component, the NPA. The problem with this, and the rationale for why the Marcos anti-subversion law was repealed, is precisely that mere membership should not be criminal. Worse, the HSA, as applied in the case of Candule, appears now to be applicable to the armed conflict between the Philippines and the NPA. This conflict has been characterised as a non-international armed conflict by the International Committee of the Red Cross (ICRC).[46] While fighters in such conflicts do not enjoy immunity from criminal prosecution (as combatants in international armed conflicts do), the armed group is not to be viewed as a group of common criminals owing to their ideological leanings and their proven adherence to the laws and customs of warfare. Assuming the government can prove that Candule is in fact a member and a fighter of the NPA, then the HSA should not apply to him, as the NPA are considered as combatants in a non-international armed conflict and not terrorists under the HSA. Further, the Arroyo government's sudden resolve to change the basis of criminal prosecution of suspected members of the NPA from rebellion to terrorism seem to be part of the government propaganda that all fighters of the NPA have now become terrorists, or a veiled warning to their supporters that regardless of ideology, to support or join the NPA would cease to be a political crime, but now constitute the crime of terrorism. Moreover, if the NPA are indeed terrorists, this raises the problem of the engagement by the government in peace talks with them. In fact, until the latest peace talks collapsed, talks were being conducted in Norway after the European state offered its good offices to facilitate the talks. The same terrorist tag raises the issue of construing the previous act of amnesty

---

[45] See *David* v. *Arroyo*, G.R. No. 171396, 3 May 2006.
[46] See International Committee of the Red Cross, *Our World: Views From The Philippines*, available at www.icrc.org/Web/eng/siteeng0.nsf/htmlall/research-report-240609/$File/Philippines.pdf.

given by the late President Corazon Aquino and its effect on future grants of amnesty against NPA fighters and supporters.

This practice of classifying fighters of the NPA as terrorists appears to be inconsistent with the very definition of terrorism under the law. The predicate crime for charging Candule appears to be the crime of rebellion, and it must be committed with the *mens rea* of 'sowing and creating a condition of widespread and extraordinary fear and panic among the populace, in order to coerce the government to give in to an unlawful demand'. Rebellion is defined under the Revised Penal Code[47] as:

> The crime of rebellion or insurrection is committed by rising publicly and taking arms against the Government for the purpose of removing from the allegiance to said Government or its laws, the territory of the Philippine Islands or any part thereof, of any body of land, naval or other armed forces, deprizing the Chief Executive or the Legislature, wholly or partially, of any of their powers or prerogatives.
>
> This practice of classifying fighters of the NPA as terrorists appears to be inconsistent with the very definition of terrorism itself under the law. The predicate crime for charging Candule appears to be rising publicly and taking arms against the government for the purpose of removing from the allegiance to said Government or its laws, the territory of the Republic of the Philippines or any part thereof, of any body of land, naval or other armed forces, or depriving the Chief Executive or the Legislature, wholly or partially, of any of their powers or prerogatives.

There does appear to be a contradiction in the elements of the crime of rebellion and the *mens rea* of terrorism. This is because in rebellion, the public taking up of arms is precisely for a specific purpose as enumerated in the law and not for the purpose of implanting fear in the minds of the civilian population. In fact, it would be foolhardy for any ideologically based insurgency, such as the NPA, to 'sow terror' in the populace when, in reality, they have become Asia's longest running insurgency partly because of the public support and sympathy they enjoy particularly in the countryside. And yet, it appears that the Philippines has classified Asia's longest running insurgency as a terrorist group.

C.   Violation of equal protection

The HSA converts ordinary crimes into acts of terrorism which are punishable with higher penalties. Convictions under the HSA are made easier

---

[47] Revised Penal Code, art. 134.

to procure since it punishes acts of terrorism as *mala prohibita*, as *mens rea* or the criminal intent is not a requirement for prosecution. The higher penalty imposed on accomplices and accessories are provided in ss. 5 and 6 of the HSA.[48]

This is in complete contrast to the imposable penalty for accomplices and accessories under the Revised Penal Code for a consummated felony.[49] To illustrate, the penalty for a person who participates in a rebellion is *reclusion temporal*, or imprisonment within the range of twelve years and one day to twenty years. An accessory is punished by imprisonment which is two degrees lower than *reclusion temporal*, or *prision correccional* in its maximum period within the range of four years, two months and one day to six years. Meanwhile, an accomplice is *prision mayor* in its medium period within the range of six years and one day to eight years. Compare this with the penalty of ten to twelve years of imprisonment for an accessory and seventeen to twenty years for an accomplice under the HSA.

Under Philippine law, there is a violation of the equal protection clause where the classification is not based on real differences.[50] But the HSA as applied creates no valid classification that could differentiate the criminal responsibility of one committing just the predicate crime in the HSA to one committing the same crime with the qualifier in HSA. To illustrate, the duration of the penalty the court can impose for an accessory to the

---

[48] **Section 5.** *Accomplice.* Any person who, not being a principal under Article 17 of the Revised Penal Code or a conspirator as defined in Section 4 hereof, cooperates in the execution of either the crime of terrorism or conspiracy to commit terrorism by previous or simultaneous acts shall suffer the penalty of from seventeen (17) years, four (4) months one day to twenty (20) years of imprisonment.

    Section 6. *Accessory.* Any person who, having knowledge of the commission of the crime of terrorism or conspiracy to commit terrorism, and without having participated therein, either as principal or accomplice under Articles 17 and 18 of the Revised Penal Code, takes part subsequent to its commission in any of the following manner: (a) by profiting himself or assisting the offender to profit by the effects of the crime; (b) by concealing or destroying the body of the crime, or the effects, or instruments thereof, in order to prevent its discovery; (c) by harboring, concealing, or assisting in the escape of the principal or conspirator of the crime, shall suffer the penalty of ten (10) years and one day to twelve (12) years of imprisonment.

[49] **Article 52.** *Penalty to be imposed upon accomplices in consummated crime.* The penalty next lower in degree than that prescribed by law for the consummated felony shall be imposed upon the accomplices in the commission of a consummated felony.

    Article 53. *Penalty to be imposed upon accessories to the commission of a consummated felony.* The penalty lower by two degrees than that prescribed by law for the consummated felony shall be imposed upon the accessories to the commission of a consummated felony.

[50] *People* v. *Vera* 65 Phil 56 G.R. No. L-45685, 16 November 1937.

crime of piracy under Article 122 of the Revised Penal Code is from six months and one day to twelve years' imprisonment. If the crime of piracy was committed as a *predicate crime under the HSA*, the penalty the court can impose for an accessory is from ten years and one day to twelve years' imprisonment. Because of the vague qualifier in the HSA, the same overt-act of an accessory to the criminal act of piracy is penalised more severely under the HSA compared to the Revised Penal Code.

All these combined could have serious ramification on the right to due process, because the definition of the crime of terrorism is vague and is coupled with undue classification as to the penalties for perpetrators of terrorism, compared with the violators of the Revised Penal Code for the same acts *sans* the qualifier under the HSA.

D.   Violation of freedom to associate

The 1987 Constitution recognises the right of the Filipino people to join associations:

> **Section 8.** The right of the people, including those employed in the public and private sectors, to form unions, associations, or societies for purposes not contrary to law shall not be abridged.

In *David* v. *Arroyo*, as aforequoted, the Supreme Court rightfully observed that a vague definition of terrorism will lead to a violation of the right to association since organisations would be classified as 'terrorist' without a clear understanding of what terrorism is. The HSA therefore is also unconstitutional for violating the right to freely associate, since s. 17[51] of the HSA is based on a vague definition of terrorism.

The HSA could also violate the right to freely associate in the event of a lunatic fringe infiltrating a legitimate movement composed of ordinary people honestly pursuing their ideals and exercising, quite properly, their democratic rights.[52] For example, some unscrupulous personalities may

---

[51]   **Section 17.** *Proscription of Terrorist Organizations, Association, or Group of Persons.* Any organization, association, or group of persons organized for the purpose of engaging in terrorism, or which, although not organized for that purpose, actually uses the acts to terrorize mentioned in this Act or to sow and create a condition of widespread and extraordinary fear and panic among the populace in order to coerce the government to give in to an unlawful demand shall, upon application of the Department of Justice before a competent Regional Trial Court, with due notice and opportunity to be heard given to the organization, association, or group of persons concerned, be declared as a terrorist and outlawed organization, association, or group of persons by the said Regional Trial Court.

[52]   Jude McCulloch, *Blue Army: Paramilitary Policing in Australia* (Melbourne University Press, 2001), p. 176.

be clandestinely pursuing their terrorist tactics within the framework of legitimate organisations such as the anti-uranium movement, Greenpeace and even the animal welfare movement.[53] Section 17 as presently written prohibits the creation of organisations with legitimate purposes so long as any of its members commit acts the HSA considers as acts of terrorism.

An equally troubling concern is the procedure by which the Anti-Terrorism Council can declare groups and associations as 'terrorist' organisations. While the law requires a judicial declaration to this effect and requires further that notice should be served on the group sought to be declared a terrorist group, the implementation of the law and its implications are in doubt. For example, the sending of notice and other processes to groups such as the NPA, which are without a regular place of business, cannot be done without assurance that these groups were properly notified. Notice here is through service of the pleadings and other processes and not by publication. Under the present set-up of the law, notice by publication is only for proceedings *in rem* or *quasi-in-rem* and the proceedings under the HSA are neither.

E.   Violation of freedom of speech and right to privacy

The HSA is also unconstitutional for violating the right to free speech. This can be clearly seen from s. 7 of HSA, which grants law enforcement agencies the power to intercept any communication described in it:

> **Section 7.** *Surveillance of Suspects and Interception and Recording of Communications.* The provisions of Republic Act No. 4200 (Anti-wire Tapping Law) to the contrary notwithstanding, *a police or law enforcement official and the members of his team may, upon a written order of the Court of Appeals, listen to, intercept and record, with the use of any mode, form, kind or type of electronic or other surveillance equipment or intercepting and tracking devices, or with the use of any other suitable ways and means for that purpose, any communication, message, conversation, discussion, or spoken or written words* between members of a judicially declared and outlawed terrorist organization, association, or group of persons or *of any person charged with or suspected of the crime of terrorism* or conspiracy to commit terrorism.
>
> Provided, That surveillance, interception and recording of communications between lawyers and clients, doctors and patients, journalists and their sources and confidential business correspondence shall not be authorized (emphasis added).

[53]   Ibid.

The HSA violates the right to free speech since any communication made by the accused may be subject to any means of interception by law enforcement agencies, thereby resulting in a chilling effect on his or her right to free speech. Such a chilling effect on the right to free speech constitutes a violation of his or her freedom of expression. This already constitutes an official prohibition of any and all forms of speech of so called terrorist members or organisations. The mere fact they are members of terrorist organisations or a *mere suspect* of the crime of terrorism and this removes from them the right to speak out their valid grievances against the government clearly constitutes prior restraint. The interception of the messages allowed *under the HSA* could not be considered as content-based regulation as the HSA lacks the required well defined standard and the significant government interest that is unrelated to the freedom of expression for its validity.[54]

There is also no 'sunset' provision in the HSA on the interception of communications. This is in contrast to the original provision of the US Patriot Act, which provides for an expiration of the sections on surveillance[55] after four years. While the same provision had been deleted or modified by subsequent laws by extending the sunset provision, the choice to still include a sunset provision in the later laws seemingly demonstrates the US Congress's caution concerning these sections.[56] This is in clear contrast with the Philippine Congress in the creation of the HSA, knowing very well the past and present violations of the right of free speech in the country. Considering that s. 17 deals directly with all forms of communications and information technology, the lack of 'sunset' provision creates the potential for intrusion to chill communications.[57]

Also, the HSA violates the right to privacy since any 'suitable' means can be used by law enforcement agencies to intercept communication. The HSA does not provide any guidelines and limitations as to the methods of interception that may be adopted by law enforcement agencies. Such vague, over-broad, and unlimited means of intruding into communications is a

---

[54] *Francisco Chavez* v. *Raul Gonzales*, G.R. No. 168338, 15 February 2008.
[55] Uniting and Strengthening America by Providing Appropriate Tools Required to Intercept and Obstruct Terrorism Act of 2001 (USA PATRIOT Act) Pub. L. 107–56, § 224. However this has been deleted or modified by later laws, the latest of which is the Department of Defense Appropriations Act 2010 (Pub. Law 111–141). This law extends the sunset provision to 28 February 2011.
[56] Todd M. Gardella, 'Beyond terrorism: the potential chilling effect on the Internet of broad law enforcement legislation' (2006) 80 *St. John's Law Review* 663.
[57] Norman Redlich, John Attanasio and Joel K. Goldstein, *Understanding Constitutional Law* (New York: Matthew Bender & Co 2nd edn, 1999).

clear violation of the right to privacy in accordance with the seminal case of *Ople* v. *Torres*,[58] which invalidated an administrative order creating a National computerised identification reference system:

> *Unlike the dissenters, we prescind from the premise that the right to privacy is a fundamental right guaranteed by the Constitution, hence, it is the burden of government to show that A.O. No. 308 is justified by some compelling state interest and that it is narrowly drawn.* A.O. No. 308 is predicated on two considerations: (1) the need to provide our citizens and foreigners with the facility to conveniently transact business with basic service and social security providers and other government instrumentalities and (2) the need to reduce, if not totally eradicate, fraudulent transactions and misrepresentations by persons seeking basic services. It is debatable whether these interests are compelling enough to warrant the issuance of A.O. No. 308. *But what is not arguable is the broadness, the vagueness, the overbreadth of A.O. No. 308 which if implemented will put our people's right to privacy in clear and present danger.*[59]

Hence, the HSA is subject to strict scrutiny, according to the holding in this case:

> *And we now hold that when the integrity of a fundamental right is at stake, this court will give the challenged law, administrative order, rule or regulation a stricter scrutiny. It will not do for the authorities to invoke the presumption of regularity in the performance of official duties. Nor is it enough for the authorities to prove that their act is not irrational for a basic right can be diminished, if not defeated, even when the government does not act irrationally. They must satisfactorily show the presence of compelling state interests and that the law, rule, or regulation is narrowly drawn to preclude abuses.* This approach is demanded by the 1987 Constitution whose entire matrix is designed to protect human rights and to prevent authoritarianism. In case of doubt, the least we can do is to lean towards the stance that will not put in danger the rights protected by the Constitution.[60]

3. HSA versus IHL Law

Almost sixty years after ratifying the Geneva Conventions and hence entering into the obligation to enact domestic laws punishing grave breaches thereof, the Philippines finally discharged this burden with the passage and coming into effect of the IHL Law,[61] which penalises crimes against

---

[58] G.R. No. 127685, 23 July 1998.
[59] Ibid. (emphasis in original).   [60] Ibid. (emphasis in original).
[61] This is a consolidation of Senate Bill No. 2669 and House Bill No. 6633, and was signed into law by then President Macapagal-Arroyo on 11 December 2009.

international humanitarian law, genocide and crimes against humanity. Although a domestic enactment, the law expressly provides that its interpretation and application must be consistent with international law and rulings of international criminal tribunals.[62] It was intended hence not just to be an implementing legislation to the Geneva Conventions, but also to the entire corpus of international humanitarian and criminal law. The law then penalises grave breaches and serious violations of international humanitarian law by restating provisions of the Geneva Conventions.[63] It thus penalises any attack directed against protected individuals and infrastructures, as well as any resort to prohibited means and methods of warfare committed in international armed conflicts.[64] Further, the law penalises the breach of Common Article 3 of the Geneva Conventions and serious violations of international humanitarian law when committed in the context of a non-international armed conflict.[65] It defines genocide pursuant to the definition provided in the Genocide Convention as an intent, in whole or in part, to destroy a nationality, ethnic race, or religious group of people;[66] and provides for the different means by which genocide may be committed, borrowing the language of the Rome Statute of the International Criminal Court (Rome Statute).[67]

---

[62] IHL Law, s. 15(i).   [63] Ibid., s. 4(a).   [64] Ibid., s. 4(c).   [65] Ibid., s. 4(b).

[66] See Convention on the Prevention and Punishment of the Crime of Genocide, art. 2, available at www2.ohchr.org/english/law/genocide.htm.

[67] IHL Law, s. 5:

> Genocide – (a) For the purpose of this Act, 'genocide' means any of the following acts with intent to destroy, in whole or in part, a national, ethnic, racial, religious, social or any other similar stable and permanent group as such:
>
> (1) Killing members of the group;
> (2) Causing serious bodily or mental harm to members of the group;
> (3) Deliberately inflicting on the group conditions of life calculated to bring about its physical destruction in whole or in part;
> (4) Imposing measures intended to prevent births within the group; and
> (5) Forcibly transferring children of the group to another group.
>
> (b) It shall be unlawful for any person to directly and publicly incite others to commit genocide.
>
> Any person found guilty of committing any of the acts specified in paragraphs (a) and (b) of this section shall suffer the penalty provided under Section 7 of this Act.
>
> In comparison, see Rome Statute, art. 6, available at untreaty.un.org/cod/icc/statute/romefra.htm:
>
> For the purpose of this Statute, 'genocide' means any of the following acts committed with intent to destroy, in whole or in part, a national, ethnical, racial or religious group, as such:
>
> (a) Killing members of the group;

It also penalises crimes against humanity pursuant to the definition provided in the Rome Statute, as well as the different means by which the crime may be committed.[68] Included in the means of committing crimes against humanity is torture and enforced disappearances, both of which are occurring in the Philippines in alarming numbers.[69] For torture as a crime against humanity, the law adopts the Rome Statute definition of the same as a crime that may be committed by anyone, not just state agents.[70] On the other hand, the definition of the crime of enforced disappearance

> (b) Causing serious bodily or mental harm to members of the group;
> (c) Deliberately inflicting on the group conditions of life calculated to bring about its physical destruction in whole or in part;
> (d) Imposing measures intended to prevent births within the group;
> (e) Forcibly transferring children of the group to another group.

[68] IHL Law, s. 6:
> *Other Crimes Against Humanity.* – For the purpose of this act, 'other crimes against humanity' means any of the following acts when committed as part of a widespread or systematic attack directed against any civilian population, with knowledge of the attack:
> (a) Willful killing;
> (b) Extermination;
> (c) Enslavement;
> (d) Arbitrary deportation or forcible transfer of population;
> (e) Imprisonment or other severe deprivation of physical liberty in violation of fundamental rules of international law;
> (f) Torture;
> (g) Rape, sexual slavery, enforced prostitution, forced pregnancy, enforced sterilization, or any other form of sexual violence of comparable gravity;
> (h) Persecution against any identifiable group or collectivity on political, racial, national, ethnic, cultural, religious, gender, sexual orientation or other grounds that are universally recognized as impermissible under international law, in connection with any act referred to in this paragraph or any crime defined in this Act;
> (i) Enforced or involuntary disappearance of persons;
> (j) Apartheid; and
> (k) Other inhumane acts of a similar character intentionally causing great suffering, or serious injury to body or to mental or physical health.
>
> Any person found guilty of committing any of the acts specified herein shall suffer the penalty provided under Section 7 of this Act.
>   In comparison, see Rome Statute, art. 7.

[69] See Task Force Detainees of the Philippines, 'Statistics of documented cases of human rights violations 2009', available at www.tfdp.net/resources/statistics; Karapatan Monitor, April-June 2010, available at www.karapatan.org/resources/statistics.

[70] IHL Law, s. 3(s): '"Torture" means the intentional infliction of severe pain or suffering, whether physical, mental, or psychological, upon a person in the custody or under the control of the accused; except that torture shall not include pain or suffering arising only from, inherent in or incidental to, lawful sanctions.' In comparison, see Rome Statute, art. 7, s. 2(e).

was borrowed from the definition provided in the Convention Against
Enforced Disappearances:[71] there has to be an abduction perpetrated by
state agents, a refusal to acknowledge such an arrest, and the *mens rea*
of intending to remove the victim from the protection of the law for an
extended period of time.

The law then provides for stiff penalties for violations thereof.[72] The
penalty of incarceration ranges from *reclusion temporal* in its medium
to maximum scale and a fine of Php 100 to Php 500,000 up to *reclusion
perpetua* and a fine of up to Php 1,000,000 in the event that the violation
leads to death or serious physical injury, or constitutes rape.

Finally, the law provides a statutory basis for principles intended to
implement the binding nature of international human rights law as they
exist under customary international law. There is to be universal jurisdiction for the crimes enumerated by the new law,[73] the principle of
non-prescriptibility,[74] and the operation of the principles of command
and superior responsibility.[75] For the first time, it has also provided that
immunity cannot be invoked as a defence for prosecutions under the
law.[76]

A first observation is that, while the law only took effect in March 2010,
the jurisdiction of Philippine courts to try individuals for war crimes had
earlier been recognised by way of jurisprudence. In two cases decided
at the end of World War II, the Supreme Court acknowledged that the
duty to prosecute war criminals is recognised by all civilised nations and
forms part of the laws of the land pursuant to the clause of the Philippine
Constitution which incorporates into domestic law generally accepted
principles of international law

In the earlier case of *Yamashita* v. *Styer*,[77] General Tomoyuki Yamashita,
known as the 'Tiger of the Malaya', was the highest ranking officer of the
Japanese Imperial Army in Southeast Asia when Japan lost the war. In his
criminal prosecution for the commission of 144 counts of war crimes, he
invoked the defence of legality since the Philippines then had no domestic law criminalising war crimes. While the majority opinion ruled that
the parties to the conflict, Japan and the United States, were under treaty
obligations which extended to the Philippines, which was a theatre for

---

[71] International Convention for the Protection of All Persons from Enforced Disappearance,
Paris, 6 February 2007, in force 23 December 2010, UN Doc. A/RES/61/177, art. 2.
[72] IHL Law, s. 7.   [73] Ibid., s. 17.   [74] Ibid., s. 11.
[75] Ibid., ss. 10, 12.   [76] Ibid., s. 9.
[77] *Tomoyuki Yamashita* v. *Wilhelm D. Styer*, G.R. No. L-129, 19 December 1945.

the armed conflict, an interesting separate concurring and dissenting opinion explained why international human rights law was binding in the Philippines even if it was not a party to the Convention:

> Impelled by irrepressible endeavors aimed towards the ideal, by the unconquerable natural urge for improvement, by the unquenchable thirstiness of perfection in all orders of life, humanity has been struggling during the last two dozen centuries to develop an international law which could answer more and more faithfully the demands of right and justice as expressed in principles which, weakly enunciated at first in the rudimentary juristic sense of peoples of antiquity, by the inherent power of their universal appeal to human conscience, at last, were accepted, recognized, and consecrated by all the civilized nations of the world.

Likewise, in the second case of *Kuroda* v. *Jalandoni*,[78] another Japanese General questioned the legality of his criminal prosecution pursuant to an Executive Order that invoked grave breaches of the Geneva Conventions and the Hague Regulations at a time when the Philippines was not a party to either. According to the Court, war crimes under both Conventions constituted generally accepted principles of international law and hence part of the laws of the land.

The first point hence is that while penal statutes do not have retroactive effect (as otherwise, it would amount to an *ex post facto* law), it could not be said that serious violations of international humanitarian law only became criminal when the IHL Law became effective. On the contrary, the cases of *Yamashita* and *Kuroda* ruled that war crimes were already criminal because the duty to prosecute war criminals is a *ius cogens* norm and subject to the duty of *aut dedere aut ajudicare*.[79] What the IHL Law really did was to address the need for a law providing specific penalties for these violations. Otherwise, there would be serious questions on what penalties could be imposed under the country's Indeterminate Sentence Law, which requires that if the offence is punished by a penal law other than the Revised Penal Code, the Court shall sentence the accused to an indeterminate sentence, the maximum term of which shall not exceed the

---

[78] *Shigenori Kuroda* v. *Major General Rafael Jalandoni*, G.R. No. L-2662, 26 March 1949.
[79] See Geneva Convention for the Amelioration of the Condition of the Wounded and Sick in Armed Forces in the Field, Geneva, 12 August 1949, in force 21 October 1950, 75 UNTS 31, art. 49; Geneva Convention for the Amelioration of the Wounded, Sick and Shipwrecked Members of the Armed Forces at Sea, Geneva, 12 August 1949, in force 21 October 1950, 75 UNTS 85, art. 50; Geneva Convention Relative to the Treatment of Prisoners of War, Geneva, 12 August 1949, in force 21 October 1950, 75 UNTS 135, art. 129; and Geneva Convention Relative to the Protection of Civilian Persons in Time of War, Geneva, 12 August 1949, in force 21 October 1950, 75 UNTS 287, art. 146.

maximum fixed by said law and the minimum shall not be less than the minimum term prescribed by the same.[80]

Second, the passage of the twin HSA and IHL Law has now given the Philippines very powerful weapons in dealing with modern day terrorism. Certainly, the IHL Law can now be utilised for acts of terrorism which occur in the context of an armed conflict[81] and for acts which qualify as crimes against humanity.[82] Ideally, the HSA, despite its possible constitutional infirmities, may be utilised for criminal acts which do not take place in the context of either an armed conflict or in a widespread or systematic manner. Still, it is uncertain how the courts would construe the relationship between these new laws. This is because in the drafting of both laws, the Philippine Congress proceeded as if the two laws would operate independently of each other. In fact, the drafting of the IHL Law was a result of concerted lobbying by non-governmental authorities such as by the UP Law Center Institute of International Legal Studies[83] and the IHL Committee of the Philippine National Red Cross.[84] The emphasis was on enacting the required enabling legislation for the Geneva Conventions. All reference to 'terrorism' may be found in the Additional Protocols to the Geneva Conventions and not in the Conventions themselves.[85]

On the other hand, the drafting intent and history of the HSA was clearly to create a new legislation that would assist state actors in the fight against terrorism. It was not intended to be supplementary, complementary, nor in any way related to the IHL Law. Otherwise, the HSA should have recognised the right of combatants to criminal immunity for taking part in hostilities in international armed conflicts, and the political context by which the Philippines has dealt with domestic armed groups

---

[80]   Act No. 4103, s.1.   [81]   IHL Law, ss. 3(d)–(e), 6.   [82]   IHL Law, ss. 4–6.
[83]   See Universal Jurisdiction Project of the University of the Philippines Law Center Institute of International Legal Studies, conducted from February 2005 to December 2006.
[84]   See Soliman M. Santos Jr., 'Backgrounder on RA 9851, IHL Law' (speech delivered at the Public Briefing on Republic Act No. 9851: Philippine Act on Crimes Against International Humanitarian Law, Genocide, and Other Crimes Against Humanity, 3 March 2010, Benito Soliven Room, First Floor, Malcolm Hall, University of the Philippines College of Law, Diliman, Quezon City).
[85]   See Protocol Additional to the Geneva Conventions of 12 August 1949 and Relating to the Protection of Victims of International Armed Conflicts, Geneva, 8 June 1977, in force 7 December 1978, 1125 UNTS 3, art. 51(2) (Additional Protocol I); Protocol Additional to the Geneva Conventions of 12 August 1949, and Relating to the Protection of Victims of Non-International Armed Conflicts, Geneva, 8 June 1977, in force 7 December 1978, 1125 UNTS 609, arts. 4(2), 13(2) (Additional Protocol II).

within its territory, which includes entering into political peace agreements with them.

Third, there appears to be a serious lapse in the definition of torture under the IHL Law and under Republic Act No. 9745, the Philippine Law against Torture.[86] The IHL Law adopts the definition of torture found in the Rome Statute; that is, that it may be committed by a person who has custody over the victim.[87] Republic Act No. 9745, on the other hand, adopts the definition found in the Convention against Torture, which provides that torture is a crime that may be committed by state agents only.[88] Again, it is still unsettled when either of these definitions of torture could apply, although a means of harmonising the two laws would be to use the IHL Law as a basis for prosecutions for torture committed as war crimes and crimes against humanity, and to use the special law for isolated acts of torture.

Fourth, it is also noteworthy that the IHL Law for the first time criminalises enforced disappearances. Borrowing the definition in the Convention against Enforced Disappearances and the Rome Statute, it now criminalises enforced disappearances as a form of a crime against humanity.[89] Its elements are: an arrest by state agents and/or with the acquiescence of state organs, refusal to acknowledge such arrest and the intent of removing the person from the protection of the law for an extended period of time.[90] Note though that what has been criminalised are enforced disappearances which are either widespread or systematic. Isolated disappearances are not yet criminal, and hence the need still exists for legislation in this regard.

Finally, while both the HSA and IHL Law have finally filled the legal vacuum in terms of legislation required to deal with terrorism, they cannot, however, address inherent weaknesses in the Philippine legal system which gives rise to disregard for the law in general. The UN Special Rapporteur on extra-legal killings, for instance, argues that the Philippines is in breach of its legal obligation to protect and promote the right to life primarily because of a lack of political will to bring the perpetrators of extra-legal killings and enforced disappearances

---

[86] See Republic Act No. 9745, available at senate.gov.ph/republic_acts/ra%209745.pdf.

[87] See above note 75.

[88] Republic Act No. 9745, s. 3(a); cf. Convention against Torture and Other Cruel, Inhuman or Degrading Treatment or Punishment, New York, 10 December 1984, in force 26 June 1987, 1465 UNTS 85, art. 1.

[89] See above notes 75 and 76.

[90] Ibid.; See IHL Law, s. 3(g).

to justice.[91] Likewise, he observed that the institutions of the criminal justice system appear to be in breach of their obligations. The prosecutors are failing in their task because of their insistence that they have no obligation to take part in the investigation of cases involving extralegal killings, the Ombudsman has been in breach of its obligation to investigate and prosecute state agents for these crimes, and the courts are also in breach because of inordinate delays in the prosecution of these cases.[92] Unless these matters are addressed by the new Aquino Administration, new legislation notwithstanding, the Philippine legal system may still prove ineffective in the fight against terrorism and disregard or non enforcement of the law.

4. Conclusion

Two new pieces of legislation were enacted by the Philippine Congress to better equip the Philippines in dealing with terrorism. The first is an anti-terror legislation, referred to as the Human Security Act, while the second is the enabling legislation to the Geneva Conventions and other international humanitarian law treaties. The anti-terror law appears to fit the mould warned against by the UN Special Rapporteur on anti-terror legislation and human rights. In fact, he had this observation on the HSA:

> On 6 March the bill, titled 'The Act to Secure the State and Protect our People from Terrorism', otherwise known as the 'Human Security Act of 2007' was signed into law by the President of the Philippines. This law is scheduled to take effect in July 2007, two months after the May elections. During this interim period, I encourage the legislative branch of Government in the Philippines to reconsider this new counter-terrorism law which was approved by Congress in a Special Session of Parliament on 19 February 2007. It is my hope that there will be further debate which may result in the introduction of specific amendments or repeal of the entire Act by the new Congress elected this spring, since implementation of this law could have a negative impact on human rights in the country and undermines the rule of law.

---

[91] See Preliminary note on the visit of the Special Rapporteur on extrajudicial, summary or arbitrary executions to the Philippines (12–21 February 2007), available at daccess-dds-ny. un.org/doc/UNDOC/GEN/G07/120/95/PDF/G0712095.pdf?OpenElement; See also Report of the Special Rapporteur on extrajudicial, summary or arbitrary executions on his mission to the Philippines, available at daccess-dds-ny.un.org/doc/UNDOC/GEN/ G08/130/01/PDF/G0813001.pdf?OpenElement, and its Addendum, available at daccess-dds-ny.un.org/doc/UNDOC/GEN/G08/130/01/PDF/G0813001.pdf?OpenElement.

[92] Ibid.

There are some positive aspects of the definition of terrorist acts in the HSA but the end result is an overly broad definition which is seen to be at variance with the principle of legality and thus incompatible with Article 15 of the International Covenant on Civil and Political Rights (ICCPR). Further, the strict application of a penalty of forty years' imprisonment undermines judicial discretion in individual cases and may result in a disproportionate punishment due to the broad definition of terrorist acts.

While there has been some improvement regarding the length of pre-charge detention in the final version of this law, there is a further concern regarding the competence of various bodies authorized to review detention of an individual since some of these are members of the executive rather than an independent judicial body. Thus, section 19 of the Human Security Act appears to lack the procedural guarantees provided by Article 9 of the ICCPR.

Another area of concern is that the Act provides for restrictions on movement including the imposition of house arrest where the legal basis is simply 'in cases where evidence of guilt is not strong' rather than positive suspicion or a higher evidentiary threshold.

The Philippines is a country facing many challenging issues and I wish to reaffirm that I am fully conscious of the need to take effective measures to prevent and counter terrorism, and of the difficulties of States in doing so without compromising the freedoms of a civil society. However, I am concerned that many provisions of the Human Security Act are not in accordance with international human rights standards.[93]

The IHL Law, while long delayed, is an enabling legislation to implement the country's treaty obligation to criminalise grave breaches of the law. This could only be a positive development. New legislation notwithstanding, impunity and terrorism may only be effectively addressed if there is a working legal system that would ensure that those who break the law would in fact be investigated, prosecuted and punished for their acts.

---

[93] See Report of the Special Rapporteur on the promotion and protection of human rights and fundamental freedoms while countering terrorism, Addendum: Communications with Governments, UN Doc. A/HRC/6/17/Add.1, 28 November 2007, [97], available at www2.ohchr.org/english/issues/terrorism/rapporteur/reports.htm.

14

Responses to terrorism in China

FU HUALING

'What I miss the most at this moment are explosives and guns.' A parent
who lost his child during the Wenchuan earthquake[1]

1. Introduction

It is convenient to divide threats to China's national security, in the form
of terrorist attacks or otherwise, into two kinds. The first and most visible kind of threat is what I shall call 'high-level threats', because of the
tremendous attention they have received from the Chinese government.
As some commentators point out, China has infinite political will and
resources to crack down on such threats.[2]

High-level threats, which include organised and highly visible challenges
to the established political order, have two inter-related components. The
first component is separatist movements fighting for independence from
China. Originating from the 'peripheries', the ethnicity-based resistance
against Han domination aims at a separatist goal, and this struggle for
separatism has taken the form of organised violence from time to time.

The second component comprises movements which threaten a regime
change: 'subversive' forces with an ostensible political goal to overthrow
the political system, i.e. to overthrow the monopoly of power held by
the Chinese Communist Party (CCP or Party). Political opposition has

The author would like to thank Albert Chen, D. W. Choy, Richard Cullen, Michael Dowdle,
Michael Hor, Eva Pils, Randy Peerenboom, Kent Roach, Joshua Rosenzweig and Victor
Ramraj for their comments on the earlier versions of this paper.

[1] Editorial, 'A stupid government making a time-bomb for itself', *Ming Bao* (*Mingpao
Daily*), 13 May 2010. The high death rate among school children was attributed to the low-
quality construction of school buildings which collapsed quickly when the earthquake
started. After the earthquake, parents of the victims organised themselves to investigate
corruption that may have occurred during the construction of the schools. The investigation was frustrated by the police.
[2] Martin I. Wayne, 'Inside China's war on terrorism' (2009) 59 *Journal of Contemporary
China* 249–61.

largely been non-violent in nature and the institutional face of these forces includes dissident communities, Falun Gong and other ad hoc resistance groups.

Then there is what may be identified as the 'low-level threats'. These include the ad hoc, individualistic violence against the society at large with certain vaguely conceived political motivations. They involve the killing of judges, police officers and other government officials as a form of protest against certain governmental action. These acts are often committed by isolated individuals and often referred to in China as 'individualistic terrorism'. Individualist violence has, however, often been neglected by the government because it does not pose a direct challenge to the Party-state. Such individualistic terrorism is increasing in intensity and frequency in China. Yet, government responses are mechanical and passive, with the public viewing its perpetrators with sympathy, if not encouragement. However, the impact of such threats cannot be underestimated, for the accumulation of individualised political violence may develop into a prototype terrorism, which may eventually develop into organised terrorism if the conditions are rights.

2.   Historical legacy and legal framework

Terrorism is not new to the CCP. Started as an underground Leninist party, the CCP had grown and developed in a hostile environment and suffered brutal repression from its inception until it came to power in 1949. Officially branded as 'Communist bandits' by its adversaries, the CCP was an insurgent force fighting for political survival, with its own territories, armed force and a political structure. Before gaining political power, the CCP also resorted to terrorism against government forces to advance its political goal.[3]

After coming to power, the CCP government immediately became the target of terrorist attacks. In the years immediately following the establishment of the new government, terrorist attacks in the form of political assassination, poisoning of water resources, bombing of bridges, factories and other facilities, and other forms of sabotage routinely occurred. The CCP-led government responded brutally and swiftly. The first

---

[3] Patricia E. Griffin, *The Chinese Communist Treatment of Counterrevolutionaries, 1924–1949* (Princeton University Press, 1976); Leng Shao-Chuan, *Justice in Communist China* (New York: Oceana Publications, 1967); James P. Brady, *Justice and Politics in People's China: Legal Order or Continuing Revolution?* (London: Academic Press, 1982).

criminal legislation was entitled the 'Regulations for the Suppression of Counterrevolution', which was in essence a counter-terrorism legislation adopted in 1951 authorising mass execution and indefinite incarceration of counter-revolutionaries, enemy agents and spies, separatists and other hostile elements which violently resisted the new regime.[4] Revolutionary justice did not permit the luxury of evidence, burden of proof, defence or other procedural niceties, nor was there any tradition of institutional-ised checks and balances against the overwhelming governmental power: both the judiciary and the congresses were weak, to say the least, and were placed under the control of the CCP.[5]

With the consolidation of political power and the elimination of poten-tial enemies outside the Party, the CCP was able to virtually eliminate regime change and separatist threats. Indeed, the CCP monopolised all political power and exercised it in a dictatorial fashion, removing the pre-conditions for any meaningful dissent, political, religious, cultural or otherwise.[6]

This revolutionary legacy foreshadowed China's legal development even when China was shifting from revolution to modernisation. When the first criminal code of the People's Republic of China – the Criminal Law of the People's Republic of China (Criminal Law) – was promul-gated in 1979, it did not have a specific offence of terrorism. However, the Criminal Law did have a specific chapter on counter-revolutionary offences including insurgency and sabotage. Some of these counter-rev-olutionary offences were in fact 'terrorist offences', given their violent nature and political motivation.

The concept of terrorism was first introduced into China's criminal law when the Criminal Law was revised in 1997. After 9/11, China further amended its criminal law to toughen its stance against terrorism in order to respond to the UN Security Council Resolution 1373 (2001).[7]

---

[4] Ibid.; Richard Curt Kraus, *Class Conflict in Chinese Socialism* (New York: Columbia University Press, 1981).

[5] Leng, *Justice in Communist China*; Brady, *Justice and Politics in People's China*; Jerome Cohen, 'The Chinese Communist Party and "Judicial Independence": 1949–1959' (1969) 82(5) *Harvard Law Review* 967–1006.

[6] Jerome Cohen, *The Criminal Process in the People's Republic of China, 1949–1963: An Introduction* (Cambridge, MA: Harvard University Press, 1968).

[7] For the details of these amendments, see the Amendment to the Criminal Law of the People's Republic of China (Third Amendment) (Adopted by the Standing Committee of the National People's Congress on 29 December 2001), available at www.chinalawinfo. com.

Although China has been drafting an anti-terrorism law for almost a decade, no legislative bill has been tabled to the Chinese legislature. Currently, there are four offences of terrorism in the Criminal Law:

(1) Article 120(1) punishes those who 'organise or lead', 'actively participate' or 'participate' in 'terrorist organisations';
(2) Article 120(2) punishes those who finance terrorist organisations or individuals who engage in terrorist activities;
(3) Article 191(1) punishes those who knowingly hide or conceal the proceeds of terrorism; and
(4) Article 291(2) punishes those who falsify terrorist information or knowingly disseminate false information.

In addition to the four offences listed above, there are also a number of offences of endangering public order which are closely related to terrorist offences. However, one fundamental problem is that the substantive criminal law does not define 'terrorism' or 'terrorist organisation'. Additionally, given the lack of a specific anti-terrorism legislation, there are no separate procedures or rules of evidence for terrorist offences and no separate tribunal to try terrorist offences. Terrorism is therefore simply treated as an ordinary criminal offence and historically has been treated as such under Chinese criminal law.

In policy documents, terrorism is largely defined as politically-motivated violence against the state. In its application, the definition is both too narrow and over-broad: it is narrow because political violence is limited to those aiming at either regime change or boundary change; it is over-broad because once a regime change threat or a boundary change threat is identified, peaceful advocacy of the changes may be regarded as associated with, and treated as an integral part of, terrorism, especially in the context of separatist movements.[8]

The rule of law reform in China in the past thirty years was to rid the country of its revolutionary legacy and to create a minimum degree of the rule of law in the anti-terrorism law and other emergency measures. The first thirty years of the PRC was defined largely by a perpetual, and often violent, revolution in which the Party imposed terror on real or imagined enemies. The Party was then perpetuating a continuous revolution in a state of exception, and political life returned to normalcy only in the late 1970s and early 1980s when the Party-state initiated an open door policy.

[8] Michael Clarke, 'China's "War on Terror" in Xinjiang: human security and the causes of violent Uighur separatism' (2008) 20 *Terrorism and Political Violence* 271–301.

Because of gradual political liberalisation – incremental legal and institution building and expansion of rights and freedoms in social and economic spheres – China began to accommodate the distinction between normalcy and emergency. It is only when a certain form of the rule of law has been established that we can speak of the need to suspend it in response to an emergency; and it is only when citizens normally have certain rights that those rights can be derogated from because of the emergency. It is only after the distinction between normalcy and exception is clearly recognised and defined that the need for the derogation of rights and departure from the rule of law can be discussed, and hopefully prevented or minimised.[9]

Interestingly, it is the increase in social volatility and unrest in the form of peaceful and violent demonstration in the new century that compelled the government to resort to law to regulate and legalise state power in an emergency. The government has moved quickly in creating a legislative framework for crisis management, including the enactment of the Martial Law in 1996 and the Emergency Responses Law in 2007.[10] While the Martial Law aims at providing a legal framework for handling riots and social unrest, the Emergency Responses Law provides a legal mechanism for handling natural disasters and public health crises.

Both the Martial Law and the Emergency Responses Law aim at enhancing governmental capacity and effectiveness during a crisis, but those power-creating/power-centralising laws also have the potential of creating a degree of certainty, transparency, regularity, as well as rights creation and rights protection even in an emergency.[11] Unfortunately, however, these two laws have so far existed in name only because the government has handled actual crises administratively (and politically) without a clear invocation of the laws.

The application of the 1996 Martial Law is an example. Before the enactment of the Martial Law in 1996, the government relied on the emergency power in the constitution to declare martial law in Lhasa and parts of Beijing in 1989 pursuant to the Constitution.[12] There were no

---

[9] Albert H. Y. Chen, 'Emergency powers, constitutionalism and legal transplants: the East Asian experiences', in Victor V. Ramraj and Arun K. Thiruvengadam (eds.), *Emergency Powers in Asia: Exploring the Limits of Legality* (Cambridge University Press, 2010), Chapter 3.

[10] Ibid.; Jacques DeLisle, 'States of exception in an exceptional state: emergency powers law in China', in Ramraj and Thiruvengadam, *Emergency Powers in Asia*, Chapter 13.

[11] Ibid.; Chen, 'Emergency powers, constitutionalism and legal transplants'.

[12] Mo Jihong and Xu Gao, *Jieyan Falü Zhidu Gaiyao* (*An Overview of the Martial Law and the Martial Law System*) (Beijing: Law Press, 1996), Chapter 1. The Chinese Constitution

specific legal provisions on the operation of martial law and the 1996 Martial Law was expected to fill in the legal gap. According to art. 2 of the Martial Law, a martial law order may be proclaimed if the following three conditions are satisfied: (1) an unrest, a rebellion or a grave riot is taking place; (2) the incident is seriously endangering the unification and security of the State or public security; and (3) it has reached a state of emergency where public order cannot be maintained and the safety of lives and property cannot be ensured unless extraordinary measures are taken.

The Martial Law provides a procedure according to which a martial law order can be lawfully imposed, but the law was not used when actual unrest took place and when the government took extreme emergency measures. The Chinese government's handling of the Tibetan riot in March 2008[13] and the Urumqi riots in July 2009[14] illustrate the primacy of political expedience in crisis-management and the marginalisation, if not irrelevance, of the Martial Law. The Xinjiang government, for instance, adopted a series of harsh and restrictive measures to suppress riots and restore order in the city without using the Martial Law.[15] The government preferred to achieve its objectives without the benefits or constraints of the Martial Law.

1982 provides the legal ground for the imposition of martial law in China. In the 2004 Amendment to the PRC Constitution, the term 'martial law' ('戒嚴') in these three provisions was replaced with the term 'state of emergency' ('緊急狀態').

[13] See, e.g., 'Mass arrest in Tibet after riot, government said 10 citizens died and ordered the rioters to voluntary surrender within the prescribed time limit', *Ming Bao*, 16 March 2008, A02; 'Monks demonstrated and lit fires, police and soldiers used tanks to suppress, corpses were found on streets, many people died and injured in the Lhasa riot', *Ming Bao*, 15 March 2008, A19; 'Journalists dissatisfied with the prohibition of covering news in Tibet', *Xinbao (Hong Kong Economic Journal)*, 18 March 2008, P08.

[14] See, e.g., 'Army marched into Urumqi to execute curfew order', *Ming Bao Zhishi Xinwen (Mingpao Daily Real Time News)*, 7 July 2009; 'Drivers refuse to enter the riot area, "people inside will kill all Han people"', *Ming Bao*, 7 July 2009, A03; 'Xinjiang riot has an impact on the anti-terrorism measures for the National Day, the greatest bloodshed after the June Fourth, at least 140 died and 828 injured', *Xianggang Jingji Ribao (Hong Kong Economic Times)*, 7 July 2009, A14; 'Han-Uighur conflict heightened, army is standing by, thousands of Han people marched to the street with knives, Urumqi is also out of control and curfew order is administered', *Xinggang Jingji Ribao*, 8 July 2009, A15.

[15] These included sending fully-equipped People's Liberation Army officers to be stationed in the city; administering curfew; administering traffic control; closing certain parts of the city to the outside world; blocking the telephone and Internet networks in the city; ordering no activities to be carried out in the city for three days; and obstructing journalists from covering the news after the riot: ibid.

3. Theoretical framework

Terrorism comes in many different shapes.[16] In the context of contemporary China, terrorism has mainly taken the form of politically motivated violence against society at large. It has been resorted to by political, religious or ethnic minorities who desire to declare and assert their rights and interests. Without any intention of joining the debate on the moral justifiability of terrorism,[17] I want to observe that terrorism is taking place in China in the particular context of rising rights-awareness and civil society forces which are asserting their rights and interests by both lawful and unlawful, or even violent, means. Terrorism is part of a general social resistance.

The thesis of rightful resistance, as developed by O'Brien and Li, is representative of the resistance literature in post-Mao China. By rightful resistance, O'Brien and Li refer to 'a form of popular contention that operates near the boundary of authorized channels, employs the rhetoric and commitments of the powerful to curb the exercise of power, hinges on locating and exploiting divisions within the state, and relies on mobilizing support from the wider public'.[18] Rightful resistance thus consists of legally sanctioned actions taken to protect one's legal rights. In carrying out rightful resistance, the resisters strategically engage the state, exploit the gaps within the state and change the society through legitimate means.

Rightful resistance emerges because of the increase in political opportunities in China, broadly the result of the widening of gaps between improved and increasing legal rights in law and policies (offered by the central authorities) and the violation of legal rights in action (by the local government). This 'structural opening' provides the context for rightful resistance to develop. In addition, the appreciation by social groups of this opportunity, and their willingness and ability to exploit the gap between law and practice, is another important condition for rightful resistance. Because of improved transportation and communication, the penetration of mass media, and many other social and economic changes brought about by economic reform in China, citizens have become more

---

[16] Gus Martin, *Understanding Terrorism: Challenges, Perspectives, and Issues* (Thousand Oaks, CA: Sage Publications, 2003).

[17] See Igor Primoratz (ed.), *Terrorism: The Philosophical Issues* (New York: Palgrave Macmillan, 2004).

[18] Kevin J. O'Brien and Lianjiang Li, *Rightful Resistance in Rural China* (Cambridge University Press, 2006), p. 2.

aware of their rights and are prepared to assert and defend these rights. Within this larger context, rightful resistance is taking place throughout China where aggrieved citizens air their complaints and use laws to assert their rights.

The theory of rightful resistance can explain the increase in the assertion of legal rights as well as the rise of ethnically based politics and claims. The structural opening is not limited to the creation of legal rights. There has been a general liberalisation in the political environment since the 1980s and an expanding freedom in social and economic spheres since the 1990s.

The theory of rightful resistance does not necessarily exclude unlawful or even violent resistance, which borders with, and has the potential to morph into, politically motivated violence. Rightful resistance transcends both 'contained' politics (i.e. political activism that is legally permissible) and 'transgressive' politics (i.e. political activism that goes beyond what is legally permissible).[19]

Disruptive collective action, or low-level rioting and social unrest, may provide a link between rightful resistance and politically motivated violence. Collective action includes a wide range of disruptive activities ranging from more peaceful types of protest, sit-ins and demonstrations, to more disruptive and violent forms such as traffic blockades, attacks on state agencies, street riots and sabotage. Cai Yongshun has argued that disruptive collective action becomes an option when legal channels are blocked or become ineffective. When rights are deprived and remedies are not forthcoming, aggrieved individuals are ready to resort to less legitimate ways to make their claims.[20] Disruptive action is used to escalate a particular conflict so that it would be placed on the political agenda. It is meant to attract attention so that authorities at a higher level would be persuaded to provide remedies which were otherwise not forthcoming.[21] The use of extreme violence could be, and has been used as, a step to achieve a political objective.

Terrorism thus grows in societies which are in social and political transition. Terrorism is first of all a criminal offence which is strongly associated with social and economic transition.[22] Economic development,

[19] Douglas McAdam, Sidney Tarrow and Charles Tilly, *Dynamics of Contention* (Cambridge University Press, 2001).
[20] Yongshun Cai, 'Disruptive collective action in the reform era', in Kevin J. O'Brien (ed.), *Popular Protest in China* (Cambridge, MA: Harvard University Press, 2008), ch. 8.
[21] Ibid.
[22] Louis I. Shelley, *Crime and Modernization: The Impact of Industrialization and Urbanization on Crime* (Carbondale, IL: Southern Illinois University Press, 1981).

marketisation and the resulting social and economic changes may improve education, alleviate poverty and upgrade transportation and communication, but they can also generate new tensions such as social disruption, economic disparity and political inequality. These changes can create entitlement but also a strong sense of deprivation.[23]

Terrorism is also a political offence. Recent studies have shown that it is not poverty but political transition which bears a strong correlation with terrorism. The research of Abadie and many others have shown that '[c]ountries with intermediate levels of political freedom are shown to be more prone to terrorism than countries with high levels of political freedom or countries with highly authoritarian regimes'.[24] Thus, neither dictatorships nor mature democracies breed domestic terrorism. Dictatorships create a suffocating environment where any form of resistance, including terrorism, is made impossible. A mature democracy has strong legitimacy, adequate resources and institutional capacity to absorb, contain and internalise social conflicts so that terrorist attacks become unnecessary.

In transitional states, there is the diversification of interests, either economic, ethnic or otherwise, and a degree of tolerance towards the identification, articulation or assertion of different interests. Society is pluralistic and is accepted as such. There is also a considerable degree of freedom in religious belief and practices, and in the social and economic spheres, including the freedom of mobility, association and expression.[25] There is improved protection of rights in the criminal process, including the rights of terrorist suspects. Terrorists tend to exploit the rights and freedom in perpetrating terrorist activities.[26] This is the reason politically motivated

---

[23] See, e.g., C. Ronald Chester, 'Perceived relative deprivation as a cause of property crime' (1976) 22(1) *Crime & Delinquency* 17–30; Iain Walker and Heather J. Smith (eds.), *Relative Deprivation: Specification, Development, and Integration* (Cambridge University Press, 2002).

[24] Alberto Abadie, 'Poverty, political freedom, and the roots of terrorism' (2006) 96(2) *The Economics of National Security* 51; Alan B. Krueger and David D. Laitin, 'Kto Kogo?: A cross-country study of the origins and targets of terrorism', *NBER Working Paper*, 11 November 2003, available at www.krueger.princeton.edu/terrorism3.pdf; Subhayu Bandyopadhyay and Javed Younas, 'Poverty, political freedom, and the roots of terrorism: a reappraisal', *Research Division of the Federal Reserve Bank of St. Louis Working Paper Series*, Working Paper 2009–023C (July 2010), available at research.stlouisfed.org/wp/2009/2009–023.pdf.

[25] Bandyopadhyay and Younas, 'Poverty, political freedom, and the roots of terrorism'.

[26] Walter Enders and Todd Sandler, *The Political Economy of Terrorism* (Cambridge University Press, 2006).

violence did not emerge in China until the early 1980s when the Chinese political system began to open up.

4. Boundary change threat

Terrorism in China has been closely associated with separatist movements in the ethnic autonomous regions, the Uighur region in particular. Violent protests against Chinese rule have been organised by the Uighur separatists and Buddhists.[27]

Violent separatist protests in Tibet and Xinjiang in particular re-emerged immediately after the commencement of the open door policy in the early 1980s. Confrontation also took place between rioters and security forces, but the state often responded swiftly and harshly. Violent confrontation in Lhasa, Tibet, eventually led to the imposition of martial law in March 1989.[28] Separatist demonstrations in Inner Mongolia between late 1989 and early 1990 were suppressed by the armed police,[29] and in Xinjiang, in particular, the armed police, backed by the army, frequently battled with the armed rioters.[30]

The crackdown on violent demonstrations was followed by frequent terrorist attacks in the mid-1990s, especially in Xinjiang. Terrorist attacks there included riots and ambushes targeting government offices and military installations, bombings of buses and the assassination of police and local officials. With few exceptions, the attacks were of a relatively low level and were dealt with by the police effectively.[31] Notwithstanding that, however, the Chinese government asserted that the cumulative impact of those attacks was significant in destabilising the whole region. Officially, more than 2,000 terrorist attacks have taken place in Xinjiang since the

---

[27] Yitzhak Shichor, 'Blow up: internal and external challenges of Uyghur separatism and Islamic radicalism to Chinese rule in Xinjiang' (2005) 32(2) *Asian Affairs: An American Review* 119–36; Ronald David Schwartz, *Circle of Protest: Political Ritual in the Tibetan Uprising 1987–92* (London: Hurst, 1994).

[28] '1989: Tibet riots, martial law was imposed on Lhasa', *Renmin Wang (People's Daily)*, 23 July 2009, available at news.qq.com/a/20090723/001567.htm.

[29] Human Rights Watch, *Crackdown in Inner Mongolia* (July 1991), available at www.smhric.org/Hada/Alban_5.htm.

[30] Wayne, 'Inside China's war on terrorism'.

[31] Ibid.; Zheng Yongnian and Lim Tai Wei, 'China's new battle with terrorism in Xinjiang', *EAI Background Brief No 446* (8 April 2009), available at www.eai.nus.edu.sg/BB446. pdf; Chien-Peng Chung, 'Confronting terrorism and other evils in China: all quiet on the western front?' (2006) 4(2) *China and Eurasia Forum Quarterly* 75–87; Shichor, 'Blow up'.

1990s, resulting in 160 deaths and 4,040 wounded.[32] While China was reluctant to publicise terrorist events in China before 2001, it started to highlight and amplify the reporting of terrorist activities after 9/11.

On the domestic front, China has launched a brutal war against separatist movements since the 1990s and ruled the affected regions with an iron fist. The standard reaction of the Chinese security forces is to launch a strike-hard campaign (*yanda*) on a specific target area or a target offence. For example, upon discovery of a large quantity of home-made grenades in Hetian in 1998, the Xinjiang CCP Committee ordered a special campaign against terrorist activities within the region. After the campaign, the security forces arrested more than 100 international and domestic terrorist suspects, confiscated more than 1,000 home-made grenades and more than 100 firearms, and destroyed more than ten terrorist training bases and fifty-one firearms-manufacturing shops.[33] Campaigns often led to mass detention, arrest, conviction and execution.

When it comes to trials of separatists, the justice system simply performs a ritual, rubber-stamping function of decisions made by the CCP. The government explicitly prohibits legal representation by lawyers not appointed by the government. Torture by law enforcers is commonly alleged and the procedural rights of suspects and defendants, although provided by the law, are violated as a matter of routine. The use of the death penalty is excessive in both Xinjiang and Tibet, especially when compared with its decline in the Han regions due to recent procedural reforms.[34]

China's war on terror is comprehensive and aims at reaching the social fabric of the Uighur society. The country has tightened the crackdown on what is referred to as the 'Three Evils' (i.e. violent terrorism, ethnic separatism and religious fundamentalism) that are putting China's national security at risk. Separatism is the ultimate goal behind this trinity: religious fundamentalism lays a cultural foundation and terrorism is the

---

[32] Information Office of State Council, '"East Turkistan" terrorist forces cannot get away with impunity', 21 January 2002, available at english.peopledaily.com.cn/200201/21/eng20020121_89078.shtml. For a critical assessment of the official claims, see James Millward, *Violent Separatism in Xinjing: A Critical Assessment* (Washington, DC: East-West Centre, Policy Studies 6, 2004).

[33] Chen Nan, 'China counter-attacking "Eastern Turkistan" for 17 years', *Xinwen Shijie* (*News World*), available at qkzz.net/article/e1c75eb5–03ee-4ba0–96ec-e618c0a70797.htm.

[34] For more recent examples, see Human Rights Watch, 'China: Xinjiang trials deny justice', available at www.hrw.org/en/news/2009/10/15/china-xinjiang-trails-deny-justice; and 'China:hundreds of Tibetan detainees and prisoners unaccounted for,' available at www.hrw.org/en/news/2009/03/09/china-hundreds-tibetan-detainees-and-prisoners. unaccounted.

instrument to achieve this ultimate goal. China treats these three forces with equal seriousness and determination.

Facilitated by the ambiguity of any definition of terrorism, a net has been cast so wide as to cover all cultural and religious affairs. The government is able to treat religion as the cause of terrorism in Xinjiang and to treat religious groups as potential terrorist organisations.[35] Two researchers of the Ministry of Public Security provided the following facts to prove an increase in religious fanaticism in Xinjiang: a sharp increase of mosques, a steady increase in Quranic schools and students, the popularity of pilgrimages to Mecca and the spread of religious publications.[36]

Their concerns are both real and imagined, of course. Religious schools which are more secretive, for example, may be used to train future separatists and terrorists, pilgrimages may be a pretext for terrorist training, fundamentalist publications may incite hatred and mobilise support for independence, and cross-border religious exchange may facilitate the infiltration of terrorist funding and weapons at China's Western borders.

Increasingly, the government is using extra-judicial measures to punish 'minor' terrorists, especially the administrative measure of re-education through labour which allows incarceration without trial for up to three years. Usually, organisers of terrorist organisations and principal perpetrators of terrorist activities are subject to severe criminal punishment, while their followers and sympathisers are subject to administrative detention for involvement with unlawful organisations, unlawful publications or unlawful religious practices.[37]

Given the geopolitics of Xinjiang, China promoted regional and multilateral co-operation against separatist terrorism. The Shanghai Co-operation Organisation (SCO) is a successful example. Founded on 15 June 2001 in Shanghai by China, the Republic of Kazakhstan, the Kyrgyz Republic, the Russian Federation, the Republic of Tajikistan and the

[35] For a discussion of the broad scope of 'splittism' in the Tibetan context, see Emily Yeh, 'Living together in Lhasa: ethnic relations, coercive amity, and subaltern cosmopolitanism', in Shail Mayaram (ed.), *The Other Global City* (New York: Routledge, 2009), Chapter 3; Emily Yeh, 'Tibetan indigeneity: translations, resemblances and uptake', in Marisol de la Cadena and Orin Starn (eds.), *Indigenous Experience Today* (Oxford: Berg, 2007), 69–97; Emily Yeh, 'Tibet and the problem of radical reductionism' (2009) 41(5) *Antipode* 1004.
[36] Shichor, 'Blow up'.
[37] Fu Hualing, 'Counter-revolutionaries, subversives, and terrorists: China's evolving national security law', in Fu Hualing, Carole J. Petersen and Simon N. M. Young (eds.), *National Security and Fundamental Freedoms: Hong Kong's Article 23 under Scrutiny* (Hong Kong University Press, 2005), Chapter 2; Shichor, 'Blow up', 126–9.

Republic of Uzbekistan, the SCO seeks to enhance the co-operation and strengthen the relationship between the member states in matters such as politics, trade and economy, science and technology, culture and education, energy and environmental protection.

Enhancing mutual benefits in these areas are important goals. However, as the borders of these member states are shared,[38] the crucial concern underlying the formation of the SCO was to maintain peace and security within the region.[39] This was also the original goal of the formation of the Shanghai Five – the predecessor of the SCO that was founded by China, Russia, Kazakhstan, Kirghizia and Tajikistan in 1996. The agenda of the first meeting of Shanghai Five was confined to developing 'some security confidence building measures in the border areas before the final resolution of the border problems'.[40]

According to the SCO's Charter, the goal of maintenance of peace and security is achieved through co-operation in transnational crime fighting (illicit narcotics, arms trafficking and illegal migration in particular) and counteracting terrorism, separatism and extremism.[41] To effectively tackle the terrorism problem, the Regional Counter-terrorist Structure (RCTS), which is a standing body under the SCO, was created.[42] Aside from liaison and exchange work, document drafting, and gathering and analysing terrorism-related information, one of the major tasks of the Executive Committee of the RCTS is to provide 'assistance in interaction among the member states in preparation and staging of counterterrorism exercises at the request of concerned member states, preparation and conduct of search operations and other activities in the field of fighting terrorism, separatism and extremism'.[43]

---

[38] Qingguo Jia, 'The success of the Shanghai Five: interests, norms and pragmatism', available at www.comw.org/cmp/fulltext/0110jia.htm.

[39] The goals of the SCO are set out in art. 1 of the Charter of the Shanghai Co-operation Organisation (SCO Charter).

[40] For details about the Shanghai Five, see Jia, 'The success of the Shanghai Five'. See also Michael Clarke, 'China, Xinjiang and the internationalization of the Uyghur issue' (2010) 22(2) *Global Change, Peace and Security* 213–29.

[41] SCO Charter, art. 1.

[42] SCO Charter, art. 10. The RCTS 'operates in accordance with the SCO Charter, the Shanghai Convention on Combating Terrorism, Separatism and Extremism, the Agreement among the SCO member states on the Regional Anti-Terrorism Structure, as well as documents and decisions adopted in the SCO framework': see 'The Executive Committee of the Regional Counter-Terrorism Structure', available at www.sectsco.org/EN/AntiTerrorism.asp.

[43] 'The Executive Committee of the Regional Counter-Terrorism Structure'.

China has used the SCO to provide energy, security and political stability in the vast Xinjiang region with cross-border activities associated with the 'Three Evils' clearly in mind. Through the co-operation and support of SCO member states, China is able to control Uighur separatist movements (the East Turkestan Islamic Movement (ETIM) in particular), cut off foreign support that separatists in Xinjiang receive from its Central Asian neighbours, and extradite separatists and terrorists back to China for prosecution. Given the size of the overseas Uighur population in the SCO member states, co-operation from hosting states becomes essential in ending the foreign connection with, and support for, any separatist movement in the region. China demanded that the Central Asian countries, Kazakhstan and Kyrgyzstan in particular, clamp down on separatist activities of the large Uighur émigré communities.[44]

China responded to 9/11 actively and has used the event to highlight and magnify the terrorist threat in Xinjiang.[45] China supported the use of international force against terrorism and played a constructive role in co-operating with the United Nations and the US in anti-terrorism matters.[46] China was successful in placing the ETIM on the US list of terrorist organisations in 2002, winning international recognition for the risk of terrorism in Xinjiang and a promise of international co-operation against separatist movements in that region.

China's state policy on ethnic separatism is at a crossroads. The government may have created overall economic prosperity and tolerated cultural diversity and social autonomy for the ethnic regions.[47] The government has also ruled the autonomous regions politically with an iron fist over the past twenty years and is prepared to crush any sign of political challenge brutally and swiftly. The riots and insurgencies in the Greater

---

[44] Clarke, 'China, Xinjiang and the internationalization of the Uyghur issue'.
[45] Shichor, 'Blow up'.
[46] China's anti-terrorism position paper states that: 'The fight against terrorism calls for protracted and concerted efforts of the international community. It is imperative to strengthen international cooperation at all levels and establish an international anti-terrorism mechanism under the auspices of the United Nations in accordance with the Charter of the United Nations'. See 'China's position paper against international terrorism', 25 September 2001, available at www.china-un.org/eng/chinaandun/securitycouncil/thematicissues/counterterrorism/t26910.htm.
[47] Barry Sautman, 'Ethnic law and minority rights in China: progress and constraints' (1999) 21(3) *Law and Policy* 283–314; Barry Sautman, 'Preferential policies for ethnic minorities in China: the case of Xinjiang' (1998) 4(1–2) *Nationalism and Ethnic Policies* 88; Barry Sautman, 'Is Tibet China's colony?: the claim of demographic catastrophe' (2001) 15 *Columbia Journal of Asian Law* 81–131.

Tibetan regions in 2008 and Xinjiang in 2009 heightened the concern for the security and vulnerability of the regions and prompted the government to rethink its iron-fist policies. The events symbolised the failure of ethnic policies that relied on economic boost and political repression. These events revealed the volatility of the situation even after sixty years of Communist rule and the lack of mutual trust and understanding between the ethnic population and the government. These events also demonstrated the organising capacity of ethnic leaders, domestic or overseas, in mobilising support and orchestrating events, as well as their readiness to resort to political violence. Beyond suppression, the CCP may have to do more soul searching and develop a new ethnic policy that is more tolerant of cultural diversity and economic equality in the future.

5. Regime change threats

Regime change threats were real and immediate in the early 1950s when the new Communist government was established. After brutal suppression, enemy forces within mainland China vanished and political dissidence of any kind simply disappeared under the dictatorial regime during the 1960s and 1970s. Open political dissidence re-emerged in the post-revolutionary era only *after* the regime shifted its priority from revolution to modernisation and adopted a reform-oriented open door policy.[48]

Political dissidence in China has evolved in three stages. The first stage was the use of speech. From the late 1970s and the 1980s, the major form of resistance was speech and publications advocating peaceful change of the political system, mostly through 'wall papers' ('*dazibao*') and underground journals calling for further political liberation and implicitly challenging the Party-state. Occasionally, there was highly emotional and harsh rhetoric against the regime and even advocacy of violent overthrow of the state. But, in the early days of political dissidence, there was little, if any, organised dissidence or action, except words uttered or published. The offence of sedition, or counter-revolutionary propaganda, in the Criminal Law became the principal tool used by the government against this generation of dissidents.

Expression-based prosecution was most intensive in the early 1980s and diminished in scope and intensity in subsequent years. After the 1997 Criminal Law amendment, the counter-revolutionary propaganda offence was abolished and replaced by the offence of inciting subversion

---

[48] Fu Hualing, 'Sedition and political dissidence: towards legitimate dissent in China?' (1996) 26 *Hong Kong Law Journal* 210–33.

of the socialist system. The new incitement offence is strikingly similar to the old counter-revolutionary propaganda offence in its statutory wording[49] and given the similarities, it is not surprising that expression-based prosecutions have continued. The incitement-based offence has been used widely to punish people for activities such as calling for a collective commemoration of the 1989 Tiananmen bloodshed, trying to set up a human rights NGO, criticising the CCP or publicising corruption scandals.

It is important to note that prosecution has become more targeted, focusing on known dissidents with a long anti-government record who had published critical comments in 'hostile' overseas media. Beyond this relatively narrow security concern, the government is more tolerant of some dissenting and critical voices, especially those coming from certain disadvantaged social groups.[50]

The second stage saw dissidents moving forward from mere speech to organisation and action. Falun Gong started as an aggrieved cult but it has become the strongest, and the most organised, political opposition to the CCP, largely because of the brutal crackdown and repression it has suffered.[51] The repression cemented a collective identity and nurtured a determination to end the one-party rule. At the same time, the China Democracy Party (CDP) emerged, representing the most direct challenge to the CCP. Symbolically, the CDP moved political dissidents from expression to political action through an attempt to register an opposition political party openly and legally. Organisationally, like Falun Gong, the CDP is a cross-regional, with preparatory committees being formed in many provinces and cities, and cross-professional organisation, with members coming from diverse professional backgrounds.[52] More recently, in 2008, political activists, led by a dissident intellectual, Liu Xiaobo, published Charter 08, a political charter which demanded further democratisation and the eventual end of the one-party rule in China.[53]

[49] Fu, 'Counter-revolutionaries, subversives, and terrorists'.
[50] Fu, 'Counter-revolutionaries, subversives, and terrorists'; 'Sedition and political dissidence'.
[51] James Tong, 'An organizational analysis of the Falun Gong: structure, communications, financing' (2002) 171 *The China Quarterly* 636–60; James W. Tong, *Revenge of the Forbidden City: The Suppression of the Falungong in China, 1999–2005* (Oxford University Press, 2009).
[52] Teresa Wright, 'The China Democracy Party and the politics of protest in the 1980s-1990s' (2002) 172 *The China Quarterly* 906–26. Merle Goldman, *From Comrade to Citizen: The Struggle for Political Rights in China* (Cambridge, MA: Harvard University Press, 2005), Chapter 6.
[53] For discussion of the prosecution of Liu Xiaobo and Charter 08, see Human Rights in China, 'Freedom of expression on trial in China' (2010) 1 *China Rights Forum*.

The change from dissident speech to dissident action was reflected in a clear shift from expression-based prosecution to action-based prosecution, with enhanced penalties for cross-region and cross-profession activity. Subversion is the primary offence which punishes any person who 'organises, plans or implements the subversion of the state power or the overthrow of the socialist system'.[54] It is clear from Chinese criminal law that the essence of sedition is to incite others to overthrow the government, while subversion requires active organisation and participation.

The third stage of political dissidence is likely to be an increase in politically motivated violence. Facing harsh government suppression, dissidents have endured and persisted with non-violent struggle. But the harsh environment and the brutal treatment have a polarizing effect in the dissident community. The vast majority of them are in exile, forced or self-imposed, advocating peaceful change of the regime from a distance.

But the harsh treatment may have had a brutalising impact on some dissidents and may have radicalised a minority of them. Frustrated with the system and desperate about furthering their causes, and suffering repeatedly for their activism, some, such as Liu Xiaobo and the Charter 08 group, will continue to organise peaceful political opposition. Others have given up hope and are ready to resort to political violence.

While the political and religious opposition in and outside China remains firmly non-violent, it is likely that some members in dissident community will break ranks and opt for a violent confrontation. Wang Bingzhang's case illustrates the process of transformation from peaceful advocacy to terrorist attacks.[55]

Wang is one from the first generation of dissidents in the post-Mao China. He went to Canada to study medicine and stayed on in North America. He published the once well-known dissident journal *China Spring* in the early 1980s, and established and led overseas dissident organisations. Frustrated by the slow-pace of political reform and, allegedly, aided by Taiwanese intelligence agencies, Wang advocated the use of political violence in promoting regime change, including the use of assassination, kidnapping, mail bombs and other forms of sabotage. He published manuals and articles in different media including the Internet, advocating violent confrontation with the government. He has allegedly

---

[54] Criminal Law, art. 105.
[55] For the judgment of Wang Bingzhang's first instance trial, see 'The case of organizing and leading terrorist organization and espionage by Wang Bingzhang', available at www. chinalawinfo.com.

incited and organised others to purchase firearms and to set up training camps in North Thailand to carry out a series of terrorist attacks against Chinese targets in and outside of China.[56]

With rare exceptions such as this, dissidents who advocate political change in China do so only through peaceful means, and the prohibition of any lawful political opposition has not so far created much political radicalism which advocates violent overthrow of the Party-state. But the situation may change if the repressive political environment remains.

6.   Individualistic terrorism in China's transitional society

The danger is to study political violence in China in isolation, without placing it in the context of China's contemporary social, economic and political transitions. The root cause for separatism and regime-change dissidence may be historical but the contemporary motivating factors evolve and are dynamic. The objectives of political dissidents and strategies to achieve them evolve, reflecting the ever-changing international environment, domestic political reality and the demands of the people they claim to represent.

The separatist movements may not be driven exclusively by an intrinsically nationalistic inclination informed by identity, culture, religion or otherwise. Political and economic frustrations as experienced by the minority population in their daily lives have also contributed significantly to the radicalising process and the readiness to resort to violence.

The point is that there are many similarities between the Han-based regime change activism and the ethnic independence movements. There have been riots and unrest in recent years in both Han and minority regions, reflecting a common structural and systemic contradiction of economic growth without political liberalisation. For example, religions have been under tight state control in both Han and ethnic regions.[57] Thus, underground churches in Han regions are very similar to the unlawful Quranic schools in minority areas. Islamic pilgrimage in Xinjiang has parallels with the growing exchange between domestic and international Christian communities, with the latter providing financial and technical support. The rise of religion reflects common social and economic changes in society and the impact of those changes on the behaviour of citizens.

---

[56] Ibid.
[57] Kunal Mukherjee, 'The Uyghur question in contemporary China' (2010) 34(3) *Strategic Analysis* 420–35.

The Party-state is facing a common problem and has responded with equal brutality. There is no clear distinction in the way the government treats unauthorised Quranic schools on the one hand and house churches on the other. Social and economic transition has awakened rights awareness of social groups and individuals in both Han and minority regions, and citizens are demanding better protection of their rights and interests through lawful or violent means.

Smith's excellent study of generational differences in the attitude of Uighurs towards independence illustrates the importance of social and economic factors in the shaping of separatist ideologies.[58] Older Uighurs, who are well-versed in the Quran and have a strong and clear Uighur identity, are cautious and less inclined to independence because of their life experiences: they grew up either during the pre-Communist chaos or suffered Communist persecution in the pre-reform period. The older generation is grateful for the economic change and relative political stability they now enjoy.

On the other hand, younger Uighurs, who are more militant and vocal in fighting for independence, know little about the Quran and have a weaker Uighur identity. 'Secular and modern',[59] the younger generation fear less because of their experience of relative stability and prosperity. They hate more because of their experience with discrimination and inequality. They hold out more hope because of the rise of the international Islamic movement and the collapse of the former Union of Soviet Socialist Republics and the subsequent formation of the Commonwealth of Independent States. Educated Uighur youth, socially, economically and politically frustrated, are the principal fighters for a separate Uighur state with a clear militant tendency.[60]

Similarly, Yeh has convincingly argued that the Tibetan uprising in the spring of 2008 may be separatist in its manifestation, but behind the nationalist rhetoric are legitimate cultural, religious and economic grievances which cannot be tidily distinguished from the separatist motive. Tibetans resorted to violence due to a combination of social, economic and political frustrations. Tibetan nationalism is a significant issue but

---

[58] Joanne Smith, 'Four generations of Uyghurs: the shift towards ethno-political ideologies among Xinjiang's youth' (2000) 2(2) *Inner Asia* 195–224. Yeh touched upon this issue in Tibet, citing a Tibetan landlord that Han prostitutes gave idle Tibetan men something to do other than thinking about political protest. See Yeh, 'Living together in Lhasa'. For a discussion of political radicalism among young Tibetans, see Yeh, 'Tibetan indigeneity'.

[59] Shichor, 'Blow up'.

[60] Smith, 'Four generations of Uyghurs'.

it 'does not ... exist as a thing, pre-formed, unchanging, and static. It is, rather, processual, and actively produced, called into existence and cultivated by the very state policies that hope to destroy it.'[61]

The same can be said about the radical dissidents in Han regions who seek regime change not because of pre-formed political idealism. Rather, they *become* radicals and *decide* to take drastic actions because of their life experiences. It is their sense of justice and their frustration with the institutions in seeking remedies that drive them to confrontation with the government and eventually to violent political outburst. Tension builds in a gradual and sequential manner and conflict escalates. Sooner or later aggrieved individuals give up making peaceful requests and resort to violence in public to make a political statement. When that happens, Han-Chinese resort to violence to effect regime change in the same way that Tibetans and Uighurs turn to violence to further their claims of independence. It is social and economic frustration and the lack of effective redress for grievances that drive the Han-Chinese and ethnic minorities to extreme measures.

Similar social and economic frustrations that have created separatists in Tibet and Xinjiang are making individualist terrorists in China. Individualised radicalism has an interesting trajectory. When legal rights are clearly provided for in law, and wantonly disregarded in practice, grievances accumulate over time and are expressed by individual and spontaneous radical action. Initially, frustration with institutions takes the form of a threatened suicide, such as construction workers threatening to jump from a construction site.[62] When these threats fail to work, they inflict harm on themselves to make a moral claim – for example, Zhang Haichao had his chest opened to make the point that he suffered from an occupational disease,[63] and Sun Zhongjie, a taxi driver in Shanghai, chopped one of his fingers off to protest against an unlawful police fine.[64]

When they realise that inflicting self-injury does not achieve their goal or attract much attention, aggrieved people turn to venting their anger on

---

[61] Yeh, 'Tibet and the problem of radical reductionism'.
[62] See, e.g., 'A society that pressurizes migrant workers', *Radio Free Asia*, 24 January 2003, available at www.rfa.org/cantonese/commentaries/97553–20030124.html.
[63] See, e.g., 'Zhang Haichao has his chest opened for lung check up: a humiliation for the grassroots people who defend their rights after getting occupational disease', *Yanzhao Dushi Bao* (*Yanzhao Metropolitan News*), 15 July 2009, available at www.clb.org.hk/chi/node/1300988.
[64] See, e.g., 'Shanghai Pudong made an open apology in the "Sun Zhongjie Incident"', *Jingji Guancha Wang* (*Economic Observer News*), 26 October 2009, available at www.eeo.com.cn/Politics/by_region/2009/10/26/153890.shtml.

government officials. There is a long record in China of victims of certain government policies and practice who killed government officials in protest. For example, Zhou Yichao killed a human resource cadre in protest against a policy which barred Hepatitis B virus carriers from joining the civil service,[65] Beijing street hawker Cui Yingjie killed one of the notorious urban management officers to protest against routine harassment[66] and Yang Jia killed six police officers in a Shanghai police station to retaliate against police abuse.[67] More recently, aggrieved parties inflicted grievous bodily harm on, or even caused the death of, judges;[68] and frustrated citizens mass-murdered the most vulnerable people: children in preschools.[69]

This kind of individualistic violence and the danger it poses has not been given the attention it deserves. They are treated as isolated individual crimes as defined by the ordinary criminal law. But the new individualist terrorism is alarming in three senses.

First, the motivation is clearly political in the sense that the crime is committed largely to vent anger against government officials or policies. The immediate grievances and demands have been limited to individual interests, but they relate to larger issues of public policy such as the discriminatory policy against Hepatitis B virus carriers, ill-treatment by the police or other government institutions, or judicial corruption.

Second, while the incidents are all isolated and do not have any sign of organisation, acts of individualist terrorism can become contagious and can spread quickly from one region to another in a short time span. The

---

[65] See, e.g., 'The case of stabbing a civil servant to death by a student of Zhejiang University: Zhou Yichao was executed by lethal injection', *Xinhua wang* (*Xinhua News Agency*), 3 March 2004, available at news.xinhuanet.com/legal/2004–03/03/content_1343729.htm.

[66] See, e.g., Li Boyu, 'Looking back on the incident of Cui Yingjie' (2007) 19 *Renmin Gongan* (*People's Police*) 13.

[67] See, e.g., 'Reflection on the case in which the Shanghai police were attacked: why do so many people acclaim Yang Jia as "hero"', *Renmin Wang* (*People's Daily*), 17 July 2008, available at society.people.com.cn/BIG5/42733/7521817.html.

[68] See, e.g., 'Six judges in Guangxi Wuzhou were splashed with sulfuric acid, the President of the Court suffers grievous injury', *Zhongguo Guangbo Wang* (*China Broadcasting Net*), 8 June 2010, available at www.hkcd.com.hk/content/2010–06/08/content_2537183.htm; 'Aggrieved by the court's unfair judgment, a man in Yongzhou of Hunan shot three judges to death before committing suicide', *Zhongguo Xinwen Wang* (*China News*), 1 June 2010, available at www.chinanews.com.cn/sh/news/2010/06–01/2317026.shtml.

[69] See, e.g., 'Suspect of Fujian Nanping murder case confessed that he originally planned to kill 30 children', *Yangzi Wanbao* (*Yangzi Daily*), 26 March 2010, available at news. xinhuanet.com/legal/2010–03/26/conent_13238218.htm; 'The society pays a heavy price for each case of school homicide', *Hong Wang* (*Red Net*), 29 April 2010, available at www. chinadaily.com.cn/hqpl/zggc/2010–04–29/content_235726.html.

series of mass murders of kindergarten children and the physical attacks on judges in 2010 clearly indicate the readiness and eagerness of some individuals to use extreme violence to make a political statement.

Third, extreme political violence, even those perpetrated against the most vulnerable members of society, has been perceived to be acts of the desperately poor against an abusive government. As such, the perpetrators have received tremendous public sympathy and support, providing legitimacy for the spread of such violence. Even in the case of the mass murder of kindergarten children, the prevailing public message to the offenders is that they should have chosen a more suitable target: 'Cowards, you should have killed corrupt officials.'[70]

China has lived with violent separatism for decades and has developed the capacity to control its growth effectively. But now, China has to face a new breed of terrorism which may be more difficult to identify and control.

7. Conclusion

China remains a one-party authoritarian state struggling with political legitimacy. It is also a multi-ethnic nation struggling with national unity. In the past thirty years, China has experienced a great social and economic transition. Old threats that challenge the regime or its boundaries have returned since the early 1980s when the reform and open-door policy started. The social and economic reform and an enhanced expectation among its citizens have generated new breeds of domestic terrorists who are determined to achieve regime change or boundary change through violence or other means.

China faces high-level threats from different sources, including the forces that demand regime change and forces that demand boundary change. The former comes from the community of political and religious dissidents, and the latter includes the Tibet and Xinjiang-based separatist forces in China's western region. The two forces are distinct in their principal political demands, their geopolitical basis and the level of threat they pose.

---

[70] See, e.g., 'People who killed corrupted officials are heroes; people who killed children are cowards', *Shijie Xinwen Wang* (*World Journal*), 2 May 2010, available at www.world-journal.com; 'How to protect our children?', *Zhongguo Pinglun Yuekan* (*China Review*), 16 May 2010, available at www.cn-rn.com/crn-webapp/mag/docDetail.jsp?coluid=27&docid=101323890&page=3.

China's reaction to the high-level threats is swift, repressive and comprehensive. The government is also adaptive in modifying its strategies and tactics in dealing directly with high-level threats and the more indirect, broad social and economic issues underlying those threats. When it comes to high-level threats, the Chinese state is strong and determined. Its counter-measures are largely regarded as effective and successful in containing and neutralising the threats. The riots and insurgencies in Tibet in 2008 and Xinjiang in 2009 represent a heightening of problems in the high-threat zone. This has placed new and serious demands on the CCP to rethink its governance strategies in the ethnic regions.

Terrorist attacks, however, are not limited to regime change and boundary change contexts. The social and economic transition has enhanced the expectations and aspirations of the people and generated new conflicts. However, the established institutions may lack the necessary legitimacy or capacity to contain and resolve these social conflicts. When institutional remedies fail to meet the needs of aggrieved people, some of them may take drastic measures and resort to extreme violence simply to make a political statement. The state is, however, less prepared for the emerging low-level threats which take the form of politically motivated, but individualistic, violence.

15

Security laws for Hong Kong

SIMON N. M. YOUNG

1. Introduction

In the decade after September 2001, Hong Kong (fortunately) avoided any terrorist or other security threats to its territory. It managed this, however, with little assistance from new legislation. Indeed it was only on 1 January 2011 that legislation enacted (and later amended) to implement UN resolutions on combating terrorism and terrorist financing entered into full force.[1] In 2003, Hong Kong tried but failed to pass national security legislation as required by art. 23 of its Constitution. In hindsight it may appear that new legislation was unnecessary to preserve the peace and stability in Hong Kong post-9/11. But for an international financial centre in Asia with a population of more than seven million people and increasing integration with mainland China, the need for effective laws to prevent and interdict security threats is obvious, not to mention as well the importance of meeting international obligations and standards. The post-9/11 experience in Hong Kong has revealed, however, that it has yet to devise and apply an effective strategy for developing and enacting security laws.

This chapter tries to understand the reasons for the difficulties and challenges that Hong Kong has experienced in enacting security laws. In respect of both the anti-terrorism and national security initiatives, the Hong Kong government's approach was misguided in many ways. For example, it failed to consult the public on genuine options for reform, adopted a defensive attitude in the consultation process and made significant concessions only at the final hour as acts of appeasement. More fundamentally, the problems can be traced to Hong Kong's constitutional framework, which, while conferring a high degree of autonomy on Hong Kong, reserves power over foreign affairs and defence

I thank Dixon Tse for his assistance with this chapter.

[1] See United Nations (Anti-Terrorism Measures) Ordinance (Commencement) Notice 2010, L.N. 133 of 2010; United Nations (Anti-Terrorism Measures) (Amendment) Ordinance 2004 (Commencement) Notice 2010, L.N. 134 of 2010.

to the central Chinese authorities. Security issues necessarily engage the foreign affairs and defence heads of power, and the challenge for the Hong Kong administration has been to implement security measures, authorised by the central authorities, in a manner consistent with the autonomy promised by The Basic Law of the Hong Kong Special Administrative Region of the People's Republic of China (Basic Law).[2] It has yet to meet this challenge, and the implementation failures are mostly attributed to the absence of a grass roots concept of security, conceived in a genuine and informed public consultation process. This chapter will also discuss ideas for developing a new and more effective implementation strategy.

2.   Initiatives to enact security laws

A.   Security regime before 9/11

While under British rule, seven of the major international treaties on terrorism were extended to Hong Kong after ratification by the United Kingdom.[3] The colonial government in turn implemented these treaties.[4] It was never considered necessary to apply the general anti-terrorism laws enacted in the United Kingdom to Hong Kong.

Following the resumption of sovereignty by China in 1997, Hong Kong's obligations under international instruments were to cease unless they continued in accordance with the new constitutional framework of

---

[2] Adopted by the 7th National People's Congress at its Third Session on 4 April 1990 (Basic Law).

[3] See Convention on the Prevention and Punishment of Crimes Against Internationally Protected Persons, including Diplomatic Agents (1973), extended on 2 May 1979; International Convention Against the Taking of Hostages (1979), extended on 22 December 1982; Convention on Offences and Certain Other Acts Committed on Board Aircraft (1963), extended on 4 December 1969; Convention for the Suppression of Unlawful Seizure of Aircraft (1970), extended on 22 December 1971, effective 21 January 1972; Convention for the Suppression of Unlawful Acts against the Safety of Civil Aviation (1971), extended on 25 October 1973; Protocol for the Suppression of Unlawful Acts of Violence at Airports Serving International Civil Aviation (1988), extended on 21 May 1997; Convention on the Marking of Plastic Explosives for the Purpose of Detection (1991), extended on 28 April 1997.

[4] See Internationally Protected Persons and Taking of Hostages Ordinance (Cap 468), originally Ord. No. 20 of 1995; Fugitives Offenders (Internationally Protected Persons and Hostages) Order (Cap 503H), originally L.N. 205 of 1997; Aviation Security Ordinance (Cap 494), originally Ord. No. 52 of 1996; Fugitive Offenders (Safety of Civil Aviation) Order (Cap 503G), originally L.N. 204 of 1997; Crimes Ordinance (Cap 200), Part VIIA, originally Crimes (Amendment) Ordinance 1994, Ord. No. 52 of 1994.

the Basic Law. This framework was similar to the previous one in that treaty obligations of China did not automatically apply to Hong Kong, but required a separate decision by the Central People's Government after seeking the views of the Hong Kong government.[5] Showing respect for Hong Kong's high degree of autonomy, the Basic Law made it possible for previously implemented international agreements to continue in force even if China was not a party to those agreements.[6] After 1997, the seven anti-terrorism instruments and their implementing legislation were allowed to continue.[7]

Hong Kong also adhered to the anti-terrorism measures contained in UN Security Council decisions made under Chapter VII of the UN Charter. On 16 July 1997, Hong Kong's Provisional Legislative Council enacted the United Nations Sanctions Ordinance (UNSO), which gave the Chief Executive a law-making power (using subsidiary legislation) for the purpose of implementing Chapter VII sanctions.[8] There were two main prerequisites to the exercise of this power. First, there had to be instructions from the Central People's Government to implement such a sanction.[9] This was consistent with the framework under the Basic Law, which reserved matters of foreign affairs to the central government.[10] Second, the sanctions had to be 'mandatory measures decided by the Security Council of the United Nations, *implemented against a place outside the People's Republic of China*' (emphasis added).[11] These two conditions were more than prerequisites since their satisfaction made it mandatory for the Chief Executive to exercise the power.[12] Strangely, regulations made under this power, unlike normal subsidiary legislation, were not subject to scrutiny by the Legislative Council of the Hong Kong Special Administrative

---

[5] Basic Law, art. 153.   [6] Ibid.

[7] At the time, China was a party to all of the instruments except for the Convention on the Marking of Plastic Explosives for the Purpose of Detection (1991). The International Convention for the Suppression of Terrorist Bombings (1997) and the International Convention for the Suppression of the Financing of Terrorism were applied to Hong Kong on 13 November 2001 and 19 May 2006, respectively.

[8] The United Nations Sanctions Ordinance (Cap 537) (UNSO) was originally Ord. No. 125 of 1997, coming into operation on 18 July 1997. Prior to 1 July 1997, Orders in Council made under English legislation (i.e. the United Nations Act 1946) were used to extend Chapter VII sanctions to British colonies. These Orders in Council were first made by Her Majesty in Council, then laid before the English Parliament, and once published in the Hong Kong Gazette, had legal force in Hong Kong.

[9] UNSO, s. 2(2).   [10] Basic Law, art. 13.   [11] UNSO, s. 2(1).

[12] Ibid., s. 3(1) provides that the 'Chief Executive shall make regulations to give effect to a relevant instruction'.

Region (LegCo).[13] As discussed below, it was the restrictiveness of this condition and also the second prerequisite that drew significant criticisms from legislators in late 2002 in the course of implementing legislation in response to 9/11.

Using the power conferred by the UNSO, Hong Kong passed a regulation, the United Nations Sanctions (Afghanistan) Regulation (UNSAR), to implement the economic sanctions against the then Taliban regime in Afghanistan required by Security Council Resolution 1267 adopted on 15 October 1999.[14] This regulation, for the first time, provided for the listing of individuals, groups and property related to the Taliban, who were designated by the Committee established by Resolution 1267, in the Hong Kong Gazette for the purpose of enforcing the sanctions. When the Security Council extended these sanctions on 19 December 2000 by applying a general arms embargo to Taliban territory and against Osama bin Laden and the al-Qaeda organisation, Hong Kong made a further regulation to implement the extended sanctions.[15]

Overall, the Hong Kong measures against terrorism before 9/11 were limited, in terms of both the type of terrorist activity proscribed and the persons targeted. There were no general criminal offences proscribing terrorists or terrorist activities. Indeed, no definition of 'terrorist' or 'terrorist activity' was ever codified. There was no offence of financing terrorism. Terrorist acts that did not come within any of the implemented offences were left to be addressed by Hong Kong's ordinary criminal laws.[16] The listing of persons in the Gazette was restricted to only Osama bin Laden and members of the Taliban and the al-Qaeda organisation. Measures to cut off the flow of funds to terrorists more generally did not come until well after September 2001.

---

[13] Normally, subsidiary legislation is subject to either positive or negative vetting according to ss. 34 and 35, respectively, of the Interpretation and General Clauses Ordinance (Cap 1) originally Ord. No. 31 of 1966. Subs. 3(5) of the UNSO provides that these sections are not to apply.

[14] United Nations Sanctions (Afghanistan) Regulation (Cap 537K), originally L.N. 229 of 2000, which came into effect on or about 15 June 2000. See generally C. H. Powell Chapter 2, this volume.

[15] See United Nations Sanctions (Afghanistan) (Arms Embargoes) Regulation, L.N. 211 of 2001, which came into effect on or about 11 October 2001 and expired on 18 January 2002.

[16] E.g. murder, kidnapping, criminal damage to property, causing explosion likely to endanger, etc.

B. Legal response to 9/11 (Part I)

i. Two-stage strategy to implementation

The Security Council's first Chapter VII response to the 9/11 attacks was in Resolution 1373, adopted on 28 September 2001. This resolution required all States to implement measures against the financing of terrorism generally and to cut off all forms of support to terrorists and terrorist groups. On 16 January 2002, the Security Council adopted further Chapter VII action in Resolution 1390, which strengthened its existing measures aimed at Osama bin Laden, members of the al-Qaeda organisation and the Taliban, and all their controlled entities and associates.[17]

Unlike other jurisdictions, Hong Kong did not respond urgently and rashly with new anti-terrorism legislation after 9/11. Since the matter concerned 'foreign affairs', Hong Kong itself was not free to enact laws until it received instructions from the central government, which were reportedly given in October 2001.[18] In late November 2001, the Security Bureau presented a paper in a LegCo joint meeting between the Panels on Administration of Justice and Legal Services and the Panel on Security outlining measures to combat terrorism.[19] During the course of the meeting, it became apparent that the administration had internally debated the possible legal responses to 9/11.[20] As Resolution 1373 was a Chapter VII measure, one might naturally have thought that the implementation would be by executive regulations made under the UNSO. However, it was not possible to do this since Resolution 1373, being a resolution adopted against terrorists anywhere in the world, did not come within the second prerequisite condition of containing measures

---

[17] Resolution 1624 adopted on 14 September 2005 is also important for calling upon states to prohibit the incitement of terrorist acts. Relevant resolutions and treaties are accessible on the Security Council Counter-Terrorism Committee website, www.un.org/en/sc/ctc/resources/res-sc.html.

[18] Security Bureau, '[LegCo] Brief: [the Bill]', SBCR 2/16/1476/74, 10 April 2002, para. 2 (LegCo Brief). This document and others from the Security Bureau or LegCo Secretariat are available at www.legco.gov.hk.

[19] See Security Bureau, 'Measures to combat terrorism', LC Paper No. CB(2)490/01–02(01) for Joint Meeting of the Panels on Administration of Justice and Legal Services, Financial Affairs and Security, 30 November 2001.

[20] See LegCo Secretariat, 'Minutes of joint meeting held on Friday, 30 November 2001 at 10:45 am in the Chamber of the [LegCo] Building', LC Paper No. CB(2) 916/01–02 for LegCo Panels on Security and Administration of Justice and Legal Services, 8 January 2002 (Minutes of Joint Meeting).

'implemented against a place outside the People's Republic of China'.[21] It was decided that this would be the first Security Council sanction to be implemented by ordinary legislation. Whether the administration intended it or not, this was a positive move, since the use of the UNSO executive power would have bypassed public scrutiny and the checks and balances of the legislative process. However, as will be seen below, the UNSO was not completely out of the picture since it was used to implement Resolution 1390.

In the November joint meeting, the then Secretary for Security, Regina Ip, announced the two-stage strategy to implementation.[22] In the first stage, the 'essential elements' of Resolution 1373 were to be implemented in a new bill to be introduced in late February 2002.[23] Those elements generally related to the financing and material support of terrorism and freezing of terrorist funds.[24] Added to the first stage was the implementation of Recommendations II, III and IV of the Special Recommendations of the Financial Action Task Force on Money Laundering (FATF).[25] While these recommendations overlapped somewhat with Resolution 1373, they widened the scope of implementation with new duties related to confiscating terrorist assets and reporting suspicious transactions related to terrorism.[26] In the second stage, the administration intended to implement the less urgent 'non-mandatory elements' of Resolution 1373 and other international conventions against terrorism, and to 'give full effect to the FATF's Special Recommendations'.[27]

While the administration had planned to introduce legislation in late February 2002, it was not until 17 April 2002 that the United Nations (Anti-Terrorism Measures) Bill (Anti-Terrorism Measures Bill) was first read in LegCo.[28] Apparently, the drafting of the bill had 'taken more time

---

[21] UNSO, s. 2(1). In the Minutes of Joint Meeting, para. 28, the Solicitor-General acknowledged this problem and made statements to the effect that the UNSO would have to be amended if it was to be used to implement Resolution 1373.
[22] Minutes of Joint Meeting, [3].   [23] Ibid., [3], [9].
[24] Mentioning paras. 1(a)–(d) and 2(a) of Resolution 1373: see LegCo Brief, [4].
[25] Ibid.
[26] On 28–30 October 2001, the FATF held an extraordinary plenary meeting on the financing of terrorism, which led to eight Special Recommendations. See the FATF website: www.fatf-gafi.org/. Hong Kong has been a member of the FATF since 1990. It held the Presidency in 2001–2.
[27] LegCo Brief, [4.]
[28] The Anti-Terrorism Measures Bill was gazetted on 12 April 2002. See the Government of the HKSAR Gazette website at www.gld.gov.hk/cgi-bin/gld/egazette/index.cgi?lang=e&agree=0.

than expected'.[29] Unfortunately, as it would turn out, this delay took away a critical amount of time for legislators and the public to scrutinise the bill. The government was determined to pass the legislation by June 2002. There appeared to be three reasons for this urgency.[30] First, the FATF had imposed a deadline of June 2002 for countries to comply with its Special Recommendations on terrorist financing. Failure to comply could have resulted in counter-measures from FATF members. As Hong Kong held the Presidency of the FATF during this period, it would have been very embarrassing and a poor example for other countries if it did not comply with this deadline.[31]

Second, China had reported to the Counter-Terrorism Committee (CTC), established by Resolution 1373, on 22 December 2001 that Hong Kong would soon be enacting legislation to implement Resolution 1373.[32] The CTC replied with preliminary comments on the report and a request 'to provide a response in the form of a supplementary report by 24 June 2002'.[33] As it is unusual for China to accept UN reporting obligations, it would have been a loss of face if by June 2002 it could not report back to the CTC that concrete measures had been enacted in Hong Kong. China eventually provided its supplementary report in a letter dated 17 July 2002, five days after the Bill had passed through LegCo.[34]

Third, China itself had implemented Resolution 1373 by enacting anti-terrorism laws for the mainland in late December 2001.[35] It would have greatly displeased China if the Hong Kong authorities excessively delayed the implementation of Resolution 1373, especially since the instruction to

[29] See reply of Secretary for Security in LegCo Secretariat, 'Minutes of special meeting held on Tuesday, 5 February 2002 at 8:30 am in the Chamber of the [LegCo] Building', LC Paper No. CB(2) 1478/01–02 for LegCo Panel on Security, 25 March 2002, [30].

[30] See also Andrew Lynch Chapter 7, this volume, for a discussion of the problems with enacting 'urgent' anti-terror legislation.

[31] The Security Bureau described the consequence for Hong Kong as 'serious reputational risk as the FATF may publicly announce the jurisdictions which fail to comply with certain Special Recommendations'. It went on to say that this would 'reflect badly on HKSAR especially given our leading role as the President of the FATF'. See '[the Bill]', Paper No. CB(2)1930/01–02(03) for the Bills Committee on [the Bill], 17 May 2002.

[32] Jeremy Greenstock, 'Letter dated 27 December 2001 from the Chairman of the [CTC] addressed to the President of the Security Council', UN Doc. S/2001/1270, Annex.

[33] Jeremy Greenstock, 'Letter dated 10 April 2002 from the Chairman of the [CTC] addressed to the President of the Security Council', UN Doc. S/2002/399.

[34] Jeremy Greenstock, 'Letter dated 31 July 2002 from the Chairman of the [CTC] addressed to the President of the Security Council', UN Doc. S/2002/884, Annex.

[35] See the Government of China's supplementary report in the Annex to Jeremy Greenstock, 'Letter dated 4 January 2002 from the Chairman of the [CTC] addressed to the President of the Security Council', UN Doc. S/2001/1270/Add.1.

Hong Kong was issued in October 2001.[36] As discussed below, these three reasons were the source of an immense amount of pressure to have the legislation passed before the 2002 summer recess.

ii.   United Nations (Anti-Terrorism Measures) Ordinance

The process   There is no doubt that the pressure to pass the bill in less than three months resulted in faulty legislation. Indeed, the second stage of implementing anti-terrorism laws, which began in May 2003, was partly devoted to correcting the flaws in the United Nations (Anti-Terrorism Measures) Ordinance (UNATMO).[37] The Bills Committee met for the first time on 17 May 2002. Although the Committee held fifteen meetings before the Bill was passed on 12 July 2002, the last twelve meetings were packed within a period of twenty-four days, leaving on average a day between each meeting. No wide public consultations were held on the Bill. While various public interest groups, media and business associations, legal academics and legal professional groups were invited to make written submissions, only two meetings were held to receive oral deputations from invited persons and groups.[38]

A common criticism amongst the commentators was the insufficient amount of time the government had allowed for review of the original Bill and the many proposed amendments that were being made. For example, in its written submission the Hong Kong Bar Association deplored 'the lack of proper time for full public consultation on the Bill when there is obviously no urgency to enact any anti-terrorist legislation in Hong Kong'.[39] From as early as the seventh meeting on 17 June 2002, the administration began introducing a set of committee stage amendments (CSAs) that was constantly being updated and altered. The

---

[36]   As these instructions have never been revealed, it is not clear if the Chinese authorities imposed any deadline or timetable for implementation.

[37]   United Nations (Anti-Terrorism Measures) Ordinance (Cap 575), originally Ord. No. 27 of 2002 (UNATMO). Only certain provisions brought into operation on 23 August 2002, see L.N. 137 of 2002, and on 7 January 2005, see L.N. 172 of 2004.

[38]   See LegCo Secretariat, 'Minutes of the second meeting held on Monday, 3 June 2002 at 8:30 am in the Chamber of the [LegCo] Building', LC Paper No. CB(2)2323/01–02 for Bills Committee on the Bill, 17 June 2002, and LegCo Secretariat, 'Minutes of the 10th meeting held on Tuesday, 25 June 2002 at 8:30 am in Conference Room A of the [LegCo] Building', LC Paper No. CB(2)2880/01–02 for Bills Committee on the Bill, 7 October 2002.

[39]   See Hong Kong Bar Association, 'Submissions on [the Bill]', LC Paper No. CB(2)2548/01–02(01) for the Bills Committee on the Bill, 9 July 2002, para. 5. To the same effect, see submissions of JUSTICE in '[The Bill]: Main Points and Suggested Draft Amendments', LC Paper No. CB(2)2390/01–02(01) for the Bills Committee on the Bill, June 2002, p. 1.

manner in which these amendments were being proposed, considered and modified was chaotic. Commentators were not properly informed of the latest changes to the proposed CSAs.[40] These sudden changes to rashly formulated proposals frustrated persons participating in the process.[41]

On the day of the ninth meeting in the Bills Committee, on 24 June 2002, the government, somewhat high-handedly, gave notice to resume the second reading on 10 July 2002.[42] This was done even though it was clear that the work of the Bills Committee was incomplete and members of the Committee objected to such notice being given.[43] This move added fuel to the already fired atmosphere of the Committee. Three days later, in a show of protest, the Bills Committee passed, without objection, a motion expressing 'deep regret' that the second reading debate was to resume before scrutiny of the Bill was complete.[44]

An 'embarrassing hiccup' with the enactment of the terrorist recruitment offence was symbolic of the defects resulting from the rushed and unconsidered passage of the Bill.[45] The original proposal made it an offence for a person to 'become a member of, or begin to serve in any capacity with, a person specified in a notice'.[46] This offence was drawn so broadly that it could have included the family members of the specified person and anyone providing a service to that person, including his or her legal counsel or someone as innocuous as a laundry delivery person. It was also problematic because it lacked express *mens rea* requirements. The government acknowledged these problems and prepared committee

[40] See generally Simon Young, 'Hong Kong's anti-terrorism measures under fire', Occasional Paper No. 7 (Hong Kong: Centre for Comparative and Public Law, 2003), pp. 8–10, available at www.hku.hk/ccpl.

[41] See, e.g., speech by legislator Audrey Eu in *Official Record of Proceedings of the Legislative Council of the Hong Kong Special Administrative Region* (HK Hansard), 11 July 2002, 8863–4.

[42] Legislators questioned whether there had been a breach of 54(5) of the LegCo Rules of Procedure, which required consultation with the chairman of the House Committee before effective notice could be given. See LegCo Secretariat, 'Minutes of the 29th meeting held in the [LegCo] Chamber at 2:30 pm on Friday, 28 June 2002', LC Paper No. CB(2) 2490/01–02 for House Committee of the [LegCo], 25 September 2002, [78]–[120].

[43] Ibid., [99].

[44] See LegCo Secretariat, 'Minutes of the 11th meeting held on Thursday, 27 June 2002 at 8:30 am in Conference Room A of the [LegCo] Building', LC Paper No. CB(2)2881/01–02 for the Bills Committee on the Bill, 7 October 2002, [2].

[45] See Ambrose Leung, Angela Li and Alyssa Lau, 'Embarrassing hiccup for terror bill', *South China Morning Post*, 12 July 2002.

[46] Anti-Terrorism Measures Bill, cl. 9(1)(b).

stage amendments to address some of them.[47] The embarrassing moment occurred in the Council meeting when, due to a dinner break, there was an insufficient number of legislators who supported the government's amendment.[48] A competing amendment proposed by legislator Margaret Ng aimed at narrowing the provision even more was also defeated. After the absent legislators had returned, there was little choice for the government supporters but to accept the original proposal, which even the government acknowledged was faulty. The enacted proposal contained another obvious anomaly in that it referred only to persons specified by the Chief Executive and not to those specified by court order, which was a second form of specification added only in the CSAs.[49] Subsequently, the administration stated that the provision would not be brought into operation until it was corrected in the second stage of implementation.[50]

The substance   In formulating its proposals, the administration stated that it was adopting a 'minimalist approach' to implementing Resolution 1373.[51] To some extent, this was true. The bill was relatively short, with only nineteen clauses and three schedules, spanning only twenty-two pages in the Gazette. Except in one respect, the proposals stayed within the aims and purposes of Resolution 1373 and the FATF Special Recommendations. None of the controversial detention powers or provisions affecting fair trial rights, as seen in other countries such as the United States and Canada, was proposed.[52] Nevertheless, the original proposals were often

---

[47] LegCo Secretariat, 'Report of the Bills Committee on [the Bill]', LC Paper No. CB(2)2401/01–02 for House Committee meeting on 28 June 2002, 28 June 2002, [44].

[48] See HK Hansard, 11 July 2002, 8990–9004; Leung, Li and Lau, 'Embarrassing hiccup for terror bill'.

[49] See UNATMO, s. 10.

[50] Legal Services Division, 'Legal Service Division Report on Subsidiary Legislation Gazetted on 23 August 2002', which is Annex III to LegCo Secretariat, 'Paper for the House Committee Meeting on 4 October 2002', LC Paper No. LS 131/01–02 for House Committee, 2 October 2002.

[51] Security Bureau, 'Legislative Proposals to Implement Anti-Terrorism Measures under United Nations Security Council Resolution (UNSCR) 1373', LC Paper No. CB(2)1021/01–02(01) for LegCo Panel on Security, January 2002, [5].

[52] See, Kent Roach, 'Canada's response to terrorism', in Victor V. Ramraj, Michael Hor and Kent Roach (eds.), *Global Anti-Terrorism Law and Policy* (Cambridge University Press, 2005); Helen Fenwick and Gavin Phillipson 'Legislative over-breadth, democratic failure and the judicial response: fundamental rights and the UK's anti-terrorist legal policy', in Ramraj, Hor and Roach, *Global Anti-Terrorism Law and Policy*; William C. Banks, 'Unites States responses to September 11' in Ramraj, Hor and Roach, *Global Anti-Terrorism Law and Policy*.

drawn in such broad terms without sufficient safeguards or clear limits that their impact on human rights seemed far from minimal.

One of the most pressing concerns with the proposals was the risk that the new specification system might be used to marginalise groups, such as the Falun Gong, that China had branded as 'terrorists' or counter-revolutionaries.[53] Whether this was possible turned on how 'terrorist act' was defined in the Bill since the definitions of 'terrorist', 'terrorist associate' and 'terrorist property' were all based on the concept of 'terrorist act'. The definition in the original Bill together with the superimposed changes in the final enacted definition is shown below:

> 'terrorist act' (恐怖主義行為)-
> (a) subject to paragraph (b), means the use or threat of action where-
>   (i) the action <u>(including, in the case of a threat, the action if carried out)</u> -
>   (A) ~~involves~~ <u>causes</u> serious violence against a person;
>   (B) ~~involves~~ <u>causes</u> serious damage to property;
>   (C) endangers a person's life, other than that of the person committing the action;
>   (D) creates a serious risk to the health or safety of the public or a section of the public;
>   (E) is ~~designed~~ <u>intended</u> seriously to interfere with or seriously to disrupt an electronic system; or
>   (F) is ~~designed~~ <u>intended</u> seriously to interfere with or seriously to disrupt an essential service, facility or system, whether public or private; and
>   (ii) the use or threat is-
>   (A) ~~designed~~ <u>intended</u> to ~~influence~~ <u>compel</u> the Government or to intimidate the public or a section of the public; and
>   (B) made for the purpose of advancing a political, religious or ideological cause;
> (b) in the case of paragraph (a)(i)<u>(D), (E) or</u> (F), does not include the use or threat of action in the course of any advocacy, protest, dissent or ~~stoppage of work~~ <u>industrial action</u>.[54]

As shown by the amendments, the original definition used imprecise language, such as 'involves' and 'designed', unfamiliar to the criminal law. Legislators also felt that the exception clause for legitimate protest and dissent had to be extended to the other non-directly violent forms of terrorism.[55]

---

[53] Minutes of Joint Meeting, para 6(b).
[54] See Anti-Terrorism Measures Bill, cl. 2(1); UNATMO, s. 2(1).
[55] LegCo Secretariat, 'Report of the Bills Committee on [the Bill]', LC Paper No. CB(2)2537/01–02 for House Committee, 9 July 2002, [12]-[17] (UNATMO Report).

Despite these improvements to the original definition, there was one issue that the administration and legislators could not agree on. Margaret Ng, one of the main critics of the Bill and legislative process, proposed that the definition of 'terrorist act' should not include threats of action.[56] It was argued that this made the definition unjustifiably broad as it could catch merely mischievous behaviour.[57] Threats and other inchoate harm were already caught by the definition of 'terrorist', i.e. a 'person who commits, or attempts to commit, a terrorist act or who participates in or facilitates the commission of a terrorist act'.[58] The Secretary for Security, however, insisted on keeping the threat component mainly because other countries had it in their definition and threats of terrorist acts would inevitably cause public panic.[59]

The originally proposed specification system contributed to concerns that it could be misused against certain groups. The original proposal gave the Chief Executive the exclusive power to specify persons and property as 'terrorists', 'terrorist associates' or 'terrorist property' on reasonable grounds to believe.[60] Once a person or property was specified and gazetted, the person or property was presumed to be a terrorist, terrorist associate or terrorist property, as the case may be, in the absence of evidence to the contrary. It was left to persons specified to bring proceedings in the Court of First Instance to contest the specification. Without a system of prior judicial authorisation, there was a real concern that Beijing might try to influence the Chief Executive on what individuals and groups to specify.

To the government's credit, it accepted these criticisms and revamped the system by introducing a number of safeguards.[61] While specification by the Chief Executive was maintained, it was restricted to only persons and property already specified by a UN sanctions committee.[62] If other persons or property were to be specified, it had to be by the Chief Executive's application to the Court of First Instance.[63] There were further judicial checks on this second form of specification by way of review and appeal.[64] Another safeguard that was added was a compensation provision for persons wrongly specified.[65] But one of the threshold preconditions for obtaining compensation required the court to be satisfied that 'there has been serious default on the part of any person concerned in

---

[56] HK Hansard, 11 July 2002, 8916–18.   [57] Ibid.
[58] UNATMO, s. 2(1).   [59] HK Hansard, 11 July 2002, 8912–14.
[60] Anti-Terrorism Measures Bill, cl. 4.
[61] See UNATMO Report, [29]–[38].
[62] UNATMO, s. 4.   [63] Ibid., s. 5.   [64] Ibid., ss. 2(7), 17.   [65] Ibid., s. 18.

obtaining the relevant specification'.[66] To many legislators and commentators critical of the Bill, this threshold was so high that it essentially nullified the provision.[67] Until mid-2004, the government had always held that the threshold was appropriate to cap government expenditure and also because it was the same standard for the compensation provisions in Hong Kong's money laundering laws.[68]

Specification facilitates the freezing and forfeiture of terrorist property, which under the Bill (later accepted unchanged in the UNATMO) was defined as:

(a) the property of a terrorist or terrorist associate; or
(b) any other property consisting of funds that –
   (i) is intended to be used to finance or otherwise assist the commission of a terrorist act; or
   (ii) was used to finance or otherwise assist the commission of a terrorist act.[69]

By virtue of the first limb of the definition, 'terrorist property' was defined very broadly. The first limb presumptively tainted all property connected to the terrorist or terrorist associate; in other words, there was no need to show that the property was in fact crime tainted. In the Bill, it was proposed that the Secretary for Security would have the exclusive power to freeze funds that were terrorist property, subject to subsequent review by a court.[70] A scheme of executive freezing was controversial not only because of the absence of prior judicial scrutiny but also because it deviated from the general approach under Hong Kong's money laundering laws of obtaining court orders to restrain suspected proceeds of crime.[71] Ultimately, the government insisted upon maintaining the scheme on grounds that urgency and swift action required executive control.[72] It was moderately mitigated by added safeguards such as the power of the

---

[66] Ibid., s. 18(2)(c).
[67] See criticisms in UNATMO Report, [83]–[91].
[68] HK Hansard, 11 July 2002, 9045–6.
[69] See Anti-Terrorism Measures Bill, cl. 2(1); UNATMO, s. 2(1).
[70] Anti-Terrorism Measures Bill, cl. 5.
[71] See Drug Trafficking (Recovery of Proceeds) Ordinance (Cap 405), s. 10 (DTROPO) originally Ord. No. 35 of 1989; Organized and Serious Crimes Ordinance (Cap 455), s. 15 (OSCO) originally Ord. No. 82 of 1994. An exception is seen in pt. IVA of the DTROPO, which allows a limited warrantless power to seize money suspected to be proceeds of drug trafficking going across the border.
[72] See Security Bureau, 'Summary of written submissions and the administration's response', Paper No. CB(2)2424/01–02(04) for Bills Committee on the Bill, 26 June 2002.

Secretary for Security and of the court to grant a licence to release frozen funds to pay reasonable living and legal expenses, the reduction in the time limit of a freeze notice from three years to two years and the need to show a 'material change in the grounds' if an application was made to re-freeze previously but no longer frozen funds.[73]

The scheme of forfeiting terrorist property was also somewhat unique to Hong Kong because it involved civil forfeiture, i.e. it was not predicated on a criminal conviction; the standard of proof was the civil standard, and hearsay evidence was admissible.[74] One important safeguard of this scheme was that not all terrorist property was forfeitable. It had to be shown to have some connection to crime, which was true for the second limb of the definition but not for the first. Merely being property of a terrorist or terrorist associate was insufficient for forfeiture, it also had to be property which:

i. in whole or in part directly or indirectly represents any proceeds arising from a terrorist act;

ii. is intended to be used to finance or otherwise assist the commission of a terrorist act; or

iii. was used to finance or otherwise assist the commission of a terrorist act.[75]

One of the implications of this narrower forfeiture power is that the power to freeze is more extensive than the power to forfeit, since the former applies to all terrorist property in the form of funds. This raises the issue of the legitimacy of allowing the government to hold on to property that it cannot forfeit. Ultimately, this is an issue of whether the first limb of the 'terrorist property' definition is too broad.

Another area of great controversy in the Bills Committee was the enactment of new criminal prohibitions.[76] The fiasco concerning the terrorist recruitment offence has already been mentioned.[77] There were five other new criminal prohibitions. Two of the new provisions concerned

---

[73] See HK Hansard, 11 July 2002, 8945–7.
[74] Civil forfeiture exists on a limited basis in pt. IVA of the DTROPO. On the use of such powers in other countries, see generally Simon N. M. Young (ed.), *Civil Forfeiture of Criminal Property: Legal Measures for Targeting the Proceeds of Crime* (Cheltenham: Edward Elgar, 2009).
[75] UNATMO, s. 13(1)(a).
[76] For a discussion on the limits of the criminal law in preventing terrorism, see Kent Roach, 'The criminal law and terrorism' in Ramraj, Hor and Roach, *Global Anti-terrorism Law and Policy*.
[77] See text accompanying note 44 above.

the financing of terrorism and appeared to overlap with each other substantially, leaving one to wonder if more time should have been given to their formulation. The first was concerned with providing or collecting funds to be supplied or otherwise used by a person known or reasonably believed to be a terrorist or terrorist associate.[78] The second was concerned with making funds or financial (or related) services available to or for the benefit of a person known or reasonably believed to be a terrorist or terrorist associate.[79] A third provision prohibiting the supply of weapons to terrorists was relatively uncontroversial.[80]

One debated issue that was common to all three offences was the repeated use of the *mens rea* standard of has or having 'reasonable grounds to believe', a standard that appears five times in these three provisions.[81] It is controversial since Hong Kong courts have interpreted it as an objective standard. Having actual belief is not required; it is enough if sufficient objective grounds for the belief exist and one is aware of those objective grounds.[82] Calls for a purely subjective standard were rebuffed by the administration primarily on the basis that the standard was well established in Hong Kong's money laundering offences.[83] In stage two of the implementation, the administration softened its position on this point. Signs of this change were already seen in respect of the *mens rea* standard for the disclosure offence. In the Bill, it was proposed that any person who knew or had 'reasonable grounds to suspect' that any property was terrorist property had a duty to make a secret disclosure to the police.[84] This was an offence that had the greatest potential impact on ordinary persons, particularly those in the financial and business sectors. After significant concerns were expressed by the business and professional community, the government yielded by replacing the objective element with the subjective standard of 'knows or suspects'.[85]

The most controversial new criminal offence introduced was the prohibition against false threats of terrorist acts.[86] Legislators and media

---

[78] UNATMO, s. 7.   [79] Ibid., s. 8.   [80] Ibid., s. 9.
[81] By comparison, see the discussion of *mens rea* standards in the Canadian and United States offences in Kevin E. Davis, 'The financial war on terrorism,' in Ramraj, Hor and Roach, *Global Anti-terrorism Law and Policy*.
[82] See *HKSAR* v. *Shing Siu Ming & Others* [1999] 2 HKC 818 at 825 (CA), leave to appeal to CFA refused, [1999] 4 HKC 452 (CFA AC); *HKSAR* v. *Ma Zhujiang* [2007] 4 HKLRD 285 (CA).
[83] HK Hansard, 11 July 2002, 8985–6.
[84] Anti-Terrorism Measures Bill, cl. 11(1).
[85] UNATMO Report, [60]–[72]. This was the formula eventually used in UNATMO, s. 12.
[86] Anti-Terrorism Measures Bill, cl. 10.

groups objected to the proposal for various reasons, including the chilling effect on press freedoms, being outside Resolution 1373 or the FATF recommendations, and being already covered by offences in the Public Order Ordinance.[87] In the words of Margaret Ng, the 'Secretary [had] not kept her word' of applying a minimalist approach.[88] While the government acknowledged that it was outside the scope of Resolution 1373 and the FATF recommendations, it nevertheless said that the offence was necessary because of the incidences of false threats of anthrax after 9/11.[89] Ultimately, without achieving any reconciliation of these divergent views, the offence provision was passed with only an amendment to confine the scope of the *mens rea* requirement.[90]

There were two other major amendments to the original bill that were important from the perspective of human rights. The first amendment removed two lengthy schedules that would have conferred controversial new police powers to enforce the provisions in the Bill.[91] The other amendment, to the relief of various legal and media groups, provided for express preservation of legal professional privilege, the privilege against self-incrimination and the protective regime governing journalistic materials in the Interpretation and General Clauses Ordinance.[92]

After all the amendments were made, the enacted legislation was significantly transformed from the original Bill.[93] One ponders why the Bill in its original form was so short-sighted and over-broad to begin with. It was certainly not for lack of preparation time since the instructions from China had arrived in October 2001, six months before the Bill was gazetted. As argued below, it was due to insufficient consultation with the public and experts at the 'bill formulation stage', instead of only at the 'bill amendment stage'. This is a problem that reoccured with the National

---

[87] Public Order Ordinance (Cap 245) originally Ord. No. 64 of 1967. See UNATMO Report, [53]–[59].

[88] HK Hansard, 11 July 2002, 8861.

[89] Ibid., 9004–16.

[90] The original proposal made it an offence to communicate information known or believed to be false to another person 'with the intention of inducing in him or any other person a false belief that a terrorist act has been, is being or will be carried out'. The enacted provision confines the added intent element to that of 'causing alarm to the public or a section of the public by a false belief that a terrorist act has been, is being or will be carried out'. See UNATMO, s. 11.

[91] Anti-Terrorism Measures Bill, schedules 2, 3.

[92] Interpretation and General Clauses Ordinance; see UNATMO Report, [26]–[27].

[93] For discussion of the legislative process see Young, 'Hong Kong's anti-terrorism measures under fire'.

Security Bill. The critical tasks of formulating policies and drafting the Bill, carried out from October 2001 to April 2002, were largely completed by government lawyers and officials with no outside participation. The willingness of the government to make concessions was more likely due to the June 2002 deadline than an earnest desire to safeguard fundamental rights and freedoms. Where the government was unwilling to change a proposal, there was a tendency to try to justify its position by reference to the same provision in other Hong Kong laws or in the laws of other countries. But this approach to justification is narrow-minded because, in respect of existing Hong Kong laws, it fails to question whether those laws are themselves illegitimate (particularly in the areas of police powers and *mens rea* standards) or otherwise inappropriate for the anti-terrorism context. In respect of the anti-terrorism laws of other countries, it cannot be assumed that what is appropriate for country A, B and C is necessarily appropriate for Hong Kong, particularly having regard to its relatively low risk of attracting terrorist related activity.

iii.   United Nations Sanctions (Afghanistan)
(Amendment) Regulation 2002

On the same date as the UNATMO was passed through LegCo, the Chief Executive made the United Nations Sanctions (Afghanistan) (Amendment) Regulation 2002 (UNSAAR), which amended the UNSAR in light of Resolution 1390, adopted by the Security Council on 16 January 2002.[94] To the outsider, this new regulation came as a bit of a surprise since it suddenly emerged as law without any prior consultation with the public or even the elected members of the legislature. It would also have been surprising for the legislators who had just completed an intense one and a half month exercise of scrutinising the UNATMO. The UNSAAR and UNATMO had much in common in terms of origin, purpose and provisions, yet the manner in which both were enacted could not have been more unique. It did not take long for legislators and the legal advisors in the LegCo Secretariat to start questioning the legal basis of the UNSAAR and the manner in which it came into being.

On 4 October 2002, legislators discussed three issues concerning the UNSAAR identified by LegCo's Legal Service Division.[95] First,

---

[94] Published in the Hong Kong Gazette on 19 July 2002, amending the United Nations Sanctions (Afghanistan) Regulation (Cap 537K) originally L. N. 229 of 2000.
[95] LegCo Secretariat, 'Minutes of the meeting held in the [LegCo] Chamber at 2:30 pm on Friday, 4 October 2002', LC Paper No. CB(2) 2886/01–02 for House Committee, October 2002, [20]–[25].

legislators questioned whether Resolution 1390 was a sanction to be implemented 'against a place' as required by the UNSO.[96] If it was not, then there had to be a legal basis for the amendment regulation other than the UNSO, possibly the Basic Law itself. While the antecedents of Resolution 1390 certainly arose out of events in Afghanistan, by January 2002, it appeared the real focus of Resolution 1390 was on certain individuals and entities linked to Osama bin Laden and al-Qaeda, persons who were probably no longer physically in Afghanistan. The Administration's position was that Resolution 1390 was a sanction implemented against a place and the use of the UNSO was appropriate.[97] In making this argument, it cited the number of references to 'Afghanistan' in Resolution 1390, and the antecedent resolutions, Resolution 1267 and Resolution 1333, which were more clearly applied against a place.[98]

The second issue identified by the Legal Service Division was the overlap of the supply of weapons offences in the UNATMO with three offences in the UNSAAR.[99] The difficulty was that the offences in the UNSAAR involved strict liability, subject to statutory defences for the accused to satisfy on a balance of probabilities. The equivalent offences in the UNATMO required proof of *mens rea*. In theory, if a relevant case arose, the prosecution could avoid this *mens rea* requirement by choosing to prosecute under the UNSAAR offences. In its response of 26 November 2002, the Administration acknowledged that there was overlap but said that this was inevitable since there was overlap between Resolution 1373 and Resolution 1390.[100] Recognising that the offence in the UNATMO was wider, it was prepared to repeal the strict liability offences in the UNSAAR.[101] The LegCo Legal Service Division later questioned whether the Hong Kong government could amend the sections in the UNSAAR

---

[96] Legco Secretariat, 'Legal Service Division Report on Subsidiary Legislation gazetted from 19 July 2002 to 27 September 2002', LC Paper No. LS 131/01–02 for the House Committee Meeting on 4 October 2002, 2 October 2002, Annex I, [5]–[7] ('Report on Regulations').

[97] Commerce, Industry and Technology Bureau, '1: Whether the [UNSAAR] (Amendment Regulation) is within the regulation making powers of the UN Sanctions Ordinance? (Raised by the Hon James TO)', Paper No. CB(2)164/02–03(01) for House Committee, October 2002.

[98] Ibid.   [99] Report on Regulations, [9].

[100] Anita Chan for Secretary for Commerce, Industry and Technology, 'Letter to Clerk to Subcommittee on UNSAAR and United Nations Sanctions (Angola) (Suspension of Operation) Regulation 2002', Paper No. CB(2)477/02–03(01), 26 November 2002.

[101] Ibid.

that overlapped with those in the UNATMO without fresh instructions from the Central People's Government.[102]

In respect of the third issue, the Legal Service Division noticed the 'wide powers of search and investigation' contained in six provisions of the UNSAAR.[103] Resolution 1390 did not expressly require the inclusion of these new police powers. The Administration's response was that these powers were necessary to facilitate the enforcement of the new sanctions in the UNSAAR and that they also existed in a previous UNSO regulation relating to Liberia.[104]

Legislators in the House Committee were not satisfied with these responses.[105] Concerns about the UNSO and its regulations dragged on in two subcommittees of the House Committee.[106] Three further issues developed. The first was whether the implementing instructions from the Central People's Government should be disclosed to legislators. While the Administration was prepared to advise as to the contents of the instructions, it refused to make disclosure on grounds that they are intended for internal use only and disclosure would be unprecedented.[107] The second issue concerned the means by which to implement United Nations sanctions, and particularly when administrative measures, regulations or primary legislation should be used.[108] Finally, the third issue, and the more fundamental one, was whether the regulations made under the UNSO should be subject to legislative scrutiny.

---

[102] LegCo Secretariat, 'Report of the Subcommittee on [UNSAAR] and United Nations Sanctions (Angola) (Suspension of Operation) Regulation 2002', LC Paper No. CB(2)3003/02–03 for the House Committee meeting on 3 October 2003, Appendix II, [6]–[10].

[103] Report on Regulations, [10].

[104] Ibid.

[105] See LegCo Secretariat, 'Minutes of meeting held on Monday, 31 March 2003 at 4:30 pm in Conference Room A of the [LegCo] Building', LC Paper No. CB(2)2064/02–03 for the Panel on Administration of Justice and Legal Services, 13 May 2003, [45]–[51]; LegCo Secretariat, Minutes of the meeting held in the LegCo Chamber at 2:30 pm on Friday, 3 October 2003, [53]–[56].

[106] The Subcommittee on UNSAAR and United Nations Sanctions (Angola) (Suspension of Operation) Regulation 2002 held four meetings from 30 October 2002 to 25 February 2003. The Subcommittee on the United Nations Sanctions (Liberia) Regulations 2003 held five meetings from 11 December 2003 to 21 June 2004.

[107] Donald Tsang, Chief Secretary for Administration, 'Letter to Hon Miriam Lau, Chairman of the House Committee' dated 13 November 2003.

[108] The problem of having multiple listing mechanisms in domestic law has also been the subject of criticism in Canada. See E. A. Dosman, 'For the record: designating "listed entities" for the purposes of terrorist financing offences at Canadian law' (2004) 62 *University of Toronto Faculty of Law Review* 1.

The debate in LegCo on the legitimacy of the UNSO continued unabated into the next two legislative terms from 2004 onwards. Quite often LegCo's Legal Service Division continued to express opinions consistent with the views of the legislators, Margaret Ng being the main critic, who had taken up the issue with the government.[109] In 2008 and clearly in defiance of the UNSO's intention to escape legislative scrutiny, LegCo established a de facto standing committee to review all regulations made under the UNSO.[110]

C. The Article 23 episode

With the first stage of the anti-terrorism initiative completed, the path was clear for the Security Bureau to commence its national security initiative in late 2002. Only two months after the enactment of the UNATMO, the Security Bureau released *Proposals to Implement Article 23 of the Basic Law: A Consultation Document* (Consultation Document).[111] Article 23 of the Basic Law requires Hong Kong to enact laws on its own to prohibit acts of treason, secession, sedition and subversion against the Central People's Government. It also requires laws against the theft of state secrets and to prevent foreign political organisations or bodies from conducting activities in Hong Kong or from forming ties with Hong Kong political organisations or bodies. It is well known that art. 23 was inserted in the Basic Law by China following the mass demonstrations in Hong Kong against the 1989 Tiananmen incident in Beijing.[112] After several months of public consultation, the National Security (Legislative Provisions) Bill (National Security Bill) was introduced in LegCo on 26 February 2003.[113]

---

[109] See Cheng Yan Ki Bonnie, 'Implementing Security Council Resolutions in Hong Kong: an examination of the United Nations Sanctions Ordinance' (2008) 7 *Chinese Journal of International Law* 65.

[110] See the House Committee's Subcommittee to Examine the Implementation in Hong Kong of Resolutions of the United Nations Security Council in relation to Sanctions.

[111] Security Bureau, *Proposals to Implement Article 23 of the Basic Law: A Consultation Document* (Hong Kong: Hong Kong Government, 2002) was released on 24 September 2002.

[112] See Fu Hualing, 'The national security factor: putting article 23 of the Basic Law in perspective', in Steve Tsang (ed.), *Judicial Independence and the Rule of Law in Hong Kong* (Hong Kong University Press, 2001), pp. 73–98.

[113] National Security (Legislative Provisions) Bill, gazetted on 14 February 2003 (National Security Bill). The events surrounding the National Security (Legislative Provisions) Bill are analysed in Fu Hualing, Carole J. Petersen and Simon N. M. Young (eds.), *National Security and Fundamental Freedoms: Hong Kong's Article 23 Under Scrutiny* (Hong Kong University Press, 2005).

The legislative exercise to implement art. 23 probably would have occurred even if 9/11 did not happen. Nevertheless, following as it did after the first stage of implementing anti-terrorism laws, the two initiatives were closely related in many ways. It was very much the same group of officials responsible for implementing both initiatives. The Secretary for Security, Regina Ip, was the person in charge of both. This can probably explain why some of the same tactics and strategies to legal drafting, consultation and concession making were employed. As well, the substance of the proposals shared many commonalities. Roach noted that the National Security Bill 'combined an older vision of security based on betrayal of the state with a newer vision of security found in post-September 11 anti-terrorism laws'.[114] Two of the more noteworthy commonalities were found in the National Security Bill's definition of 'serious criminal means' and its use of the proscription mechanisms to ban local organisations.

As was true with the Anti-terrorism Bill, though for different reasons, there was a significant amount of criticism of both the consultation and legislative processes. Two critical observations were generally made about the Consultation Document.[115] Although a significant amount of research from international sources was reflected, the document presented what seemed to be a set of *fait accompli* proposals rather than different options for reform. The second critical observation was that the sixty-two-page document contained proposals often described in vague and ambiguous language. One of the most common sayings floated by commentators at the time was that the 'devil was in the details'; until the details were revealed, it was difficult to come to any final opinions on the proposals. It was not long after the publication of the Consultation Document that commentators began asking the government to publish a 'White Bill' before presenting the 'Blue Bill' for first reading in LegCo.

The government ultimately declined to issue a White Bill, saying that amendments would still be possible when the Blue Bill was scrutinised.[116] Legislators and public interest groups, aware of how difficult it was to

---

[114] Kent Roach, 'Old and new visions of security: article 23 compared to post-September 11 security laws', in Hualing, Petersen and Young, *National Security and Fundamental Freedoms*.

[115] See generally, Carole Petersen, 'Hong Kong's spring of discontent: the rise and fall of the national security bill' in Hualing, Petersen and Young, *National Security and Fundamental Freedoms*; Carole Petersen, 'National security offences and civil liberties in Hong Kong: a critique of the government's "consultation" on article 23 of the Basic Law' (2002) 32 *Hong Kong Law Journal* 457–70.

[116] Ravina Shamdasani and Jimmy Cheung, 'Officials stand firm against white bill', *South China Morning Post*, 24 December 2002, 2.

amend a Blue Bill without support from the government, were greatly disappointed. Before the Bill was issued in February 2003, the government suffered another blow to its credibility with the Compendium of Submissions fiasco, which led some legislators to condemn the Administration for compiling a compendium 'in a slipshod, incomplete and inequitable manner, distorting the views expressed by the public and organizations'.[117]

There was much in the substance of the National Security Bill that was indeed positive from the viewpoint of modernisation and rationalisation of the law. Hong Kong's laws concerning treason and sedition have not been updated since they were introduced pre-World War II.[118] If some of these offences and related police powers were to be applied now, they would surely be challenged on constitutional human rights grounds, e.g. freedom of expression.

Unlike with the anti-terrorism initiative, the Administration never claimed to take a 'minimalist approach' to implementation. There were at least three main proposals that were not expressly required by art. 23.[119] The first related to the creation of a new offence of illegal access to protected information and a new category of protected information related to 'international relations or affairs concerning the Hong Kong Special Administrative Region which are, under the Basic Law, within the responsibility of the Central Authorities'.[120] This proposal was of great concern to journalists.[121] The second overreaching proposal was to give the Secretary for Security a new power to proscribe organisations endangering national security.[122] The power could be exercised if the organisation was subordinate to an organisation proscribed on the mainland. With this proposal, the earlier fears that the anti-terrorism laws might be used to marginalise religious groups undesired by the mainland were re-emerging in a new and real way.[123] The third proposal was to give the

---

[117] Words taken from a condemnatory motion, introduced by legislator Sin Chung Kai, which did not pass. See debates in HK Hansard, 26 February 2003, 4182–257. See also Press Release, 'Transcript of remarks by Secretary for Security', 6 February 2003.

[118] See generally Crimes Ordinance (Cap 200) originally Ord. No. 60 of 1971, pts. I, II.

[119] See generally Benny Y. T. Tai, 'The principle of minimum legislation for implementing article 23 of the Basic Law' (2002) 32 *Hong Kong Law Journal* 579–614.

[120] See National Security Bill, cll. 10, 11.

[121] See Doreen Weisenhaus, 'Article 23 and freedom of the press: a journalistic perspective' in Hualing, Petersen and Young, *National Security and Fundamental Freedoms*.

[122] National Security Bill, cl. 15.

[123] See Lison Harris, Lily Ma and C. B. Fung, 'A connecting door: the proscription of local organizations', in Hualing, Petersen and Young, *National Security and Fundamental Freedoms*.

police a new warrantless entry and search power to gather evidence in urgent circumstances.[124] The difficulty with this proposal was that there was no empirical necessity for the power or anything to suggest that existing powers were inadequate.[125]

Although the Administration had always said that amendments to the Blue Bill were possible during the legislative process, it became clear as the work of the Bills Committee progressed that the Administration would only agree to minor changes and not budge on the main proposals.[126] Indeed, it was this very defensive attitude taken by the Secretary for Security and other staff and colleagues that angered legislators and commentators, causing much resentment.

The boiling point of this anger and resentment was reached on 1 July 2003 (a public holiday celebrating Hong Kong's reunification with China) when approximately half a million people marched in protest primarily against the National Security Bill but also against the Administration generally.[127] At the time of the march, the Bills Committee for the National Security Bill had already completed its work, and the Second Reading debate on the Bill was scheduled to continue on 9 July 2003.[128] Four days after the march, the Chief Executive announced three significant amendments to the bill: (1) deletion of the 'subordinate to a mainland organisation' triggering condition to the proscription power; (2) introduction of a 'public interest' defence for unlawful disclosure of certain protected information; and (3) deletion of the warrantless entry and search power.[129] Having made these major concessions at the last minute, the Chief Executive still insisted on proceeding with the Second Reading on 9 July.[130]

It soon became apparent that these concessions raised further issues, particularly the scope and definition of the public interest defence.

---

[124] National Security Bill, cl. 18B.
[125] See Simon Young, '"Knock, knock. Who's there?" Entry and search powers for article 23 offences', in Hualing, Petersen and Young, *National Security and Fundamental Freedoms*.
[126] LegCo Secretariat, 'Report of the Bills Committee on [National Security Bill]', LC Paper No. CB(2)2646/02–03 for House Committee on 27 June 2003, 27 June 2003 (BC Art. 23 Report).
[127] Ambrose Leung, Klaudia Lee and Ernest Kong, 'Hopes for freedom float upon a sea of political discontent', *South China Morning Post*, 2 July 2003, 3; Jimmy Cheung and Klaudia Lee, 'Turnout piles the pressure on Tung administration', *South China Morning Post*, 2 July 2003, 3.
[128] BC Art. 23 Report, [156].
[129] Press Release, 'Chief Executive's transcript on Basic Law article 23', 5 July 2003.
[130] Ibid.

Legislators and members of the public expressed concerns over the insufficient amount of time they had to consider the new amendments. These concerns escalated until they climaxed when James Tien, legislator and leader of the Liberal Party, resigned from the Executive Council, an unelected body of special advisors to the Chief Executive.[131] This hurt the Administration because the Liberal Party, representing mostly business and corporate interests, held a sizeable number of votes in LegCo.

On the day after Tien's resignation, 7 July 2003, the Chief Executive announced that the Second Reading would be deferred and efforts would be stepped up to explain the amendments to the public.[132] Nine days later, the Secretary for Security and another principal official, who had been embroiled in a car buying scandal, announced their decisions to resign.[133] Shortly afterwards, the Chief Executive said that the government was going to 'put forward the Bill to the whole community for consultation again.'[134] He promised a 'more extensive [consultation exercise] than the previous one' and 'to win the maximum understanding and support of the community as a whole'.[135] The timeline was to 'depend very much on how the consultation [went]'.[136] After the summer recess, however, the Chief Executive announced, on 5 September 2003, that the National Security Bill was being withdrawn to allow the public sufficient time to 'study the enactment question' and for the Security Bureau to establish a special working group to review the legislative work afresh.[137] In September 2004, the Chief Executive announced that there were no immediate plans to resume the legislative exercise.[138] With two years left in his mandate, the same Chief Executive resigned in March 2005, claiming health issues, but for reasons more likely due to his unpopularity and a string of governance problems, the art. 23 debacle being but one.[139]

It has never been disclosed how much of a role the Chinese authorities played in the making of the three amendments and the withdrawing of the Bill. The general perception is that the Chief Executive consulted the

---

[131] Press Release, 'Statement by CE', 7 July 2003.   [132] Ibid.
[133] Press Release, 'Statement by Secretary for Security', 16 July 2003.
[134] Press Release, 'CE's transcript', 17 July 2003.
[135] Ibid.   [136] Ibid.
[137] Press Release, 'CE's opening remarks on Basic Law article 23', 5 September 2003.
[138] Press Release, 'Chief Executive comments on Basic Law article 23', 16 September 2004.
[139] See Simon N. M. Young and Richard Cullen, *Electing Hong Kong's Chief Executive* (Hong Kong University Press, 2010), p. 24. See also Joseph Y. S. Cheng (ed.), *The July 1 Protest Rally: Interpreting a Historic Event* (City University of Hong Kong Press, 2005); Christine Loh and Carine Lai, *Reflections on Leadership: Tung Chee Hwa and Donald Tsang 1997–2007* (Hong Kong: Civic Exchange, 2007).

central authorities as these decisions were being made. It became rather clear that the Hong Kong government was not fully in charge of the legislative exercise when, shortly before his resignation, James Tien travelled to Beijing to determine from officials that there was no deadline to implementing art. 23.[140]

From time to time there have been calls in Hong Kong and on the mainland for the legislative exercise to be restarted. In February 2009 after relatively little controversy, Macau's legislative assembly passed national security legislation to implement art. 23 of its Basic Law.[141] Despite strong calls by prominent pro-Beijing figures to resume the legislative process in the summer of 2010, the Chief Executive, Donald Tsang, made clear in his October 2010 policy address that his administration, which continues to 2012, would not legislate on art. 23.[142]

D. Legal response to 9/11 (Part II)

Even before the march on 1 July 2003, stage two of the implementation of anti-terrorism laws had commenced with the introduction of the United Nations (Anti-Terrorism Measures) (Amendment) Bill 2003 (Amendment Bill) in LegCo on 21 May 2003.[143] The Amendment Bill contained proposals to expand the freezing power, to implement three additional anti-terrorism treaties,[144] to replace the recruitment offence provision with a new one, to add a new warrant-based power to search and seize terrorist property, to add three additional investigation powers involving prior

---

[140] See Albert Chen, 'Hong Kong's Political Crisis of July 2003' (2003) 33 *Hong Kong Law Journal* 265, 267; Petersen, 'Hong Kong's spring of discontent'.

[141] Suki Leong, 'Lawmakers approve article 23 bill', *Macau Post Daily*, 26 February 2009.

[142] Chief Executive, *2010–11 Policy Address – Sharing Prosperity for a Caring Society*, 13 October 2010, [163], available at www.policyaddress.gov.hk. See also Gary Cheung, 'Beijing eyed new article 23 push, research says', *South China Morning Post*, 15 October 2010.

[143] Gazetted on 9 May 2003. The Amendment Bill was passed on 3 July 2004, and signed and promulgated by the Chief Executive on 8 July 2004. The United Nations (Anti-Terrorism Measures) (Amendment) Ordinance, Ord. No. 21 of 2004 (Amendment Ordinance) was only partly brought into operation on 7 January 2005, see L.N. 173 of 2004.

[144] The International Convention for the Suppression of Terrorist Bombings (1997), Convention for the Suppression of Unlawful Acts against the Safety of Maritime Navigation (1988), and Protocol for the Suppression of Unlawful Acts against the Safety of Fixed Platforms Located on the Continental Shelf (1988). See LegCo Secretariat, 'Legal Service Division Report on [Amendment Bill]', LC Paper No. LS 107/02–03 for House Committee Meeting on 23 May 2003, 21 May 2003, [2].

judicial authorisation and to provide for limited international sharing of information obtained using the new powers.

In this second stage, there were a number of signs that the administration, with its new Secretary for Security, Ambrose Lee, had modified its approach after learning from the failings and problems of the two earlier legislative exercises. Indeed, the change was so apparent that it attracted the following complimentary comments from the staunchest critic of the original Bill, Margaret Ng:

> Thankfully, the Government changed its attitude in the end, and worked together with the Bills Committee with a more open mind. The many amendments to be introduced by the Government is a result of that process. Although it has caused us much effort, I am pleased that it has happened, and I do sincerely thank the Government for its co-operation.
>
> I took some time to revisit the Committee stage amendments I proposed last year. I am pleased to say that many of them are now being effected through the Government's amendments. I would like to mention the most significant improvements from the point of view of better legislation and better regard for human rights.[145]

This time there was no externally imposed deadline and more time was given to legislators and the public to study the Amendment Bill. A total of sixteen Bills Committee meetings were held over the course of eight months from 10 October 2003 to 18 June 2004. The rushed and confused atmosphere that marked the first stage of implementation was not repeated, and interested groups had ample opportunity to comment on both the original Amendment Bill and the draft CSAs to that Bill. The deadline of the end of the 2003–4 session was mutually acceptable as it also coincided with the conclusion of LegCo's first complete four-year term since the transfer of sovereignty.

The open public consultation process this time contributed to an informed, balanced and acceptable piece of legislation. The administration showed a willingness to revisit the UNATMO to correct and improve defects resulting from the rushed enactment. The United Nations (Anti-Terrorism Measures) (Amendment) Ordinance (Amendment Ordinance) narrowed the definition of 'terrorist act' with new *mens rea* qualifiers,[146] enacted a narrower recruitment offence with subjective *mens*

---

[145] HK Hansard, 3 July 2004, 470.

[146] Under pt. (a)(i) of the definition, a terrorist act must now involve the use or threat of action where the action 'is carried out with the intention of, or the threat is made with the intention of using action that would have the effect of' realising one of the harmful consequences enumerated in clauses (A) to (F). See s. 3 of the Amendment Ordinance.

rea requirements,[147] removed some of the objective *mens rea* standards in the existing criminal prohibitions[148] and removed the 'serious' from the 'serious default' precondition to obtaining compensation.[149] Important amendments were also made to clarify and restrict some of the new police powers introduced in the original Amendment Bill.[150]

E. Long delay to entry into force

By January 2005, only some of the provisions of the UNATMO and Amendment Ordinance had been brought into force. The court-ordered specification mechanism and the powers for freezing, seizing and forfeiting terrorist property could not be brought into operation until there was in place prescribed rules of court setting out the required court procedures. The offence of making funds and financial services available to terrorists except by a licence granted by the Secretary for Security or by a court also had to await the necessary rules of court. The new investigative power to compel persons to answer questions and produce materials had to await the legislative approval of a code of practice before it could enter into force. One would have expected the rules and code to be ready and approved within a reasonably short time after the principal Ordinance had been passed; instead, it took almost six years to pass these subsidiary instruments and to bring the main Ordinances into full operation.[151]

In a 2008 joint evaluation of Hong Kong by the FATF and Asia/Pacific Group on Money Laundering, Hong Kong was criticised for having delayed the entry into force of enacted anti-terrorism legislation.[152] The FATF

---

[147] Section 10 of the UNATMO now makes it an offence to (1) recruit another person to become a member; or (2) become a member, of a specified terrorist body knowing that, or being reckless as to whether, it is a body so specified. See s. 9 of the Amendment Ordinance.

[148] The objective standard of 'having reasonable grounds to believe' in ss. 7–9 of the UNATMO have now been replaced with fault standards of recklessness, knowledge and intention. See ss. 6–8, 14 of the Amendment Ordinance.

[149] See s. 17 of the Amendment Ordinance.

[150] See ss. 3, 5 and 12 of the Amendment Ordinance, the significance of which is explained in LegCo Secretariat, 'Report of the Bills Committee on [Amendment Bill]', LC Paper No. CB(2)2915/03–04, 25 June 2004.

[151] See Rules of the High Court (Amendment) Rules 2009, L.N. 186 of 2009, which were made by the Rules Committee of the High Court on 28 September 2009 and entered into force on 1 January 2011; Code of Practice for Requiring Persons to Furnish Information or Produce Material under Section 12A of the United Nations (Anti-Terrorism Measures) Ordinance (Cap. 575), G.N. 4250, was approved by LegCo on 7 July 2010, see G.N. 4249.

[152] FATF/OECD, *Third Mutual Evaluation Report: Anti-Money Laundering and Combating the Financing of Terrorism – Hong Kong, China*, 11 July 2008, available at www.fatf-gafi.org (FATF Report).

report described the delays as 'inordinate' and recommended the authorities prioritise the work required to bring the then remaining provisions into force.[153] The evaluation found that Hong Kong was in full compliance of none of the nine FATF Special Recommendations, largely compliant in only one, partially compliant in five and non-compliant in one.[154]

The government has never provided an explanation for the six-year delay. Margaret Ng in the debate on the Code of Practice made reference to legislators 'developing a habit of transferring their dissatisfaction with the original Ordinance to its subsidiary legislation by striving to delay the implementation of an unsatisfactory piece of legislation', but the legislative record did not show that legislators were to blame for the delay.[155]

3.   Ideas for a new implementation strategy

The defects with Hong Kong's security laws and policies have been more procedural than substantive. It is not so much the substance of the laws (in its final enacted or proposed form) that is problematic. And it is not so much the policy behind the law that is troubling because most Hong Kong people accept the reasons for having to implement anti-terrorism and national security laws. Instead, this chapter has shown that the problems directly arose from how the laws and policies were formulated, debated, subjected to public consultations, reformulated and finally enacted. In other words, the implementation strategy was problematic, and the constitutional framework that does not clearly define the roles of the Hong Kong executive authorities, LegCo and central authorities in matters concerning defence and foreign affairs aggravated the problems. If the administration is to win the public's trust and confidence for future legislative initiatives, it must first understand the reasons why the public resisted and frustrated its previous attempts at implementation. These reasons and possible ways of addressing them are discussed under the following three headings.

A.   External imposition without internal need

With both the anti-terrorism and national security initiatives, there was no empirical necessity in Hong Kong for new laws. Unlike the need for

---

[153]   Ibid., [158].   [154]   Ibid., [220]–[222].
[155]   HK Hansard, 7 July 2010, 11034.

measures during the SARS (servere acute repiratory syndrome) crisis in 2003.[156] Instead, the public perception was that these new measures were being externally imposed on Hong Kong, in which case adopting a 'minimalist approach' seemed to follow logically. Closer examination revealed that the external imposition came from China in both cases. This form of imposition touches upon a particularly sensitive area for Hong Kong people. The Basic Law promised a 'high degree of autonomy' for Hong Kong, which meant that China's socialist political system would not be applied in Hong Kong. Naturally any steps taken by China that appear to interfere with this high degree of autonomy are viewed with mistrust by Hong Kong people.[157]

Both security initiatives were matters under the Basic Law that required intervention from the central authorities who were obviously very interested in both matters. The Hong Kong Administration had the responsibility of mediating between China and the Hong Kong people. This was a challenging task since it required, on the one hand, upholding Hong Kong's autonomy, while, on the other hand, carrying out the mainland's instructions.[158] Judging from its performance and the public reaction, the Administration failed to strike the proper balance by insufficiently upholding Hong Kong's autonomy. Indeed, the manner in which the proposals were initiated, the inability to compromise on certain issues until the final hour and the imposition of artificial deadlines were strategies that clearly reinforced the external imposition perception.

Contributing to the mistrust were two other factors: the internal policy not to disclose the instructions from China in respect of UN sanctions and the proposal to make information concerning Hong Kong and China affairs protected information under the Official Secrets Ordinance.[159] Without transparency about China's instructions to Hong Kong in respect of both initiatives, there would always be a lingering suspicion that the administration's hard bargaining and imposed deadlines were a product of Chinese interference.

---

[156] On SARS Crisis, see Chritine Loh and Civic Exchange (eds.) *At the Epicentre: Hong Kong and the SARS Outbreak* (Hong Kong University Press, 2004).

[157] This mistrust was exacerbated in early 2004 when the Standing Committee of the National People's Congress adopted an Interpretation of the Basic Law and made a Decision that ruled out universal suffrage for 2007/2008, which was an aim that many in Hong Kong had hoped to realise.

[158] In respect of the national security initiative, it is unknown if China gave further instructions beyond art. 23.

[159] Official Secrets Ordinance (Cap 521).

B. Faulty consultation processes

Where there is no apparent empirical need for new criminal laws and police powers, the need for genuine public consultation at the earliest possible moment is greatest. Even where there is an empirical need, subject matters such as anti-terrorism and national security can involve very technical legal proposals, which is another reason for ensuring early and full consultations. A third reason for having early consultation is that it helps to remove the perception of external imposition. When the public is involved as early as the proposal formulation stage then the public can take ownership in the final product. This is a strategy that engenders autonomy over the initiatives.

Unfortunately this has not been a strategy used by the administration. Some have criticised the Administration for not using the Hong Kong Law Reform Commission (HKLRC) in developing the art. 23 proposals.[160] Using the HKLRC would have involved the public in a wide consultation during the proposal formulation stage. However, the HKLRC may not be the best vehicle for implementing laws on security in Hong Kong. It is not unknown for governments to ignore completely the recommendations of an independent law reform agency.[161] When this is the case, the initiative goes back to the drawing board, although with the benefit of the work done by the law reform body. To avoid this potential roadblock, it may be necessary to include some of the responsible government officials and legislators in the law reform process. By having them actively involved in the formulation process (but not in any leading role), there is a greater chance that the formulated proposals will later be accepted. More importantly, the officials and legislators will have the opportunity to gain broader perspectives by interacting directly with the independent experts forming part of the body. The present system of consultation, in the formal and politically charged atmosphere of a Bills Committee, leaves very little room for focused and rational discussion and exchange. A plurality of expert views in the drafting process is very important in order to avoid the formulation of short-sighted and overreaching proposals, as was seen in the initial drafts of the Anti-terrorism and National Security Bills.

Another limitation of the HKLRC is that its subcommittees are generally non-permanent, and are made up of the volunteer services of

---

[160] See Petersen, 'Hong Kong's spring of discontent'.
[161] This has also been a challenge for the HKLRC: see, e.g., Ludwig Ng, 'Law for the times', *South China Morning Post*, 29 September 2010.

members of the community. Typically the subcommittee is disbanded once the specific law reform reports are complete. There are no standing committees in the HKLRC devoted to the study of specific areas of law. In the area of security laws, it is a good idea to have a standing committee of experts that not only proposes new laws when needed but also reviews existing ones. This will help to avoid some of the delays to implementation that the Administration has experienced. This standing committee will also be able to formulate policies and principles governing security issues in Hong Kong. The aim is to develop a new discourse on security that arises from the grass roots rather than from outside of Hong Kong.[162]

The government's new Central Co-ordinating Committee (CCC), which was put together in response to the 2008 FATF review, is not the kind of standing committee being recommended here.[163] The CCC is chaired by the Financial Secretary and made up only senior officials without any membership from the public or LegCo.

C. Defects in policy and practice

The anti-terrorism initiative revealed some serious defects in the Administration's present policies and practices in implementing Security Council sanctions. The UNSO is in dire need of a complete overhaul.[164] The triggering condition of implementing sanctions 'against a place' needs to be reconsidered for at least two reasons. First, it falsely assumes that Chapter VII decisions are always against a particular place. Resolution 1373 proved this assumption was false, and increasingly, there is a greater tendency to employ 'smart sanctions' that target specific persons or subject matters without territorial boundaries.[165]

---

[162] Although it has not been a problem in Hong Kong, this informed Standing Committee can also help to avoid the problem, which Ramraj discusses, of having an overreacting populist democracy motivated by misperceptions of risk and public fear. See Victor V. Ramraj, Terrorism, risk perception and judicial review', in Ramraj, Hor and Roach, *Global Anti-Terrorism Law and Policy*.

[163] FATF Report, p. 229.

[164] The UNSO was originally enacted in a matter of days without question or dissent in the first few weeks after the resumption of sovereignty. The expediency was a product of the need to ensure that the existing UN sanctions continued to apply in Hong Kong after 1 July 1997. Unfortunately, it was enacted by the Provisional Legislative Council, an unelected body put in place by China to facilitate the resumption of sovereignty. The body was notoriously known to be uncritical of legislation put forward by the government.

[165] See Security Council Resolution 1540 (2004) (non-proliferation of weapons of mass destruction) and Peter L. Fitzgerald, 'Managing "smart sanctions" against terrorism wisely' (2002) 36 *New England Law Review* 957.

The other difficulty with the condition and the general scheme is that Chapter VII sanctions against a place must necessarily require implementation using the UNSO (assuming instructions from the central authorities have been received). In other words, regardless of the urgency of the matter, the Chief Executive has no choice but to implement the measure by making regulations that are not subject to scrutiny by the legislature. This raises important issues concerning the accountability of the executive and the separation of powers.[166] It has been seen that these implementing regulations can contain wide police powers and strict liability offences. There is no reasonable justification on policy grounds for why Resolution 1390 was implemented with a UNSO regulation while Resolution 1373 was implemented with primary legislation. Having these two overlapping laws tends to confuse due to their separate terrorist listing mechanisms.[167] Currently there are two lists published in the Gazette on a regular basis as required by both the UNATMO and UNSAR. While the names on the two lists have been the same, this will not always be the case since the power to specify under the UNATMO is broader than the power under the UNSAR. With the Security Council continuing to find favour with listing mechanisms, Hong Kong is now also required to gazette lists of persons and entities in respect of sanctions against Eritrea, Somalia, Côte d'Ivoire, the Democratic Republic of the Congo, Liberia and the Democratic People's Republic of Korea.

The urgency in having the sanction implemented may be one explanation for why executive regulations should be used over primary legislation, but presently this is not a triggering condition in the UNSO. Even if regulations are the desired method of implementation in urgent circumstances, it still does not explain why there cannot be tabling of the subsidiary legislation before LegCo for negative vetting. Ironically, even with the present scheme of executive regulations under the UNSO, there has still been considerable delay in implementing UN sanctions.[168] Some of this delay may be explained by the existing practice of the Chief Executive seeking views from the Executive Council. Conferring this task on the proposed standing committee may very well lead to a more expeditious process of implementation.

---

[166] See further Cheng, 'Implementing Security Council Resolutions in Hong Kong' for an elaboration of the separation of powers point.

[167] See similar problems in Canada, E. A. Dosman, 'For the record'.

[168] See elaboration of this point in Cheng, 'Implementing Security Council Resolutions in Hong Kong'.

In reforming the UNSO Hong Kong can learn from the enabling legislation used in Canada and Singapore, both of which share the same name
and are very similar in nature.[169] Both laws give the executive a discretionary power to implement Chapter VII sanctions by regulations 'as
appear to him to be necessary or expedient for enabling the measure to
be effectively applied'.[170] Neither have the anomaly of restricting the law-
making power to Chapter VII resolutions implemented 'against a place'.
Both laws also preserve legislative scrutiny by requiring the regulations to
be tabled before their respective parliament within a short time after they
are made.[171]

4. Conclusion

In April 2010, to justify the expense of creating a Counter-Terrorism
Response Unit with 100 new police posts, the Secretary for Security made
reference to Hong Kong being at medium risk of a terrorist attack (Level
2 on a three-level alert system) stating that it was necessary to 'maintain
a high level of alertness at all times'.[172] Paradoxically, the Secretary's concerns about terrorism were not matched by a resolve to have an improved
process to develop and implement security laws effectively and efficiently.
If terror was to strike Hong Kong, the public calls for action could well
lead to rushed and ill-conceived legal measures that overreach. But if,
before terror strikes, there is a permanent body of officials and experts
that has kept security laws under review, there is a greater chance for the
response to terror to be reasoned, informed, balanced and kept in good
measure.

---

[169] See the United Nations Act, R.S.C. 1985, c. U-2 (Can) originally enacted in 1945 (Canada
UNA), and the United Nations Act, ch. 339, originally No. 44 of 2001, Republic of
Singapore Government Gazette, which was enacted on 17 October 2001 (Singapore
UNA).
[170] See s. 2 of the Canada UNA and s. 2(1) of the Singapore UNA. However, this formulation is not without its difficulties: see criticisms of the Singapore UNA in C. L. Lim,
'Executive lawmaking in compliance of international treaty' [2002] *Singapore Journal
of Legal Studies* 73–103. See also Cheng, 'Implementing Security Council Resolutions in
Hong Kong'.
[171] See s. 4 of the Canada UNA and s. 2(4) of the Singapore UNA.
[172] HK Hansard, 21 April 2010, 7198.

16

Japan's response to terrorism post-9/11

MARK FENWICK

1. Introduction

In responding to the 9/11 attacks on the US, many liberal democracies substantively expanded the scope of the criminal law as well as the investigative powers of law enforcement and intelligence agencies. In some cases, constitutional rights have been curtailed or even suspended. In Japan, however, no significant changes to the Criminal Code or the Code of Criminal Procedure were enacted as a result of 9/11. Although legislative measures related to terrorist financing were introduced to ensure that Japan complied with obligations in international law and some controversial changes were made to immigration procedures for foreign nationals, no comprehensive anti-terrorism law of the kind passed in many other jurisdictions was enacted. In fact, the principle legal instrument for countering terrorism, the Subversive Activities Prevention Law, was not amended in spite of various well-documented deficiencies. At first glance, the Japanese response to 9/11 appears to be a controlled one, at least when compared with other states.

And yet, although Japan's response to 9/11 has been relatively uncontroversial insofar as it relates to domestic counter-terrorism law and policy, 9/11 did instigate a significant shift in Japanese legal and political culture. However, unlike many jurisdictions where discussion of counter-terrorism focused on balancing the civil liberties of suspect populations with national security interests, the Japanese debate primarily involved a different issue, namely what is an appropriate *military* contribution for a sovereign nation to make in the global war on terrorism. More practically, this has meant delimiting the role for the Japanese Self-Defense Forces (SDF) in counter-terrorism operations overseas, particularly in Afghanistan.

The legal context for this discussion is, of course, art. 9 of the Japanese Constitution, which on an initial reading seems to explicitly renounce war and prohibit the maintenance of military forces. Rather than embrace the values of art. 9, however, successive Japanese governments came to regard the provision as being incompatible with Japan's national security interests and international obligations, and, in particular, the demands of the US–Japan security framework.

This chapter will suggest that in a Japanese context the primary significance of 9/11 has been to change the terms of the domestic debate on art. 9. Prior to 9/11, there were, broadly speaking, two views of this provision. On the one hand, the view of the Liberal Democratic Party (LDP) was that art. 9 did not infringe upon Japan's sovereign right to self-defence and that maintaining a military for purely defensive purposes was constitutional. Since the LDP governed Japan constantly between 1955 and August 2009 (apart from eleven months in 1993–4) this view was the official government position for most of the post-World War II period, and had facilitated the expansion of Japan's military capacity. On the other hand, various left-wing opposition parties (notably the Communists and Social Democratic Party) tended towards a more literal reading of art. 9 and regarded the SDF as unconstitutional. As we shall see, the courts preferred to avoid tackling this sensitive political question and tended to defer to the executive.

An effect of 9/11 was to change the terms of the discussion by facilitating a controversial new interpretation of the Constitution that permitted the overseas deployment of the SDF in the context of international counter-terrorism operations. That is to say, 9/11 prompted the LDP to abandon the earlier justification for the constitutionality of the SDF based around a narrowly defined concept of self-defence in favour of a more expansive and ambiguous standard based around international co-operation in eradicating terrorism.

This new interpretation was given legal effect in the Anti-Terrorism Special Measures Law of 2001 (ATSML) and, after 2008, in the Replenishment Support Special Measures Law (RSSML). As we shall see, both pieces of legislation and the military operations they authorised proved to be highly controversial and were a significant factor in the LDP's loss of power in August 2009. The new DPJ-led Administration of Yukio Hatayama did not seek to renew the RSSML and it ceased to be law on 15 January 2010. Nevertheless, the apparent failure of post-9/11 legislation to win popular support should not be interpreted as marking a return to a pre-9/11 situation with regard to art. 9. Rather, this chapter will suggest that the main legacy of 9/11 in Japan has been to introduce further uncertainty into debates surrounding this provision and to highlight once again that constraints on the Japanese deployment of its military remain political rather than legal.

2.   Failure to revise counter-terrorism laws after 9/11

Immediately after the 9/11 attacks the then Prime Minister Junichiro Koizumi pledged his government's strong support for the United States.[1] Within one week a 'Ministerial Meeting Concerning Measures against Terrorism' was convened and a package of counter-terrorism measures – 'Japan's Measures in Response to the Simultaneous Terrorist Attacks in the United States' – was confirmed.[2] As 'Basic Policy' it provided that Japan would 'actively engage' in the fight against terrorism, which it regarded as 'Japan's own security issue', and that Japan would strongly support the US, its most important ally in both a military and humanitarian capacity. Seven 'Immediate Measures' were outlined.[3]

A striking feature of these immediate measures and the Japanese response to 9/11 more generally has been the absence of any attempt to use 9/11 as a justification to revise domestic security laws or to enact the kind of comprehensive counter-terrorism law introduced in other jurisdictions. An apparent unwillingness to enact and enforce such comprehensive legislation is a more general feature of Japanese responses to political violence post-1945 and has resulted in an ad hoc selection of laws that are, it could be argued, in need of rationalisation or reform. This section will offer a brief overview of Japanese counter-terrorism law, and examine possible reasons for the failure to revise these laws post-9/11.

---

[1] The role of Koizumi in immediate post-9/11 events was particularly important. After the resignation as Prime Minister of the error-prone Yoshiro Mori in early 2001, Koizumi was elected leader of the ruling Liberal Democratic Party (LDP) under a new system in which ordinary members of the party were given a greater role. Koizumi had a reputation as both a populist and a political outsider. In his domestic policies he supported structural reform, a policy that often placed him in direct conflict with many conservatives within the LDP. In his foreign policy, however, Koizumi focused on strengthening relations with the US and expanding the role of the SDF. Moreover, he offended many Asian countries by repeatedly visiting Yasukuni Shrine in Tokyo, where Japan's war dead – including Class A war criminals – are enshrined. Although this has been criticised internationally, it enabled Koizumi to retain the support of his own party and remain in office until 26 September 2006, despite opposition within the LDP to his domestic reform agenda.

[2] An English language version of this document is available at www.mofa.go.jp/region/n-america/us/terro0109/measure.html.

[3] The seven 'Immediate Measures' were: (1) SDF 'support for US response to terrorist attacks'; (2) SDF assistance in 'securing US facilities inside Japan'; (3) dispatch of SDF ships for 'information' (i.e. surveillance) purposes; (4) greater 'information sharing' with other countries, particularly in the context of immigration; (5) humanitarian aid to regions effected by the war on terrorism; (6) assistance to displaced persons, including 'the possibility of humanitarian assistance by SDF'; and (7) measures to 'avoid confusion in the international and domestic economic systems'.

Japanese law does not prohibit 'terrorism' as such but relies on various provisions of the Criminal Code.[4] In addition, a number of special laws related to terrorism have been enacted post-1945 in response to particular terrorist incidents. This highlights an often-overlooked point, namely that in spite of having relatively low rates of 'street crime', political violence has been a recurring problem in modern Japanese history, at least until relatively recently. The image of Japan as a harmonious, well ordered and 'crime free society' is somewhat at odds with the Japanese experience of politically and religiously motivated violence post-1945.[5]

After 1945, the Japanese Communist Party and the North Korean League engaged in radical protest against pro-US policy and increased anti-communism. Between 1948 and 1952 there were a series of violent clashes with the police resulting in thousands of arrests.[6] Such demonstrations flared up again in 1959–60 when 4.7 million demonstrators confronted a mobilised police force of around 900,000, and 1967–70 when 18.7 million demonstrators clashed with security forces numbering 6.7 million.[7] In the late 1960s, the activities of extreme left groups became increasingly violent. The most well known of these groups, the Japanese Red Army Faction, carried out a series of attacks both domestically and abroad.[8] Between 1969 and 1989, over 200 bombing incidents occurred and 570 'guerilla attacks' were recorded between 1978 and 1989. Right wing extremists also engaged in violent campaigns, including a series of political assassinations and attempted *coups d'etat* (including the incident in November 1970 when novelist Yukio Mishima committed ritual suicide after failing to persuade SDF recruits to join his attempted revolution). More recently there has been religiously motivated violence,

---

[4] Many acts commonly associated with terrorism such as insurrection (arts. 77–80), homicide (arts. 199–203), kidnapping (arts. 224–9), destruction of property (arts. 258–263) and rioting (arts. 106–7) are prosecutable as ordinary crimes under the Criminal Code. Furthermore, the Criminal Code's extra-territorial jurisdiction provisions, which were significantly revised in 1987 in order to comply with the International Convention Against the Taking of Hostages, can also be used to bring certain acts of terrorism committed abroad (both by Japanese and non-Japanese nationals) within the jurisdiction of Japanese courts (art. 4(2)).

[5] See P. J. Katzenstein, *Cultural Norms and National Security: Police and Military in Post-War Japan* (New York: Cornell University Press, 1996).

[6] The following statistics derive from P. J. Katzenstein and Y. Tsujinaka, *Defending the Japanese State: Structures, Norms and the Political Responses to Terrorism in Post-war Japan* (New York: Cornell University Press, 1991), Appendix.

[7] Ibid., pp. 8–9.

[8] For a general account of the Red Army, see A. Gallagher, *The Japanese Red Army* (New York: Rosen, 2003).

notably that associated with the cult Aum Shinrikyo.[9] Aum is well known for the attack on the Tokyo Subway in March 1995 that killed seventeen and injured more than 5,000. However, prior to this incident Aum members had been implicated in as many as eighty individual murders and a string of attempted chemical and biological attacks.[10] In fact, Aum began developing weapons of mass destruction in 1990 and successfully manufactured anthrax and botulinus toxin, in addition to sarin.[11]

The Japanese experience – from the Red Army to Aum – thus mirrors the well-documented shift from 'old' to 'new' style terrorism. The broad contours of this argument are now familiar.[12] In the context of the Cold War and the twilight of European imperialism, terrorism was fairly settled in its form. It was connected to either national liberation struggles or Marxist ideologies of revolution. The so-called 'old terrorism' involved clearly identifiable, state-sponsored terrorist groups with clear political goals who engaged in the premeditated and controlled use of force against 'legitimate' targets in order to bring the state to the negotiating table. In contrast, newer forms of terror have no borders, no clear ideology, no state or government involvement, no clear structure and amorphous apocalyptic objectives. Such groups are not only interested in guns and bombs, but also in chemical, biological and even nuclear weapons. Controlled attacks against the state are replaced by terrorist spectaculars of the kind associated with 9/11 and Aum. Although commentators often over-emphasise the difference between these two forms of terrorism, this distinction nevertheless points to an important shift that appears to track the Japanese experience.

The legal framework that emerged in Japan to respond to political violence has consisted of a number of special laws, most of which have been enacted in response to specific terrorist incidents. For example, after a series of bomb attacks involving 'Molotov cocktails' the Law for the Punishment for the Use of Glass-Bottle Grenades was enacted in 1972. This law criminalised the use, possession or manufacture of gasoline bombs. More recently, the Law Concerning the Prevention of Bodily Harm

---

[9] For general accounts of Aum see D. A. Metraux, *Aum Shrinrikyo and Japanese Youth* (New York: University Press of America, 1999); I. Reader, *Religious Violence in Contemporary Japan: The Case of Aum Shinrikyo* (New York: Curzon, 1999).

[10] R. J. Lifton, *Destroying the World to Save It: Aum Shinrikyo, Apocalyptic Violence and the New Global Terrorism* (New York: Metropolitan, 1999), pp. 37–9.

[11] Ibid., p. 39.

[12] On this distinction, see W. Lacquer, *The New Terrorism: Fanaticism and the Arms of Mass Destruction* (Oxford University Press, 1999).

Caused by Sarin Gas was enacted in 1999 in response to the Tokyo subway attack orchestrated by Aum. The use of sarin or other lethal chemicals warrants a maximum penalty of penal servitude for life, while production or possession carries a sentence of imprisonment of up to seven years.

Perhaps the most important and controversial of the special laws relating to terrorism is the Subversive Activities Prevention Law of 1952 (SAPL). It is worth considering this law and the attempt to utilise it against the Aum cult after the 1995 Tokyo subway attack because it illustrates many of the difficulties associated with security laws in Japan. Enacted during the Korean War and escalating US–Soviet tensions, the SAPL was initially intended to suppress the Japanese Communist Party and other left-wing groups. In principle, however, it can be utilised against any 'subversive' organisation or individual belonging to such an organisation. The purpose of the SAPL is 'to contribute to the preservation of public safety by establishing regulatory procedures for taking action against organizations which have carried out terrorist activities as organizational activities and supplementing the Criminal Code with additional penalties'.[13] Certain designated crimes (including riot, arson, the use of explosives, endangering the passage of public conveyances, murder, robbery, interference in the exercise of duties of public officials) normally prosecuted under the Criminal Code can be prosecuted under the SAPL if committed with a 'political purpose' by 'a person or persons affiliated with a subversive organization'.[14] Those prosecuted under the terms of the SAPL are liable for more severe punishments than if prosecuted under the Criminal Code. However, there have been less than fifteen prosecutions under this law and all related to minor offences carried out by members of radical left-wing groups in the 1950s, 1960s and early 1970s.[15] In each case the legal proceedings were extremely protracted. For example, several left-wing radicals arrested between 1969–71 only had their convictions confirmed by the Supreme Court twenty years later in 1990.[16]

The SAPL also contains provision for an organisation to be banned or restricted from engaging in certain activities.[17] An intelligence agency was established – the Public Security Investigation Agency (PSIA) – which may designate an organisation as 'a danger and appropriate for surveillance and investigation', and may implement proceedings for the banning

---

[13] SAPL, art. 1.   [14] Ibid., art. 4.
[15] See P. J. Katzenstein and Y. Tsujinaka, *Defending the Japanese State*, pp. 70–5.
[16] See *Mainichi Shimbun*, 29 September 1990, pp. 1–2. This judgment was important because the Supreme Court confirmed the constitutionality of the SAPL.
[17] SAPL, arts. 5–9.

of such an organisation.[18] The process is initiated when the Director-General of the PSIA makes an application to dissolve an organisation. A government committee on security matters reviews the application. Details of the application, including the rationale for applying the law, are then printed in the government gazette and representatives of the targeted group are allowed to state their views at public hearings. Finally, the Public Security Commission (PSC) – a different and independent administrative body – decides whether to apply the law against the organisation. The legal standard for the decision to ban a group involves three elements, namely that the targeted organisation has (1) engaged in 'destructive activities' that (2) they have 'a political purpose' and (3) that the organisation 'poses an on-going threat'. Even then the law will only be applied 'within the minimum extent necessary to assure public safety'.[19]

Although a number of groups have been, and continue to be, placed under surveillance by the PSIA (including Korean Japanese groups, as well as radical left-wing and nationalist groups) no organisation has ever been dissolved under the terms of the law. The most recent case of dissolution proceedings being initiated against an organisation involved the Aum cult. After it carried out the sarin gas attack on the Tokyo subway, proceedings were initiated to dissolve Aum. However, the PSC on 31 January 1997 rejected the PSIA's application for a dissolution order. Although the PSC acknowledged that the cult had a political motive in carrying out the attacks, they concluded that Aum no longer posed an on-going threat: as a result of the post-1995 police crackdown on the cult there was no longer a danger that Aum would continue to repeat the subversive activities in the future. Consequently, the request for a dissolution order was rejected. However, the PSC went on to note that 'it is only natural that the PSIA's future performance of its duties as they concern Aum should be strictly separated from this decision, and it should conduct itself accordingly'. The PSIA, therefore, continues to monitor Aum's activities. This kind

---

[18] The PSIA is an external branch of the Ministry of Justice. It specialises in the investigation and surveillance of domestic subversive organisations. It is the successor to the Special Investigation Bureau of the Ministry of Justice, set up in 1949 to follow up on the GHQ Ordinance of the Regulation for Associations. Under the direct supervision of the US occupation forces, this bureau investigated suspected militarists and communists and purged them from office. For an historical account of the activities of the latter organisation in post-World War II Japan, see J. Dower, *Embracing Defeat: Japan in the Aftermath of World War II* (London: Penguin, 1999), ch. 14.

[19] SAPL, art. 2. Moreover, art. 3(1) prohibits the 'unreasonable restriction to freedom of thought, association', and art. 3(2) prohibits the 'restriction of and interference with the legitimate activities of any organization through the abusive use of the SAPL'.

of PSIA intelligence-gathering work would appear to be the only aspect of the SAPL that is currently in operation, and this is largely because it (necessarily) occurs outside the glare of publicity.

Given the degree of public anger directed against the cult in the wake of the 1995 attack, one might imagine that the decision of the PSC not to ban Aum would have been criticised. However, the decision was met with cautious approval, at least in the mainstream news media. For example, the *Mainichi* newspaper labelled the ruling 'sound',[20] while the left-leaning *Asahi* newspaper praised the commission for their 'calm appraisal of the facts'.[21] An editorial in *Asahi* went so far as to call into question the very existence of the SAPL and the PSIA. It was suggested that the law was 'draconian' and 'likely to violate basic human rights'.[22] An analogy was made to the repressive conditions of pre-World War II Japan and the SAPL compared to the Peace Preservation Law of 1925, under which a number of religious and other groups were suppressed. Finally, the most conservative of the dailies, the *Yomiuri* newspaper, pointed out that 'the judgment shows that the SAPL is almost useless in stemming the rising tide of organized crime … Japan has no law that effectively prevents or checks organized crime or terrorism'.[23]

The Japanese Civil Liberties Union and National Bar Association joined those critical of the SAPL. They argued that the SAPL violates the due process provisions of the Constitution because any decision made by the PSC regarding the dissolution of an organisation is made by an administrative agency and not a court, and it excludes the application of the Administrative Procedure Law, as well as the appeal system provided for under the Administrative Appeal Law. Moreover, the fact that the law allows for the dissolution of an organisation infringes upon the freedom of association, the freedom of expression and mental freedom provisions of the Constitution.

The government nevertheless felt that some reform of the SAPL was necessary and in 1999 a number of amendments were made.[24] The

---

[20] *Mainichi Shimbun*, 1 February 1999, p. 2.
[21] *Asahi Shimbun*, 1 February 1999, p. 5.   [22] Ibid.
[23] *Yomiuri Shimbun*, 1 February 1999, p. 4.
[24] A number of other laws were introduced in response to Aum's activities, including the Wiretapping in Criminal Investigations Law (which for the first time in Japanese criminal procedure authorised the lawful use of wiretapping), and an amendment to the Religious Corporation Law (which tightened up the review and inspection process for groups accorded, as Aum had been, the status of religious corporation). On these changes, see S. M. Lenhart, 'Hammering down nails: the freedom of religious groups in Japan and the United States: Aum Shinrikyo and the Branch Davidians' (2001) 29 *Georgia Journal of*

amendments provide that if members of a group have committed 'mass murder' in the past, the group is subject to various additional restrictions, including search without warrants, eviction from land and seizure of group assets in order to compensate victims. Additionally, any group found to have violated the SAPL would lose its status as a religious organisation. Obviously, these reforms were specifically designed to target Aum, and are a further example of the Japanese preference for reactive and limited law making in this area.

In the absence of a specific threat or actual attack, Japanese authorities have been cautious in enacting counter-terrorism legislation. The result of this approach is an ad hoc collection of laws whose utility is sometimes difficult to discern. These laws are rarely, if ever, enforced and seem designed to appease public anxieties during periods of uncertainty rather than as elements of a coherent counter-terrorism strategy. And yet, such laws are rarely, if ever, repealed. They remain on the statute books for possible future use as and when it may be necessary or expedient. Of course, as the attempt to ban Aum reveals, legislation conceived in the context of the Cold War may be ineffective for terrorism in its modern forms.

It is against this background that one must consider Japan's response to 9/11. Surprisingly perhaps, given the disparate state of the law, no comprehensive anti-terrorism law was enacted and existing special laws, such as the SAPL, were not amended.[25] In explaining this omission, a number of factors should be mentioned. First, unlike in many jurisdictions, there was no public outcry demanding counter-terrorism legislation in the immediate aftermath of 9/11. This may reflect a general perception that Islamic terrorism is not a Japanese problem or at least not a problem *within* Japan. In addition, there has been little external political pressure placed on the Japanese government, either from the United States or from any other

---

International and Comparative Law 491. It is also worth noting that more than ten leading figures within the cult – including the guru Shoko Asahara – have been sentenced to death as a result of their role in the 1995 attack.

[25] This is not to suggest that nothing happened domestically. In fact, a number of operational activities and organisational reforms were implemented post-9/11. The most significant organisational reform was the creation of a Foreign Policy Bureau, an International Counter-Terrorism Co-operation Division within the Ministry of Foreign Affairs. The principle task of this agency is to facilitate closer co-operation amongst government agencies concerned with terrorism, as well as with the international community. Operationally, key activities included the tightening of immigration controls and the more active pursuit of illegal immigrants. It is perhaps significant that the government has been able to adopt this kind of operational reform away from the glare of the mass media. On these issues, see H. Mizukoshi, 'Terrorists, terrorism and Japan's counter-terrorism policy' (2003) 53 *Gaiko Forum* 53.

countries, to enact more comprehensive domestic security laws. Such pressure – so-called *gaiatsu* – is often an important factor in Japanese law making. As we shall see in the next section, the pressure that has been placed on successive governments since 9/11 has involved the overseas deployment of the SDF rather than a call for tougher internal security laws.

The government may also have felt that a more comprehensive anti-terror law is unnecessary because existing laws already provide the authorities with sufficient powers. Most obviously, the Code of Criminal Procedure permits suspects to be detained for up to twenty-three days prior to indictment.[26] During this time investigators have constant access to suspects, legal representation is limited and interrogations are not recorded. Although the Constitution provides for an extensive range of rights for suspects and defendants, the courts, and particularly the Supreme Court, have tended to favour the investigating authorities. With such extensive powers at their disposal, it may be not be necessary to enact further counter-terror laws.

And yet, it is a noteworthy feature of the Aum case that the police were often unwilling to utilise these extensive powers in spite of widespread evidence of criminal activity, including the production of weapons of mass destruction. This points to one final factor why a comprehensive counter-terrorism law has not been enacted. An important legacy of the history of state abuse of power that occurred pre-1945 in Japan is an ongoing concern with possible infringements of civil liberties by state agencies, at least in cases involving questions of political and religious freedom.[27] A painful history of state-sponsored terror means that it is often politically difficult to enact and then enforce counter-terrorism laws without being exposed to criticism from the mass media. One reason for the failure to act against Aum was that the cult had been a designated religious corporation in 1989. Such a designation may well have shielded Aum from the gaze of the authorities who would have been criticised for violating religious freedoms if they had aggressively pursued Aum. In the continued

---

[26] For more on Japanese criminal justice, see D. Foote, 'The benevolent paternalism of Japanese criminal justice' (1992) 80 *California Law Review* 317; D. T. Johnson, *The Japanese Way of Justice: Prosecuting Crime in Japan* (Oxford University Press, 2002); S. Miyazawa, *Policing in Japan: A Study on Making Crime* (State University of New York Press, 1992).

[27] For general accounts of pre-1945 repression, see R. Tipton, *The Japanese Police State: The Tokko in Inter-war Japan* (Honolulu: University of Hawaii Press, 1991); R. M. Mitchell, *Janus Faced Justice: Political Criminals in Imperial Japan* (Honolulu: University of Hawaii Press, 1992); P. Steinhoff, *Tenko: Ideology and Social Integration in Pre-War Japan* (New York: Garland, 1999).

absence of an attack, there seems to be an apparent lack of political will to enact or enforce counter-terrorism law.

This is not to say that there were no domestic legal reforms post-9/11. In fact, changes were made to laws concerned with terrorist financing and immigration procedures.

The measures related to terrorist financing are interesting insofar as they highlight another feature of Japanese policy towards terrorism, namely that the government is keen to be seen as a responsible and co-operative member of the international community, and that when an international instrument concerning terrorism is concluded and a clear international consensus exists, the government will act to implement the necessary domestic measures.[28]

At the time of the 9/11 attacks, Japan had signed but not ratified the International Convention for the Suppression of the Financing of Terrorism. As a result of the events of 9/11, the ratification process was accelerated and the process of incorporating the Convention into domestic law was concluded on 11 June 2002. In order to implement the Convention, as well as various UN Security Council Resolutions, a series of reforms were introduced that considerably strengthened surveillance and control of money flows related to terrorism, together with the targeting of terrorist financing. Most significantly, a series of amendments were made to the Foreign Exchange and Foreign Trade Law in order to implement the more effective control of criminal assets. Under the amended law, financial institutions are required to identify customers in foreign exchange transactions, including capital transactions, and to identify a customer's name, address and date of birth in case of a natural person, and customer's name and main office in the case of a juridical person.[29] Moreover, financial institutions are now obliged to record the data on customer identification and maintain the records for seven years.[30] The law

---

[28] For example, in ratifying the 1970 Convention for Suppression of Unlawful Seizure of Aircraft and the 1971 Convention for the Suppression of Unlawful Acts Against Safety of Civil Aviation, Japan enacted the Law Concerning Punishment for Unlawful Seizure of Aircraft and Similar Crimes 1970 and the Law Concerning Punishment of Activities Endangering Aircraft 1974. Japan also ratified the 1973 Convention for the Prevention and Punishment of Crimes Against Internationally Protected Persons, Including Diplomatic Agents and the 1979 International Convention Against the Taking of Hostages by Enacting the Law Concerning Punishment for Hostage-Taking 1979. In 1988, Japan amended the Law for Control of Nuclear Source Material, Nuclear Fuel Material and Reactors to ratify the Convention on the Physical Protection of Nuclear Material.

[29] The Foreign Exchange and Foreign Trade Law, as amended 2002, arts. 18 and 22.

[30] Ibid., art. 22.

also requires 'close co-operation' among relevant government agencies, to designate terrorists whose assets should be frozen (for example, by speedily exchanging information).[31] These powers have been utilised to freeze assets of groups identified by the UN Security Council as associated with the Taliban and al-Qaeda. By aggressively targeting terrorist financing, the Japanese authorities have followed the lead of the international community post-9/11.

The other area of post-9/11 domestic reform was in immigration law, where changes were made to immigration procedures for foreign nationals. Again, this was a measure justified by reference to international – particularly US – practice and the war on terrorism. A bill revising the Immigration Control and Refugee Recognition Law passed the Diet in May 2006. The new law obliged the estimated 6 to 7 million foreigners entering Japan every year to have their fingerprints and photographs taken, as well as to provide other personal identification information. The collected data is then electronically registered and cross-checked with a list of past deportees and internationally wanted criminals, including terrorists. The measure exempts people under the age of sixteen, ethnic Koreans and other special permanent residents, those invited by the government and people entering Japan for diplomatic or official purposes. The new system was launched on 20 November 2007.

One might be tempted to conclude from the above that Japan's response to 9/11 was controlled and relatively uncontroversial. Certainly, if one focuses on domestic counter-terrorism measures then one can make a case for this argument, particularly if the Japanese situation is compared with legislative developments in other jurisdictions. For those accustomed to the kind of aggressive counter-terrorism measures adopted by the US, Canadian or UK governments after 9/11, the stance of the Japanese government appears to be something of an anomaly. Stated somewhat starkly, there has been an apparent unwillingness on the part of the Japanese government to mobilise the full force of state authority against terrorism, preferring instead a more cautious, or at least less visible, approach. In this respect, the post-9/11 response is a continuation of what has gone before. Of course, the continued absence of an al-Qaeda-sponsored attack in Japan or on Japanese interests is a major consideration, and were such an attack to occur one imagines – based on previous experience – that this situation might quickly change.

---

[31] Ibid., art. 69(4).

It would be a mistake, however, to conclude from this brief review of the domestic situation that 9/11 has not had an impact upon Japanese law or politics. Quite the contrary, 9/11 resulted in a significant shift in government policy and policy debates related to the role of the SDF and in the government position regarding art. 9 of the Constitution.

3. The Anti-Terrorism Special Measures Law and art. 9 of the Constitution

When the then Prime Minister Koizumi met with President Bush on 25 September 2001 he confirmed his government's decision to deploy the SDF abroad in support of US retaliation for the attacks. In fact, four of the seven 'immediate measures' adopted by the Ministerial Meeting Concerning Measures against Terrorism in the days following 9/11 directly related to the activities of the SDF.[32] Amongst these measures was the declaration that the government would enact legislation to allow for the SDF to provide support for US forces overseas. On 5 October the government agreed to the text of three bills that would facilitate such deployments and submitted them to the Diet. After legislative deliberation in both the House of Representatives and the House of Councillors, the package of bills was passed on 29 October. The principle piece of legislation was the Anti-Terrorism Special Measures Law (ATSML), which came into effect on 2 November 2001.

This section describes the main features of the ATSML and examines the reasons why it proved to be so controversial, notably the new interpretation of art. 9 that it seemed to contain. It then examines the political problems that the Fukuda Administration had in renewing the ATSML in 2007, and the 2008 enactment of a new, more restrictive law designed to allow SDF support for the US in the Indian Ocean to continue.

Three weeks was an extremely short period of legislative deliberation, particularly for legislation concerning the SDF. This was largely because the opposition parties – and in particular, traditional opponents of an expanded role for the SDF, namely the Communist Party and Social Democratic Party – felt unable, given the circumstances surrounding 9/11, to adopt the kind of stalling tactics that they customarily utilise.[33]

---

[32] See above note 3.

[33] The politics of pacifism in Japan are complex and cut across party political lines. For example, former Cabinet Secretary Hiromu Nonaka, one of the more influential conservative members of the LDP, was well known for his strong objection to Japan's assumption of a greater security role. Moreover, one of the three governing coalition parties, the

The quick passage of the law invited the suggestion that the government had used the events of 9/11 in order to enact legislation that would have been extremely difficult, if not impossible, under ordinary circumstances. Critics pointed to the fact that the Diet had taken nine months to enact the Peacekeeping Law in 1992 and over a year to enact legislation to provide US forces with logistic support under the revised defence guidelines in 1999. This is not to mention earlier efforts to legislate in this area that had to be abandoned due to political and public opposition.[34]

Unlike in other jurisdictions, however, the speed of the legislative process post-9/11 should not be regarded as a case of populist democracy. The ATSML was not enacted on a wave of public anger over the attacks, but as a result of Prime Minister Koizumi's ideological commitment to expand Japan's security role and, it seems, direct pressure from the United States. It has been suggested that the decision to involve the SDF in international counter-terror operations was prompted, at least in part, by comments made to the Japanese Ambassador in Washington by Deputy Secretary of State Richard Armitage, who apparently suggested that Japan should 'show the flag' in any future military action.[35] Given that Koizumi constructed his foreign policy around strengthening ties with the United States often at the expense of relations with his regional neighbours, he may well have been keen to comply with this request. Nevertheless, the fact that this kind of story is given credence indicates the degree to which Japanese security policy is subject to US influence. The dilemma for Japanese governments – particularly post-9/11 – has been in reconciling the reality of the US–Japan security relationship with the often competing desire to be a responsible member of the international community.

And yet, read in isolation the ATSML appears – even a decade later – to be an uncontroversial piece of legislation. The purpose of the law was defined as 'specifying certain "response measures" that enable Japan to contribute actively and effectively to the efforts of the international community to prevent and eradicate international terrorism, thereby ensuring the peace and security of the international community including Japan'.[36]

New Komei Party – the political wing of Buddhist sect Sokka Gakkai – also had serious reservations about Koizumi's security policy.

[34] A detailed review of failed attempts to enact legislation pertaining to the SDF is beyond the scope of this chapter. For an overview, see Katzenstein, *Cultural Norms and National Security*, Chapter 5.

[35] See G. MacCormack, 'Japan's Afghan expedition', *Japan World*, 5 November 2001, available at www.iwanami.co.jp/jpworld/text/Afghanexpedition01.html.

[36] ATSML, art. 1.

This included (1) 'measures Japan implements in support of the activities of the armed forces of the US and other countries which aim to eradicate the threat of the terrorists responsible for the 9/11 attacks and thereby contribute to the purpose of the Charter of the UN'; and, (2) 'measures Japan implements in a humanitarian spirit based on the relevant resolutions of the UN'.[37]

Response measures included three broad categories of activity, namely 'co-operation and support activities', 'search and rescue activities' and 'assistance to affected peoples'.[38] Each of these three broad categories was then defined. Co-operation and support activities included the provision of materials and services and other measures in support of foreign forces;[39] search and rescue activities included measures implemented by Japan to search for and rescue combatants in distress due to combat in the case of the activities of foreign forces.[40] Assistance to affected peoples was defined as the transportation of necessary provisions, including food, clothing and medicine, medical services and other humanitarian activities implemented by Japan with regard to terrorist attacks.[41]

All the above measures could be carried out by various government agencies including the SDF,[42] but crucially they could not involve the 'threat or use of force'.[43] Members of the SDF responsible for any measures could proportionately use weapons only when an 'unavoidable and reasonable cause exists for their use in order to protect the lives of SDF members or those who have come under SDF control during the implementation of operations'.[44]

Response measures could be adopted in the following areas: '(a) the territory of Japan; (b) the high seas and airspace above; and, (c) the territory of foreign countries' (subject to the condition that the country consents to the presence of Japanese forces).[45] Significantly, in the case of (b) and (c), implementation was limited to cases where 'combat is not taking place or expected to take place, while Japanese activities are being implemented'.[46] The ATSML required that the Prime Minister 'seek the approval of the Diet for all response measures within three weeks of their initiation'. In the event that the Diet did not approve, any response measure must be 'terminated immediately'.[47] Finally, the law was subject to periodic legislative renewal.

---

[37] Ibid., art. 1.   [38] Ibid., arts. 2–3.   [39] Ibid., art. 3(1).   [40] Ibid., art. 3(2).
[41] Ibid., art. 3(3).   [42] Ibid., art. 3(4).   [43] Ibid., art. 2(2).   [44] Ibid., art. 12.
[45] Ibid., art. 2(3).   [46] Ibid., art. 2(3).   [47] Ibid., art. 5.

Measures adopted under the ATSML in the immediate period after 9/11 were, from a military point of view, small-scale. On 9 November 2001, two destroyers and a supply ship were deployed in the Indian Ocean in support of US Navy operations. On 25 November, a destroyer, a supply ship and a minesweeper were also deployed. More controversially, on 16 December 2002 Japan sent a surveillance class destroyer to the Indian Ocean. Other operations have been of a similar scale, mostly involving re-supply of US and UK vessels, as well as intelligence gathering. Re-supply of NATO boats and intelligence work in the Indian Ocean continued to be the only activities conducted under the ATSML. The modest nature of SDF deployments in the 'war on terrorism' highlights that what was at stake was not a revival in Japanese militarism, but rather the Japanese Constitution.[48]

Complicating discussion of the ATSML is art. 9 of the Constitution and the history of Japanese aggression that preceded its promulgation. The renouncing of war and the concomitant prohibition of maintaining any war potential together constitute one of the fundamental principles that the occupying US forces imposed on the defeated Japanese government in August 1945.[49] This principle is given effect by Chapter III, art. 9 of the Constitution:

(1) Aspiring sincerely to an international peace based on justice and order, the Japanese people forever renounce war as a sovereign right of the nation and the threat or use of force as means of settling international disputes.

(2) In order to accomplish the aim of the preceding paragraph, land, sea, and air forces, as well as other war potential, will never be maintained. The right of belligerency of the state will not be recognized.

There are other examples of how this principle informs the Constitution, and Japanese law more generally. For example, art. 66(2) of the Constitution states that the PM and other Cabinet posts must be held by civilians. The prohibition on 'involuntary servitude' found in art. 18

---

[48] There are two main arguments as to why Japanese re-militarisation is unlikely: first, the extreme dependence of Japan on the US for security, and second, the genuine culture of anti-militarism that exists amongst a significant proportion of the population in Japan. On the latter issue, see I. Buruma, *The Wages of Guilt: Memories of War in Germany and Japan* (London: Phoenix, 1994); N. Field, *In the Realm of a Dying Emperor: Japan at Century's End* (New York: Vintage, 1992).

[49] The other principles were the sovereignty of the people – as opposed to the Emperor – and the guarantee of fundamental human rights.

is understood by constitutional scholars to include conscription to the military and no legal provision in the Constitution provides for martial law or for dealing with acts of war such as declaring war or concluding peace. The pre-war Criminal Code – which in contrast to the Code of Criminal Procedure was not completely revised during the US occupation – was subject to minor amendments, notably, those offences that were predicated on the existence of a war situation were deleted.

It is well known that art. 9 has been an ongoing source of controversy since the Constitution came into effect on 3 November 1947. A literal interpretation of art. 9 would seem to suggest that the existence of the SDF is unconstitutional because art. 9(2) contains a clear prohibition on the maintenance of any kind of military forces or 'other war potential'. Certainly, this is the view of most mainstream Japanese constitutional law scholars and left-leaning political parties. They regard Japan's acceptance of the terms of the Potsdam Declaration on 2 September 1945 as crucial. Under the terms of the Potsdam Declaration, Japan was to be 'completely disarmed' and the authority of those who 'misled the people' would be eliminated 'for all time'.[50] As John Dower, the most prominent English language historian of post-World War II Japan, puts it, Potsdam 'made clear that disarmament and demilitarization were not merely to be "complete" but also "permanent"'.[51]

In the 1950s, however, and with the explicit support of a US government concerned about Soviet expansion in East Asia, Japan began a programme of rearmament that has continued through to the present.[52] The procedural obstacles to constitutional reform as well as the political sensitivities surrounding art. 9 meant that an amendment to the Constitution was

---

[50] Quoted in Dower, *Embracing Defeat*, p. 74.

[51] Ibid, p. 75. See also K. Inoue, *MacArthur's Japanese Constitution: A Linguistic and Cultural Study of its Making* (University of Chicago Press, 1991); S. Koseki, *The Birth of Japan's Postwar Constitution* (Denver, CO: Westview Press, 1998).

[52] For details of this expansion, see P. J. Katzenstein, *Cultural Norms and National Security*, chapters 5–6. Fearful of Communist insurrection, the occupying US forces authorised the creation of a 75,000 National Police Reserve (NPR) to safeguard internal security in the late 1940s. Following the end of the US occupation in 1952 and the conclusion of the US–Japan Security Treaty, the NPR was transformed into the SDF. It seems the name SDF was adopted to indicate the defensive nature of the force. It is often suggested that Japan has the second largest military budget in the world: see, for example, D. Hayes, *Japan: The Toothless Tiger* (Tokyo: Tuttle, 2003), p. 131, although such claims are difficult to verify. The SDF currently consists of 150,000 ground troops, a maritime force of 43,000 troops and 160 vessels, and an air force of 45,000 troops and 51,000 planes.

unlikely.[53] In fact, it is worth noting that no amendment of the Japanese Constitution has ever been enacted. Instead, the government adopted an interpretation of art. 9 in which they denied that the SDF constituted 'forces' or 'other war potential' prohibited by art. 9(2). The logic of this position derives from the argument that all sovereign nations – including Japan – enjoy an 'inherent right' of self-defence in international law.[54] This principle is expressly stated in art. 51 of the UN Charter although it also has a basis in customary international law.[55] Since the Constitution does not expressly prohibit the possession of a minimum level of armed strength necessary to exercise the right of self-defence, the maintenance of the SDF for the purpose of self-defence is constitutional.

In order to understand the Japanese government's position (i.e. the position of the Liberal Democratic Party 1955–2009) it is important to distinguish between an individual right of self-defence and a right of collective self-defence. An individual right of self-defence refers to the right of a country which is directly attacked (i.e. Japan) to repel such an attack whereas the right of collective self-defence refers to the right of Japan, in a situation where Japan is not directly attacked, to deem an attack against another country that is an alliance with Japan (i.e. the US) as an attack on itself and then counter-attack. Over the course of the last five decades, the Japanese Government and Defense Agency have consistently taken the position that maintaining military force necessary for individual self-defence is constitutional but that collective self-defence is not permissible under art. 9. The following is an indicative statement of the government view:

> The Constitution, upholding pacifism, sets forth in Article 9 the renunciation of war, non-possession of war potential and denial of the right

---

[53] The procedure for amending the Constitution is to be found in art. 96: 'Amendments to this Constitution shall be initiated by the Diet, through a concurring vote of two-thirds or more of all the members of each House and shall thereupon be submitted to the people for ratification, which shall require the affirmative vote of a majority of all votes cast thereon, at a special referendum or at such election as the Diet shall specify. (2) Amendments when so ratified shall immediately be promulgated by the Emperor in the name of the people, as an integral part of this Constitution.'

[54] See generally I. Brownlie, *International Law and the Use of Force by States* (Oxford University Press, 1963), pp. 231–80; I. Brownlie, 'The Nicaragua case', 1986 *ICJ Reports* 14.

[55] 'Nothing in the present Charter shall impair the inherent right of individual or collective self-defence if an armed attack occurs against a Member of the United Nations': Charter of the United Nations, San Francisco, 26 June 1945, in force 24 October 1945, 1 UNTS XVI, art. 51.

to belligerency of the state, As long as Japan is a sovereign state, *it is recognized beyond doubt that the provision in the article does not deny the inherent right of self-defense that Japan is entitled to maintain as a sovereign nation.*

Since the right is not denied, the government remains firm in the belief that *the Constitution does not inhibit the possession of the minimum level of armed strength necessary to exercise the right of self-defense.* On the basis of such understanding the government has adopted the *exclusively defense-oriented policy* as its basic policy of national defense and has maintained self-defense as an armed organization, and has taken steps to improve its capabilities and to ensure their efficient operation. These measures do not present any constitutional problem.[56]

Although official translations such as this do not explicitly refer to *individual* self-defence, the phrase 'exclusively defense-oriented policy' has always been understood in this way both by the government and its critics. The government interpretation of art. 9, therefore, derives the constitutionality of the maintenance of the minimum necessary level of armed strength for individual self-defence from the existence of Japan's right in international law to defend itself if directly attacked.

Further support for the government's view can be found in the legislative history of art. 9. Of crucial importance in this discussion is the fact that the original draft of art 9 was amended – with, it should be noted, the consent of the occupying US authorities – during the final stages of its deliberation in the Diet.[57] The original English language version of art. 9 drafted by the occupying forces and presented to the Diet was as follows:

(1) War as a sovereign right of a nation, and threat or use of force, is forever renounced as a means of settling disputes with other nations.
(2) The maintenance of land, sea and air forces, as well as other war potential, will never be authorized. The right of belligerency of the state will never be recognized.

Discussion of the amendment process is complex and involves rather subtle questions of language, but the government position is that the effect of the so-called Ashida amendment was to clearly establish a right to individual self-defence in contrast to the original draft. According to this argument, the first clause of the revised version of art. 9 establishes

---

[56] Japanese Defense Agency, *Annual Report* (Tokyo: Japan Times, 1993), pp. 63–7, 127–8 (emphasis added).
[57] The 1947 Constitution was formally enacted as an amendment to the 1889 Meiji Constitution, and so was subject to limited legislative review. For more on the history of legislative debate surrounding art. 9, see Dower, *Embracing Defeat*, pp. 75–90.

international peace as the article's objective. The words added to the second clause as a result of the Ashida amendment – namely 'In order to accomplish the aim of the preceding paragraph' – indicate that what was being renounced was, in contrast to the earlier draft, not the maintenance of military force *per se*, but the maintenance of a capacity for an aggressive war that would disturb international peace. This, according to the government view, left open the possibility that military force necessary for self-defence would be constitutional.

Although historians and constitutional lawyers have repeatedly criticised the government's position on art. 9, the courts have taken a more cautious view.[58] The leading cases on this question have generally accepted the government position that art. 9 does not proscribe the country's right of individual self-defence. On the question of whether a right to maintain military force can be derived from this right of self-defence, there is something of a division between courts of first instance who have rejected the government position on a number of occasions, and appeal courts who have consistently refrained from ruling on this matter on the grounds that it is a political matter.

The 'exclusively defense oriented' interpretation of art. 9 thus provided the justification with which Japanese governments conducted defence policy during the Cold War. This proved to be both an enabling and disabling interpretation of art. 9. On the one hand, the 'minimum level of armed strength necessary to exercise the right of individual self-defense' is an unclear standard that on a critical view has allowed the Defense Agency to construct a military capability free from any kind of restriction on the scale or composition of the SDF. And yet, although this justification for the existence of the SDF has imposed little in the way of quantitative restriction on Japanese rearmament, it has imposed limits of a different

---

[58] The leading Supreme Court judgments relating to art. 9 can all be found in translation in L. W. Beer and H. Itoh (eds.), *The Constitutional Case Law of Japan 1970 through 1990* (Seattle, WA: University of Washington Press, 1996). On the topic of judicial independence in Japan more generally, see J. Haley, 'Judicial independence in Japan revisited' (1995) 25 *Law in Japan* 1; M. J. Ramseyer and E. Rasmussen, *Measuring Judicial Independence: The Political Economy of Judging in Japan* (University of Chicago Press, 2003). Japan has a career judiciary in which judges are allocated new posts every three to five years. Ramseyer and Rasmussen argue that those judges who make decisions that are deemed to be politically controversial find themselves suffering in their subsequent career postings. The fifteen Supreme Court justices, however, come from a variety of backgrounds, including the judiciary, the legal profession, bureaucracies and academia. In spite of this diversity in intake, the Supreme Court has a reputation for political conservatism, particularly in cases involving central government.

order, namely in restricting the areas and circumstances where the SDF may be deployed. By formulating the justification for the SDF's existence in terms of individual self-defence, the government has been limited in how the SDF may be utilised. Most significantly, this has meant that any overseas deployment of the SDF, including the use of the SDF in support of an ally who is under attack (i.e. collective self-defence) has been considered to be unconstitutional even by the government.

However, over the course of the 1990s the self-defence justification became increasingly strained in the face of the changing geo-political situation. Of particular importance in this context was international criticism of the Japanese role in the first Gulf War of 1990–1. Although Japan made significant financial contributions, they did not contribute any military assistance to Coalition forces on the grounds that it was incompatible with the 'exclusively defense oriented policy'. Stung by US criticism of this so-called 'cheque book diplomacy', the government introduced a number of new measures. Foremost amongst these were the Law Concerning Co-operation with UN Peacekeeping Operations and Other Operations Law of 1992 (the PKO Law) and the Law Concerning Measures to Maintain the Peace and Security of Japan in Situations Surrounding Japan Law of 1999 (SASJL).

The purpose of the PKO Law was to provide appropriate and prompt co-operation for UN peacekeeping operations and humanitarian relief operations. Under the terms of the PKO Law, the overseas deployment of the SDF became legally possible for the first time on condition that five conditions were met, including the existence of a UN Security Council resolution authorising the peacekeeping operation and the existence of a ceasefire agreement. Moreover, the use of weapons is limited to the minimum necessary in order to protect the lives of SDF personnel. Based on this law, the SDF have participated in PKOs in Cambodia (September 1992–September 1993), Mozambique (May 1993–January 1995), the Golan Heights (February 1996–present) and East Timor (March 2002–present).[59] SASJL was enacted in 1999 and made it possible for the SDF to provide so-called 'Rear Area Support', i.e. the provision of logistical support in co-operation with US forces in

---

[59] It is worth noting the shift in public opinion that has occurred as a result of these activities. According to government surveys, only 20.6 per cent of the population 'approved' of Japan's participation in PKOs in 1991 compared with 40.5 per cent in 2000. The number of those opposed decreased from 18.8 per cent in 1991 to 2.7 per cent in 2001. See National Institute for Defense Studies Japan, *East Asian Strategic Review 2003* (Tokyo: Japan Times, 2003), p. 311.

areas 'surrounding Japan' that may lead to a direct military attack on Japan if they are not addressed.[60]

However, under the terms of the PKO Law and the SASJL it was not possible for the government to take measures in support of US forces outside of Japan or 'areas surrounding Japan'. Under the PKO Law there were clear limits to the overseas deployment of the SFD, notably the existence of a specific UN resolution and a cease-fire agreement. Under the terms of SASJL, SDF activities were limited to 'areas surrounding Japan'. Although these reforms facilitated the overseas deployment of Japanese forces – which in itself is clearly controversial from the point of view of the 'exclusively defense oriented policy' – the situations authorised were still clearly restricted. The ATSML removed these limits and enabled the government to deploy the SDF on completely new grounds, based neither on co-operation with the UN nor solely on the basis of US–Japan co-operation in defending Japan and surrounding areas. The key question then is whether the new law is inconsistent not only with the clear meaning of art. 9, but also – perhaps more significantly – with the previously held government interpretation of art. 9.

In addressing how the ATSML marks a break with earlier policy, critics of the law pointed to a number of issues.[61] Most significantly, art. 2 of the ATSML added the open-ended category of the 'territory of foreign countries' and 'the high seas and space above' to the areas where the SDF could lawfully operate. This went beyond the PKO Law and the SASJL and made it possible for the government to deploy the SDF overseas in the name of international co-operation against terrorism without any geographical restrictions or a clear UN mandate. Although SDF deployment was limited to activities that aimed to 'eradiate international terrorism' and thereby 'contribute to the purpose of the UN Charter', this was an open-ended and unclear standard, particularly when one considers that international terrorism is not clearly defined and the reference is to the UN Charter rather than specific Security Council Resolutions.

The ATSML would also appear to be incompatible with the previously held government interpretation of art. 9 as it would seem to permit

---

[60] This law gave legal effect to the 1997 Guidelines negotiated between Japan and the United States under the terms of the US–Japan Security Agreement.

[61] The following discussion draws upon the contents of an open letter of 9 October 2001 signed by over fifty Japanese constitutional law scholars written in protest over the ATSML. The Japanese language version is available at www.jca.apc.org/~kenpoweb/appeal.html. It also uses arguments found in a special issue of the Japanese language law journal, which discusses art. 9 post-9/11: (2004) 1260 *Jurist*.

'response measures' in support of collective self-defence and perhaps even pre-emptive attacks if they are conducted with the goal of eradicating terrorism. This would involve stretching the earlier concept of self-defence – which is already a contentious one given the plain meaning of art. 9 – to breaking point. The law also provided that implementation should be limited to cases where combat is not taking place. However, it can be difficult to distinguish between areas of combat and areas of non-combat, particularly in cases of terrorism.[62]

In addition, the ATSML emphasised that 'response measures' did not constitute the use of force as prohibited by art. 9 by providing in art. 2(2) that these measures must not constitute a 'threat or use of force'. The issue here relates to the kind of activities that are specified as co-operation and support activities. As mentioned above, these included supply, transportation, repair and maintenance, medical services and communication. These would generally be thought of as logistical activities. However, since the use of force is impossible without such logistical support – that is to say, logistical support is a necessary pre-condition for the exercise of military force – the distinction that the law makes between 'response measures' and the 'use of force' has been questioned. A rather graphic illustration of this particular argument was posed by one newspaper editorial when it wondered whether a Japanese vessel would be permitted to provide fuel to US destroyers launching cruise missiles against terrorist training camps in Northwest Pakistan.[63]

Finally, under the ATSML the implementation of response measures by the SDF could be taken without advance parliamentary approval and an after-the-event validation of the Diet is permitted. This is to be contrasted with the PKO Law and the SASJL, which both provide for advance Diet approval for the overseas deployment of the SDF. The argument has been made that in this regard civilian control of the SDF was diminished. Given the history of the Japanese military, this is an extremely sensitive question and it is not surprising that this was one aspect of the law that was contested in the brief parliamentary deliberations.

The government was clearly aware that in enacting the ATSML they were stretching the self-defence justification, and acknowledged that a

---

[62] A similar restriction exists in the Special Law relating to Iraq. SDF forces can only be deployed if combat has ceased. In spite of the worsening security situation in Iraq, the Japanese government has argued that combat is not taking place in the *area* where the SDF forces are deployed, and that the deployment is therefore lawful.

[63] *Nihon Keizai Shimbun*, 11 November 2001.

different justification for the constitutionality of the SDF was required. The argument that the government proposed was a new one and focused on the suggestion that there is a 'gap' between the preamble of the Constitution and the earlier interpretation of art. 9. The government's recourse to the preamble is interesting, not least because the preamble has often been utilised in support of the argument that art. 9 amounts to an absolute prohibition and the conclusion that the SDF is unconstitutional. However, the new government position was to suggest that a fundamental principle underlying the preamble is the principle of international co-operation.[64] It was argued that when read in the context of the preamble, art. 9 can legitimately justify the use of force not only in the case of individual self-defence but also in the broader case of international co-operation in pursuit of peace and security (i.e. collective self-defence). Overseas deployment of the SDF in support of operations aimed at eradicating terrorists was now to be considered constitutional by the Japanese government.

Most constitutional scholars met this suggestion with scepticism, arguing that the new government position meant that art. 9 is meaningless as almost any joint deployment of the SDF could be justified on the grounds of international co-operation. Critics argued that there is no 'gap' between the preamble and art. 9. Quite the contrary, the principles of the preamble – namely pacifism and an absolute rejection of military force – are enshrined in every article of the Constitution, including art. 9. According to this view, it is a unique feature of the so-called 'Peace Constitution' that it adopts international co-operation based on pacifist principles. As such, critics questioned both the legality of the government's position and the belief that military force, even if it is co-operative, can ever succeed in eradicating terrorism.

One further point of discussion concerned the relationship between international law, art. 9 and the ATSML. As was mentioned above, successive Japanese governments relied upon the existence of an 'inherent right' of self-defence in international law in arguing that the SDF is constitutional insofar as it adopts an 'exclusively defense oriented policy'. As

---

[64] It has been suggested that this can be found most clearly, for example, in the following section of the Preamble: '*We desire to occupy an honored place in an international society striving for the preservation of peace, and the banishment of tyranny and slavery, oppression and intolerance* for all time from the earth … We recognize that all peoples of the world have the right to live in peace, free from fear and want. *We believe that no nation is responsible to itself alone*, but that laws of political morality are universal; and that obedience to such laws is incumbent upon all nations' (emphasis added).

such, the government view of art. 9 imposed a more severe standard than art. 51 of the UN Charter since only acts of individual self-defence are permitted. Given the fact that art. 51 explicitly mentions collective self-defence, was it possible for the government to rely upon international law as a legal basis for the ATSML?

Chapter X (Articles 97–9 of the Constitution) establishes the hierarchy of norms in Japanese law. Of crucial importance in this context is art. 98:

(1) This Constitution shall be the supreme law of the nation and no law, ordinance, imperial rescript or other act of government, or part thereof, contrary to the provisions hereof, shall have legal force or validity.

(2) The treaties concluded by Japan and established laws of nations shall be faithfully observed.

The 'prevailing view' is that the effect of this provision is that the Constitution has priority over international law.[65] The Cabinet's power to conclude treaties and the Diet's power to approve them derive from the Constitution, therefore it is logically not possible to justify the superiority of a treaty.[66] On this view, art. 51 of the UN Charter cannot provide a legal basis for the exercise of collective self-defence, if art. 9 is understood (as it has been even by the government) to exclude such acts.

The alternative (minority) view is to suggest that art. 98(2) constitutes a limitation on art. 98(1).[67] That is to say, treaties and the 'established laws of nations' (i.e. customary international law) have priority over the Constitution. This view leads to the conclusion that art. 51 of the UN Charter would have superiority over the provisions of art. 9 and that collective self-defence is permitted as a result of Japan's ratification of the Charter. It is interesting to note that the Japanese government did not adopt this line of argument, preferring instead the re-interpretation of art. 9 discussed above.

Although international law may provide a legal basis for acts of *collective* self-defence, it is a much more controversial question whether it would be of assistance to the Japanese government if the response measures adopted under the ATSML were in support of *pre-emptive* attacks,

---

[65] H. Oda, *Japanese Law* (Oxford University Press, 2001), p. 50.
[66] A further argument in support of this view is that the procedure for amending the Constitution is much more difficult than that for concluding treaties.
[67] See, e.g., K. Sorimachi, 'Internationalization and globalization demand changes in judicial interpretation', *21st Century Shape of Japan, No.3* (2003), available on-line at www.lec-jp.com/speaks/info_003.htm.

e.g. if the SDF were to re-fuel a US aircraft involved in a pre-emptive strike against a terrorist group located in a third country. As is well documented, post-9/11 the Bush Administration sought to extend the scope of the right of self-defence to include action in anticipation of a terrorist attack against any state that willingly harbours such terrorists.[68] Such acts would appear to be problematic from the point of view of art. 51 of the UN Charter, as well as customary international law.[69] If the Japanese government had relied upon international law as the basis for action under the ATSML they would have been obliged to defend the view that such pre-emptive strikes were permissible in international law. Given the delicacy of this issue within the international community, this is a course of action that any Japanese government would have been unwilling to take. Re-interpreting the Constitution to broaden the scope of art. 9 thus seemed to be a more expedient approach.

The ATSML thus resulted in a re-interpretation of art. 9 that was hard to reconcile with the plain meaning of the text or, perhaps more importantly, the previous government position that limited the SDF's activities to defending Japan in the event of a direct attack. This more assertive approach reflected, in part, the ideological preferences of the Koizumi Administration at that time, as well as the demands of the US–Japan security relationship post-9/11. By presenting military force as a legitimate and effective means of responding to terrorism, the Koizumi Administration seems to have agreed with the then dominant US thinking that regarded terrorists as hybrid paramilitaries engaged in a form of quasi-warfare rather than thinking of terrorist acts as crimes and terrorists as criminals. The message that was communicated to the Japanese public by the ATSML about the nature of the current terrorist threat and the most effective response to that threat seems to have been designed to confirm anxieties that may lead many to question the values found in art. 9.

The policy of strong support for US military measures against suspected terrorists and their supporters continued with the enactment of The Law Concerning Special Measures on Humanitarian and Reconstruction Assistance in Iraq in July 2003.[70] Under the terms of this

---

[68] See, e.g., M. Byers, 'Terrorism, the use of force and international law after 9/11' (2002) 51 *International and Comparative Law Quarterly* 401.

[69] Ibid., 413–14.

[70] Japan was quick to express its support for the US-led attack on Iraq. In February 2003, when many members of the UN Security Council were expressing reluctance to approve a new resolution that would have authorised an attack, Japan declared its backing for

law, the SDF were permitted to undertake humanitarian and reconstruction assistance in 'non-combat zones' in support of the US-led occupation.[71] The decision to actually deploy troops was repeatedly postponed largely as a result of public opposition to such a move. However, after the killing of two Japanese diplomats on 29 November 2003 in a terrorist attack inside Iraq, the government decided to push ahead with the deployment, citing the importance of maintaining Japan's alliance with the US and co-operating with the international community. In March 2004, 550 ground troops arrived in Samawah, Southeast Iraq where they engaged in 'reconstruction activities', principally involving the reconnection of water supplies. These deployments continued until June 2006, when the Japanese government concluded that a 'new stage' had been reached in the reconstruction process and that Japanese forces were no longer required. All Japanese ground forces had left Iraq by September 2006, although air operations in support of multinational forces continued until December 2008.

The Iraq mission proved extremely controversial, with at least eleven lawsuits filed by citizens groups who contested the constitutionality of the law and claiming damages for the psychological pain caused by the dispatch of forces. All of these suits were dismissed but in an unusual turn of events, the Nagoya High Court in April 2008 held that the expansion of air support operations to airspace above Baghdad and Arbil in Northern Iraq violated the Iraq Special Law since both areas could be considered 'combat zones' because killings and subversive activities were taking place. The Court reasoned that the SDF's act of transporting armed soldiers of the multinational forces to Baghdad, a combat zone, is integral to the use of force by other countries and therefore must be regarded as use of force on the part of the SDF. It concluded that the SDF's transport mission included activities that violate the special law's clauses prohibiting

such a move. And in May 2003, when Koizumi met with President Bush, he promised Japanese help with the post-war reconstruction effort, implicitly suggesting that this would include dispatch of the SDF. The negative effects of this policy were highlighted after the 11 March 2004 train bombings in Madrid when the group with alleged links to the al-Qaeda terrorist network that claimed responsibility for the attack named Japan as a potential future target: *Japan Times*, 13 March 2004, p. 2. Public anxiety in Japan has been raised by the kidnapping of Japanese civilians and the murder of journalists in Iraq and the recent disclosure that a French citizen, Lionel Dumont, who is suspected of having links with al-Qaeda, had been attempting to form a terrorist cell inside Japan: see *Time*, 7 June 2004, 37.

[71] The Law Concerning Special Measures on Humanitarian and Reconstruction Assistance in Iraq, 2003, art. 2.

the use of force and activities in a combat zone, as well as art. 9(1) of the Constitution. The ruling undermined the claims consistently made by the Koizumi Administration that the SDF was not, and had never, conducted operations in combat zones.

A final illustration of the government's more aggressive stance on security issues occurred in July 2003 when a package of measures, notably the Law to Respond to Armed Attacks (so-called emergency legislation), were enacted. As mentioned above, the Constitution contains no provision for the suspension of the rule of law in wartime or other national emergency. Since 1977 LDP governments had unsuccessfully attempted to pass laws that would delimit the domestic powers of the PM and the role of the SDF in the event of an armed attack on Japan. An escalation of tensions with North Korea highlighted the need for some contingency plans. After failing once in the 2002 legislative session, the Koizumi Administration succeeded in 2003 in passing a package of measures that delimited the powers of the state and the role of the SDF in the event of such an emergency situation.[72]

As indicated by these other measures, the ATSML was part of a series of measures on the part of the Koizumi Administration designed to expand the role of the SDF using the new global security situation as a justification. However, after Koizumi stepped down as PM in September 2006 three successive LDP prime ministers struggled to maintain political support for such a stance, notably for the ATSML.

A significant feature of the ATSML was that it contained a 'sunset clause' and required the approval of the Diet for any extension. On 10 October 2003, the Diet confirmed a government request to extend the law for a further two years.[73] A similar extension was granted in 2005. However, when the law came up for a further extension in 2007 (after Koizumi's resignation), the then leader of opposition Democratic Party (DPJ), Ichiro Ozawa, decided to oppose the extension. Such opposition was possible as the DPJ at that time enjoyed a majority in the Upper House of the Japanese Diet. The DPJ position was to argue that the operations being conducted under this law – namely the re-supply of US forces in the Indian Ocean – should be terminated, as they constituted collective self-defence operations lacking a basis in international law.

---

[72] See Mark Fenwick, 'Emergency powers and the limits of constitutionalism in Japan', in Victor V. Ramraj and A. K. Thiruvengadam (eds.), *Emergency Powers in Asia: Exploring the Limits of Legality* (Cambridge University Press, 2010).

[73] *Japan Times*, 11 October 2003, 2.

Whether this was political opportunism on the part of Ozawa and other senior members of the DPJ (many of whom – including Ozawa – were former members of the LDP and had a record of supporting the LDP's stance on art. 9) is open to argument. With the popular Koizumi off the scene – replaced as LDP leader and PM by Yasuo Fukuda – the DPJ clearly sensed an opportunity to strike a damaging blow to the government on an issue where opinion polls consistently showed strong public opposition to activities conducted under the ATSML. In spite of the fact that there were inconsistencies in the DPJ position – notably the claim that the operation in Afghanistan lacked UN backing[74] – the debate continued for several months before it became clear that an extension could not be achieved.

In November 2007, therefore, the ATSML expired and all support activities in the Indian Ocean ceased. The Japanese government came under pressure from the US to resume these operations and so the Fukuda Administration enacted a new law in January 2008, the Replenishment Support Special Measures Law (RSSML). The RSSML was a more limited version of the ATMSL designed to facilitate the resumption of operations in the Indian Ocean that had previously been authorised by the ATMSL.

The purpose of the new law was similar to the ATMSL, namely 'to make an active and proactive contribution to the efforts of the international community to prevent and eradicate international terrorism and to contribute to ensuring peace and security of the international community, including Japan'.[75] Activities permitted under the act were restricted to supply operations and the areas of activity were explicitly limited to areas around Japan and – crucially – the Indian Ocean.

The Fukuda Cabinet approved an implementation plan to supply vessels in the Indian Ocean but on a greatly reduced scale. In the first phase of the mission (i.e. that conducted under the framework of the ATSML) between December 2001 and November 2007, the maritime SDF supplied 490,000 kilolitres of oil to vessels in the Indian Ocean. In the second phase, from February 2008 to January 2010 (i.e. within the framework of the RSSML), the SDF supplied only 27,000 kilolitres.

Nevertheless, the law continued to be a source of domestic political controversy and was one factor in the elector defeat of the LDP by the DPJ in August 2009. The new administration of Yukio Hatoyama decided not

---

[74] For an interesting discussion of the confusion of the DPJ position, see Craig Martin, 'Japan's Anti-Terrorism Measures Law and confusion over UN authority': *Japan Times*, 8 March 2007, 8.
[75] RSSML, art. 1.

to seek a renewal of the RSSML and the law expired on 15 January 2010 when all replenishment activities in support of the global war on terrorism were finally terminated.[76] On the day of expiration, the government announced that it had opted to increase direct aid to Afghanistan and pledged US$5 billion in civilian aid over five years.

4. Conclusions

Formulating an appropriate response to terrorism presents all governments with an acute political dilemma. On the one hand, by failing to act decisively, a government runs the risk of providing terrorist groups with the opportunity to consolidate in order to launch further and more devastating attacks. On the other hand, there is the opposite danger of overreacting. After all, one of the key objectives of terrorism is to provoke states into adopting policies that expose the commitment to constitutional rule as being shallow, hypocritical and contingent upon circumstances. By inviting a 'terror against terror', the terrorist hypothesis is that violent attacks can cause governments to derogate from key constitutional principles, and that such a suspension of norms exposes the limits of the rule of law and undermines the moral authority of the state. Striking an appropriate balance in responding to terror between the need for action and the dangers of over-reaction has become one of the central political challenges of the post 9/11 world order.

This chapter has suggested that, although the Japanese response to 9/11 did not involve the adoption of aggressive domestic counter-terrorism policies of the kind introduced in other jurisdictions, it did result in the introduction of a new interpretation of art. 9 that is hard to reconcile with the plain meaning of the text or even the earlier 'exclusively defense oriented' interpretation. Although this interpretation of art. 9 and the military activities it justified proved to be politically controversial, it highlighted once again that constraints on the Japanese deployment of its military remain political rather than legal, and that debates around the scope of this crucial provision of the Japanese Constitution remain unresolved and mired in uncertainty.

[76] See *Japan Times*, 19 January 2010, 2.

17

Mapping anti-terror legal regimes in India

UJJWAL KUMAR SINGH

1. Introduction

The Indian Parliament has so far enacted three anti-terror laws: the Terrorist and Disruptive Activities (Prevention) Act 1985 and 1987 (TADA), the Prevention of Terrorism Act 2002 (POTA) and the Unlawful Activities Prevention Act 1967 (UAPA) as amended in 2004 and 2008. TADA lapsed in 1995 and POTA was repealed in 2004. The repeal of POTA took place alongside the amendment of an existing law – the UAPA – to include POTA provisions pertaining to punishment for terrorist activities and organisations and interception of telephone and electronic communications. In December 2008, the UAPA was amended yet again to import POTA provisions relating to bail and remand which had not been included in the 2004 amendment. UAPA, as amended in 2004 and 2008, may therefore well be considered the third anti-terror law in India.[1]

This chapter argues that the three laws – TADA, POTA and UAPA – may be seen as embodying three distinct legal and political regimes for addressing terrorism in India. While all the three laws have provisions that relayed from one to the other, suggesting continuity, each regime is also marked out by innovations which are peculiar to it. The association of the term 'regime' with each law is crucial for the argument that the law is to be seen not only in terms of its bare provisions, but also examined for its political and ideological embeddedness, and the discursive practices which accumulate around it. Thus, while it is important to identify the specificity of the law in each case, it is also critical to see the significance of the law in terms of its contextual frame and the effects it produces. This chapter will, therefore, present each anti-terror law as a legal regime, *focusing not only on the law's words*, i.e. the nature of rules, principles and

---

[1] For an exhaustive analysis of anti-terror laws in India, see Ujjwal Kumar Singh, *The State, Democracy and Anti-Terror Laws in India* (New Delhi: Sage, 2007). This chapter covers later developments in the anti-terror legal regimes in the country, taking off from where the book ended.

procedures, and their interpretation in judgments, *but also on the law's deeds and effects*, which is to say, on its implications for conceptions of justice, for the lives of people, for democratic governance and for the legal and penal structures of the state.

The TADA, it is argued, manifests a phase where a single federal or central law was enacted with the specific purpose of countering the separatist movement in Punjab and its adjoining states. With the events of 9/11 in the United States, followed closely by the attack on the Indian Parliament on 13 December in the same year, the anti-terror legal regime in India aligned itself with the burgeoning 'international consensus' over the Bush doctrine of 'making the world safe for democracy'. Significantly, POTA brought to an end the interregnum that had ensued in the absence of a 'national' law to deal with terrorism following the lapse of TADA in 1995. Unlike TADA which lapsed, POTA was repealed by the Indian Parliament in 2004.

In what may perhaps be seen as the first example of a legislative or political withdrawal of an anti-terror law in the context of the international consensual regime of the 2000s, the repeal of POTA would represent, albeit in a limited way, a triumph for democratic forces. The repeal was, however, followed by two interrelated phenomena. First, it was synchronous with the amendment of the UAPA 1967, importing into it specific features of the repealed POTA. Second, coincident with the announcement of the repeal, a process of decentralisation of the legal regime for countering terror unfolded, with states like Chhattisgarh and Madhya Pradesh, among others, enacting their own anti-terror laws. Other states like Jharkhand resorted to s. 17 of the Criminal Law Amendment Act (1908) (CLA). Also significant is the Maharashtra Control of Organised Crime Act (MCOCA), which has been in operation in Maharashtra and Delhi since February 1999 and January 2002, respectively. MCOCA is seen as a precursor of POTA, providing the model for an 'efficient' law, and has outlived POTA.[2]

---

[2] In the joint sitting of the two houses of Parliament on 26 March 2002, when the Prevention of Terrorism Bill 2002 was being considered after it was rejected by the Rajya Sabha, MCOCA, which was being used by the Mumbai Police to curb organised crime, was projected as the model for the proposed legislation. While TADA was projected as an inefficient law for its low rates of conviction, the success of MCOCA in this regard was put forward as a reason for emulating the act. Sections 36–48 of POTA followed ss. 13–16 of MCOCA, which authorised interception of wire, electronic or oral communication. MCOCA and POTA, like TADA, had extraordinary provisions pertaining to confessions.

This chapter is organised into four sections. The first three sections focus on the specificities of the legal regimes surrounding the TADA, POTA and UAPA respectively. Yet, while each law represents a specific regime of anti-terror legislation, all of them are also inextricably woven into a cumulative narrative of extraordinary laws in India. The last section presents this narrative and argues that, beyond the specifics of each legal regime, an aggregate trajectory of anti-terror laws may be traced, which is characterised by a continuous unfolding towards the normalisation of extraordinary laws. The normalisation of the extraordinary, it is argued, has taken place in India through a network of processes, involving an unending string of extraordinary laws which do not just accumulate exponentially, but also have an 'after-life' beyond their statutory 'deaths'. There has also been an interlocking of ordinary and extraordinary laws, providing a permanence to these extraordinary measures. The trail of anti-terror legislation in India leads up to the 'strengthening' of UAPA, which has converted the UAPA into a surrogate for POTA, thus confirming a dangerous trend, whereby extraordinary laws have become a model for remapping ordinary criminal jurisprudence.

2. TADA 1985 and 1987: securing the state

TADA manifests a phase in the history of anti-terror laws in India, when for the first time a federal or central law was enacted with the specific purpose of addressing 'terrorist' and 'disruptive' activities. Enacted in May 1985 in the context of the separatist movement for Khalistan, the Act was initially enacted as a temporary measure for two years and was confined to Punjab and some adjoining states.[3] It was, however, re-introduced in 1987 through an Ordinance, with a provision for an extension for periods of two years after legislative review. TADA 1987 was extended periodically, the last being the two-year extension in 1993. During the course of subsequent extensions, TADA not only became more stringent, it also assumed a more general geographical application. Its area of operation was extended to cover most of the country by 1993, so that eventually more than 95 per cent of the citizens of the country came under its purview.[4]

---

[3] Before the introduction of TADA, the Terrorist Affected Areas (Special Courts) Act 1984 was promulgated through an Ordinance on 14 July 1984, empowering the central government to declare an area to be terrorist-affected and to constitute special courts for the speedy trial of suspected terrorists.

[4] In 1985 the government cited two union territories and four states in its statement of objects and reasons. Two years later, two more were added. In 1991 the total number of

As has been a characteristic feature of anti-terror laws, TADA gave enormous and overriding powers to the executive, conferring special powers on the central government to make rules for executing its provisions and for constituting Designated Courts to try TADA cases. Again, in keeping with the feature of such laws, TADA introduced extraordinary provisions pertaining to matters such as the definition of 'terrorist acts', arrest, bail, remand, investigation, trial and enhanced punishments for offences under the Act by laying down specific exceptions in the Criminal Procedure Code 1973 (CrPC) and the Indian Evidence Act 1872.

Prescribing exceptions to the ordinary law, TADA facilitated prolonged detention by providing for arrests without warrant, extending the period of police and judicial custody and the period within which the charge sheet is to be drawn.[5] Ordinarily, under art. 22(2) of the Constitution of India, every person who is arrested and detained should be brought before the nearest Magistrate within a period of twenty-four hours of arrest, excluding the time required for travelling from the place of arrest to the Magistrate's Court. Under s. 167 of the CrPC, the Magistrate is authorised to extend this detention for a maximum period of fifteen days, after which the accused must be produced before the magistrate, who can, if there are adequate grounds for further detention in judicial custody, extend the detention further for fifteen days. The total period of detention cannot, however, exceed sixty days, whether or not the investigation of the offence has been completed.[6] Modifying the application of s. 167 of CrPC, s. 20(4)(b) of TADA extended the period of pre-trial remand to a period of up to one year, thus facilitating the

states became seventeen. In 1993, TADA was in force in twenty-two out of the twenty-five states and two out of the seven union territories. The exceptions were Kerala, Orissa, Sikkim, Andaman and Nicobar, Dadra and Nagar Haveli, Daman and Diu, Lakshadweep and Pondicherry.

[5] As confirmed by the Supreme Court in *Sanjay Dutt* v. *State through the CBI Bombay (II)* (1994), once the period for completion of investigation and filing the charge sheet has expired, the accused is entitled to be released on bail. The Court, however, is under no obligation to release the accused on bail on its own. The accused has to make an application for bail under s. 20(4) of TADA, read with s. 167 of the CrPC, following which a notice is to be issued to the public prosecutor. The public prosecutor can oppose the release of the accused on bail and seek an extension beyond 180 days, up to a period of one year, by filing a progress report of the investigation and giving reasons for further extension: *Sanjay Dutt* v. *State through the C.B.I. Bombay (II)* (1994) SCC 410.

[6] The Magistrate may extend the period of detention to ninety days in cases where the investigation relates to offences punishable with death, imprisonment for life or imprisonment for a term of not less than ten years.

long-term detention of large numbers of suspects without charges being brought against them.[7]

Similarly, TADA introduced exceptions in ss. 436 to 450 of Chapter XXXIII of the CrPC which provide the framework for granting bail. Bail provisions under TADA were stringent, to the extent that in its ten-year life, and beyond its lapse, TADA prisoners continue to languish in jails across the country. Section 8 of TADA made the granting of bail subject to the public prosecutor being given the opportunity to oppose the application for release (s. 8(a)), and the satisfaction of the court that there are reasonable grounds for believing that the applicant is not guilty of the offence and not likely to commit such an offence while on bail (s. 8(b)).[8]

In what was perhaps its most striking provision, TADA made an exception to the law of evidence, and gave evidentiary status to confessions before the police. Specific guarantees and safeguards against self-incrimination are provided in the Indian Constitution.[9] The CrPC (s. 161) and the Indian Evidence Act (ss. 25–30) as a norm do not allow any a confessional statement made to any police officer under any circumstances to be

---

[7] Section 20(4)(b) of TADA laid down an exception to s. 167 (2) of the CrPC, providing that the references to 'fifteen days', 'ninety days' and 'sixty days', wherever they occur, be construed as 'sixty days', 'one year', and 'one year', respectively.

[8] While looking into the public interest litigation brought by Shaheen Welfare Association on behalf of under-trial prisoners charged under TADA (*Shaheen Welfare Association* v. *Union of India and Others* 1995) the Supreme Court examined the data regarding the number of TADA cases pending in various states, and the number of designated courts entrusted with the trial of these cases, on the basis of affidavits submitted by states (Gujarat, Rajasthan and Maharashtra) and the central government, and the statement furnished by the NHRC. Going specifically into the question of a right to bail, the Court emphasised the importance of: (1) seeing release on bail as embedded in the right to speedy trial to meet the requirement of art. 21 of the Constitution, and (2) balancing the rights of the accused with those of the victims, and the collective interests of the community and the safety of the nation as emphasised by the Supreme Court in *Kartar Singh* v. *State of Punjab* (1994). The Court concluded that, since the stringent bail provisions under TADA made release difficult, it was necessary that the trial 'proceed and conclude within a stipulated time'. Moreover, the invocation of the provisions of TADA in cases where the facts did not 'warrant its invocation' was to be construed as 'nothing but sheer misuse and abuse of the Act by the police'.

[9] Article 20(3) of the Constitution of India declares that 'no person accused of any offence shall be compelled to be a witness against himself', embodying thereby the principle of protection against self-incrimination. A number of decisions by the Supreme Court have examined art. 20(3), viz., *M. P. Sharma* v. *Satish Chandra, District Magistrate, Delhi* (1954 SCR 1077; AIR 1954 SC 300; 1954 Cri LJ 865); *Raja Narayanlal Bansilal* v. *Maneck Phiroz Mistry* (1961 1 SCR 417; AIR 1961 SC 29; 1960 30 Comp Cas 644); *State of Bombay* v. *Kathi Kalu Oghad* (1962 3SCR 10; AIR 1961 SC 180; 1961 2 Cri LJ 856); *Nandini Satpathy* v. *P. L. Dani* (1978 2SCC 424: 1978 SCC Cri 236).

admissible as evidence.[10] Since such confessions are excluded generally, the courts are not required to go into the question of whether or not they were extracted under coercion.[11] Making a departure from the ordinary law and constitutional principles, s. 15 of TADA allowed 'certain confessions made to police officers to be taken into consideration'.[12]

The constitutional validity of TADA was upheld by the Supreme Court in *Kartar Singh* v. *State of Punjab*,[13] generally on the grounds of 'necessity' and 'overwhelming need' not covered by the existing law, and specifically on grounds of 'legislative competence'. The principle of legislative competence for the validation of an anti-terror law was reiterated by the Supreme Court in *PUCL* v. *Union of India* where the constitutional validity of POTA was contested. In this case, the Supreme Court held that terrorism fell within the category of residuary power not defined in the Constitution, but conferred on Parliament under art. 248, read with Entry 97 of the Union List in the constitution.

Subscribing to what may be called the *principle of legislative classification and rule of differentiation*, the majority decision of the Supreme Court in *Kartar Singh* justified the prescription of a special procedure under TADA. The special provision pertaining to confession, which was contested by the petitioner, was approved by the Supreme Court, which appealed to the specific contexts and concerns of the Act (viz., terrorism). In the process, the court affirmed the existence of a class of *offenders* under TADA, viz., 'terrorists and disruptionists', distinct and separate from ordinary criminals who ought to be tried only under 'normal' laws,

---

[10] The inadmissibility of confessions to the police has been justified by the need to protect the accused from coercion and torture by police, a purpose which has been explained and approved in different judgments by the Supreme Court (e.g., *Raja Ram Jaiswal* v. *State of Bihar* (1964) 2 SCR 752).

[11] Section 25 makes all confessions made to a police officer inadmissible as evidence, s. 26 makes admissible only those confessions which are made before a magistrate and s. 27 provides that, although confessional statements are not admissible, any material evidence discovered in relation to such a confession is admissible along with that part of the confession relating to the discovery. Under s. 30 a confession (under s. 27) may be used as corroboration against other persons who are being tried jointly for the same offence.

[12] Section 15(1) of TADA provides that, 'notwithstanding anything in the Code or in the Indian Evidence Act 1872 (1 of 1872), but subject to the provisions of this section, a confession made by a person before a police officer not lower in rank than a Superintendent of Police and recorded by such police officer either in writing or on any mechanical device like cassettes, tapes or sound tracks from out of which sounds or images can be produced, shall be admissible in the trial of such person for an offence under this Act or rules made thereunder'.

[13] *Kartar Singh* v. *State of Punjab*, Writ petition no. 1833 of 1984 (decided on 11 March 1994), SCC 569, 569–791 (*Kartar Singh*).

as well as a distinct class of terrorism *offences* for which the special provisions of TADA were justified.

Starting from the premise that the objective of TADA was to target a distinct and aggravated form of crime and category of offenders, the majority decision of the Supreme Court held that the provisions of s. 15 were 'non-discriminatory', and not 'in the circumstances unjust unfair or oppressive'.[14] The court chose to acknowledge but yet overlook the danger that confessions are more often than not extracted by coercion. Justifying the provision as an 'overwhelming need', the court adhered to the position that a confession obtained by a police officer is to be presumed to have been in accordance with what is legally permissible. It did go on to provide certain procedural safeguards along the lines of the 'fruit of the poisonous tree' doctrine. These safeguards, it argued, would ensure that a 'confession obtained in the pre-indictment interrogation' by a police officer would not be 'tainted with any vice', and would be 'in strict conformity with the well-recognised and accepted aesthetic principles and fundamental fairness'.

Notably, the National Human Rights Commission (NHRC), set up under a Parliamentary statute in 1993, in the discharge of its statutory function of reviewing safeguards for the protection of human rights, set out to adopt what it expressed as 'a well-informed and unambiguous position on TADA'.[15] Identifying this position as premised on a non-negotiable 'central preoccupation' of 'protection of civil liberties',[16] the NHRC conducted a 'full-fledged examination of all aspects of TADA', especially as reports and complaints of its arbitrary and abusive use 'began flooding the Commission within weeks of its establishment'.[17]

Inscribing the question of TADA on its regular agenda, the Commission 'invited periodic meetings' with officers of the central and state governments, and visited various states on its own fact-finding investigations. As early as 6 June 1994, the Commission declared in Srinagar that it had 'learnt enough to have serious doubts about the worth and terms of the Act', and began contemplating seeking a review of the Supreme Court judgment which had upheld the constitutional validity of TADA. It followed thereafter a 'three-pronged strategy', whereby it continued to monitor the implementation of the Act, prepared a dossier for possible recourse to the Supreme Court and, as the date for the renewal of the Act drew near, resorted to a 'direct approach' of sending letters to

---

[14] Ibid., [218].   [15] Protection of Human Rights Act 1993, s. 12.
[16] NHRC, Annual Report (1994–5), p. 8.   [17] Ibid., p. 9.

parliamentarians recommending that the life of the Act should not be renewed when it expired on 23 May 1995.[18] The letter made it clear that the Act made 'considerable deviations from the normal law', was 'draconian in effect and character' and 'incompatible with [India's] cultural traditions, legal history and treaty obligations'. The NHRC concluded with the crucial observation that it found it difficult to maintain human rights – a charge with which the Parliament entrusted it – 'unless the draconian law was removed from the statute books'.[19]

Indeed, the manner in which TADA was implemented shows how the 'prevention of terrorist and disruptive activities' became effectively an instrument to contain and repress minorities. More significant perhaps is the manner in which the Act came to be perceived widely as communal and sectarian, not only because it was used against identity struggles of the Sikhs in Punjab and the Kashmiri Muslims, but also because it came to be used generally against minorities not associated with these movements, and who were arrested under the Act simply because they were Muslims or Sikhs. To illustrate this, in 1991, the Home Minister Digvijay Singh reported in the Rajasthan Assembly that of the 228 arrested, 101 were Muslims, 96 Sikhs, and three Hindus. No charges were established in 178 cases. In July 1993, the government withdrew cases against seventy-two persons. By 1993 Gujarat had climbed ahead of Punjab (14,457) in the number of TADA detainees, with 3,452 more TADA arrests adding to its 1992 total of 14,094. In Gujarat, arrests under TADA were made in cases associated with communal violence where most of the persons arrested were Muslims.

The selective application of the Act against minorities was apparent from the fact that, whereas TADA was not brought into force when large-scale violence against Muslims took place in the Bombay riots, Muslims became the first to be brought under the purview of TADA after the bomb blasts. The use of TADA against ethnic minorities has resulted in the use of epithets such as 'extremists', 'terrorist' and 'anti-national', turning them into objects of suspicion. Movements to assert democratic self-determination – e.g. tribal movements in Vidarbha, Telangana, Godavari and Bastar Forests – were also brought under the scope of the Act. In the Northeastern states, the assertion of ethnic specificity was characterised as a threat to national security, sovereignty and integrity. In Tripura, the Act was brought into force in the wake of violence by the All Tripura Tribal Force (ATTF) in October 1991. In Assam, three MLAs of the

---

[18] Ibid.   [19] Ibid., pp. 55–6.

UJJWAL KUMAR SINGH

Bodoland Legislature Party were arrested in connection with bomb blasts in Guwahati and Dispur.[20] According to the Union Home Ministry figures of October 1993, the total number of detentions under TADA was 52,268; the conviction rate of those tried by Designated Courts under it was 0.81 per cent ever since the law came into force. Punjab had a conviction rate of 0.37 per cent out of its 14,557 detainees. On 24 August 1994, then Minister of State for Home Rajesh Pilot stated that of the approximately 67,000 individuals detained since TADA came into force, 8,000 were tried and only 752 were convicted. *Some 59,509 people had been detained with no case being brought against them.*[21] The Review Committees of TADA stated that other than in 5,000 cases, the application of TADA was wrong. Thus TADA was wrongly applied in more than 50,000 cases.

3. POTA: the national security state and the global consensus on securing democracy

Efforts to enact an anti-terror law had been afoot for quite some time and various draft bills were considered intermittently before and, particularly, after TADA lapsed in 1995. Attempts to enact a TADA-like law proved desultory until the 173rd Report of the Law Commission submitted what it called a modified version of TADA to the government in April 2001.[22] POTA entered the statute books on 24 October 2001, first as an Ordinance by the BJP-led National Democratic Alliance (NDA) government. The Prevention of Terrorism Ordinance (POTO) was promulgated in the wake of the 9/11 attack on the World Trade Centre Towers in the United States and the subsequent campaign for concerted and consensual global action against terrorism, spearheaded by the United States and expressed

---

[20] See People's Union for Democratic Rights, *Lawless Roads* (Delhi, September 1993). For details of the invocation of TADA in the Vidarbha region see Punya Prasun Vajpayee, *'TADA': Vidarbha Mein* (New Delhi, 1995). In the adivasi-dominated forest areas of Betul a long resistance has been waged over several years to the World Bank-funded Madhya Pradesh Forestry Project, which has prevented poor tribes from cultivating what are known as 'newad' or untitled: 'Draconian Shades', *The Hindu*, 21 January 2001.

[21] See A. G. Noorani, 'Banality of Repression', *Frontline*, 23 September 1994, p. 12; South Asia Human Rights Documentation Centre, *Prevention of Terrorism Ordinance 2001: Government Decides to Play Judge and Jury* (New Delhi: South Asia Human Rights Documentation Centre, November 2001), p. 31.

[22] In the meantime, consistent with its stand against TADA, the National Human Rights Commission (NHRC) rejected the draft Bill submitted by the Law Commission for consideration.

in a resolution (1373) to that effect passed by the Security Council of the United Nations. The 'international consensus' against terror and the Security Council resolution became the most frequently quoted justification for an anti-terror law in India.

In the meantime, with the attack on the Parliament building in New Delhi on 13 December 2001, the chorus of a global war on terror became shrill in India. Since the Parliament was adjourned following the bomb attack, the Prevention of Terrorism Bill, which was to replace the first POTA Ordinance, could not be passed. A second Ordinance was, therefore, promulgated on 30 December 2001.[23] The Prevention of Terrorism Bill was presented in the Parliament in the Budget Session amidst an absence of political consensus. The opposition by the Congress and the Left Parties among others, and reservations by several state governments, resulted in the rejection of the Bill in the Rajya Sabha, the Upper House (of States) of Parliament. Eventually, the Bill replacing the Ordinance was passed on 26 March 2002 in an extraordinary joint sitting of Parliament, bringing to an end the interregnum of an absence of a 'national law' to deal with terror that had ensued.

The legal regime to counter terrorism which was ushered in by POTA adopted the stringent measures of arrest, investigation and trial, including the admission of confessions to police officers as evidence which TADA had initiated. However, the maximum period allowed for investigation, after which bail was permissible, was reduced from one year under TADA to 180 days in POTA. The truncation of this period was, nonetheless, counterbalanced by the imposition of TADA-like conditions that had to be satisfied for securing bail, viz., the consent of the public prosecutor, and the satisfaction of the POTA court of the innocence of the accused. In a large number of POTA cases, therefore, bail was refused.

Moreover, ss. 20, 21 and 22, which concerned the curbing of terrorist activities, contained a broadened definition of terrorism which extended to membership, support and financial assistance, thus injecting vagueness into the definition and allowing for a much wider use of the law.

---

[23] An ordinance, which is basically an executive/presidential order, has a temporary life, and needs to be subsequently put before the Parliament to become a duly enacted law. Art. 123 of the Constitution of India, which gives the President the power to promulgate ordinances when the Parliament is in recess, says that every ordinance will be laid before the Parliament and will cease to operate at the expiration of six weeks from the reassembly of Parliament. Since the legislation enacted by Parliament to replace the ordinance could not be passed due to the adjournment of Parliament, another ordinance was promulgated. The Bill was eventually passed in the budget session after significant opposition.

Section 21(2), for example, provided that 'a person commits an offence if he arranges, manages or assists in arranging or managing a meeting' in which the speaker is a member of a banned organisation, Such a person would be guilty of supporting terrorist activities, an offence punishable by a sentence of up to ten years. Ironically, a meeting under the Act means 'three or more persons whether or not the public are admitted', creating the distinct possibility of over-extensive use.

The specific innovation of POTA, however, was the introduction of provisions pertaining to the interception of electronic communication and their admissibility as evidence in court, and the banning of 'terrorist organisations'. TADA had no provision for telephone tapping.[24] Significantly, in State v. Mohammad Afzal, commonly known as the Parliament Attack case,[25] the evidence against the four accused was built largely around the interception of telephonic communication, apart from the confessional statements made by three of them.

Before POTA introduced the banning of terrorist groups (Chapter III, ss. 18–22), a procedure for banning unlawful organisations existed under the UAPA 1967. Under UAPA, the identification of an 'unlawful organisation' required a notification in the Official Gazette by the central government, and the notification had to be normally accompanied by the grounds for the decision to ban along with 'conspicuous and adequate publicity' of the same. POTA, however, changed the manner in which an organisation banned under UAPA could now be treated in law. Under section 18(1) of POTA, an organisation was a terrorist organisation if it was listed in the Schedule of UAPA, or operated under the same name as an organisation listed in that schedule. Under s. 18(3), an organisation could be declared a terrorist organisation if the central government believed that it was one. Thus, the government was no longer required to issue a statement explaining the reasons for issuing a ban. A gazette notification merely adding an entry to the Schedule of UAPA was sufficient. Moreover, unlike UAPA,

---

[24] Borrowing from provisions existing under MCOCA, POTA allowed electronic interceptions, which were otherwise not admissible as evidence, to be presented in a Special Court as evidence against the accused. Chapter V of POTA (ss. 36–48) laid down the provisions pertaining to 'Interception of Communication in Certain Cases': its definition (s. 36); appointment of competent authority (s. 37); the procedure for application and authorisation of interception (ss. 38–9); and safeguards including a review procedure (ss. 40 and 46) and the submission of an annual report of interception (s. 48).

[25] On 13 December 2001 five armed men drove into the precincts of the Parliament House, killing nine members of the Parliament, watch and ward staff and injuring sixteen others, before they fell to the bullets of the security men. This attack was widely portrayed as an attack on Indian democracy.

there was no provision for judicial redress. While the period of proscription under the UAPA was two years (s. 6), POTA provided no such period after which the ban would cease to be effective.

Immediately after the promulgation of the first POTA Ordinance on 24 October 2001, the government announced a list of twenty-three banned organisations, including groups from Jammu and Kashmir,[26] the Northeast,[27] and others like the Liberation Tigers of Tamil Eelam (LTTE), the Students Islamic Movement of India (SIMI), the Deendar Anjuman, the Babbar Khalsa International, the Khalistan Commando Force, the Khalistan Zindabad Force and the International Sikh Youth Foundation. On 5 December 2001, the Communist Party of India (M-L), People's War, and the Maoist Communist Centre (MCC) along with all their 'Formations and Front Organisations' were added to the list. Several other organisations were added later and, by 21 July 2002, the number of banned organisations had reached thirty-two.[28] Several of these banned organisations are associated with political movements. Moreover, in a manifestation of selective application, SIMI, an Islamic organisation, was banned when the corresponding organisations of the Hindu Right were given a long leash by the government, despite their role in the demolition of the Babri Mosque at Ayodhya in 1992 and in the killing of Muslims in Gujarat in February 2002.[29]

[26] These included the Jaish-E-Mohammed/Tahrik-E-Furqan, Lashkar-E-Taiba/Pasban-E-Ahle Hadis, Harkat-Ul-Mujahideen/Harkat-Ul-Ansar/Harkat-Ul-Jehad-E-Islami, Hizb-Ul-Mujahideen-Hizb-Ul-Mujahideen Pir Panjal Regiment, Al-Umar-Mujahideen, Jammu and Kashmir Liberation Front.

[27] These were the United Liberation Front of Assam (ULFA), the National Democratic Front of Bodoland (NDFB), the People's Liberation Army (PLA), the United National Liberation Front (UNLF), the People's Revolutionary Party of Kangleipak (PREPAK), the Kangleipak Communist Party (KCP), the Kanglei Yaol Kanba Lup (KYKL), the Manipur People's Liberation Front (MPLF), the All Tripura Tiger Force and the National Liberation Front of Tripura (NLFT).

[28] The later additions were Al Badr, Jamiat-Ul-Mujahideen, al-Qaeda, Dukhtaran-E-Millat (DEM), the Tamil Nadu Liberation Army (TNLA), the Tamil National Retrieval Troops (TNRT) and Akhil Bharatiya Nepali Ekta Samaj (ABNES).

[29] On 27 February 2002, a coach of the Sabarmati Express was burnt in Godhra, in the state of Gujarat, leading to the gruesome death of fifty-nine persons, some of whom were 'karsevaks' or Hindu volunteers returning from Ayodhya. This was followed immediately by a communal onslaught against Muslims in several districts of Gujarat. The Sabarmati train burning incident at Godhra was investigated and tried under POTA, with 125 Muslims charge-sheeted. The POTA review committee, which was constituted after the repeal of POTA, concluded that the case did not fall under the scope of POTA and should be tried under the ordinary law.

A significant distinction between TADA and POTA, indicative of the political context within which POTA was brought, was that POTA was embedded within the ideological discourse of global Islamic terrorism and the national-security state. The various judgments which were delivered in POTA cases, may be seen as following a line of argument where procedural infirmities were often ignored in the quest for securing the nation-state.

In a POTA judgment delivered on 21 July 2003 – *State v. Mohd. Yasin Patel alias Falahi and Mohd. Ashraf Jaffary* – the Special Court sentenced the accused Falahi, an American national, and Ashraf, an Indian national, to five years under POTA s. 20 (membership of a terrorist organisation), and to seven years under s. 124-A (sedition) of the Indian Penal Code (IPC). In May 2002, both the accused, who were members of the SIMI, an organisation banned in September 2001 under the UAPA 1967, were arrested from a road near Jamia Milia Islamia University library in Delhi, where they were sticking posters carrying the following slogan in English: 'Destroy Nationalism Establish Khilafat', accompanied by a picture of a closed fist. The fist was described in the judgment as crushing a missile with an 'Indian sign, and flags of several countries like Russia, America, including that of India'. Below the fist, and above the name of the organisation (SIMI), were shown several Muslim youths with raised hands.

It is significant that the POTA court also found the accused guilty under s. 124-A of IPC that deals specifically with charges of sedition. While sentencing under this section, the judgment reasoned that '[t]he motive of SIMI as stated in the Constitution of SIMI is to bring into force Islamic Order and to destroy nationalism in India and other countries'.[30] Since s. 124-A explicitly removes 'criticism of government' from its purview, the judgment went on to say that 'a person may affix posters criticizing the Government. He or she can do it freely and liberally but it must be without an effort to incite the people to break the nation or to destroy the nation … But when a person attacks the very nationalism, he acts as a fundamentalist and his motive are not to criticize the government but to act against the very fabric of society [sic]'.[31]

A similar spectre of an Indian nation threatened by transnational-Islamic terrorism was raised in the opening paragraphs of the judgment in *State v. Mohammad Afzal*. The judgment began by identifying terrorism

---

[30] *State v. Mohd.Yasin Patel alias Falahi and (2) Mohd.Ashraf Jaffary*, Judgment dated 21 July 2003, 36.

[31] Ibid., p. 37.

with 'religious fanatics', without naming the religion: 'terrorism is a scourge of all humanity. It is being perpetuated and propagated by religious fanatics, to poison the minds of their followers and generate mercenaries and terrorists to kill innocent persons'.[32] That the reference here is to Muslim fundamentalism is clear from the fact that the judgment specifically mentions three instances of terrorist attacks, viz., the attacks on World Trade Centre, on a theatre in Russia and on Akshardham temple. Care is taken also to show that the attack on Parliament was part of global network of terrorism that thrived on its nexus with 'under-world criminal organization[s]'.[33]

More significant perhaps is the manner in which the new context of 'global Islamic terrorism' was cited in the Supreme Court judgment in the TADA case *Devender Pal Singh* v. *State of NCT of Delhi and Another*.[34] Coming several years after the institution of the case, the judgment referred to the *new contexts* of terrorism to justify the stringent interpretation of provisions pertaining to 'confession', and the decision to sentence the accused to death.[35] 'The menace of terrorism', the judgment stated, 'is not restricted to our country, and it has become a matter of international concern and the attacks on the World Trade Centre and other places on 11–9–2001 amply show it. Attack on Parliament on 13–12–2001 shows how grim the situation is'.[36] The spectre of the besieged nation, and the perception of global risk affirmed by an international consensus, form the context of a judgment that is temporally removed from the circumstances in which the 'terrorist act' in the case was originally committed

---

[32] *State* v. *Mohd. Afzal and others*, Judgment of the Special POTA Court, dated 18 December 2002, 1.

[33] Ibid., p. 3, [4].

[34] The judgment was delivered on 22 March 2002 in the case where an explosion of a car bomb, on 11 September 1993, at a place close to where the car of the then President of the Indian Youth Congress (I) was passing, resulted in the death of nine persons and injury to several others. The investigations implicated five persons, all members of the Khalistan Liberation Front (KLF), in a conspiracy to assassinate the Youth Congress leader. Devender Pal Singh was awarded the death sentence by the designated TADA Court on 24 August 2001, which was upheld by the Supreme Court by a 2:1 majority, in the above judgment: see *Supreme Court Cases* (Criminal), Part 7, July 2002, pp. 978–1014.

[35] Like POTA (s. 32), s. 15 of TADA permits certain confessions made to police officers to be taken into consideration. Unlike POTA, however, under s. 21(C) of TADA, if a confession was made by a co-accused that the accused had committed the offence, 'the Designated Court shall presume, unless the contrary is proved, that the accused had committed such an offence'.

[36] *Devender Pal Singh* v. *State of NCT of Delhi*, p. 978.

and brought to trial. This gloss on historical specificity is fed by the overwhelming discourse of global terrorism.

Significantly, while upholding the constitutional validity of POTA
in *PUCL* v. *the Union of India*, the Supreme Court not only *emphasised
the legislative competence* of the central government in matters concerning 'national security' (reiterating the argument in *Kartar Singh* where
it upheld TADA) but also *secured the central government's control* over
all such cases in future. The People's Union for Civil Liberties (PUCL)
had challenged the constitutional validity of POTA on the ground that
Parliament lacked legislative competence over it, since the provisions of
POTA fell under 'Public Order', which was Entry 1 of the State List (List
II). Making a distinction between subjects that fell ordinarily in what
was termed 'public order' in the State List and situations of terrorism, the
Court yet again gave the Parliament legislative competence in the latter.
While outlining its reasons for establishing the legislative competence of
Parliament, it decided that the fight against terrorism was not a 'regular criminal justice endeavour', or an issue pertaining to 'public order
or security' relating only 'to a particular state'. Given the nature of the
'undeclared war by the epicenters of terrorism' with the 'aid of well-knit
and resourceful terrorist organisations', it was a challenge to India's 'sovereignty and integrity', to 'the constitutional principles' it held dear, to 'the
democratically elected government', and to its 'secular fabric'. It went on
to argue that that none of these concerns which were addressed by POTA
were covered by any of the entries of List II.[37] Significantly, the question
whether the law could be allowed to impinge on respect for human rights
and the principles of fair trial was resolved by the court in favour of an
'overwhelming need' for such a law, which in turn justified a strong role
for the central government.[38]

---

[37] *People's Union for Civil Liberties and Another* v. *Union of India*, judgment dated 16
December 2003, in W.P. No. 389 of 2002.

[38] While examining judicial review of anti-terrorism activities of the state after 9/11, Roach
argues that in the case of the judicial review of POTA, even as it recognised the implications for human rights and the need for basic restraints to ensure that only the guilty are
punished, the Supreme Court generally relied on the severity of the problem of terrorism
in India and the importance of preventing it. In the process, however, it did not conduct a 'proportionality analysis' along the lines of what the House of Lords in the United
Kingdom and the Supreme Court of Canada did when faced with similar issues. Such
an analysis requires going into the question whether the law was proportionate to the
objective, especially with respect to the question whether a less rights-invasive approach
would have been equally effective. See Kent Roach, 'Judicial review of the state's anti-
terrorism activities: the post-9/11 experience and normative justifications for judicial
review' (2009) 3 *Indian Journal of Constitutional Law* 152.

Consistent with its stand on TADA, the NHRC addressed two questions: was there a need for the enactment of the proposed law (POTA) and, if there was, what should it be? The NHRC's 'considered unanimous opinion' as stated in its Annual Report 2001–2 was that there was 'no need' to enact POTA since the concerns identified by the bill were 'substantially taken care of under the existing laws'.[39] The problem, which the criminal justice system in India faced, related to (1) proper investigation of crimes, (2) efficient prosecution of criminal trials and (3) delays in adjudication and punishment in courts. None of these problems, however, could be solved 'by enacting laws that did away with the legal safeguards that were designed to prevent innocent persons from being persecuted and punished', nor by 'providing for a different and more drastic procedure for prosecution of certain crimes'.[40] The NHRC also concluded that the bill would 'hinder rather than enhance, the effective implementation of treaties and other international instruments on human rights' and that, in particular, the provisions of the bill 'would not be in consonance with many provisions of the International Covenant on Civil and Political Rights (ICCPR) to which India is a State Party'.[41]

Interestingly, debates concerning TADA, during its lifetime and beyond, focused not so much on its misuse, but on its 'inefficiency'. These were fuelled by the large number of arrests under TADA, which resulted in prolonged detention, but did not result in convictions. When POTA was debated in Parliament, apologists for the law argued that POTA was a more efficient law, stronger than TADA, and had sufficient safeguards. The manner in which POTA was implemented, however, buttressed the position of its detractors, including the Congress and the left parties, that POTA had an enormous potential for misuse. An examination of the manner in which POTA was employed in particular states shows a pattern of institutional erosion, caused in turn by a politics of intolerance and distrust. In Tamil Nadu and Uttar Pradesh, for example, the much

---

[39] In its opinion on the Prevention of Terrorism Bill, the NHRC pointed out that 'any action which threatens the unity, integrity, security or sovereignty of India' was already covered by s. 153-B of the Indian Penal Code (IPC). 'Offences against the state' was dealt with in Chapter VI of the IPC, especially ss. 121-A (conspiracy to overawe by means of criminal force or show of criminal force), 122 (collecting arms and ammunitions with the intention of waging war against the government of India), and 124-A (sedition). Chapter XVI likewise dealt with 'offences against the human body'. Apart from the IPC, the Arms Act 1959, Explosives Act 1884, Explosive Substances Act 1908 and the Armed Forces (Special Powers) Act 1958 were other existing laws that were available to deal with specific situations (Annual Report 2001–2, pp. 322–3).

[40] Ibid., pp. 323–4.   [41] NHRC, Annual Report 2000, Annexure 4.

publicised and 'officially recognised' cases of 'misuse' of POTA, viz., the arrest of the MDMK (Marumalarchi Dravida Munetra Kazhagam) leader and Member of Parliament Vaiko by the AIDMK (All India Dravida Munnetra Kazhagam) government in Tamil Nadu and the Samjvadi Party leader Raghuraj Pratap Singh's arrest by the then BSP (Bahujan Samaj Party) government in Uttar Pradesh, showed how POTA was used in electoral politics, the politics of attrition within states, and between the centre and particular state governments. The use of POTA in Gujarat and Maharashtra showed the manner in which the official justifications of extraordinary laws and emergency powers as necessary correctives directed against a clear enemy, namely the 'terrorists', unfolded in such a way as to draw lines of conflict between communities. The BJP government, led by Narendra Modi in Gujarat, invoked POTA in the *Godhra* (train burning) case and arrested fifty-nine persons, all of whom were Muslims, for 'terrorist activities'. Incidentally, bail was denied to them and they continue to be in detention under various IPC charges, even after the POTA Review Committee set up under the POTA Repeal Act decided that POTA was wrongly applied in this case.

The repeal of POTA figured prominently in the Common Minimum Programme of the Congress Party-led United Progressive Alliance (UPA) government that replaced the National Democratic Alliance (NDA), led by the BJP in May 2004. The repeal of POTA was effected through an Ordinance in September 2004, a rare occasion when an extraordinary law was repealed. Yet, the repeal of POTA was synchronous with the enactment of the Unlawful Activities Prevention (Amendment) Act 2004, which imported into UAPA 1967, an ordinary and long-standing statute, specific features of the repealed POTA.

4.   The UAPA (1967, 2004, 2008): normalisation and expansion

The contemporary anti-terror legal regime, dominated by the UAPA and decentralised state anti-terror laws, shows the complex ways in which the war against terror has unfolded in India. Employed in a process of normalisation of extraordinary laws, UAPA has become a receptacle for a law forced into disuse due to political or democratic pressure. Following the 26 November 2008 terror attacks in Mumbai, UAPA was amended yet again in December 2008, increasing its resemblance to POTA. The process of normalisation has also deepened with the enactment of the National Investigating Agency Act 2008 (NIA Act), which provided for the setting up of the National Investigating Agency (NIA) to investigate terror-related offences for trial in special courts.[42] The provision of special courts existed in TADA and POTA but did not figure in the 2004 amendments to UAPA.

Simultaneously, a process of expansion of the legal regime against terror may be seen as taking place through a process of decentralisation. Numerous state and provincial extraordinary laws have been enacted to address specific 'terror' concerns of states, with the result that state governments have arrested suspects under the provisions both of UAPA and specific state laws.

While UAPA has become a repository for extraordinary measures for anti-terror and security laws, these measures have come without the safeguards of legislative review and temporal limits which accompanied overtly anti-terror laws like TADA and POTA. Significantly, while TADA and POTA unleashed a debate concerning the 'extreme' measures they employed, UAPA has been able to elude a larger debate and political contest, escaping the public scrutiny to which POTA and TADA were constantly subjected. On the other hand, there still exists the ubiquitous refrain from some quarters that UAPA is not quite like POTA in that it is not strong, effective and lethal enough to counter terrorism.

UAPA has an interesting pre-2004 history. It was enacted in 1967 in the context of the Naga rebellion, and the need felt in that context for an effective law to deal with 'associations' whose activities were 'prejudicial to the maintenance of harmony between different groups on grounds of religion, race, place of birth, residence, language etc.'.[43] Significantly, following the recommendations made by the National Integration Council, the Constitution (Sixth Amendment) Act 1963 empowered the Parliament 'to impose, by law reasonable restrictions' on the fundamental rights guaranteeing freedom of speech and expression, the right to assemble peaceably and without arms; and the right to form associations or unions 'in the interest of the sovereignty and integrity of India'. While the UAPA 1967 applied to the entire country, its application to Jammu and Kashmir, which has a special status under art. 370 of the Constitution, was made

---

[42] The National Investigation Agency (NIA) was set up through an act of Parliament in December 2008, at the same time as the UAPA (Amendment) Act 2008 was passed. The NIA was empowered to take up terror-related cases from across the country, on the behest of the central government. While in its statement of objects, the Act refers to the setting up of the NIA to investigate and prosecute offences affecting the sovereignty and integrity of India and the security of state, it emphasises in particular friendly relations with foreign countries, implementation of international treaties, agreements, conventions and resolutions of the United Nations and its agencies.

[43] The Unlawful Activities Prevention Act 1967, Objects and Reasons.

possible through the Constitution (Application to Jammu and Kashmir) Amendment Order 1969 issued by the central government on 1 September 1969. UAPA 1967 identified unlawful activity and organisations, and provided the procedure for banning unlawful organisations.

In the context of the demolition of the Babri Mosque in Ayodhya in December 1992, and the surge in the separatist movement in Kashmir, a range of organisations were declared unlawful under the Act in the 1990s. These included the Jamaat-e-Islami Hind, Islamic Sewak Sangh, Vishwa Hindu Parishad, Rashtriya Swayam Sewak Sangh, Bajrang Dal and Jammu and Kashmir Liberation Front. While the Jamaat was 'banned' for its conviction that the 'separation of Kashmir from India was inevitable', and for 'questioning the sovereignty and territorial integrity of India', the Islamic Sewak Sangh was declared unlawful because of the 'inflammatory speeches' that its leaders had been giving 'with a view to promoting on grounds of religion, disharmony or feelings of enmity, hatred or ill-will between different communities'. The Vishwa Hindu Parishad was banned for advocating the 'demolition of the Babri Masjid' to build a temple on Ram Janma Bhoomi, and public speeches by its leaders exhorting 'that Muslims would be taught the language of force in case they would fail to understand the language of reasoning'.[44]

With the enactment of POTA in 2002, as discussed in the previous section, the provisions of POTA pertaining to banning of 'terrorist organszations' under s. 18 of the Act were to apply to organisations which were listed in the Schedule of UAPA. These organisations continue to be on the list after the repeal of POTA under the provisions of the 2004 amendments to UAPA. More than 100 organisations listed in the Schedule to the UN Prevention and Suppression of Terrorism (Implementation of Security Council Resolutions) Order 2007 were added at entry number thirty-three on the list of banned organisations. On 4 June 2010 the Government of India issued an order adding 'Indian Mujahideen, all its formations and front organizations' to the list. Significantly, the amendments made to UAPA in 2004, introduced an anomaly in the Act, in that the procedure for banning a terrorist organisation prescribed by the Act is considerably easier than the procedure for banning an organisation under a less substantial charge of being an unlawful organisation.

---

[44] Declared unlawful through notification numbers, S.O. 898 (E), S.O. 899 (E) and S.O. 900 (E), all dated 10 December 1992, and published in the Gazette of India, Extraordinary, Pt. II, s. 3(ii).

Following the repeal of POTA and the amendment of UAPA in 2004, UAPA metamorphosed into the foremost national anti-terror law in India. The Unlawful Activities Prevention (Amendment) Ordinance 2004 inserted new Chapters IV, V, VI, and VII, substituting Chapter IV of the original Act, broadening its scope to include 'terrorist activities' alongside 'unlawful activities', and specifying procedures for dealing with each. Moreover, the amendments brought into the Act specific provisions of POTA pertaining to the definition of, and enhanced penalties for, 'terrorist activities', specific procedures for banning 'terrorist organizations', and the interception of telephone and electronic communications. Yet, the 2004 amendments to UAPA did not merely *replicate* the broad and vague definition of terrorist activities in POTA, it also *extended* it by introducing an element of extraterritoriality, and *enlarged* its scope by including in its ambit the 'likelihood' of death and injury. The 2008 amendments lowered the threshold further, from the 'likelihood of causing death' introduced in 2004, to the 'likelihood of causing terror'. Moreover, while the 2008 amendments to UAPA maintained the provision relating to the admissibility in evidence of telephone and e-mail intercepts, it dispensed with the elaborate safeguards provided by the repealed POTA.

When POTA was repealed, its provisions pertaining to confessions, bail, remand and presumption as to guilt were not included in UAPA by the 2004 amendments, restoring to some extent the principles of fair trial. Yet in 2008, fresh amendments reinstated these provisions into UAPA. Chapter VII of the Unlawful Activities (Prevention) Amendments Act 2008, titled 'miscellaneous', has the longest list of insertions in the form of ss. 43A to 43F, all of which have made exceptions to the usual procedures of arrest, bail and pre-charge detention, and presumption as to offence under the CrPC.[45] Indeed the 2008 Act made the belief of a police officer sufficient ground for arrest, increased the period of detention before the charges could be framed from 90 to 180 days, and made the bail provisions as stringent as they were under POTA. The changes in introduced 2008 have made it possible for governments to arrest people with ease and deny them bail over long periods of time.

---

[45] Under s. 43E of UAPA 2008, if it is proved during prosecution that arms, explosives or any other substances were recovered from the possession of the accused, and if the evidence of an expert (e.g. a finger-print expert) provides definitive evidence suggesting the association of the accused with the substance found at the site of the offence, the Court shall presume, unless it is proved to the contrary, that the accused has committed such an offence.

Moreover, the 'fishing' strategy adopted by specific state governments has enabled it to cast its net wide, including persons who may have had a past association with organisations which are *now* declared unlawful or terrorist. This has been used to threaten academics and activists for 'sympathising' with the Maoist cause. 'Omnibus' FIRs,[46] for example, have been filed under UAPA and sections of the IPC against unspecified persons in order to arrest activists engaged in grass-roots movements involving the rights of the poor, dalit and adivasi groups in Gujarat. One such omnibus FIR reads like a general essay, making unsubstantiated allegations with no specific details against activists for 'carrying out false propaganda among tribal/forest people as well as religious minorities like Christians and Muslims to separate them from the mainstream of the nation, to create civil war and to encourage revolt against the constitutionally established government'.[47]

Another innovation introduced into UAPA in 2008 has been s. 51A relating to the 'prevention of, and coping with terrorist activities'. Under this section, the central government is empowered 'to freeze, seize or attach funds and other financial assets or economic resources held by, on behalf of or at the direction of individuals or entities listed in the schedule to the government order giving effect to this provision, or any other person engaged in or suspected to be engaged in terrorism and prohibit any individual or entity from making any funds, financial assets or economic resources or related services available for the benefit of individuals or entities listed in the schedule'.[48] The provisions of s. 51 introduced provisions to curb and rein in sources of funding for terrorist organisations, bringing it in consonance with anti-terror laws elsewhere in the world. Yet, the orders of the Reserve Bank of India to invoke the Prevention of

---

[46] The First Information Report or the FIR is a written document prepared by the police about the commission of a cognisable offence, on the basis of the information which it receives from the victim. The FIR becomes the essential first step for setting in motion the legal process in the case.

[47] FIR no. 1–37/2010, dated 26 February 2010, in a letter by PUCL to the NHRC, New Delhi, dated 3 June 2010.

[48] Under an Order issued by the Reserve Bank of India (dated 16 November 2009) banks were instructed to 'strictly follow the procedure laid down in the' UAPA Order dated 27 August 2009 and ensure meticulous compliance to the same'. The Orders were seen as complying with Security Council Resolution 1373 obligations: RBI/2009–10/222, Circular no.21/12.05.001/2009–10, available at www.rbi.org.in. Incidentally, this was a follow up to a similar instruction issued by the RBI to all banks to comply with the instructions issued by the RBI under the guidelines on 'Know Your Customer' norms and anti-money laundering measures laid down by the Prevention of Money-Laundering Act, 2002. See RBI circular dated 2 July 2008 (RBI/2008–2009/86, NO.1/12/05.001/2008–09).

Money-Laundering Act 2002, which is primarily an Act to deal with economic offences, while implementing the provisions of UAPA dealing with terrorist activities, have opened up the possibility of blurring economic with terrorist crimes.

UAPA and the NIA Act, together with other laws that continue to be in operation in parts of India (viz., MCOCA, the Disturbed Areas Acts and the Armed Forces Special Powers Act (AFSPA),[49] and several state laws, like the Chhattisgarh Special Public Safety Act 2006 (CSPSA) constitute a network of anti-terror laws spanning the breadth of the country. AFSPA is particularly significant as an example of a 'permanent' law that was justified at the time of its enactment for merely shifting, under logistical compulsion, powers of ordinary policing to the army in Jammu and Kashmir and the Northeast. MCOCA is generally considered as the precursor of POTA, contributing some of its more 'effective' features, like the interception of wire, electronic or oral communication, and continuing with TADA provisions pertaining to confessions. Unlike POTA, which did not permit a confession by the co-accused as evidence, MCOCA and TADA allowed a confession of a co-accused implicating the accused to be considered as evidence of the guilt of the accused, by the Special Court (under MCOCA) or the Designated Court (under TADA).

A similar widening of the legal net may be seen in the Chhattisgarh Special Public Safety Act, (CSPSA) 2006.[50] While the need for such an Act was declared by the state Home Minister in the context of a Maoist attack in the state in September 2005, all 'Naxalite' groups are already banned and declared unlawful under the UAPA amendments made in 2004. The CSPSA broadened the ambit of what constitutes 'unlawful' by going well beyond the definitions of 'unlawful activity' and 'terrorist act' in UAPA, including in its purview any communication, verbally or in writing or by

---

[49] The Armed Forces (Special Powers) Regulation 1958 was promulgated in April 1958 to suppress the Naga movement. The Regulation gave special powers 'to officers of the armed forces in disturbed areas in the Kohima and Mokokchung districts of Naga Hills-Yuensang Area' while making the officers at the same time immune from 'prosecution, suit or other legal proceedings in any court of law' in respect of anything done in any part of Kohima or Mokokchung district of the Naga Hills-Tuensang Area with retrospective effect from 23 December 1957. A similar Act was passed for the states of Assam and Manipur (The Armed Forces (Assam and Manipur) Special Powers Act 1958 No. 28 of 1958 (11 September 1958)). A disturbed areas legislation was enacted for Punjab in December 1983 (The Punjab Disturbed Areas Act 1983 amended in 1989) to put down the movement for a separate state.

[50] The Chhattisgarh Vishesh Jan Suraksha Vidheyak 2005 was introduced by the ruling BJP in the state and passed by the State Assembly in December 2005. It received Presidential assent in March 2006.

representation by a person or organisation.[51] Moreover, by making the definition of 'unlawful' vague and imprecise with the inclusion of a 'tendency' to do certain acts[52] the Act gives an arbitrary over-reach to especially empowered district authorities.[53] Several organisations have been banned under the Act, and it has been used extensively in the past years against adivasis in Chhattisgarh (allegedly for being Maoists themselves or for helping them) and civil rights activists, including Dr Binayak Sen, General Secretary, Chhattisgarh PUCL, and Vice-President, National PUCL, who was detained on 14 May 2007 for his alleged links with the Communist Party of India (Maoist).[54]

On the other hand, Jharkhand, a state like Chhattisgarh which is rich in mineral and forest resources, with a substantial adivasi population and a region which falls within the official category of the 'red corridor' where Maoist groups have a social base, has resorted to s. 17 of the Criminal Law Amendment Act (1908) (CLA), to curb 'unlawful' associations. Section 17 lays down that a person who is a member of an unlawful association, notified as such under the CLA, or takes part in its meetings, contributes or solicits any contribution for the association, assists in any way in its operation, and commits a cognisable offence which is non-bailable, is liable to imprisonment extending to three years.

5.   Extraordinary laws: exception or norm?

Beyond the specific regime of each law lies a cumulative trajectory of anti-terror laws in India towards a deepening reliance on extraordinary laws through a process of normalisation and expansion. Anti-terror laws like the TADA 1985 and POTA 2002 were presented as problem-solving measures, surrounded by discourses asserting their indispensability and assurances that, because they were in response to specific situations, they were not meant to be everlasting. The experience with anti-terror laws in India has shown that the persistent lament of the existence of a pernicious

---

[51] CSPSA 2006, s. 2(e).   [52] CSPSA 2006, sub-ss. 2(e)(ii) and (iii).
[53] For a detailed discussion of the Act, see People's Union for Democratic Rights, *Casting the net wider! The Chhattisgarh Special Public Security Act 2006* (Delhi, April 2006).
[54] Sen languished in Raipur Central Jail for almost two years, until the Supreme Court of India gave him bail. For details, see People's Union for Democratic Rights, *Through the Lens of National Security: A Case Against Dr. Binayak Sen and the Attack on Civil Liberties* (Delhi, January 2008). On 24 December 2010, the Sessions Court at Raipur convicted Dr Sen under ss. 120(B) (Conspiracy), 124(A) (Sedition) of the IPC, ss. 1, 2, 3 and 5 of CSPSA, and s. 39(2) of the UAPA, sentencing him to life imprisonment.

internal enemy, and the fear of a legal system being unable to cope with it, have produced the context for the normalisation of extraordinary laws.

Constantly re-enacted and extended, these laws have become a consistent feature of criminal jurisprudence. Beginning with the Preventive Detention Act 1950, used against the Communists in Telengana, the Defence of India Act, re-introduced in the context of the Indo-China War of 1962, and the Maintenance of Internal Security Act 1971 (MISA), extraordinary laws have allowed the government to detain a wide range of people. With the declaration of a state of national emergency in 1975, the right of access to the courts for the protection of the fundamental freedoms of the people was suspended. The Constitution (39th Amendment) Act 1975 placed MISA in the ninth schedule of the Constitution, taking it beyond judicial review. The Constitution (42nd Amendment) Act 1976 further strengthened the powers of the central government by providing that no law for the prevention of anti-national activities could be declared invalid on grounds that it violated the fundamental rights in Part III of the Constitution.

In 1977 MISA was repealed by the Janata Party government, but other extraordinary laws, including the AFSPA 1958, UAPA 1967 and preventive detention laws in the states of Madhya Pradesh, Jammu and Kashmir, Bihar and Orissa, continued to be in force. A subsequent attempt made by the Janata government to bring in a mini MISA in the form of a Criminal Procedure (Amendment) Act proved futile. When the Congress returned to power, the National Security Act 1980 (NSA) was brought onto the statute books. The NSA was followed by TADA 1985 and 1987 and POTA 2002. The repeal of POTA, as discussed earlier, was followed by amendments to UAPA and the enactment of NIA Act 2008.

Significantly, while all anti-terror laws are enacted for an ostensibly limited duration, they also carry self-perpetuating provisions. The life of the Preventive Detention Act 1950 was initially for a year, i.e., until 1 April 1951, but it was extended every year until 1969, making it a normal feature of Indian political life, even though the number of persons detained under this Act decreased. Similarly, TADA provided for its own extension every two years, and continued to exist on the statute books until 1995. In 1993, when TADA was renewed for what turned out to be the last time, the extension process had became so much of a 'routine' and part of the 'ordinary' that only eight Members of Parliament (excluding the Minister presenting the Bill) participated in a discussion that lasted an hour and ten minutes. It is significant that the period after which extension could be sought was increased in the first POTA Ordinance to five years. The second Ordinance promulgated in December 2002, following a wave of criticism, reduced the period to three years. The period, for which such an Act can remain on the statute books without being subjected to legislative review, is indicative of a fear that non-renewal would create a 'legislative vacuum' for responding to terrorism. This manifested itself more recently in the recommendation of the Malimath Committee that 'a comprehensive and inclusive definition of terrorist acts, disruptive activities and organised crimes be provided in the Indian Penal Code, 1860 *so that there is no legal vacuum* in dealing with terrorists, underworld criminals and their activities after special laws are permitted to lapse, as in the case of TADA, 1987'.[55] This wish to make extraordinary laws permanent has come true in the form of the amendments to UAPA.

Indeed, even when an extraordinary law apparently expires or is supposedly repealed, it continues to live though provisions which allow 'investigation, legal proceeding or remedy' to be 'instituted, continued or enforced', 'as if this Act has not expired'.[56] The experience with TADA and POTA has shown that the provision of continuation after expiry, imparts a prolonged 'life after death' to the Act. Cases under TADA and POTA continue to be tried in various designated or special courts and the Supreme Court several years after those laws are supposed to have expired.

Ever since the enactment of the PDA in 1950, as Baxi points out, the Indian legal system has had to manage the co-existence of the Preventive Detention System (PDS), an institution authorised by the Constitution of India itself, as a parallel legal system in aid of the Criminal Justice System (CJS).[57] While laws like TADA and POTA were *not* preventive detention laws, despite the long periods of detention they permit, the parallels are easily drawn.

A distinctive pattern has emerged, however, in the operation of extraordinary laws. Through a subtle symbiosis, laws pertaining to 'ordinary crimes', and those dealing with extraordinary situations, intertwine and interlock in specific contexts. Not only is this evident in the letter of the law, and in judicial pronouncements, but more importantly, it has also had an impact on ordinary laws: much of the extraordinary gets accepted, ideologically and procedurally, in normal criminal justice jurisprudence, normalising the exceptional.

---

[55] Government of India, Ministry of Home Affairs, *Report of the Committee on the Reform of the Criminal Justice System* (March 2003), vol. I, p. 294 (emphasis added).
[56] See POTA, s. 1(6) and TADA, s. 1(4).
[57] See Upendra Baxi, *The Crisis of the Indian Legal System* (New Delhi: Vikas, 1982), p. 30.

The interlocking takes diverse forms. Anti-terror laws may amend specific statutes of the ordinary law, or there may be a mutual sharing of provisions between the ordinary and extraordinary laws. Extraordinary laws often carry specific provisions whereby the accused may be simultaneously charged and tried for a violation of other (ordinary) laws by special or designated courts with expansive and overriding powers to try cases in a common trial, and to hand out enhanced penalties on the basis of evidence that is considerably diluted under extraordinary laws.[58] In other words, an accused under ordinary law would get a different treatment if POTA or TADA provisions were added to the charges.

As a result of this symbiotic relationship, as Hillyard calls it, between ordinary criminal law and emergency legislation, there is a general tightening up throughout statutory law.[59] This standardisation of law becomes symptomatic of 'an insidious circular process in which draconian laws soften us up to similar laws which become the desired standard for further measures'.[60]

6. Conclusion

The anti-terror legal regime in India claims to be addressing specific forms of organised violence or what has been termed terrorist activities. These pertain to the autonomy or separatist movements of various hues and dispensations in large parts of Northeast India, Jammu and Kashmir, earlier in Punjab, and what the government calls Left Wing Extremism (LWE) encompassing the earlier Naxalite movement and the present Maoist movement in several states in India, including Andhra Pradesh, Chhattisgarh, Jharkhand, Bihar, West Bengal and parts of Maharasthra. Religious fundamentalist groups, mostly Muslim and more lately Hindu, who have been involved in bomb blasts, constitute another set of terrorists. Significantly, while the government uses the activities of these groups as justification for extraordinary measures, the laws are employed generally to curb political opposition and to constrain popular movements.

In the context of the 26 November terror attack in Mumbai, the amendments to UAPA in December 2008 came amidst a political consensus

---

[58] Section 26 of POTA pertained to the power of Special Court with respect to other offences.
[59] Paddy Hillyard, *Suspect Community: People's Experience of Terrorism Acts in Britain* (London: Pluto Press, 1993), p. 263.
[60] See J. Sim and P. A. Thomson, 'The Prevention of Terrorism Act: normalizing the politics of repression' (1983) 10 *Journal of Law and Society* 75.

among political parties (Congress-led UPA and BJP-led NDA) over the need to strengthen the law to deal with terrorism. This was markedly different from the enactment of prior anti-terror laws when there was political opposition to such laws because of a fear that they might be misused. While POTA was repealed because it was misused, as the Common Minimum Programme of the UPA stated, TADA was allowed to lapse, and was largely seen as having failed to achieve substantial conviction rates.

There has been a continuous and ubiquitous chant for an effective and strong anti-terror law, which became more belligerent with every fresh terrorist attack. While subsequent governments have continued to grapple with strategies for strengthening the law, they have simultaneously responded to nationalist movements in Kashmir and the Northeast, and Maoist violence in large tracts of India, particularly in the central Indian state of Chhattisgarh, by the use of the armed police, the paramilitary (Central Reserve Police Force and Border Security Force) and specialised policing. Thus where the army occupies large parts of Kashmir and Northeast, buttressed by extraordinary laws like AFSPA, the Maoist violence is dealt with through special police forces like the Greyhound and Cobra, specialising in jungle warfare. In the case of Chhattisgarh, the civil militia is drawn from the local adivasi population, pitting adivasis against each other.[61]

In civil war-like situations, where the armed might of the state and armed insurgent groups generate a cumulative threshold of violence to the extent that they make the situation insoluble by any legal regime, whether of extraordinary laws or of the ordinary criminal justice system, the debate on what the law should be starts to sound irrelevant. Ultimately, anti-terror legal regimes play only a transitory role, until a political resolution is sought though cultural, socio-economic and developmental measures evolved through a dialogue.

---

[61] This civil militia is called *salwa judum* in the local Gondi language, which translates literally as 'purification hunt'. The *salwa judum* had it precursors in sporadic *jan jagaran abhiyans*, which were then enforced as a compulsory campaign by the government: see Nandini Sundar, *Subalterns and Sovereigns: An Anthropological History of Bastar (1854– 2006)* (Delhi: Oxford University Press, 2nd edn, 2007).

PART IV

Anti-terrorism law and policy in the West

18

The United States a decade after 9/11

WILLIAM C. BANKS

1. Introduction

Ten years out, the world as seen from the perspective of the United States continues to look like a scary place. Indeed, the 9/11 attacks were 'more like a bolt of lightning that illuminated essential contours of the international landscape than an earthquake that reconfigured it'.[1] Countering terrorism and other global threats had occupied the United States during the final decades of the twentieth century, yet 9/11 showed their novel and more potent dimensions and signalled an especially combustible combination of threats and challenges that the United States would have to face in the years ahead. Although the threat posed by al-Qaeda and related groups is less severe than that highlighted by the 9/11 attacks, the threats have become more complex and more amorphous than at any time in the past decade. More US citizens and residents have played important roles in planning and carrying out terrorist attacks on behalf of al-Qaeda and its allies, and a diverse range of domestic-based jihadist groups have proliferated during the same period.[2]

Over the last decade, instead of the time-tested strategy of using its overwhelming military might to respond to conventional foes, the United States has been confronted with a mismatch between its power and a range of asymmetric threats. In response, new laws and policies created after 9/11 marked radical changes for the United States. Considerable controversy surrounded several of the new initiatives, at home and abroad. Now, a decade out from that defining moment, it is possible to assess the ways that the United States has attempted to counter the threat of terrorism. Treating the response to the 9/11 attacks as war was a deliberate choice

---

[1] Josef Joffe, 'Hubs, spokes and public goods', *The National Interest*, 30 October 2002, available at nationalinterest.org/article/hubs-spokes-and-public-goods-2159.

[2] Peter Bergen and Bruce Hoffman, *Assessing the Terrorist Threat: A Report of the Bipartisan Policy Center's National Security Preparedness Group*, Bipartisan Policy Center, 10 September 2010.

made by the Bush Administration and was endorsed by Congress a few days after 9/11. The war paradigm made sense to most observers at the time and it helped mobilise support for a military invasion of Afghanistan. In the major military campaigns in Afghanistan and Iraq, and in the more episodic uses of force by the United States in Pakistan, Somalia and Yemen, among other places, since 9/11, the United States has sought to win battles and gain the tactical advantage over an elusive, amorphous, and non-state enemy.

From the beginning, however, the legal and policy implications of choosing to characterise the strategy to counter al-Qaeda and the Taliban as war were troubling. In effect, by labelling the conflict as a 'new kind of war',[3] President Bush provided himself with the power to unilaterally initiate several new measures to detain, interrogate, transfer and try suspected terrorists, launch pre-emptive war against Iraq, target strikes against terrorists outside traditional battlefields, and conduct wholesale warrantless electronic surveillance in the hopes of thwarting terrorist plots. For the most part, the new policies and laws have had remarkable staying power. As a result, the United States is now creating more durable structures, processes and institutions to undertake and control efforts to counter terrorism. Judging from the counter-terrorism programmes that have become part of our codified laws in the last decade, it appears that a longer term realignment of the relative importance of security among our government's objectives may be taking place.

Predictably, the aggressive assertion of executive power that mark out Bush Administration policies and programs in the first few years after 9/11 was pushed back eventually by the courts (on surveillance, detention and military commissions), to some extent by Congress (on coercive interrogation), and eventually by the voters. Although the legal regime began to mature in the last years of the Bush presidency, the modifications were driven by judicial decisions and occasional actions of Congress. The executive arm, by and large, continued to view the co-ordinate branches as standing in its way.

The Obama Administration has changed the music of countering terrorism – no more 'global war on terror', for example – but it continues to rely on military force (drone strikes in numbers far outstripping the prior administration, including at least one US citizen target), the

---

[3] Telephone Interview with Rudolph Giuliani (Mayor of New York City) and George Pataki (Governor of New York), 13 September 2001, available at www.whitehouse.gov/news/releases/2001/09/20010913–4.html.

practice of extraordinary rendition and support for the use of the state secrets doctrine to block judicial review of the practice. In addition, the Administration has stalled in its commitment to close the Guantánamo Bay detention facility, has modified only slightly the criteria for who may be subjected to military detention, has blocked access to lawsuits in the United States by detainees in Afghanistan, has forged ahead with plans for military commission trials, and backs sweeping surveillance authorities. The institutions and processes supporting the maturing strategy are part war (targeted killing of identified terrorists by drone attacks) and part law enforcement (pursuing prosecutions in the regular courts for accused terrorists). Even now, continuing detentions and military commission decisions are subjected to judicial review based in part on international humanitarian law principles. At the same time, programmatic surveillance is overseen by the courts and Congress. These evolving arrangements may represent the emergence of a new counter-terrorism paradigm, the shape and dimensions of which are slowly beginning to appear.

This chapter will selectively examine developments in the counter-terrorism programmes of the United States since 9/11, and it will offer an assessment of their legal efficacy. In a concluding section, it will note briefly some unmet challenges that confront the United States as its counter-terrorism regime matures.

2. The continuing war against al-Qaeda

Within a few days of the World Trade Centre and Pentagon attacks, Congress passed the Authorization for the Use of Military Force (AUMF)[4] empowering the President to 'use all necessary and appropriate force' against those responsible for for 9/11 attacks 'in order to prevent any future acts of international terrorism against the United States by such ... persons'. No geographic or temporal limit was placed on the authority granted by the AUMF, and the authorisation to 'prevent any future acts' raises the possibility that military and other activities could take place against an unidentified enemy anywhere they are found in the foreseeable future. The scope of the discretion given by Congress to the Commander-in-Chief is unprecedented in US history.

The AUMF cemented the war paradigm as the dominant strategic response to 9/11 and it facilitated the Bush Administration's unilateral

---

[4] Authorization for the Use of Force, Pub. L. No. 107–40, 115 Stat. 224 (2001).

moves to set up military detention at Guantánamo Bay and elsewhere (including inside the United States), create military commissions, order coercive interrogations, render suspects to third countries for coercive interrogation and implement wholesale warrantless surveillance. Yet the AUMF did not represent a sharp break from the recent past in US counter-terrorism policies. Indeed, the war paradigm had been emerging as the leading policy option in countering terrorism throughout most of the Clinton terms as President, and to some degree even earlier.[5] Military strikes against terrorists have been carried out since the 1980s, and unilateral executive branch programmes such as extraordinary rendition have also been practised, covertly, long before 9/11. Still, the breadth of the AUMF supported the Bush Administration's argument that Congress approved any and all of the executive branch measures taken in the global war on terror.

The unleashing of the Commander-in-Chief through the AUMF was understandable and appropriate at the time of enactment. Ten years out, however, the AUMF has become too blunt an instrument. The absence of location or duration limits on the original authorisation contributes to legal ambiguities that continue to surround a range of counter-terrorism actions. Although the Congress eventually established limits on coercive interrogation, military commissions and electronic surveillance, the use of military force and a longer term system for the detention of terrorist suspects continues unguided by clear legal prescription.

Early on, the Obama Administration revised how it would interpret the AUMF standard, restricting it to someone who was 'part of, or substantially supporting' Taliban, al-Qaeda or associated forces.[6] The phrases 'associated forces' and 'substantially supporting' remain quite broad, but achieving more definitional precision is complicated in part by the difficulties of distinguishing dangerous terrorists from the civilians they blend with, by the non-hierarchical structures of terrorist groups and by the different operations that are legally justified by the AUMF. Detaining and targeting suspected terrorists with lethal force are, of course, very different tactics. In any case, it may be possible to narrow the authorising language by focusing on the command structure of al-Qaeda and

---

[5] Benjamin Wittes, *Law and the Long War: The Future of Justice in the Age of Terror* (New York: Penguin, 2008), pp. 25–6.

[6] In Re: Guantanamo Bay Detainee Litigation, Respondent's Memorandum Regarding the Government's Detention Authority Relative to Detainees Held at Guantanamo Bay, No. 08–442 (TFH) (US Dist Ct for the DC 2009), available at www.scotusblog.com/wp/wp-content/uploads/2009/03/doj-detain-authority-3-13-09.pdf.

associated organisations or by focusing on terrorists who directly participate in armed conflict against the United States, a standard borrowed from international humanitarian law.[7] To date, there is no indication that the Obama Administration has sought a more nuanced authority or any evidence that Congress will propose reforms.

3.   Problems of detention and trial, including trial by military commission

In the weeks after 9/11, the Bush Administration crafted a legal scheme for detaining and then trying suspected al-Qaeda and Taliban operatives captured in the war on terrorism. Perceiving that it would have far more latitude to detain, interrogate and decide the fate of suspected terrorists, or financiers of terrorism, if it fashioned an off-shore military-type regime for holding and trying those it characterised as 'enemy combatants', the Bush Administration promulgated a Military Order and claimed the authority to detain without time limit any non-citizen whom the President has 'reason to believe' is a member of al-Qaeda, is involved in international terrorism or has knowingly harboured such members or terrorists.[8] The same Order authorised trials of suspected non-citizens accused of committing 'violations of the laws of war and other applicable laws' by military commissions, outside the traditional civilian and military justice systems. By early 2002 the United States military removed several hundred persons from Afghanistan to the United States Naval Base at Guantánamo Bay, Cuba.

The Bush Administration acted during the same period to detain indefinitely three US citizens it labelled as enemy combatants, without charges and without access to counsel. Unable to rely on the Military Order for authority, the administration justified the citizen detentions on the basis of the AUMF and on the President's authority as Commander-in-Chief. Yaser Hamdi was allegedly captured on the battlefield in Afghanistan, transferred to Guantánamo Bay, and then to a military brig in South Carolina once his US citizenship was determined. Jose Padilla was detained as he stepped off a commercial flight in Chicago. At first, Padilla was held in civilian confinement in New York City as a material witness

---

[7] Jack Goldsmith, 'Long-term terrorist detention and our national security court' in Benjamin Wittes (ed.), *Legislating the War on Terror: An Agenda for Reform* (Washington, DC: Brookings Institution Press, 2009), p. 84.

[8] Military Order: Detention, Treatment, and Trial of Certain Non-Citizens in the War Against Terrorism, 66 Fed. Reg. 57,833, 13 November 2001.

to the 9/11 attacks, but was later declared an enemy combatant and transferred to the same military facility as Hamdi. Ali Saleh Kahlah al-Marri is a Qatari national who earned a bachelor's degree during the 1990s from Bradley University in Illinois and who returned to the United States with his family to pursue a master's degree on 10 September 2001. Al-Marri was subsequently arrested on 12 December of the same year, as a material witness to the 9/11 conspiracy and later indicted for making false statements and for credit card fraud before being designated an enemy combatant by President Bush in June 2003. The criminal case was dismissed, and al-Marri was transferred to the South Carolina military brig.

In a first round of challenges to their detention, several of the noncitizen detainees at Guantánamo Bay and their representatives petitioned courts in the United States for habeas corpus, on the grounds that the detentions violated a range of protections provided by the US Constitution. They asked for release from custody, access to legal counsel and freedom from coercive interrogation. On the same day that it announced in *Rasul* v. *Bush*[9] that federal habeas corpus statutes permit the Guantánamo Bay detainees to sue in federal court, the Supreme Court ruled on the appeals of Yaser Hamdi and Jose Padilla. The Court ruled in *Hamdi*[10] that Congress had authorised the detention of enemy forces captured in battle by enacting the AUMF, regardless of citizenship or nationality. At the time, the question was not one of the President's authority, but whether the detention of US citizens without judicial review violated the Fifth Amendment command that no 'life, liberty, or property' be taken without 'due process of law'. After balancing the competing interests of Hamdi and the government, Justice O'Connor found that the detainee 'must receive notice of the factual basis for his classification, and a fair opportunity to rebut the Government's factual assertions before a neutral decisionmaker'. Rather than take their chances in further legal proceedings with Hamdi, the government made a deal that deported Hamdi to Saudi Arabia in return for him giving up his US citizenship and agreeing not to return to the United States.[11]

The case of Jose Padilla was more difficult for the government to defend and for the Court to decide because Padilla was not captured on a battlefield and, once detained, never presented a security danger to the United States. After he was transferred from civilian detention, as a material witness in New York, to a military detention facility in South Carolina, his

---

[9] *Rasul* v. *Bush*, 542 US 466 (2004).   [10] *Hamdi* v. *Rumsfeld*, 542 US 507 (2004).
[11] *Hamdi* v. *Rumsfeld*, Case No. 2:02CV439 Motion to Stay Proceedings.

lawyer filed a habeas corpus petition in New York federal court. However, the Supreme Court held that Padilla's lawyer sued the wrong person in the wrong court.[12] Padilla started over in the federal courts in South Carolina, and while his case was again pending in the Supreme Court (where this time the Court would likely be forced to decide the merits of his claim) the government announced that Padilla had been indicted on charges considerably less serious than those for which he was militarily detained. The government then moved successfully to transfer Padilla *back* to civilian custody. Eventually, Padilla was convicted of providing material support to terrorism as part of a conspiracy unrelated to 9/11.[13]

A second generation of challenges continued to limit the executive's claimed powers over detention and trial by military commission. Al-Marri challenged his military detention by arguing that his criminal detention was sufficient to thwart any terrorist acts and that there was no necessity for military detention. After lower courts found that the government met its burden of providing credible evidence that al-Marri was an enemy combatant, the Court of Appeals ruled that al-Marri was entitled to additional process to contest the government's determination that he is an enemy combatant.[14] While the government's appeal was pending in the Supreme Court, the government once again successfully avoided an unfavourable decision in the Supreme Court by seeking the transfer of al-Marri *from* military to civilian custody.[15] He was indicted and pleaded guilty to providing material support to terrorism.[16]

Selim Hamdan, a Yemeni national, was captured in November 2001 by militia forces in Afghanistan and turned over to the US military. In June 2002, he was transported to Guantánamo Bay, and in 2003 he and five other detainees were determined by President Bush to be subject to the November 2001 Military Order and therefore triable by a military commission. Among the overt acts listed in the charges against Hamdan was the claim that he acted as bin Laden's bodyguard and personal driver. Before a trial could begin, Hamdan challenged the legality of the commission process. In 2006, the Supreme Court held in *Hamdan* v. *Rumsfeld*[17]

---

[12] *Rumsfeld* v. *Padilla*, 542 US 426 (2004).

[13] Robert M. Chesney, 'Optimizing criminal prosecution as a counterterrorism tool', in Wittes, *Legislating the War on Terror*, pp. 108–9.

[14] *Al-Marri* v. *Pucciarelli*, 534 F 3d 213 (4th Cir. 2008).

[15] *Al-Marri* v. *Spagone*, 129 S Ct 1545 (2009).

[16] *United States* v. *Al-Marri*, Plea Agreement and Stipulation of Facts, US District Court (CD III 2010), available at www.slideshare.net/LegalDocs/findlaw-almarri-guilty-plea.

[17] *Hamdan* v. *Rumsfeld*, 126 S Ct 2749 (2006).

that the Bush Military Order authorising trial of an enemy combatant by a military commission violated applicable statutes and the Geneva Conventions. The President and Congress responded by enacting the Military Commissions Act, which created processes for trial by military commission that, as amended in 2009, remain to be tested. Meanwhile, a 2008 Supreme Court decision, *Boumediene* v. *Bush*,[18] determined that Guantánamo detainees are constitutionally entitled to pursue habeas corpus relief in the federal courts and, thus, statutes that sought to curtail that review after the Court's 2004 decision in *Rasul* could not be enforced. The Court did not explain what legal standards must guide a lower court in making the habeas corpus decisions and the *Boumediene* decision did not say whether those detained by the United States in other locations are similarly entitled to habeas corpus.

Significant questions remain unanswered. Do the Guantánamo detainees enjoy due process protections? Must they be allowed to confront their accusers? Do detainees in Afghanistan and in other locations abroad have habeas rights, and if not, what processes will determine their continued detention?[19] After the Guantánamo facility is closed, what rules will govern the continued detentions of those who cannot be tried? Judges in the lower courts are making the law in these uncharted waters, case by case. Although Guantánamo detainees have prevailed in most of their habeas petitions so far, detainees in Afghanistan have not fared so well. In one decision, a Court of Appeals ruled that detainees picked up and detained in Afghanistan have no habeas corpus rights.[20] As the Obama Administration continues a mostly political struggle to close the Guantánamo Bay detention facility, it is inevitable that the federal courts in the District of Columbia are becoming an equivalent 'national security court' for the United States. However, it remains incumbent on Congress and the President to spell out, in statutory terms, the limits of their jurisdiction, the substantive bounds of detention authority for those who may be held until the conflict is over and the processes for review.[21]

At present, the developing counter-terrorism paradigm is beset with political squabbles over the means for detaining and interrogating suspects in domestic terrorism crises. As the 2009 and 2010 cases of the would-be Christmas Day bomber and the would-be Times Square

---

[18] *Boumediene* v. *Bush*, 128 S Ct 2229 (2008).
[19] See, e.g., *Boumediene* v. *Bush*, 579 F Supp 2d 191 (DDC 2008); Goldsmith, 'Long-term terrorist detention', pp. 75–94.
[20] *Al Maqaleh* v. *Gates*, 605 F 3d 84 (DC Cir. 2010).
[21] Goldsmith, 'Long-term terrorist detention', pp. 75–94, note 19.

bomber demonstrated, if the executive branch treats the suspect as a criminal, a body of long-standing legal precedent provides protections for the accused that can disrupt interrogations. If the suspect stops talking, valuable intelligence about co-conspirators or other plots may be lost. If the government treats the suspect as an enemy combatant and thus subjects him to lengthy interrogations without the benefit of counsel or an early proceeding before a judge, officials run the risk that the courts will rule against the executive and order release of the suspect. The Attorney-General has proposed legislation that would provide officials greater flexibility in crisis cases to have time to extend interrogations of suspects before making pivotal decisions about their eventual treatment in the law enforcement or military justice systems. Creating a statutory mechanism for counter-terrorism detention and initial interrogations would advance the new paradigm and at least partially quiet the political sniping in times of crisis.

4. Coercive interrogation

As early as December 2002, US military and civilian interrogators are reported to have abused individuals captured and detained in the war on terrorism, by beating them, subjecting them to prolonged sleep and sensory deprivation and sexual humiliation. The abuse began in Afghanistan, migrated to Guantánamo Bay and other offshore US interrogation centers, and then later to Iraq. Investigations of these abuses revealed[22] that serious injuries and deaths occurred among the detainees. By any standard, the scandal generated by the abuse did considerable harm to the national image of the United States.

Common Article 3 of the Geneva Conventions requires that detainees protected by it 'shall in all circumstances be treated humanely' and bans 'violence to life and person, in particular … cruel treatment and torture; [and] outrages upon personal dignity, in particular humiliating and degrading treatment'.[23] This language likely applies to all the coercive interrogation methods employed at the instance of the Bush Administration in the first few years after 9/11. Yet the President purported to overcome the legal obstacle when he determined in February 2002 that Taliban

---

[22] See Senate Armed Services Committee Inquiry into the Treatment of Detainees in US Custody, 11 December 2009, available at levin.senate.gov/newsroom/supporting/2008/Detainees.121108.pdf.

[23] Geneva Convention Relative to the Treatment of Prisoners of War, Geneva, 12 August 1949, in force 21 October 1950, 75 UNTS 135, art. 3 (common to all four conventions).

and al Qaeda detainees were not entitled to Geneva protections.[24] The President issued his memorandum after being advised by then-Counsel to the President Alberto Gonzales that 'this new paradigm [the war on terror] renders obsolete Geneva's strict limitations on questioning of enemy prisoners and renders quaint some of its provisions'.[25] Apart from the Geneva protections, the Convention against Torture (CAT) is implemented in United States legislation criminalising 'torture', defined as any 'act ... specifically intended to inflict severe physical or mental pain or suffering ... upon another person within [an official's] custody or physical control'.[26] The CAT also bans 'cruel, inhuman, or degrading treatment', although this category of abuse was not forbidden by US law until statutes were amended after the abuse scandal came to light.

The abusive treatment was set in motion by leaders determined to break the resistance of a few captured al-Qaeda leaders, but the wholesale decision by the President to deny Geneva protections to al-Qaeda and the Taliban led to applying the harsh techniques to hundreds of low-level detainees. At the centre were the civilian lawyers that crafted strained, overblown and often simply incorrect legal opinions that purported to sanction the coercive treatment. Legal opinions in 2002 went so far as to claim that for treatment to meet the standards for 'torture', as prohibited by the CAT, a detainee would have to suffer the equivalent of 'pain accompanying serious physical injury, such as organ failure, impairment of bodily function, or even death'.[27] The opinion maintained that interrogation activities 'may be cruel, inhuman, or degrading, but still not produce pain and suffering of the requisite intensity'[28] to violate the law.

After the photos of abuses at Abu Ghraib prison in Iraq came to light in the spring of 2004, the Administration discontinued its most abusive

---

[24] George W. Bush, 'Re: the humane treatment of Al Qaeda and Taliban detainees' (Memorandum dated 7 February 2002), in Karen Greenberg and Joshua Dratel (eds.), *The Torture Papers: The Road to Abu Ghraib* (New York: Cambridge University Press, 2005), pp. 134–5.

[25] Alberto R. Gonzales, 'Re: Decision re application of the Geneva Convention on Prisoners of War to the conflict with al Qaeda and the Taliban', Memorandum dated 25 January 2002, in Greenberg and Dratel, *The Torture Papers*, p. 119.

[26] Convention Against Torture and Other Cruel, Inhuman or Degrading Treatment or Punishment, New York, 10 December 1984, in force 26 June 1987, 1465 UNTS 85, art. 1.

[27] Memorandum from Alberto R. Gonzales to the President, 'Re: Standards of conduct for interrogation under 18 USC §§ 2340–2340A' (1 August 2002), available at www.justice.gov/olc/docs/memo-gonzales-aug2002.pdf.

[28] Ibid.

practices and in 2005 and 2006 Congress adopted restrictions on inter-rogation in the Detainee Treatment Act and the Military Commissions Act. At about the same time, the US military promulgated a revised field manual strictly forbidding coercive measures. However, the CIA was per-mitted by a 2007 Presidential Order to hold detainees in secret sites and to subject them to coercive interrogation tactics that were at least in tension with if not in violation of legal limits.[29]

Once the abuses were stopped, and the legal maelstrom was quieted by the legislative prohibitions on torture and cruel, degrading, and inhumane treatment, the more difficult question facing the Obama Administration, Congress and other civilian and military leaders is what precise rules should govern interrogations in the future. The Convention against Torture, Geneva Conventions and US implementing laws are notoriously open-textured and lacking in detailed guidance. Are there circumstances where some degree of coercion should be permitted, for some prisoners, in limited circumstances? What techniques might be allowed, subject to whose approval and review? When President Obama stated in his inaugural address that he can 'say without exception or equivocation that the United States of America does not torture',[30] he implemented his new policies in the form of an Executive order.[31] Such orders may be changed at any time by this President or the next one, and exceptions may be made by the President, unilaterally and in secret, if needed. Instead of relying on a list of approved techniques in the Army Field Manual, Congress should also determine whether the CIA should in all circumstances be subject to the same restrictions on coercion as military and other civilian interrogators, and it should clearly criminal-ise all violations of the statutory limits.[32]

The efforts by the Obama Administration to reclaim the moral high ground for the United States are anchored in law, albeit in an executive order that may be rescinded or altered at any time. In any case the legal architecture remains incomplete. At the same time, proposals to prosecute

---

[29] Exec Order No. 13,340, 72 Fed Reg 40,707 (20 July 2007) (interpreting Common Article 3 and the MCA to permit coercive interrogation so long as the purpose is to gain intelli-gence and not humiliate or degrade the detainee). See Stuart Taylor and Benjamin Wittes, 'Refining US interrogation law', in Wittes, *Legislating the War on Terror*, pp. 307–8.

[30] Barack Obama, President of the United States, Inaugural Address, 20 January 2009; Barack Obama, President of the United States, Address to Joint Session of Congress, 24 February 2009.

[31] Exec Order No. 13,491, 74 Fed Reg 4893 (22 January 2009).

[32] Taylor and Wittes, 'Refining US interrogation law', pp. 329–30.

or at least publicly condemn officials in the Bush Administration responsible for the abusive treatment have not been supported by the Obama Administration. Meanwhile, there have been ongoing efforts to assess what effective interrogation means, and whether coercion produces better or worse intelligence.[33] Going forward, it is likely that US counterterrorism laws will require greater specificity in elaborating permissible techniques and yet allow for flexibility to employ more coercive measures in extreme circumstances, subject to vigorous oversight.

5.   Extraordinary rendition

Rendition is generally understood as the surrender of a person from one state to another state that has requested him, typically pursuant to an agreement or extradition treaty, for the purpose of criminal prosecution. Since the 1990s, however, the United States began transferring detainees to foreign countries for detention and interrogation without the request of the transferee country, sometimes where it is possible that the individuals will be subjected to torture or cruel, inhuman or degrading treatment. This 'extraordinary rendition' is so labelled because it involves no treaty or formal agreement and is attended by no judicial process. Whether authorised by secret presidential directive or simply done by government officials without authorisation, extraordinary rendition has been utilised as an integral adjunct to coercive interrogation since 9/11.

Beginning in 2004, journalists described CIA transport of suspected terrorists to various undisclosed locations for coercive interrogations, outside public view and beyond the apparent reach of US courts. Sightings of agency use of Gulfstream turbojets at military air fields in Pakistan, Indonesia and Jordan were reported, along with scenes of hooded suspects being handcuffed before boarding. Human rights groups complained that the CIA purpose was to transfer detainees to countries that employed brutal interrogation techniques that were expressly unlawful in the United States and in clear violation of the Convention against Torture.[34] One unnamed US official with experience in so rendering

---

[33]   See Intelligence Science Board, *Educing Information – Interrogation: Science and Art – Foundations for the Future* (Phase 1 Report), December 2006, available at www.fas.org/irp/dni/educing.pdf; Intelligence Science Board, *Intelligence Interviewing: Teaching Papers and Case Studies – A Report from the Study on Educing Information*, April 2009, available at www.fas.org/irp/dni/isb/interview.pdf.

[34]   Dana Priest, 'Jet is an open secret in terror war', *Washington Post*, 27 December 2004.

detainees explained: 'We don't kick the [expletive] out of them. We send them to other countries so they can kick the [expletive] out of them.'[35] The countries apparently receiving suspects, including Syria, Egypt, Saudi Arabia and Jordan, had been identified by the State Department as purveyors of torture.

Bush Administration officials declined to confirm or deny the CIA programme, although the President insisted that the United States did not deliver people to other nations to face torture.[36] The Administration also insisted that the CIA followed legal requirements in receiving assurances from the receiving country that it would treat the detainee humanely. Yet former prisoners who were subject to extraordinary rendition stated that they were tortured, shackled, humiliated in various ways and subjected to electric shocks.[37]

European rights groups called attention to the apparent practices and some European governments began investigations of their own, prompting Secretary of State Condoleezza Rice to seek to deflect the investigations by issuing a statement in December 2005. Among other things, Secretary Rice asserted that 'the United States does not transport, and has not transported, detainees from one country to another for the purpose of interrogation using torture'.[38] The wriggle room in her statement is obvious, and its ambiguity was not lost on US allies.

After the Supreme Court held in *Hamdan* v. *Rumsfeld* that detainees must have protections of the Geneva Conventions, including the Common Article 3 prohibition on torture and cruel, inhuman and degrading treatment, the Bush Administration decided to close CIA prisons abroad and transfer fourteen so-called 'high value detainees' held in those facilities to Guantánamo, where their interrogations would comply with new US army rules.[39] A November 2006 European Parliament report confirmed that many governments co-operated with the CIA and knew

[35] Dana Priest and Barton Gellman, 'U.S. decries abuse but defends interrogations, "stress and duress" tactics used on terrorism suspects held in secret overseas facilities', *Washington Post*, 26 December 2002.

[36] Jennifer K. Elsea and Julie Kim, 'Undisclosed US detention sites overseas: background and legal issues' (CRS Report for Congress, 12 September 2006), available at www.law.umaryland.edu/marshall/crsreports/crsdocuments/RL33643_09122006.pdf.

[37] See US Department of State, 'Egypt: country reports on human rights practices' (2003), available at www.state.gov/g/drl/rls/hrrpt/2003/27926.htm.

[38] Secretary Condoleeza Rice, 'Remarks upon her departure for Europe', 5 December 2005, available at merln.ndu.edu/archivepdf/terrorism/state/57602.pdf, p. 3.

[39] Elsea and Kim, 'Undisclosed US detention sites overseas'.

that individuals were being abducted and transported to countries where they would be tortured.[40]

Two prominent examples came to light as the result of failed lawsuits against US officials. Khalid el-Masri brought suit in the United States against the CIA director and private companies and individuals who assisted the CIA in detaining, interrogating, and torturing him during an extraordinary rendition. El-Masri, a German national, alleged that he was kidnapped while travelling on holiday in Macadonia, handed over to CIA agents and then flown to a secret detention centre in Afghanistan where he was detained and tortured. El-Masri was eventually released when the government learned that he had a similar name but was not the suspected terrorist they were interested in. El-Masri's lawsuit was dismissed after the government invoked the state secrets privilege and the lower courts agreed that privileged national security information would be central to the litigation.[41] (The state secrets privilege permits the government to request that the courts dismiss a case, prevent the use of evidence in it, or both on the grounds that national security information would be compromised in the lawsuit.[42])

Maher Arar, a dual citizen of Syria and Canada, was returning to Canada from a vacation with his wife and children in Tunis. After landing at JFK airport in New York on his transit back to Montreal, Arar's name was entered into a computer and he was then pulled aside at immigration, where he was fingerprinted, photographed and detained. He was held virtually incommunicado for thirteen days and then removed to Syria, where he was repeatedly tortured by Syrian officials. After falsely confessing that he had received military training in Afghanistan to end the torture, he was eventually returned to Canada. Syria was widely known to have a record of abusing detainees in its prisons and a Commission created by the Canadian government later found no evidence that Arar had committed any crime or that his activities threatened the security of Canada. The Commission found that Canadian investigators erroneously placed Arar and his wife on a 'terrorist lookout' list, which led the Mounted Police to include them in a database that alerts United States border officers to suspect individuals.[43] During the period of Arar's detention in New

---

[40] Brian Knowlton, 'Report rejects European denial of CIA prisons', *New York Times*, 29 November 2006.

[41] *El-Masri* v. *United States*, 479 F 3d 296 (4th Cir. 2007).

[42] *Mohamed* v. *Jeppesen Dataplan*, No. 08–15693, 2010 WL 3489913 (9th Cir. 2010).

[43] Ian Austen, 'Canadians fault US for its role in torture case', *New York Times*, 19 September 2006.

York, Canadian officials communicated to United States officials that they had found no connection between Arar and al-Qaeda and that he would be subject to surveillance but not arrested if he returned home to Canada. The Canadians did not know that, at the time, US officials were planning to render Arar to Syria.[44] Although the Canadian government compensated Arar for his suffering, his lawsuit against US officials in the US Federal Court was dismissed at the trial and appellate levels, on the grounds that statutes protecting victims of torture and treaty protections do not create a right of action in court, and that separation of powers considerations prevent the judiciary from interfering in the national security and foreign policy considerations that attend such renditions.[45]

The Obama Administration has not renounced the practice of extraordinary rendition. Indeed, the Obama Justice Department adhered to a Bush Administration legal position and successfully argued for the dismissal on state secrets grounds of a case against a private company allegedly involved in CIA renditions.[46] The possibility that the CIA may continue the rendition practice may as a practical matter confer back-door discretion to engage in coercive interrogations, despite US laws, through its foreign subcontractors.[47] It is not publicly known whether the United States continues to render suspected terrorists to third countries for interrogation. The distrust engendered by Bush Administration denials of its involvement in extraordinary renditions contributed to the erosion of US standing in world opinion and to a loss of trust in government at home. Torture is unlawful and morally repugnant. Extraordinary rendition is an end run around legal accountability for lawless acts and it should be disavowed by the United States. To close the legal loop, Congress should proscribe the practice by statute.

6.   Targeted killing

In October of 2001, on the first night of the campaign against al-Qaeda and the Taliban in Afghanistan, the United States nearly had a major success. Officials believed that they had pinpointed the location of the supreme leader of the Taliban, Mullah Muhammad Omar. While patrolling the roads near Kabul, an unmanned but armed drone trained its

---

[44]   Scott Shane, 'Canadian to remain on US terrorist watch list', *New York Times*, 23 January 2007.
[45]   *Arar* v. *Ashcroft*, 585 F 3d 559 (2d Cir. 2009).
[46]   *Mohamed* v. *Jeppesen Dataplan*, No. 08–15693, 2010 WL 3489913 (9th Cir. 2010).
[47]   Taylor and Wittes, 'Refining US interrogation law', p. 310.

crosshairs on Omar in a convoy of cars fleeing the capital. Under the terms of an agreement, the CIA controllers did not have the authority to order a strike on the target. Likewise, the local Fifth Fleet commander in Bahrain lacked the requisite authority. Instead, following the agreement they sought approval from United States Central Command (CENTCOM) in Tampa to launch the Hellfire missile from the Predator drone positioned above Omar.

The Predator followed the convoy to a building where Omar and about 100 guards sought cover. Some delay ensued in securing General Tommy R. Franks' approval. One report indicated that a full-scale fighter-bomber assault was requested and that General Franks declined to approve the request on the basis of on-the-spot legal advice.[48] Another report suggested that the magnitude of the target prompted General Franks to run the targeting by the White House.[49] Media reports indicated that President Bush personally approved the strike, although the delay permitted time for Mullah Omar to change his location and thus disrupt the attack.[50] F-18s later targeted and destroyed the building, but Omar escaped.[51] Some speculated that the Predator attack was aborted because of the possibility that others in a crowded house might be killed.

The decision to target specific individuals with lethal force after 9/11 was neither unprecedented nor surprising. In appropriate circumstances the United States has engaged in targeted killing, at least since a border war with Mexican bandits in 1916.[52] In a time of war, subjecting individual combatants to lethal force has been a permitted and lawful instrument of waging war successfully.

The components of the targeted killing policy quickly took on a sharper focus soon after 9/11. After the near miss on Mullah Omar, on 3 November 2001, a missile-carrying Predator drone killed Mohammed Atef, al-Qaeda's chief of military operations, in a raid near Kabul.[53] Then, in early May 2002, the CIA tried but failed to kill an Afghan factional

[48] See Seymour Hersh, 'King's ransom', *The New Yorker*, 10 October 2001.
[49] Michael R. Gordon and Tim Weiner, 'A nation challenged: the strategy', *New York Times*, 16 October 2001.
[50] Eric Schmitt, 'US would use drones to attack Iraqi targets', *New York Times*, 6 November 2002.
[51] Gordon and Weiner, 'A nation challenged'.
[52] See William C. Banks and Peter Raven-Hansen, 'Targeted killing and assassination: the US legal framework' (2003) 37 *University of Richmond Law Review* 688.
[53] James Risen, 'A nation challenged: the terror network', *New York Times*, 13 December 2001.

leader, Gulbuddin Hekmatyar, an Islamic fundamentalist who had vowed to topple the government of Hamid Karzai and to attack US forces.[54] The calculus for targeted killing changed dramatically on 3 November, 2002, when a drone fired a Hellfire missile and killed a senior al-Qaeda leader and five low-level operatives travelling by car in a remote part of the Yemeni desert.[55] In the first use of an armed Predator outside Afghanistan or, indeed, the first military action in the war against ter-rorism outside Afghanistan, Qaed Salim Sinan al-Harethi was killed. Al-Harethi was described as the senior al-Qaeda official in Yemen, one of the top ten to twelve al-Qaeda operatives in the world, and a suspect in the October 2000 suicide bombing of the US destroyer *USS Cole*, where seventeen American Navy personnel were killed. US intelligence and law enforcement officials had been tracking his movements for months before the attack. Along with al-Harethi, killed in the Predator strike were five other al-Qaeda operatives, including an American citizen of Yemeni des-cent, Kamal Derwish, who grew up in the Buffalo suburb of Tonawanda and who, according to FBI intelligence, recruited US Muslims to attend al-Qaeda training camps.

Now, after years of fighting in Iraq and Afghanistan, the focus of atten-tion for lethal targeting has shifted to other areas, principally Pakistan, including Waziristan and neighbouring border areas. On 5 August, 2009, Baitallah Mehsud was killed when two Hellfire missiles were fired from a Predator drone piloted by someone at CIA headquarters in Virginia. Mehsud was the commander of the Pakistan Taliban. He had terror-ised the Pakistani government for years, kidnapped Pakistani soldiers, deployed suicide bombers into the streets of Pakistan, master-minded the assassination of Prime Minister Benazir Bhutto, and was implicated in attacks on US forces in Afghanistan. The missiles struck while Mehsud was lying on the roof of his father-in-law's house, apparently while receiv-ing an intravenous drip for his diabetes or a kidney condition. His wife and uncle were killed, along with his in-laws and eight others, including Mehsud's bodyguards. It was significant that Mehsud was in Pakistan, not Afghanistan, and that the trigger was pulled by the CIA, not the US military. Was Mehsud a combatant involved in an armed conflict with the United States in Pakistan? Alternately, was he a civilian who was taking a

---

[54] Thom Shanker and Carlotta Gall, 'U.S. attack on warlord aims to help interim leader', *New York Times*, 9 May 2002.

[55] John J. Lumpkin, 'Al-Qaida suspects die in US missile strike', *Associated Press*, 5 November 2002.

direct part in hostilities during an armed conflict? If there was no armed conflict in Pakistan when Mehsud was targeted, did the United States nonetheless possess the US and/or international legal authority to target Mehsud with lethal force?

In 2009 alone, President Obama ordered more drone strikes than President Bush ordered in two terms as President. In the first months of 2010, the pace quickened, as more than a dozen strikes were carried out in the first six weeks of the year, killing up to ninety suspected militants. The Administration's legal position was outlined by State Department Legal Adviser Harold Koh in a March 2010 speech. Koh offered a vigorous defence of the use of force against terrorists, including the targeting of persons 'such as high-level al Qaeda leaders who are planning attacks'.[56] Koh indicated that each strike is analysed beforehand based on 'considerations specific to each case, including those related to the imminence of the threat, the sovereignty of the states involved, [and] the willingness and ability of those states to suppress the threat the target poses'.[57] Koh indicated that the operations conform to 'all applicable law',[58] and are conducted consistent with the principles of distinction and proportionality.

It was understood long before 9/11 that under the Constitution, the President may order targeted killing in defence of the United States in war. The President's authority as Commander-in-Chief to 'repel sudden attacks'[59] has traditionally had a real-time dimension, or a sort of imminence requirement, by analogy to the doctrine of self-defence at international law. Yet a terrorist attack is usually over before it can be repelled in real time, and when the attack is a suicide attack, it is impracticable to strike back. In addition, the United States has learned to expect terrorists to pursue a course of continuing attacks. As such, over time, a domestic law anticipatory self-defence custom has emerged that permits the President to use deadly force against a positively identified terrorist if he has exhausted other means of apprehending him.[60] Congress has the legal authority to regulate the use of force in this setting and it has done so.

---

[56] Harold Hongju Koh, 'The Obama Administration and international law', Keynote Speech delivered at the Annual Meeting of the American Society of International Law, 24 March 2010, available at www.state.gov/s/l/releases/remarks/139119.htm.
[57] Ibid.
[58] Ibid.
[59] Max Farrand (ed.), *The Records of the Federal Convention of 1787* (New Haven, CT: Yale University Press, first published 1911, 1937 edn.) vol. II, p. 318.
[60] Banks and Raven-Hansen, 'Targeted killing and assassination', 677–81.

The National Security Act of 1947 authorised the CIA to 'perform such other functions and duties related to intelligence affecting the national security as the President or National Security Council may direct'.[61] Although the original grant of authority in 1947 likely did not contemplate targeted killings, the 1947 Act was designed as a dynamic authority to be shaped by practice and necessity, and by the 1970s, the practice came to include targeted killing. After the Church Committee[62] learned of and disapproved of assassination plots of the CIA, or its agents, in the mid-1970s, President Ford issued an executive order prohibiting CIA involvement in assassinations (but notably not restricting targeted killing) and Congress enacted intelligence oversight legislation that, as amended, continues to require reporting to Congress by the President of significant anticipated intelligence operations.

In the weeks after 9/11, President Bush signed an intelligence finding giving the CIA broad authority to pursue terrorism around the world.[63] The 2001 finding was apparently modified in 2006 by President Bush to broaden the class of potential targets, beyond bin Laden and his close circle, and extend the boundaries beyond Afghanistan.[64] A finding contains the factual and policy predicates for the intelligence activities authorised in any significant operation and the document must be personally approved by the President. By statute,[65] a finding must accompany any covert operation approved by the President, including those that permit targeted killing. In the classified finding, the President delegated targeting and operational authority to senior civilian and military officials. Revised findings, including any prepared by President Obama, along with their precise approval mechanisms, remain classified. The authority given in these presidential findings is surely the most sweeping and most lethal since the founding of the CIA. In part, the findings contemplate a high and unprecedented degree of co-operation between the CIA and Special Forces, as well as other military units.

To some it seemed that the 2001 finding ran counter to the long-standing ban on political assassination. Enshrined in an executive order first

---

[61] Pub. L. No. 80–253, §102(d)(5), codified as amended at 50 USC §403–4a(d)(4).

[62] Select Committee to Study Governmental Operations (known as the Church Committee after its Chair, Senator Frank Church), S. Rep. No. 94–755, Book I (1976).

[63] James Risen and David Johnston, 'Bush has widened authority of CIA to kill terrorists', *New York Times*, 15 December 2002.

[64] David Johnston and David E. Sanger, 'Fatal strike in Yemen was based on rules set out by Bush', *New York Times*, 6 November 2002.

[65] 50 USC §413 *et seq.*

issued by President Gerald Ford and unchanged since President Reagan's version in 1981, the directive forbids political assassination but does not define the term.[66] Just what does distinguish lawful targeted killing from unlawful political assassination? The answer turns upon which legal framework applies. During war, whether authorised by Congress or fought defensively by the President on the basis of his authority, targeted killing of individual combatants is lawful, although killing by treacherous means – through the use of deceit or trickery – is not. In peacetime, any extra-judicial killing by a government agent is lawful only if taken in self-defence or in defence of others. But what rules apply when the United States is engaged in a non-traditional war on terrorism, or war against al-Qaeda? The evolving customary law of anticipatory self-defence and intelligence legislation regulating the activities of the CIA supply adequate, albeit not well articulated or understood legal authority, for the drone strikes.

In addition to the President's constitutional authorities as Commander-in-Chief and his authorities over intelligence activities authorised by statute, the President's finding may also be supported by the AUMF. As suggested earlier in this chapter, Congress should revisit the AUMF and provide a more fine-grained authorisation for the use of military force against terrorists. Criteria should be supplied for the use of force in self-defence, including targeted killings, within and outside what are regarded as traditional battlefields. Congress should debate the criteria for triggering the use of lethal force against suspected terrorists. Is functional membership in al-Qaeda or a related group sufficient? Must the target be taking a direct part in hostilities, or is providing financial or logistical support to terrorists enough to permit targeting with lethal force? To what extent should the consent of a sovereign state be required before military force is used against terrorists who seek refuge in that state?

The defensive use of force – targeting a known al-Qaeda leader, for example – also has firm legal roots in customary international law.[67] In making operational decisions like the one made to strike with Predators in Afghanistan, Yemen or Pakistan, the international and US laws concerning self-defence permit targeting al-Qaeda combatants. Yet carrying out the strike in an alleged terrorist sanctuary (Pakistan or Yemen, for

---

[66] Barton Gellman, 'CIA weighs "targeted killing" missions', *Washington Post*, 28 October 2002.

[67] W. Hays Parks, *Memorandum of Law: Executive Order 12333 and Assassination*, Dept. of the Army Pamphlet 27–50–204, from Army Law. 4 (December 1989).

example), rather than on a traditional battlefield complicates the international legal issues.

Within this twilight zone of threat from terrorist attacks, it is not clear exactly what distinguishes a combatant and, thus, a proper target, from a civilian who may not be targeted. Also, it is not known what evidence suffices to implicate someone who does not wear a uniform and does not fight for a sovereign state in terrorist activities, so as to warrant targeting with lethal force. Clearly someone who is positively identified as an al-Qaeda operative is an enemy combatant, one who may be targeted with lethal force.

Under international humanitarian law, during an armed conflict the selection of individuals for targeted lethal force is lawful if the targets are combatant forces of another nation, a guerilla force, or a terrorist or other organisation whose actions pose a threat to the security of the United States. The United States is surely engaged in an armed conflict in Afghanistan, but the absence of sustained fighting over a significant period of time in Yemen means that there is no armed conflict going on there. Pakistan is a closer case. Until sometime in 2009, fighting in the border region of Pakistan did not likely rise to the level of an armed conflict under the laws of war. By 2010, however, the conditions on the ground changed so dramatically that the laws of armed conflict likely apply in Pakistan, in relation to the United States and its use of military force against al-Qaeda or Taliban insurgents.

In the decade since 9/11, the use of military force against terrorists has evolved and matured. The 2001 invasion of Afghanistan was in some ways a continuation of long-standing US projection of overwhelming force. Civilian casualties were high, and the forces were not always well prepared to fight their non-traditional enemies. As the use of drones and targeted killing as a tactical option expanded outside the Afghanistan battle space, operational successes were tempered by widespread criticism that legal boundaries were crossed and that the policy of using lethal force beyond the traditional battlefield could lead to escalating and uncontrolled violence. As counter-insurgency emerged late in the last decade as the favoured strategy in Iraq and then Afghanistan, targeted killing has become a key tool. The Obama Administration stepped up drone attacks at least in part because their potential for precision and diminished civilian casualties meshes well with the 'hearts and minds' strategy in counter-insurgency. The laws of the United States may be read to support targeted killing wherever the United States is fighting a defensive war, yet questions persist about the scope and dimensions of the battlefield and compliance with international law and the laws of war. At the same time the Obama Administration defended its use of drone strikes in Pakistan and Yemen in 2010, it defended successfully against a lawsuit seeking to enjoin the targeting of US citizen Anwar al-Aulaqi who is believed to be hiding in Yemen.[68]

7. The USA PATRIOT Act

A few weeks after 9/11, after minimal hearings and scant debate, Congress enacted the Patriot Act.[69] Perhaps more than any other legal development, the Patriot Act became a symbol for galvanising supporters and defenders of the Bush Administration response to 9/11. Yet anyone who took the time to read the 352-page act would have recognised the more modest and incremental changes in law and policy that were actually reflected in the legislation. The Patriot Act is hardly a code for fighting the war on terrorism, nor one for saving the US homeland from another attack. Instead, it is an amalgam of often unrelated pieces of authority, most of which simply amend existing laws, and the larger share of which are unremarkable complements to existing authority.

That is not to say that the Patriot Act lacks importance. The few really significant changes in investigative authorities and criminal law were initially made subject to a three-year sunset provision, and controversy really surrounded only several pages of the 352. An entire subtitle of the Act that would have authorised lengthy detention of any alien immigrant on the say-so of the Attorney-General[70] has not been utilised, because existing immigration statutes and regulations conferred equally expansive authority.

Three categories of Patriot Act changes in law merit separate mention: records searches, foreign intelligence gathering and criminalising material support for terrorism. The Patriot Act permits the FBI secretly to compel internet service providers, libraries, banks and credit card companies to turn over sensitive information about their customers without having to show that the target of the investigation has any involvement in espionage or terrorism. Commercial vendors may be compelled to produce the requested records following a statement from the FBI that the information

---

[68] *Al-Aulaqi* v. *Obama*, 727 F. Supp. 2d 1 (US D Ct, DC 30 August 2010).
[69] Uniting and Strengthening America by Providing Appropriate Tools Required to Intercept and Obstruct Terrorism (USA PATRIOT) Act, Pub. L. No. 107–56, 115 Stat. 272 (2001).
[70] Ibid., §§ 411–418, 8 USC § 1226a, ff.

is 'relevant' to an investigation 'to protect against international terrorism or clandestine intelligence activities'. No showing is required that the target has anything to do with terrorism, much less that the target is an agent of a foreign power. Provisions requiring a limited judicial approval before exercising this expanded authority to examine business records were later eliminated, when Congress in 2003 amended the law again to permit the Attorney General to issue administrative subpoenas (with no judicial role) in these investigations, and expanded the categories of those subject to the subpoenas to include securities dealers, currency exchanges, car dealers, travel agencies, post offices, casinos and pawnbrokers, among others.[71]

Since the Patriot Act, the volume of administrative subpoenas, known as national security letters (NSLs), has increased dramatically. Beginning in 2004, the American Civil Liberties Union (ACLU) sued the Justice Department, challenging the constitutionality of the expansion of this authority to obtain personal records as it applies to electronic service providers. The ACLU claimed that the FBI can obtain information from traditional Internet service providers (ISPs), as well as universities, businesses, public interest organisations and libraries. The ACLU argued that the expanded authority chills protected expression, that it invades personal privacy and that it constitutes a search that should be attended by a probable cause determination and warrant procedure to meet constitutional Fourth Amendment requirements.

In a series of judicial decisions in litigation still ongoing in late 2010, the lower federal courts found that provisions forbidding disclosure by the recipient that an NSL was received violated the First Amendment, and that ISP subscribers have First Amendment interests that must be subject to judicial review before enforcing a NSL, but that the broad authority conferred by the Patriot Act is otherwise lawful.[72] Government reports confirm that more than 14,000 secret demands for records concerning US persons are issued each year.[73]

A second controversial Patriot Act provision amended the Foreign Intelligence Surveillance Act (FISA),[74] the authority that has, since 1978,

---

[71] Intelligence Authorization Act for FY 2004, Pub. L. No. 108–177, x 374, 117 Stat. 2599, 2628 (2003).

[72] Doe v. Ashcroft, 334 F Supp. 2d 471, vacated and remanded; Doe v. Gonzales, 449 F 3d 415 (2d Cir. 2006); Doe v. Holder, 2010 WL 1253522, SDNY (2010).

[73] US Department of Justice, Office of Legislative Affairs, Letter to Congress, 30 April 2010, available at www.fas.org/irp/agency/doj/fisa/2009rept.pdf.

[74] Foreign Intelligence Surveillance Act of 1978, Pub. L. No. 95–511, 92 Stat. 1783 (codified in scattered sections of the United States Code).

allowed intelligence investigators to bypass the regular law enforcement warrant process by obtaining authorisation for electronic surveillance or (since 1994) a physical search from a special secret court. Instead of having to demonstrate to a magistrate probable cause to believe that a crime is being or has been committed before being given permission to conduct electronic surveillance or a physical search, the judge of the secret court has merely to find probable cause that the requested surveillance is to obtain 'foreign intelligence' from an 'agent of a foreign power'. In other words, there should be a reasonable belief that the target is connected to an international terrorist organisation.

Of course, intelligence and law enforcement investigations often overlap, utilise the same methods and may concern the same targets. Because of the importance attached to personal privacy as enshrined in the Fourth Amendment requirements for probable cause of a criminal act and a warrant issued by a neutral magistrate, law enforcement and intelligence officials have historically walked a fine line. To gather foreign intelligence, agents could forego the traditional Fourth Amendment processes, but if they were intending to build a criminal case against the target, the probable cause and warrant requirements had to be followed. Until amended by the Patriot Act, to avoid tainting a criminal prosecution, investigators who found criminal activity in the course of a FISA investigation effectively had to show that the primary purpose of the surveillance approved by the secret FISA court was to obtain foreign intelligence. Once that showing was made, the fact that evidence turned up that could be used in building a criminal case would not undermine the rights of the accused.

This 'wall' between law enforcement and intelligence investigations permitted parallel law enforcement and intelligence investigations to coexist and protected the constitutional rights of the potential accused, but the government argued that the various procedures designed to insure the integrity of the wall stood in the way of effective co-operation and information sharing between the law enforcement and intelligence investigators. The Patriot Act thus changed FISA to permit an investigation to proceed by means of the secretive and less burdensome FISA procedure so long as a 'significant purpose' of the investigation is to gather foreign intelligence.[75] Thus, a terrorism investigation that is seeking to build a criminal case from the beginning may bypass the traditional law enforcement warrant process and attendant Fourth Amendment protections for

---

[75] Patriot Act, §218, 115 Stat. 291.

individuals[76] through use of the FISA procedures, so long as some foreign intelligence is also sought.[77] The wall has been dismantled, and the comingling of law enforcement and foreign intelligence investigations is now routine.

Finally, the Patriot Act amended an earlier criminal statute that criminalises providing 'material support' to terrorists, and extended the crimes to include providing 'expert advice or assistance' to terrorists.[78] After a lower federal court struck down the Patriot Act amendment as unconstitutionally vague,[79] Congress clarified that 'expert advice or assistance' means advice or assistance 'derived from scientific, technical or other specialized knowledge'.[80] The amendment was designed to overcome the fear expressed by some, including the federal judges, that the Patriot Act provision could be construed to include speech and advocacy protected by the First Amendment. In 2010 the Supreme Court upheld the amended 'material support' provisions against a challenge that the law remained unconstitutionally vague and continued to violate the First Amendment.[81]

As amended, nearly all of the Patriot Act provisions of consequence have become part of the permanent laws of the United States. As such, the new authorities for records searches, foreign intelligence surveillance and criminalising 'material support' to terrorism have contributed to an emerging counterterrorism paradigm in the United States.

8.   Investigating in the digital age

As noted above, beginning in 1978, FISA authorised the means for electronic collection of foreign intelligence that served the nation well for many years. The basic idea was simple. Government may conduct

---

[76] The Fourth Amendment of the US Constitution provides: 'The right of the people to be secure in their persons, houses, papers, and effects, against unreasonable searches and seizures, shall not be violated, and no Warrants shall issue, but upon probable cause, supported by Oath or affirmation, and particularly describing the place to be searched, and the persons or things to be seized.'

[77] See *In re: Sealed Case*, 310 F 3d 717 (Foreign Intelligence Surveillance Court of Review 2002).

[78] Patriot Act, §805(a)(2)(B), 18 USC §2339A.

[79] *Humanitarian Law Project* v. *United States Department of Justice*, 352 F 3d 382 (9th Cir. 2003).

[80] Intelligence Reform and Terrorism Prevention Act of 2004, Pub. L. No. 108–458, §6603(c)–(f), 118 Stat. 3638, 3763 (2004).

[81] *Holder* v. *Humanitarian Law Project*, 130 S. Ct. 2705 (2010).

intrusive electronic surveillance of Americans or others lawfully in the United States without traditional probable cause to believe that they had committed a crime if it could demonstrate to a special Article III court that it had a different kind of probable cause: reason to believe that targets of surveillance are acting on behalf of foreign powers.[82] Over time, FISA was amended several times to extend its procedures to conduct physical searches,[83] monitor suspected lone-wolf terrorists[84] and accommodate evolving threats.[85]

Particularly since the 9/11 attacks, critics have argued that the patch-work-like architecture of FISA has become too rigid, complicated and unforgiving to enable effective intelligence responses to crises.[86] The computerisation of communications that has so enriched our capabilities has also facilitated stealth and evasion by those seeking to avoid detection.[87] Would-be targets of surveillance are communicating in ways that stress or evade the FISA system. Because of the pervasiveness of US telecom switching technology, collection *inside* the United States is now often the best or only way to acquire even foreign-to-foreign communications that were originally left unregulated by FISA.[88] Meanwhile, powerful computers and data-mining techniques now permit intelligence officials to select potential surveillance targets from electronic databases of previously unimaginable size.[89] Instead of building toward an individual FISA

[82] Foreign Intelligence Surveillance Act, Pub. L. No. 95–511, § 105(a), 92 Stat. 1783, 1790 (codified at 50 USC § 1805(a)).

[83] Intelligence Authorization Act for Fiscal Year 1995, Pub. L. No. 103–359, sec. 807, §§ 301–309, 108 Stat. 3423, 3443–53 (codified as amended at 50 USC §§ 1821–1829).

[84] Intelligence Reform and Terrorism Prevention Act of 2004, Pub. L. No. 108–458, sec. 6001(a), 118 Stat. 3638, 3742 (codified as amended at 50 USC § 1801(b)(1)(C)).

[85] See FISA, Pub. L. No. 95–511, § 105(b)(2)(B), 92 Stat. 1783, 1791 (codified at 50 USC § 1805(c)(2)(B)) (roving wiretaps); FISA, Pub. L. No. 95–511, § 105(b)(1)(B), 92 Stat. 1783, 1790 (codified at 50 USC § 1805(c)(1)(B)) (requiring an application to identify the facilities where surveillance will be sought 'if known').

[86] See, e.g., Richard A. Posner, 'A new surveillance act', *Wall Street Journal*, 15 February 2006 (arguing that FISA is 'dangerously obsolete'); K. A. Taipale and James J. Carafano, 'Fixing surveillance', *Washington Times*, 24 January 2006; Richard A. Posner, 'Privacy, surveillance, and law' (2008) 75 *University of Chicago Law Review* 245, 252 (claiming that FISA 'remains usable for regulating the monitoring of communications of known terrorists, but it is useless for finding out who is a terrorist …').

[87] See William C. Banks, 'The death of FISA' (2007) 91 *Minnesota Law Review* 1209, 1275–6 (observing that, in the world of technological surveillance, evasion and logistical difficulties force the government to continually play 'catch-up').

[88] See David S. Kris, 'Modernizing the foreign intelligence surveillance Act: progress to date and work still to come', in Wittes, *Legislating the War on Terror*, p. 217.

[89] See, e.g., James Bamford, *The Shadow Factory: The Ultra Secret NSA from 9/11 to the Eavesdropping on America* (New York: Anchor, 2008), pp. 12–14 (describing the vast data-collection capabilities of the NSA).

application by developing leads on individuals with some connection to an international terrorist organisation, for example, officials now develop algorithms that search thousands or even millions of collected e-mail messages and telephone calls for indications of suspicious activities.[90] At the same time, more Americans than ever are engaged in international communications and there is far greater intelligence interest in communications to and from Americans.[91] Both circumstances increase the likelihood that the government will be intercepting communications of innocent Americans, raising as many questions about the adequacy of FISA safeguards as they do about the adaptability of FISA architecture.

After 9/11, President Bush ordered an expanded programme of electronic surveillance by the National Security Agency (NSA) that simply ignored FISA requirements.[92] In December 2005 the *New York Times* reported that President Bush had secretly authorised the NSA to eavesdrop on Americans and others inside the United States to search for evidence of terrorist activity without obtaining orders from the FISA court.[93] Although the details of what came to be called the Terrorist Surveillance Program (TSP) have not been made public, NSA apparently monitored the telephone and e-mail communications of thousands of persons inside the United States where one end of the communication was outside the United States and where there were reasonable grounds to believe that a party to the international communication was affiliated with al-Qaeda or a related organisation.

From subsequent accounts and statements by Bush Administration officials, it appears that the TSP operated in stages. With the co-operation of telecommunications companies, the NSA first engaged in wholesale collection of all the traffic entering the United States at switching stations (so-called 'vacuum cleaner surveillance'). Second, those transactional

---

[90] See Shane Harris, 'FISA's failings', *National Journal*, 8 April 2006, p. 59 ('[T]he NSA's warrantless eavesdropping program also involves looking for suspicious patterns in a sea of communications').

[91] See Leslie Cauley, 'NSA has massive database of Americans' phone calls', *USA Today*, 11 May 2006, available at www.usatoday.com/news/washington/2006–05–10-nsa_x.htm ('[T]he National Security Agency has been secretly collecting the phone call records of tens of millions of Americans … [T]he spy agency is using the data to analyze calling patterns in an effort to detect terrorist activity …').

[92] Except where otherwise noted, this section relies on Offices of Inspectors General of the Department of Defence, Department of Justice, Central Intelligence Agency, National Security Agency and Office of the Director of National Intelligence, *Unclassified Report on the President's Surveillance Program* (10 July 2009), available at www.fas.org/irp/eprint/psp.pdf.

[93] James Risen and Eric Lichtblau, 'Bush lets US spy on callers without courts', *New York Times*, 16 December 2005.

data – addressing information, subject lines, and perhaps some message content – were computer mined for indications of terrorist activity. Third, as patterns or indications of terrorist activity were uncovered, intelligence officials at NSA reviewed the collected data to ferret out potential threats, at the direction of NSA supervisors. Finally, the targets selected as potential threats were referred to the FBI for further investigation, pursuant to FISA, and the human surveillance ended for the others.

Throughout most of 2006 the Bush Administration defended the legality of the TSP vigorously, but it was an uphill struggle. In the face of mounting criticism and litigation challenging TSP, the Administration persuaded the FISA court to take over supervision of the programme, presumably within the statutory parameters of FISA. When the Foreign Intelligence Surveillance Court (FISC) took over administration of the TSP programme in January 2007, Attorney General Alberto Gonzales advised that a FISC judge 'issued orders authorizing the Government to target for collection international communications into or out of the United States where there is probable cause to believe that one of the communicants is a member or agent of al Qaeda or an associated terrorist organization'.[94] According to the Attorney General, all surveillance that had been occurring under the TSP would now be conducted with the approval of the FISC.

A different FISC judge decided in April 2007 not to continue approval of what had been the TSP under FISC supervision, and apparently determined that at least some of the foreign communications acquired in the United States pursuant to the programme are subject to individualised FISA processes.[95] After a backlog of FISA applications developed, the Bush Administration successfully persuaded Congress to pass statutory authorisation for programmatic surveillance outside the case-specific FISA processes.

As enacted in August 2007 the Protect America Act[96] (PAA) determined that the definition of 'electronic surveillance' in FISA would not apply to surveillance of a person reasonably believed to be outside the United

---

[94] Letter from Alberto R. Gonzales, Attorney General, to Senator Patrick Leahy and Senator Arlen Specter (17 January 2007), available at www.fas.org/irp/congress/2007_cr/fisa011707.html (implicitly conceding that TSP did fall within the scope of FISA).

[95] See J. Michael McConnell, Director of National Intelligence, evidence given to Senate Committee on the Judiciary, *Hearing on the Foreign Intelligence Surveillance Act and Implementation of the Protect America Act* (25 September 2007), p. 11, available at www.dni.gov/testimonies/20070925_testimony.pdf.

[96] Pub. L. No. 110–55, 121 Stat. 552.

States. The PAA also permitted the Director of National Intelligence and the Attorney General to authorise collection of foreign intelligence from within the United States 'directed at' persons reasonably believed to be outside the US, without obtaining an order from the FISC, even if one party to the communication was a United States citizen inside the United States. Because a FISA 'person' may include groups or foreign powers, surveillance 'directed at' al-Qaeda permitted warrantless surveillance of the telephones and e-mail accounts of any US person if the government was persuaded that the surveillance was directed at al-Qaeda.

Although the PAA was temporary legislation, in 2008 Congress enacted the FISA Amendments Act of 2008 (FAA).[97] The FAA codified a procedure to permit broad, programmatic surveillance focused on patterns of suspicious activities and not on a specific individual or the contents of their communications through changes in FISA that overcame the case-specific orientation of the original statute.[98] As a result, the FAA also codifies, until 31 December 2012, potentially intrusive electronic surveillance unaccompanied by safeguards to protect personal privacy and free expression. The amended FISA also institutionalises operations that are prone to inaccuracy and chronic over collection. The Obama Administration has endorsed the programmatic features of FISA and continues to defend lawsuits challenging the TSP.

From its beginnings, the overarching FISA question has been how to evaluate and weigh the basic values of security and individual liberties when intrusive electronic surveillance is used to collect foreign intelligence. Modern communications and surveillance technologies have so complicated policy discussions, however, that the values debate has drowned in a sea of misapprehension about the means to implement the policies. Meanwhile, FISA has become so complex that the law further occludes informed policy choices. Programmatic surveillance adds considerably to complexity, has already produced implementation problems and casts doubt on the lawfulness and efficacy of FISA's techniques. The high-speed digital world may have made inevitable the need for similarly nimble government capabilities to monitor the communications of suspected terrorists. To date, however, neither Congress nor the Obama Administration has revisited FISA nor attempted to insert safeguards and other oversight mechanisms that would ensure that the open-ended

[97] Pub. L. No. 110–261, 122 Stat. 2436, 50 USC §§1881a et. seq.
[98] See FISA Amendments Act, Pub. L. No. 110–261, § 702(a)–(e), 122 Stat. 2436, 2438–40 (to be codified at 50 USC § 1881a).

discretion conferred by programmatic surveillance does not undermine the privacy and free expression interests of innocent persons.

9. Conclusions: shifting paradigms and institutional roles

The United States now finds itself fighting non-state terrorist groups in asymmetric military conflicts that were not the subject of the extensive international framework for warfare negotiated after the World Wars. This chapter has shown that, even as our legal and policy regime for combating terrorism matures, the laws of the United States have not kept pace with changes in the dynamics of military conflicts. The relevant spheres of authority overlap: the laws of the United States (constitutional, statutory, executive and customary), international laws (treaty-based and customary) and international humanitarian law (a subset of international law that applies during armed conflicts). The relationship of the spheres of authority to one another, and their application as binding law, is fraught with dispute and contentiousness. In part, the lack of consensus on the legal rules reflects the changing nature of asymmetric warfare. These new battlefields require adaptations of old laws.

President Obama's May 2010 National Security Strategy, the first of his administration, departs from the strategy documents issued by his predecessor in part by emphasising that efforts to counter violent extremism (his replacement for the Bush phrase 'Islamic terrorism') are not the single-minded focus of the US strategy, and by emphasising that the United States will seek broad international support for its actions, although it will reserve the right to act unilaterally if necessary.[99] The Strategy does commit to 'engage and modernize international institutions and frameworks',[100] and it promises to 'submit decisions to checks and balances and accountability'.[101] Time will tell whether these promises result in the adaptations and accommodations that are required to meet the changing dynamics of countering terrorism.

A few years after 9/11, the policies of warrantless surveillance, military commissions, the Guantánamo Bay detention camp, coercive interrogation, extraordinary rendition and the detention as enemy combatants of US citizens, taken together constituted an argument for a separate track, law-free zones outside the rule of law and constitutional protections, for

---

[99] Barack Obama, *National Security Strategy* (May 2010) available at www.whitehouse.gov/sites/default/files/rss_viewer/national_security_strategy.pdf.
[100] Ibid., at 12.   [101] Ibid., at 21.

those adjudged by the administration not to be worthy of the protections our system otherwise provides. Principally, though not exclusively, the law-free zones applied in our government's dealings with non-citizens suspected of terrorist activities.

Ten years after 9/11, the courts have helped restore the rule of law in the US counter-terrorism strategy. Yet, unsurprisingly, most of the time the courts have deferred to the actions of the elected branches. Indeed, it has been Congress far more than the judiciary that has been quiescent in responding to the executive branch adventures and to the new challenges faced by the nation. Congress did react to the Abu Ghraib scandal with legislation that goes some distance in regulating interrogation of suspected terrorists and it has prescribed broad policy contours for military commissions and rules for the conduct of what was the TSP. While the FISA changes may create more legal and policy problems than they solve, and the efficacy of the military commission will depend heavily on agency rules and practices not yet fully developed, detention, rendition and targeted killing continue to lack critical legislative guidance.

Perhaps of even greater importance has been the evolving tendency of US military forces and CIA or other intelligence personnel to blend their roles and missions, blurring their operational responsibilities. The 'shadow war' that has found the United States involved in at least twelve nations since 9/11, threatens to leave our Congress and the courts outside the oversight and accountability picture in significant ways, as the military do not face detailed oversight of their intelligence operations and the CIA may conduct its paramilitary operations under the rubric of broad findings that do not mention the specifics.[102]

Meanwhile, the merging of national security and law enforcement spheres of governance in the United States has inculcated in the citizenry the idea that emergency conditions that arose on 9/11 have become routine, and that adding the national security emblem to terrorism-related law enforcement renders extraordinary measures legitimate. As developed in this chapter, the United States is some distance along a path toward developing a new counter-terrorism paradigm, neither one of law enforcement nor war as those domains are conventionally understood. To the extent that a counter-terrorism paradigm supplies transparent processes, safeguards against abuses of powers, and institutions and mechanisms to

---

[102] Scott Shane, Mark Mazetti and Robert F. Weurth, 'Secret assault on terrorism widens on two continents', *New York Times*, 15 August 2010.

ensure that the government is held legally accountable for its actions, the new paradigm may represent a step forward.

Finally, asymmetric warfare against non-state actors and the now widespread use by states of contractors to wage the wars and provide their logistical and technical support foreshadows the spectre of loss of sovereign control over the projection of violence against civilians.[103] In the United States, contracting for security and related services skyrocketed after 9/11, two large-scale wars and global threats. The outrage provoked by the Blackwater rampage against civilians in Baghdad in 2007 awakened officials in the State Department, Defense Department and members of Congress to the relatively untethered nature of the relationships between the United States and its contractors. Legislative and administrative reforms began in US law and practice, but contractors continue to populate critical counter-terrorism positions for the United States around the world. In general, contractors' actions are not subject to the same effective legal controls as military personnel and they are not bound to obey the laws of armed conflict, nor human rights laws.

Because the global battlefields are increasingly populated by contract agents of one sort or the other, the absence of regulation for the global security industry portends a loss of sovereign control by the United States and other nations over the very sphere of governing meant to justify governments' existence. The United States should take a lead position in determining to reassert sovereign control over the battle space, wherever it is, and over those who occupy it.[104]

---

[103] Dana Priest, 'National Security Inc.', *Washington Post*, 20 July 2010.
[104] James Cockayne *et al.*, *Beyond Market Forces: Regulating the Global Security Industry* (International Peace Institute, 2009), available at www.ipinst.org/media/pdf/publications/beyond_market_forces_final.pdf.

19

UK counter-terror law post-9/11: initial acceptance of extraordinary measures and the partial return to human rights norms

HELEN FENWICK AND GAVIN PHILLIPSON

1. Introduction

Three main governmental policy responses to terrorism have been identified:[1] a military one, treating the fight against terrorism as a form of warfare; a police-based one, treating it as a form of criminal activity, to be detected and then defeated using an existing or modified version of the criminal justice system; and a political one, viewing it as a form of armed rebellion to be resolved through negotiation and the political process. In contrast to its eventual approach to resolving the Northern Ireland conflict, the British government has not so far tried the political route in response to the threat from Islamist terrorism, although it has used the military approach in Afghanistan. At home, however, the response has been largely police-based: it has involved a very significant ratcheting up of the state's coercive powers in terms of criminal law, police powers, and extraordinary 'pre-emptive' measures.[2] The UK has thus continued to ensure post-9/11 that even exceptional state measures to combat terrorism are clothed in legal authority; it has also sought to achieve face-value adherence to key norms laid down by the European Convention

---

[1] Noel Whitty, Therese Murphy and Stephen Livingstone, *Civil Liberties Law: The Human Rights Act Era* (London: Butterworths, 2001), pp. 128–9.

[2] We prefer the term 'pre-emptive' to the more commonly used 'preventive' for the reasons given by Jude McCulloch and Sharon Pickering, 'Counter-terrorism: the law and policing of pre-emption' in Nicola McGarrity, Andrew Lynch and George Williams (eds.), *Counter-Terrorism and Beyond: the Culture of Law and Justice after 9/11* (Oxford: Routledge, 2010), pp. 13–17: essentially (at 17), 'the concept of pre-emption focuses attention on the *strategy* behind the legislation: targeting threats before they emerge. The term prevention, by way of contrast, asserts an *outcome* that is not supported empirically and is challenged by historical experience and a range of scholarship'.

on Human Rights (ECHR).[3] Its exceptional measures contain three main strands: first, broad substantive counter-terror offences; second, a criminal justice response that lies at the absolute outer edge – or beyond – of ECHR toleration; and third, the creation of a parallel pre-emptive system running in tandem with the continuing criminal justice approach – what Walker terms the 'executive measures' model.[4]

All three strands form part of what Zedner has termed 'an emerging genre of preventive justice'.[5] While Zedner was describing measures lying outside the normal criminal law and criminal justice system, all three strands discussed in this chapter are in essence pre-emptive or investigatory rather than punitive. All are characterised by 'the shift to intelligence-based and proactive methods [with] the primary aim of preventing terrorist attacks, rather than responding to events and attempting to solve crimes after they occur'.[6] A fourth strand of the UK's anti-terrorism policy – the so-called 'Prevent' strategy, aiming to intervene at a still earlier stage by combating radicalisation in Muslim communities – is considered in Chapter 10 of this volume .

While the 'control orders' scheme, which we consider first, represents the most obviously 'exceptional' measure, the substantive offences are also designed to allow intervention at such an early stage in any engagement

---

[3] The exception is the UK's complicity – the extent of which is still unknown – in so-called 'extraordinary rendition' carried out by the US government. There are related allegations of complicity in the torture of citizens by other countries; these are to be investigated in a judicial inquiry chaired by Sir Peter Gibson.

[4] Clive Walker, 'The treatment of foreign terrorist suspects' (2007) 70(3) *Modern Law Review* 427, 430. There is a further strand – only applying to terror suspects who are foreign nationals – which we do not consider here for reasons of space. This is what Walker terms the 'exit strategy'; namely deportation, and detention with a view to deportation, which is one of the exceptions to the right to liberty in art. 5(1)(f) of the ECHR (see below note 15). This strategy has been used in relation to certain suspects who were detained in Belmarsh prison and then placed in 'immigration detention' or under control orders. Where there is a real risk that deportees would be subject to torture, contrary to art. 3 (see note 19 below), or treatment in flagrant breach of the right to a fair trial (*Chahal* v. *UK* App no 22414/93, 1996-V) diplomatic assurances have been sought from the receiving country that such treatment will not be accorded (see *RB (Algeria)* v. *SSHD; OO (Jordan)* v. *SSHD* [2009] UKHL 10). This is clearly a doubtful basis for the detentions since acceptable assurances do not appear to have been obtained in all instances and were not obtained before the detention began. See generally Walker, 'The treatment of foreign terror suspects', 433–57.

[5] Lucia Zedner, 'Preventive justice or pre-punishment? The case of control orders' (2007) 60 *Current Legal Problems* 174.

[6] Whitty, Murphy and Livingstone, *Civil Liberties Law*, p. 143. See also Clive Walker, 'Terrorism and criminal justice: past, present and future' [2004] *Criminal Law Review* 311, 314; R. V. Ericson and K. D. Haggerty, *Policing the Risk Society* (Oxford: Clarendon Press, 1997); McGarrity, Lynch and Williams, *Counter-Terrorism and Beyond*.

or potential engagement with terrorist-related activity or support for it as to fall more readily within the category of pre-emptive measures. The criminal justice measures discussed below are in effect designed to allow unacknowledged racial or religious profiling and to maximise the scope for information-gathering rather than acting as aspects of the investigation of offences. These aims are contentious enough, but they have been legislatively realised via an executive discretion so uncontrolled as to create an ultimately irresolvable tension with the ECHR: indeed, we argue in this chapter that the previous Labour government was only prepared to introduce measures that apparently complied with international human rights norms on the basis of creating, in effect, minimal interpretations of certain Convention rights that stripped them of much of their content; in the worst cases this amounted to a form of unacknowledged, and therefore 'stealthy', derogation. This chapter sets out to explore the Labour government's use of the threat of terrorism to persuade Parliament and the judiciary to co-operate in this process and to consider how far each branch nevertheless provided some resistance to the executive. We examine in particular the constant invocation by the executive of the need for judicial deference in the area of national security and the judicial response to this. We conclude that the role of both branches has been less significant than that of the European Court of Human Rights in Strasbourg, which has played a decisive part in upholding human rights and rule of law norms in the face of executive attack, legislative compliance and a very mixed judicial response.

Britain now has a Liberal–Conservative coalition government promising to reform counter-terrorist legislation, a highly pertinent stance in the face of the defeats the UK has suffered at Strasbourg in this area. This is, therefore, an opportune moment at which to consider the tensions between the measures at issue and the ECHR norms, and reappraise certain apparently failing strategies such as control orders and mass, random stops and searches. Plainly, in a chapter of this length, it is not possible to cover the huge array of criminal offences and other measures that may be used against terrorism suspects[7] introduced under the five anti-terrorism

---

[7] We do not consider here another significant measure: the asset freezing of terrorism suspects. It was successfully challenged, but only on the *vires* basis that it could not be introduced as subordinate legislation: *Ahmed et al.* v. *HM Treasury* [2010] 2 WLR 378; see also Angus Johnston and Eva Nanopoulos, 'The new UK Supreme Court, the separation of powers and anti-terrorism measures' (2010) 69(2) *Cambridge Law Journal* 217. A Bill placing this power on a permanent legislative basis was passed by Parliament in December 2010.

Acts passed between 2000 and 2008.[8] We select those we view as the most significant in human rights terms.

2. The definition of terrorism and key provisions of the Human Rights Act

Before going any further it is necessary to set out certain basic provisions referred to throughout this chapter. The anti-terrorism powers and offences discussed herein all use the basic definition of terrorism set out in s. 1(1) of the Terrorism Act 2000 (TA 2000). This provides that 'terrorism' means the use or threat, 'for the purpose of advancing a political, religious or ideological cause', of action 'designed to influence a government or to intimidate the public or a section of the public', which involves serious violence against any person or serious damage to property, endangers the life of any person, 'creates a serious risk to the health or safety of the public or a section of the public', or is 'designed seriously to interfere with or seriously to disrupt an electronic system'. Under s. 1(4), this extraordinarily wide definition covers such action occurring anywhere in the world; moreover, because it covers damage to property, it could clearly encompass direct action by protest groups, such as causing criminal damage to GM crops or air force bases used for military attacks on other countries. As discussed in other chapters in this volume, such groups were expressly exempted when Australia and South Africa borrowed their definitions of terrorism from the UK.[9]

The rights guaranteed under the ECHR are given domestic effect through the UK's Human Rights Act 1998 (HRA), under which, however, the courts are given no power under to strike down statutory provisions that violate fundamental rights guaranteed under the ECHR. They are limited instead to a duty to *interpret* legislation compatibly with such rights 'so far as is possible',[10] and if they cannot do so, to make a formal declaration of incompatibility between the provision in question and the ECHR right,[11] which has no effect upon the legal validity or enforceability of the incompatible provision.[12] Executive action that

---

[8] David McKeever, 'The Human Rights Act and anti-terrorism in the UK' (2010) *Public Law* 110, 113–22, notes that forty-six new terrorism offences were created between 2000 and 2008; for full details see Clive Walker, *The Anti-Terrorism Legislation* (Oxford University Press, 2nd edn, 2009).

[9] See George Williams, Chapter 21, this volume; Chris Oxtoby and C. H. Powell, Chapter 22, this volume.

[10] Human Rights Act 1998, s. 3(1).   [11] Ibid., s. 4(2).   [12] Ibid., ss. 3(2) and 4(6).

violates Convention rights is unlawful under s. 6(1) of the Act, unless required by primary legislation or plainly authorised under legislation that cannot itself be interpreted compatibly with the Convention rights.[13]

3. Directly pre-emptive measures: control orders

The directly pre-emptive aspects of the UK's counter-terrorism law consisted at first of a form of executive detention,[14] which required derogation from the right to liberty guaranteed by art. 5 of the ECHR.[15] Following widespread domestic and international criticism, and after the legislative provisions were declared incompatible with arts. 5 and 14 of the ECHR by the House of Lords in *A and Others*,[16] the UK Government abandoned this scheme, withdrew its derogation from art. 5 and introduced 'Control Orders' under the Prevention of Terrorism Act 2005 (POTA). These apply to British and non-British suspects alike, but again do not require proof of criminal activity and hence operate outside the ordinary criminal courts. Two types of orders are provided for in POTA. *Derogating* orders – which would allow full house arrest and so would require derogation from art. 5 of the ECHR – have been placed on the statute books but have not yet been authorised for use by Parliament. Non-derogating orders are those judged by the Home Secretary *not* to be incompatible with the suspect's rights under art. 5. They are imposed by the Home Secretary and subject to judicial review by a court,[17] but under s. 2(1) of POTA the standard of proof required is low: it relies on asking only whether there are reasonable grounds for suspecting that an individual is or has been involved in 'terrorism-related activity'; additionally, the Secretary of State must consider each obligation imposed to be necessary for the purpose of protecting the public from a risk of terrorism. *Any* obligations that the Secretary of State considers necessary for the purpose of preventing or restricting

---

[13] Ibid., s. 6 (2).   [14] Under Anti-terrorism, Crime and Security Act 2001, pt. IV.

[15] Article 5(1) provides that: 'Everyone has the right to liberty and security of person. No one shall be deprived of his liberty save in the following cases and in accordance with a procedure prescribed by law' and then provides for a number of specific exceptions in paras. (a)–(f). Article 5(3) provides for the right to be brought 'promptly' before a judicial authority upon arrest and to trial within a reasonable time; art. 5(4) provides for habeas corpus.

[16] [2005] 2 AC 68 (the *Belmarsh* case).

[17] Under ss. 3(10) and (11), the Court, at the full hearing on the order, must decide whether the Secretary of State's decision is 'flawed', applying judicial review principles, which include compliance with Convention rights.

involvement in terrorist activity may be imposed,[18] except obligations that would breach art. 5 (or art. 3, the anti-torture guarantee).[19] In what follows we analyse briefly the judicial response to this scheme.[20]

A.　Imposing article 5 compliance in the courts?

When the control orders were introduced they initially included: an eighteen-hour curfew (house detention); electronic tagging; house searches at any time; forced relocation; stringent geographical restriction; bans on visits by non-approved persons and prohibitions on all electronic communication. Evidence provided by solicitors who represent controlled persons to Parliament's Joint Committee on Human Rights (JCHR) was to the effect that control orders 'amount to virtual house arrest … [T]he homes of controlled persons [are] being turned into "domestic prisons"'.[21] The obligations imposed could only be viewed as avoiding the creation of a 'deprivation of liberty' by relying implicitly on a very narrow interpretation of that concept.[22] Our central argument is that the executive has made use of the discretion accorded under the core provisions of POTA in effect to redefine and minimise the ambit of art. 5, and that the domestic courts have resisted this tendency to an extent – but have been partly drawn into acceptance of it.

The House of Lords considered the question of when a range of restrictions on liberty under a control order will amount to an art. 5 'deprivation of liberty' in three cases. In JJ[23] the appellants were subjected to house detention for eighteen hours. Visitors had to provide identifying details to the Home Office. Their residences were subject to spot searches at any time and they were restricted to confined urban areas. The Secretary of State argued that, within the current security climate, the concept of deprivation of liberty in art. 5 should be interpreted with

---

[18]　Sub-sections 1(3) and (4) provide a non-exhaustive list of conditions.

[19]　Article 3 provides that: 'No one shall be subjected to torture or to inhuman or degrading treatment or punishment.' No exceptions are provided.

[20]　We are able to provide here only an outline sketch of the complex case law. For a full account, on which sections A and B are partly based, see Helen Fenwick and Gavin Phillipson, 'Covert derogations and judicial deference: redefining liberty and due process rights in counte-terrorism and beyond' (2011) 56(4) *McGill Law Journal*, 865.

[21]　Keith Ewing and Joo-Cheong Tham, 'The continuing futility of the Human Rights Act' (2008) *Public Law* 668, 675.

[22]　It was apparent that none of the exceptions in art. 5 could apply to the non-derogating control orders scheme: see above, note 15.

[23]　*Secretary of State for the Home Department* v. *JJ* [2007] UKHL 45; [2007] 3 WLR 642.

especial narrowness.[24] The majority in the Lords rejected this stance, relying on the leading Strasbourg case, *Guzzardi* v. *Italy*,[25] in which the Court found that, outside the paradigm instances of physical detention such as imprisonment, the difference between deprivation of and restriction on liberty was one of degree, not of substance; that account must be taken of a whole range of criteria such as the type, duration, effects and manner of implementation of the measure in question; and that the result depended on an assessment of the cumulative impact of the restrictions on the person in the context of the life he or she might otherwise have been living. Applying these criteria, the majority found a breach of art. 5; Lord Brown, however, thought that a sixteen-hour curfew would have been acceptable.[26] The minority found no deprivation of liberty: Lord Hoffmann (with whom Lord Carswell agreed) argued that the concept should be seen as referring to 'literal physical restraint', as in prison,[27] in order to avoid imposing 'too great a restriction on the powers of the state to deal with serious terrorist threats to the lives of its citizens'.[28] The minority therefore acceded to the executive view that the national security context should influence the ambit of art. 5. The Lords by a 3:2 majority agreed that the order should be quashed.

Two further cases followed: *E*,[29] which concerned a less onerous set of restrictions and curfews of twelve hours, and *MB and AF*,[30] which concerned a fourteen-hour curfew plus electronic tagging, police searches of the premises, strict restrictions on visitors and restriction to an area of about nine square miles. In both cases, the House of Lords unanimously found that there was no breach of art. 5. The finding in particular in *MB and AF*, coupled with the rejection of an eighteen-hour curfew in *JJ*, appeared to imply that the Lords gave some – albeit, reluctant and qualified – support to the finding of Lord Brown in *JJ* that sixteen hours may be the upper limit. The three decisions were interpreted by the government in various public statements to mean that the House of Lords had supported the control orders scheme and that the scheme was still relatively intact, but that orders would have to impose curfews of sixteen hours or

---

[24] See JUSTICE, *Written Submission on behalf of Justice* (intervening in *MB* and *AF* before the House of Lords), available at www.justice.org.uk, A22.

[25] [1980] 3 EHRR 333, especially [92]–[93].

[26] *JJ* [2007] 3 WLR 642, [105]. He considered that twelve- or fourteen-hour curfews were consistent with physical liberty.

[27] Ibid., [36] (Lord Hoffmann).   [28] Ibid., [44].

[29] [2007] UKHL 47, [2007] 3 WLR 720.

[30] *Secretary of State for the Home Department* v. *MB and AF* [2007] UKHL 46; [2007] 3 WLR 681.

less.[31] Four or more control orders were indeed modified so that their curfew periods were *raised* to that point from twelve hours.[32]

Since sixteen hours house detention was on the cusp of acceptability according to Lord Brown in *JJ*, it might have been expected that where the controlee suffered the added factor of forced relocation, away from all his family and friends in a form of internal exile,[33] this would have tipped the situation into deprivation of liberty, particularly given the appalling impact of such exile on the controlees. However, when the Court of Appeal had to consider such a control order in *AP* v. *Secretary of State for the Home Department*,[34] it refused to find a violation of art. 5, arguing first that the isolation was mitigated as the controlee's family could visit occasionally; and second, that the issue of interference with family life was an art. 8 issue only.[35] However, the Supreme Court in 2010 overruled this decision and quashed the control order.[36] Lord Brown, with whom the other Justices agreed, found that control orders with a curfew of sixteen hours or less would only be struck down under art. 5 where the other conditions imposed were 'unusually destructive of the life the controlee might otherwise have been living'.[37] However, he went on to find that the forced relocation of AP had led to his social isolation, due to the particular difficulties his family had in visiting him and the consequent profound adverse impact of such isolation on him. This narrowly focused decision of the Supreme Court thus gave support to a number of the core aspects of the control order scheme, but did embrace a more holistic approach towards the adverse impacts of control orders, in particular taking account of their destructive effect upon family life and friendship.

So the net result appears to be that art. 5 has been interpreted in domestic law to mean that sixteen, but not eighteen, hours house detention can be imposed and may well not breach art. 5, even when combined with other restrictions on liberty and movement, so long as such restrictions do not have the stringent effect on the controlee described in *AP*. The combined effect of these decisions is, we argue, to redefine and minimise

---

[31] See Government Reply to Joint Committee on Human Rights, *Tenth Report of Session 2007–8*, HL paper 57, HC 356, Cm 7368, p. 4.

[32] See JCHR, *Tenth Report of 2007–8*.

[33] Creating some parallels with the *Guzzardi* situation (note 25 above), in which the applicant was exiled on a small island for sixteen months.

[34] [2009] EWCA Civ 731.

[35] Article 8 provides for respect for private and family life, subject to lawful and proportionate restrictions, where there is a pressing social need to safeguard one or more of a broad range of specified social interests including national security and public safety.

[36] *Secretary of State for the Home Dept* v. *AP* [2010] UKSC 24.   [37] Ibid., [4].

the ambit of art. 5, since the obligations imposed could only be viewed as avoiding the creation of a 'deprivation of liberty' by relying implicitly on a narrow interpretation of that concept.[38] In particular, too much emphasis has been placed on the idea of restriction of physical liberty analogous to arrest; there has also been insufficient focus on the long *duration* of the interference with liberty in many control order cases (some orders have been imposed for three or four years, with detention for over three years in Belmarsh prison prior to that).[39] In conclusion, the non-derogating orders scheme as originally envisaged by the executive relied on an obviously attenuated version of art. 5 that the judges did not accept; however, we argue that the judges *have* nevertheless been drawn into accepting an overly restrained concept of deprivation of liberty.

B.   Due process and article 6

We now turn to consider the second key human rights issue raised by the control order scheme, namely due process and the use of secret, or 'closed' evidence and 'special advocates' to deal with it. We address this issue in the context of control orders in the UK but it has far wider significance than this. First of all, it is but one example of a general problem: how to use information in criminal or quasi-criminal proceedings that the government considers sensitive. This issue arises in a huge number of areas concerned with anti-terrorism, including inquiries, deportation decisions and bail proceedings,[40] to name only a few. Second, the use of special advocates as a means of dealing with the disclosure of secret evidence is used in other countries.[41] It originated in Canada, and is again being used for the new Canadian procedure for challenges to deportation and detention decisions[42] following the suspended strike-down by the Supreme Court of the old procedure in *Charkaoui*.[43] It has also been used in New Zealand.[44] The significance of this issue therefore extends well

---

[38] The interpretation of this concept at Strasbourg has been analysed elsewhere: see note 20 above.

[39] See JCHR, *Fifth Report of Session 2008–9*, HL Paper 37, HC282, p.10 [31].

[40] See *R (on the application of Cart)* v. *Upper Tribunal* [2009] EWHC 3052 (QB), finding the use of closed evidence in bail proceedings in relation to a deportee to breach art. 5(4).

[41] See generally, John Ip, 'The rise and spread of the special advocate' (2008) *Public Law* 717.

[42] An Act to amend the Immigration and Refugee Protection Act (certificate and special advocate) and to make a consequential amendment to another act, SC 2008, c.3.

[43] *Charkaoui* v. *Canada (Citizenship and Immigration)* [2007] 1 SCR 350, [64].

[44] JUSTICE, *Secret Evidence* (2009), [365], [366]; Ip, 'The rise and spread of the special advocate', 728–31.

beyond the UK – as discussed in more detail by McGarrity and Santow in their chapter in this volume. Finally, as in so many other areas of criminal procedure, what was trailled as an exceptional measure to deal with specific situations raising acute national security concerns has spread very quickly to no less than twenty-two different types of legal proceedings in the UK,[45] including Parole Board Hearings, asset-freezing cases, and some employment and immigration hearings. This phenomenon of creep and contamination – the undermining of ordinary criminal justice standards by special provisions spreading outwards from the anti-terrorism context – is now well known in the United Kingdom and abroad.[46]

The use of such special procedures in control order cases was challenged under art. 6(1), which provides for 'a fair and public hearing … by an independent and impartial tribunal established by law'.[47] Article 6 contains no stated exceptions to the basic right to a fair trial;[48] however, Strasbourg, compromising somewhat with the bare text of the article, has found that limited departures from some of the component aspects of a fair hearing – such as full disclosure of evidence and equality of arms[49] – may be permissible, provided that these are *strictly necessary* to protect other vital interests, such as the safety of witnesses or national security,[50] and that the proceedings overall are fair. The due process problems raised under the control orders scheme are four-fold. First the statutory rules themselves provide that the court *must not* allow open disclosure of material (even redacted summaries) that it considers would be contrary to the public interest.[51] The rules themselves thus provide for no irreducible minimum of disclosure of the incriminating material to the suspect to allow him directly to challenge it. This problem is exacerbated by the second factor, which is that, under the scheme as originally practised, the detail of the grounds for suspicion were normally contained in 'closed material' that was not disclosed to the suspect. In many cases, including those of *AF* and *MB*, as one judge put it: 'The basis for the Security

---

[45] *Hansard*, HC, vol. 506, col. 739, 1 March 2010 (Andrew Dismore).
[46] See McCulloch and Pickering, 'Counter-terrorism', pp. 13–17.
[47] Paragraph 2 provides for specific minimum rights in criminal proceedings (found not to be applicable to control order hearings).
[48] It allows the public to be excluded from trials in certain circumstances.
[49] For a concise account, see *Kress* v. *France* no. 39594/98, 7 June 2001, [72].
[50] *Rowe* v. *United Kingdom* (2000) 30 EHRR 1, [61]; *Botmeh and Alami* v. *United Kingdom*, no. 15187/03, (2007) at [37]; *Van Mechelen* v. *The Netherlands* (1997) 25 EHRR 647, [58].
[51] Prevention of Terrorism Act 2005, sch. 1, cl. 4(3)(d)–(f) and Civil Procedure Rules 76.2(2) and 76.29(8).

Service's [suspicion of terrorism-related activity] is wholly contained within the closed material ... The open case before him is no more than a bare assertion.'[52] In the same case, Lord Bingham agreed that in such cases the suspect 'was confronted by a bare, unsubstantiated assertion, which he could do no more than deny'.[53]

Third, in order to adduce some level of protection for the suspect, the closed case may be challenged but only by special security-cleared counsel (termed 'special advocates').[54] Their role is to argue for greater disclosure to the suspect and to seek to challenge the evidence that remains closed, searching for inconsistencies and weaknesses in the case for suspicion made out by the evidence. However, in both instances, their abilities are severely limited,[55] since they cannot take instructions from the suspect on the closed material or indeed communicate about it with the suspect in any way.[56] The combination of the second and third features together raised a very clear risk that the scheme would fall foul of the principle declared at Strasbourg that where material is relied on in coming to a decision which the person at risk of an adverse ruling has had no adequate opportunity to challenge or rebut, the proceedings will be unfair.[57]

Fourth, and equally important, the notion of 'public interest' relied on in POTA as grounds for refusing disclosure to the suspect goes far beyond guarding against actual danger to national security: to avoid disclosure it must merely be shown that disclosure is likely to harm the public interest; this is defined extremely broadly to include damage to the international relations of the UK, the detection or prevention of crime, or 'in any other circumstances where disclosure is likely to harm the public interest'.[58] Thus, the rules do not even *purport* to confine infringements of due process rights only to circumstances in which national security so requires.[59] The scheme on its face therefore appears over-broad and

---

[52] *Re MB*, [2006] EWHC 1000 (Admin), [67] (Sullivan J).

[53] [2007] UKHL 46; [2008] 1 AC 440, [41].

[54] Civil Procedure Rules 76.23, 76.24.

[55] JCHR, *9th Report of 2009–10*, HL Paper 64, HC 395, [60]–[65]; Constitutional Affairs Select Committee, *Ev 38: Evidence submitted by a number of special advocates* (7 February 2005), [9].

[56] CPR 76.25, 76.28(2).

[57] See, e.g., *Edwards and Lewis v. UK* (2005) 40 EHRR 593; *Doorson v. the Netherlands* (1996) 22 EHRR 330.

[58] Civil Procedure Rules, 76.1(4).

[59] For the corresponding provisions applying to Australian control order procedures and other judicial proceedings, see George Williams, Chapter 21, this volume.

disproportionate as tested against the Strasbourg case law, which, as indicated, allows departures from full disclosure of evidence *only where this is strictly necessary*.[60]

Nevertheless, in *MB*[61] the Court of Appeal held that the special advocate procedure as it stood afforded sufficient safeguards for a controlee to satisfy art. 6(1). In *MB* and *AF*, by four to one, the House of Lords overturned the Court of Appeal's judgment on this point.[62] It read into the rules a proviso that the procedures overall must be such as to ensure a fair trial under art. 6. But this apparently straightforward outcome masked the highly significant difference and divergence within the judgments: while Lord Bingham considered the system fundamentally unfair and would clearly have liked to declare it incompatible with art. 6,[63] Lord Hoffmann in dissent fully accepted the government position, turning art. 6 on its head by assuming that the risk of damage to the public interest should automatically override the right to due process.[64] Baroness Hale, Lord Brown and Lord Carswell occupied an uneasy middle ground, holding that procedural fairness was fact-specific and did not always depend on minimum disclosure, while more of what was being withheld at present could and should be disclosed and the special advocates could do more to challenge whatever *was* disclosed. But these judgments also were heavily weighted with distorting deference, in particular from Lord Carswell, who appeared to lay the burden on the suspect to explain why his right should prevail over the public interest, rather than the other way around.[65] Most dangerously, perhaps, Lord Brown indicated that there may be cases in which disclosure would not in any event have made any difference, since simply by seeing the evidence the court could find that it was so compelling that the suspect would not have been able to rebut it, whatever he might have said.[66]

The lower courts could not then agree on what *MB* had decided; in particular, as Bates points out,[67] judges found it hard to see whether the Lords had or had not concluded that there was an irreducible minimum of disclosure that needed to be given to ensure the fairness of

---

[60] See above note 50.
[61] [2007] QB 415.
[62] *Secretary of State for the Home Department* v. *MB and AF* [2007] UKHL 46; [2007] 3 WLR 681.
[63] Ibid., [34]–[35].   [64] Ibid., [50]–[54], especially [54].
[65] Ibid., [85].   [66] Ibid., [90].
[67] Ed Bates, 'Anti-terrorism control orders: liberty and security still in the balance' (2009) 29 *Legal Studies* 99, 114.

proceedings. A divided Court of Appeal[68] then concluded that it had not, relying on the 'makes no difference' exception earlier put forward by Lord Brown, which was heavily criticised by Lord Justice Sedley in dissent as 'dangerous and wrong'.[69] However, before the appeal came back to the House of Lords, Strasbourg intervened in its seminal decision in *A v. UK*[70] on the 2001 system of detention without trial. Its findings as to the fairness of the procedure under the 2001 Act were plainly of direct relevance to the procedure in control order cases, since the two were substantially identical. Unlike the House of Lords, the Grand Chamber was clear and unanimous. If the case was based mainly on the open evidence, or where it was not, if the allegations in the open material were sufficiently specific, the proceedings could be fair, since, in either case, the suspect would be reasonably able to challenge the case against him.[71] But where the open material consisted purely of general assertions, and the decision to uphold detention was based solely or to a decisive degree on closed material, the proceedings *could not be fair*. In such instances, the role of the special advocates, unable to take instructions on the secret evidence, was rendered effectively nugatory and could not render the system ECHR-compliant.[72]

This judgment was then applied to the control order procedure by the House of Lords, when it gave its unanimous judgment on the appeal from *AF*.[73] Their Lordships accepted that it was now clear that art. 6 required that the suspect have knowledge of the essence of the case against him, so as to be able to give effective instructions to the special advocates and that this was so 'however cogent the case based on the closed materials may be'.[74] Article 6 thus provided for an irreducible minimum disclosure of the case against the suspect and the procedural rules governing control orders had to be read and given effect under s. 3(1) of the HRA in a way that provided for this. However, the fact that it took an international court to show the UK's highest court the way is an eloquent and sobering illustration of the dangers of excessive judicial deference. It is now apparent that the combined effect of the above judgments, together with the growing perception that control orders have proved unsatisfactory from a security point of view, has led to the demise of the control orders regime, at least as conceived of under the 2005 Act, a matter we address in the conclusion to this chapter.

---

[68] *Secretary of State for the Home Department* v. *AF and Others* [2008] EWCA Civ 1148.
[69] Ibid., [113].   [70] (2009) 49 EHRR.   [71] Ibid., [120].   [72] Ibid.
[73] *Secretary of State for the Home Department* v. *AF (No 3)* [2009] 3 WLR 74.
[74] Ibid., [59] (Lord Phillips).

4.   Special criminal justice police powers

A.   Stop and search

In the area of stop and search, the UK courts also failed to provide any kind of check to the hugely broad executive discretion granted by Parliament; it was again left to Strasbourg to rescue the rule of law. There are clear parallels between these powers and the control order scheme: both are pre-emptive measures; in both cases, Parliament was persuaded to grant very wide powers that assume an ungenerous or narrow conception of art. 5; and in both cases, the executive then proceeded to use the discretionary powers granted to it in an extraordinarily draconian way that was eventually found to violate fundamental rights under the ECHR.

Special powers of stop and search without the need for reasonable suspicion for use in the anti-terrorism context arise under ss. 44–7 of the TA 2000. Despite there being clearly room for doubt, it was in effect assumed when the powers were presented to Parliament that stop and search did not fall within the ambit of art. 5(1), or that if it did, one of the stated exceptions would apply. The same assumption was made in relation to art. 8; in the result, the Minister introducing the TA made a statutory statement of its compatibility with the ECHR under s. 19 of the HRA. Such promises of compatibility were partly based on the fact that the powers require special authorisation: these must be made by a very senior police officer, confirmed by the Secretary of State[75] and last for a maximum of twenty-eight days, although that period can be continually renewed.[76] The provisions thus appeared to envisage that the special powers would be used 'sparingly, where other police powers were inadequate',[77] only for a temporary period and in geographically limited areas where there were specific reasons to fear terrorist attacks. However, from early 2001 onwards, the power to stop and search without reasonable suspicion was imposed continuously throughout the whole of Greater London[78] under a succession of rolling authorisations and used extensively throughout

---

[75] This confirmation must be made within forty-eight hours of an authorisation being made, or it will cease to have effect.

[76] Terrorism Act 2000, s. 46(7).

[77] As argued by the applicants in *Gillan*, note 87 below, 311.

[78] See, e.g., Lord Carlile of Berriew, *Report on the Operation in 2005 of the Terrorism Act 2000* (May 2006), p. 27. During 2009 it was withdrawn to smaller selected areas in central London – this appeared to be in the hope of avoiding an adverse ruling in the case of *Gillan* (below) which was about to be heard at Strasbourg.

the rest of the country. Once an authorisation is in place, s. 44 allows for stop and search of persons[79] or vehicles without reasonable suspicion in the designated area; the term used allowing for its authorisation is that it would be 'expedient' to prevent acts of terrorism.[80] The word 'expedient' is obviously carefully chosen to maximise the discretion of the officer making the authorisation: it is not necessary to demonstrate that terrorist acts are likely to occur or even that they are more likely to occur in the area covered by the authorisation than in other areas. Moreover, it clearly connotes a much less rigorous requirement than necessity, once again demonstrating the way in which executive discretion to use counter-terror powers is given the broadest possible scope. Section 45(1)(a) provides that the powers under s. 44 'may be exercised only for the purpose of searching for articles of a kind which could be used in connection with terrorism', but in order to ensure that this is not interpreted as a limiting requirement, s. 45(1)(b) provides that the powers 'may be exercised whether or not the constable has grounds for suspecting the presence of articles of that kind'. Further, it is an imprisonable offence in itself to refuse to comply with the search.[81]

Once an authorisation is in place, police officers are given an almost limitless discretion as to who to search within the authorised area, since there is no need to show reasonable suspicion. There is evidence that s. 44 has been used in a racially and religiously discriminatory fashion, in particular against black people and Asians,[82] meaning that informal profiling has been operated by police officers on the ground. Indeed, the Home Office acknowledged in 2004 that it was inevitable that the Muslim community would be disproportionately targeted for such searches.[83] Since the statutory provisions do not specify what a police officer must have in

---

[79] The search only authorises a constable to require a person to remove headgear, footwear, outer coat, jacket or gloves (Code A, para. 4A).

[80] Under s. 44(3), such an authorisation 'may be given only if the person giving it considers it expedient for the prevention of acts of terrorism'.

[81] Terrorism Act 2000, s. 47.

[82] 'Statistics on Race and the Criminal Justice System 2007/8', published in April 2009, recorded an increase of 215 per cent in the use of the power (Table 4.6). Searches increased for all ethnic groups but the biggest rise was for black people (322 per cent), and the Asian group (277 per cent), compared to white people (185 per cent). See also the report of the Equality and Human Rights Commission, available at www.equalityhumanrights.com/uploaded_files/raceinbritain/ehrc_stop_and_search_report.pdf. For an analysis of the evidence around the use of stop and search, its efficacy and deleterious effects, see B. Bowling and C. Phillips, 'Disproportionate and discriminatory: reviewing the evidence on police stop and search' (2007) 70(6) *Modern Law Review* 936.

[83] Home Affairs Select Committee, *Sixth Report of Session 2004–5*, HC165-I, 46.

mind before exercising the power, it is clearly non-transparent and not based on objectively justifiable criteria, thus creating a clear lack of police accountability. It has also been used to harass protesters, and it was criticised in 2009 by the JCHR,[84] which found that a significant number of witnesses had expressed serious concerns about the use of s. 44 in relation to protestors,[85] and suggested that the breadth of the powers contravened OSCE/ODIHR Guidelines.[86]

In one of the most disappointing UK judgments of the post-9/11 era, *R (on the application of Gillan) v. Commissioner of Metropolitan Police*,[87] the House of Lords found that neither the powers themselves, nor their blanket use, nor the particular actions complained of, contravened arts. 5, 8 or 10[88] of the ECHR or common law standards. The search in question had taken place close to a protest against an arms fair; one of those searched was a protester, the other a journalist reporting on the protest. Both could be stopped and searched under the s. 44 power, since an authorisation under that provision was in force, covering the area where the protest was taking place (since it was in London's Docklands area and the whole of London was covered). There was nothing in relation to those searched to suggest any connection with terrorism. Lord Bingham, giving the leading judgment, appeared to be minded to carry out a minimalist audit of UK law against Convention law, imposing a restrained ambit on art. 5. His Lordship had to consider whether a stop and search created a deprivation of liberty, something on which there has been no clear finding by Strasbourg. As in the control order cases, Lord Bingham relied on the general principles expounded in *Guzzardi* v. *Italy*[89] and found that the stop and search procedure did have some features of a deprivation of liberty.

---

[84] JCHR, *Demonstrating Respect for Rights? A Human Rights Approach to Policing Protest* (March 2009), [86]–[87].

[85] The National Union of Journalists complained that the police had relied on the Terrorism Act 2000 to prevent journalists from leaving demonstrations: ibid., [87].

[86] These were produced by the Organisation for Security and Co-operation in Europe, and the Office for Democratic Institutions and Human Rights. The Guidelines provide: 'domestic legislation designed to counter terrorism or "extremism" should narrowly define these terms so as not to include forms of civil disobedience and protest; the pursuit of certain political, religious, or ideological ends; or attempts to exert influence on other sections of society, the government, or international opinion': see www.osce.org/odihr/item_11_23835.html.

[87] [2006] UKHL 12; [2006] 2 AC 307 (*Gillan*).

[88] Article 10 provides that: 'Everyone has the right to freedom of expression'. The second paragraph contains broadly the same exceptions as for art. 8: see note 35 above.

[89] (1980) 3 EHRR 333. See above, text to note 25. He also relied on *HL* v. *United Kingdom* (2004) 40 EHRR 761, [89].

However, he noted that the procedure would 'ordinarily be relatively brief' and the person stopped 'would not be arrested, handcuffed, confined or removed to any different place'. He considered that 'in the absence of special circumstances', the person should not be regarded as being detained in the sense of being confined or detained, but in the sense of being 'kept from proceeding or kept waiting', and therefore the process did not create a deprivation of liberty.[90] At one level, his Lordship was simply relying on a gap in the Strasbourg jurisprudence. But it has also been pointed out that to compare being compulsorily detained by the police on the street to an anodyne short delay, like waiting to cross the road at a pedestrian crossing, is scarcely convincing.[91] Lord Bingham went on to find that even if there had been a deprivation of liberty, it would have been justified as within art. 5(1)(b) – detention 'to secure the fulfilment of any obligation prescribed by law'.[92] This was because, as he found, the statutory regime and the authorisation itself were 'prescribed by law' and 'the public are … subject to a clear obligation' not to obstruct constables carrying out such lawful searches.[93]

In considering the interference with the art. 8 guarantee of respect for private life, Lord Bingham also took a minimalist stance. Finding it 'clear Convention jurisprudence that intrusions must reach a certain level of seriousness to engage the operation of the Convention', he 'incline[d] to the view that an ordinary superficial search of the person … can scarcely be said to reach that level'.[94] This, however, is a very difficult proposition to sustain: indeed, given that Strasbourg has found that the taking of a photograph of a person in an everyday situation in the street engages Article 8,[95] it would seem almost startling to contend that a stop and search – on any sensible view a more intrusive interference with the person than merely being photographed on the street – does not. Again, his Lordship went on to find that even if art. 8(1) were to be engaged, art. 8(2) would be readily satisfied. He dealt with this issue briefly and dismissively, finding that there would be a legitimate aim under para. 2 and going on:

> The search must still be necessary in a democratic society, and so proportionate. But if the exercise of the power is duly authorised and confirmed, and if the power is exercised for the only purpose for which it may

---

[90] *Gillan* [2006] 2 AC 307, 343.
[91] Case Comment: [2006] *Criminal Law Review* 751, 755.
[92] Article 5(1)(b): 'arrest or detention for non-compliance with the lawful order of a court or in order to secure the fulfilment of any obligation prescribed by law'.
[93] *Gillan* [2006] 2 AC 307, 344.   [94] Ibid.
[95] *Von Hannover* v. *Germany* (2004) 40 EHRR 1.

permissibly be exercised (i.e. to search for articles of a kind which could be used in connection with terrorism: section 45(1)(a)), it would in my opinion be impossible to regard a proper exercise of the power, in accordance with Code A [the Code of Practice for searches], as other than proportionate when seeking to counter the great danger of terrorism.[96]

Clearly, there is no real proportionality review here: in particular, no inquiry at all is made into the *effectiveness* of the power, something that has been doubted by many expert observers.[97] But, aside from the manifest superficiality of the reasoning, there are two further serious problems here. First, the statutory provisions themselves mean that one of the factors said in this passage to limit the power – that the search should have the purpose of finding articles that could be used in connection with terrorism – is effectively unenforceable, since it is based entirely on trusting in the good faith of the police: s 45(1)(b) provides that the powers 'may be exercised whether or not the constable has grounds for suspecting the presence of articles of that kind'. Thus a key plank in Lord Bingham's desultory consideration of proportionality proves upon examination to be illusory. Second, Lord Bingham's argument at this point appears entirely inconsistent with a finding made earlier in his judgment in relation to the standard required to allow authorisations to be made:

> The claimants submitted that section 44(3) should be interpreted as permitting an authorisation to be made only if the decision-maker has reasonable grounds for considering that the powers are necessary and suitable, in all the circumstances, for the prevention of terrorism. I would … reject this argument.[98]

Given that Lord Bingham finds here that the statute did *not* require the use of the powers to be proportionate, only 'expedient', and that it had been admitted that the blanket authorisation in London was done on a 'precautionary' basis only, the inevitable conclusion would appear to be that stops and searches carried out under such blanket authorisations *could not* constitute a proportionate restriction under Article 8(2).[99]

Articles 10 and 11[100] also had to be considered, because the stop and search affected persons reporting on or going to a protest at an arms fair.

---

[96] *Gillan* [2006] 2 AC 307, 344.
[97] See, e.g., the views of Lord Carlile, *Report on the Operation in 2006 of the Terrorism Act 2000* (2007), [114].
[98] *Gillan* [2006] 2 AC 307, [13]–[14].
[99] As Strasbourg subsequently found: below notes 115–17 and accompanying text.
[100] The right to freedom of assembly and association, subject to similar restrictions as art. 10: see above note 88.

However, these two important rights received even more cursory treatment, rating only a single short paragraph. In this instance, Lord Bingham doubted so strongly whether the rights were even engaged that assessment of the proportionality of the restrictions on them vanished from the analysis completely: the only finding his Lordship made was that he '*would expect* the restriction to fall within the heads of justification provided in articles 10(2) and 11(2)'.[101]

There also remained the issue of the rule of law, given the requirement in the Convention that interferences with the rights must be 'prescribed by law' of sufficient quality. Lord Bingham said that this requirement 'addresses supremely important features of the rule of law',[102] finding it to connote that:

> the law must be accessible [and] foreseeable ... giving an adequate indication of the circumstances in which a power may be exercised ... [T]he scope of any discretion conferred on the executive ... must be defined with such precision, appropriate to the subject matter, as to make clear the conditions in which a power may be exercised; and ... there must be legal safeguards against abuse.[103]

In response to this, his Lordship found that the combination of the statutory provisions and Code A on stop and search set out the law and procedures to be followed in detail. He addressed the potential for random or arbitrary stop and searches only very briefly, saying:

> In exercising the power the constable is not free to act arbitrarily, and will be open to civil suit if he does. It is true that he need have no suspicion before stopping and searching a member of the public. This cannot, realistically, be interpreted as a warrant to stop and search people who are obviously not terrorist suspects, which would be futile and time-wasting. It is to ensure that a constable is not deterred from stopping and searching a person whom he does suspect as a potential terrorist by the fear that he could not show reasonable grounds for his suspicion. It is not suggested that the constables in these cases exercised their powers in a discriminatory manner (an impossible contention on the facts), and I prefer to say nothing on the subject of discrimination.[104]

The notion expressed here, that a requirement of reasonable suspicion might deter a constable from searching someone whom he suspects of being a terrorist, is particularly revealing. Such deterrence might normally be thought of as a *virtuous* property of law: the requirement to

---

[101] *Gillan* [2006] 2 AC 307, 344–5 (emphasis added).   [102] Ibid., 346.
[103] Ibid., 345.   [104] Ibid., 346–7.

show *reasonable* suspicion acts as a check upon an individual officer's suspicion – which might be based on flimsy, instinctive or prejudiced grounds – thus ensuring that invasions of liberty only occur at the point at which objectively justifiable grounds for such intervention arise. Such a constraint, in other words, is normally perceived as a desirable attribute of the rule of law – a bulwark against individual prejudice and arbitrariness in the exercise of state power, and thus an assurance that the rule of law, not men, is enforced in such situations. Lord Bingham, indeed, has written eloquently of these virtues.[105] But in this context, his Lordship *assumed* that such a constraint would be undesirable. One can doubtless make an argument that, for example, where there is a very strong risk, or immediate threat of an attack that would cause large-scale fatalities, the ability of police officers to search on instinct would be a necessary price to pay for preventing loss of life. But to accept so casually that this discarding of core rule of law norms was justified throughout the whole of Greater London for an indefinite period, without any argument at all, cannot be seen as showing anything but a lack of due care for a basic principle that the judiciary, above all, are committed to uphold.[106] His Lordship also considered, and rejected, the argument that the practice since 2001 of continuous, rolling extensions to the power throughout the London area was *ultra vires* as a misuse of discretionary powers contrary to the intention of Parliament, despite the fact that it had been admitted by the police that such use was 'precautionary', so that the powers were there 'just in case' they might be needed.[107] What had happened complied with the letter of the statute, or so his Lordship said.[108]

Employment of such a weak standard of review, coming close to ensuring only that the view taken of the need for the restriction was not unreasonable, provided huge scope for the Lords to defer to the judgment of the executive while appearing to subject the power and its use to structured Convention scrutiny. In this sense, arts. 8, 10 and 11 were in effect emptied of part of their content: the interference was so readily found to be justified that the structured proportionality test they require was in effect discarded. Their Lordships might have been expected to ask

---

[105] Lord Bingham of Cornhill, 'The rule of law' (2007) 66(1) *Cambridge Law Journal* 67.
[106] Lord Bingham also found (*Gillan* [2006] 2 AC 307, 339) that the common law principle of 'legality' was satisfied: this is the notion that restrictions of fundamental rights must be authorised by clear provisions in primary legislation (see, e.g., *R v. Secretary of State for the Home Department ex parte Simms* [2000] 2 AC 115, 130–1). The plain wording of the 2000 Act was found to answer to this requirement.
[107] *Gillan* [2006] 2 AC 307, 312.   [108] Ibid., 430–41.

whether s. 44 had led to minimal impairment of the rights in question, consistent with the need to combat terrorism, asking whether the interference went beyond the aim in question, and whether sufficient relevant evidence of its effectiveness had been advanced by the State.[109] But Lord Bingham's approach in *Gillan* demonstrates that proportionality review can readily be rendered an empty exercise. His findings at every stage in the reasoning were in harmony with the familiar tendency of judges to defer heavily to police decision-making on the ground, especially in the anti-terrorism context.[110] While the overt language of deference was not used in this case, an acquiescent stance was taken to the minimalist approach to the ECHR rights adopted in the statutory power itself. It is fair to say that Lord Hope appeared much more troubled by the thought that the powers were open to being used in an arbitrary way, which could include discriminatory use,[111] as was Lord Brown.[112] But both in the end appeared satisfied, on remarkably little evidence, that the law provided sufficient safeguards about both possibilities. Thus both Parliament and the judiciary failed to create a check on the excessive executive discretion created under s. 44, accepting a minimised version of art. 5; both also almost presupposed – and certainly gave no effective scrutiny to – the crucial requirement that interferences with arts. 8, 10 and 11 be necessary and proportionate.

As with the control orders saga, reanimation of the ECHR rights was left to the Strasbourg Court. The stance taken at Strasbourg in the resulting decision in *Gillan and Quinton* v. *UK*[113] could hardly present a stronger contrast to that taken by the House of Lords. The Court did not need to make a definitive finding as to whether stop and search did engage art. 5(1), since it found a violation on other grounds. However, it appeared to view the s. 44 process as closer to the paradigm cases of deprivation of liberty – where the deprivation is total, as in arrest and detention – rather than to the non-paradigm instances, such as *Guzzardi*.

---

[109] These are proportionality tests used by Strasbourg: see, e.g., *Sunday Times* v. *UK* (1979) 2 EHRR 245; cf. the similar test set out by the Canadian Supreme Court in *R* v. *Oakes* [1986] 1 SCR 103, 137, 138.

[110] See further J. Jowell, 'Judicial deference: servility, civility or institutional capacity?' (2004) *Public Law* 592, 600.

[111] *Gillan* [2006] 2 AC 307, 347–52. Neither applicant alleged racial or religious discrimination in this case.

[112] Ibid., 355–62. For criticism of the reasoning of Lords Hope, Brown and Scott on the discrimination point, see D. Moeckli, 'Stop and search under the Terrorism Act 2000' (2007) 70(4) *Modern Law Review* 659, especially 663–9.

[113] Application no. 4158/05, 12 January 2010.

The Court focused on the element of coercion, rather than on the range of criteria from *Guzzardi*:

> [Those searched] were obliged to remain where they were and submit to the search and if they had refused they would have been liable to arrest, detention at a police station and criminal charges. This element of coercion is indicative of a deprivation of liberty within the meaning of Article 5(1).[114]

In the event, however, the Court did not finally have to determine that question in the light of its findings in relation to art. 8: it refused to determine more than it had to in order to resolve the issue before it.

Strasbourg went on to hold that art. 8 had been breached; but what is striking is its reason for doing so: that ss. 44–7 did not satisfy the 'in accordance with the law' test, under which interferences with rights must first of all be shown to be prescribed by existing domestic law of reasonable clarity.[115] That was an unprecedented move in relation to a *modern* British statute – the first time it had happened in the course of the history of the UK's engagement with the ECHR.[116] The Court began by finding that art. 8(1) *was* engaged by the use of s. 44: such searches were a 'clear interference with the right to respect for private life'. The words used indicated that this was not a borderline case, as Lord Bingham had thought. The Court then turned to the question whether the interference was in accordance with the law and necessary in a democratic society under art. 8(2). Upholding the claimants' contention, the Strasbourg judges found that the powers vested in the police under ss. 44–7 could not be regarded as 'in accordance with the law', precisely because of the key controversial element of the power – that it dispensed with the condition of reasonable suspicion: 'The powers of authorisation and confirmation as well as those of stop and search under sections 44 and 45 of the 2000 Act are neither sufficiently circumscribed nor subject to adequate legal safeguards against abuse', the Court found. It pointed, in particular, to the breadth of the discretion conferred on the individual police officer whose decision to stop somebody could be 'based exclusively on the "hunch" or "professional intuition" of the officer concerned'. The Court concluded

---

[114] The Court noted in support the example of *Foka* v. *Turkey*, no. 28940/09, §§ 74–9, 24 June 2008.

[115] *Sunday Times* v. *UK* (1979) 2 EHRR 245.

[116] For the previous occasions, see *Malone* v. *UK* (1985) 7 EHRR 14 (no authorising statute present); *Hashman* v. *Harraup* (2000) EHRR 24 (test in fourteenth century statute insufficiently clear).

that '[t]here is a clear risk of arbitrariness in the grant of such a broad discretion to the police officer'.[117]

As a result of this judgment, it became apparent that s. 44 would have to be significantly modified to connect it much more closely with suspicion of carrying something linked to terrorist activity, thereby curbing the discretion of the officer on the ground. In July 2010 the Home Secretary announced[118] that s. 44 would be modified to provide that stop and search powers could only be used where 'necessary' – not 'expedient' – for the prevention of terrorism. She further decided that the police would no longer be allowed to use s. 44 to stop and search individuals, but only vehicles, a less intrusive use. She announced that, in the meantime, police officers who want to use the Act to stop and search individuals would have to use s. 43,[119] which, unlike s. 44, provides that officers must have a 'reasonable suspicion' that someone is a terrorist. Thus, for the time being, authorisations to stop and search within certain areas under s. 44 will be confined to vehicle searches.

Gillan provides one of the two important instances documented in this chapter in which Strasbourg has upheld higher human rights standards than the domestic judiciary, and insisted upon acceptance of the full content of the rights in question. In each case the failure by the domestic courts to subject the contested powers to rigorous human rights review meant that neither Parliament, which had granted the broad powers, nor the judiciary, which had failed to restrain them, had contributed significantly to the checking of executive discretion to invade fundamental rights.

B.   Lengthy periods of detention without charge – seeking to minimise article 5

We next turn to consider briefly the UK government's persistent and partially successful attempts to extend the period for which terrorist suspects can be held before being charged. The original maximum time limit for which a person could be held, on suspicion of being involved in the commission, preparation or instigation of a terrorist offence, was seven days under the TA 2000; as a safeguard, and to ensure compliance

---

[117] Quotations from [83], [85], [87].
[118] *Hansard*, HC, vol. 513, col. 540, 8 July 2010.
[119] Terrorism Act 2000, s. 43 provides a further stop and search power but subject to reasonable suspicion of terrorism activity in relation to the person searched.

with art. 5(3),[120] extensions after forty-eight hours must be authorised by a magistrate. This compares with a maximum of four days in ordinary criminal law. This was doubled only three years later to a maximum of fourteen days by the Criminal Justice Act 2003; three years later it was doubled again to twenty-eight days by the Terrorism Act 2006 (TA 2006). These increases are striking enough: but the key point is that, by accepting an increase to twenty-eight days in 2006, the government was forced into a major compromise with Parliament: it had wanted an increase to ninety days. The government's pursuit of a ninety-day and, later, a forty-two-day detention without charge period rested in effect on an attempt to impose once again an attenuated version of art. 5 in the domestic sphere. Despite the flexibility with which Strasbourg is prepared to approach art. 5 in this context,[121] it is argued that such long periods of pre-charge detention are compatible with art. 5 only if the ambit of the right is minimised and the exceptions maximised in a manner that is not clearly supported by the Strasbourg jurisprudence. That jurisprudence does not set clear limits on the period of pre-charge detention, as long as judicial authorisation is obtained after four days,[122] but there clearly must be a point at which, even with judicial authorisation, the detention violates art. 5(1) read with art. 5(2) on the basis that the length of detention is disproportionate to the aim pursued.

The lack of a clear time limit may be due to the absence of a common definition of what is meant by 'charge' that is applicable in all contracting state parties to the ECHR. Nevertheless, the unanimous opinion of human rights groups was that the planned extensions were incompatible with art. 5.[123] Clearly, the question of ECHR compatibility was not the only matter at issue, and the Commons debate turned far more on matters of traditional civil liberties, habeas corpus and the rule of law. Nevertheless, compatibility with art. 5 had in fact been claimed by the government via a statement under s. 19 of the HRA, and therefore the executive had clearly espoused a minimalist conception of that article. That conception was given no backing by the JCHR[124] and – in effect – rejected by the House of Commons. In the vote on the ninety-day period in the Terrorism Bill 2006 on 9 November, Tony Blair suffered his first legislative defeat in the

---

[120] See note 15 above.
[121] See JCHR, *Twenty-Fourth Report of Session 05–6*, HL Paper 240, HC 1576, [22].
[122] *Brogan* v. *United Kingdom* (1988) 11 EHRR 117.
[123] See the Law Society's *Parliamentary Briefing HC 2nd Reading* (26 October 2005) and JUSTICE, *Preliminary Briefing* (September 2005), [60].
[124] JCHR, *Twenty-Fourth Report of Session 2005–6*, HL Paper 240, HC 1576.

Commons as Prime Minister. MPs voted against the proposal by 322 votes to 291, with forty-nine Labour MPs rebelling.

The proposal to extend the detention without charge period to forty-two days under Gordon Brown's regime was also condemned by the JCHR[125] and in a report from the Council of Europe.[126] Both bodies considered that the forty-two day period was very likely to be incompatible with art. 5. Nevertheless, the Counter-Terrorism Bill 2008 was introduced into the Commons on the basis that it was compatible with the rights under the ECHR. Again, there was a strong campaign against it: the government just got it through the House of Commons in June but was defeated decisively in the unelected second chamber of Parliament, the House of Lords, in October of that year. Thus, the Brown government succeeded in changing the law so that terrorism suspects could be held in detention without charge for almost a month, in strong contrast to non-terrorist suspects, who can only be held for ninety-six hours, even for the most serious offences. But this is the one example provided in this chapter in which Parliament refused to accept the minimised version of art. 5 upon which post-arrest detention for ninety days (or forty-two days) was inevitably predicated, in the absence of a derogation. As we note in the conclusion, in this area also, the Cameron-led Coalition government has liberalised the law, reducing the period of detention back to fourteen days.

5.   Substantive offences

A.   Proscription-related and information-withholding offences

Even before the controversial and very broad new offences introduced in 2006, the JCHR had found that 'the UK's armoury of anti-terrorism legislation is widely regarded as the most rigorous in Europe'.[127] The fact that such offences do not go as far as those in Australia, considered by George Williams in this volume, is perhaps due in part to the greater growth of a human rights culture in the UK, itself the result of long-standing adherence to the ECHR, the Human Rights Act and in particular the role of the JCHR in scrutinising legislation in draft or when before Parliament. Nevertheless, the sheer breadth of some of the offences, and

---

[125] JCHR. *Twentieth Report of Session 2007–8*, HL 108 HC 554.
[126] 'Proposed 42-day pre-charge detention in the United Kingdom', 30 September 2008. See assembly.coe.int debate on 2 October 2008 (35th Sitting Doc 11725).
[127] JCHR, *Second Report of Session 2001–2*, HC 37, HL 372, [35].

their effectively pre-emptive character, remains striking. What follows is only a brief sketch of a very substantial body of law.[128] Under the TA 2000, the power of proscription[129] for groups 'concerned in terrorism' anywhere in the world and all the proscription-related offences[130] are retained from previous legislation, and their impact is greatly extended. As has been pointed out, such offences 'aim to pre-empt terrorist acts by disrupting the networks that are seen to support or foster terrorist activity'.[131] Further offences also have a pre-emptive nature: these include failing to report to the police information coming to a person's attention in the course of their trade or employment, which might be of material assistance in preventing an act of terrorism or in arresting someone carrying out such an act.[132] Section 38B of the Anti-Terrorism Crime and Security Act 2001 broadened this provision immensely by extending this offence to persons generally, subject to an un-explicated defence of reasonable excuse; family members are not exempted from the duty. A further wide range of people are potentially subject to criminal penalties under s. 58(1) of the TA, the provision relating to the collection of information 'likely to be of use' to terrorists.[133] Section 57(1) is particularly draconian in imposing a reverse burden of proof: it provides that a person is guilty of an offence if he has an article in his possession in circumstances giving rise to a reasonable suspicion that the article is in his possession for a purpose linked to terrorism. Under s. 57(2), the accused can rebut this presumption of guilt by proving that the article was not in his possession for that purpose.[134] These offences are plainly aimed at activity that is very far removed from

---

[128] See note 8 above.
[129] Exercised by the Home Secretary, but subject to Parliamentary approval: s. 3(3) and s. 123.
[130] Including belonging to such an organisation, subject to certain defences (s. 11), soliciting support for it (s. 12(1)) and, under ss. 12(2) and 12(3), arranging, managing or speaking at meetings designed to support or further the activities of it, or wearing badges or uniforms signalling support (s. 13).
[131] McCulloch and Pickering, 'Counter-terrorism' p. 19.
[132] Section 19(5) preserves an exemption in respect of legal advisers' privileged material.
[133] Section 58(1) provides: 'A person commits an offence if (a) he collects or makes a record of information of a kind likely to be useful to a person committing or preparing an act of terrorism, or (b) he possesses a document or record containing information of that kind.' The offence lacks any requirement of *knowledge* regarding the nature of the information or any requirement that the person *intended* to use it in order to further the aims of terrorism, though a defence of 'reasonable excuse' is provided: see *R* v. *K* [2008] QB 82; *R* v. *G* [2010] 1 AC 43.
[134] See also the adverse presumption introduced under s. 57(4). The decision in *R* v. *Malik (Samina Hussain)* [2008] EWCA Crim 1450 narrowed the scope of the possession offence slightly.

actually engaging in terrorist acts. However, as we explore in the next section, two new offences introduced in 2006 went even further.

B.   *Acts preparatory to terrorism and incitement or glorification of terrorism*

Section 5 of the TA 2006 introduced a new offence of 'acts preparatory to terrorism', designed to capture potential terrorists at a very early stage. The offence requires intention, but the *actus reus* is exceptionally broad. Under s. 5(1), '[a] person commits an offence if, with the intention of (a) committing acts of terrorism, or (b) assisting another to commit such acts, he engages in *any conduct* in preparation for giving effect to his intention' (emphasis added). Such preparation can be directed at particular acts or terrorism generally (s. 5(2)) and the maximum penalty is life imprisonment (s. 5(3)). Section 5 is obviously intended to be a catch-all offence, designed to allow intervention in relation to would-be terrorists at a very early stage, before any conduct linked to the actual preparation of a terrorist attack has occurred.[135] Lord Carlile, the government-appointed reviewer of terrorism legislation, supported the introduction of this offence as a means of dealing with at least some of those under suspicion as potential terrorists rather than using control orders.[136] This is clearly laudable in principle, but as the broadest early intervention offence introduced so far in the counter-terrorist scheme, it again relies heavily on executive discretion in deploying it. At the time of writing, there has been no appellate decision challenging the breadth of this offence, suggesting that it has not so far been used in relation to borderline behaviour. This is perhaps because the evidence to be adduced in cases of very early-stage preparation would be highly likely to be intelligence based and thus something that the prosecuting authorities would not be willing to expose in open court.[137] Hence, whether this offence will actually enable those currently subject to control orders to be prosecuted instead seems doubtful: it has not so far.[138]

---

[135] See also the comments made by Whealy J. in *R* v. *Elomar*, discussed by George Williams, Chapter 21, this volume.

[136] Above note 78, [33].

[137] It might also be statute barred: evidence obtained by telephone taps is inadmissible in all UK criminal proceedings under s. 17 of the Regulation of Investigatory Powers Act 2000.

[138] See below, note 161.

The TA 2000 had created new offences of inciting terrorism abroad, under ss. 59 and 60, aimed at incitement of specific and serious acts of violence.[139] But the 2006 Act went much further, by introducing a new offence of *indirect* encouragement of acts of terrorism, which can include the 'glorification' of terrorism. The new offence does not require actual incitement, since it includes the condoning or praising of acts that have already occurred; indeed, it was plainly intended to go well beyond incitement to commit particular offences, which was thought to be covered by existing law.[140] The basic offence, per s. 1(1), applies to a statement 'that is *likely* to be understood by some or all of the members of the public to whom it is published as a direct or indirect encouragement or other inducement to them to the commission, preparation or instigation of acts of terrorism'.[141] The 'public' includes people living anywhere in the world, immensely broadening the scope of the offence. The person making the statement must intend such encouragement or be subjectively reckless to that consequence,[142] but it is not necessary to show that anyone was actually 'encouraged or induced' to commit any relevant offence by the statement (s. 1(5)). Webmasters and media bodies engaging merely in reportage of another's words are also protected by a defence of innocent publication (s 1(6)).[143] Conviction on indictment carries a hefty maximum sentence of seven years.

Against considerable opposition from the House of Lords, the government insisted on including within the offence of indirect encouragement the notion of 'glorification'. Per s. 1(3), liability extends to every statement which:[144]

(a) glorifies the commission or preparation (whether in the past, in the future or generally) of such acts or offences; and
(b) is a statement from which those members of the public could reasonably be expected to infer that what is being glorified is being glorified as conduct that should be emulated by them in existing circumstances.

---

[139] The ordinary law of solicitation to murder had been used against extremist preachers: see, e.g., *R* v. *El-Faisal* [2004] EWCA Crim 456.
[140] See JCHR, *Third Report of Session 2005–6*, HL Paper 75–1, HC 561–1, [21].
[141] There is a like offence of dissemination of terrorist publications under s. 2.
[142] Section 1(2) (and 2(1) in relation to the dissemination offence).
[143] Unless there has been a failure to remove an offending statement after notice has been given to the web controller by a police constable of its violation of the Act (s. 3).
[144] The like definition appears in other relevant parts of the Act.

The last few words of the definition are significant in excluding statements purely in praise of historical events, such as the Easter Rising in Ireland. But the definition remains extraordinarily broad nevertheless: glorification, s. 20 tells us, '*includes* any form of praise or celebration'.[145] While the JCHR thought that there was on balance a case for a 'narrowly defined criminal offence of indirect incitement to terrorist acts',[146] it was deeply concerned about the potential breadth and vagueness of the actual offence introduced,[147] as well as its potential incompatibility with freedom of expression protected under art. 10 of the ECHR.[148] Hence, the JCHR opposed using 'glorification', pointing out that the use of such a term opened up 'enormous uncertainty'.[149] It thought there was a risk that those engaged in legitimate political debate about armed action by resistance groups, for example in Palestine,[150] or against oppressive regimes around the world, could be caught by the offence.

This aspect of the offence is perhaps its most extraordinary one. Since it uses the definition of 'terrorism' in the TA 2000, the government conceded in Parliament that, 'the effect of the [offence] is to criminalise expressions of support for the use of violence [including violence against property] as a means of political change anywhere in the world'. However, the government argued that, 'there was nowhere in the world where resort to violence, including violence against property, could be justified as a means of bringing about change'.[151] What is bizarre about this is not just that the government here embraced an entirely pacifist world view, but that it pushed through Parliament a measure which means that anyone who disagrees with this view, and expresses support for violence or property damage directed against, say, a military dictatorship like the Burmese junta, may by doing so commit a serious crime. It thus elevates one view of contemporary global politics – essentially a pacifist one – into dogma, the challenge to which may be a criminal offence. Such an offence represents an extraordinary attack upon freedom of expression and there must be serious doubts as to whether it is compatible with art. 10 of the ECHR.[152]

---

[145] Terrorism Act 2006, s. 20(2) (emphasis added).

[146] JCHR, *Third Report of Session 2005–6.*   [147] Ibid., [25].   [148] Ibid., at [20].

[149] Hansard, HL, vol. 680, col. 248, 22 March 2006.   [150] Ibid.

[151] JCHR, *Third Report of Session 2005–6*, [29].

[152] It has not yet been tested against art. 10. Many commentators took the view that it was incompatible at the time; however, the much-criticised decision in *Leroy* v. *France* (App. No.36109/03), 6 April 2009, makes that judgment more uncertain: see S. Sottiaux, '*Leroy v France*: apology of terrorism and the malaise of the European Court of Human Rights' free speech jurisprudence' (2009) *European Human Rights Law Review* 415.

6.   Conclusion

While extraordinary pre-emptive measures in the form of control orders continue to be used in the United Kingdom, we have seen that the judiciary, eventually, and albeit with heavy assistance from Strasbourg, have achieved significant amelioration of the system, in terms both of the severity of the restrictions imposed on suspect controlees and the fairness of the procedure by which they may be challenged. This in turn has forced the British government out of its preferred post-*Belmarsh* strategy of engaging in stealthy derogations of Convention rights, as opposed to the open derogation necessary to run the Belmarsh scheme, that incurred much domestic and international opprobrium. During 2010, the re-application of more rigorous ECHR standards by a combination of domestic and Strasbourg judgments made the control orders scheme look precarious.[153] While it continued to use control orders, and imposed fresh orders since taking office,[154] it became clear that the new government was considering alternatives. Eventually, in January 2011, the government announced its intention to replace control orders with 'Terrorism Prevention and Investigation Measures', or TPIMS; such measures will replace house detention with an 'overnight residence requirement';[155] travel restriction orders and other surveillance measures will also be retained under the current proposals.[156] Clearly, TPIMS are indistinguishable from 'light touch' control orders: the measures to be introduced under them could have been introduced under such orders. But it appears that TPIMS will not be used to impose forced relocation or house detention for more than around eleven hours per day. Thus the most draconian aspects of the control orders scheme are to be abandoned. It remains to be

---

[153] A few orders have been revoked; in other cases, the government was forced to disclose more evidence, or water down the conditions in the hope that the new light touch orders would not be seen to engage art. 6, a strategy that has so far failed when challenged in the courts: *Re BC; Re BB* (11 November 2009, unreported).

[154] This followed the ruling in *Nasseer and Khan* v. *SSHD* (18 May 2010), appeal no. C/77/80/81/82/83/09 that two Pakistani students created a threat to security but could not be returned to Pakistan due to the risk of torture. Control orders were imposed on the two students: see news.bbc.co.uk/1/hi/8688501.stm. But at present only eight orders are in place.

[155] See Counter-Terrorism Review, published on 26 January 2011 www.homeoffice.gov.uk/publications/counter-terrorism/review-of-ct-security-powers/. The Coalition government asked Parliament to renew the PTA for the last time, for a period of less than a year, in March 2011 while the legislation introducing the TPIMS scheme was under preparation to replace it.

[156] Ibid; see also 6th Report of the Independent Reviewer pursuant to s14(3) of the PTA 2006, Lord Carlile of Berriew, 6 February 2011.

seen whether the courts will accept that the *AF* principle of disclosure is not engaged by the procedure for imposing TPIMS.

As we have seen, the last government also radically extended the state's powers of stop and search and detention before charge, giving itself draconian tools with which to disrupt terrorist plots, in a way that also made significant incursions into normal liberty-based rights. While it succeeded in giving itself a much longer period to detain terror suspects before charge than ordinary criminals, its attempts to extend this to mini-internment of three months were decisively checked in Parliament, while political sentiment appears to have coalesced around the conviction that the proposed extension was unnecessary. Indeed, as this book goes to press, the extended period of twenty-eight days detention has been allowed to lapse,[157] returning the maximum length of pre-charge detention to fourteen days; meanwhile, provisions in the long-awaited Protection of Freedoms Bill 2011 will, if enacted, prevent the power to detain for twenty-eight days being reactivated: to take the powers back up to twenty-eight days would now require fresh legislation.[158] Moreover, the special stop and search powers discussed above were so widely and arbitrarily used by police forces around the United Kingdom, especially in London, that even though the domestic courts wholly failed to check them, or even subject them to any kind of searching review, Strasbourg's rescue of rule of law norms in *Gillan* v. *UK* found enough political support, with the change of government, to result in the disapplication of what had become a discredited and unpopular power.

Finally, while many extraordinarily broad criminal offences have been introduced, the most draconian of these do not yet appear to have been used in the full range of circumstances to which they potentially apply, continuing the ironic trend, noted in the first edition of this chapter, in which 'the special terrorist offences are viewed by the government as ineffective in relation to those who pose the greatest security threat'.[159] The continuance of the control orders scheme in fact amounts to an

---

[157] It was subject to a sunset clause: the power to detain for twenty-eight days lapsed on 25 January 2011. As the Explanatory Notes to the new Bill explain, subsection 1 of clause 57 amends para. 36(3)(b)(ii) of Schedule 8 to the 2000 Act so as to make the current (as of 25 January 2011) maximum period of pre-charge detention of 14 days permanent.

[158] The government has prepared draft primary legislation, to be presented to Parliament if the event of an emergency, which would temporarily re-raise the limit to twenty-eight days.

[159] Helen Fenwick and Gavin Phillipson, 'Legislative over-breadth, democratic failure and the judicial response: the UK's anti-terrorism law and human rights' in Kent Roach, Michael Hor and Victor Ramraj (eds.) *Global Anti-Terrorism Law and Policy* (Cambridge University Press, 2005), p. 488.

admission of the failure of the criminal law to deal with this threat. So far the UK government has not sought to introduce modifications to the criminal trial itself[160] – such as allowing the use of intercepted material in evidence – with a view to bringing persons currently on control orders to trial.[161] To do so would require bold new thinking of a kind plainly *not* represented by the over-cautious approach of the Chilcot Report,[162] and the continuing somewhat absurd notion, held by many in what Walker calls the 'securitocracy',[163] that the United Kingdom, uniquely, cannot use such evidence in criminal trials without doing serious damage to its national security or public safety.[164] The continuing failure to lift the intercept ban has fatally undermined the UK government's previously stated priority of prosecuting terrorist suspects wherever possible. Indeed, the current Director of Public Prosecutions, Keir Starmer, argued before he took office that the real reason for the government's reliance on pre-emptive measures like detention without trial and control orders is not pressing security needs but the unreasonable resistance of the Security Services to preparing phone tap evidence that could be used as evidence in criminal trials.[165] As Lord Lloyd said, when he reviewed the UK's counter-terrorism powers back in 1996: 'We know who the terrorists are, but we exclude the only evidence which has any chance of getting them convicted; and we are the only country in the world to do so.'[166] The suspicion remains that, as McGarrity, Lynch and Williams have put it, when the state can choose between a range of legal measures to deploy against suspect individuals, it 'may deliberately select [those] which demand less of it – in terms of due process and respect for individual liberties – than other means of achieving substantially the same end'.[167]

Thus adverse court judgments, together with unremitting pressure from the JCHR, and the much-publicised government defeats on pre-charge detention in Parliament, have cumulatively resulted in a noticeable

---

[160] Save for the introduction, in places, of reverse burdens of proof, as in Terrorism Act 2000 (UK) s. 57: above, text to and note 133.

[161] No-one subject to a control order has yet been prosecuted for an offence, save for breach of their control order.

[162] On intercept evidence: Cm 7324, 30 January 2010.

[163] 'The threat of terrorism and the fate of control orders' (2010) (Winter) *Public Law* 4, 6.

[164] See, e.g., JUSTICE, *Secret Evidence* (2009), [94].

[165] K. Starmer, 'Setting the record straight: human rights in an era of international terrorism' (2007) 2 *European Human Rights Law Review* 123, especially 128–32.

[166] Quoted in Starmer, 'Setting the record Straight', 129–30. See also the comments in Fenwick and Phillipson, 'Legislative over-breadth', pp. 483–5.

[167] McGarrity, Lynch and Williams (eds.,), *Counter-Terrorism and Beyond*, p. 6.

shift back towards human rights and rule of law norms. The new government, as seen above, is engaged in proactively shifting the balance back towards civil liberties as a result of its review of counter-terrorism powers and the Protection of Freedoms Bill. At the time of writing, it remains unclear whether this broad political and judicial trend is likely to accelerate and consolidate; however, it appears to justify ending this chapter on a more optimistic note than the bleak one struck in the conclusion to our chapter in the first edition of this book.

20

Canada's response to terrorism

KENT ROACH

1. Introduction

Canada's response to terrorism has been dramatically affected by 9/11. Canadians died in the horrific attacks on the World Trade Centre, but so did the citizens of many other countries. What was unique about Canada's response was the border it shares with the United States. The border meant that Canada felt the repercussions of the swift US response in an immediate and profound manner. When the United States closed its air space that terrible day, Canada accepted over 200 aeroplanes destined for the United States. Canada was affected by erroneous claims that some of the terrorists had entered the United States through Canada, as indeed had occurred before and could occur again given the millions who cross the border each day.[1] It was singled out in the Patriot Act,[2] which contained a whole section entitled 'Protecting the Northern Border' providing for increased border guards and scrutiny of those entering the United States.

Canada drafted broad new anti-terrorism laws and developed a new public safety department of government in response to 9/11, but also with an eye to US perceptions that Canada might provide a safe haven for terrorists. Important components of Canada's anti-terrorism and immigration policies were established in border agreements with the United States signed at the end of 2001, including a safe third country agreement that prohibits refugees from applying for asylum in Canada's more liberal system if they have reached the US first. In response to concerns about a thickening border for trade and continued threats from terrorists, Canada and the United States agreed in February 2011 to a shared

---

[1] See Kent Roach, *September 11: Consequences for Canada* (Montreal: McGill-Queen's University Press, 2003) for a fuller account of the immediate consequences of the 9/11 terrorist attacks on Canada.

[2] Uniting and Strengthening America by Providing Appropriate Tools to Intercept and Obstruct Terrorism (USA PATRIOT) Act of 2001, HR 3162, Title 4, sub-s. A, 'Protecting the Northern Border'.

vision for perimeter security and economic competitiveness including increased intelligence sharing, integrated cross-border law enforcement, joint emergency response, protection of critical infrastructure, cyber security and trade facilitation.[3]

Canada refused to ask the US to repatriate a Canadian citizen held at Guantánamo despite two rulings by the Supreme Court of Canada that Canadian officials had violated his rights when they questioned him at Guantánamo Bay. In the second case, the Supreme Court reversed a lower court order that Canada be required to ask for Omar Khadr's repatriation because of concerns that such a remedy would interfere with Canada's delicate diplomacy with the United States.[4] In the end, Khadr pled guilty in US military commission proceedings to murdering a US soldier in Afghanistan when he was fifteen years old. Khadr remains the only citizen of a Western democracy still imprisoned at Guantánamo, but Canada, at the request of the United States, has indicated that it will accept a prison transfer of Khadr, probably later in 2011.[5]

Canada was not immune from terrorism before 9/11. In response to kidnappings by two cells of the Front de Libération du Québec in 1970, it invoked extraordinary emergency powers to declare that organisation to be illegal and to detain suspected supporters and associates of that organisation without ordinary legal safeguards. In 1985, a Vancouver-based conspiracy of Sikh Canadians bombed two Air India planes, killing 331 people in what until 9/11 was the most deadly act of aviation terrorism. Only one person has been convicted for the bombings. Two people were acquitted in 2005 after one of the longest trials in Canadian history. A 2010 public inquiry concluded that the bombings were related to problems in the distribution of intelligence, converting intelligence into evidence, witness protection and aviation security that to some extent continue to this day.[6]

In the first part of this chapter, I examine Canada's Anti-Terrorism Act (ATA) that was quickly enacted in the months after 9/11 and compare it to Canada's previous response to terrorism. I focus on the breadth of the

---

[3] Beyond the Border: A Shared Vision for Perimeter Security and Economic Competitiveness: A Declaration by the Prime Minister of Canada and the President of the United States, 4 February, 2011 available at www.pm.gc.ca/eng/media.asp?id=3938.

[4] *Canada* v. *Khadr* [2008] 2 SCR 125; *Khadr* v. *Canada* [2010] 1 SCR 44.

[5] A similar procedure was used to allow David Hicks to return to Australia: see George Williams, Chapter 21, this volume.

[6] Commission of Inquiry into the Investigation of the Bombing of Air India Flight 182 (Air India Commission), *Air India Flight 182: A Canadian Tragedy* (2010), 5 volumes.

definition of terrorism in the new law, its reliance on executive proscription of groups and individuals, its authorisation of novel investigative powers and its status as permanent legislation. I also examine how the law has been used since 9/11, including how it resulted in guilty verdicts and guilty pleas, as well as the continuing challenges facing terrorism prosecutions in Canada.

One of the reasons why Canada's 2001 anti-terrorism law did not result in its first conviction until 2008 was that Canadian authorities used immigration law as a means to detain suspected international terrorists. Although the ATA departs from some traditional criminal law principles, it still requires proof of guilt beyond a reasonable doubt and prohibits the use of secret evidence. In contrast, the Immigration and Refugee Protection Act[7] (IRPA) allows the removal of non-citizens on the basis of secret evidence not disclosed to the deportee. In the second part of this chapter, I examine how Canada's immigration law has been used as anti-terrorism law. I also assess successful legal challenges that have resulted in the introduction of special advocates to challenge secret evidence. I will also examine how the Canadian courts have refused to rule out the possibility of deportation to torture and how Canada's sharing of information with some foreign countries has contributed to torture.

In the last part of the chapter, I will examine the effectiveness of Canadian anti-terrorism law and policy. In 2004, Canada enacted the Public Safety Act,[8] which features administrative regulations designed to secure sites and substances vulnerable to terrorism. It also created a new Department of Public Safety and devised a new national security policy. This 'all-risk' policy has the potential to allow a more rational and effective approach to multiple security risks including not only terrorism but also disaster and disease. It also presents less of a threat to due process and equality than reliance on immigration or even criminal law.

2.   The criminal law response: Canada's Anti-Terrorism Act

Canada responded to 9/11 and Security Council Resolution 1373 by enacting a massive new law that for the first time created and defined crimes of terrorism under Canada's Criminal Code. The act's definition of terrorism was inspired by the UK's Terrorism Act 2000 in requiring proof of religious, ideological or political motive and the commission of a broad range of harms that went well beyond violence against civilians.

---

[7] SC 2001 c. 27.   [8] SC 2004 c. 15.

Many civil society groups voiced concerns that the act would brand many illegal protests and strikes as terrorism.[9] This concern led to amendments before the bill became law that dropped the requirement that protests and strikes must be lawful to be exempted from the definition of terrorism. It also provided that the expression of religious, political or ideological thought or opinions would not normally be considered terrorism.[10] In the first prosecution brought under the ATA, the trial judge struck down the political or religious motive requirement as a disproportionate and unnecessary burden on freedom of speech and religion.[11] This decision was unique in the many Commonwealth countries that have followed the lead of the UK Terrorism Act 2000 in requiring proof of political and religious motive, but it has now been reversed on appeal.

Canada's definition of terrorism is much broader than the functional definition of terrorism that was used during the 1970 October Crisis. In 1970, groups that advocated 'the use of force or the commission of crime as a means of or as an aid in accomplishing governmental change within Canada' were declared to be unlawful associations under emergency regulations.[12] The ATA was enacted as permanent legislation as opposed to the emergency orders of the October Crisis. Two of the ATA's most controversial provisions relating to preventive arrest and investigative hearings were, however, subject to a renewable sunset after five years. These provisions expired in 2007, but the expiry was related more to partisan politics than principles. Canada's minority Conservative government has unsuccessfully attempted several times to re-introduce these powers.[13]

The ATA was defended as a necessary means to prevent terrorism. It criminalised a broad array of activities in advance of the actual

---

[9] For essays largely critical of the proposed Bill and this aspect of the definition of terrorism in particular, see Ronald J. Daniels, Patrick Macklem and Kent Roach (eds.), *The Security of Freedom: Essays on Canada's Anti-Terrorism Bill* (University of Toronto Press, 2001). See also 'Special Issue' (2003) 14 *National Journal of Constitutional Law*, 1*et seq.* For an account of how various groups, including unions, churches, charities and Aboriginal people, criticised the Bill and the impact these criticisms made on the legislative process see Roach, *September 11: Consequences for Canada*, chapter 3.

[10] Criminal Code, s. 83.01(1.1).

[11] *R* v. *Khawaja* (2006) 214 CCC (3d) 399 (ONSC) rev'd 2010 ONCA 862 [64ff.], leave to appeal to Supreme Court of Canada granted, 30 June 2011.

[12] Public Order Regulations 1970 SOR/70–444, s. 3. For an examination of the October Crisis, see Dominique Clement 'The October Crisis: Human rights abuses under the War Measures Act' (2008) 42 *Journal of Canadian Studies* 160.

[13] Kent Roach, 'The role and capacities of courts and legislatures in reviewing Canada's anti-terrorism law' (2008) 24 *Windsor Review of Legal and Social Issues* 5. See also Andrew Lynch, Chapter 7, this volume.

commission of a terrorist act, including the provision of finances, property and other forms of assistance to terrorist groups, participation in the
activities of a terrorist group and instructing the carrying out of activities
for a terrorist group. There are no requirements of a proximate nexus to
any planned act of terrorism or the planning of a specific act of terrorism.
Some of the financing provisions of the ATA were required to implement
Canada's obligations under the 1999 Convention for the Suppression of
the Financing of Terrorism, but the other offences were not necessarily
required to apprehend and punish either the Air India bombers or the
9/11 terrorists. The failure in both cases was more with intelligence gathering and co-ordination than with the ambit of the criminal law.[14]

The ATA applies to a broad range of acts committed inside or outside
Canada. This was done to make clear that Canada was implementing various international conventions concerning specific forms of terrorism. The
only exemptions are for armed conflict conducted according to customary
or conventional international law or the official activities of a state military force 'to the extent that those activities are governed by other rules
of international law'.[15] This would not necessarily apply to all resistance
efforts against repressive regimes. Difficult issues have already emerged
when people in Canada are charged with sending financial or other forms
of support to struggles against repressive governments in foreign lands.
In 2010, a Tamil-Canadian pled guilty to providing CAN $3000 to the
Tamil Tigers in Sri Lanka, but argued outside of court that the Sri Lankan
government were the real terrorists. He received a sentence of only six
months' imprisonment. The sentence reveals some ambiguity about the
criminalisation of the financial support for the Tamil Tigers.[16]

The armed conflict exception was argued by the accused in Canada's
first prosecution under the ATA, but rejected on the grounds that support
for al-Qaeda in Afghanistan was a terrorist activity that did not satisfy
the exception for armed conflict conducted in accordance with the laws of

---

[14] Kent Roach, 'Trading rights for security' (2006) 27 *Cardozo Law Review* 2151, 2203ff. But
for arguments that the new offences were required to respond to cell-based terrorism, see
Richard Mosley, 'Preventing terrorism: Bill C-36, the Anti-terrorism Act' in D. Daubney
and Canadian Institute for the Administration of Justice (eds.), *Terrorism, Law and
Democracy: How is Canada Changing After September 11* (Montreal: Les Editions Themis,
2002).

[15] Anti-Terrorism Act 2001, s. 83.01(1)(b).

[16] The sentence was appealed by the prosecutor but upheld on appeal. See *R v. Thambaithurai*
2011 BCCA 137. In Australia, those who have provided financial support to the Tamil
Tigers have also received light sentences. See Kent Roach, *The 9/11 Effect: Comparative
Counter-Terrorism* (Cambridge University Press, 2011) pp. 320–2.

war.[17] These first charges were laid against Mohammad Momin Khawaja in 2004. He was eventually convicted in 2008 of having participated in the activities of a terrorist group and having facilitated terrorist activity in Canada, England and Pakistan as part of a London-based cell.[18] Khawaja's trial was delayed by his largely unsuccessful challenge to the constitutionality of the new ATA offences under the Canadian Charter of Rights and Freedoms and by two trips to a separate administrative court, the Federal Court, to determine that secret intelligence not used in his trial did not have to be disclosed to him. The litigation of such public interest immunity applications in a court separate from the trial court weakens Canada's ability to conduct terrorism prosecutions. A trial judge in a subsequent Toronto terrorism prosecution held that a statute that prevented trial judges from seeing secret information and determining whether it should be disclosed to the accused violated the Charter rights of the accused and the inherent powers of a superior court. This decision was, however, overturned by the Supreme Court which stressed that trial judges could stay proceedings if they concluded that a non-disclosure order made a fair trial impossible even though the trial judges would not necessarily have access to the secret material that was not disclosed to the accused and could not revise any non-disclosure order made in the Federal Court. The Supreme Court was aware that no other democracy uses a bifurcated system and that the system had been criticised, but held that this was a policy matter for the legislature.[19]

In 2006, eighteen people including four youths were arrested in Toronto on the grounds that they were involved in plots to storm Parliament and behead politicians until Canada withdrew from Afghanistan and to use three truck bombs in Toronto. Most of the accused were born abroad, but had grown up in Canada. The case was based on extensive wiretaps, two informers within the Muslim community and controlled deliveries by undercover agents of twenty-five bags of a substance held out to be

---

[17] *R* v. *Khawaja* (2008) 238 CCC (3d) 114, [132] (ONSC) aff'd 2010 ONCA 862 [152–69].

[18] Khawaja was sentenced to ten years and six months' imprisonment in addition to the five years he was detained in pre-trial custody, but this sentence was raised on appeal to life imprisonment. The companion British case is *Khyam* v. *The Queen* [2008] EWCA 1612 (CA) and the offenders also received life sentences.

[19] *R* v. *Ahmad* 2011 SCC 6. The Air India Commission also recommended that trial judges be allowed to make public interest immunity disclosure decisions: Air India Commission, *Air India Flight 182*, vol. 3, recommendation 19. It also stressed the challenges of terrorism prosecutions with multiple accused and voluminous disclosures and recommended more prosecutorial specialisation, increased trial management powers for judges and the use of more alternative jurors.

ammonium nitrate. In the end, seven of the eighteen pled guilty, seven had charges dropped by the prosecution, two were convicted of various terrorism offences in a judge-alone trial and two were convicted of participating in a terrorist group after a trial by jury. The case represented a major challenge to the ATA and to co-operation between the Royal Canadian Mounted Police (RCMP) and the Canadian Security Intelligence Service (CSIS). Unlike in the Air India case where the RCMP and CSIS clashed over access to sources and other intelligence, two human sources were successfully transferred from CSIS to the RCMP with one of them being paid CAN $4 million and being placed in witness protection.[20] The Ontario Court of Appeal increased the sentences of a number of accused who pled guilty in this case stressing the need to deter terrorism and and high sentences awarded in similar cases in the United Kingdom and Australia. It also stated that rehabilitation was of marginal importance in terrorism cases even though the accused were young and remorseful.[21]

Canada has limited experience with so-called Al Capone strategies of prosecuting suspected terrorists for non-terrorist crimes. A child pornography prosecution collapsed after a judge held that CSIS had flagrantly violated a terrorist suspect's rights when they required him to turn over his computer without a warrant to demonstrate that he was not a terrorist. CSIS then searched and found child pornography on the computer even though they do not have law enforcement powers.[22] A recent report has raised concerns about a lack of guidelines and ministerial knowledge about CSIS's attempts to disrupt suspected terrorists.[23]

Like the emergency regulations enacted during the October Crisis, a central feature of the ATA is the ability of the cabinet of elected ministers to designate groups and even persons as terrorists.[24] So far forty-two groups have been listed in this fashion. Executive designation of a group as a terrorist is deemed to be conclusive proof in a criminal trial that the

[20] See generally, 'The Toronto 18', available at www3.thestar.com/static/toronto18/index. html.

[21] R v. *Amara* 2010 ONCA 858 (life imprisonment for twenty-year-old mastermind of truck bomb plot who pled guilty and expressed remorse); R v. *Khalid* 2010 ONCA 861 (twenty-year sentence for a nineteen-year-old first offender who was willfully blind but not fully aware of the details of the truck bomb plot and who had renounced violence); R v. *Gaya* 2010 ONCA 860 (eighteen-year sentence for a eighteen-year-old first offender who was willfully blind but not fully aware of the details of the truck bomb plot and was genuinely remorseful). For discussion of sentencing and terrorism, see Kent Roach, Chapter 5, in this volume.

[22] R v. *Mejid* 2010 ONSC 5532.

[23] Security Intelligence Review Committee, *Annual Report 2009–2010* (2010).

[24] Criminal Code, s. 83.05.

group is in fact a terrorist group.[25] The government did not, however, rely on such listing in recent prosecutions of home grown terrorists who lack formal connections with al-Qaeda.

In addition to the above listing, over 450 groups and individuals have been listed as terrorists under regulations enacted under the United Nations Act which is used to implement the asset freeze and travel ban in Security Council Resolution 1267.[26] These lists are distributed to financial institutions and within government. Executive designation of terrorist groups and individuals follows the 1267 process, but can be criticised as a challenge to judicial powers to decide in a particular case who is a terrorist. Soon after 9/11, Liban Hussein was wrongfully listed as a terrorist by the US, but he was eventually removed from the US, Canadian and 1267 lists and attempts to extradite him from Canada to the United States were also abandoned.[27] In another case, a Canadian court found that a Canadian citizen's listing by the UN 1267 Committee did not justify Canada refusing to grant him documents to allow him to return to Canada from Sudan. In making this decision, the judge stated that the 1267 process was 'a situation for a listed person not unlike that of Josef K. in Kafka's *The Trial*, who awakens one morning and, for reasons never revealed to him or the reader, is arrested and prosecuted for an unspecified crime'.[28]

Another important feature of the ATA was its expansion of police powers. One provision provided for preventive arrest when there were reasonable grounds to believe that a terrorist activity will be carried out and reasonable suspicion to believe that detention or the imposition of conditions was necessary to prevent the carrying out of the terrorist activity. The period of preventive arrest was limited to seventy-two hours, but the arrestee could be required by a judge to enter into a recognisance or peace bond for up to a year with breach of the peace bond being punishable by up to two years imprisonment and a refusal to agree to a peace bond punishable by a year's imprisonment.[29] This provision was more restrained than

---

[25] But for an argument that this would violate the presumption of innocence see David Paciocco, 'Constitutional casualties of September 11' (2002) 16 *Supreme Court Law Review* (2d) 199.

[26] United Nations Suppression of Terrorism Regulations, SOR 2001–360, 2 October 2001. On the Resolution 1267 process, see C. H. Powell Chapter 2, this volume.

[27] E. Alexandra Dosman, 'For the record: designating "listed entities" for the purposes of terrorist financing offences at Canadian law' (2004) 62 *University of Toronto Faculty Law Review* 1, 15–19.

[28] *Abdelrazik v. Canada* 2009 FC 580, [53]. For similar criticisms of the UN listing process, see *Kadi v. Council of Europe* [2009] AC 1225; *Treasury v. Ahmed* 2010 UKSC 2.

[29] Anti-Terrorism Act 2001, s. 83.3

the comparable UK provision, which at the time provided for a maximum of seven days preventive arrest, a period subsequently raised to twenty-eight days. No preventive arrests were made and the authorising sections of the ATA were allowed to expire in 2007. It is still possible to order peace bonds in terrorism cases,[30] but none has been ordered.

Another new investigative power was a power to compel a person to answer questions relating to terrorist activities either in the past or the future. The subject could not refuse to answer on the grounds of self-incrimination, but the compelled statements and evidence derived from them could not be used in subsequent proceedings against him or her. In 2004, the Supreme Court upheld the constitutionality of investigative hearings, but stressed that compelled evidence should not be used against the person in any subsequent proceedings including immigration and extradition proceedings.[31] Three judges dissented on the basis that investigative hearings violated the institutional independence of the judiciary by requiring judges to preside over police investigations.[32] The Court also held that the presumption in favour of open courts applied to the conduct of investigative hearings, but two judges dissented on the basis that such a presumption 'would normally defeat the purpose of the proceedings by rendering them ineffective as an investigative tool'.[33]

Even though upheld as constitutional and more constrained than comparable US grand jury provisions or questioning warrants available to Australia's security intelligence agency,[34] investigative hearings represented an undesirable incursion on the adversarial traditions of criminal justice. The law assumed that unco-operative persons will suddenly co-operate and tell the truth because they are threatened with contempt of court or a prosecution for refusing to co-operate at an investigative hearing. The only attempt to use an investigative hearing was made during the Air India trial that culminated in acquittals in 2005.[35] The use of

---

[30] Criminal Code, s. 810.01. The grounds for such peace bonds would be that there were reasonable grounds to fear that a person would commit a terrorist offence. Similar peace bond provisions in relation to sexual offences have been upheld under the Charter. *R v. Budreo* (2000) 142 CCC(3d) 225 (ONCA).

[31] *Re Application under Section 83.28 of the Criminal Code* 2004 2 SCR 248.

[32] Ibid., [180].

[33] *Re Vancouver Sun* [2004] 2 SCR 332, [60].

[34] Kent Roach, 'The consequences of compelled self-incrimination' (2008) 30 *Cardozo Law Review* 1089; George Williams, Chapter 21, this volume.

[35] *R v. Malik and Bagri* 2005 BCSC 350. Reyat was convicted of making the bomb for the simultaneous bombing in Narita and subsequently pled guilty to manslaughter in relation to the Air India bombing. He was also convicted of perjury and sentenced to nine

investigative hearings in the Air India investigation was a blunt and coercive shortcut around the proper development of human sources and witness protection during that lengthy investigation. The Air India inquiry did not recommend that investigative hearings which expired in 2007 be revived, but rather focused on improvements to witness protection and recommendations that a National Security Advisor be able to resolve any disputes between the RCMP and CSIS, including over the handling of human sources.[36] Attempts by the minority Conservative government to re-introduce investigative hearings and preventive arrests continue, however, and the RCMP has expressed a desire to use investigative hearings in the ongoing Air India investigations.

The ATA also included provisions making it easier to obtain wiretap warrants in terrorism investigations. These changes were not subject to a sunset and have been upheld from Charter challenge in the Toronto case where wiretaps of over 80,000 phone conversations were obtained.[37] Intercepts are obtained by the police on crime-related grounds, but it is also possible that intercepts obtained by CSIS might be accepted as evidence.[38]

As criminal law the ATA is administered by police officers throughout Canada. The McDonald Commission concluded in 1981 that the RCMP had engaged in illegalities and had trouble distinguishing radical dissent from terrorism in the wake of the 1970 October Crisis.[39] In 2006, the Arar Commission found that RCMP officers without adequate national security training had exchanged inaccurate information about Maher Arar with the US in a manner that likely played a role in his 2002 rendition by the US to Syria and Arar's torture in Syria.[40]

---

years' imprisonment for his false testimony in the 2005 trial. His perjury conviction also underlines the risk that those compelled to speak at investigative hearings might not necessarily tell the truth.

[36] Air India Commission, *Air India Flight 182*, vol. 3, Chapter 8.

[37] *R* v. *NY*, 2008 CanLII 15908 (ONSC).

[38] *R* v. *Atwal* (1986) 36 CCC(3d) 161 (FCA). For discussion of the use of intelligence as evidence see Kent Roach, *The Unique Challenges of Terrorism Prosecutions* (Ottawa: Public Works, 2010).

[39] Commission of Inquiry Concerning Certain Activities of the Royal Canadian Mounted Police, *Second and Third Reports* (Ottawa: Queen's Printer, 1981).

[40] Commission of Inquiry into the Activities of Canadian Officials in Relation to Maher Arar, *Analysis and Recommendations* (Ottawa: Public Works, 2006). See also *Internal Inquiry into the Actions of Canadian Officials in Relation to Abdullah Almalki, Ahmad Abou-Elmaati and Muyayyed Nureddin* (Ottawa: Public Works, 2008), that also finds similar errors in the RCMP processes for sharing information and sending questions to be asked of Canadians detained in Syria and Egypt on suspicion of terrorism. Both inquiries also found deficiencies in the conduct of CSIS and foreign affairs officials.

The Arar Commission recommended in 2006 that the body that hears complaints against the RCMP be given broad powers to audit national security investigations and examine secret information.[41] The Canadian Government in 2010 introduced a Bill to enhance review of the RCMP, but contrary to the Arar Commission's recommendations, the Bill would still allow the RCMP to deny the reviewer access to material claimed to be secret.[42] Both the Arar and Air India commissions criticised over-broad secrecy claims made by the government in an attempt to avoid review and embarrassment. The review of both the propriety and effi-cacy of national security activities has not kept pace with intensified national security activities since 9/11.[43]

3.   The use of immigration law as anti-terrorism law and Canada's foreign anti-terrorism activities

Consistent with the US's initial reliance on immigration and military detention,[44] and the UK's use of indeterminate immigration detention without trial,[45] Canada relied on immigration law as anti-terrorism law in the immediate aftermath of 9/11.

Unlike the ATA which only had a now expired seventy-two-hour pre-ventive arrest period, the IRPA authorises indeterminate investigative detention on the basis that the Minister is taking necessary steps to inquire into a reasonable suspicion that non-citizens are inadmissible on secur-ity grounds.[46] These broad powers were used in August 2003 to detain twenty-two non-citizens from Pakistan. A media release claimed that the men had indirect al-Qaeda associations and that one of them took fly-ing lessons that took him over a nuclear plant outside of Toronto.[47] Not surprisingly, the case made headlines, but the terrorism allegations were

---

[41]   Commission of Inquiry into the Activities of Canadian Officials in Relation to Maher Arar, *A New Review Mechanism for the RCMP's National Security Activities* (Ottawa: Public Works, 2006).

[42]   Bill C-38, an act to amend the RCMP Act (first reading, 14 June 2010).

[43]   Kent Roach, 'Review and oversight of national security activities' (2007) 29 *Cardozo Law Review* 53; Reg Whitaker and Stuart Farson 'Accountability in and for national security' (2009) 15(9) *Institute for Research on Public Policy Choices* 1.

[44]   David Cole, *Enemy Aliens* (New York: New Press, 2003).

[45]   Anti-Terrorism Crime and Security Act 2001(UK), pt. 4, which was repealed after it was held to be incompatible with the European Convention on Human Rights in *A v. Secretary of State* [2004] UKHL 56.

[46]   Immigration and Refugee Protection Act, s. 55 (3)(b).

[47]   Project Thread Backgrounder: Reasons for Detention Pursuant to 58(1)(c) (undated).

not pursued and the men were eventually released as not being a security threat with many of them being deported on other grounds. A number of them, however, made refugee applications on the basis that the highly publicised but false allegations made against them would lead to torture if they were deported to Pakistan.

A. Security certificates: broad liability rules, secret evidence and deportation to torture

The use of security certificates under the IRPA allowed Canadian officials to use a lower standard of proof and wider liability rules than available even under the ATA. Under immigration law, the state's burden of proof falls well short of the criminal law standard of proof beyond a reasonable doubt.[48] In addition, secret evidence that is not disclosed to the noncitizen can be used even though such evidence cannot be used in criminal prosecutions. Canada's robust use of immigration law as anti-terrorism law has been legally and politically controversial.

Security certificates enable the Ministers of Immigration and Public Safety to declare that a permanent resident or foreign national is inadmissible on security grounds. These grounds include engaging in terrorism[49] or being a member of a group when there are reasonable grounds to believe that it has, does or will engage in terrorism,[50] even though membership in a terrorist group is not a crime in Canada. The security certificate is subject to judicial review in the Federal Court to determine its reasonableness, but such review pre-empts other proceedings, including applications for refugee status.

The procedure for reviewing security certificates is extraordinary because it involves the use of secret evidence. In 2002, Justice Hugessen of the Federal Court stated that the judges of his Court:

> 'do not like this process of having to sit alone hearing only one party and looking at the materials produced by only one party and having to try to figure out for ourselves what is wrong with the case that is being

---

[48] *Chiau* v. *Canada* [2001] 2 FC 207 (CA); *Almeri* v. *Canada* [2009] FC 1263.

[49] The courts have defined terrorism under the IRPA more narrowly than under the ATA but also found that a person may be a security threat because he or she poses an indirect threat to Canada's security. In addition, the courts have adopted a deferential posture when deciding whether the Ministers erred by declaring a non-citizen to be a security threat: *Suresh* v. *Canada* [2002] 1 SCR 3.

[50] Immigration and Refugee Protection Act, s. 34.

presented before us and having to try for ourselves to see how that
witnesses that appear before us ought to be cross-examined.'[51]

He ended his extra-judicial speech with an extraordinary confession: 'I
sometimes feel a little bit like a fig leaf'.[52]

Justice Hugessen's plea for reform of the secret evidence process was
vindicated by a 2007 Supreme Court decision that held that the absence
of any adversarial challenge to the secret evidence submitted to the judge
violated the Charter. The Court stressed that the judge acting alone could
not 'bear the heavy burden' of assuring that the case was properly decided
on the facts and the law. Moreover, the Court stressed that there were
more proportionate ways of reconciling fairness with secrecy.[53] The Court
delayed its declaration of invalidity for a year to give the government time
to devise a new scheme.

The government complied by amending the IRPA to allow security-
cleared special advocates to have access to the secret evidence. These
advocates act on behalf of the detainee, but are not allowed to speak to
the detainee without judicial permission once they have seen the secret
evidence.[54] Nevertheless, they have enjoyed success both in challenging
the government's claims of secrecy and the accuracy and significance
of the secret evidence. For example, they have been successful in having intelligence excluded on the basis that it is unreliable because it was
derived from the use of torture in countries such as Egypt and that it was
obtained from unreliable human sources. In 2008, the Supreme Court
also ruled that CSIS should retain relevant raw intelligence in order to
allow for more accurate decision-making and adversarial challenge. This
ruling may increase the fairness of proceedings, but at costs to privacy
through increased retention of intelligence.[55] Canadian courts have not

---

[51] James Hugessen, 'Watching the watchers: democratic oversight' in Daubney et al.,
Terrorism, Law and Democracy, p. 384.

[52] Ibid., 386.

[53] *Charkaoui* v. *Canada* [2007] 1 SCR 350. See generally the collection of essays in (2008) 42
Supreme Court Law Review (2d) 251–440.

[54] Immigration and Refugee Protection Act, s. 85.4(2). Under a previous act, security-cleared
counsel for the Security Intelligence Review Committee challenged the secret evidence in
security certificates and did consult with those subject to security proceedings even after
they had seen the secret evidence. See Murray Rankin, 'The Security Intelligence Review
Committee: reconciling national security with procedural fairness' (1990) 3 *Canadian
Journal of Administrative Law and Practice* 173. The European Court of Human Rights
in *Chahal* v. *United Kingdom* (1996) 23 EHHR 413 wrongly assumed a special advocate
system was used in Canada's Federal Court. In any event, such a system is now in place.

[55] *Charkaoui* v. *Canada* [2008] 2 SCR 326. The head of CSIS has predicted that 'within several years, someone will accuse us of acting like the Stasi because of the information

confronted the same problems relating to disclosure of the gist of allegations as in the United Kingdom,[56] because of more robust disclosure practices under the Canadian system.

Although there is increased adversarial challenge to secret evidence, Canada's use of immigration law as anti-terrorism law remains problematic because it continues to detain people who would encounter a substantial risk of torture if they were deported to their country of citizenship. In *Suresh* v. *Canada*,[57] the Supreme Court decided that the Charter would generally prohibit deportation to torture, but it also regrettably suggested that deportation to torture could be justified in undefined 'exceptional circumstances'[58] under the Charter even though it would breach Canada's international obligations.[59] The government has relied on this exception to justify continued detention and attempts to deport terrorist suspects to countries such as Egypt and Syria.

Six security certificates have been issued against men suspected of terrorism. The decision in *Suresh* did not result in Manickavasgam Suresh's deportation to Sri Lanka. Mohamad Mahjoub, an Egyptian, was detained on 26 June 2000. He is alleged to have worked for bin Laden, but in 2007 was released on strict conditions after a judge found that he would not be returned to Egypt within a reasonable amount of time and his controlled release would not threaten the security of Canada. His conditions of release include electronic monitoring, house arrest, no access to telephones or the Internet and only approved visits.[60] Special advocates have

---

we are now compelled to keep' Richard Fadden 'Remarks', 29 October 2009, available at www.csis-scrs.gc.ca/nwsrm/spchs/spch29102009-eng.asp. On the implications of this ruling see Kent Roach, 'When secret intelligence becomes evidence' (2009) 47 *Supreme Court Law Review* (2d) 147.

[56] See Helen Fenwick and Gavin Phillipson, Chapter 19, this volume.

[57] [2002] 1 SCR 3.

[58] Ibid., [78]. The Canadian courts have also refused to stay deportations to allow UN Committees such as the Human Rights Committee and the Committee Against Torture to hear complaints that non-citizens will be tortured if deported from Canada: *Ahani* v. *Canada* (2002) 58 OR (3d) 107. The United Nations Human Rights Committee subsequently indicated that the deportation of Ahani before it had decided the complaint violated Canada's obligations under the International Covenant on Civil and Political Rights and reaffirmed the absolute prohibition on torture under international law: *Ahani* v. *Canada*, Communication No.1051/2002, UN Doc. CCPR/C/80/D/1051/2002 (15 June 2004).

[59] Although a refugee applicant facing the risk of torture is entitled to heightened due process in terms of written reasons from the Minister for the deportation, the Minister's decisions as to whether a person faces a substantial risk of torture or is a threat to the security of Canada will only be overturned by the courts if they are patently unreasonable.

[60] *Mahjoub* v. *Canada* [2007] FC 171.

had evidence derived from terrorism prosecutions in Egypt excluded in Mahjoub's case on the basis that it was not reliable because it was probably obtained through torture.[61] The requirement that the government demonstrate that the secret evidence is reliable is more protective than the House of Lords' requirement that a person establish that evidence was obtained through torture.[62] Mahmoud Jaballah, alleged to have terrorist ties with the Egyptian Al Jihad, had been detained since August 2001. The government argued that he would not be tortured if deported to Egypt or alternatively that deportation to torture was justified by 'exceptional circumstances'. Fortunately, the courts have rejected both claims.[63] In 2007, he was also released on a very strict form of house arrest.[64] Mohammed Harkat was detained on 10 December 2002, with allegations that he has ties to al-Qaeda.He was released in 2006 on strict conditions and his security certificate was confirmed as reasonable at the end of 2010,[65] but it remains to be seen whether the government will attempt to deport him to Algeria.[66]

Two security certificate cases have so far collapsed. Adil Charkaoui from Morocco was detained in May 2003 on suspicions of involvement with al-Qaeda. Following his fourth detention review in 2005 he was released on strict conditions. In 2008, the government found that CSIS had misinterpreted its statutory mandate and violated Charkaoui's rights by destroying raw intelligence that was said to support the allegations that he was a security threat.[67] In 2009, the government abandoned proceedings against him rather than follow a judge's ruling that more intelligence be disclosed to Charkaoui.[68] Hassan Almrei, from Syria, was detained on 19 October 2001. In 2005, he staged a hunger strike for more than sixty days in protest against his conditions of confinement in a remand centre designed for prisoners awaiting trial. At the end of 2009, a judge quashed the security certificate as unreasonable, holding that there was no evidence that Almeri had engaged in terrorism, was a member of a terrorist group or a threat to the security of

---

[61] *Re Mahjoub* [2010] FC 787 [48]; *Re Mahjoub* [2010] FC 937.
[62] *A v. Secretary of State* [2005] UKHL 71.
[63] *Jaballah v. Canada* [2006] FC 1230, [83].
[64] *Jaballah v. Canada* [2007] FC 379.   [65] *Harkat v. Canada* [2010] FC 1241.
[66] See *RB (Algeria) v. Secretary of State* [2009] UKHL 10 applying a deferential standard of judicial review to hold that terrorist suspects could be deported to Algeria with assurances that they would not be tortured.
[67] *Charkaoui v. Canada* [2008] 2 SCR 326. On the implications of this ruling, see Roach, 'When secret intelligence becomes evidence', 147.
[68] *Charkaoui v. Canada* [2009] FC 1030.

Canada.[69] In the *Almeri* case the judge gave special advocates permission to communicate with the affected person that the government was not relying on information obtained at Guantánamo or CIA black sites and also allowed special advocates on different cases to communicate on common issues.[70]

The prolonged legal proceedings in these security certificates cases[71] reveal the difficulties that result from indeterminate detention, the use of secret intelligence as evidence and attempts to deport terrorist suspects to countries where they may be tortured. Security certificates in Canada have failed as an anti-terrorism policy: they have morphed into a de facto restrictive control order regime and they have been much more politically controversial than criminal prosecutions. No new security certificate has been issued in a terrorism case since 2003 and the remaining security certificates will probably collapse eventually. Nevertheless, the government of Canada has taken the official position that the men detained on security certificates cannot be rehabilitated. This is in contrast to Singapore which imposes indeterminate detention on suspected terrorists, but has released many of them on generally light conditions.[72] Both in its approach to sentencing terrorists and security certificates, Canada, like other Western democracies, has demonstrated little interest in attempts to rehabilitate alleged terrorists.

B. Changes in refugee policy and multiculturalism

In December 2001, Canada and the United States agreed to implement a 'safe third country agreement' as part of a smart border agreement to

---

[69] *Almeri v. Canada* [2009] FC 1263. The judge did hold that the certificate was reasonable when originally issued in 2001.

[70] Ibid., [41]. See also *Re Harkat* [2010] FC 1242 holding the special advocate regime to be constitutional in part because of full disclosure of the allegations and the frequently exercised ability of the special advocate to obtain judicial permission to contact the detainee. This decision is now being appealed. *Re Harkat* [2011] FC 75.

[71] The *Charkaoui* case resulted in thirty-eight decisions in the Federal Court and two separate decisions in the Supreme Court before the security certificate was abandoned. The *Almeri* case resulted in fourteen judgments before the security certificate was quashed. The *Harkat* case has so far resulted in thirty-four judgments with more appeals launched; the *Jaballah* case in thirty-two judgments; and the *Mahjoub* case in twenty-four judgments.

[72] Angel Rabasa, Stacie L. Pettyjohn, Jeremy J. Ghez and Christopher Baucek *Deradicalizing Islamic Extremists* (Santa Monica: Rand Corporation, 2010), pp. 100–2; Zachary Abuza 'The rehabilitation of Jemaah Islamiyah Detainees in South East Asia' in Tore Bjorgo and John Horgan (eds.), *Leaving Terrorism Behind* (London: Routledge, 2009). See also Michael Hor, Chapter 11, this volume.

increase security and ease the flow of goods and people at the border. The agreement responded to perceptions that Canada's refugee policy was too liberal and generous and contributed to dramatic decreases in the number of refugee applicants entering Canada. Although there have been some recent increases, the numbers of refugees have not returned to pre-9/11 levels.[73]

The reduction in refugees demonstrates that the use of immigration law as anti-terrorism law can be blunt and over-inclusive. Conversely the use of security certificates underlines the under-inclusive nature of relying on immigration law as anti-terrorism law. As in the 1985 Air India bombings, Canadian citizens are quite capable of being terrorists. The courts have resisted challenges to Canadian immigration laws including security certificates and the safe third country agreement as a violation of the equality rights of non-citizens. They have stressed that non-citizens do not have the same Charter rights to be in Canada as citizens without really engaging, as the House of Lords did in the *Belmarsh* case,[74] with whether the use of immigration law as anti-terrorism law is a rational and proportionate response to the terrorist threat.[75]

Some cautious linkages have been drawn between multiculturalism and security policy. The 2001 ATA included a new offence of hate-motivated mischief against religious property and expanded powers to remove hate literature from the Internet. These provisions were defended on the basis of the connection between racial and religious hatred and terrorism. Canada has not, however, created new glorification of terrorism offences in response to UN Security Council Resolution 1624 and maintains that existing laws on incitement are adequate. In 2004, the government created a Cross-cultural Roundtable on National Security Issues. The roundtable has not emerged as an active presence,[76] but it does link security issues with multiculturalism and radicalisation.

Concerns have been raised in Canada about racial and religious profiling, but the Canadian government refused to introduce an anti-discrimination clause in the ATA.[77] Such a clause might provide

[73] In 2001, over 44,457 refugee applicants entered Canada but that figure declined to 19,691 in 2005 and then rose again to 36,851 in 2008. See Total Entry of Refugee Claimants 2008, available at www.cic.gc.ca/english/resources/statistics/facts2008/temporary/21.asp.
[74] *A v. Secretary of State* [2004] UKHL 56, as discussed in Helen Fenwick and Gavin Phillipson, Chapter 19 this volume.
[75] *Charkaoui v. Canada* [2007] 1 SCR 350; *Canada v. Council for Refugees* [2008] FCA 229.
[76] Kent Roach, 'Multiculturalism, Muslim minorities and security policy' [2006] *Singapore Journal of Legal Studies* 405.
[77] Those who advocated such a clause included Irwin Cotler, a noted human rights lawyer, who subsequently was appointed Canada's Minister of Justice. See Irwin Cotler,

symbolic reassurance to those who have expressed concerns that they will be subject to heightened scrutiny because they may have the same origins and religion as some terrorists. The importance of maintaining good relations with multicultural communities is underlined by the fact that informers within Canada's Muslim community played an important role in the prosecution of the Toronto terrorism plots.

C.   Canada's foreign anti-terrorism activities

Canada's anti-terrorism activities extend beyond its borders. Canada continues to participate in the occupation of Afghanistan, but did not participate in the invasion of Iraq. Canadian courts have imposed restrictions on the extra-territorial application of the Charter and the Federal Court of Appeal held that the Charter would not apply in Afghanistan even if Canadian Forces transferred detainees to a substantial risk of torture at the hands of Afghan intelligence agencies.[78] Parliamentary committees have encountered difficulties gaining access to secret documents relating to Canada's Afghan detainee policy and the government has refused to appoint a public inquiry into this matter.

Two public inquiries were appointed to examine the actions of Canadian officials in relation to Canadian citizens suspected of involvement in terrorism who were detained and tortured in Syria. The Maher Arar inquiry concluded that Canadian officials had passed on inaccurate intelligence about Arar, were not sufficiently aware of his mistreatment in Syria and sent mixed signals about whether they wanted him returned to Canada.[79] A subsequent inquiry found that Canadian officials indirectly contributed to the torture of three other Canadian citizens held abroad by sending questions to Syrian and Egyptian officials for them to answer.[80] These inquiries, as well as a subsequent court case that stayed a US extradition request on the grounds that the United States has participated

---

'Thinking outside the box: foundational principles for a counter-terrorism law and policy' in Daniels, Macklem and Roach, *The Security of Freedom* (2001).

[78] *Amnesty International* v. *Canada* [2008] FC 336 (affd [2008] FCA 401; leave denied SCC). For further discussion see Kent Roach '"The Supreme Court at the bar of politics"': the Afghan Detainee and Omar Khadr cases' (2011) 28 *National Journal of Constitutional Law* 115.

[79] Commission of Inquiry into the Actions of Canadian Officials in Relation to Maher Arar, *Report of the Events Relating to Maher Arar* (Ottawa: Public Works, 2006).

[80] *Internal Inquiry into the Actions of Canadian Officials in Relation to Abdullah Almalki, Ahmad Abou-Elmaati and Muayyed Nureddin* (Ottawa: Public Works, 2008). See also Kerry Pither, *Dark Days* (Toronto: Viking, 2008).

in the abuse of the fugitive when detained in Pakistan,[81] underline the transnational nature of Canadian anti-terrorism efforts. They also reveal the dangers of torture, mistreatment and inaccurate intelligence when Canada co-operates with countries with poor human rights records. The inquiries themselves were an extraordinary exercise in accountability for secret national security activities,[82] but the appointment of an inquiry remains at the discretion of the government.

Canada's treatment of Omar Khadr, a Canadian citizen detained at Guantánamo since 2002, who in 2010 pled guilty to murder, attempted murder, material support of terrorism, conspiracy and spying, has also been the subject of much political and legal controversy. In 2005, a judge issued a temporary injunction that prevented Canadian intelligence officials from continuing to go to Guantánamo to question Khadr.[83] The Supreme Court twice held that Canadian interrogations of Khadr at Guantánamo in 2003 and 2004 violated both the Canadian Charter and international law. In 2008, the Court ordered disclosure of the results of the Canadian interviews as a remedy subject to the government making a case for state secrets.[84] In 2010, it held that the effects of the violation continued, but reversed a lower court order that required Canada to request Khadr's repatriation to Canada as a remedy on the grounds that it interfered with the government's prerogatives over diplomacy.[85] The government responded to this decision with a diplomatic note requesting that the United States not use evidence obtained by Canadian officials, but this was rejected by US officials. In subsequent litigation, a lower court concluded that Khadr had still not received an effective remedy but the government obtained a stay of this decision.[86]

Despite doubts about the fairness of his treatment or the jurisdiction of military commissions to adjudicate crimes such as murder, conspiracy or material support of terrorism,[87] Khadr's guilty plea reflected his

---

[81] *AG of Canada* v. *Abdullah Khadr* [2010] ONSC 4338, aff'd [2011] ONCA 358

[82] The inquiries were denounced by a former CSIS official whose conduct was examined by them as 'legal jihad' and by a former RCMP official who headed an integrated national security enforcement team in Toronto as 'judicial terrorism.' Pither *Dark Days*, p. 400. These disrespectful remarks also revealed a deep seated aversion among high security officials about external and independent review of their work. Such attitudes may help explain why the government has resisted inquiry proposals for increased review of either the propriety or efficacy of security activities.

[83] *Khadr* v. *Canada* [2005] FC 1076.   [84] *Khadr* v. *Canada* [2008] 2 SCR 125.

[85] *Khadr* v. *Canada* [2010] SCC 3.

[86] *Khadr* v. *Canada* [2010] FC 715; *Canada* v. *Khadr* [2010] FCA 199. This appeal is now moot given Khadr's plea agreement: *Canada* v. *Khadr* [2011] FCA 92.

[87] See William C. Banks, Chapter 18, this volume.

desire to return to Canada as well as the weakness of his case after the military commission ruled that confessions he made were admissible despite the fact that he had been threatened with rape in a US prison if he did not co-operate.[88] Khadr agreed to a sentence of eight additional years that included his transfer back to Canada after one more year in Guantánamo. This sentence is much lighter than the forty years that the jury of military officers at Guantánamo would have imposed after hearing victim impact statements and contested expert evidence that Khadr was dangerous.[89] Khadr will receive the benefit of his more lenient plea agreement, but he remains the only citizen of a Western democracy still imprisoned at Guantánamo.

D. Summary

Most academic and civil society concerns in the immediate aftermath of 9/11 focused on the ATA even though provisions of the IRPA and Canada's extra-territorial anti-terrorism activities presented a much greater threat to the values of due process and equality. As my colleague Audrey Macklin has suggested, 'laws that arouse deep concerns about civil liberties when applied to citizens are standard fare in the immigration context'.[90] Canada's extensive use of immigration law as anti-terrorism law has resulted in long-term and indeterminate detention of non-citizens suspected of terrorism. Although some legal challenges have resulted in reforms such as the use of special advocates to challenge secret evidence and increased retention of raw intelligence, the threat of deportation to torture still hangs over the remaining cases. Security certificates have failed as anti-terrorism policy and no security certificate has been issued with respect to a terrorist suspect since 2003.

Two public inquiries have provided extraordinary accountability for Canada's indirect role in the torture of Canadians held in Syria. These inquiries reveal the challenge of holding governments to account for whole of government responses to international terrorism because they had an extraordinary ability to see all the secret information and to review the conduct of all Canadian officials. At the same time, concerns remain over Canada's treatment of its Afghan detainees and of Omar

---

[88] *United States* v. *Khadr*, Ruling on Suppression Motion, 17 August 2010, available at www.defense.gov/news/D94-D111.pdf.

[89] 'Plea nets 8 years for Khadr', *Toronto Star*, 1 November 2010.

[90] Audrey Macklin, 'Borderline security' in Daniels, Macklem and Roach, *The Security of Freedom*, p. 393. See also Colin Harvey, Chapter 9, this volume.

Khadr who has been imprisoned at Guantánamo since he was fifteen years of age.

4. Canada's evolving anti-terrorism policy: the emphasis on public safety and security

There are reasons to doubt the effectiveness of the ATA as an instrument to deter acts of terrorism. Even before its enactment, most acts of terrorism were already punished as serious crimes. The ATA may marginally increase the severity and certainty of punishment, but determined terrorists are not rational actors readily amenable to deterrence. The ATA will probably be most useful when it is directed at third parties, such as financial institutions, that could provide services to terrorists. These entities may well be encouraged to cease dealing with suspected terrorists. At the same time, there may be problems of over-deterrence and inflicting harm on the innocent. Terrorism financing lists may include innocent people by containing those with names similar to those of terrorists. They may also deter legitimate charitable giving to Muslim charities and charities that work in countries where there is terrorism.

Reliance on immigration law as anti-terrorism law is both over-inclusive and under-inclusive. Policies such as the safe third country agreement will turn away many more legitimate refugees than deflect terrorists. The type of long-term detention allowed under immigration law security certificates may incapacitate suspected terrorists, but without a clear finding of guilt. The head of CSIS has criticised NGOs, journalists and lawyers who he claims sympathise with suspected terrorists.[91] Unfortunately, he failed to recognise that many of those he criticises are reacting to the unfairness of his agency's use of foreign and domestic intelligence as secret evidence in security certificate proceedings as well as the government's attempt to deport such persons to a substantial risk of torture in countries such as Egypt and Syria. In contrast, there is much less sympathy for those whose guilt has been proven beyond a reasonable doubt with public

---

[91] Richard Fadden alleged that suspected terrorists are 'given tender-hearted profiles, and more or less taken at their word when they accuse CSIS or other government agencies of abusing them … It sometimes seems that to be accused of having terrorist connections in Canada has become a status symbol, a badge of courage in the struggle against the real enemy, which would appear to be, at least sometimes, the government. To some members of civil society, there is a certain romance to this. This loose partnership of single-issue NGOs, advocacy journalists and lawyers has succeeded, to a certain extent, in forging a positive public image for anyone accused of terrorist links or charges': 'Remarks', 29 October 2009.

evidence. Even if the detainees could be deported to a safe country, it is not clear that deportation of suspected international terrorists will actually increase security. It may simply displace the problem of global terrorism. Finally, immigration law cannot be used against terrorist suspects who are Canadian citizens and may have contributed to Canada's relative inexperience in the difficult task of terrorism prosecutions.

Reliance on military force such as Canada's participation in the war against the Taliban regime in Afghanistan may play some role in disrupting terrorist cells and state sponsors of terrorism. Nevertheless, the war has not incapacitated al-Qaeda-inspired terrorism or even the Taliban. Reliance on war also results in loss of innocent lives and has costs in terms of human rights. Canadian troops in Afghanistan participated in the transfer of some prisoners to Guantánamo Bay at a time when it was a 'legal black hole'[92] and they continue to transfer detainees to the Afghan intelligence agency despite concerns that this may result in torture.

What then ought Canada and other countries do to respond to the very real risk of terrorism? Clearly doing nothing is not an option because of the dire consequences of even one successful act of biological, chemical or nuclear terrorism or the poisoning of food or water supplies. In 2004, Canada enacted the Public Safety Act[93] which increased controls over dangerous materials such as explosives and toxins and provided for increased aviation security measures. Administrative and environmental controls that help secure sites and substances that can be used to commit acts of terrorism are promising anti-terrorism measures that present less of a threat to due process and equality values than reliance on immigration or criminal law.[94] It is unfortunate that defining as crimes of terrorism much that was already illegal before 9/11 was a priority for the Canadian government while administrative measures to reduce the damage that could be caused by terrorists were not. At the same time, the criminal law approach taken in the ATA, as well as the immigration law approach that was subsequently relied upon, was partially encouraged by

---

[92] Johan Steyn, 'Guantanamo Bay: The Legal Black Hole' (2004) 53 *International and Comparative Law Quarterly* 1. The Supreme Court of Canada recognised in *Khadr* v. *Canada* [2008] 2 SCR 125 that indeterminate detention without resort to habeas corpus at Guantánamo violated international law. It did so in large part by relying on *Hamdan* v. *Rumsfeld* 126 S Ct. 2749 (2006). For discussion of *Hamdan* see William C. Banks, Chapter 18 this volume.

[93] SC 2004 c.15.

[94] For example, Canadian police monitor the sale of large quantities of fertiliser that can be used in bombs: 'How a terror plot turned into a "gardening incident"', *Globe and Mail*, 10 June 2010.

United Nations Security Council Resolution 1373, which called for criminalisation of financing and participation in terrorism, better border controls and attention to the risk of refugee status being used by terrorists.[95]

An administrative and environmental approach designed to prevent
terrorists from gaining access to substances such as explosives, chemical
or nuclear materials or sites vulnerable to terrorism such as aeroplanes
and nuclear plants has a number of benefits. Such softer but smarter strategies do not rely upon punishment and detention to the same extent as
criminal and immigration law. They help implement the mandate in UN
Security Council Resolution 1540 to take steps to ensure that terrorists do
not gain access to nuclear, chemical or biological material. They also work
as a failsafe should it prove impossible to deter, incapacitate or identify all
the terrorists. More effective security screening may also limit or at least
equalise damage done to liberty, privacy and equality.

Technology can be used to screen all passengers and all shippers and
not just those who fit into a perhaps faulty profile of a terrorist. To be sure,
technology, such as the use of biometrics, could have a negative impact
on privacy. When applied to large-scale populations, it will also produce
a considerable number of false positives and false negatives. It will not be
possible to screen all passengers of mass transit, but it should be possible to
provide better controls on explosives and other materials that can be used
for bombs. Terrorists can adjust to target hardening. For example, better
controls over air passengers have underlined the urgent need to better
screen cargo that is shipped on planes including passenger airlines.[96]

Some environmental measures such as better monitoring of public
health and the safety of food and water have the important additional
benefit of providing protections against diseases and accidental contamination of food and water, as well as terrorism. Better security for computer systems would protect them not only from a cyber-terrorism attack,
but also from random attacks by hackers. Better emergency preparedness
also serves similar all-risk functions as it better prepares society to deal
with a wide range of natural and man-made disasters such as earthquakes
and black-outs. The Public Safety Act[97] contains provisions that allow

---

[95] For a critique of these UN initiatives see Kent Roach, 'Sources and trends in post-9/11
anti-terrorism law' in Liora Lazurus and Benjamin J. Goold (eds.), *Human Rights and
Security* (Oxford: Hart, 2007).

[96] The Air India Commission stressed the threat to aviation security caused by cargo carried on passenger planes that is not screened: Air India Commission, *Air India Flight 182*,
vol. 4.

[97] Part 1 allows emergency directions when necessary to deal with immediate risks to
safety, security, health and the environment in relation to aeronautics; part 3 in relation

Ministers of Transport, the Environment, Health and Defence to take temporary measures in a wide range of emergencies, not just with respect to terrorism. The American National Research Council has concluded in a post-9/11 report that we should invest in strategies that will make us safer not only from terrorist attacks, but from disaster, disease and accidents.[98] Such strategies also present less of a risk, both for the targets and for society, of targeting the wrong people. The 2011 border declaration between Canada and the United States contemplates a common all-risk approach to security by recognising common interests not only in preventing terrorists from entering a common perimeter, but also in responding to a wide range of natural and man-made emergencies and protecting 'health security'. [99]

Many provisions in the Public Safety Act[100] facilitate the collection and sharing of information within governments and between governments. Although this may respond to some concerns that security information is not appropriately communicated within government, the information-sharing provisions also raise concerns about privacy and transparency, as well as practical concerns about decision-makers being swamped by too much information. Vast databases can undermine privacy while producing information about potential terrorists that may not be accurate or helpful. The lack of a federal Ombudsperson and broad protections of information that the government claims is secret make it difficult to review the propriety of increased information sharing within and among governments. The challenge for the government will be to make optimal uses of its resources to protect the security of Canadians and to ensure that review keeps pace with increased national security activities so as to minimise intrusions on important democratic values such as equality, fairness and the right to engage in religious or political dissent.

---

to environmental protection; part 6 in relation to health; part 9 in relation to food and drugs; part 10 in relation to hazardous products; part 15 in relation to navigable waters; part 18 in relation to pest control products; part 20 in relation to quarantines; part 21 in relation to radiation emitting devices; and part 22 in relation to shipping. In subsequent years, Parliament has enacted new laws for emergency management and quarantines. See Craig Forcese *National Security Law* (Toronto: Irwin Law, 2008), Chapter 9.

[98] National Research Council, *Making the Nation Safer: The Role of Science and Technology in Countering Terrorism* (Washington, DC: National Academy Press, 2002).

[99] Beyond the Border: A Shared Vision for Perimeter Security and Economic Competitiveness.

[100] SC 2004 c. 15. For example, part 5 of the Act amends the Department of Citizenship and Immigration Act to permit the sharing of information with other governments and foreign organisations, and part 11 allows the collection and disclosure of information for national security purposes under the IRPA. Part 17 extends the government databases and agencies that can be consulted in relation to terrorist financing.

In response not only to 9/11, but also to the SARS crisis, black-outs, and contamination of food and water, a new Ministry of Public Safety was created in late 2003. The Minister has responsibilities for a new Canada Border Services Agency and the Office of Critical Infrastructure and Emergency Preparedness. The new Ministry was designed in part to allow for better integration with the new US Department of Homeland Security[101] and it has seen significant increases in its budget in large part to deal with its new emergency preparedness mandate. The Public Safety Ministry has the potential to develop a more comprehensive and rational approach to the various risks that Canadians face to their well-being. It could allow for cost-effective distribution of limited resources with a premium placed on strategies that protect Canadians not only from terrorism but other harms. This all-risk approach was adopted in a national security policy released in April 2004 that includes commitments to better emergency preparedness, better public health, better transport security and better peacekeeping, as well as the more traditional terrorism-specific proposals relating to better intelligence and better border security.[102] This national security policy, which was not repealed by Canada's Conservative government that has ruled since 2006, can be contrasted with the post-9/11 Bush policy of pre-emptive use of military force. At the same time, it is consistent with a renewed emphasis in the United States on emergency preparedness in the wake of problems recovering from Hurricane Katrina.

The above developments do not, however, guarantee that Canada's security policy will be effective. There has been increased spending on security intelligence in Canada since 9/11, but problems remain with the co-ordination of multiple intelligence agencies in Canada and their sometimes uneasy relation with the police. The 2010 Air India inquiry found problems with the transfer of intelligence and co-ordination of security activities within government. It recommended enhanced powers for the Prime Minister's National Security Advisor in order to co-ordinate whole of government responses to terrorism.[103] This role would involve

---

[101] See William C. Banks, Chapter 18, this volume

[102] 'This system is capable of responding to both intentional and unintentional threats. It is as relevant in securing Canadians against the next SARS-like outbreak as it is in addressing the risk of a terrorist attack': Canadian Government, *Securing an Open Society: Canada's National Security Policy* (April 2004), p. 10. See also Kent Roach, 'Canada's responses to terrorism: human security at home?' in Nik Hynek and David Bosold, *Canada's Foreign and Security Policy* (Oxford University Press, 2010).

[103] Air India Commission, *Air India Flight 182*, vol. 3, pp. 26–47. The government's response to the Commission did not include an enhanced role for the National Security Advisor. Canada, Action Plan The Government of Canada Response to the Commission of

not only determining when intelligence should be turned over to the police, but also the effectiveness of how many ministries respond to the threat of terrorism. These review proposals complement those of the Arar Commission which stressed the need to review the propriety of whole of government responses to terrorism. Review of both the propriety and efficacy of anti-terrorism activities has not caught up to the increased intensity and integration of such activity. Unlike in most democracies, no legislative committee in Canada has regular access to secret information.[104] Effective review should be welcomed as a means of improving security activities and ensuring public confidence in such activities. Too often, however, review is seen as a threat to the vested interests of agencies responsible for security. The Canadian government has rejected both the Arar and Air India Commission's recommendations for increased review of national security activities.

5. Conclusion

Canada is an interesting case study of how a democracy can counter terrorism. Canada did not declare a state of emergency after 9/11 as it did in response to the terrorism in October 1970 but rather enacted a broad new ATA. There was a fairly robust civil society debate about the effect of this permanent legislation on civil liberties and some controversial provisions were amended and subject to sunsets. Provisions for preventive arrests and investigative hearings expired in 2007 and Canada's minority government has failed in several attempts to re-instate these police powers.

In the initial years after 9/11, Canada relied on immigration law as anti-terrorism law as opposed to criminal prosecutions under the new ATA. The use of security certificates were successfully challenged and special advocates can now challenge the secret evidence. More emphasis has now been placed on criminal prosecutions, including successful prosecutions of a transnational plot and serious plots in Toronto. Canada's foreign anti-terrorism activities have also been controversial and resulted in two public inquiries that have found that Canadian officials have contributed to the torture of Canadians held abroad on suspicion of terrorism.

Inquiry into the Investigation of the Bombing of Air India Flight 182 December, 2010 (Ottawa: Her Majesty the Queen in Right of Canada, 2010).

[104] It appears that a few parliamentarians may be given access to secret information in relation to the treatment of Canada's detainees in Afghanistan, but only subject to oversight by an ad hoc committee of judges.

Finally, Canada proclaimed an all-risk national security policy and re-organised the lead public safety ministry around emergency preparedness as a means to respond not only to terrorism but other threats to security. This is a promising policy, but one that needs to be complemented by more effective review of both the propriety and efficacy of the government's intensified and integrated national security activities.

21

Anti-terror legislation in Australia and New Zealand

GEORGE WILLIAMS

1. Introduction

Australia and New Zealand may seem unlikely targets for a terrorist attack. They are geographically isolated and only minor players in the global response to the threat of terrorism. It is therefore unsurprising that the New Zealand Security Intelligence Service (NZSIS) assesses the level of terrorist threat in that nation as 'low',[1] and the Australian National Counter-Terrorism Alert system has since 2003 set its threat level at 'medium' (a terrorist attack 'could' occur).[2] Nonetheless, governments in both nations continue to emphasise the dangers posed by the 'global violent jihadist movement'.[3] In its 2008 annual report, NZSIS stated that the country 'continually faces threats from espionage, sabotage, subversion, terrorism, and clandestine and damaging actions'.[4] In 2010, the Australian government reiterated that '[t]he threat of terrorism to Australia is real and enduring. It has become a persistent and permanent feature of Australia's security environment'.[5]

Anthony Mason Professor and Foundation Director, Gilbert & Tobin Centre of Public Law, University of New South Wales; Australian Research Council Laureate Fellow. I thank Nicola McGarrity for her comments on an earlier draft, and Keiran Hardy and Jesse Galdston for their research assistance.

[1] New Zealand Security Intelligence Service, *Our Work: Protecting New Zealand from Terrorist Attacks* (2010), available at www.nzsis.govt.nz/work/terrorism.html.
[2] Australian National Security, *National Counter-Terrorism Alert System* (2010) www.nationalsecurity.gov.au.
[3] See Australian Government, *Counter-Terrorism White Paper: Securing Australia – Protecting Our Community* (2010).
[4] New Zealand Security Intelligence Service, *Annual Report* (2008), p. 5.
[5] Australian Government, *Counter-Terrorism White Paper: Securing Australia – Protecting our Community* (2010), p. ii.

These comments might seem exaggerated in light of the fact that there has not been a successful terrorist attack on Australian or New Zealand soil for more than twenty years. In the last decade, however, many Australians and New Zealanders have died in terrorist attacks overseas. In the 9/11 attacks, ten Australians and two New Zealanders were killed. A year later, on 12 October 2002, eighty-eight Australians and three New Zealanders were among the 202 dead when two bombs exploded in the Sari Club and Paddy's Bar in Bali, Indonesia. In July 2005, one Australian and one New Zealander were killed in the London bombings. Most recently, in July 2009, three Australians and one New Zealander were killed in the Jakarta hotel bombings. While these numbers may seem small compared to the death toll of other nations, they have had a major impact on the politics of these two countries.

This chapter examines the new laws enacted after 9/11 by the Australian and New Zealand parliaments. Its focus is on the laws introduced into Australia for three main reasons. First, Australia has enacted many more anti-terror laws than New Zealand: an extraordinary forty-four pieces of legislation in the six years following 9/11. Second, and perhaps because of the extraordinary scope of its legislation, Australia has had substantial experience in prosecuting terrorism offences. To date, thirty-seven men have been charged with preparatory and group-based terrorism offences in Australia, and two men have been made subject to control orders imposing restrictions on their liberty. In contrast, no one has been charged with a terrorism offence in New Zealand. Third, Australia provides a useful counterfactual scenario as a democratic nation without a national human rights instrument. This provides a unique contrast to nations such as the United Kingdom[6] and Canada,[7] which have similar human rights instruments to the New Zealand Bill of Rights Act 1990.

2.   Human rights law in Australia

Terrorism is an attack on our most basic human rights. It can infringe our right to life and our ability to live our lives free of fear. Our response to terrorism also raises important human rights issues. Indeed, it poses some of the most important questions of law and policy of our

---

[6] See Helen Fenwick and Gavin Phillipson, Chapter 19, this volume, for a discussion of key human rights under the European Convention and their impact on the United Kingdom's control order scheme through the UK Human Rights Act 1998.

[7] See Kent Roach, Chapter 20 this volume.

time. Should the death penalty be reintroduced into Australia and New Zealand for terrorism offences? Should, as Dershowitz has argued,[8] the law provide for a 'torture warrant' whereby a terrorist suspect might be tortured to gain information about a large-scale, imminent danger to the community? Should the police be able to detain terrorist suspects for weeks without charge? Should governments be able to access our emails without our knowledge to search for information about pending attacks? The list goes on.

Unfortunately, unlike every other Western democratic nation, Australia must search for answers to these questions without the benefit of a national human rights law like a Bill of Rights.[9] The task is even more difficult when, after 9/11, new laws have often been made in great haste.[10] In the aftermath of a terrorist attack, when public hysteria is at its highest, a Bill of Rights can potentially play an important role. They are certainly far from foolproof,[11] and indeed their capacity to make a difference at such a time has been doubted.[12] Nevertheless, such instruments

---

[8] Alan Dershowitz, *Why Terrorism Works* (New Haven, CT: Yale University Press, 2002).

[9] See generally George Williams, *Human Rights under the Australian Constitution* (Oxford University Press, 1999); George Williams, *A Charter of Rights for Australia* (University of New South Wales Press, 2007). A National Human Rights Consultation was commissioned by the Commonwealth government in December 2008. The *National Human Rights Consultation: Report*, released to the public in October 2009, recommended the enactment of a statutory Bill of Rights at the national level. This recommendation has been rejected by the Commonwealth government. The government instead proposes to: (1) establish a Joint Parliamentary Committee on Human Rights, which will engage in scrutiny of Bills against the human rights set out in the core United Nations human rights treaties; and (2) require all new Bills and disallowable legislative instruments introduced into the Commonwealth Parliament to be accompanied by statements assessing compatibility with those human rights. See Human Rights (Parliamentary Scrutiny) Bill 2010 and Human Rights (Parliamentary Scrutiny) (Consequential Provisions) Bill 2010.

[10] See Andrew Lynch, Chapter 7, this volume, for a discussion of the 'urgency' paradigm affecting the passage of anti-terror laws since 9/11. See also Andrew Lynch, 'Legislating with urgency – the enactment of the Anti-Terrorism Act [No 1] 2005 (Cth)' (2006) 30 *Melbourne University Law Review* 747; Anthony Reilly, 'The processes and consequences of counter-terrorism law in Australia: 2001–2005' (2007) 10 *Flinders Journal of Law Reform* 81; Greg Carne, 'Hasten slowly: urgency, discretion and review – a counter-terrorism legislative agenda and legacy' (2008) 13 *Deakin Law Review* 49.

[11] See Andrew Lynch, Chapter 7 this volume, and Kent Roach, 'The dangers of a charter-proof and crime-based response to terrorism' in Ronald J. Daniels, Patrick Macklem and Kent Roach (eds), *The Security of Freedom: Essays on Canada's Anti-Terrorism Bill* (University of Toronto Press 2001), pp. 131–50, for a discussion of the negative effect Charters of Rights can have on the pre-enactment scrutiny of anti-terror legislation.

[12] See Tam Campbell, 'Emergency strategies for prescriptive in legal positivists: anti-terrorist law and legal theory' in Victor V. Ramraj, (ed.), *Emergencies and the Limits of Legality* (Cambridge University Press, 2008), pp. 201, 220–2.

can remind governments and communities of a society's basic values and of the principles that might otherwise be compromised at a time of grief and fear. After new laws have been made, a Bill of Rights can also allow courts to assess them against human rights principles.[13] This provides a final check on laws that, with the benefit of hindsight, ought not to have been passed. The absence of such a check is one reason why Australian law after 9/11 can be unusually severe, as compared to other nations, in its impact upon individual rights. The situation differs in New Zealand, in part because the New Zealand Bill of Rights Act 1990 shapes legislative, executive and judicial decision-making in this and other fields.

In Australia, the absence of a Bill of Rights means that there is rarely a role for judges in assessing new terrorism laws, and what role they do have is usually at the margins of the debate. When it comes to constitutional constraints, judges are generally limited to applying the structural features of the Constitution – for example, limitations on legislative power derived from federalism or the separation of judicial power. In almost all cases, there is simply no constitutional remedy for the violation of human rights, such as discrimination on the basis of race. Where there is a rare example of the Constitution recognising a human right, such as freedom of religion, Australia's final court of appeal, the High Court, has tended to interpret the right so narrowly as to be of little use.[14]

The most significant role played by the courts occurs in the context of statutory interpretation. According to Chief Justice Mason and Justices Brennan, Gaudron and McHugh of the High Court of Australia in *Coco* v. *The Queen*,[15] '[t]he courts should not impute to the legislature an intention to interfere with fundamental rights. Such an intention must be clearly manifested by unmistakable and unambiguous language'. Hence, 'a statute or statutory instrument which purports to impair a right to personal liberty is interpreted, if possible, so as to respect that right'.[16]

The result is that parliaments can usually depart from fundamental rights so long as their law is clear in its expressed intent and operates within the structural limits set out in the Australia Constitution. In general, there is no mechanism through which the courts can analyse whether

---

[13] See, e.g., Helen Fenwick and Gavin Phillipson, Chapter 19 this volume, for a discussion of the 2010 *Gillan* v. *Quinton* case, in which the Strasbourg court held that the UK stop and search powers under ss. 44 and 45 of the Terrorism Act 2000 were contrary to art. 8 of the European Convention on Human Rights.

[14] See generally Williams, *Human Rights under the Australian Constitution*.

[15] (1994) 179 CLR 427, 437.

[16] *Re Bolton; Ex parte Beane* (1987) 162 CLR 514, 523 per Justice Brennan.

the abrogation of human rights is necessary or proportionate. Unlike in every other Western democratic nation, the absence of a Bill of Rights in Australia means that the issue can be purely political. The extent to which human rights are considered when enacting legislation is up to the legislators themselves. As is demonstrated by the legislation introduced into the federal Parliament after 9/11 (discussed below), the contours of debate will frequently match the majoritarian pressures of Australian political life rather than the principles and values upon which the democratic system depends. This means that any check upon the power of parliaments or governments to abrogate human rights derives from political debate and the goodwill of political leaders. This is not a check that is regarded as acceptable or sufficient in other nations.

It is possible that clear, prospective emergency powers laws might blunt the need for new legislation after a major terrorist attack in a nation like Australia,[17] but that is doubtful. The experience in Australia is that the political imperative for action after a terrorist incident has been so strong, and so unconstrained by a political or legal culture of human rights protection, that even an existing regime of emergency powers would not likely prevent the passage of significant extra legislation. Certainly, the presence of a large number of anti-terror statutes on the books has not deterred government from seeking major new powers after further terrorist attacks.

The lack of a domestic reference point for basic rights in Australia means that it is difficult to determine the extent to which, if at all, particular human rights and the rule of law should be compromised in the name of national security and in the fight against terrorism. As in many other debates, the absence of a domestic Bill of Rights means that Australians can turn to international law. The United Nations has been a focus of debate and activity in responding to terrorism, and a number of international instruments are important, such as UN Security Council Resolution 1373, made on 28 September 2001, which determines that States shall '[p]revent and suppress the financing of terrorist acts' and '[t]ake the necessary steps to prevent the commission of terrorist acts'. Other instruments ratified by Australia – such as the International Covenant on Civil and Political Rights – recognise that governments must protect their citizens from terrorism, but that any such action must be in accordance with accepted human rights principles.

Although such international instruments can provide useful assistance on human rights issues and national security, they have not been

---

[17] See, generally, Campbell, 'Emergency strategies for prescriptive legal positivists', p. 201.

incorporated into Australian law and so lack legal force and political legitimacy. Australia is replete with examples of the latter.[18] For example, when there was criticism in 2000 from the United Nations Human Rights Committee of the mandatory sentencing regime for minor property offences then in operation in the Northern Territory, its Chief Minister, Denis Burke, stated: 'This is designed to cause embarrassment. This is designed to shame Australians. And to my mind an opportunity for Australians to tell them to bugger off.'[19] The response of the then federal government was less direct, but the message was the same. Prime Minister Howard rejected any international pressure, stating on Perth radio that 'we are mature enough to make decisions on these matters ourselves full stop'.[20] By contrast, the Howard government felt the need to respond quickly to the 'international pressure' created by United Nations Security Council Resolution 1373 to criminalise terrorist acts. The current Labor government led by Prime Minister Julia Gillard is more open to engaging with international human rights bodies, but nonetheless there is little evidence that such bodies and international human rights principles have much impact on policy and law-making in Australia.

3.   Australia's anti-terror laws

Australia has a short history of enacting laws aimed at terrorism.[21] In fact, before 9/11, only the Northern Territory had such a law,[22] and in other Australian jurisdictions politically-motivated violence was instead dealt with by the ordinary criminal law. The Australian government's response to 9/11 was similar to that of many other countries. It emphasised the need to deviate from the ordinary criminal law – with its emphasis on punishment of individuals after the fact – by pre-empting terrorist acts from occurring in the first place.

---

[18] See Devika Hovell, 'The sovereignty stratagem: Australia's response to UN human rights treaty bodies' (2003) 28 *Alternative Law Journal* 6.

[19] 'NT under fire again for mandatory sentencing', Australian Broadcasting Corporation Radio, *PM Program*, available at www.abc.net.au/pm/stories/s154694.htm.

[20] Interview on Perth Radio 6PR, available at www.abc.net.au/worldtoday/stories/s103292.htm.

[21] For a history of terrorism laws in Australia, see Jenny Hocking, *Terror Laws: ASIO, Counter-Terrorism and the Threat to Democracy* (University of New South Wales Press, 2003).

[22] Criminal Code Act (NT), Pt. III Div. 2. The provisions were modelled on the Prevention of Terrorism (Temporary Provisions) Act 1974 (UK).

The result was an extraordinary burst of law-making by the Australian Parliament. From 2002 to 2007 under the conservative Howard Coalition government, Parliament enacted forty-eight separate anti-terrorism statutes – an average of one new law every seven weeks. That government lost office at the November 2007 election to the Australian Labor Party led by Kevin Rudd. Rudd was then replaced as Prime Minister by his own party in mid-2010 by Prime Minister Julia Gillard.

Since 2007, only six pieces of anti-terror legislation have been passed during the time of the Rudd/Gillard Labor Governments. The Independent National Security Legislation Monitor Act 2010 creates a new office to report on the operation and effectiveness of Australia's regime of anti-terror legislation, although the office has not yet been formally established. Most recently, the National Security Legislation Amendment Act 2010 was passed by both Houses of the Australian Parliament. It includes a large number of changes to Australia's counter-terror laws. Many of these are technical amendments, and some are improvements in human rights tenus on previous legislation: for example, the Act sets a new seven-day cap on 'dead time' authorised by magistrates in terrorism investigations,[23] and raises the threshold for the offence of 'advocating' terrorist activity.[24] Most contentiously, however, the Act gives the Australian Federal Police (AFP) the power to enter premises without a warrant where an officer reasonably suspects that this is necessary to 'prevent a thing that is on the premises from being used in connection with a terrorism offence' and 'there is a serious and imminent threat to a person's life, health and safety'.[25] While on the premises, officers will then have the power to seize any other thing not specified in the warrant if they reasonably suspect that it is necessary to do so because the circumstances are 'serious or urgent'.[26] The officers may also re-enter the premises at a later time if an emergency situation suspends the exercise of the warrant.[27]

A.   The definition of a 'terrorist act' and terrorism offences

Australia's first two packages of national anti-terrorism legislation were introduced into the federal Parliament by the Howard government in March 2002 as part of its response to United Nations Security Council

---

[23] See below note 49.   [24] See below note 38.
[25] National Security Legislation Amendment Act 2010 (Cth) sch. 4, cl. 3UEA(1).
[26] Ibid., sch. 4, cl. 3UEA(5).   [27] Ibid., sch. 5.

Resolution 1373.[28] The most important statute in the first package was the Security Legislation Amendment (Terrorism) Act 2002 (Terrorism Act).[29] Section 100.1 introduced a definition of 'terrorist act' into the Criminal Code Act 1995 (Cth) (Criminal Code). The definition has both intentional and physical elements. The intentional elements are that the act or threat of action must be done with the intention of: (1) 'advancing a political, religious or ideological cause'; and (2) coercing or influencing by intimidation an Australian or foreign government or intimidating the public or a section of the public. The first of these has been particularly controversial. The concerns about such an element were set out by Justice Rutherford of the Ontario Superior Court of Justice in the Canadian case of *R* v. *Khawaja*. He concluded that:

> [T]he focus on the essential ingredient of political, religious or ideological motive will chill freedom [of] protected speech, religion, thought, belief, expression and association, and therefore, democratic life; and will promote fear and suspicion of targeted political or religious groups, and will result in racial or ethnic profiling by governmental authorities at many levels.[30]

Nevertheless, the Security Legislation Review Committee, in reviewing Australia's anti-terrorism laws in 2006, recommended that this element be maintained. It regarded it as a 'specific and narrowing provision in defining the scope of the "terrorist act"', thereby ensuring that it was not a disproportionate limitation on the rights guaranteed by the International Covenant on Civil and Political Rights.[31]

---

[28] See generally C. H. Powell, Chapter 2, this volume.

[29] The other Bills were the Suppression of the Financing of Terrorism Bill 2002; Criminal Code Amendment (Suppression of Terrorist Bombings) Bill 2002; Border Security Legislation Amendment Bill 2002; Telecommunications Interception Legislation Amendment Bill 2002.

[30] [2006] OJ 4245, [73]. For both sides of the debate about the inclusion of a motivational element, see Ben Saul, 'The curious element of motive in definitions of terrorism: essential ingredient or criminalising thought?' and Kent Roach, 'The case for defining terrorism with restraint and without reference to political or religious motive' in Andrew Lynch, Edwina MacDonald and George Williams (eds.), *Law and Liberty in the War on Terror* (Sydney: Federation Press, 2007).

[31] Security Legislation Review Committee, *Report of the Security Legislation Review Committee* (2006) p. 57. In at least one instance, the specific nature of the definition may have affected the ability to secure a successful prosecution. In the case of Zeky Mallah, a basis for acquittal may have been that the accused committed the relevant act not for a political, religious or ideological purpose, but for purely personal reasons. See Nicola McGarrity, '"Testing" our counter-terrorism laws: the prosecution of individuals for terrorism offences in Australia' (2010) 34 *Criminal Law Journal* 92, 96.

In terms of the physical elements of the definition of a 'terrorist act', the act or threat of action must satisfy one of the following criteria:

(a) involves serious physical harm to a person;
(b) involves serious damage to property;
(c) causes a person's death;
(d) endangers a person's life, other than the life of the person taking the action;
(e) creates a serious risk to the health or safety of the public or a section of the public; or
(f) seriously interferes with, seriously disrupts, or destroys, an electronic system.

Furthermore, advocacy, protest, dissent or industrial action (whether lawful or not) is excluded so long as it is not intended to, among other things, cause serious physical harm to a person or create a serious risk to the health or safety of the public.[32]

The definition of a 'terrorist act' provides the basis for the individual terrorism offences in Division 101 of the Criminal Code. Division 101 makes it an offence to engage in a terrorist act as well as to engage in conduct in preparation for a terrorist act. This conduct includes making a document or possessing a 'thing' connected with preparation for a terrorist act or doing any act in preparation for a terrorist act. The preparatory offences reflect the deliberate legislative policy of the Commonwealth Parliament to shift the focus in the anti-terrorism context from the punishment and deterrence of criminal conduct to the *prevention* of such conduct. Amendments to the Criminal Code in 2005 reinforced this policy by providing that an offence is committed even if 'a terrorist act does not occur'.[33] The preparatory offences therefore go significantly further than the inchoate offences of 'attempt', 'incitement' and 'conspiracy' in the Criminal Code by eliminating the requirement that the prosecution prove that a defendant planned to commit a specific terrorist act.

---

[32] No amendments have been made to the definition of a 'terrorist act' since the enactment of the Security Legislation Amendment (Terrorism) Act 2002. The Commonwealth government has, however, announced that it is negotiating with the Australian states to make amendments to the definition to include psychological (rather than merely physical) harm. See House of Representatives, Australian Parliament, 18 March 2010, 2922 (Robert McClelland).

[33] Anti-Terrorism Act 2005 (Cth).

B. Proscription of organisations

The Terrorism Act empowered the federal Attorney-General to proscribe organisations.[34] Nineteen such organisations are currently banned.[35]

Under the law as first enacted, the Attorney-General was not granted a unilateral power of proscription but was only permitted to proscribe organisations identified as such by the United Nations Security Council.[36] This limitation was removed by the Criminal Code Amendment (Terrorist Organisations) Act 2004, which gave the Attorney-General the power to determine that a body is a terrorist organisation if 'satisfied on reasonable grounds that the organisation is directly or indirectly engaged in preparing, planning, assisting in or fostering the doing of a terrorist act (whether or not the terrorist act has occurred or will occur)'. An organisation may also be declared to fall within the definition of a 'terrorist organisation' by a court.

The Anti-Terrorism Act (No 2) 2005 (Cth) added an additional ground upon which an organisation can be proscribed, namely, if it 'advocates the doing of a terrorist act (whether or not the terrorist act has occurred or will occur)'. The definition of 'advocates' applies to an organisation that directly or indirectly urges, counsels or provides instruction on the doing of a terrorist act, or even an organisation that 'directly praises the doing of a terrorist act in circumstances where there is a risk that such praise might have the effect of leading a person (regardless of his or her age or any mental impairment that the person might suffer) to engage in a terrorist act'.[37] The National Security Legislation Amendment Act 2010 now restricts this latter element to conduct that creates a 'substantial' risk of subsequent terrorist activity.[38] Nonetheless, the scope of this definition

---

[34] For a detailed discussion of the history of this power, see Andrew Lynch, Nicola McGarrity and George Williams, 'The proscription of terrorist organisations in Australia' (2009) 37 *Federal Law Review* 1.

[35] Australian Government National Security website www.nationalsecurity.gov.au/agd/ www/nationalsecurity.nsf/AllDocs/95FB057CA3DECF30CA256FAB001F7FBD?Open Document.

[36] See C. H. Powell, Chapter 2, this volume, for a critique of the UN listing regime under Security Council Resolution 1267. See also Christopher Michaelsen, 'The Security Council's Al Qaeda and Taliban sanctions regime: "essential tool" or increasing liability for the UN's counterterrorism efforts?' (2010) 33 *Studies in Conflict & Terrorism* 448–63.

[37] Criminal Code, s. 102.1(1A). The Terrorist Material Act 2007 (Cth) also introduced a new s. 9A into the Classification (Publications, Films and Computer Games) Act 1995 (Cth) which provides that a publication, film or computer game that advocates the doing of a terrorist act must be refused classification (that is, banned). The definition of 'advocates' is in the same terms as s. 102.1(1A).

[38] National Security Legislation Amendment Act 2010 (Cth) sch. 2, pt. 1, cl. 2

remains extremely wide and problematic. It is arguable, for example, that an organisation could be proscribed as a terrorist organisation if just one member of that organisation praised liberation struggles in East Timor or against a colonial power.

Proscription does not have any automatic consequences for the organisation itself. The organisation is not, for example, declared to be unlawful or required to forfeit its property to the Commonwealth. The Criminal Code instead makes it an offence for a person to participate in the activities of a terrorist organisation. For example, it is an offence to: (1) direct the activities of a terrorist organisation; (2) provide training to, or receive training from, a terrorist organisation; (3) provide funds to, or receive funds from, a terrorist organisation; and (4) give support or resources to a terrorist organisation. While some of these offences are clearly justifiable, others fail adequately to target activities related to the threat of terrorism.[39] The training and funding offences, for example, make no distinction between the purposes for which the training or funding are made or used. It may be justifiable to criminalise training members of a terrorist organisation in the use of explosives or firearms, but not to criminalise training in the use of office equipment.

Controversially, the Criminal Code not only criminalises the involvement of individuals in the *activities* of a terrorist organisation. It also establishes two status offences. First, it is an offence to be a member of a terrorist organisation. The definition of membership is extremely broad and includes a person who is an informal member of a terrorist organisation or has taken steps to become a member of a terrorist organisation. Second, the Anti-Terrorism Act (No 2) 2004 (Cth) made it an offence to intentionally associate, on two or more occasions, with a member of a terrorist organisation.

C.   Expanded investigatory powers for intelligence-gathering and law enforcement agencies

The second package of anti-terrorism legislation introduced into the federal Parliament in March 2002 contained only the Australian Security Intelligence Organisation Legislation Amendment (Terrorism) Act 2002 (ASIO Act). It sought to confer unprecedented intelligence gathering

---

[39] Andrew Lynch and Nicola McGarrity, 'Australia's counter-terrorism laws: how neutral laws create fear and anxiety in Muslim communities' (2008) 33(4) *Alternative Law Journal* 225, 226.

powers on the Australian Security Intelligence Organisation (ASIO). In its original form as introduced into Parliament, the law would have allowed adults and even children who were *not* terrorist suspects, but who may have useful information about terrorism, to be strip searched and detained by ASIO for rolling two-day periods that could be extended indefinitely. While the Bill stated that detainees 'must be treated with humanity and with respect for human dignity', there was no penalty for ASIO officers who subjected detainees to cruel, inhuman or degrading treatment. The author of this chapter described the ASIO Bill as 'rotten to the core' and one of the worst Bills ever introduced into the federal Parliament.[40] Similarly, the Parliamentary Joint Committee on ASIO, Australian Secret Intelligence Service and Defence Signals Directorate unanimously found that the ASIO Bill 'would undermine key legal rights and erode the civil liberties that make Australia a leading democracy'.[41]

The ASIO Bill was only passed after one of the longest – fifteen months – and most bitter debates in Australian parliamentary history. The final Act is still directed at people who are not terrorist suspects, but does differ in important respects from the original Bill. The detention regime only applies to people aged sixteen years and over. As a general rule, detainees have access to a lawyer of their choice; ASIO may request that access be denied to a particular lawyer where the lawyer poses a security risk and communications between a detainee and his or her lawyer may be monitored. Australians may be questioned by ASIO for twenty-four hours, and may only be detained for a maximum of one week. They must then be released, but can be questioned again if a new warrant can be justified by fresh information. A person can only be held and questioned under the Act when ordered by a judge, and the questioning itself will be before a retired judge. The questioning must be video-taped and the whole process will be subject to the ongoing scrutiny of the Inspector-General of Intelligence and Security (who is effectively the Ombudsman for ASIO).

These additional protections in the hands of independent people blunted some of the worst excesses of the original ASIO Bill. However, even in this form, the ASIO Act could be justified only as a temporary response to the threat that terrorism poses to national security. Acceptance of this was reflected in the three-year sunset clause included in the Act. However,

---

[40] George Williams, 'Why the ASIO Bill is rotten to the core', *The Age* (Melbourne), 27 August 2002, 15.
[41] Parliamentary Joint Committee on ASIO, ASIS and DSD, Parliament of Australia, *An Advisory Report on the Australian Security Intelligence Organisation Legislation Amendment (Terrorism) Bill 2002* (2002) p. vii.

the difficulty of repealing anti-terrorism laws is evident in the fact that, in 2006, the Act was renewed for a further ten years.[42] This was despite the recommendation of a parliamentary committee that the Act should not be renewed for more than five years.[43]

Far from winding back the provisions of the ASIO Act, amending legislation since 2003 has expanded the period of time for which a person requiring an interpreter may be questioned to forty-eight hours and created two new offences regarding the disclosure of information about a warrant.[44] It is an offence, while a warrant is in effect, to disclose even the fact that a warrant has been issued or a person questioned or detained. It is also an offence, for up to two years after the expiration of a warrant, to disclose operational information obtained in connection with the issue of a warrant.

Major changes have since been made through legislation to the powers of the AFP. The Anti-Terrorism Act 2004 (Cth), for example, doubled the detention time for terrorism suspects to twenty-four hours.[45] In determining compliance with this time limit, any 'dead time' is to be disregarded.[46] 'Dead time' includes periods during which questioning is suspended to allow a person to communicate with a legal practitioner, receive medical attention or sleep. It also, however, gives judicial officers a broad power to declare periods of time within which 'the questioning of the person is reasonably suspended or delayed' to be 'dead time'. As demonstrated by the case of Dr Mohamed Haneef, this provision effectively enabled indefinite detention of terrorism suspects.

Haneef was detained at Brisbane Airport on 2 July 2007 after Australian authorities became aware that he had given a partially used SIM card to his second cousin in England, who was subsequently connected to an attempted car bombing at Glasgow Airport. The AFP made four separate applications to the courts for time to be specified as 'dead time'. As a result, it was not until 14 July 2007 (twelve days after he was first detained)

---

[42] See also Andrew Lynch, Chapter 7, this volume, for a discussion of the pernicious effects of sunset clauses and the tendency of anti-terror legislation to become normalised in domestic jurisdictions.

[43] Parliamentary Joint Committee on ASIO, ASIS and DSD, *Review of Division 3 Part III of the ASIO Act 1979 – ASIO's Questioning and Detention Powers* (2005) Recommendation 19.

[44] ASIO Legislation Amendment Act 2003 (Cth).

[45] A person may be detained for an initial period of four hours, which may then be extended by a judicial officer for an additional twenty hours: see Crimes Act 1914 (Cth) ss. 23CA, 23DA.

[46] Ibid. s. 23CA.

that Haneef was charged with the offence of recklessly providing support to a terrorist organisation. On 27 July 2007, the charge against Haneef was withdrawn. An independent inquiry into the *Haneef* case reported in November 2008 that:

> [T]here was no evidence that Dr Haneef knew he was giving his SIM card to a terrorist organisation or knew facts that would have demonstrated that he was reckless in giving his SIM card to Sabeel. In short, the material was completely deficient in the most important respect.[47]

The inquiry also noted that 'the most important deficiency in Part 1C of the Crimes Act is the absence of a cap on, or limit to, the amount of dead time that may be specified'. This is because 'the concept of uncapped detention time is unacceptable to the majority of the community and involves far too great an intrusion on the liberty of citizens and non-citizens alike'.[48] In response, the Commonwealth government included in the National Security Legislation Amendment Act 2010 a seven-day limit on 'dead' time that can be authorised by judicial officers.[49] While this cap is significantly longer than human rights organisations and academics have suggested (commonly between one and three days), it nevertheless represents a significant improvement on the prospect of indefinite detention. The new legislation also clarifies that dead time will only be counted once where multiple delays overlap, and that a suspect may be questioned during an administrative delay, although such questioning time will not be disregarded (for example, if a suspect is questioned while officers seek an extension of the investigation period from a magistrate).[50] This latter change is designed to ensure that police officers cannot take advantage of any 'free' questioning time during procedural delays.

D.   Control orders and preventative detention orders

The most important change to the powers of the AFP has been the introduction of control order and preventative detention order regimes by the Anti-Terrorism Act (No 2) 2005 (Cth). Division 104 of the Criminal Code permits an AFP officer, with the consent of the Commonwealth

---

[47] The Hon John Clarke, *Clarke Inquiry into the Case of Dr Mohamed Haneef* (2008) p. x.
[48] Ibid., 249.
[49] See National Security Legislation Amendment Act 2010 (Cth), sch. 3, cl. 16, inserting ss. 23DB(9)(m),(11), 23DD into the Crimes Act 1914 (Cth).
[50] See National Security Legislation Amendment Act 2010 (Cth), sch. 3, cl. 16, inserting ss. 23DB(9),(10) into the Crimes Act 1914 (Cth).

Attorney-General, to apply to the Court for a control order. Before granting either an interim or confirmed control order, the Court must be satisfied either that: making the order would substantially assist in preventing a terrorist act; or the person subject to the order has provided training to or receiving training from a terrorist organisation. The Court must also be satisfied that any obligations, prohibitions or restrictions imposed on a person under a control order are both reasonably necessary and reasonably appropriate and adapted for the purpose of protecting the public from a terrorist act.

Since 2005, only two control orders have been issued. Australia's first control order was issued against Joseph Thomas in August 2006. This was issued after Thomas's conviction for receiving money from al-Qaeda was overturned by an appeal court, which found that admissions made by Thomas in Pakistan had not been made freely. The conditions of Thomas's control order included a ban on communicating with a member of a terrorist organisation or any one of fifty specified people, including Osama bin Laden. The use of a control order in these circumstances has previously been criticised as demonstrating 'how the Government is willing to use these schemes in addition to the normal trial process, and even to have a second attempt at detaining a person where there has not been a conviction'.[51] A similar criticism could be levelled in relation to the issuing of a control order against David Hicks. Hicks, who had been detained at Guantánamo Bay since December 2001, pleaded guilty before a US military commission in March 2007 to the offence of providing material support to terrorism. He was transferred to Adelaide's Yatala Prison to serve the remaining nine months of his sentence, and became the second subject of an Australian control order upon his release in December 2007. The control orders against both Thomas and Hicks have since expired, and thus there is no control order currently in force in Australia.[52]

By contrast, the preventative detention order regime in Division 105 of the Criminal Code has never been used. Preventative detention orders enable the AFP to detain a person on the basis that detention will either aid in preventing the commission of an act of terrorism expected to occur within the next fourteen days or preserve evidence of a terrorist act which has occurred within the last twenty-eight days. The preventative detention

---

[51] Edwina MacDonald and George Williams, 'Combating terrorism: Australia's Criminal Code since September 11, 2001' (2007) 16 *Griffith Law Review* 27, 50.

[52] Compare with the approach of the United Kingdom, which has used substantially larger numbers of control orders as an alternative to prosecution and imprisonment: see Helen Fenwick and Gavin Phillipson, Chapter 19, this volume.

order regime imposes strict time limits upon the period of detention – an initial order (which is issued by a senior AFP officer) lasts up to twenty-four hours and a continued order (which is issued by retired judges, tribunal members or federal judges acting in their personal capacity) may last for a further period not more than forty-eight hours from the time the person was first detained. The regime was framed in this manner to avoid constitutional challenges based on the separation of powers doctrine in the Commonwealth Constitution.[53] However, complementary regimes in the Australian states and territories, which are not so constrained by that doctrine, permit an application to be made to a judge for a person to be detained for up to fourteen days. Australia's control order and preventative detention regimes have been viewed as problematic on the basis that they illustrates

> the tension in employing the law as a tool of preventative policy. They challenge the traditional purpose of legal regulation. Under neither order is there a need for a person to have been found guilty of, or even be suspected of committing, a crime. Yet both orders enable significant restrictions on individual liberty. This is more than a breach of the old 'innocent until proven guilty' maxim: it ignores the notion of guilt altogether.[54]

E.   National security information

In 2004, the federal Parliament enacted a new regime governing the disclosure of national security information in judicial proceedings. The National Security Information (Criminal and Civil Proceedings) Act 2004 (NSIA) enables the Commonwealth Attorney-General to issue a certificate if he or she believes that the disclosure of information is likely to prejudice national security. This triggers a requirement that the Court hold a closed hearing to determine what orders to make in relation to the disclosure of the information. Such orders may include: that a summary or statement of facts may only be disclosed in a redacted document or that a witness may not be called to give evidence.

There are two aspects of this regime which are particularly concerning. First, in deciding what orders to make, s. 31(8) of the NSIA requires

---

[53] This doctrine mandates a strict separation of judicial power from the legislative and executive arms of government. In particular, it means that only federal courts can be conferred with judicial power, and that federal courts cannot be conferred with power other than judicial power. See *R* v. *Kirby; Ex parte Boilermakers' Society of Australia* (1956) 94 CLR 254.

[54] Andrew Lynch and George Williams, *What Price Security? Taking Stock of Australia's Anti-Terror Laws* (University of New South Wales Press 2006) 42.

the Court to give greater weight to any risk to national security than the effect that the orders would have upon the defendant's right to a fair trial. Second, a defendant and even his or her legal representative may be excluded from the closed hearing if the Court regards their presence as prejudicing national security and the legal representative does not possess a security clearance at the level considered appropriate by the Secretary of the Attorney-General's Department. This means that defendants may be convicted when they have not been able to mount effective challenges to the admissibility of evidence. The NSIA, in allowing defendants to be convicted on the basis of national security intelligence provided in summary or redacted form, can make it very difficult for defendants to challenge the reliability of evidence submitted against them.

F. Sedition

The Anti-Terrorism Act (No 2) 2005 updated Australia's sedition offences and extended them to cover the actions of those who urge violence or assistance to Australia's enemies. The original sedition offences in s. 24A of the Crimes Act 1914 (Cth) criminalised words or conduct used to incite rebellion against the state, and had fallen into disuse in the latter half of the twentieth century. Under s. 80.2 of the Criminal Code, however, it is now an offence to urge another person to overthrow by force or violence the Constitution, a government of Australia or the lawful authority of the Commonwealth government. It is also an offence to urge a person to interfere in parliamentary elections, use violence in the community or assist an 'enemy' at war with the Commonwealth. A person does not commit an offence if he or she acts in 'good faith' in a set of specified circumstances – pointing out errors in legislation, for example, or urging someone to attempt lawfully to bring about a change to a law or publishing a report or commentary on a matter of public interest. Under the 2005 Amendments, each offence attracted a maximum penalty of seven years imprisonment.

Much criticism has been levied at these offences, which risk creating a 'chilling' effect on political expression in Australia. In 2006 the Australian Law Reform Commission (ALRC) reported that the broad and vaguely drafted offences were in danger of breaching Article 19 of the International Covenant on Civil and Political Rights.[55] Others have expressed concern that the provisions would be used to target 'suspect'

[55] See Australian Law Reform Commission, *Fighting Words: A Review of Sedition Laws in Australia* (2006) pp. 115–17.

minority groups who advocate resistance against everyday violence and discrimination by Anglo-Saxon Australians.[56]

In response to this criticism, the sedition offences were amended more by the National Security Legislation Amendment Act 2010. The legislation now expressly requires that an individual 'intentionally' urges another person to use such force or violence, and does so 'intending' that force or violence will occur. It also creates an offence for urging violence against members of groups distinguished by national or ethnic origin, and reduces the maximum penalties to five years where the use of violence is not likely to threaten the peace, order or good government of the Commonwealth.[57]

4. Australia's anti-terrorism laws in practice

A. Prosecutions

Thirty-seven men have been charged with terrorism offences in Australia.[58] A further forty Australians have had their passports revoked or applications denied for reasons related to terrorism. In a number of instances, law enforcement agencies have justified terrorism-related raids or arrests on the basis that attacks on Australian military installations or significant public events were 'imminent'.[59] However, as discussed above, such a claim is not necessary for a terrorism prosecution to succeed. In many of Australia's terrorism trials, it has been acknowledged that the laws are designed to stop the earliest planning of terrorist acts. For example, in sentencing five Sydney men for terrorism offences in February 2010, Justice Whealy stated:

> The broad purpose of the creation of offences of the kind involved in the present sentencing exercises is to prevent the emergence of circumstances which may render more likely the carrying out of a serious terrorist act ... The legislation is designed to bite early, long before the preparatory acts

---

[56] Simon Bronitt and James Stellios, 'Sedition, security and human rights: "unbalanced" law reform in the "war on terror" (2006) 30 *Melbourne University Law Review* 949–50, 959–60.

[57] See National Security Legislation Amendment Act 2010 (Cth), sch. 1.

[58] See McGarrity, '"Testing" our counter-terrorism laws', 125.

[59] 'Pre-Dawn Raids Net Terrorism Suspects' Australian Broadcasting Corporation Television, *The 7:30 Report*, 8 November 2005 (Carl Scully) available at www.abc.net.au/7.30/content/2005/s1500743.htm; 'Sydney terrorist attack was "imminent"' Australian Broadcasting Corporation News, 4 August 2009, available at www.abc.net.au/news/stories/2009/08/04/2645794.htm.

mature into circumstances of deadly or dangerous consequence for the community.[60]

The breadth and indeterminacy of the terrorism offences was particularly apparent in this case. The five men were charged with a combination of preparatory and inchoate offences, namely, conspiracy to do an act connected with preparation for a terrorist act. There was evidence that the offenders had purchased large amounts of ammunition, chemicals and laboratory equipment. Each of the offenders was also in possession of extremist propaganda and military instructional material.

In sentencing the five offenders, Justice Whealy noted that they had not reached any firm conclusion as to the nature of the attack they intended to carry out, and that they had not necessarily intended to kill innocent civilians. Nonetheless, he held that their actions fell only just short of the most serious case, because their 'collective disdain for the Australian Government and their intolerant animosity towards members of the community' made it 'inevitable' that they would be willing to take human life.[61] It is this kind of predictive approach, exemplified in the doubly pre-emptive offence of 'conspiracy to do an act in preparation for a terrorist act', which gives Australian anti-terror laws an extraordinary reach into the earliest stages of criminal responsibility.

B.   Constitutional challenges

As noted above, the absence of a Bill of Rights in Australia means that there are limited opportunities for the courts to assess or strike down anti-terrorism laws. As a result, despite the many novel and far-reaching aspects of such laws, there have only been two major challenges to them on constitutional grounds.

In *Thomas* v. *Mowbray*[62] the High Court rejected a challenge to the control order regime in Division 104 of the Criminal Code. Significantly, the case was not argued before the High Court on the basis that the regime violated an individual's human rights. Instead, it was argued that the legislation did not fall within one of the enumerated heads of federal legislative power in the Australian Constitution and that it also breached the strict separation of judicial from legislative and executive power. The majority judges rejected these arguments and gave considerable discretion to

---

[60]   *R* v. *Elomar* [2010] NSWSC 10, [79].   [61]   Ibid., [60], [69].
[62]   (2007) 233 CLR 307.

the executive to determine the level of threat posed by terrorism and the action which should be taken in response.

In R v. *Lodhi*,[63] the defendant sought to challenge the NSIA on the ground that it allowed those accused of committing terrorist offences to be sentenced through a process that was incompatible with the exercise of judicial power (and therefore in breach of the separation of powers implied through the structure of the Australian Constitution). Justice Whealy in the Supreme Court of New South Wales held that the legislation was not inconsistent with the exercise of judicial power because it primarily set down a procedure for determining the pre-trial disclosure of evidence rather than one for excluding evidence during the trial itself.[64] On appeal in the New South Wales Court of Criminal Appeal, Chief Justice Spigelman upheld Justice Whealy's decision, stating that the NSIA merely 'tilted the balance' in favour of national security without rendering the legislation invalid.[65] In 2008, an application for special leave to appeal to the High Court was denied.[66]

C. 'Soft' approaches

While most analysis of Western responses to 9/11 has focused on statute law, the Australian government has also taken a 'softer' approach to addressing the underlying causes of extremist terrorism. In the wake of the London bombings in July 2005, the Council of Australian Governments held a special meeting on counter-terrorism at which it resolved to combat intolerance and violence within Australian Muslim communities by establishing a National Action Plan.[67] That plan was released in July 2006, with its primary goal being to 'reinforce social cohesion, harmony and support the national security imperative in Australia by addressing extremism, the promotion of violence and intolerance, in response to the increased threat of global religious and political terrorism'.[68] It appears that similar initiatives will continue under the Labor government's more recent 'Social Inclusion Agenda', although the results of this initiative are not yet known. In May 2008,

---

[63] [2006] NSWSC 571.   [64] Ibid., [82]–[85].

[65] *Lodhi* v. *R* [2007] NSWCCA 360, [66]–[67].

[66] *Lodhi* v. *The Queen* [2008] HCATrans 225.

[67] See Council of Australian Governments Communiqué, 'Special Meeting on Counter-Terrorism', 27 September 2005, 3.

[68] Ministerial Council on Immigration and Multicultural Affairs, *A National Action Plan to Build on Social Cohesion, Harmony and Security* (2006), p. 6.

the Australian Social Inclusion Board was established, with one of its key goals being to 'eliminat[e] the threats to security and harmony that arise from excluding groups in our society'.[69]

5. The New Zealand response

Unlike Australia, New Zealand already had significant anti-terrorism laws[70] in place prior to 9/11.[71] These included the International Terrorism (Emergency Powers) Act 1987, which was enacted in part as a response to the 1985 bombing of the *Rainbow Warrior* in Auckland harbour by French agents. This Act confers 'emergency powers' upon the police and the armed forces after an 'international terrorist emergency' has been declared. Section 2 provides that such an emergency can only arise in regard to terrorist acts undertaken 'for the purpose of furthering, outside New Zealand, any political aim'. A controversial aspect of the Act is that, under s. 14, the Prime Minister may prohibit publication or broadcasting of matters relating to the international terrorist emergency. This power has never been used because a declaration of an international terrorist emergency has not been made under the Act.

Prior to 9/11, New Zealand had passed legislation implementing eight of the dozen major international conventions on terrorism.[72] A further Bill that sought to implement two more of the conventions, the Terrorism (Bombings and Financing) Bill 2001, was before the New Zealand Parliament on 9/11. After the attack, it became a 'convenient vehicle'[73] to respond to the requirement imposed on nations to combat terrorism by

---

[69] Australian Social Inclusion Board, *Social Inclusion in Australia: How Australia is Faring* (2010), p. 1.

[70] Indeed, one study found that 'a comprehensive legislative and substantive counter-terrorist framework had been established by the New Zealand state prior to New Zealand having any "real" contact with terrorism'. This was attributed to factors including 'a degree of caution' and 'a desire to be part of a broader anti-terrorist effort to strengthen ties with other "like-minded" states': B. K. Greener-Barcham, 'Before September 11: a history of counter-terrorism in New Zealand' (2002) 37 *Australian Journal of Political Science* 509, 514.

[71] For accounts of the evolution of New Zealand's anti-terrorism laws, see Greener-Barcham, 'Before September 11'. For an overview of New Zealand law on terrorism before and after September 11, see J. E. Smith, *New Zealand's Anti-Terrorism Campaign: Balancing Civil Liberties, National Security, and International Responsibilities* (December 2003), available at www.fulbright.org.nz/voices/axford/docs/smithj.pdf.

[72] Alex Conte, 'A clash of wills: counter-terrorism and human rights' (2003) 20 *New Zealand Universities Law Review* 338, 340, fn 7.

[73] M. Palmer, 'Counter-terrorism law' (2002) *New Zealand Law Journal* 456.

United Nations Security Council Resolution 1373. Indeed, a focal point of the debate became how the Bill could be redrafted to comply with the Resolution, and the Resolution was added as a Schedule to the Bill. The Bill was renamed and was ultimately enacted in October 2002[74] with overwhelming cross-party support[75] as the Terrorism Suppression Act 2002.[76] Before its enactment, the Bill was vetted by the government's Crown Law Office for compliance with the New Zealand Bill of Rights Act. Section 70 of the Terrorism Suppression Act 2002 also required a parliamentary review of the Act before 1 December 2005. In November 2005, the Foreign Affairs, Defence and Trade Committee presented its report to the New Zealand Parliament and recommended that further attention be given to certain aspects of the offence and proscription regimes. Section 70 of the Act was thereafter repealed, and there is no ongoing requirement for review of the Act.

Section 5 of the Terrorism Suppression Act defines a 'terrorist act' in three alternative ways.[77] First, under s. 5(1)(a), an act is a 'terrorist act' if it satisfies three criteria: it must be carried out for the purpose of advancing an ideological, political or religious cause; it must be intended to induce terror in a civilian population or unduly compel or force a government or international organisation to do or abstain from doing any act; and it must cause one of five possible harms. These possible harms are listed in sub-s. (3), namely:

(a) the death of, or other serious bodily injury to, 1 or more persons (other than a person carrying out the act):
(b) a serious risk to the health or safety of a population:
(c) destruction of, or serious damage to, property of great value or importance, or major economic loss, or major environmental damage, if likely to result in 1 or more outcomes specified in paragraphs (a), (b) and (d):
(d) serious interference with, or serious disruption to, an infrastructure facility, if likely to endanger human life:

---

[74] Concerns raised prior to enactment included the definition of terrorism, the scope for designating terrorist organisations and the effects of such a designation: Treasa Dunworth, 'Public International Law' [2002] *New Zealand Law Review* 255, 270.
[75] The Bill was passed with a margin of 106 to 9 votes, with only the Greens voting against it: Smith, *New Zealand's Anti-Terrorism Campaign*, p. 30.
[76] As amended by the Terrorism Suppression Amendment Act 2003 (NZ).
[77] Under s. 25(1), 'planning or other preparations to carry out the act, whether it is actually carried out or not', a 'credible threat to carry out the act' or an 'attempt to carry out the act' also constitute a terrorist act.

(e) introduction or release of a disease-bearing organism, if likely to devastate the national economy of a country.

There are a number of notable differences between the listed possible harms in the New Zealand and Australian definitions. The New Zealand definition does not include acts that merely 'endanger' a person's life. The New Zealand definition also provides that any property seriously damaged by a terrorist act must be 'of great value or importance', whereas in Australia serious damage to *any* property is sufficient. A terrorist act against property in New Zealand must also be likely to result in one of the other harms contained in sub-ss. (a), (b) or (d). The New Zealand definition also provides that serious interference with, or disruption to, an infrastructure facility must be 'likely to endanger human life', whereas an attack against an electronic system in Australia has no additional requirements. New Zealand also includes a 'bio-terrorism' provision in sub-s. (e). These factors tend to suggest that the New Zealand definition sets a higher standard of required harm than the Australian provision. However, both lists include as a lowest common denominator acts that create a 'serious risk to the health or safety' of a population, meaning that the coverage of the two lists may not significantly differ in practice.

Subsection (4) exempts acts that occur during situations of armed conflict in accordance with applicable international law. Subsection (5) provides an exemption for acts of protest, advocacy, dissent or other industrial action.

Second, an act qualifies as a 'terrorist act' under s. 5(1)(b) of the Terrorism Suppression Act if it is an act 'against a specified terrorism convention'.[78] Section 4(1) defines a 'specified terrorism convention' as any of the nine treaties listed in Schedule 3, such as the Convention for the Suppression of Unlawful Seizure of Aircraft or the Convention for the Suppression of Unlawful Acts against the Safety of Maritime Navigation.

Third, an act qualifies as a 'terrorist act' under s. 5(1)(c) if it is a 'terrorist act in armed conflict'. Section 4(1) defines a 'terrorist act in armed conflict' as an act that occurs in a situation of armed conflict, is designed to intimidate a population or compel a government to act in a particular way, and is intended to cause death or serious bodily injury to civilians. The act must also not be excluded from the application of the International Convention for the Suppression of the Financing of Terrorism by article 3 of that Convention.

---

[78] The use of 'against' in this context is certainly awkward: see M. Palmer, 'Counter-terrorism law' [2002] *New Zealand Law Journal* 456, 457.

Surprisingly, prior to 2007, committing a 'terrorist act' was not itself made an offence under statute. This oversight was remedied by the Terrorism Suppression Amendment Act 2007 (NZ).[79] The concept of a 'terrorist act' is also central to other offences, such as the financing of terrorism (s. 8) or harbouring or concealing terrorists (s. 13A).

The Terrorism Suppression Act criminalises certain types of involvement by individuals with designated terrorist entities. Since 2007, this has included involvement with terrorist organisations designated by *either* the New Zealand Prime Minister *or* the United Nations Security Council (most notably under Resolution 1267).[80] In its original form, the 2002 Act only applied to organisations listed by the New Zealand Prime Minister under ss. 20 or 22 of that Act. This meant that the Prime Minister could choose to designate a United Nations designated entity for the purposes of the Act, but could also later revoke that under s. 34. The High Court also had the power to revoke, or refuse to extend, the proscription of a UN designated entity by the Prime Minister under the 2002 Act (ss. 33 and 35). This regime was altered by the Terrorism Suppression Amendment Act 2007 on the basis of a 2005 report of the Foreign Affairs, Defence and Trade Committee. The Committee had expressed concern that the power of the Prime Minister and High Court to overturn a United Nations listing was inconsistent with New Zealand's international obligations.[81] After the passage of the 2007 Amendment Act, the Prime Minister and the High Court still retain their powers of revision in relation to organisations designated under ss. 20 and 22, but cannot affect the operation of the Act in relation to United Nations listed entities.

Under s. 22 of the amended Terrorism Suppression Act, the New Zealand Prime Minister now has the power to make designations *in addition* to United Nations listed entities if he or she believes on reasonable grounds that the entity 'has knowingly carried out, or has knowingly

---

[79] Terrorism Suppression Act 2002 (NZ), s. 6A.
[80] See the definition of 'designated terrorist entity' in s. 4 of the Terrorism Suppression Act 2002 (NZ), inserted by s. 5 of the Terrorism Suppression Amendment Act 2007 (NZ). See also the United Nations Sanctions (Afghanistan) Regulations 2001, as amended by the United Nations Sanctions (Afghanistan) Amendment Regulations 2002, and replaced by the United Nations Sanctions (Al-Qaida and Taliban) Regulations 2007, which have provided a range of other restrictions on designated terrorist entities since 2001. See also C. H. Powell, Chapter 2, this volume, for a critique of the Resolution 1267 regime.
[81] See House of Representatives Foreign Affairs, Defence and Trade Committee, Parliament of New Zealand, *Review of the Terrorism Suppression Act 2002* (2005), pp. 5–6; New Zealand, *Parliamentary Debates*, House of Representatives, 24 October 2007, 12668 (Mark Burton).

participated in the carrying out of, 1 or more terrorist acts'. In making this decision, he or she 'may take into account any relevant information, including classified security information' (s. 30). A decision to designate an organisation under s. 22 is classified as 'final', but is nonetheless subject to judicial review and will expire after three years unless renewed by the Prime Minister (ss. 33, 35). Interim designations may also be made under s. 20, which expire after a period of 30 days unless converted into a final designation. Once designated, an organisation is subject to a number of consequences, such as having its property seized and being unable to gain financial or related services.[82] To date, only four final designations under s. 22 have been made.[83]

A second major piece of terrorism legislation, the Counter-Terrorism Bill 2002, was introduced into the New Zealand Parliament two months after the enactment of the Terrorism Suppression Act. The Act covered a wide range of matters in seeking to close gaps in the legislative framework. It sought to amend a range of New Zealand statutes and contained important changes relating to, for example, search warrants and tracking devices.[84] It also sought to implement the requirements of the remaining international treaties on terrorism yet to be legislated for in New Zealand. After nearly a year of debate and committee inquiry, the Bill was split into six separate Bills[85] and then passed in October 2003 with the overwhelming support of Parliament.

Most recently, in October 2009, the Anti-money Laundering and Countering Financing of Terrorism Act 2009 was given royal assent in the New Zealand Parliament. In being directed at detecting and deterring money laundering and the financing of terrorism, the Act creates obligations on business organisations to conduct due diligence assessments on customers and other persons, report suspicious transactions, keep records, store and destroy records in certain ways and maintain

---

[82] For a more detailed discussion of the New Zealand proscription regime, see Alex Conte, *Counter-Terrorism and Human Rights in New Zealand* (New Zealand Law Foundation, 2007) pp. 300–9. For a discussion of UN designations, see pp. 309–15.

[83] For a current list of New Zealand proscriptions, see New Zealand Police website, available at www.police.govt.nz/service/counterterrorism/designated-terrorists.html.

[84] See Alex Conte, 'Tracking devices, search warrants and self-incrimination' (July 2003) *New Zealand Law Journal* 235.

[85] Namely, the Crimes Amendment Act 2003 (NZ), Misuse of Drugs Amendment Act (No 2) 2003 (NZ), New Zealand Security Intelligence Service Amendment Act 2003 (NZ), Sentencing Amendment Act 2003 (NZ) and Summary Proceedings Amendment Act 2003 (NZ), Terrorism Suppression Amendment Act 2003 (NZ).

other codes of practice for preventing money laundering and the financing of terrorism.

6.   Australia and New Zealand compared

A primary aim of the New Zealand response has been to bring its law into compliance with UN conventions and other international responses to terrorism. Rather than being a direct and necessary response to a domestic terrorist threat, the New Zealand legislative effort appears often to be directed at New Zealand playing its part in the international community. For example, when debating the Counter-terrorism Bill in the House of Representatives, National Member for Rangitikei, Simon Power, argued:

> This bill is really about New Zealand doing its bit. This bill is about recognising that one of this country's obligations in being part of the international community is to take a stand on issues that are serious and difficult, and that require the commitment of the country.[86]

Similar pressures have played a part in the enactment of anti-terror legislation in Australia.[87] However, Australia has tended to look more towards the United States (rather than just the United Nations and other multilateral bodies) for leadership, to the extent of taking part in pre-emptive (and arguably illegal[88]) military action in Iraq. New Zealand did eventually contribute a small force of army engineers to the coalition force in that nation, but withdrew these troops in September 2004. This difference in approach explains in part why New Zealand has not sought to replicate some of the more controversial and far-reaching proposals put forward in Australia, such as the detention of non-suspects by a security intelligence service. Indeed, amendments to the New Zealand Security Intelligence Service Act 1969 have been relatively minor[89] and the focus has instead been on the proscription of terrorist organisations combined with more traditional law enforcement processes. Indeed, in the one case where charges under the Terrorism Suppression Act 2002 might have been laid (after raids on camps in the Ruatoki Valley and the Uruwera

---

[86] New Zealand, *Parliamentary Debates*, House of Representatives, 1 April 2003, 9158 (Simon Power).

[87] See, e.g., Commonwealth, *Parliamentary Debates*, House of Representatives, 12 March 2002, 1041 (Daryl Williams).

[88] See Devika Hovell and George Williams, 'Advice on the use of force against Iraq' (2003) 4 *Melbourne Journal of International Law* 183.

[89] See New Zealand Security Intelligence Service Amendment Act 2003 (NZ).

Ranges found stocks of ammunition), the government elected to instead charge the offenders under the Arms Act 1983.[90]

A recent similarity between the responses of the two nations to the threat of terrorism is the relationship between anti-terrorism measures and the regulation of immigration.[91] In its 2010 Counter-Terrorism White Paper, the Australian government identified '[t]he ability to identify and prevent the movement of individuals who try to enter or transit Australia to conduct terrorist acts or terrorism-related activities' as 'vital to Australia's security'.[92] The government therefore committed to introduce a biometric-based visa system (involving the collection of fingerprints and facial images) from non-citizens from high risk countries. One particularly notorious incident demonstrating the close relationship between Australia's response to terrorism and regulation of immigration occurred during the course of the Haneef case discussed above. *Haneef* was released on bail by a Brisbane magistrate; however, the Minister for Immigration and Citizenship, Kevin Andrews, nevertheless proceeded to cancel Haneef's visa on the basis that he failed the 'character test' in s. 501 of the Migration Act 1958 (Cth). The Minister's decision to cancel Haneef's visa was later overturned by the Federal Court of Australia,[93] but Haneef had since been deported from Australia.

In New Zealand, a similar blunder occurred with Algerian asylum seeker Ahmed Zaoui, who was held in detention from two years from December 2002 on the basis of a 'security risk certificate' issued by the New Zealand Director of Security under the Immigration Act 1987.[94] That controversy revealed several problems with Part 4A of the 1987 legislation, not least the lack of human rights protection for persons seeking judicial review of such a certificate. Zaoui was appointed a security-cleared lawyer to view classified information not previously released by NZSIS, but this regime was not fully tested by the time the certificate was withdrawn in September 2007.[95]

---

[90] See *Paraha and Ors v. New Zealand Police HC AK CRI 2007-092-5673* [2008] NZHC 582.

[91] See Kent Roach, Chapter 20, this volume, for a discussion of immigration law as an alternative to criminal law in countering terrorism.

[92] Australian Government, *Counter-Terrorism White Paper: Securing Australia – Protecting our Community* (2010) 35.

[93] *Haneef* v. *Minister for Immigration and Citizenship* (2007) 161 FCR 40 (Federal Court); *Minister for Immigration and Citizenship* v. *Haneef* (2007) 163 FCR 414.

[94] See Conte, *Counter-Terrorism and Human Rights in New Zealand*, pp. 343–5.

[95] See, generally, Lani Inverarity, 'Immigration Bill 2007: special advocates and the right to be heard' (2009) 40 *Victoria University of Wellington Law Review* 471.

These issues led the New Zealand Parliament to create the Immigration and Protection Tribunal and to introduce a 'special advocate' regime under the Immigration Act 2009. The latter mirrors regimes in the UK and Canada by allowing security-cleared lawyers to challenge classified information in review, appeal or detention proceedings.[96] While the regime appears to aid individuals in challenging such decisions, it raises significant problems for the requirements of natural justice under the New Zealand Bill of Rights Act. In particular, one Māori Member of Parliament criticised the government for hiding that the Bill was really intended to 'build a case for upping the ante in the fight against terrorism'.[97]

7. Conclusion

Australia and New Zealand have passed important new laws in response to 9/11 that challenge settled assumptions about the role and proper limits of public and criminal law. Australia in particular has a record of passing an extraordinary range of new statutes that confer powers on agencies like ASIO that had been unthinkable prior to the attack. Some of these laws are explicable only by the fact that Australia has no national human rights framework that requires Parliament to pay due attention to basic rights such as freedom of speech.

Australia's long run of anti-terror lawmaking ended with the defeat of the Howard government in late 2007. While new anti-terror legislation has been little seen since, this also means that new laws have yet to be passed that revise earlier statutes and deal with some of their more problematic aspects. The most positive sign in Australia since 2007 is the introduction of the Independent National Security Legislation Monitor, an office that may have the capacity to identify and provide the catalyst for much needed changes.

New Zealand has taken a different path, leading Minister of Justice and Minister of Foreign Affairs and Trade, Phil Goff, to even suggest in 2003 that '[a]t this point, legislatively, I think we've pretty much got it covered'.[98] This has not proven to be correct, as subsequent New Zealand statutes show, but it nonetheless points to a difference in approach between the two nations. Much more so than Australia, anti-terror legislation in New

---

[96] See Nicola McGarrity and Edward Santow, Chapter 6, this volume, for a discussion of the special advocate regimes in Canada and the United Kingdom.
[97] New Zealand, *Parliamentary Debates*, House of Representatives, 16 August 2007, 11245 (Tariana Turia).
[98] Smith, *New Zealand's Anti-Terrorism Campaign*, p. 35.

Zealand has been made as a response to international pressures and a desire to be good international citizen. While raising its own issues, such legislation has also proven to be more compatible with basic human rights standards, as is required by the New Zealand Bill of Rights Act.

In both Australia and New Zealand, the law has played a front line role in the fight against terrorism. It is not surprising that political leaders in both nations, as Members of Parliament and law-makers, have turned to new laws after 9/11 and the more recent attacks overseas. New legislation is at least within their control and is a symbolic and potentially practical response. However, it is important to acknowledge that new laws will not provide long-term solutions. Legislation is unlikely to tackle the causes of terrorism and will not deter a terrorist from a premeditated course of action. Law-making can also direct attention away from debate over other responses to terrorism. Worse still, enacting draconian laws may lead to a sense of complacency on the part of the public while also contributing to the radicalisation of some sections of the community. Such laws may compromise the very democratic freedoms that they are meant to protect. This is of particular concern in Australia, which lacks the national state-ment of human rights needed to navigate through the fight against terror-ism while still maintaining basic democratic and other freedoms.

This is not to suggest that a nation's response to terrorism should be timid. Indeed, all nations have an obligation to protect their community from terrorism. However, when the law is used as a primary tool in the war on terror, it can also pose a threat to the rule of law, especially when such law is unconstrained by fundamental principles of human rights. Passed in haste and rapid succession, such laws can undermine values and assumptions developed over the course of centuries.

PART V

Anti-terrorism measures in the
Middle East and Africa

22

Terrorism and governance in South Africa and Eastern Africa

CHRIS OXTOBY AND C. H. POWELL

1. Introduction

Because of its sheer scale, terrorism is seen as the kind of crime which states should prevent rather than prosecute. Many therefore accord the state special leeway against it. Anti-terrorism legislation accordingly curtails individual rights, allowing action against terrorist suspects before their guilt is proven. It may also relax the requirements for proving guilt if the suspect gets to court. Proponents of this view argue that any harsh treatment which may result is the price which society has to pay to protect the general public.

Here we find a paradox of the anti-terrorism debate, because a second argument sees, in this same legislation, protection for the terrorist *suspects*. This argument accepts that additional powers, beyond those in ordinary criminal and procedural law, may be needed in order to combat terrorism. However, it then demands that the government articulate exactly when these powers will arise and what their extent will be. Under such an argument, legislation must define clearly what terrorism is and establish the limits of executive action against it. In this way, the government will be constrained by the anti-terrorism legislation, rather than acting extra-legally, and its exercise of power will be subject to review.

In this chapter, we explore this debate in the context of the anti-terrorism programme of four African states: South Africa and the East

The authors would like to thank Anton du Plessis, Annette Hübschle, Livingstone Sewanyana, Caroline Adoch, Laibuta Mugambi, Gertrude Wamala and Paddy Clark for providing information on developments in East Africa; Joshua Mendelsohn for providing hard-to-find South African cases; Dilshaad Brey and the staff at the Government Publications section of the University of Cape Town library for their assistance in locating Ugandan and Kenyan government documents; and the participants in the August 2010 Anti-Terrorism Symposium in Sydney, in particular Theunis Roux, for their comments on earlier drafts.

African countries of Kenya, Tanzania and Uganda. We ask whether anti-terrorism legislation is, indeed, necessary for the effective prevention and prosecution of terrorism, referring to examples of anti-terrorism action taken in the absence of anti-terrorism laws (Kenya) or within the apparent framework of ordinary criminal procedure when an alternative anti-terrorism framework is available (South Africa). We also investigate whether anti-terrorism legislation protects the rights of suspects. Comparing the human rights protection of systems with and without anti-terrorism legislation, we identify a gap between the legislation and the situation on the ground. This gap suggests that the legislation in itself may play a negligible role in countering terrorism and is inadequate to protect human rights. Anti-terrorism legislation could, however, be effective at both attempts if it is accompanied by respect for the rule of law.

2.   Background to the anti-terrorism legislation of South Africa and Eastern Africa

The 2005 version of this chapter considered the international anti-terrorism regime in some detail, as well as the anti-terrorism legislative framework in South Africa, Kenya, Uganda and Tanzania. The international context is now dealt with elsewhere in this edition.[1] We will deal only briefly with the content of the legislation in the surveyed states, highlighting changes and aspects relevant to the thematic discussion to follow.[2] To discuss how the legislation has been implemented, we analyse anti-terrorism practice in the surveyed states in terms of various themes, namely: the geographical location and significance of the states in the context of the global 'war on terror'; the internal legitimacy of anti-terrorism laws; human rights concerns, particularly the suppression of political opposition, the conduct of security forces and renditions of terrorism suspects; and, finally, court decisions dealing with the anti-terrorism laws.

   The four countries surveyed in this chapter share a legal heritage, having adopted, albeit to slightly different extents, the common law tradition. As this chapter demonstrates, however, the legal responses to contemporary terrorism are in some ways markedly different. In 2005, both Uganda and Tanzania had anti-terrorism legislation in force, but Kenya's Suppression of Terrorism Bill of 2003 had encountered considerable opposition from

---

[1] See C. H. Powell, Chapter 2, this volume.
[2] A more detailed discussion of the content of the legislation may be found in this chapter in the first edition of this volume.

politicians and civil society, and had not been passed.[3] South Africa's anti-terrorism legislation came into force in 2005.[4] It had a long and difficult birth, taking eight years to come into law. It was criticised from two perspectives: one on the basis of principles of constitutionalism and human rights, the other based on fears of victimisation, similar to those raised in East Africa, with criticisms coming particularly from the Muslim community and from trade unions.[5]

The status of the legislation remains largely unchanged. The South African Act has not been amended. Kenya continues to lack specialist anti-terrorism legislation. In May 2006, the Kenyan government drafted a further suppression of terrorism bill, but did not submit it to Parliament,[6] and it is thought to be unlikely that legislation will be reintroduced in the near future.[7] The Kenyan position will thus be discussed with reference to the 2003 Bill. Efforts are underway to update the Tanzanian Act,[8] but at the time of writing it remains unchanged. No amendments to the Ugandan legislation have been tabled,[9] although provisions on surveillance have been supplemented by other legislation.[10]

3.   The anti-terrorism regimes of South Africa and Eastern Africa

This section analyses the anti-terrorism legislation of South Africa and the East African states under two themes. The first examines legislative provisions which empower the state to prevent acts of terrorism. The second deals with provisions governing the trial of those charged with terrorism-related offences. An additional section discusses possible challenges to the constitutionality of the South African legislation, drawing

---

[3] C. H. Powell, 'Terrorism and governance in South Africa and Eastern Africa', in Victor V. Ramraj, Michael Hor and Kent Roach (eds.), *Global Anti-Terrorism Law and Policy* (Cambridge University Press, 2005), p. 566.

[4] The Protection of Constitutional Democracy against Terrorist and Related Activities Act 33 of 2004. The Act was passed by the National Assembly on 12 November 2004, assented to by the President on 4 February 2005 and became law on 20 May 2005.

[5] Powell, 'Terrorism and governance in South Africa and Eastern Africa', pp. 566–7.

[6] Authors' survey of bills presented to Parliament on www.kenyalaw.org; US Department of State, *Country Reports on Terrorism*, Chapter 2 – Country Reports: Africa Overview (2006), available at www.state.gov/s/ct/rls/crt/. The Kenyan government seemed to lack the political capital to pass such a controversial measure.

[7] Anton du Plessis, Institute for Security Studies, Correspondence with the authors, 20 September 2010.

[8] Du Plessis, Correspondence with authors, 20 September 2010.

[9] Authors' search of Ugandan Government Gazettes.

[10] The Regulation of Interception of Communications Act was passed in September 2010.

on comparisons with South Africa's anti-organised crime legislation. For ease of reference, the legislation of the three East African states is discussed together.

A. South Africa's anti-terrorism legislation

i. Prevention

The South African anti-terrorism act links the investigation and prevention of terrorism with South Africa's anti-organised crime legislation, extending the ambit of the Prevention of Organised Crime Act (POCA) to include terrorism. POCA thereby provides for the civil forfeiture of property 'associated with terrorist or related activities'. Property which was 'acquired, collected, used, possessed, owned or provided for the benefit of, or on behalf of, or at the direction of, or under the control of an entity which commits or attempts to commit or facilitates the commission' of the crimes in the anti-terrorism act may be forfeited. It is not necessary to institute a criminal prosecution against any person involved in such an 'entity', but the civil forfeiture requires a court order.[11]

Section 22 of the anti-terrorism act activates Chapter 5 of the National Prosecuting Authority (NPA) Act,[12] which gives investigating officers in terrorism cases the same powers as officers investigating organised crime. The Investigating Director of the Directorate of Special Operations (the DSO)[13] was empowered to conduct a particular investigation and assign officers to it.[14] Such officers were given expanded powers of search and seizure. While required to obtain a court order to search a suspect's property, officers are not required to specify the particular articles they hope to find.[15]

One change came in 2008, when the DSO was controversially disbanded, a move attributed to the unit's investigation and prosecution of several senior political figures. In its stead, the Directorate for Priority Crime Investigation, a specialist unit of the South African Police Service (colloquially known as the 'Hawks'), has assumed the DSO's powers.[16]

---

[11] Powell, 'Terrorism and governance in South Africa and Eastern Africa', pp. 569–70.
[12] Act No. 32 of 1998.
[13] Colloquially known as the 'Scorpions', the DSO had special powers to investigate organised crime: J. Redpath, *The DSO: Analysing the Scorpions* (Pretoria: Institute for Security Studies Monograph no. 93, 2004).
[14] NPA Act, s. 28.   [15] Ibid., s. 29.
[16] See the National Prosecuting Authority Amendment Act 56 of 2008.

Although these powers are now wielded by a different organisation, they remain substantively unchanged.

ii. Trial

The first edition of this volume noted that terrorist suspects faced trial under some of the most broadly and vaguely defined crimes in South African law.[17] The Act codified a range of treaty crimes, and introduced two new main offences: terrorism, and the 'offence connected with terrorist activities', which provides for extensive accomplice liability.[18] The offence of terrorism consists of three broadly defined elements: an act, an intention and a motivation. The act may be set out in detail, but is nonetheless unclear and broad. For example, the 'systematic, repeated or arbitrary use of violence' constitutes 'terrorist activity'. Most forms of violence would be qualified by one of these three adjectives, meaning that only the elements of intention and motivation distinguish the serious crime of terrorism from any other act of violence. The remainder of the activities listed generally cause severe harm.[19]

The three terrorist intentions are: to threaten the unity and territorial integrity of a state, to intimidate or cause feelings of insecurity in the public, and unduly to compel or induce a person, the government or the general public to do or abstain from any act. These intentions are broad and require a lower burden of proof. The state can establish either that the accused had the intention, or that such intention can, by its nature and context, reasonably be inferred. In drawing that inference, a court may rely on an accused's 'constructive knowledge' of a fact.[20] As far as the element of motivation is concerned, an act which satisfies one of the criteria in the definitions of act or intention becomes a terrorist activity if it is carried out for an individual or collective political, religious, ideological or philosophical cause.[21] The act contains significant duplication, with a wide range of treaty-based offences being created which could easily be covered under the offence of terrorism.[22] The offence of terrorism itself

---

[17] Powell, 'Terrorism and governance in South Africa and Eastern Africa', pp. 572–8.

[18] Sections 1, 2 and 3.

[19] Powell, 'Terrorism and governance in South Africa and Eastern Africa', pp. 573–4.

[20] Under s. 1(6), a person is deemed to have knowledge of a fact if he or she had actual knowledge, failed to obtain information to confirm the existence of a fact or believed that it was reasonably possible that the fact existed.

[21] Powell, 'Terrorism and governance in South Africa and Eastern Africa', p. 574.

[22] Ibid., pp. 574–6.

includes numerous existing crimes, and accomplice liability is provided for at least four times.[23]

Maximum sentences upon conviction for terrorism or a related offence are very high.[24] As with POCA, the anti-terrorism act increases the ordinary sentencing limits of magistrates' courts. The basis for doing so is unclear, as is the advisability of the change.[25] On conviction, the anti-terrorism act provides for the mandatory forfeiture of assets connected to the crime.[26] Third parties have the usual prescription period of three years to claim restitution or compensation for their interests in the property.[27] Third parties must establish that they acquired the property in good faith, and for consideration.[28] Furthermore, they must show either that the surrounding circumstances were not such as to arouse a reasonable suspicion of terrorist use of the property, or that they could not prevent such use.

iii.   Constitutionality

In the first edition it was argued that the constitutionality of the anti-terrorism act could face similar challenges to POCA. It was suggested that POCA might be challenged for infringing various constitutional rights, in particular the right to silence, the presumption of innocence, the right not to be deprived of property, the right to privacy and the right to dignity.[29] By 2005, no such challenges to the constitutionality of POCA had succeeded, although the challenges had been limited in their scope and had not produced judgments that pronounced decisively on the issue. It was suggested that courts might respond more favourably to legislation aimed at organised crime than to legislation against terrorism, due to the greater threat organised crime is perceived to pose to South African society. It was noted that in considering POCA, South African courts had acknowledged the threat to the international community posed by organised crime, and that if the perceived needs of the international community were to influence South African courts, they might accept that terrorism is an even greater threat. In light of the generally sympathetic response

---

[23] Ibid., pp. 575–6.   [24] Ibid., pp. 576–7.   [25] See further ibid. pp. 576–7.
[26] See further ibid., p. 578.   [27] Section 20.
[28] This may be contrasted with s. 17(6), under which those accused of financing terrorism under s. 4 may defend themselves by showing that they dealt with the property in question purely to preserve its value.
[29] Sections 35(1), 35(3)(h), 25, 14 and 10 of the Constitution of the Republic of South Africa Act 108 of 1996. See Powell, 'Terrorism and governance in South Africa and Eastern Africa', pp. 578–9.

to POCA, this suggested that the anti-terrorism act might pass constitutional muster.[30] It was also argued that the courts were likely to interpret the act restrictively, as has been done to preserve the constitutionality of some sections of POCA.[31]

The Constitutional Court has since dealt with POCA on several occasions,[32] although few cases presented a direct attack on the legislation. In *Prophet*, a direct challenge was made to the provisions of POCA relating to asset forfeiture. It was argued that the rights of dignity, privacy, fair trial, silence, the presumption of innocence and the right not to be arbitrarily deprived of property were infringed. However, this challenge was dismissed on procedural grounds.[33] The Constitutional Court appears to accept the constitutionality of POCA in principle, while being aware of its potentially harsh impact. The objective of civil forfeiture of assets, namely, curbing serious crime, has been described as 'worthy and noble',[34] but judges are alive to the potentially draconian nature of the remedy, especially in light of a lower burden of proof and the fact that it is not necessary to show that the owner of property has committed an offence in order to obtain a forfeiture order.[35] If forfeiture were to amount to an arbitrary deprivation of property, it would be unconstitutional.[36] In *Shaik*, the Court considered the restraint and seizure of property provisions of POCA. It identified the primary purpose of this part of the Act as being to ensure that no-one could benefit from his or her own wrongdoing, with subsidiary purposes of general deterrence and crime prevention. The Court found these to be legitimate under South Africa's constitutional order.[37]

The courts will, however, subject the constitutionality of the particular forfeiture to close scrutiny. The test applied by the courts considers firstly whether the property is an 'instrumentality' of an offence; and then assesses whether the forfeiture is proportional, by balancing the severity of the interference with individual property rights against the extent to which the property has been used in the commission of the offence.[38]

---

[30] Ibid., pp. 578–81.   [31] Ibid., pp. 580–1.

[32] *Mohunram and Another* v. *National Director of Public Prosecutions and Another (Law Review Project as* Amicus Curiae) 2007 (4) SA 222 (CC) (*Mohunram*); *Prophet* v. *National Director of Public Prosecutions* 2007 (6) SA 169 (CC) (*Prophet*); see also *S* v. *Shaik and Others* 2008(5) SA 354 (CC) (*Shaik*).

[33] *Prophet*, [49]–[53].

[34] *Mohunram*, [118] (Moseneke DCJ).   [35] See ibid.

[36] Ibid., [141] (Sachs J).   [37] *Shaik*, [51]–[52] and [57].

[38] See *Prophet*, [55], [57]–[58].

The Court will be more likely to grant a forfeiture order the more closely related the criminal activities in question are to the objectives of POCA, and vice-versa. Courts are required to weigh the deterrent purpose of POCA against the impact on the individual owner – a disproportionate impact would violate the principle of dignity.[39] This analysis is far from straightforward,[40] and is fact and context sensitive.[41] In *National Director of Public Prosecutions* v. *Rautenbach*,[42] a majority of the Supreme Court of Appeal held that where there was good reason to believe that the value of the restrained property would materially exceed the prospective confiscation order, the Court must limit the scope of the restraint. In *Mohunram*, a majority of the Constitutional Court found that the forfeiture under consideration was disproportionate, as no link had been shown between the underlying offence and the purpose of POCA.[43]

These decisions suggest an implicit acceptance of the constitutionality of POCA, and it seems unlikely that further challenges would now succeed. However, the decisions bear out the suggestion that it would be open to the courts to interpret anti-terrorism legislation restrictively, and in light of constitutional rights and values, in order to ameliorate potential harshness in the application of the legislation. The POCA case law suggests that it is possible that the courts may accept the aims of a legislative scheme, and yet be careful to ensure that it is not applied without constraint.[44]

As for the substantive aspects of the act, the chapter in the first edition of this volume suggested that the vagueness of the definition of terrorism could conceivably be cured by a very restrictive reading of the text. It was also argued that s. 23, which adopts the Security Council's list of terrorist organisations for the purposes of asset forfeiture, could be seen as an unconstitutional delegation of legislative power to an international body.[45] It would be interesting to see, were such an issue to arise, whether the South African courts might be emboldened to take such an approach

---

[39] *Mohunram*, [145]–[146] (Sachs J).
[40] As is demonstrated by *Mohunram*, where the Constitutional Court split 6:5 on whether the forfeiture order was disproportionate, with a plurality formed by two separate judgments.
[41] See Sachs J's distinguishing of *Prophet* in *Mohunram*, [147]–[149].
[42] 2005 (4) SA 603 (SCA).
[43] *Mohunram*, [129] (Moseneke DCJ).
[44] See the discussion of *Minister of Safety and Security and Others* v. *Mohamed*, below.
[45] Powell, 'Terrorism and governance in South Africa and Eastern Africa', pp. 581–2. See also C. Powell, 'Terrorism and the separation of powers at the national and international level' (2005) *South African Journal on Criminal Justice* 151.

in future following the example of the European Court of Justice in *Kadi*.[46] In this case, the Grand Chamber of the European Court of Justice overturned the European implementation of a listing decision against a Saudi Arabian national, on the basis that the European measures violated European constitutional law and the rights treaties applicable to members of the EU.

B. Anti-terrorism legislation and draft legislation in Eastern Africa

i. Prevention

The executive in Kenya, Tanzania and Uganda enjoys a far wider discretion in identifying terrorism suspects and in deciding how to proceed on that suspicion. All three countries allow the relevant Cabinet Ministers to declare groups to be terrorist organisations or people to be terrorists, with Uganda granting the legislature some powers to annul changes to the list of organisations set out in the Act. Tanzania's legislation provides for some judicial oversight, but reference in guidelines to the view of the UN Security Council may effectively mean that the view of the executive will prevail. In Kenya, the draft legislation would have allowed the Minister of National Security to declare an organisation terrorist merely on the belief that it met the guideline criteria of terrorism provided in the Bill, although the declaration would be subject to judicial review.[47]

Once an organisation is declared to be a terrorist organisation, provision is made for funds to be frozen and assets to be forfeited to the state. The Kenyan draft legislation would grant less discretion to the executive in this respect, as pre-trial asset forfeiture is only permitted on an *ex parte* application to a court.[48] Regarding investigation and powers in respect of suspected persons and objects, the Ugandan Act does not provide for any special powers of arrest and search and seizure. The Tanzanian Act contains fairly unexceptional provisions allowing for arrest without a warrant on reasonable suspicion, and for search and seizure without a warrant, if applying for a warrant would cause a prejudicial delay.[49]

All three states allow for the seizure of property upon suspicion of terrorist connections, but with varying degrees of executive discretion. The

---

[46] Judgment of the European Court of Justice in Joined Cases C-402/05 P and C-415/05 P, *Yassin Abdullah Kadi and Al Barakaat International Foundation* v. *Council of the European Union and Commission of the European Communities* (3 September 2008).
[47] Powell, 'Terrorism and governance in South Africa and Eastern Africa', pp. 583–4.
[48] Ibid., p. 584.   [49] Ibid., pp. 584–5.

Ugandan legislation requires court orders to search for and seize property on reasonable grounds. In Tanzania, detention orders against vehicles or aircraft may be issued by the Inspector-General of Police, but may be varied by the Minister. The police may seize property on suspicion of a terrorist connection, but must then apply for a court order to authorise further detention of the property. In Kenya, the draft legislation would allow for search and seizure only in specifically defined circumstances and on order of a court, unless obtaining such an order would cause a delay prejudicial to public safety and public order.[50]

Unlike the South African legislation, all three East African states make provision for the surveillance of terrorism suspects. Authorisation is given by the Minister in Uganda, the Minister or a court in Tanzania, and, in Kenya, the draft Bill would require a court order. The Ugandan legislation specifically requires the Minister to protect, *inter alia*, the public interest and the national economy when authorising the monitoring. In Tanzania, private bodies may be co-opted in the interception of information.[51]

Beyond criminal investigations, the legislation grants powers to the executive to control access to the respective states. The Tanzanian legislation empowers the Minister to make regulations to prohibit the entry of persons to Tanzania, and provides for the refusal of entry to suspected terrorists, and the deportation of suspected terrorists already in Tanzania. The Minister may also refuse refugee status to applicants suspected of terrorist involvement. Similarly, the Kenyan Bill would allow the Minister to issue exclusion orders against non-nationals suspected of terrorist involvement, and even against Kenyan nationals with dual nationality. This would prevent the entry of persons and allow the removal of persons already present in Kenya.[52] Finally, and especially controversially, immunity was granted for members of the executive who act against terrorist suspects, which covers damage to property and the causing of injury, or even death.[53]

ii.   Trial

The legislation in all three states creates the offence of terrorism, and a range of ancillary and convention crimes. The definition of terrorism is generally organised around constituent elements of act, purpose and

---

[50] Ibid., pp. 585–6.   [51] Ibid., p. 586.

[52] Ibid., pp. 586–7. This is a potentially significant power in the context of Kenya's porous borders, as discussed under section III A.

[53] Powell, 'Terrorism and governance in South Africa and Eastern Africa', p. 587.

motivation, although these are not always set out systematically, and it is sometimes unclear whether all three elements are required. The definitions in the legislation and draft legislation of all three states are unclear to varying degrees.[54]

In all three states, the rules of evidence are relaxed in order to assist the state in proving these charges, most notably through the introduction of reverse onuses of proof for many offences.[55] Uganda and Tanzania impose harsh penalties for terrorist offences. In Uganda, the Act provides that the death penalty is mandatory for acts of terrorism which result in death, and may be imposed for all lesser forms of terrorism.[56] However, in *Susan Kigula and Others* v. *Attorney-General*,[57] the Constitutional Court of Uganda found, by a 3:2 majority, that provisions of Ugandan law prescribing mandatory death sentences were inconsistent with the Constitution.[58] In Tanzania, the only offence which carries a minimum sentence of less than fifteen years' imprisonment is that of arranging a terrorist meeting,[59] for which the sentence range is between ten and fifteen years' imprisonment.

Kenya's draft legislation seems milder, providing for a maximum sentence of ten years' imprisonment for ancillary offences such as weapons training, possessing articles for terrorist purposes, collecting and transmitting information and membership of a terrorist organisation.[60] It is a curious anomaly that no penalty is attached to terrorism as such, as the Bill does not expressly render terrorism an offence.[61] This is especially strange since the Bill does provide for a term of life imprisonment for the offence of directing the activities of a terrorist organisation,[62] but yet fails to make terrorism itself a criminal offence.

In both Kenya and Uganda, courts have discretion to order the forfeiture of property on conviction for a terrorist or terrorist-related offence. The draft Kenyan Bill provides no guidance on how a court should exercise this discretion, but Uganda allows the forfeiture order to be made if the Court believes that the property will be used for further terrorist

---

[54] Ibid., pp. 587–90.　　[55] See ibid., pp. 590–2.
[56] Sections 7(1)(a) and (b) of the Ugandan Act.
[57] Constitutional Petition No 6 of 2003, available at www.ulii.org//cgi//cgi-bin/uganda_disp.pl?file=ug/cases/UGCC/2005/8.html&query=terrorism.
[58] See p. 45. The judgment expressly identified s. 7(1)(a) of the Anti-Terrorism Act as one of the impugned pieces of legislation.
[59] Tanzanian Act, s. 26.　　[60] Kenyan Bill, cll. 4, 6 and 10.
[61] Powell, 'Terrorism and governance in South Africa and Eastern Africa', pp. 592–3.
[62] Clause 3.

offences. The onus is on the person attempting to preserve the property to show that it will not be used in this way.[63] Kenya and Uganda allow third parties to assert their rights in the property.[64]

4. Domestic politics and terrorism in Africa since 2005

Having set out the provisions of anti-terrorism legislation in the region, we now turn to examine post-2005 developments and anti-terrorism practice in the surveyed countries under four themes: the significance of the geographical location of the countries surveyed; the public perception and legitimacy of anti-terrorism legislation; the impact of anti-terrorism measures on human rights; and the application of anti-terrorism legislation by courts.

In the first edition of this volume it was noted that, despite a long and difficult history of violence and civil war, the African continent in general had not experienced much terrorism, in the sense of ideologically motivated, 'peacetime' attacks on civilians with the intention of causing terror within the targeted community.[65] Terror attacks had generally manifested themselves as attacks by organised groups engaging in criminal activities or as violations of the laws of armed conflict, whereby rebel groups terrorised, robbed and coerced civilians to assist in military campaigns.[66] However, South Africa and Eastern Africa had had experience of terror attacks against civilian targets in peacetime.[67] Perhaps the most infamous of these was the 1998 bombing of the US embassies in Nairobi and Dar es Salaam, but there have been other high-profile incidents, such as an attack on an Israeli hotel in Mombasa, Kenya in 2002. South Africa experienced a series of bombings between 1994 and 2000, although these were felt to be criminally rather than ideologically motivated.[68] This trend

---

[63] Section 16(5) of the Ugandan Act.

[64] The Ugandan Act seems to expect interested parties to make application immediately upon conviction of the person who used the property for terrorist purposes: see s. 16(6). The Kenyan Bill would allow third parties six months to bring an application: see cl. 22 and sch. 3.

[65] C.H. Powell, 'Defining terrorism: how and why', in N. LaViolette and C. Forcese (eds.), *The Human Rights of Anti-Terrorism* (Toronto: Irwin Law, 2008).

[66] Powell, 'Terrorism and governance in South Africa and Eastern Africa', p. 563.

[67] See A. Oloo, 'Domestic terrorism in Kenya', in W. Okumu and A. Botha (eds.), *Domestic Terrorism in Africa: Defining, Addressing and Understanding its Impact on Human Security* (Pretoria: Institute for Security Studies, 2007), pp. 85–94.

[68] Powell, 'Terrorism and governance in South Africa and Eastern Africa', pp. 563–4; A. Botha, 'Domestic terrorism in South Africa', in Okumu and Botha, *Domestic Terrorism in Africa*, pp. 65–76.

has continued post-2005, with the most high-profile incident of terrorism being the recent bomb blasts in Kampala, Uganda during the 2010 World Cup football final, which killed seventy-six people.[69]

A. Geographical location

The three East African states surveyed are of particular significance in the global anti-terrorism context due to their geographical location. The states are in close proximity to the 'Horn of Africa', which consists of Sudan, Ethiopia, Eritrea, Djibouti and Kenya itself. This region is regarded as especially vulnerable to recruitment by al-Qaeda affiliated groups, which in turn poses a threat to the stability of the African countries in surrounding areas.[70] This instability is attributed in large part to Somalia, which has lacked an effective central government since the early 1990s and is regarded as a focal point for growing Islamic extremism in the region. This dynamic is further complicated by the presence of large communities of ethnic Somalis in many other countries in the region.[71] Kenya is regarded as having unsecured borders, which makes it vulnerable to possible infiltration by terrorist groups.[72] Tanzania is also regarded as being vulnerable to terrorism, with the network alleged to be responsible for the 1998 embassy bombings said to remain active in the region.[73]

Uganda is a particularly complex case, as it is exposed to terrorism threats which have been attributed to extremist organisations based in Somalia,[74] and also has extensive experience of armed conflict. Two rebel

---

[69] BBC news, '"Somalia link" as 74 World Cup fans die in Uganda blasts', 12 July 2010, available at news.bbc.co.uk/2/hi/africa/10593771.stm; Ben Simon, 'Uganda charges 32 over World Cup bombings', 18 August 2010, available at www.mg.co.za/article/2010–08–18-uganda-charges-32-over-world-cup-bombings.

[70] US State Department, *Annual Terrorism Report*, cited in VOANews.com, 'US Anti-Terror Report cites potential Al-Qaida link to African insurgencies', 1 May 2008.

[71] See 'Horn of Africa could become major front for anti-terrorism efforts', *USA Today* 21 October 2006; Institute for Security Studies, *Africa Terrorism Bulletin*, December 2008 (quoting Ugandan military officials warning the Somali community in the Kisenyi region not to become involved in terrorist activities).

[72] US Department of State, *Country Reports on Terrorism*, Chapter 2 – Country Reports: Africa Overview (2007).

[73] US Department of State, *Country Reports on Terrorism*, Chapter 2 – Country Reports: Africa Overview (2008).

[74] Uganda's geographical proximity to Somalia, as well as its support for Somalia's vulnerable interim government, has made it vulnerable to such threats. Ugandan peacekeepers are based in Mogadishu, and the al-Qaeda linked group al-Shabab has previously threatened attacks on Kampala. This is seen as the most likely explanation for the World Cup final day bomb blasts in Kampala. See BBC news, '"Somalia link" as 74 World Cup

forces, the Lord's Resistance Army (LRA) and the Allied Democratic Forces (ADF),[75] conduct military campaigns in the country and have been declared 'terrorist organisations' by the government.[76] Notwithstanding arrest warrants issued by the International Criminal Court against several LRA leaders, and some tentative peace negotiations, the activities of these groups continue.[77] As with Kenya, Uganda's borders are regarded as vulnerable, and combined with the insecurity in the region, this leaves it vulnerable to terrorist activity. Reports suggest that Uganda has been used as a transit point for extremists moving between the Horn of Africa, and North Africa and Europe.[78]

The heightened threat of terrorism from Eastern Africa – both real and imagined – suggests that the region will continue to be an important arena in the global anti-terrorism context.

B.   The public perception and legitimacy of anti-terrorism laws

In the first edition of this volume, the hypothesis was put forward that the presence of terrorist threats within the four states might indicate that there would be a strong internal need and support for anti-terrorism legislation. However, there was significant opposition to the new anti-terrorism regime, with critics in East Africa accusing governments of introducing measures in response to foreign pressure, in particular from the United States.[79]

Since 2005, in addition to incidents of traditional 'terrorist' activity, there have been outbreaks of violent instability in some of the states which, although they would not normally be considered to constitute terrorism, might have been expected to have created public support for counter-terrorism style measures. Examples include the violence that followed

---

fans die in Uganda blasts'. Al-Shabaab has claimed responsibility for the attack: Simon, 'Uganda charges 32 over World Cup bombing'.

[75] The ADF, a dissident group with bases in the DRC, was blamed for a series of attacks between 1997 and 1999 characterised by bomb throwing in pubs, markets, taxi stops and other public places. Privacy International, 'Terrorism Profile – Uganda', 19 December 2004, available at www.privacyinternational.org/article.shtml?cmd%5b347%5d=x-347-359656.

[76] See Powell, 'Terrorism and governance in South Africa and Eastern Africa', p. 564.

[77] W. Okumu, 'Domestic terrorism in Uganda', in Okumu and Botha, Domestic Terrorism in Africa, pp. 77–84; K. Apuuli, 'The ICC arrest warrants for the Lord's Resistance Army leaders and peace prospects for Northern Uganda' (2006) 4 Journal of International Criminal Justice 179.

[78] US Department of State, Country Reports (2007), (2008).

[79] Powell, 'Terrorism and governance in South Africa and Eastern Africa', pp. 564–5.

Kenya's elections in 2007, violent service delivery protests in South Africa, and the wave of xenophobic violence in South Africa in 2008. However, there does not appear to have been any discernable shift in public attitudes towards anti-terrorism legislation; international terrorism still tends to be viewed as a Western problem and is seen as less pressing than domestic issues such as the threat of HIV/AIDS and violent crime.[80] This attitude is evident from continued opposition to anti-terrorism legislation in Kenya. Whitaker remarks that:

> Kenyans still see terrorism largely as an American (or Israeli) problem. In this view, Kenyans are just collateral damage in a conflict between these countries and terrorists. Kenyans are not involved nor are they the intended targets; they are innocent bystanders. Without the recognition of terrorism as a local problem, there is little homegrown demand for stronger counterterrorism measures.[81]

Scepticism has been exacerbated by the tendency of local anti-terrorism units to be heavily funded by Western powers, particularly the United States.[82] Even in the absence of anti-terrorism legislation, these groups conduct operations against terrorism suspects which have created considerable resentment within local communities.[83] In 2007, the United States announced that it would provide US $14 million worth of training and equipment to Kenyan security forces, to counter terrorist activities in the Horn of Africa.[84] The following year, Kenyan anti-terrorism police conducted raids to search for suspects in the 1998 US Embassy bombings. The raid failed to capture the suspects, and was criticised as a publicity-

---

[80] Center on Global Counter-Terrorism Cooperation and Institute of Security Studies, *Implementing the UN Global Counter-Terrorism Strategy in Southern Africa* (Discussion Paper, 2007), p. 3.

[81] Beth E. Whitaker, 'Reluctant partners: fighting terrorism and promoting democracy in Kenya' (2008) 9 *International Studies Perspectives* 266. There are exceptions, with some Members of Parliament supporting the anti-terrorism Bill: see, 'MPs support anti-terrorism bill', *Kenyan Broadcasting Corporation* 11 November 2008, available at www.kbc.co.ke/story.asp?ID+53746.

[82] The United States Africa Command (AFRICOM) makes funding available to support African states in combating terrorist threats. See 'US anti-terror report cites potential al-Qaida link to African insurgencies', *voa.news.com* 1 May 2008.

[83] Notably Kenyan Muslims: see Stephanie McCrummen, 'Hunt for suspects in embassy bombings elicits anger in Kenya', *Washington Post*, 15 August 2008.

[84] BBC News, 'Kenya gets US anti-terror funds', *BBC News* 4 May 2007, available at news.bbc.co.uk/go/pr/fr/-/2/hi/africa/6623635.stm. A significant portion of the US $100 million East African Counter-Terrorism initiative was assigned to Kenya, and the US provided training for Kenya's anti-terrorism police. Beth E. Whitaker, 'Exporting the Patriot Act? Democracy and the "war on terror" in the Third World' (2007) 28(5) *Third World Quarterly* 1024.

seeking exercise by the anti-terrorism units to ensure continued US fund-ing.[85] Aid and other financial support, particularly from the United States, has increasingly been perceived as being contingent on the receiver states implementing anti-terrorism legislation. The impact of foreign aid can-not be underestimated, as it often makes up a significant proportion of the budget of African states.[86]

This has led to strong perceptions that anti-terrorism legislation is sim-ply being implemented at the behest of the United States.[87] This percep-tion was apparent in the reaction to the 2006 Kenyan draft bill. Politicians promised to block the bill on the basis that it was being promoted by the United States, and the public perception that the legislation was being imposed by the United States continued.[88] In Tanzania, while the Act encountered fairly limited opposition when it was passed, provisions allowing government to share information with foreign state author-ities regarding Tanzanian citizens provoked widespread protests against the United States when FBI officials were involved in the arrests of two Muslim leaders in Tanzania.[89]

C.   Anti-terrorism measures and violations of human rights

The first edition of this volume noted fears that anti-terrorism laws were not used to protect citizens of the surveyed countries, but to suppress par-ticular groups, with Muslims, in particular, feeling targeted. Concerns were expressed that the legislation would be abused by governments in order to crack down on opposition, particularly in light of allegations that the Tanzanian government had tortured members of opposition groups, and the Ugandan government had engaged in widespread mistreatment of its opponents.[90]

---

[85] McCrummen, 'Hunt for Suspects'.

[86] Donors are estimated to fund close to half of Uganda's budget: see W. Ross, 'Museveni: Uganda's fallen angel', *BBC News*, 30 November 2005, available at news.bbc.co.uk/go/pr/fr/-/2/hi/africa/4482456.stm.

[87] See International Summit on Democracy, Terrorism and Security, 3 March 2005, avail-able at summit.clubmadrid.org/contribute/democracy-and-terrorism-the-impact-of-the-ant.html, alleging that recipients of USAID assistance were being required to sign agreements conforming to anti-terrorism conditions. However, the US has expressed concerns about the human rights implications of the Kenyan draft Bill, and has given significant military aid to Kenya, Uganda and Tanzania – therefore military aid, at least, is not necessarily contingent on anti-terrorism legislation. Whitaker, 'Exporting the Patriot Act?' 1022, 1024.

[88] Ibid., 1024.   [89] Ibid., 1028–9.

[90] Powell, 'Terrorism and governance in South Africa and Eastern Africa', pp. 565–6.

These concerns remain, as was illustrated by the 2008 raids in Kenya, and by criticisms that the 2006 Kenyan Bill singled out Muslim members of the population.[91] Kenya's Muslim and Somali communities have complained of being targeted and harassed by counter-terrorism units.[92] Analysts note that allegations of human rights violations have increased since 2007, with security forces in northeast Kenya intensifying efforts to capture terrorism suspects fleeing the conflict in Somalia.[93]

Another serious human rights issue is the unlawful removal of terrorism suspects to other states or locations. Kenyan civil society organisations contend that, while large numbers of Kenyans are arrested on suspicion of terrorist activities, very few are successfully tried. However, large numbers of people, including Kenyan nationals, are alleged to have been sent to Ethiopia or Somalia for questioning, without charge or access to legal representation, and allegations of torture in Kenyan and Ethiopian custody have been recorded.[94] During the period between December 2006 and February 2007, reports document at least 150 people, many having fled the conflict in Somalia, being arbitrarily detained in Kenya and held for several weeks without charge.[95] Most were denied access to a lawyer or consular assistance, and were unable to challenge the legality of their detention or to assert possible refugee status.[96] A large number of the detainees are alleged to have been 'rendered' to Somalia without any legal process being followed; the rest are believed to have been transferred to Ethiopia.[97]

Uganda is also facing serious allegations of abuse and misconduct by anti-terrorism forces. In 2009, Human Rights Watch accused Uganda's Joint Anti-Terrorism Task Force (JATT)[98] of systematic and serious

---

[91] US Department of State, *Country Reports* (2006), (2007).

[92] William Church, 'Somalia: CIA blowback weakens East Africa', 23 October 2006, available at www.sudantribune.com/spip.php?page=imprimable&id_article=18301.

[93] McCrummen, 'Hunt for suspects'; Whitaker, 'Reluctant Partners', 258, 264–5.

[94] McCrummen, 'Hunt for suspects'; BBC News, 'Kenya gets US anti-terror funds'; Redress and Reprieve, *Kenya and Counter-Terrorism: A Time for Change* (2009) (alleging mass arbitrary detentions, deportations and transfers).

[95] Redress and Reprieve, *Kenya and Counter-Terrorism*, p. 1. Similar allegations were made by Human Rights Watch: see *Why Am I Still Here? The 2007 Horn of Africa Renditions and the Fate of those Still Missing* (2008), which reports at least ninety people as having been unlawfully rendered from Kenya to Somalia and then to Ethiopia during 2007. A year later, at least ten were alleged to remain in Ethiopian prisons, and the fate of several more was unknown.

[96] Redress and Reprieve, *Kenya and Counter-Terrorism*, p. 1.   [97] Ibid., p. 1.

[98] The JATT is described as a paramilitary group operating under the authority of the Chieftaincy of Military Intelligence, although it lacks a codified mandate. It draws its

human rights abuses, including the incommunicado detention of suspects and the routine use of torture during interrogations.[99] The report documents 106 cases of illegal detention by the JATT over a two-year period, and more than twenty-five instances of torture or other ill treatment.[100] Uganda's Human Rights Commission has been thwarted in its attempts to inspect the safe houses of the JATT.[101] Human Rights Watch charged that JATT personnel 'typically operate in unmarked cars, carry out arrests wearing civilian clothes with no identifying insignia, and do not inform suspects of the reasons for their arrest'.[102]

According to the Human Rights Watch report, detainees are often not told where they are being taken, and are frequently blindfolded, handcuffed and beaten. They are denied access to lawyers or family members. The detention centre on which the Human Rights Watch investigation focused is not a legal detention centre, as the requisite notice required by the Ugandan Constitution has not been given. In contravention of ordinary rules of Ugandan constitutional law and criminal procedure, suspects are not handed over to the police or brought before a magistrate within the required time and detainees are held for long periods of time in poor conditions. Incidents of deaths and enforced disappearances of detainees have also been recorded.[103] It should be noted that, in respect of officials authorised to carry out interceptions of communication or surveillance activities under the Act, the Act specifically criminalises torture, inhuman and degrading treatment, illegal detention and intentional harm to property.[104]

General concerns have been expressed about the increasing influence of the army in Ugandan society and politics. This concern was illustrated during the 2005 trial of Kizza Besige, a prominent opposition politician seen as a likely challenger to Ugandan President Yoweri Museveni. Besige and his fellow accused had been granted bail, but opted to remain in prison after a group of armed men in civilian clothes surrounded the

---

members from the Ugandan Defence Force, the police and Uganda's internal and external security organisations: US Department of State, *2009 Human Rights Report: Uganda*, 11 March 2009.

[99] Human Rights Watch, *Open Secret: Illegal Detention and Torture by the Joint Anti-terrorism Task Force in Uganda* (2009).

[100] Ibid., p. 3.

[101] G. Bareebe, 'Uganda: rights body blocked from safe houses', *The Monitor*, 23 February 2010.

[102] Human Rights Watch, *Open Secret*, p. 3.   [103] See ibid., p. 3

[104] Section 21(e) read with s. 1. It is notable that the Act does not criminalise these offences more generally.

court building. An army statement claimed they were members of the anti-terrorism unit.[105] Such activities seem to fall some way outside a normal understanding of the role of anti-terrorism forces,[106] and indeed were subsequently found to have been unconstitutional by the Ugandan Constitutional Court.[107] Ugandan authorities have also been accused of using the threat of prosecution under the Anti-Terrorism Act to intimidate journalists and stifle dissent.[108] Critics have accused Ugandan President Museveni of using the threat of terrorism as a pretext for delaying political reforms and silencing opposition.[109]

The experience in these countries demonstrates that the often draconian powers granted by anti-terrorism legislation may be turned against suspects whose alleged offences in fact bear little relation to 'terrorism', as it is traditionally understood. In many of the Ugandan cases described above, the anti-terrorism legislation has failed either to protect human rights or to prevent and prosecute terrorism. However, the problem clearly goes deeper than the anti-terrorism legislation itself. Kenya has carried out several anti-terrorist operations, despite having no legislation targeting terrorism at all. These operations may have disrupted terrorist activities.[110] However, they have also violated individual rights. The mass arbitrary arrests and transfers in Kenya can be seen as a significant part of Kenya's anti-terrorism operations.[111]

Even South Africa, often lauded as a shining example of constitutionalism and the rule of law on the African continent, has struggled to

---

[105] Ross, 'Museveni'; *Uganda Law Society* v. *Attorney General of the Republic of Uganda – Constitutional Petition No. 18 of 2005* [2006] UGCC 11 (31 January 2006) (*Uganda Law Society*).

[106] It should also be noted that the Ugandan military has been accused of human rights abuses in other contexts, apparently unrelated to counter-terrorism. See, 'Uganda army accused of Karamoja torture abuses', *BBC News* 17 August 2010, available at www.bbc.co.uk/news/world-africa-10996764; International Press Institute, *In Wake of Deadly Uganda Riots: Journalist Beaten and Detained; Four Radio Stations Closed*, available at www.freemedia.at/site-services/singleview-master/4546/.

[107] *Uganda Law Society* [2006] UGCC 11 23.

[108] International Federation of Journalists, 'IFJ condemns spying allegations against journalists in Uganda', 25 January 2004, available at www.ifj.org/en/articles/ifj-condemns-spying-allegations-against-journalists-in-uganda.

[109] Whitaker, 'Exporting the Patriot Act', 1027.

[110] US Department of State, *Country Reports on Terrorism*, Chapter 5 – Country Reports: Africa Overview (2005); US Department of State, *Country Reports on Terrorism*, Chapter 2 – Country Reports, Africa Overview (2006); US Department of State, *Country Reports* (2007).

[111] Redress and Reprieve, *Kenya and Counter-Terrorism*, p. 2.

reconcile counter-terrorism with its human rights obligations. A high-profile example is the case of Pakistani national Khalid Rashid, who disappeared from South Africa in November 2005 in circumstances that remain unclear. The Department of Home Affairs maintained that Rashid was legally deported from South Africa, on the basis that he was a foreigner illegally present in South Africa. While acknowledging allegations that Rashid was connected to international terrorist cells, the Department maintained that there had been insufficient grounds on which he could be extradited.[112]

This explanation has caused commentators to question why, if Rashid was indeed a terrorist suspect, he was not arrested and dealt with under anti-terrorism legislation. Allegations have been made that the Department requested the Police to 'provide legal cover' for Rashid's arrest and handover to Pakistani authorities, and suspicions linger that Rashid may have been subjected to an extraordinary rendition.[113] In 2009, the Supreme Court of Appeal found that while Rashid's initial arrest had been lawful, his subsequent detention and deportation had been unlawful due to failure to comply with South Africa's immigration legislation (the case does not mention anti-terrorism legislation).[114] The applicants did argue that Rashid's deportation was also unlawful for having been a disguised extradition because of allegations of Rashid's links to terrorist groups. However, the Court found that this argument had not been successfully made out.[115]

The event nonetheless raises the concern that, like their East African counterparts, South African authorities may be conducting anti-terrorism operations outside the framework of the country's terrorism legislation, thus placing individuals subject to these actions outside the protections provided for in the legislation. The Kenyan and South African examples also appear to provide support for the argument that 'democracy can make it difficult for governments to cooperate *publically* with the United States in the "war on terror", though *private* cooperation often continues behind the scenes'.[116]

---

[112] Institute of Security Studies, *African Terrorism Bulletin*, June 2006, Issue 006.
[113] D. Strumpf and N. Dawes, 'Khalid Rashid: Govt's cover is blown', *Mail & Guardian*, 9 June 2006, available at www.mg.co.za/article/2006–06–09-khalid-rashid-govts-cover-is-blown; Institute of Security Studies, *African Terrorism Bulletin*.
[114] *Jeebhai* v. *Minister of Home Affairs* 2009 (5) SA 54 (SCA), esp. [37], [53] (*Jeebhai*).
[115] *Jeebhai*, [40]–[45], [64]–[66].
[116] Whitaker, 'Reluctant partners' 256.

D. Application of anti-terrorism legislation by the courts

It is perhaps not surprising, given this context, that courts have begun to resist certain aspects of the anti-terrorism regime. In the *Uganda Law Society* case, the Ugandan Constitutional Court found that the trial of individuals on charges of terrorism before a General Court Martial, while they were simultaneously awaiting trial on charges of treason arising from similar facts before the High Court, was unconstitutional. A key component of this finding was s. 6 of the Act, which gives the High Court exclusive jurisdiction over the offence of terrorism.[117]

While there have yet to be any reported judgments handed down under the South African anti-terrorism Act,[118] some support can be seen for the hypothesis that the courts will be likely to subject anti-terrorism measures to close scrutiny, as seen in the *Jeebhai* case, discussed in the previous section. In *Minister of Safety and Security and Others* v. *Mohamed and Another*,[119] a majority of the Court set aside a search warrant used to raid the homes of two men suspected of terrorist activities. Police suspected the men of having formed an Islamic terrorist group, but the Court found that the warrant was over-broad, and that the magistrate had failed to apply his mind properly in issuing the warrant. The Court reacted strongly against the state not placing the full affidavit on which the warrant was issued before the reviewing courts, remarking that it 'smacks of

---

[117] *Uganda Law Society* [2006] UGCC 11, 20–1, 74.

[118] There have been cases decided under the Act, mostly relating to the activities of the right wing 'Boeremag' group, but as decisions of Magistrates' Courts in South Africa are not published, it is difficult to obtain judgments if the case is not heard by a High Court. The 'Boeremag' is a white right-wing group, twenty-one members of which are being tried for offences of high treason, murder and terrorism after a series of bomb blasts in 2001. See Institute for Security Studies, *Assessing South Africa's Commitment to Prevent and Combat Terrorism*, 21 July 2008. A possible high-profile prosecution which may take place in South Africa is that of Henry Okah, a former MEND (Movement for the Emancipation of the Niger Delta) leader, who was arrested in South Africa under the country's anti-terrorism legislation following the October 2010 car bombings in Abuja, Nigeria: Ola Awoniyi, 'Nigerian police name suspects in deadly blasts', *Mail & Guardian*, 4 October 2010, available at www.mg.co.za/article/2010-10-04-nigerian-police-name-suspects-in-deadly-blasts. At the time of writing, Okah had been charged with engaging in terrorist activities, conspiracy to do so, and delivering, placing and detonating an explosive device. His application for bail has been denied: 'Okah case postponed for decision', *Independent Online*, 5 November 2010, available at www.iol.co.za/news/crime-courts/okah-case-postponed-for-decision-1.722306; L. Faull, 'Terror-accused Henry Okah denied bail', 19 November 2010, available at www.mg.co.za/article/2010-11-19-okah-denied-bail.

[119] Unreported judgment, Case No. A 228/09, 30 April 2010 (*Mohamed*).

executive interference with a matter which is the exclusive confines [sic] of the judiciary'.[120] The Court also emphasised the need for judicial officers, in issuing search warrants, to ensure that constitutional rights are protected. [121]

Another notable feature of the *Mohamed* case was that the warrant in question had been issued under normal laws of criminal procedure.[122] In light of the majority's finding that the warrant was too general, over-broad and unclear in setting out the documents sought,[123] it is puzzling that the anti-terrorism legislation was not relied on to activate the broader search and seizure powers provided for in the NPA Act.[124]

5. Conclusion

In this section, we return to the contradictions which emerge from the anti-terrorism programmes of these regions and investigate what they can tell us about the role of anti-terrorism in preventing terrorism and protecting rights.

As noted above, some commentators support anti-terrorism legislation as an essential instrument against terrorism. These commentators accept the rights restrictions that may result for terrorist suspects as a necessary evil in protecting the broader society. Others support anti-terrorism legislation because, while limiting certain rights, it can establish those limitations with legal certainty, allowing suspects to call on law for protection should the executive act beyond its powers.[125]

If we measure these arguments against the experience of the countries in this study, both appear inadequate. First, the Kenyan experience suggests that anti-terrorism legislation may not even be necessary for an anti-terrorism programme. The South African practice discussed through

---

[120] Ibid., [12], [15]–[17].   [121] Ibid., [18], [45].

[122] Namely the Criminal Procedure Act 51 of 1977. See the judgment of Louw J in *Mohamed*, unreported judgment, [2]–[3].

[123] Ibid., [38], [41] and [42] (Moosa J).

[124] See note 15 above. To illustrate the scope this would allow, s. 29(1)(d) of the NPA Act provides that an investigating officer may 'seize ... anything on or in the premises which has a bearing or might have a bearing on the investigation'.

[125] See D. Dyzenhaus, 'Accountability and the concept of (global) administrative law', in H. Corder (ed.), *Global Administrative Law: Development and Innovation* (Cape Town: Juta, 2009), pp. 22–3, for an illustration of how, even under oppressive apartheid laws in South Africa, officials implementing the laws were operating in terms of powers vested by statute. This allowed decisions to be challenged in order to establish some protection of the rights of South Africans affected by the apartheid laws, however limited these rights might be.

the *Jeebhai* and *Mohamed* cases might also appear to suggest that anti-terrorism law is unnecessary, since both cases were dealt with in terms of 'normal' immigration and criminal procedure laws. What, it might be argued, is the purpose of specialised anti-terrorism legislation if states are not going to make use of it?

On the other hand, the Kenyan operations in particular appear to have violated human rights. This suggests that it may be desirable to enact anti-terrorism laws, not so much because such laws are essential to combat terrorism, but because they can set limits on the executive's extraordinary powers.

When we turn to Uganda, however, we find support for the traditional critique that anti-terrorism legislation increases the potential for human rights abuses. Allegations of human rights abuses levelled against anti-terrorism units in the security forces appear to demonstrate the danger of anti-terrorism legislation failing to provide protection for individual rights, and allowing for repressive actions by law enforcement agencies.

Perhaps the solution lies in the fact that, in many of these examples, the 'ordinary laws' were violated as well as, occasionally, the anti-terrorism laws themselves. There is, in other words, a gap between the proclaimed law and governmental conduct – whether it relates to terrorism or not. The larger this gap, the more questionable the value of anti-terrorism legislation will be. We submit that, in any system where the rule of law is not respected, governmental obedience to its own legislation will be piecemeal. Government is likely, in other words, to rely on the extra powers which anti-terrorism legislation grants it, but ignore the legal restriction of those powers. In such cases, anti-terrorism legislation is more likely to become an alibi for the abuse of power than an instrument to prevent terrorism within a clear legal framework.

We do not mean, through this argument, that anti-terrorism legislation should be abandoned. We do, however, argue that it must proceed hand-in-hand with the strengthening of the rule of law. In this regard, we suggest that a primary goal of any anti-terrorism programme should be the clarity of its scope. We suggest that there is a need for a clear legal framework, whether through specialist anti-terrorism legislation or otherwise, that has as its basis a clear definition of terrorism. Over-broad and unclear definitions of terrorism seem to be at the heart of the problematic instances of anti-terrorism discourse being misused by the executive, as a means of clamping down on opposition and dissent.[126] If additional

---

[126] Whitaker, 'Exporting the Patriot Act', 1028.

powers, beyond those in ordinary criminal and procedural law, are really needed in order to combat terrorism, then safeguards can be provided by forcing governments to articulate exactly what they mean by terrorism and defining what powers they will employ to combat terrorism, and the limits on those powers. The legal framework ought to allow for some form of judicial review of executive action, even if this only occurs after the fact. Sometimes, the exigency of a terrorist threat may make it genuinely impossible and undesirable to constrain the executive's ability to act by requiring judicial oversight beforehand. None of this, however, disposes of the essential role of law itself – and therefore of the courts – in containing the power of the organs of government.

Finally, there is no reason why a legislative framework for counter-terrorism should not expressly be aligned with human rights. Any attempt to see these two legal regimes as mutually exclusive ought to be rejected, as common ground can be found between the two. After all, the preservation of human rights is, or at least should be, one of the motivating factors behind efforts to prevent terrorism in the first place.[127]

---

[127]   See *The Ottowa Principles on Anti-Terrorism and Human Rights* (2006), available at aix1. uottawa.ca/~cforcese/hrat/principles.pdf; Powell, 'Defining terrorism: why and how'.

23

Israel's anti-terrorism law: past, present and future

DAPHNE BARAK-EREZ

1. Introduction

The state of Israel has been confronting terrorism and other harsh security threats since its establishment in 1948. Parallel to changing security conditions, law-makers have gradually updated relevant laws and regulations to fit changing circumstances. The following analysis aims to discuss the development of Israeli anti-terrorism law by reviewing the main issues and tensions confronting the Israeli legal system in this area, evaluating the allocation of power and control between the various branches of government, analysing the impact of anti-terrorism law on the protection of human rights and pointing to the main dilemmas and challenges faced by the system.

Israeli anti-terrorism law is an interesting laboratory for evaluating some of the basic tensions of this area of law.[1] This has been the result of the intensity of terrorism threats in the Israeli context, on the one hand, and the centrality of law to the implementation of Israeli anti-terrorism policies, on the other hand. The legal aspects of anti-terrorism policies have always been important in Israel since legislative authorisations are considered vital for executive action in this area. In addition, such

I thank Gershon Gontovnik, Liav Orgad and Kent Roach for their comments on earlier drafts and Naomi Scheinerman for her assistance.

[1] One technical shortcoming in terms of taking advantage of the richness of this laboratory is that the formal language used in Israel, and in the legal context as well, is Hebrew. The legal materials reviewed here have all been published first and foremost in Hebrew (except legal materials from the period of the British Mandate in Palestine, when all laws and judicial decisions were published in English). In the past, all Israeli legislation was also published in an English series cited in some of the footnotes (LSI – Laws of the State of Israel). The publication of this series was stopped. However, translations of some of the laws mentioned here are available on the websites of the Israeli Knesset (www.knesset.gov. il), the Israeli Ministry of Justice (www.justice.gov.il) or the Israeli Ministry of Foreign Affairs (www.mfo.gov.il). Important decisions of the Israeli Supreme Court are translated into English and made available on the website of the Israeli Supreme Court (www.court. gov.il). The footnotes mention references to relevant translations.

executive action is subject to judicial review. The framework of anti-terrorism law is composed of norms which have been formed in different historical periods. In general, it is based on the enforcement of criminal law (both ordinary offences which protect life and property and special offences connected to activities related to terrorist organisations) alongside special laws which grant the government powers to take administrative preventive measures (such as the detention of suspected terrorists). Part of these laws have been drafted to apply only when a special declaration of emergency situation is in place, but in fact have become part of the regular framework of law due to the prolonged emergency situation which has never been abolished. In addition to the specific laws in this area, currently, the regulation of anti-terrorism policies is shaped also by the application of constitutional (domestic) standards and norms derived from international law.

2.   Historical background and the gradual evolution of special legislative schemes

Israeli legislation concerning terrorism finds its roots in the days of the British Mandate in Palestine.[2] Faced with resistance, the British government enacted a detailed anti-terrorism law, the Defence (Emergency) Regulations 1945.[3] This law contained draconian provisions, including powers to demolish houses, decide on administrative detentions and deportations, and administer criminal justice before a military rather than an ordinary civilian court.

After declaring independence in 1948, Israel was confronted with new security challenges. First, it had to fight attacks by both surrounding Arab countries and local Palestinians, who opposed the establishment of the state. Second, the government was also compelled to confront Jewish extremist groups, which had retained underground methods used against British rule. For example, in September 1948, Jewish activists from the Lehi underground (known also as the Stern Group) murdered the United Nations delegate to the region, Count Bernadotte, to

---

[2] For a more detailed description of this history, see: Claude Klein, 'On the three floors of legislative building: Israel's legal arsenal in its struggle against terrorism', (2006) 27 *Cardozo Law Review* 2223.

[3] Defence (Emergency) Regulations 1945, Palestine Gazette no. 1442, Supp. No. 2, 1055 (Defence Regulations). Despite their misleading title, the Defence Regulations are primary legislation, as opposed to merely administrative regulations.

pre-empt his anticipated recommendations, which they perceived as a threat to Israel's position at that stage of the War of Independence. Acknowledging the danger of these activities, the new Israeli government pursued anti-terrorism measures, at first using its special powers to promulgate emergency regulations that would carry legal force for up to three months.[4] Soon after, the government moved forward to enact these powers in ordinary legislation: the Prevention of Terrorism Ordinance 1948[5] authorised the government to declare a group a terrorist organisation, making both membership and support for such a group criminal offences. The Prevention of Terrorism Ordinance has been used over the years against both Palestinian anti-Israeli organisations, including the PLO and Hamas, and Jewish extremist groups. It is still in force, but has been amended several times and is supposed to be replaced by an updated anti-terrorism law, as described later.

Given steady and persistent security threats, Israel chose not to abolish the old and much criticised Defence Regulations, but rather considered specific changes and reforms. About thirty years after its creation, Israel abolished the power to deport originally eminent in the Defence Regulations and introduced a reform in the area of administrative detentions, by legislating the Emergency Powers (Detentions) Law 1979.[6] The new law granted the Minister of Defence, not the military commanders, the power to issue orders to subject an individual to an administrative detention.[7]

Anti-terrorism law in Israel is the result of this complex legislative scheme which has developed during the decades since its establishment. In principle, Israel adheres to a legislative model of anti-terrorism law, which means that anti-terrorism measures must be based on legislation, rather than on executive residual power.[8]

In addition to specific legislation, the government also has the power to enact special emergency regulations, contingent on the existence of an 'emergency situation' for a period not exceeding three months (which can

---

[4] See below note 9.   [5] 1 LSI 76 (Prevention of Terrorism Ordinance).

[6] 33 LSI 89 (Detentions Law). An English translation is available at: (1990) 21 *Columbia Human Rights Law Review* 510. As explained below in Section 3, these changes apply only to Israel proper, and not to Israel's Occupied Territories.

[7] For more information on Israel's administrative detentions legislation, see: Baruch Bracha, 'Judicial review of security powers in Israel: a new policy of the courts', (1991) 28 *Stanford Journal of International Law* 39, 50–5. For more details see below, Section 3.

[8] See Daphne Barak-Erez, 'Terrorism law between the executive and legislative models' (2009) 57 *American Journal of Comparative Law* 877.

then be prolonged only by the legislature).[9] Due to Israel's security conditions, the state of emergency in force since its very first days has never been repealed and is in fact being continually renewed on a standard basis. At the same time, in practice, the government more often resorts to the anti-terrorism measures already enacted in current legislation (either laws which apply only when a declaration of emergency situation is in force or other laws) rather than to promulgating emergency regulations.[10]

Another factor which currently shapes Israeli anti-terrorism law is the move toward the constitutionalisation of the legal system. Traditionally, Israel had followed the British approach to parliamentary sovereignty. It did not adopt a formal written constitution and did not allow for judicial review of legislation (in contrast to judicial review of administrative action which was always available). Indeed, it has enacted a series of 'Basic Laws' intended to serve as chapters in the future constitution of the country, but for many years they were not considered as having a special normative status. In addition, the first Basic Laws enacted dealt only with structural and institutional matters and did not address the issue of protecting of human rights against infringing legislation. The turning point has been the enactment of two Basic Laws on human rights in 1992 – Basic Law: Freedom of Occupation and Basic Law: Human Dignity and Liberty.[11] These Basic Laws have been interpreted by the Israeli Supreme Court as protecting the human rights they recognise from infringing legislation.[12]

---

[9] An 'emergency situation' has to be declared by the legislature (the Israeli Knesset). The executive branch may declare an 'emergency situation' only when there are objective obstacles for calling a Knesset session, for a period not exceeding a week. See s. 38 of Basic Law: The Government (English translation is available on the Knesset website). This provision is the updated (and more balanced) version of earlier legislation which regulated the declaration of a state of emergency, (s. 9 of the Law and Administration Ordinance, 1948, 1 LSI 7 which was repealed).

[10] Note that the application of the several anti-terrorism laws enacted after the establishment of the state – the Prevention of Terrorism Ordinance and the Detentions Law – has been contingent on the existence of a declared state of emergency. However, it seems that due to the prolonged nature of anti-terrorism threats, as well as to the possibility that the emergency declaration would not be prolonged, new laws in this area are drafted as permanent legislation not contingent on the existence of such declaration. An example of this new approach can be found in the Incarceration of Unlawful Combatants Law 2002 (Unlawful Combatants Law) discussed in the text accompanying note 25 below (English translation available on the website of the Israeli Ministry of Justice).

[11] For more background on Israeli constitutional law, see Daphne Barak-Erez, 'From an unwritten to a written Constitution: the Israeli challenge in American perspective' (1995) 26 *Columbia Human Rights Law Review* 309.

[12] CA 6821/93 *United Mizrahi Bank v. Midgal Cooperative Village* 49(4) PD 221.

The more relevant of the two to the subject matter at hand is Basic Law: Human Dignity and Liberty.[13] Indeed, the application of this Basic Law was limited to new laws enacted after its coming into force. Accordingly, past legislation, including the very complex legislative scheme in the area of anti-terrorism law which was in existence at the time, is immune from judicial review.[14] However, every new law in this area does not enjoy this immunity. Taking into consideration the need to constantly update existing legislation for the purpose of meeting present-day terrorist threats, the Basic Laws are expected to fulfill an ever-growing role.

Currently, in the presence of the growing scope of terrorism threats as well as the development of new anti-terrorism laws in a post-9/11 world, Israel's Ministry of Justice has been working on a project of enacting a consolidated and updated anti-terrorism law. The proposed Bill is currently being debated.[15] This Bill will also have to meet these constitutional standards.

3. Criminal justice versus special administrative anti-terrorism law

The distinction between prevention and punishment is pivotal to the understanding of the structure of Israel's anti-terrorism law. While Israeli law criminalises terrorist activities and other activities supportive of terrorism, it significantly emphasises prevention and thus uses preventative administrative measures as well.

A. Prevention and administrative detentions

A major example for the use of preventive measures is that of administrative detentions. As mentioned, Israel inherited provisions allowing for administrative detentions for security reasons from the pre-independence legal system governing British Mandatory Palestine,

---

[13] Basic Law: Human Dignity and Liberty awards constitutional protection to the following rights: the preservation and the protection of the one's life, body and dignity; the right to property; the right to liberty; the right to leave the country (and the right of citizens to enter it) and the right to privacy. According to s. 8 of the Basic Law: 'There shall be no violation of rights under this Basic Law except by a law befitting the values of the State of Israel, enacted for a proper purpose, and to an extent no greater than is required.'

[14] According to s. 10 of Basic Law: Human Dignity and Liberty: 'This Basic Law shall not affect the validity of any law (din) in force prior to the commencement of the Basic Law'.

[15] For more details see below Section 7.

as enacted in the Defence Regulations.[16] This regime was later replaced by a Detentions Law in 1979, which, while preserving the possibility of preventive administrative detentions, possessed better procedural safeguards. According to the 1979 law: 'Where the Minister of Defence has reasonable cause to believe that reasons of state security or public security require that a particular person be detained, he may, by order under his hand, direct that such person be detained for a period, not exceeding six months, stated in the order'.[17] This order may be extended from time to time.[18] The detainee has the right to have his detention reviewed by a President of a District Court within forty-eight hours,[19] and after that at least every three months.[20] In principle, the procedure for the review of the detainee's status enables the state to refrain from full disclosure of the underlying evidence.[21] However, the Israeli Supreme Court has developed an activist approach to its review role of the non-disclosed evidence[22] that, to a large extent, immitates the practice of inquisitorial legal systems. This practice of the court has been described by Professor Itzhak Zamir, a scholar of Israeli public law and later a Justice on the Israeli Supreme Court, in the following manner:

> Due to the gravity of this situation, the Supreme Court instituted a practice which has no basis in law. The court dealing with the case suggests to the applicant that the administrative authority, which keeps the evidence under a cloak of secrecy, present the evidence only to the judges, behind closed doors, not in the presence of the applicant. If the applicant agrees to this proposal, the court will then examine the confidential evidence".[23]

It is important to add that the active role the Israeli Supreme Court has taken upon itself is not supposed to replace the duty to disclose to the detained person the gist of the allegations against him. In recent decisions, the Supreme Court has made it clear that the state has to disclose

---

[16] See above note 3.   [17] Detentions Law, s. 2(a).
[18] Ibid., s. 2(b).   [19] Ibid., s. 4.   [20] Ibid., s. 5.
[21] According to s. 6(c) of the Detentions Law: 'In proceedings under section 4 or 5, the President of the District Court may accept evidence without the detainee or his representative being present and without disclosing the evidence to them if, after studying the evidence or hearing submissions, even in their absence, he is satisfied that disclosure of the evidence to either of them may impair state security or public security.'
[22] For the role of the Surpeme Court in the area of anti-terrorism law, see further Section 6 below.
[23] Itzhak Zamir, 'Human rights and national security' (1989) 23 *Israel Law Review* 375, 399.

the basic allegations to the detained, as an independent duty, alongside the full disclosure of evidence to the court.[24]

In addition to the Detentions Law, Israel enacted the Unlawful Combatants Law, which applies to the detention of foreigners who reside outside Israel and are caught in the context of military-type confrontations with Israeli forces.[25] This law contains similar mechanisms of judicial review, with adjustments that reflect a consideration of the different context – such as allowing the first judicial review to take place within fourteen days,[26] and then allowing that every additional review will take place at least every six months.[27] This law also expressly provides for the possibility of using secret evidence disclosed only to the court:

> It shall be permissible to depart from the laws of evidence in proceedings under this Law, for reasons to be recorded; the court may admit evidence, even in the absence of the prisoner or his legal representative, or not disclose such evidence to the aforesaid if, after having reviewed the evidence or heard the submissions, even in the absence of the prisoner or his legal representative, it is convinced that disclosure of the evidence to the prisoner or his legal representative is likely to harm State security or public security.[28]

Accordingly, similar principles of judicial review alongside authorised limits on the disclosure of evidence to suspects apply to detentions conducted in the Occupied Territories based on military orders. As explained by Chief Justice Beinisch also in the context of the new law from 2002:

> In view of the problems inherent in submitting privileged evidence ex parte, the court that conducts out a judicial review of an administrative detention is required to act with caution and great precision when examining the material that is brought before it for its eyes only. In such

---

[24] See HCJ 2595/09 *Sofi* v. *State of Israel* (not published, 2009). In this case, Justice Rubinstein stressed that the limitation on disclosure should be 'narrowed … to the necessary minimum': ibid. See also HCJ 1510/09 *Atamana* v. *State of Israel* (not published, 2009). In *Atamana*, Justice Hayut stressed that eventually all the relevant allegations were revealed to the detainee. At the same time, it is clear from these two decisions that the authorities tended to hide the main points of the accusations from the detained individuals, eventually revealing them only under the pressure of the Court.

[25] The distinction between the two detention laws was analysed in Crim. A. 6659/06 *A* v. *Israel* (not published, 2008) (*The Unlawful Combatants* decision) (English translation is available on the website of the Israeli Supreme Court). The enactment of this law has a special history that will be discussed below – based on the Supreme Court's decision in the *Bargaining Chips* affair that Israel cannot detain individuals for other purposes other than prevention according to its regular Detention Law.

[26] Unlawful Combatants Law, s. 5(a).   [27] Ibid., s. 5(c).   [28] Ibid., s. 5(e).

circumstances, the court has a duty to act with extra caution and to examine the privileged material brought before it from the viewpoint of the prisoner, who has not seen the material and cannot argue against it.[29]

It is worthwhile adding that the Unlawful Combatants Law, which was enacted after Basic Law: Human Dignity and Liberty, was the subject of judicial review by the Israeli Supreme Court and was eventually approved as meeting its constitutional standards.[30]

B. Criminal law

The use of preventive measures was never intended to replace the enforcement of criminal law. Upon the discovery of reliable evidence regarding crimes committed, terrorists are submitted to criminal justice measures based on their involvement in these crimes.

The most pronounced cases featuring the implementation of criminal law are the trials of people charged with direct involvement in terrorist attacks. In these cases, the relevant offences are classical provisions of violent crimes, such as murder and attempted murder.[31] The *Bargouti* case is an example of the use of criminal law to punish a leader of a terrorist group found responsible for attacks conducted by individuals he ordered to perform terrorist actions.[32] Marwan Bargouti, one of the leaders of the PLO in the West Bank, was found guilty for five murders and an attempted murder, alongside other crimes.[33]

In addition to offences which are part of the 'core' of criminal law, supporters and aids of terrorist organisations are brought to justice for specific offences such as transportation of terrorists (very relevant to suicide bombings),[34] membership of terrorist organisations[35] and

---

[29] The *Unlawful Combatants* decision, [43]. For further analysis of judicial review of detentions in Israel, in a comparative context, see: Daphne Barak-Erez and Matthew C. Waxman, 'Secret evidence and the due process of terrorist detentions' (2009) 48 *Columbia Journal of Transnational Law* 3.

[30] The *Unlawful Combatants* decision.

[31] Penal Law, 1977, 8 LSI 133, s. 300 (Penal Law).

[32] Cr C (TA) 1158/02 *State of Israel* v. *Bargouti* (not published, 2004).

[33] Ibid.

[34] Transportation of individuals who have no legal status in Israel is a separate offence according to s. 12A of the Entrance to Israel Law, 1952. In addition, drivers who transported suicide bombing terrorists were also found guilty of negligently causing the death of people. See: CA 263/07 *Rajbi* v. *State of Israel* (not published, 2007).

[35] Prevention of Terrorism Ordinance, s. 3.

possession of weapons.[36] Relatively new criminal prohibitions in the area of terrorist financing were created by the Prohibition on Terror Financing Law 2005.[37]

The criminal prohibition on speech supportive of terrorist actions is considered a borderline case, due to its potential to freeze political speech. While Israeli law has allowed for criminalisation of speech supportive of terrorism, in practice this legislation is enforced with great restraint, and only narrowly interpreted by the courts. Incitement to terrorism was in fact covered by a criminal prohibition enacted in the days of the British Mandate – the offence of 'sedition', which addressed incitement to engage in activities that stood in opposition to the government or the peace of the country.[38] Later, the Prevention of Terrorism Ordinance specifically criminalised incitement to terrorism in s. 4.[39] The most significant part of this provision for the issue of incitement was sub-s. 4(a), which applied to 'words of praise, sympathy or encouragement for acts of violence calculated to cause death or injury to a person or for threats of such acts of violence'. However, when these prohibitions were applied in the courts, the judiciary adopted a narrow and balanced view on the implemention of anti-incitement norms. The Israeli Supreme Court had to contend with these provisions in two important cases it handled soon after the assasination of Prime Minister Itzhak Rabin on 4 November 1995 (although the events

---

[36] Penal Law, s. 144.
[37] Prohibition on Terror Financing Law (English translation availalable on the website of the Israeli Ministry of Justice).
[38] Originally the prohibition was enacted in Mandatory Palestine as ss. 59–60 of the Criminal Code Ordinance 1936, Palestine Gazette no. 652, Supp no. 1,399. It is currently found in ss. 133–4 of the Israeli Penal Law. The provisions on sedition do not expressly mention the word 'terrorism' but are broad enough to apply also to acts of terrorism aimed at the government or the peace of the country. According to s. 136(4) of the Israeli Penal Law: 'For the purpose of this article, "sedition" means ... to promote feelings of ill-will and enmity between different sections of the population.'
[39] Section 4 of the Prevention of Terrorism Ordinance stated: 'A person who – (a) publishes, in writing or orally, words of praise, sympathy or encouragement for acts of violence calculated to cause death or injury to a person or for threats of such acts of violence; or (b) publishes, in writing or orally, words of praise or sympathy for or an appeal for aid or support of a terrorist organisation ... (g) commits an act that expresses identification with a terrorist organisation or sympathy to it, by waving a flag, displaying a symbol or a slogan or reciting a hymn or a slogan or any similar overt act which clearly discloses identification or sympathy in a public place or in a manner that people who are present in public place can see or hear such an expression of identification or sympathy; shall be guilty of an offence and shall be liable on conviction to imprisonment for a term not exceeding three years or to a fine not exceeding one thousand pounds or to both such penalties.'

leading to the indictments had preceeded it) – the *Jabareen* case[40] and the *Benjamin Kahana* case.[41] Eventually, Israel replaced s. 4 of the Prevention of Terrorism Ordinance with a new s. 144D2 added to the Israeli Penal Law, which clarifies that the prohibition applies also to terrorist actions not necessarily connected to a designated terrorist organisation.[42]

In the context of criminal trials, attention should be given also to special questions in the context of the criminal process. Criminal trials of

[40] CFH 8613/96 *Jabareen* v. *State of Israel*, 54(5) PD 193. The *Jabareen* case concerned a newspaper column that praised attacks against Israeli soldiers in the Occupied Territories. In its decision, the Court adopted a narrow interpretation, whereby s. 4(a) of the Prevention of Terrorism Ordinance applied only to utterances that encouraged violent acts commited by a terrorist organisation but not to utterances that encouraged violent acts of individuals who do not act as agents of a terrorist organisation. This limitation proved crucial in the circumstances of the case and, accordingly, the defendant was acquitted. The Ordinance did not include any such express condition and the Israeli Supreme Court adopted it by intepreting the Ordinance narrowly in light of the right to freedom of speech.

[41] CFH 1789/98 *State of Israel* v. *Benjamin Kahana*, 54(5) PD 145. The Supreme Court issued the *Benjamin Kahana* decision on the same day on which it gave the *Jabareen* decision. Formally, this decision did not apply the provision on incitement to terrorism but rather the general provision on 'sedition'. Substantively, however, the decision dealt with utterances that encouraged violence against civilians. Specifically, the decision dealt with the publications of the right-wing Jewish extremist, Benjamin Kahana, who called for the bombing of Arab villages in Israel in retaliation for terrorist attacks against Jewish Israelis. Kahana was charged with 'sedition', and the Court had to confront the challenge of interpreting this very broad offence, originally drafted by the non-democratic legislature of the British Mandate period. The question was mainly whether the values protected by this offence were the stability of the government or social stability as well. After deliberation, the majority of the Court decided to convict Kahana (although Jabareen was acquited). The Court's rationale for this distinction was that the offence of sedition contains appropiate safeguards against misuses or overuses of it (i.e. a short time limitation and indictment only apon the approval of the Attorney General). The need to interpret it narrowly is therefore less urgent than is true of the offence of incitement to terrorism under the Prevention of Terrorism Ordinance discussed in the *Jabareen* case: *Benjamin Kahana* case, [36]. For further analysis of this case, see: Mordechai Kremnitzer and Liat Levanon-Morag, 'Limiting freedom of speech for the prevention of violence' (2004) 7 *Law and Government* 305 (Hebrew).

[42] Section 144D2 of the Israeli Penal Law (added to the law in 2002) states: 'A person who publishes a call to commit a violent act of terror, or expressions of praise, support or encouragement for violent acts of terror (for the purpose of this section, an inciting publication), that, according to its content and the circumstances of its publication could lead to an actual violent act or to an act of terror, shall be liable to a five year term of imprisonment'. For an evaluation of the Israeli approach in this area from a comparative perspective (taking account also of Security Council Resolution 1624), see also: Daphne Barak-Erez and David Scharia, 'Freedom of speech and support for terrorism: a case study of global constitutional law' (2011) 2 *Harvard National Security Journal* 1.

suspects of terrorism are typically held in standard civil, not military, courts.[43] However, it is important to note that special legislation concerning the preliminary stages of the investigation allows for postponing the time for meeting between the suspect and his attorney when the investigation involves security offences (under the assumption that such investigations should not be interrupted).[44] However, the Supreme Court clearly stated limitations to its willingness to accept different rules of procedure in this area. The Court did so in a decision that invalidated a statutory provision which professed to authorise a court to prolong an arrest of a suspect of terrorist activity without his presence in court[45] (this provision was subject to judicial review as a new law enacted after Basic Law: Human Dignity and Liberty). The Court stated that such a provision infringes the basic right to due process, which in the context of Israeli constitutional law, is derived from the right to human dignity.[46]

4. The challenge of the Occupied Territories and other neighbouring territories

The uniqueness of Israel's position in the context of anti-terrorism is also related to the fact that most of the potential attacks on its civilians come from people who do not reside in Israel itself, but rather in neighbouring territories – either territories occupied by Israel in the 1967 Six Days War and still governed by it according to the international law of occupation (the West Bank) or other territories that are controlled de facto by terrorist organisations (South Lebanon which is in fact controlled by the Hezbollah, or – with a different background – the Gaza Strip which was also occupied by Israel, but is currently governed by the Hamas organisation). When Israel counters terrorist threats from these territories, the

---

[43] In principle, according to the Emergency Regulations enacted during the time of the British Mandate, people accused of offences against these regulations may be tried in special military courts. However, currently, the policy of Israeli authorities is to try terrorists in ordinary courts. In contrast, in the territories occupied by Israel criminal trials are held in military courts, according to the law of belligerent occupation. See also Section 4.

[44] Criminal Procedure (Arrested Individuals Suspected of a Security Offence) (Temporary Provisions) 2006.

[45] More specifically, the law stated that a terrorist activity suspect whose arrest was authorised by a court for a period shorter than twenty days (following a hearing in which he was present) may be subject to a decision to prolong this arrest for a period that will not exceed twenty days in total.

[46] Crim R A 8823/07 *A* v. *State of Israel* (not published, 2010).

relevant laws are not Israel's domestic legislation but rather, in most cases, international law – the rules applicable to occupied territories (especially the West Bank) or, at any rate, to armed conflicts. The situation is also different from other military conflicts associated with anti-terrorism efforts – such as the wars in Iraq and in Afghanistan, which are wars conducted far from the civilian areas of the fighting armies (the Western countries involved). More concretely, the threats on Israeli population connected to these territories are manifested in the sending of suicide bombers to Israeli civilian areas and, more recently, the firing of missiles into Israeli civilian areas (without engaging in a formal war).

Although Israeli law as such does not apply in territories that are beyond the state of Israel proper,[47] the policy of the Israeli Supreme Court has always been that it will hear petitions on acts of the Israeli military as well as of other government officials outside Israeli territory, based on a view devoted to securing the rule of law in government action. It is worth noting that it was relatively easy for the Supreme Court to adopt this view when Israeli forces indeed had effective control in all the territories occupied by Israel since 1967 and when the military activities in these areas were more similar to ordinary law enforcement and not to full military operations of the kind developed later on.

Examples of anti-terrorism measures used by Israel in the Occupied Territories and reviewed by the Israeli Supreme Court, residing as the High Court of Justice, include:

(1) Assigned residence[48] – In search of new ways of deterring terrorists, the military commander of the West Bank decided to subject people who assist terrorists to the relocation of their place of residence. At the time, Israel still controlled the Gaza Strip and the plan was to order the move of such individuals to Gaza. Israel decided to adopt this initiative since other possibilities of deterring terrorists had proved to be either ineffective or illegal. In addition, it was apparent that the relocation of individuals from the Occupied Territories to other countries, such as Lebanon, would be deemed illegal under the Fourth Geneva Convention. The new amendment was understood as a pragmatic compromise between the country's security needs and the constraints

---

[47] Accordingly, administrative detentions in the Occupied Territories are conducted based on the legislation which applies there, in contrast to the Israeli legislation discussed above in Sections 2 and 3.

[48] HCJ 7015/02 *Ajuri* v. *IDF Commander* 56(6) PD 352 (English translation is available on the website of the Israeli Supreme Court).

of international law. The Israeli Supreme Court accepted the view that Article 78 of the Fourth Geneva Convention allows a military commander to issue orders to assign residence and that, as such, the decision did not constitute forbidden deportation under Article 49 of the Convention (as it was limited to areas occupied by Israel). However, the Court held that an essential condition for exercising this power is the existence of a reasonable possibility that the candidate for assignment presents a real threat and that assigning his/her place of residence will help avert this danger. Assigning the residence of an innocent relative who does not pose a danger or of someone who no longer does is forbidden, even if this measure may deter others from carrying out terrorist acts or collaborating with active terrorists.[49]

(2) 'Neighbour procedure' or 'early warning' – Another important Supreme Court precedent prohibited the Israeli army from using civilians for the purpose of advising terrorists to surrender.[50] The army officially declared that it had exercised this procedure only with regard to civilians who had expressed their willingness to convey the message and subject to the condition that they were guaranteed safety. The procedure thereby professed to distance itself from the use of civilians as 'human shields', which is patently illegal under international law. Yet, the Israeli Supreme Court invalidated the practice. The Court doubted the possibility of respecting or securing the fulfillment of these two conditions in real life scenarios, and emphasised the importance of generally distancing civilians from military forces.

5.   The growing influence of international law

Another major characteristic of Israeli anti-terrorism law has been the growing influence of international law on its development and implementation.[51] This has been the result of several factors. First, as already indicated, since major threats to national security come from the Occupied Territories and other territories beyond the sovereign area of

---

[49] For more details, see: Daphne Barak-Erez, 'Assigned residence in Israel's administered territories: the judicial review of security measures' (2003) 33 *Israel Yearbook on Human Rights* 303.

[50] HCJ 3799/02 *Adala: The Legal Center for the Rights of the Arab Minority in Israel v. Commander of the Central Region* 60(3) PD 67 (English translation is available on the website of the Israeli Supreme Court).

[51] See also: Daphne Barak-Erez, 'The international law of human rights and constitutional law: a case study of an expanding dialogue' (2004) 2 *ICON* 611.

Israel, the application of international law is highly relevant. Second, the Israeli Supreme Court has been especially open to the interpretation and enforcement of anti-terrorism law in a manner informed by international law. The interpretation of international law by the Israeli Supreme Court attracts much international attention. This attention has been the result of the new nature of the issues decided by the Court, the quality of its decisions, the professional controversies around some of these decisions and the prominence of the Israeli–Palestinian conflict in the international arena. The cases discussed earlier with regard to the Occupied Territories were certainly decisions of this nature.[52] Other major examples include:

(1) Targeted killings[53] – This decision concerned the Israeli policy of killing active terrorists when other less harmful measures cannot be taken (because they are beyond the reach of Israeli forces) – as a preventive measure (thus preventing them from instigating terrorist attacks against Israeli territory and Israeli civilians). Formally, this policy has been limited to active terrorists who are not present in territories in which Israel has direct control (that is, neither in Israel nor in Palestinian territories which are under Israeli rule). The Israeli Supreme Court affirmed the legality of this measure when used against active terrorists beyond Israeli territory, based on the rules of international law concerning people taking 'direct part' in hostilities.[54] In addition, in order to regulate the scope of the use of this practice, the decision of the Court details four mandatory conditions the military has to fulfill: first, well based, strong and convincing information is needed before categorising a civilian as falling into one of the relevant categories. Innocent civilians are not to be harmed. Information which has been most thoroughly verified is needed regarding the identity and activity of the civilian who is allegedly taking a direct part in the hostilities. The burden of proof on the army is, as such, rather heavy. In the case of doubt, careful verification is needed before an attack can be made. Second, a civilian directly participating in hostilities cannot be attacked if a less harmful means can be employed. A civilian directly participating in hostilities is not an outlaw (deprived of legal rights and protection). Thus, if an individual directly participating in

---

[52] See above Section 4.
[53] See: HCJ 769/02 *The Public Committee against Torture in Israel* v. *The Government of Israel* (not published, 2006) (*Targeted Killings* decision) (English translation is available on the website of the Israeli Supreme Court).
[54] Article 51(3) of the 1977 Additional Protocol I to the Geneva Conventions.

hostilities can be arrested, interrogated and tried, those are the means that should be employed. However, arrest, investigation and trial are not means which can always be used. Occasionally, these possibilities do not exist whatsoever; at times they involve great risks to the lives of the soldiers. Third, after an attack on a civilian suspected of taking an active part in hostilities, an investigation regarding the precision of the identification of the target and the circumstances of the attack upon him must be performed (retroactively). That investigation must be both thorough and independent. In appropriate cases, compensation should be paid for the harm caused to innocent civilians.[55] Fourth, every effort must be made to minimise the harm to innocent civilians (collateral damage). Attacks should be carried out only if the expected harm to innocent civilians is not disproportionate to the military advantage to be achieved by the attack. For example, shooting at a terrorist sniper who is firing at soldiers or civilians from his porch is permitted, even if an innocent passerby might be harmed. Such harm conforms to the principle of proportionality. However, that is not the case if the building is bombed from the air, harming a plentitude of residents. Between these two extremes are the difficult cases. Thus, a meticulous examination of every case is required.

(2) The security barrier – The analysis of the effect of international law is especially interesting in the context of the security barrier built by Israel in the Occupied Territories in a manner designed to create a barrier against terrorist attacks on Israeli civilians. This initiative has led not only to decisions of the Israeli Supreme Court but also to an advisory opinion of the International Court of Justice. The Israeli decisions in this matter were all based on the precedent laid down by the Supreme Court in its first decision on the barrier – the *Beit Sourik* case.[56] In contrast to the International Court of Justice which gave one opinion on the legality of the barrier (which the opinion refers to as a 'wall'), the Israeli court insisted on reviewing the issue by analysing every section of the barrier separately and evaluating its contribution to the security of the area. In the *Beit Sourik* case, the petitioners were affected landowners and village councils. They argued that the seizure orders promulgated with regard to their

---

[55] It should be noted that according to this approach the evaluation of operations of targeted killings will be conducted first and foremost by inner military bodies.

[56] HCJ 2056/04 *Beit Sourik Village Council v. The Government of Israel*, 58(5) PD 807 (English translation is available on the website of the Israeli Supreme Court).

lands were illegal. The Israeli Supreme Court examined the issue within the framework of the law of belligerent occupation and Israeli administrative law. In essence, the Supreme Court considered two questions: whether the military commander was authorised to build a security barrier in occupied territories and, if so, the legality of the barrier's location. Addressing the first question, the Court accepted the petitioners' argument that the military commander cannot order the construction of the barrier if his reasons are political, that is, aimed at annexation. The Court determined, however, that the aim of the barrier was indeed to protect Israel's civilian population. Having determined this, the Court proceeded to discuss the second question, dealing with the very route of the barrier. Applying the principle of proportionality, the Court balanced the public interest in security against the rights of the local residents according to international humanitarian law. In the circumtances of the case, the Court indicated that the harm to the local residents was disproportionate and therefore held that the military commander was under a duty to consider alternative routes.

In juxtaposion to this decision, the International Court of Justice opined on the legality of the barrier in the form of an advisory opinion, which was in fact handed down only ten days later.[57] The Advisory Opinion took a completely different approach. First, the International Court of Justice held that the barrier was built in order to achieve political rather than military purposes (by pointing to the correlation between its route and the location of Israeli settlements in the Occupied Territories).[58] Second, it stated, quite sweepingly, that the barrier infringed humanitarian law and human rights law, without conducting a detailed review of each of the barrier's sections.

Without getting into a detailed comparison of these two different views, it is worthwhile to see them as an example of the problems related to the application of international law – which is often contingent on the institution applying it. In the context of the Advisory Opinion it is worthwhile to note that Israel declined to participate in the process since it disputed the authority of the Court in this case, a

---

[57] *Legal Consequences of the Construction of a Wall in the Occupied Palestinian Territory*, Advisory Opinion (2004) 43 *International Legal Materials* 1999 (July 9) (Advisory Opinion).

[58] Specifically, according to the International Court of Justice, 'the Court, from the material available to it, is not convinced that the specific course Israel chose for the wall was necessary to attain its security objectives': Advisory Opinion, [137].

fact that probably had an impact on the factual basis of the opinion. Most importantly, the International Court of Justice failed to address seriously the security motivation behind the barrier project (even if its implementation may merit criticism).[59]

From a broader perspective, it is interesting to point out the central role Israel plays in developing and challenging traditional international law in the area of confonting terrorism. On the one hand, the Israeli judicial decisions are informed and shaped by international law. On the other hand, Israel serves as a laboratory for the application of international law norms to new anti-terrorism challenges. In this sense, some of the decisions of the Israeli Supreme Court, like the decision on *Targeted Killings*, are considered precedents world-wide, pioneering areas in which there are yet no judicial decisions (in contrast to legal scholarship or expert opinions). The new nature of these issues is reflected also in debates in the international legal community on the terminology and categories to be used in some of these cases (e.g. targeted killings versus extra-judicial killings or assassinations).

6. The role of the Supreme Court

It is impossible to discuss Israeli anti-terrorism law without addressing the central role that the Supreme Court has played in shaping it by presenting a counter-balance to security and political pressures to broaden anti-terrorism measures.[60]

The most well-known example is the decision on the General Security Services (GSS)'s use of special methods to interrogate terrorists. The debate around this matter began in the 1980s, when these methods were first disclosed to the general public. The controversy regarding their use led to the appointment of a special committee headed by Moshe Landau, a

---

[59] The difference in the factual background was later presented by the Israeli Supreme Court as a reason for its different decisions in the matter – which only rejected specific choices regarding the building of the route, in contrast to the sweeping negative view of the International Court of Justice on the barrier as such. See: HCJ 7957/04 *Mara'abe* v. *The Prime Minister of Israel* 60(2) PD 477 (English translation is available on the website of the Israeli Supreme Court). For further analysis, see: Daphne Barak-Erez, 'The security barrier: between international law, constitutional law, and domestic judicial review (2006) 4 *ICON* 540.

[60] For the challenges made to this rule of law approach to anti-terrorism law, see Pnina Lahav, 'A barrel without hoops: the impact of counterterrorism on Israel's legal culture' (1988) 10 *Cardozo Law Review* 529.

former Chief Justice of the Israeli Supreme Court. The Landau Committee concluded that the GSS has the power to use 'moderate physical pressure' in its interrogations, relying on the defence of necessity available in criminal law.[61] The heavy criticism of the Landau report led to changes in the legal doctrine. Several years later, the Israeli Supreme Court accepted a petition against the use of force in GSS interrogations. The Court held that the GSS does not possess the power to use special interrogative measures, different from the ordinary methods used in police criminal investigations. The Court added that any broadening of the GSS' interrogation powers would necessitate legislation. The only exception to this rule may be the *ex post* application of the criminal defence of necessity with regard to an interrogator who had used force for the sake of preventing the loss of human lives.[62]

Another precedent that highlights the significant role of the Supreme Court in shaping anti-terrorism law within an admittedly stressful and emotional public sphere is the so-called *Bargaining Chips* affair. In this matter, the Israeli Supreme Court faced the question whether Israel could hold Lebanese prisoners solely to use them as 'bargaining chips' in future negotiations regarding Israeli soldiers held by terrorist groups. In the first decision in this matter, the Supreme Court upheld the legality of this practice. Chief Justice Barak explained that Israeli legislation on administrative detentions should be interpreted as authorising the holding of prisoners for this purpose, adding that he would not elaborate on the international law aspects of the case, since specific local legislation supersedes international law.[63] Soon afterwards, the Court opted to use its special capacity to rehear the case, due to the novelty and complexity

---

[61] *Report of the Commission of Inquiry in the Matters of Investigation Methods of the General Security Service Regarding Hostile Terrorist Activity* (1987) (Landau Commission Report). Excerpts from the Report were translated into English and published in (1989) 23 *Israel Law Review*. For a critical analysis of the Landau Commission Report, see: Mordechai Kremnitzer, 'The Landau Commission Report: was the Security Service subordinated to the law, or the law to the "needs" of the security service?' (1989) 23 *Israel Law Review* 216.

[62] HCJ 5100/94 *The Public Committee against Torture in Israel* v. *The Government of Israel* 53(4) PD 817 (*Torture* case) (English translation is available on the website of the Israeli Supreme Court). For an analysis of this decision see: Mordechai Kremnitzer and Re'em Segev, 'The legality of interrogational torture: a question of proper authorization or a substantive moral issue?' (2000) 34 *Israel Law Review* 509.

[63] Administrative Detentions App. 10/94 *John Does* v. *Minister of Defense* 53(1) PD 97. For criticism on this decision, see: Orna Ben Naftali and Sharon Gliechgevitch, 'Missing in legal action: Lebanese hostages in Israel' (2000) 44 *Harvard International Law Journal* 185.

of the questions it raised.[64] The Court based its new decision on a different, stricter interpretation of Israeli law. In addition, it cited in detail the position of international law on this matter, which served as an additional basis for the decision. Chief Justice Barak stated that international law prohibited holding hostages, and that this prohibition applied to holding persons as 'bargaining chips'. An example, related to the *Bargaining Chips* case and the Unlawful Combatants Law, was the *Red Cross Visits* decision.[65] In this case, the petition dealt with the demand of two of the Lebanese 'bargaining chips' prisoners to meet with delegates of the International Committee of the Red Cross, based on Article 143 of the Fourth Geneva Convention. Counsel for the respondents contested the customary nature of this provision. Chief Justice Barak acknowledged the possibility of denying meetings with Red Cross representatives for security reasons, but held that, considering the long detention of the petitioners, it would be unreasonable to deny them that right at this stage. The decision was issued despite public opinion which was critical of the lack of reciprocity in the matter, as Israeli soldiers held in Lebanon and other unknown locations were denied the same right.

These landmark cases are not stand-alone examples. The Israeli Supreme Court, which has the power to review all government actions, routinely hears petitions that deal with a variety of instances of anti-terrorism measures, as many decisions discussed earlier (on the security barrier, targeted killings and more) reflect. The Court had paved the way for its involvement in these matters by narrowing preliminary barriers such as the standing and justiciability doctrines, which serve as obstacles to judicial review in these matters in other countries.[66]

The unique role played by the Israeli Supreme Court derives not only from its willingness to subject anti-terrorism measures to the rule of law, but rather from its deep involvement in these issues even with regard to military operations taking place on the ground. The *Almadani* decision,[67] for example, dealt with a petition to the Supreme Court in the midst of a military operation against the Palestinian terrorist infrastructure in the

---

[64] Crim. Further Hearing 7048/97 *John Does* v. *Minister of Defense*, 54(1) PD 721 (English translation is available on the website of the Israeli Supreme Court).

[65] HCJ 794/98 *Oubeid* v. *Minister of Defense* 55(5) P.D. 769.

[66] On the lowering of preliminary barriers by the Israeli Supreme Court, see: Daphne Barak-Erez, 'Broadening the scope of judicial review in Israel: between activism and restraint' (2009) 3 *Indian Journal of Constitutional Law* 119.

[67] HCJ 3451/02 *Almadani* v. *Minister of Defence*, 56(3) PD 30 (English translation is available on the website of the Israeli Supreme Court).

West Bank. IDF forces entered the city of Bethlehem in order to locate wanted terrorists. The operation became convoluted when several dozen wanted terrorists broke into Bethlehem's Church of the Nativity and used the holy site, full of priests and worshippers, as a shelter. After surrounding the Church's site, the IDF commander announced that if they surrendered, the terrorists would be given the option of a fair trial in Israel or deportation. At the height of the negotiations, the Palestinian governor of Bethlehem brought a petition to the Supreme Court, demanding that the IDF provide food, water, medicine and medical teams, to be positioned in the church's courtyard. The Supreme Court did not refrain from intervening and the result has been a decision that approved the declaration of the IDF regarding its willingness to supply necessary humanitarian aid.

Another example is the *Physicians for Human Rights* decision.[68] In this case, the Supreme Court allowed access to court and awarded relief in the midst of fighting during another military operation intended to damage terrorist infrastructure, arrest wanted terrorists and locate hidden weapons in the Gaza Strip. The petitioners asked the Court to order the IDF to permit the Palestinian residents of Rafiah to evacuate their dead, conduct burials and provide a steady supply of water, food and medical services. In this case as well the Supreme Court held the hearing as the battle raged, while noting that 'the military's operations were not conducted in a legal vacuum' and that every IDF soldier must behave fairly, reasonably and proportionately, while maintaining a balance between individual rights and national interests.[69] The practical result of this litigation was, once again, that the military has taken upon itself to correct most of the infringements pointed out by the petitioners, and thus the petition proved effective, although the Court did not make a formal order in this matter.

It is possible to conclude that the Israeli Supreme Court is intensively involved in shaping the balance between national security and human rights in the area of anti-terrorism law.[70]

[68] HCJ 4764/04 *Physicians for Human Rights* v. *The Commander of the IDF Forces in the Gaza Strip*, 58(5) PD 385 (English translation is available on the website of the Israeli Supreme Court).

[69] Ibid., [10].

[70] The Court is indeed highly aware of its responsibility to strike a suitable balance between human rights and national security, and has explicitly expressed the challenge it is facing in its judgments. In concluding the decision which prohibited the use of physical measures in the interrogations of terrorists, Chief Justice Barak wrote: 'We are aware that this decision does not make it easier to deal with that reality. This is the fate of democracy, as not all means are acceptable to it, and not all methods employed by its enemies are open

7. Proposed reforms: the new bill from 2011

The centrality of terrorist threats in the Israeli context, on the one hand, and the nature of current legislation in the area (scattered and relatively old), on the other hand, have motivated the Israeli Ministry of Justice to prepare a new anti-terrorism bill, aimed at reforming and updating current legislation – proposed Bill: Struggle Against Terrorism Law 2011. In fact, in contrast to most systems, Israel did not introduce an overall reform to its anti-terrorism legislation following the events of 9/11,[71] and there is no question that the time for that has come.

This Bill is relevant, obviously, only to anti-terrorism law in Israel proper, and cannot have any direct relevance to anti-terrorist activities in Israel's Occupied Territories and beyond, ruled mainly by international law. The new Bill intends to offer a comprehensive and updated mechanism with regard to terrorism, and is intended to repeal many, but not all, of the present laws in this area. It is intended to replace the Prevention of Terrorism Ordinance, but not the legislation on detentions. It is especially worthwhile to note the following reforms included in the bill:

(1) New and consistent definitions of the terms 'terrorist organisation' and 'an act of terrorism' – the Bill includes new definitions of these terms. Currently, these terms have varying definitions in different legislative contexts – such as the Prevention of Terrorism Ordinance and the Prohibition on Terror Financing Law. Basically, the Bill builds on the definitions included in the more modern Prohibition on Terror Financing Law. The definition proposed for the term 'terrorist organization' is directly adopted from the text of this law: 'an association of people which acts to perpetrate an act of terrorism or has as its goal enabling or promoting the perpetration of an act of terrorism'.[72]

---

to it. Sometimes, a democracy must fight with one hand tied behind its back. Nonetheless, it has the upper hand. Preserving the rule of law and recognition of individual liberties constitute an important component of its understanding of security. At the end of the day, they strengthen its spirit and strength and allow it to overcome its difficulties'. See: *Torture* case, 845. For Barak's analysis of the role of the Court in an age of terrorism, see also: Aharon Barak, 'Foreword: a judge on judging: the role of a Supreme Court in a democracy' (2002) 116 *Harvard Law Review* 16, 148–60.

[71] In contrast to legislating reforms with regard to specific areas, e.g. the legislation of the Prohibition on Terror Financing Law.

[72] The definition goes on to state that 'for this purpose it is immaterial – (1) whether or not the members of the organisation know the identity of the other members; (2) if the

This definition seeks to emphasise that organisations which secure civil infrastructure for terrorist activities (such as offering financial support to the families of terrorists) are also within the scope of the legislation.

(2) New provisions on the designation of terrorist organisations (replacing the provisions of the Prevention of Terrorism Ordinance).

(3) New and detailed offences regarding activities relating to terrorist organisations (including giving services to such organisations and fulfilling an active role in them).

(4) New terrorist-related offences – including incitement to terrorism (replacing the current offence included in the ordinary penal law), failing to prevent a terrorist act, preparation of a terrorist act, several offences related to the financing of terrorism and more. Another proposed provision concerns the aggravation of the punishment for terrorist-related offences.

(5) Special provisions regarding criminal procedure for terrorist-related trials (including longer periods before bringing a suspect before a judge) replacing current provisional legislation on the matter.[73]

(6) A new chapter on terrorist financing that will replace the relatively new Prohibition on Terror Financing Law.

(7) The Bill proposes to broaden the scope of the Detentions Law from 1979, in a manner that will authorise the promulgation of 'limiting orders', an equivalent to the 'control orders' regime used in the UK. Such orders will make it possible to take relatively less restrictive means such as imposing the duty to report to the police on planned activities or limitations on access to certain places.[74]

(8) The Bill is designed to be part of Israel's standard legislation, and its application was not confined only to periods in which an 'emergency situation' has been declared according to the provisions of Basic Law: The Government. This choice reflects current understandings that anti-terrorism is a constant threat, that applies also in 'regular' times.[75]

---

composition of the members of the organisation is fixed or changes; (3) if the organisation also carries out legal activities and if it also acts for legal purposes'.

[73] See above note 44.

[74] The Israeli Supreme Court decided in the past that the current law does not recognise the possibility of making recourse to these less restrictive measures, since it only mentions the power to detain. See e.g. ADA 8788/03 *Federman* v. *Minister of Defence*, 58(1) PD 176, 190–191; HCJ 4101/10 *Hacohen* v. *IDF Commander in Judea and Samaria* (not published, 2010).

[75] It is worth noting in this context that in fact an 'emergency situation' had been declared in Israel in May 1948 when the War of Independence was taking place, and has since

8. Conclusion

Israeli anti-terrorism policies can best be described by referencing the following distinctions:

(1) Time – Israel's anti-terrorism law comprises legislation enacted by the British during the time of their Mandate in Palestine as well as later Israeli legislation that evolved since the establishment of the state to confront and combat ongoing threats.

(2) Legal paradigms – Israel's anti-terrorism law utilises both ordinary criminal law and special administrative powers aimed at prevention. The choice between these alternative paradigms serves as a background source of tension.

(3) Territory – An important distinction should be noted between Israeli law in the strict sense of the term and the law that carries force or weight in the territories under Israeli occupation, where international law plays a significant role and Israeli law, except for some public law norms, does not apply.

(4) Institutions – In principle, Israel's anti-terrorism law is based on legislation rather than on a broad concept of executive power. The relevant legislation gives significant albeit expressly defined powers to administrative authorities. In addition, this legal field has been significantly determined by the Israeli Supreme Court, which applies judicial review to matters of national security and to military actions.

(5) Domestic law versus international law – Due to Israel's involvement with terrorist attacks coming from foreign territories as well as from territories occupied by Israel, the role of international law in shaping its anti-terrorism law has been significant. The recourse to international law has posed serious challenges, due to the lack of clarity inherent in the norms of international law which are still being gradually adapted to the challenge of modern day terrorism.

With an eye into the future, the plan to enact a comprehensive new anti-terrorism law, designed to replace many of the scattered laws in this area, poses a substantial challenge to current Israeli anti-terrorism law.

continued. In this sense, conditioning the new Bill on the existence of an 'emergency situation' would not have made a practical difference. Therefore, the choice not to include such a condition in the proposed law reflects a principled view that anti-terrorism efforts should be part of the standard scheme of legislation in the country. In fact, the bill also proposes to abolish the conditioning of the application of the Detentions Law on the existence of such declaration.

However, this initiative is not intended to replace all the extant layers of anti-terrorism law. Prime reasons for this include the applicability of any future legislation only to Israeli territory in the narrow sense and the influence of international law. At any rate, any new law will be subject to interpretation, as well as judicial review, by the Israeli Supreme Court which is expected to keep on playing a major role in this area also in the future.

24

Rocks, hard places and human rights: anti-terrorism law and policy in Arab states

LYNN WELCHMAN

1. Introduction

This chapter provides an overview of legislative developments in Arab states following the passage of Security Council Resolution 1373, focusing on definitions of 'terrorism' and 'terrorist offences'. It considers the Arab Convention for the Suppression of Terrorism before proceeding to review the responses of a number of individual states. Moves at the beginning of the century towards political reform and the opening of public space for dissent and criticism are challenged by the exigencies of the 'war on terror'. Certain practices in violation of human rights in Arab states have apparently been endorsed by the US alongside a stated policy focus on 'democratisation' in the region. Dissonance between law-related word and deed of the states leading the global counter-terrorism effort – particularly the United States, but also the United Kingdom – sustains the arguments of those who seek to undermine the discourse of rights and rule of law, complicates the considerable challenges posed to local and regional human rights groups, and seriously undermines the credibility of international law in the region; the efficacy of all of which in the 'global war on terrorism' must surely be open to question.

2. Regional context

The US overview of Patterns of Global Terrorism for 2003 confirmed that '[t]he Middle East continued to be the region of greatest concern in the global war on terrorism'.[1] At the same time, it is the lives and freedoms of the populations of Arab states in the region that are among the most

---

[1] Office of the Coordinator of Counter-Terrorism, *Patterns of Global Terrorism – 2003*, Washington, DC, 29 April 2004, p. 58, available at www.state.gov.

directly affected by the anti-terrorism laws and policies being implemented and promoted by the United States since 9/11. Uncounted thousands of non-combatants were killed by US-led forces in Iraq. Hundreds
of Arabs of different nationalities were held in Guantánamo Bay (and
some are still there), and Arab men have been major targets of various
domestic 'counter-terrorism' arrest and detention procedures in the
United States which have been roundly criticised.[2] In the region, thousands have been arrested in Arab states, many held for prolonged periods
without trial and others sentenced after trials that failed to meet international standards of due process.

Nationals from different states in the region have been implicated in
attacks attributed to or claimed by al-Qaeda and various groups associated with it, both before and after 9/11. Since 2001, the Arab region has
seen major bombings and other fatal armed attacks in states such as Egypt,
Jordan, Algeria, Tunisia, Saudi Arabia and Morocco, with scores of dead
and injured. Previous decades also saw considerable 'domestic' political
violence, with thousands of lives lost. Arab states have underlined their
prolonged exposure to terrorism and promoted the ways in which they
have sought to deal with it as potential models which others in the international community might do well to follow. The then Egyptian Prime
Minister, Hosni Mubarak, said that 'maybe Western countries should
begin to think of Egypt's own fight against terror as their new model', and
Syria's President Bashar al-Asad pressed the United States to 'take advantage of Syria's successful experiences'.[3] As a regional grouping, 'Arab
states were among the first to reach an anti-terrorism agreement' and
were 'the first to warn against the danger of terrorism and the importance
of taking collective measures to combat it'.[4] All twenty-two state members
of the Arab League have signed up to the 1998 Arab Convention on the
Suppression of Terrorism.

---

[2] See, e.g., Human Rights Watch, *United States: Abuses Plague September 11 Prosecutions*,
(15 August 2002); and *United States: Ensure Protection for Foreign Detainee*, (1 December
2001); Neil Hicks, 'The impact of the September 11 attacks on civil rights in the United
States', in Ashild Kjok (ed.), *Terrorism and Human Rights after September 11* (Cairo
Institute for Human Rights Studies, 2002), pp. 55–64.
[3] Joe Stork, 'The human rights crisis in the Middle East in the aftermath of September 11', in
Kjok, *Terrorism and Human Rights*, pp. 43, 45.
[4] Respectively, the Secretary-General of the League of Arab States 'Amr Mousa, in Kjok,
Terrorism and Human Rights, p. 21 and the Saudi Arabian Interior Minister quoted after
the May 2003 Riyadh bombings in the *Kingdom of Saudi Arabia* (Newsletter, London
Embassy), 28 July 2003.

Implicit in these statements are rebukes to states now seen to be leading the global counter-terrorism effort for their past criticisms of the Arab states; both Syria and Egypt have been heavily criticised for human rights abuses involved in precisely the approaches that they have presented as potential models of efficacy. There is also reproach for a less than vigorous engagement with the 'terrorist threat' until the attacks of 9/11. In its first report to the Counter-Terrorism Committee (CTC), Algeria opened:

> Having long suffered the ravages of terrorism often in the face of indifference and occasional complaisance on the part of certain sectors of the international community, Algeria welcomes the adoption of the resolution [1373] insofar as it reflects a welcome acknowledgement by the international community of the potential threats both to national stability and to international peace and security represented by the scourge of terrorism. On 11 September, the world paid the price of underestimating the dangers posed by the terrorist threat and its potential for destruction. ... As a victim of terrorism, Algeria urges the international community to firmly commit itself to definitively abandoning erroneous and selective perceptions surrounding the phenomenon of terrorism.[5]

A particular concern voiced by Algeria, shared by other states in the region, concerns a feature of most new anti-terrorism legislation which criminalises 'supporting actions abroad which satisfy the definition of terrorism'.[6] As the Algerian government put it, '[t]he need for rigorous counter-terrorism efforts concerns first and foremost the countries whose territories are known to harbour support networks and to be used by terrorist groups as staging areas'.[7] States such as Algeria and Egypt had long been objecting to the activities of dissident Algerians and Egyptians in the United Kingdom, urging the introduction of measures finally realised in the UK's Terrorism Act 2000 – according to Roach, 'something of a gold standard after September 11' in Commonwealth countries.[8] Considerable scepticism has been voiced as to whether the critical distinction between 'dissident/opposition/resistance' and 'terrorism' is adequately preserved in new anti-terrorism legislation; practice (not only judicial but executive and security practice) rather than textual analysis alone is likely to be the

---

[5] First Report of Algeria to the Counter-Terrorism Committee: UN Doc. S/2001/1280 (27 December 2001), p. 4.

[6] Kent Roach, 'The world wide expansion of anti-terrorism laws after September 11', (2004) CXVI (III Serie. LIII) Fasc 3. *Studi Senesi* 492. I am grateful to Kent Roach for providing me with this text.

[7] UN Doc. S/2001/1280, 27 December 2001, p. 4

[8] Roach, 'World wide expansion', 491

key. Algeria went on to propose a 'series of concrete proposals' for a global counter-terrorism strategy.[9]

US officials have on various occasions indicated that they are listening. In 2004, the deputy commander of the US European command noted that 'we think we have a lot to learn from the Algerians'.[10] The then US Secretary of State, Colin Powell, agreed that Egypt was 'really ahead of us on this issue' and that the US had 'much to learn' from Egypt's anti-terrorist tactics, although Joe Stork of Human Rights Watch points out that such tactics 'have been used against non-violent critics as well'.[11] At the end of 2002, it was reported that CIA agents in Bagram and Diego Garcia were 'contracting out their interrogation to foreign intelligence agencies known to routinely use torture'; specifically, it was reported that 'low-level suspects have been handed over to Jordanian, Egyptian and Moroccan agencies [...] with a list of questions from the CIA'.[12] As the decade drew on and more information came out about the CIA's 'extraordinary rendition' and secret detention practices, it was established that a number of Middle Eastern states had been collaborating: a 2010 report by four UN experts found that 'the consistency of many of the detailed allegations provided separately by detainees adds weight to the inclusion' of Jordan, Egypt, Morocco and the Syrian Arab Republic 'as proxy detention facilities where detainees have been held on behalf of the CIA'.[13] For its part, the UK government has concluded agreements with four

---

[9] UN Doc. S/2001/1280, Appendix 1: Aide-mémoire.

[10] Giles Tremlett, 'US sends special forces into north Africa,' *The Guardian*, 15 March 2004. Tremlett observes that '[s]tates previously shunned by the international community, such as Algeria, are being provided with arms and military training and may become a cornerstone of US military interests in the region'. On plans by US Defense Secretary Donald Rumsfeld to 'thrust special forces into the lead role in the war on terrorism, by using them for covert operations around the world', see Jennifer D. Kibbe, 'The rise of the shadow warriors' (2004) 83(2) *Foreign Affairs* 102–15.

[11] Stork, 'The human rights crisis', p. 45.

[12] Suzanne Goldenberg, 'CIA accused of torture at Bagram base: some captives handed to brutal foreign agencies', *The Guardian*, 27 December 2002. Original Washington Post report 'US denies abuse but defends interrogations', 26 December 2002; see Human Rights Watch press release and intervention, 'United States: reports of torture of al-Qaeda suspects', 27 December 2002.

[13] A/HRC/13/42 19 February 2010, 'Joint study on global practices in relation to secret detention in the context of countering terrorism of the Special Rapporteur on the promotion and protection of human rights and fundamental freedoms while countering terrorism, Martin Scheinin; the Special Rapporteur on torture and other cruel, inhuman or degrading treatment or punishment, Manfred Nowak; the Working Group on arbitrary detention represented by its vice-chair, Shaheen Sardar Ali; and the Working Group on enforced or involuntary disappearances represented by its chair, Jeremy Sarkin', [143].

Arab states – Jordan, Libya, Lebanon and Algeria – by way of a 'policy of obtaining assurances as a means of facilitating deportations in national security cases'.[14] Such arrangements have been criticised in human rights circles, while the Foreign and Commonwealth Office author of a response to the criticisms notes that '[t]he States with which the UK has negotiated assurances are inevitably those whose human rights records have been criticized'.[15]

These developments indicate particular challenges for the Arab human rights movement. Implicit in Arab states' reports to the CTC is a vindication of existing draconian legislation and practice, in defiance of sustained criticism by domestic and regional human rights groups as well as by international human rights organisations and the dedicated UN mechanisms. The threat perceived to human rights in the counter-terrorism effort is of course not limited to the Middle East. Irene Khan, then Secretary General of Amnesty International, has said that '[i]n a world engaged in the so-called "war on terrorism", human rights were seen as an obstacle to ensuring victory and human rights defenders as defenders of "terrorists"'.[16] As mass arrests began after the Casablanca bombings in May 2003, the official Moroccan discourse accused human rights activists of being 'soft on terrorism' by indulging in 'knee-jerk criticism of the security services'.[17] In Egypt just after 9/11, the Prime Minster took the human rights movement to task for its long-standing campaigns against torture and unfair trials, criticising groups for 'calling on us to give these terrorists their "human rights"'.[18] And in Yemen, Amnesty International reported a climate of fear in the period directly following 9/11 that stifled internal dissent to an unprecedented degree – fear of a possible US military attack or economic sanctions.[19]

This last example illustrates one of the specificities of the Arab world: a fear of being 'next on the list'. Another is the long-standing and profound grievance in the region at the treatment of the Israel/Palestine dispute

---

[14] Kate Jones, 'Deportations with assurances: addressing key criticisms' (2008) 57(1) *International and Comparative Law Quarterly* 183–94, 184. See also Colin Harvey, Chapter 9, this volume.

[15] Jones, 'Deportations with assurances', 188.

[16] Irene Khan, 'Human rights challenges following the events of September 11 and their impact on universality and the human rights movement', in Kjok, *Terrorism and Human Rights*, p. 35.

[17] Eileen Byrne, 'Escaping from the chains of history', *Financial Times*, 16 April 2004.

[18] Stork, 'The human rights crisis', p. 44.

[19] Amnesty International, 'Yemen: the rule of law sidelined in the name of security', AI Index: MDE 31/006/2003 (24 September 2003).

by the major Western powers: specifically, the failure to hold Israel, as
the Occupying Power, to its established duties under international law
over the decades, including Israel's ever-expanding settlements (colonies)
in the Occupied Palestinian Territories (including East Jerusalem) and,
most recently, the attack on Gaza 2008/9 (Israel's Operation Cast Lead)
and the 2010 attack on the international civilian flotilla carrying humanitarian supplies for Gaza.[20] The Director of the Cairo Institute for Human
Rights Studies, Bahey el-Din Hassan, outlines the impact of such actions
in producing an 'accumulated feeling of injustice' which: 'undermines the
credibility of international human rights law and international humanitarian law and increases the reservation of many people in the Arab and
Islamic worlds as to the universality of human rights principles and
values.'[21] The Iraq war increased these reservations, particularly the conduct of US troops towards Iraqi detainees, and the situation of detainees
in Guantánamo Bay was a further exacerbating factor. Governments of
Arab states were likely to feel less pressure in regard to their own abusive
practices. Domestic actors seeking socio-political reform were considerably constrained by the resulting dynamics.

3. Legislative themes

A regional overview of the Arab states presents a varied picture. It will
clearly be important to have detailed country studies on a number of
states in the region in order to meaningfully inform a 'global' comparative process and to integrate the Arab experience into the development of
mainstream paradigms in this emerging area of study.

With this caveat, certain legislative themes can be identified across
the region. All Arab states are party to the Arab Convention on the
Suppression of Terrorism and to a growing number of related international conventions. All are party to two or more of the UN human rights
treaties, although some are not yet party to the ICCPR or the ICESCR[22]
and others have not yet signed up to the Convention against Torture.[23]

---

[20] See respectively, Human Rights Council, 'United Nations fact finding mission on the
Gaza conflict', A/HRC/12/48 (15 September 2009); and 'Report of the international fact-
finding mission to investigate violations of international law, including international
humanitarian and human rights law, resulting from the Israeli attacks on the flotilla of
ships carrying humanitarian assistance', A/HRC/15/21 (27 September 2010).
[21] Bahey el-Din Hassan, 'Opening remarks', in Kjok, *Terrorism and Human Rights*, p. 15.
[22] These include Oman, Qatar, Saudi Arabia and the United Arab Emirates.
[23] Oman and the United Arab Emirates.

Most Arab states have yet to ratify the Statute of the International Criminal Court.[24] A number of Arab states are party to the African Charter on Human and Peoples' Rights. A regional human rights instrument, the Arab Charter on Human Rights, was criticised by international human rights groups for serious flaws and gaps upon its adoption in 1994 by members of the League of Arab States. The Charter failed to secure any ratifications in the years following.[25] In 2003 a process of review for the 'modernisation' of its contents was initiated in the Arab League, matching a number of governmental initiatives on human rights 'institutionalisation'. A revised text was opened for signature in 2004, and the new text came into force in 2008. Mervat Rishmawi describes the document as 'among the remnants of the wave of reform that is said to have hit the Arab world earlier in this decade'.[26]

Domestically, individuals are rarely able to realise human rights protections by directly invoking international human rights instruments in national courts. Weak and unempowered national judiciaries are usually unable to assert their independence against the executive to secure judicial protection of human rights, even though the rights enshrined in international instruments are also guaranteed in most of the constitutions of the region. The prospect of a 'dialogue' between courts and legislatures on the limits being set to rights and freedoms, particularly on 'security' issues, is minimal. Moreover, state security courts or other 'special tribunals' – including military courts – are often assigned jurisdiction over perpetrators accused of offences against state security. Such courts have fewer procedural protections than the ordinary court system. Unfair trials that fail to meet the standards set by international law or required in domestic law have been documented across the region well before 9/11.[27] Political opponents and non-violent critics have been the targets of such procedures, including alleged or suspected Islamists and Communists, human rights defenders, journalists, newspaper editors and bloggers. There are widespread reports of torture by police and security services, and all Arab states retain the death penalty, although it is used more commonly in certain states and some are de facto abolitionist.

[24] Those that have are currently Jordan, the Comoros and Djibouti. Tunisia also ratified in June 2011.
[25] See Mona Rishmawi, 'The Arab Charter on Human Rights: a comment' (1996) 10 *INTERIGHTS Bulletin*.
[26] Mervat Rishmawi, 'The Arab Charter on Human Rights', *Arab Reform Bulletin*, 6 October 2009.
[27] See Amnesty International, 'State injustice: unfair trials in the Middle East and North Africa', AI Index: MDE 01/002/1998 (16 April 1998).

Some states have semi-permanent 'states of emergency' in force, and several face the threat of serious political violence from groups included in the 'proscribed' or 'terrorist' organisations listed by the United States or the EU. Tempering this picture in the early years of the century were a set of developments indicating moves towards political and social reform with greater space for debate and dissent; later in the decade this space was closing tight in a number of states – hence Rishmawi's reference to 'the remnants of reform'. The events of early 2011 in Tunisia and Egypt have opened a new chapter.

Legislatures in the region have generally acceded to the executives' determination of the exigencies of security in matters of new or amended legislation; civil society groups have been more critical. Some states already had extensive and explicit anti-terrorism legislation, such as Egypt and Algeria; others introduced amendments to their Penal Codes addressing the issue of terrorism, such as Jordan, which later issued a separate anti-terrorism law following triple hotel bombings in Amman in 2005. Tunisia, which already exercised particularly tight political control through its criminal legislation and press law, promulgated a new Law Against Terrorism and Money Laundering. Syria at first gave the impression of not being in need of amending its laws or regulations, satisfied that its existing penal code already met the requirements of Security Council Resolution 1373, but subsequently promulgated a law on money laundering, as did Egypt.

This examination focuses on the definition of terrorism in legislative instruments, as well as measures taken that would not appear critical to the anti-terrorism mandate, but that have the potential to considerably restrict the scope for non-violent political dissent. It is unlikely that the Arab states present an exception; as Harding has observed, it is 'in the interest of governments to take advantage of any opportunities for extending the scope of their measures of legal control when political circumstances are conducive to such developments'.[28]

Legislative responses of Arab states match those of the Anglo-American systems examined by Roach:[29] the expansion of the definition of terrorism; the introduction of new offences, particularly regarding funding and financing activities, that apply 'long before an act of terror is committed'; the expansion of crimes of 'association'; and the expansion

[28] Christopher Harding, 'International terrorism: the British response,' [2002] *Singapore Journal of Legal Studies* 16–29, 18.
[29] Roach, 'The world wide expansion', 492.

of police powers, in particular the extension of pre-arraignment detention (*garde à vue*) with counsel excluded. There are detailed listings of potential offences, frequently with 'catch-all' phrases, and an increase in penalties where 'ordinary crimes' are classified as 'terrorist offences'. Terrorism is not defined by identification of the act or threat with advancing a 'political, religious or ideological cause'; indeed, the phrase 'whatever the motives' may be added, to emphasise that the accused's possible political or ideological motive is not an element in the offence. In certain cases, the definition of 'terrorism' appears to be dissociated also from the 'much less controversial'[30] purpose of intimidation or causing fear to the public as well as from seeking to influence the actions of government or public bodies. The acts through which terrorism is established do not, in some cases, appear to have to be of particular severity or danger. There is a fairly standard exemption or reduction in penalty for those who inform the appropriate authorities of the preparation of an act of terrorism. In none of the legislation reviewed in this chapter is there an exemption such as Roach notes to be contained in Canadian and Australian laws for certain acts of 'advocacy, protest, dissent or stoppage of work'.[31] Ramraj observes that 'in jurisdictions where political opposition is otherwise minimally restricted, a broadly worded definition of terrorism may well have a chilling effect'.[32] In the Arab states, where political opposition is considerably restricted, such definitions may be more than chilling. On the other hand, they may be met with resilience by non-violent opponents and critics as 'more of the same', stronger tools in harder times, which may or may not be off-set by the discourse of democratisation running parallel. Their 'effectiveness' in relation to actual or would-be violent groups or individuals is open to question.[33]

4.   The Arab Convention for the Suppression of Terrorism

The Arab Convention for the Suppression of Terrorism, adopted by member states of the Arab League in 1998, came into force in 1999. It is pointed to by Arab states in their reports to the CTC as evidence of forward-thinking and responsible action by governments in the region. The Convention defines 'terrorism' in art. 1(2) as:

---

[30] Ibid.   [31] Ibid., 493–4.
[32] Victor V. Ramraj, 'Terrorism, security and rights: a new dialogue' [2002] *Singapore Journal of Legal Studies* 1–15, 4.
[33] Ibid.

> Any act of violence or threat thereof, whatever its motives or purposes, that occurs in execution of an individual or collective criminal undertaking, and is aimed at sowing fear among people, or causing fear by harming them or exposing their lives, liberty or security to danger, or causing damage to the environment or to a public or private installation or property, or occupying or taking over the later, or exposing a national resource to danger.

This definition requires the element of violence or threat thereof, together with an undertaking that is criminal under national legislation and aimed at one of the list of purposes or actions. The phrasing in Arabic does not seem to require that the element of 'sowing fear among people' or 'causing fear' condition the remainder of the purposes, which potentially renders many ordinary criminal activities acts of terrorism. However, if the intention is in fact that the clauses following the word 'danger' are to be read as conditioned by a necessary element of causing fear, the definition is still extremely broad.

At the time of the Convention's promulgation, an Amnesty International report held that the definition was so broad that it 'does not satisfy the definition of legality in international human rights law' and that it could be read as posing a threat to the freedoms of association and of expression.[34] The definition could be applied to certain forms of attack not prohibited by international humanitarian law regulating non-international armed conflict, and that if it were indeed to render such conduct 'terrorism', 'armed political groups will lose an important incentive to comply with international humanitarian law'.[35] Three elements have been identified by the UN's Office of the High Commissioner for Human Rights that could be included in a definition of terrorism: 'criminal acts intended or calculated to provoke a state of terror in the general public, a group of persons or particular persons for political purposes'.[36] In the Arab Convention's definition, the only definite overlap is with the first element of 'criminal acts', although it adds the element of violence or threat thereof. A 'terrorist offence' is defined in art. 1(3) as:

> Any offence or attempted offence committed for a terrorist purpose in any of the Contracting states, or against their nationals, property or interests,

[34] Amnesty International, 'The Arab Convention for the Suppression of Terrorism; a serious threat to human rights', AI Index: MDE 01/002/2002 (21 January 2002), 8.

[35] Ibid.

[36] OHCHR, *Digest of Jurisprudence of the UN and Regional Organizations on the Protection of Human Rights while Countering Terrorism*, Geneva, undated, p. 3, citing the Declaration on Measures to Eliminate International Terrorism annexed to GA Res. 49/60.

that is punishable by their domestic law. The offences stipulated in the following conventions shall be considered terrorist offences unless such offences have been excepted by the legislation of the Contracting State or the state has not ratified the said convention.

The 'terrorist purpose' here presumably relates to the definition of 'terrorism' in the preceding clause, and there follows a list of international terrorism-related conventions.[37] In art. 2(a) comes a clarification and a caveat:

> Cases of struggle by whatever means, including armed struggle, against foreign occupation and aggression for the sake of liberation and self-determination, in accordance with the principles of international law, shall not be considered an offence. Such cases shall not include any act prejudicing the territorial integrity of any Arab state.

This clause reflects the concern to exclude from the definition acts done in the Palestinian struggle for self-determination, while at the same time not to exclude acts committed in any self-determination struggle against any existing Arab state – implicitly even if such claims were recognised 'in accordance with the principles of international law'. This caveat clearly sits uneasily with the prior invocation of the general principle of self-determination.

The insistence on the distinction of resistance to occupation and aggression from terrorism, with the question of Palestine as central, is a cornerstone of the Arab states' promotion of a definition of international terrorism. The CTC asked Saudi Arabia a follow-up question:

> The CTC would welcome an indication of how Saudi Arabia would deal with a request by a state that is not party to that [Arab] Convention for the extradition of a person accused of an offence against, say, the International Convention for the Suppression of Terrorist Bombings committed in circumstances of the kind attracting the above-mentioned special exception.[38]

Saudi Arabia's response was to deny that there was such a thing as an exception, since struggles against foreign occupation and aggression

---

[37] A proposed amendment to this list is noted by Egypt in its 6th report to the CTC, reporting that the Egyptian legislature had approved a Presidential decision (no 235/2005) to approve an amendment to art. 1(3). The new provision 'conforms to security council resolution 1624, which calls on all states to "prohibit by law incitement to commit a terrorist act or acts" and condemns "attempts at the justification or glorification (*apologie*) of terrorist acts that may incite further terrorist acts"' S/2006/351 (31 May 2006), [2.1].

[38] UN Doc. S/2003/583 (third report of Saudi Arabia to the CTC), p. 13.

are in accordance with the principles of international law as reaffirmed by the United Nations, and 'inasmuch as what is involved is the right of peoples to engage in armed struggle for self-determination'.[39] Stork critically observes in this regard that without any conditioning language on the framework of international humanitarian law, the affirmation of 'any means of armed struggle ... politically represents merely a mirror image of the Israeli contention that all forms of militant struggle, and certainly armed struggle, are indistinguishable from terrorism'.[40]

The Convention then proceeds to the concept of political offences, which would clearly be excluded from the provisions on extradition and rogatory procedures with which much of the remainder of the text deals. Anything already defined as a 'terrorist offence' is not to be considered a political offence, along with a list of other specific offences which are also not to be so considered 'even if they are politically motivated' (art. 2(b)). Offences excluded from the 'political offence exception' for purposes of extradition include 'attacks' on the kings and heads of contracting states, their rulers, wives (sic), ascendants or descendants, crown princes, deputy heads of state or government ministers, and persons enjoying 'international protection' including ambassadors and diplomats (art. 2(b) (i)-(iii)). Also excluded are 'intentional murder and theft accompanied by force against individuals, or the authorities, or means of transport and communications'; 'acts of sabotage and destruction of public property assigned to a public service, even if owned by another Contracting State', and offences related to weapons, munitions or explosives or other items 'that may be used to commit terrorist offences'. In the first three clauses, the word used for 'attack' (ta'adda 'ala) is unqualified; that is, it is not necessarily restricted to physical attacks, or attacks on the lives or liberty of such persons. Some Contracting States have legislation criminalising the 'defamation' or lampooning or otherwise 'undermining' of their leaders.

There is much to comment on in the remainder of the text, including particular concerns over the lack of guarantees of fair trial or rights of detainees, extended surveillance authorities threatening the right to privacy, and an absence of reference to international law standards on any of these or other issues.[41] Despite the urging by Arab

---

[39] Ibid. Compare Jordan's response to a similar question by the CTC, reproducing the government's statement on ratifying the International Convention for the Suppression of the Financing of Terrorism (S/2006/212, [1.14]).

[40] Stork, 'The human rights crisis', p. 49. [41] See above note 34.

states that an international definition of torture include a definition of state terrorism, the Arab Convention includes no such text, and fails to clarify that state officials or other agents of the state are capable of committing the crimes defined therein as 'terrorist offences'.[42] Some state parties however provide in their domestic legislation for increased penalties if terrorist offences are committed by agents of the state, notably members of the police or armed forces. The focus of such provisions appears to be hostile activities against the state by such individuals or groups, rather than state accountability for actions of its agents as 'state terrorism'.

5.   State responses
A.   Egypt

The definition of terrorism in the Arab Convention is taken almost word for word from pre-existing (1992) Egyptian legislation.[43] Egypt tends to play a leading role in legislative matters in the region, and politically is one of the 'big three' (along with Saudi Arabia and Syria) in the Arab League. Egypt has officially been in a state of emergency since 1981, when President Anwar Sadat was assassinated, and has since suffered other attacks by domestic armed groups. Concern at 'the effects on the human rights situation' caused by this prolonged state of emergency and various 'security' measures associated therewith has been voiced by the UN Human Rights Committee.[44] The Committee had similar concerns when the Egyptian government legislated Law no. 97 of 1992 in direct response to 'the emergence of the phenomenon of terrorism'.[45] It declared:

> The definition of terrorism contained in that law is so broad that it encompasses a wide range of acts of differing gravity. The Committee is of the opinion that the definition in question should be reviewed by the Egyptian authorities and stated more precisely especially in view of the

---

[42] Amr Mousa, Secretary-General of the League of Arab States, told the Cairo meeting on terrorism and human rights that the UN should draft a convention 'including a definite definition of terrorism that discerns between terrorism and peoples' legitimate right to combat occupation and aggression and a definition of state terrorism' (in Kjok, *Terrorism and Human Rights*, p. 23). See also Amnesty International, above note 34, p. 16.

[43] Egypt's first report to the CTC: UN Doc. S/2001/1237 (29 May 2002), p. 13.

[44] CCPR/10/76/EGY 2002, [16]. See also UN Doc. CCPR/C/79/Add.23 of 9 August 1993, [7], [9].

[45] UN Doc. S/2001/1237 (29 May 2002), p. 3.

fact that it enlarges the number of offences which are punishable with the death penalty…[46]

Law no. 97 of 1992 introduced amendments to a number of laws.[47] It introduced the following definition of 'terrorism' as art. 86 of the Egyptian Penal Code:

> In application of the provisions of this law, terrorism shall mean any use of force or violence or threat or intimidation resorted to by the perpetrator in implementation of an individual or collective criminal undertaking aimed at disturbing[48] public order or jeopardizing the safety and security of society, which is of such nature as to harm persons or sow fear among them or imperil their lives, liberty or security; or [of such a nature as] to damage the environment, or to damage, occupy or take over communications, transport, property, buildings or public or private realty (*amlak*); or to prevent or impede the exercise of their functions by public authorities or places of worship or institutions of learning; or to thwart the application of the Constitution or the laws or regulations.

The similarities with the definition adopted by the Arab Convention are evident, but certain revisions were made. In the Arab Convention, causing fear or terror to persons is not an element of the definition, but in Egypt, the aim of violating public order or endangering public safety and security is. The first of these, violation of public order, is extremely wide. In contrast to the Convention, in the Egyptian text, a 'threat' is not necessarily of use of force or violence. The list of possible prohibited acts is similar but rather longer and considerably wider, in particular the final two clauses which are absent from the Arab Convention. The definition of terrorism cited in Egypt's first report to the CTC is a summary of the relevant article rather than the full text.[49]

Law no. 97 of 1992 set out a series of offences as ordinary crimes, with increased penalties (including the death penalty and hard labour for life) if 'terrorism' is among the means used. For example:

> The penalty shall be prison for whosoever establishes, founds, organizes or directs, in violation of the law, an association or body or organization or group or gang the purpose of which is to call [*da'wa*] by any means for

---

[46] UN Doc. CCPR/C/79/Add.23 (9 August 1992), [8].
[47] Law no. 97 of 1992, *Official Gazette* No. 29*bis* of 18 July 1992. The legislation amended by the provisions of law no. 97 of 1992 included Penal Code and Code of Criminal Procedure, Law No. 105 of 1980 regarding the Establishment of State Security Courts, Law no. 205 of 1990 regarding the Confidentiality of Bank Accounts and Law no. 394 of 1954 regarding Weapons and Explosives.
[48] Or 'violating': *ikhlal bi.*   [49] UN Doc. S/2001/1237, pp. 3–4.

thwarting the provisions of the Constitution or the laws or preventing one of the government institutions or public authorities from exercising its functions, or attacking the personal freedom of the citizen or other public rights and freedoms guaranteed by the Constitution and the law, or injuring national unity or social safety. The penalty shall be temporary hard labour for whosoever, with knowledge of the purpose for which it calls, holds any kind of leadership within it, or supplies it with material or financial provisions.

The penalty shall be prison for a period of not more than five years for whosoever, with knowledge of its purpose, joins one of the associations, bodies, organizations, groups or gangs set out in the previous paragraph, or participates in it in any manner.[50]

This article already renders illegal mere membership in associations that have no necessary link with violence, let alone with terrorism, and poses a considerable risk to freedom of expression and association. The following article (art. 86*bis* (a)) stipulates that for offenders covered by the first paragraph of the previous article, the penalty shall be death or hard labour for life 'if terrorism is one of the means used in the realisation or implementation of the purposes called for' by the association. For offenders under the second paragraph of art. 86*bis*, the penalty in such circumstances becomes a sentence of hard labour if terrorism is among the means used.[51] There is further a prison sentence of up to ten years for anyone disseminating the purposes of such associations in any way or possessing materials for such dissemination, if terrorism is one of the means used by the association.[52] The accusation of terrorism may be made on the basis of the extremely broad terms of its definition. The UN Special Rapporteur on the promotion and protection of human rights and fundamental freedoms while countering terrorism, Martin Scheinin, has held that the definition was so broad as to run 'the risk of including acts that do not comprise a sufficient relation to violent terrorist crimes'.[53]

In 2004, Egypt reported amendments to its provisions on forced labour and the possible penalties at re-trial 'in order to avoid the difficulties which prevented certain countries from acceding to Egypt's requests for

---

[50] Article 86*bis* of the Penal Code as amended by art. 2 of Law no. 97 of 1992.

[51] Article 86*bis*(a) as amended by art. 2 of Law no. 97 of 1992. Offenders under art. 86*bis* are also liable to hard labour for membership in such an association if they are members the police or armed forces.

[52] Article 86*bis* para. 3 and Article 86*bis*(a) para. 3 as amended by Article 2 of Law no. 97 of 1992.

[53] Report of the Special Rapporteur, Martin Scheinin, on his Mission to Egypt: A/HRC/13/37/Add. 2 (14 October 2009), [11].

the extradition of terrorists'.[54] New legislation was introduced on money laundering.[55] Political violence hit Egypt again in the mid-2000s with a number of terrorist attacks directed at hotels in the Sinai, while at the very end of 2010 a bomb left over twenty mortalities at a Coptic church in Alexandria. In 2005, during the presidential election campaign, the Egyptian authorities announced their intention to put in place a prevention of terrorism law that would allow the lifting of the state of emergency.[56] Constitutional amendments of 2007 were presented as facilitating the introduction of the new law, but the state of emergency was renewed in 2008, to criticism from Martin Scheinin and others,[57] and again in 2010 against a background of protests.[58] The 2007 amendment to art. 179 of the Constitution was particularly criticised:

> The State shall seek to safeguard public security and discipline to counter dangers of terror. The law shall, under the supervision of the judiciary, regulate special provisions related to evidence and investigation procedures stipulated in paragraph 1 of Articles 41 and 44, and paragraph 2 of Article 45 shall in no way preclude such counter-terror action.
>
> The President may refer any terror crime to any judicial body stipulated in the Constitution or in law.[59]

The listed articles protect against arbitrary arrest and detention, house searches and violations of privacy. With regard to the amended art. 179, Brown and Dunne observe that:

> Some Egyptians have complained that the constitution will now enshrine what was technically a temporary (if ongoing) state of emergency as a permanent part of Egypt's political structure and wall off security practices from constitutional oversight. It is difficult to challenge this interpretation.[60]

---

[54] S/2004/343 (23 April 2004) p. 9. The reference is to Law no. 95 of 2003; the English translation of the Penal Code supplied to UNODC shows no change to the penalties in art. 86*bis*.

[55] Law to Combat Money Laundering, Law no. 80 of 2002 (*Official Gazette* no. 20 of 22 May 2002) and Law Amending Certain Provisions of the Law to Combat Money Laundering, Law no. 78 of 2003. See Sherif Sayyid Kamil, *Mukafihat jara'im ghasal al-amwal fi al-tashri' al-misri* (Cairo: Dar al-nahda al-'arabiyya, 2002).

[56] See Nathan J. Brown and Michele Dunne, 'A textual analysis' in Nathan J. Browne, Michele Dunne and Amr Hamzawy, *Egypt's Controversial Constitutional Amendments* (Carnegie Endowment for International Peace, 23 March 2007), p. 2.

[57] Report of the Special Rapporteur on his Mission to Egypt, [6].

[58] Yolande Knell, 'Egypt opposition to emergency law' (12 May 2010), available at news.bbc.co.uk/1/hi/world/middle_east/8675301.stm.

[59] Translation from www.unodc.org/tldb/pdf/Egypt_const_1971.pdf.

[60] Brown and Dunne, 'A textual analysis', p. 2.

Special Rapporteur Martin Scheinin has agreed: 'article 179 of the Constitution carries features of a permanent state of emergency, although under a new name'.[61] In 2009, the Cairo Institute for Human Rights Studies noted that the emergency law 'had been used against a number of political activists and bloggers' and that the anti-terrorism law 'will likely be used against critics and political opponents who are not accused of using violence'.[62]

Human rights concerns have included the violent suppression of anti-war demonstrations in Cairo in the spring of 2002 and the arrest of alleged 'ringleaders', the arrest of bloggers and of human rights activists as well as political opponents and the continued excessive use of force and torture. In addition, Egypt's past criticisms of other states for refusing to hand over or curtail the activities of those it accuses of offences against Egyptian security appear to be bearing fruit, giving rise in some cases to fears for the safety of those extradited or returned to Cairo. In December 2001 two Egyptian asylum-seekers were forcibly repatriated by Sweden – which took up the CIA's offer of air transport to take them – after secret evidence was relied on to dismiss their asylum claims; they then 'disappeared' into the system for more than three weeks with no access to family or counsel. Human Rights Watch reported other forcible repatriations from Jordan, Canada, Bosnia and Uruguay.[63] The Committee against Torture subsequently found Sweden's expulsion of Ahmad Agiza to have violated its obligations under art. 3 of the Convention against Torture, given that the Swedish authorities either knew or should have known that he was 'at real risk' of torture should he be returned to Egypt; the CIA involvement and treatment of Agiza by the US security personnel on Swedish territory (at the airport) should, in the Committee's view, have confirmed that risk.[64]

Egyptian human rights groups have pointed out that they were among the first to focus the attention of the international NGO community on

---

[61] Report of the Special Rapporteur on his Mission to Egypt, [13].

[62] Cairo Institute for Human Rights Studies, *Bastion of Impunity, Mirage of Reform. Human Rights in the Arab Region, Annual Report 2009* (Cairo Institute for Human Rights Studies), p. 112

[63] Stork, 'The human rights crisis', p. 46.

[64] *Agiza v. Sweden*, Communication No. 233/2003, CAT/C/34/D/233/2003 (20 May 2005), [13.2], [13.4]. See also A/HRC/13/42 (Joint Study on Global Practices, 2010), [222]–[225] with regard to practices of secret detention in Egypt, and to reports by a British national of Egyptian security agents facilitating his interrogation by British security officials after he was arbitrarily detained in Egypt in 2008. The cases of Ahmed Agiza and Mohammed Alzery are also reported in Dick Marty's 2006 report to the Council of Europe (see further below) [150]–[161].

political violence by non-state actors.[65] The country has a diverse and active non-governmental human rights community, whose many activities, such as an energetic campaign against torture, rarely, if ever, receive coverage in the domestic press. On the governmental side, and in line with other 'reform-minded' moves in the region after the turn of the century, the National Council for Human Rights was established in 2003. In what was considered its first real challenge in 2004, some observers saw a setback for the Council's potential in the apparently last-minute refusal by a majority of its members to endorse a memorandum prepared by its Legal Committee requesting the government to end the long-standing state of emergency.[66] In January 2011, as thousands poured into the streets of Cairo and other Egyptian towns and cities in unprecedented protests against President Mubarak's rule, UN High Commissioner for Human Rights, Navi Pillay, made the link, stating that she believed that 'the lifting of the emergency law is long overdue and it lies at the root of much of the frustration and anger that has now boiled over into the streets'.[67]

B.   Syria

For the United States, Syria remains one of four designated state sponsors of terrorism, in view of 'its continuing support and safe haven for terrorist organizations'.[68] Concerns that Syria might be the next target of the 'neo-cons' for invasion and 'regime change' after the invasion of Iraq reduced over 2003–4, and Syria, for its part, made positive moves to ensure it was not aligned with the 'enemy' in the 'global war on terror'. In its 2003 report, the United States formally recognised Syrian co-operation 'against al-Qaida, the Taliban, and other terrorist organizations and individuals'[69] before announcing the imposition of sanctions against the country a fortnight later. Syria remains among the most

---

[65] Bahey el-din Hassan, 'Opening Remarks' 18, p. 13.

[66] *Al-Wafd*, 6 May 2004, 'Al-majlis al-qawmi li-huquq al-insan yataraji' taht al-dughut al-hukumiyya'. See further Arab Program for Human Rights Activists, Press Release of 25 May 2004, 'Egypt: the National Council for Human Rights'.

[67] OHCHR, 'United Nations High Commission for Human Rights urges government restraint and respect for human rights in Egypt,' Geneva, 28 January 2011. In August 2011, Egypt's post-Mubarak government said it planned to lift the state of emergency and the Emergency Law.

[68] US Department of State, *Country Reports on Terrorism 2009 – Background Note: Syria* (8 September 2010) available at www.state.gov/r/pa/ei/bgn/3580.htm.

[69] *Patterns of Global Terrorism 2003*, p. 85. Other states on the list in 2010 are Cuba, Iran and Sudan; Syria has been longest on the list, featuring since its inception in 1979. The 2003 report noted (at p. 93) that 'Syrian officials have publicly condemned international terrorism but continue to make a distinction between terrorism and what they consider

tightly controlled of the Arab states, and reports of discontent by Syrian Kurds in the north in March 2004, followed in April by 'mysterious gun battles' in Damascus, made uncommon news in the region.[70] The second half of the decade – particularly following Syria's withdrawal of its forces from Lebanon – saw a determined closing of the limited opening of the public space to civil society actors (including bloggers and human rights activists, political opponents and Kurdish rights activists) that had been witnessed in the few previous years. The 2009 report from the Cairo Institute for Human Rights Studies calls Syria 'a graveyard for reformers and human rights defenders'. Syria remains under a state of emergency first declared in 1963.[71]

The Syrian Penal Code of 1949[72] was modelled on the Lebanese Penal Code, which was in turn inspired by French criminal law. The Syrian code contains three articles on 'terrorism' within the chapter on 'crimes against internal state security'. The following definition of terrorism in art. 304 is almost unchanged since the original promulgation of the law:

> Terrorist acts shall mean all deeds that aim at creating a state of panic (*dhu'r*) and which are committed by means such as explosives, weapons of war,[73] inflammable materials, poisonous or incendiary products or epidemic or microbe agents of a nature to cause public danger.

The Syrian definition makes the creation of fear an element in the definition of the offence, although it does not specify among whom. It does not specify any further purpose, and although the means listed tend to a high degree of potential danger and damage, they are not presented as exhaustive ('means such as').

---

to be the legitimate armed resistance of Palestinians in the Occupied Territories and of Lebanese Hizballah'.

[70] Trouble between Kurdish and Arab supporters at a football match in Qamlish, and the reported killing of some twenty persons by the security forces, were followed by clashes between Kurds and the security forces in March 2004; Amnesty International cited reports of hundreds of Syrian Kurds arrested.

[71] UN Doc. CCPR/CO/71/SYR, [6]; see OHCHR Digest, pp. 18–19. The Committee referred to Legislative Decree no. 51 of 9 March 1963 declaring a state of emergency. See also Human Rights Watch, 'Far from justice: Syria's Supreme State Security Court', 2009, on the measures against suspected Islamists in Syria.

[72] Promulgated by Legislative Decree no. 148 on 22 June 1949 (*Official Gazette* no. 37 of 18 July 1949 p. 2025); with fifteen laws amending it, the latest in 1979. Text annotated by Mamduh 'Atari, *Qanun al-'uqubat: mu'addalan wa madubtan 'ala'l-asl* (Damascus: Mu'assasat an-nuri, 2003).

[73] The phrase 'weapons of war' was added by Law no. 36 of 26 March 1978, 'Atari, *Qanun al-'uqubat*, 118.

Article 305 imposes a penalty of hard labour of between fifteen and twenty years for 'every terrorist act' (not further defined) and of between ten and twenty years of hard labour for conspiracy. The death penalty is mandated if such an act 'results in the destruction – even partial – of a public building, industrial establishment, vessel or other installation or disruption of means of information, communication or transport, or if it leads to the death of a person'.

The third of the three articles in the section on terrorism deals with associations that are established 'with the intention of changing the social or economic character of the state or the basic mores of society by one of the means set out in Article 304'. Such an association is to be dissolved and its members sentenced to hard labour, with a minimum seven-year sentence for founders and directors. This description includes a political purpose missing from the definition of terrorism. Membership in such an association is here, as in Egypt, a punishable offence even if no specific terrorist act has been planned, attempted or carried out.

In its second report to the CTC, Syria sets out legislation imposing 'severe penalties for all acts relating to terrorism'.[74] The first provision it sets out is art. 278, which comes in a section entitled 'crimes affecting international law' and criminalises the violation of arrangements made to maintain neutrality in a war, and punishes 'the author of acts, writings, or speeches for which the Government has not granted permission and which expose Syria to the risk of acts of hostility or disturb its relations with a foreign state or exposes Syrians to acts of revenge against their person or property'.[75] In an annotated copy of the Penal Code, this article is cross-referenced to art. 65 of the General Publications Law 1949,[76] which concerns the communication or publication of false news or falsified documents and imposes a criminal sentence of up to a year and/ or a fine 'if such act was ill-intentioned or disquieted the public or disturbed international relations or undermined the standing or dignity of the state'. This provision adds to the constraint of political dissent and criticism of the government. In 2010, lawyer Muhannad al-Hasani – the head of the Syrian Organisation for Human Rights – was sentenced by the State Security Court to three years in prison 'for having reported on legal proceedings' before the court.[77]

---

[74] Second report of Syria to the CTC: UN Doc. S/2002/1046 (19 September 2002), p. 3.
[75] The penalty is a prison sentence.
[76] Law no. 53 of 8 October 1949; 'Atari, Qanun al-'uqubat, 111.
[77] Human Rights Watch, World Report 2011: Syria, available at www.hrw.org/middle-eastn-africa/syria.

Having initially taken the position that its existing legislation was sufficient to comply with Resolution 1373, Syria did subsequently promulgate a law on money laundering in 2005.[78] In addition, it has become clear that what the US State Department calls Syria's 'limited cooperation with US counter-terrorism efforts'[79] after 9/11 extended to collaboration with the extraordinary rendition and proxy detention practices of the CIA.[80] In perhaps the best known case (that of Maher Arar), Rapporteur Dick Marty's report to the Council of Europe noted that '[i]n this specific case, the transfer of Mr Arar to Syria seems to be a well established example of the "outsourcing" of torture, a practice mentioned publicly by certain American officials'.[81]

C. Jordan

In Jordan, an opportunistic expansion of government control was passed at the same time as legislation responding to Security Council Resolution 1373, only to be changed back again after negotiations between the executive and key civil society actors. Many provisions of Jordan's Penal Code 1960[82] reproduce the Syrian text. This was the case in the three provisions in the Jordanian code on terrorism until their amendment in 2001; the only differences were that, in its definition, Jordan had not followed Syria's

---

[78] Decree no. 33 of 1 May 2005.
[79] US Department of State, *Country Reports on Terrorism 2009*.
[80] A/HRC/13/42 (Joint Study on Global Practices, 2010), [143].
[81] Dick Marty, 'Alleged secret detention and unlawful inter-state transfers of detainees involving Council of Europe member states': Report to the Committee on Legal Affairs and Human Rights at the Council of Europe's Parliamentary Assembly (Doc. 10957), 12 June 2006, [179]. Maher Arar was arrested in 2002 at JFK airport and subsequently transferred (apparently via Italy and Jordan) to Syrian military intelligence; a Canadian citizen of Syrian descent, his case became the subject of a Canadian commission of enquiry. For further discussion of the Canadian response to this case see Kent Roach, Chapter 20, this volume. See also Amnesty International, 'Below the radar: secret flights to torture and "disappearance"', 5 April 2006, 17–19, on the case of Muhammad Zammar; and A/HRC/13/42 (Joint Study on Global Practices, 2010) at [127] on the case of Mustafa Setmariam Nassar.
[82] Law no. 16 of 1960 as amended 1988, 1991, 2001, 2003; *Official Gazette* no. 1487 of 11 May 1960. This Code replaced an earlier Temporary Penal Code of 1951 (Temporary Law no. 85 of 1951, *Official Gazette* no. 1077 of 17 July 1951). On the choice made by the newly independent and sovereign state of Jordan to follow French-based models from neighbouring states rather than adopting the 1936 Criminal Code issued by the British in Palestine (and which had therefore been in force in the Palestinian West Bank, incorporated into the territory of Jordan after the war), see E.T. Mogannam, 'Developments in the legal system of Jordan' (1952) 6 *Middle East Journal* 196.

amendment of its listed means of committing terrorism to include 'weapons of war', while in the second article stipulating penalties the Jordanian text substituted life hard labour for the death penalty in one case and a slightly lighter prison sentence in another.[83]

In October 2001, Jordan's government rushed out amendments to the Penal Code by way of a royal decree issued in accordance with a decision of cabinet, during an extended delay in convening Parliament that saw over a hundred such 'temporary laws' issued.[84] Temporary Law no. 54 of 2001[85] introduced a new definition of terrorism based on a combination of the Arab Convention and its Egyptian model. The element of 'causing panic' is no longer a necessary part of the definition of terrorism, and the 'means' listed in the above-cited Syrian art. 304 as part of the definition are transformed in the new Jordanian provision into aggravating factors at sentencing, giving rise to the death penalty when an act of terrorism under the new definition is committed.[86] The new definition of terrorism in art. 147 is as follows:

> Terrorism shall mean the use of violence or threat of use thereof, whatever its motivations or purposes, occurring in implementation of an individual or collective act aimed at disturbing public order or jeopardizing the safety or security of society, where such is of a nature to spread fear among the people and frighten them or to expose their lives and security to danger, or to cause damage to the environment, or to cause damage to, occupy or take over public facilities and realty or private realty, international facilities and diplomatic missions, endangering national resources or thwarting the provisions of the Constitution and laws.

This definition adopts the broader Egyptian text in some respects (including 'disturbing public order'), while staying closer to the Arab Convention definition in others (including the threat being of the use of force). Curiously, it omits the qualification of such acts as 'criminal'.

Article 148 adds to the original text penalties of hard labour for life for terrorist offences resulting, *inter alia*, in 'damage, even partial, to a public

---

[83] Articles 147, 148, 149 of the Jordanian Penal Code 1960 before its amendment in 2001; paralleling arts. 304, 305 and 306 of the Syrian Code.

[84] Legislation issued in this manner is classified as 'temporary' and is required to be submitted for parliamentary scrutiny and decision when parliament is reconvened.

[85] Temporary Law no. 54 of 2001 amending the Penal Code of 2 October 2001, *Official Gazette* no. 4510 of 8 October 2001.

[86] Article 148(4)(c) of the Jordanian Penal Code as amended by Article 3 of Temporary Law no. 54 of 2001.

or private building'[87] or 'disabling means of communication and computer systems, or disrupting their networks, or the total or partial disabling or damaging of means of transport'. The death penalty is mandated where the act leads to death or is committed using means (such as explosives) that were previously included in the definition of terrorism.

The third of the three articles in the section on terrorism, art. 149, is also amended to show key differences from the Syrian text:

> A penalty of temporary hard labour shall be imposed on whosoever embarks upon any act of a nature to destroy the system of political rule in the Kingdom, or to incite to oppose it (*munahida*), and whosoever embarks on any individual or collective act with the intention of changing the economic or social character of the state or the basic mores of society.

The original wording of this provision was a word for word reproduction of the Syrian text. The new Jordanian text no longer refers to associations but to individual or collective acts, does not require that such acts be carried out by means elsewhere identified with the definition of terrorism, and adds as new the first half of the provision regarding the destruction of the system of political rule or incitement to opposition thereof. [88]

In the same temporary law, Jordan changed a text punishing 'every writing, speech and act intended to or resulting in the provocation of sectarian or racial chauvinism or urging discord between the sects and different elements of the nation' by a prison sentence of six months to three years plus a fine to the following:

> Regardless of any other law, a prison sentence shall be imposed for any writing, speech or any act broadcast by whatever means, or publication of news in press or any publication, where such is of a nature to injure national unity or to incite commission of crimes or spread rancour and hatred and discord between individuals of the society or provoke racial or sectarian chauvinism, or injure the dignity, personal freedoms and reputation of individuals, or shake the basic foundations of society by promoting deviant behaviour or immorality or by publishing false information or rumours or incitement to agitation or vigils or the holding of public meetings in a manner contravening the applicable law, or by any other act liable to undermine the prestige, reputation or dignity of the state.[89]

---

[87] Thus adding 'private' buildings to the Syrian text which stipulated 'public' buildings in art. 305.

[88] Subsequent clauses deal with hostage taking and with infiltration to and from the territory of the Kingdom. Articles 147(2) and (3) of the Penal Code 1960 as amended by arts. 4 of Temporary Law no. 54 of 2001.

[89] Article 150 of the Penal Code 1960 as amended by art. 5 of Temporary Law no. 54 of 2001.

The second paragraph of this article as amended provided for the punishment of the editor-in-chief and owner of any publication used in such an act, plus the temporary or permanent closure of the newspaper or press 'in accordance with a decision of the court'. International human rights groups voiced concern at the attack on the right to freedom of expression and of the press represented by the extremely sweeping terms of this amended provision. In January 2002 the editor-in-chief of a political weekly was described by Amnesty International as 'the first known victim of the amendment of Article 150' when he was charged with 'writing and publishing false information and rumours that may harm the prestige and reputation of the state and slander the integrity and reputation of its members' after publishing a piece critical of the government.[90] The Jordanian Press Association and a number of newspaper editors and owners challenged the constitutionality of the amended article but the High Court of Justice rejected the suit for lack of interest of the petitioners;[91] interventions and negotiations about the role of the media and its regulation continued, with the Press Association drafting its own 'code of honour assuring objectivity and freedom of expression' and the Prime Minister promising that the article would be repealed.[92] In another temporary law issued in June 2003, the text of art. 150 was changed back to its original reading apart from an increase in the fine that could be imposed.[93]

In its first report to the CTC, Jordan set out in some detail examples of sentences passed by its State Security Court on persons convicted of terrorism-related offences, including the death penalty and life sentences with frequent *in absentia* judgments.[94] The State Security Court has been

---

[90] The case of Fahd al-Rimawi, Editor-in-Chief of *al-Majd* weekly. See Amnesty International, 'Security measures violate human rights', AI Index MDE 16/001/2002, 5 February 2002. See also Stork, 'The human rights crisis', p. 43.

[91] 'High Court rejects JPA lawsuit contesting Penal Code provisions', *Jordan Times*, 17 July 2002. See further AMAN News Center (the Arab Regional Resource Center on Violence Against Women), available at www.amanjordan.org.

[92] 'Government announces procedures to repeal Article 150', *Jordan Times*, 9 April 2003.

[93] Temporary Law no. 45 of 2003 amending the Penal Code, *Official Gazette* no. 4600 of 1 June 2003. The potential prison sentence of between six months to three years remains the same, while the fine rises from a maximum of 50 dinars in the original 1960 text to 500 in the new version. Another change made by Temporary Law no. 54 of 2001 however remains: this is an amendment to art. 195 of the Penal Code, which deals with insults to the King; a new clause added to the list of offences that provoke a prison sentence of from one to three years for 'whosoever gossips about His Majesty the King or commits calumny by attributing to him words or deed which the King did not say or do, or acting to broadcast such or spread it among the people'.

[94] First Report of Jordan to the CTC: UN Doc S/2002/127 (29 January 2002), pp. 9–12.

the focus of criticisms from human rights groups since it was re-introduced in 1991.[95] Already in August 2001 there had been an amendment (through a temporary law) to the Law establishing the State Security Court expanding its jurisdiction (for example to include 'any other crime related to economic security that the prime minister decides to transfer to the Court').[96] The amendment also permitted the police to detain a suspect for up to seven days before bringing him or her before the Prosecutor, as compared to the twenty-four hours permitted under the regular Code of Criminal Procedure.[97] The Jordanian Bar Association voiced particular objections to the removal of the right to appeal for those convicted of 'misdemeanours' in the State Security Court.[98]

The State Security Court is a key feature of the Law on the Prevention of Terrorism promulgated in Jordan in 2006.[99] The country had suffered the bombing of its embassy in Baghdad in 2003, just weeks before the attack on the UN headquarters there. In 2005, bombings hit three hotels in Amman, carried out by Iraqi suicide bombers and claimed by the group led by Jordanian Abu Mus'ab al-Zarqawi. Reflecting on the event and its impact, the International Crisis Group asserted 'two important messages':

> No security apparatus, however efficient, can prevent each and every attack by a person prepared to die as they kill others. And any security

[95] The State Security Court was first established in 1952, replaced by military martial courts from 1967–90, and re-introduced (replacing the military martial court system) in 1991.
[96] Article 3(a)(iii) of Temporary Law no. 44 of 2001 amending the Law establishing the State Security Court, *Official Gazette* no. 4503 of 28 August 2001. An examination is made in a 'Working paper on law no. 16 of 2001 amending the Code of Criminal Procedure no. 9 of 1961' (Arabic text) by Advocate Abdel Ghaffar Freihat to a workshop of the Jordanian Banks Association in Amman, 15 October 2001.
[97] Article 7 of the Law establishing State Security Courts as amended by art. 3 of Law no. 44 of 2001. Freihat, 'working paper', 10.
[98] The Bar Association took an 'unprecedented decision' to call on all its members to refrain from appearing before the Court for a week in June 2002, to protest against the 2001 amendments: Saad Hattar, *Jordan Times*, 12 June 2002.
[99] Law no. 55 of 2006, *Official Gazette* no. 4264 of 1 November 2006, p. 4790. An English translation of the text of this law is available at the Terrorism Legislation Database of the United Nations Office on Drugs and Crime (www.unodc.org/tldb). The law's definition of 'terrorist act' is given there as: 'Every intentional act, committed by any means and causing death or physical harm to a person or damage to public or private properties, or to means of transport, infrastructure, international facilities or diplomatic missions and intended to disturb public order, endanger public safety and security, cause suspension of the application of the provisions of the Constitution and laws, affect the policy of the State or the government or force them to carry out an act or refrain from the same, or disturb national security by means of threat, intimidation or violence'.

response must be complemented by a genuine opening of the political system and more equally shared economic opportunity if Jordan is to minimise the risk of further attacks and instability.[100]

The 2006 law explicitly included in 'terrorist acts' financing and recruitment or mobilisation activities and provides for a range of measures against suspects including surveillance, travel ban, the search of homes and the seizure of funds suspected to be associated with the acts.[101] A law against money laundering followed in 2007.[102]

Jordan, rather like Morocco, emphasises its positioning as a 'moderate middle course'.[103] In November 2004, King Abdullah had announced an 'Amman Message' insisting that 'on religious grounds, on moral grounds, we denounce the contemporary concept of terrorism'.[104] Until around that time, Jordan had been actively collaborating with the CIA rendition programme, providing 'proxy detention' of non-nationals and transferring others to secret US custody. Human Rights Watch tracked at least fourteen non-Jordanians sent by the United States to Jordan 'for interrogation and likely torture' over the period 2001–4, and observes in this regard that 'while a few other countries have received individuals rendered by the United States in recent years (that is, transferred without formal legal process), no country is known to have detained as many as Jordan'.[105] Of the three Yemeni men reported by Amnesty International in 2006 to have provided at that time 'the only public testimony from those who have been held in "black sites"' by the US, two were arrested in Jordan and transferred there to US custody.[106]

During the second half of the decade, the institutionalisation of human rights mechanisms has proceeded apace. A National Centre of Human Rights was established in 2006,[107] and Jordan has gazetted a number of international human rights instruments to which it is party. On the level of practice, however, the UN Special Rapporteur on torture visited Jordan

---

[100] International Crisis Group, 'Jordan's 9/11: dealing with Jihadi Islamism', 23 November 2005, p. 1.
[101] Articles 3 and 4 of Law no. 55 of 2006. In its fifth report to the CTC, Jordan had identified these provisions as fulfilling its obligations regarding measures to prohibit incitement to terrorist acts according to Resolution 1624 (S/2006/212, 4 April 2006, [2.1]).
[102] Law no. 46 of 2007, *Official Gazette* no. 4831 of 17 June 2007, p. 4130.
[103] Jordan's first report to the CTC: UN Doc. S/2002/127 (29 January 2002), p. 3.
[104] S/2006/212 (4 April 2006), [2.4].
[105] Human Rights Watch, 'Double jeopardy: CIA rendition to Jordan', 2008, 1–2.
[106] Amnesty International, 'Below the radar', 9.
[107] Law no. 51 of 2006 (Law of the National Centre for Human Rights), *Official Gazette* no. 4787 of 16 October 2006, p. 4026.

and concluded in 2006 that 'the practice of torture is routine' in two security directorates: one the general Criminal Investigations Directorate and the other the General Intelligence Directorate, which is responsible for national security and counter-terrorism, and was described by Human Rights Watch as having 'served as a proxy jailor' for the CIA at the start of the decade.[108] In 2008, 'in the first event of its kind' in the region, Jordan hosted a Regional Seminar on Upholding Human Rights While Countering Terrorism organised by the OHCHR and the UNDP in Jordan.[109]

D. Tunisia

Tunisia's Law no. 2003–75 regarding Support for International Effort to Combat Terrorism and the Repression of Money Laundering[110] had already been prepared in draft when in April 2002 a truck exploded outside a Djerba synagogue, killing twenty-one people. The Tunisian authorities have observed that they had 'long warned of the terrorist threat', but at the same time human rights groups voiced concern at Tunisia's established use of the security discourse 'as a pretext for repression of political dissent and critical discourse across the political spectrum'.[111] Thus, while the official narrative of modernity, stability and rights (including substantial emphasis on women's rights) is fiercely promoted at home and abroad, Tunisia's public space remained extremely restricted in relation to criticism of the president or the government throughout the decade. 'Anyone who is critical of the Tunisian authorities', said Amnesty International in July 2010, 'or speaks out for human rights in Tunisia is at risk'.[112] In January 2011, unprecedented anti-government protests built into the people's revolution that forced the departure of President Ben Ali.

---

[108] Report of the Special Rapporteur on his Mission to Jordan: A/HRC/4/33/Add. 4 (5 January 2007); Human Rights Watch, 'Double jeopardy', 1.

[109] OHCHR, 'Middle East and North Africa region to discuss upholding human rights while countering terrorism', 21 October 2008.

[110] Law no. 2003–75 of 10 December 2003, *Journal Officiel de la République Tunisienne* no. 99 (12 December 2003), pp. 3592–601 (French translation by the Tunisian government for purposes of information). The French text is also available at www.jurisitetunisie. com/tunisie/codes/terror (under the title Lutte contre le Terrorism et le Blanchiment d'Argent). I do not yet have the Arabic text.

[111] Amnesty International, 'Tunisia: new draft "anti-terrorism" law will further undermine human rights', briefing note to the European Union, AI Index MDE 30/021/2003.

[112] Amnesty International, 'Independent voices stifled in Tunisia', AI Index: MDE 30/008/2010, July 2010, 2.

Tunisia's 2003 law reflects its official image in an aspirational opening statement:

> The current law guarantees society's right to live in security and peace, far from all that is of a nature to undermine its stability, to reject all forms of deviance, violence, fanaticism, racial segregation and terrorism which menace peace and the stability of societies. It contributes, moreover, to supporting the international effort to combat all forms of terrorism, to confront sources of finance that support it and to the repression of money laundering, within the framework of international, regional and bilateral conventions ratified by the Tunisian Republic and respect for constitutional guarantees (Article 1).

This is the longest of the post-Security Council Resolution 1373 legislative instruments under consideration here, and its first immediate effect was to amend the pre-existing definition of 'terrorist offence' under the Tunisian Penal Code, as follows:

> Shall be categorized as terrorist, every offence, regardless of its motives,[113] related to an individual or collective undertaking liable to intimidate a person or group of persons or spread alarm among the population with the intention of influencing the policy of the state and prompting it to do or abstain from doing any action, disturbing public order or international peace and security, causing harm to persons or property, damaging the headquarters of diplomatic and consular missions and international organizations, inflicting serious harm on the environment so as to endanger the life or health of inhabitants, or damaging vital resources, the infrastructure, transport, communications, information systems or public amenities (Article 4).

In this wording, prospective intimidation of a person or group of persons or spreading fear among the population is a necessary element;[114] also necessary is intention, but while this includes influencing state policy, it may also include 'disturbing public order', or 'causing harm to property' or 'damaging public amenities'. There is no requirement of use of violence, nor, in some phrases, of the level of damage that has to be done.

The following art. (5) provides that 'terrorist offences' in the sense of the current law shall include terrorist offences in the real sense but also 'offences dealt with under the same regime'. Article 6 then provides that '[a]cts of incitement to hatred or religious fanaticism shall also be dealt

---

[113] 'Quels qu'en soient les mobiles'. This phrase is not included in the translation in Tunisia's third report, which is otherwise used here from the phrase 'to intimidate' onwards.

[114] In the French text this is not necessarily the case, but I assume the Arabic original will confirm the meaning rendered in the English text of the UN report.

with as terrorist offences, whatever the means used'.[115] This was taken from art. 52*bis* of the Penal Code which governed the categorisation of offences as terrorist prior to Law 2003–75. [116]

Amnesty International at the time voiced particular concern over what it considers a further broadening of the definition of 'terrorist offence' in Law 2003–75 in the light of the past use of the pre-existing art. 52*bis* of the Penal Code against non-violent opponents of the Tunisian authorities. The organisation notes that 'the Tunisian authorities have been casting the net of "terrorism" charges so wide as to include prisoners of conscience. Article 52*bis* has been used to criminalize peaceful opposition activities'. The reinstatement since 1999 of the trial of civilians by military court has resulted in 'scores of civilians … sentenced on charges of "terrorism" to heavy prison sentences after unfair trials'.[117]

A large number of accomplice offences are provided for, some of them requiring intention and some not. Membership of whatever form in any sort of group or organisation which 'even coincidentally or incidentally'[118] has adopted terrorism as a means of achieving its goals is criminalised, as is putting any 'capabilities or expertise' at the disposal of such a group or supplying or disseminating information 'with the intention of assisting in the commission of a terrorist offence'.[119] A prison sentence of five to twelve years can be imposed on whosoever:

> procures a meeting place for members of an organization, group or persons connected with terrorist offences, helps to lodge them or hide them or helps them to escape or ensures they are not discovered or punished, or benefits from the outcome of their misdeeds.[120]

[115] In this case I am using the translation provided by the English text of Tunisia's second report to the CTC (S/2002/1024 of 13 September 2002).

[116] Article 52*bis* of the Penal Code was abrogated by art. 103 of Law no. 2003–75.

[117] See further Amnesty International, 'Tunisia: the cycle of injustice', AI Index MDE 30/001/2003, 9 June 2003. A particularly notorious attempt to apply art. 52 *bis* – although ultimately the conviction was not made under the 'terrorist offences' terms of this article – came in the 1999 prosecution of Radhia Nasraoui, a prominent human rights lawyer, along with twenty-one co-defendants. For details of the charges against Nasraoui and her co-defendants, and of the trial proceedings, see Amnesty International, Human Rights Watch, and the Observatory for the Protection of Human Rights Defenders, *The Administration of Justice in Tunisia: Torture, Trumped-up Charges and a Tainted Trial*, AI Index 30/04/00. March 2000 For a more recent analysis see report by Amnesty International, 'Independent Voices Stifled in Tunisia', AI Index MDE 30/008/2010 13 July 2010.

[118] Wording from S/2003/1038, p. 11.

[119] Articles 13 and 17. The penalty is five to twelve years in prison for the first offences and five to twenty for the second set, plus a fine of 5,000 to 50,000 dinars in both cases.

[120] Article 18 of Law no. 2003–75.

There is apparently no requirement here of knowledge or intention. In the parallel provision of the pre-existing Penal Code broadly the same list of actions is criminalised, with a maximum penalty of six years in prison for whosoever 'knowingly and voluntarily' commits them in relation to members of a criminal gang.[121] It is an offence under Tunisian law not to give immediate notification to the relevant authorities of information regarding a terrorist offence, even where the person is bound by professional confidentiality; here, an exception is made for ascendants, descendants, brothers, sisters and spouse.[122] Article 12 of Law no. 2003–75 provides for a penalty of five to twelve years in prison for:

> whosoever, by any means, calls for the commission of terrorist offences or for joining an organization or group connected with terrorist offences, or uses a name, a term, a symbol or any other sign with the goal of condoning[123] a terrorist organization, one of its members or its activities.[124]

In Canada, Roach notes a new offence regarding 'knowingly participating in or contributing to any activity of a terrorist group', and the evidential use of frequent association with members of a terrorist group and of the use of terrorist-related symbols and representations.[125] In Tunisia, such use of terrorist-related symbols itself constitutes an offence.

In its last public report to the CTC in 2005, Tunisia defended its antiterrorism law as 'based on precise and broad concepts of terrorist crime' and at the same time guaranteeing 'respect for human rights and universal freedoms including, in particular, the right to a fair trial and the presumption of innocence'.[126] Human rights organisations and international mechanisms disagree. In 2008, the UN Human Rights Committee concluded its consideration of Tunisia's fifth periodic report with concerns regarding the treatment of allegations of torture, the lack of exclusion from evidence of confessions obtained under torture, and the exceeding of time limits on *garde à vue* detention and other violations of the rules

---

[121] Article 133 of the Penal Code as amended by Law no. 89–23 of 27 February 1989. Article 28 of Law no. 2003–75 provides for the minimum penalty for the initial offence in the event that the perpetrators of a terrorist offence establish they were drawn into the act *inter alia* by abuse of their situation.

[122] Article 22 of Law no. 2003–75.

[123] The French text is '*faire l'apologie de*'.

[124] The last part of this provision, from 'or uses a name', is not included in Tunisia's third report to the CTC.

[125] Roach, 'World wide expansion', 502. See also Kent Roach, Chapter 20, this volume.

[126] Tunisia's Fourth Report to the CTC: S/2005/194 (24 March 2005), p. 4.

of police custody.[127] It also declared itself 'concerned at the lack of precision in the particularly broad definition of terrorist acts'.[128] The following year, Tunisia abrogated arts. 5 and 6 of Law 75–2003,[129] a move welcomed by Special Rapporteur Martin Scheinin in a statement issued at the end of his official visit to the country.[130] Nevertheless, the Special Rapporteur continued:

> [T]he 2003 counter-terrorism law still contains deficiencies, which, as in many other countries, are rooted in the definition of terrorism. […] As I have systematically emphasized, deadly or otherwise serious physical violence against members of the general population or segments of it should be a central feature of any definition of terrorism. This is clearly not the case in Tunisia where in the majority of cases since 2003 mere intentions are punished, be it in terms of 'planning' or in terms of 'membership', the latter often within vaguely defined organizations or groups.[131]

In January 2011, in one of its first statements after the departure of President Ben Ali, Amnesty International called on the caretaker government in Tunis to 'review all sentences for those convicted under the controversial and much-criticised 2003 Anti-Terrorism Law'.[132]

6. Conclusion

Reform and 'democratisation' in the Arab states were emphasised as a policy focus in developing US engagement with states in the region in a series of 'initiatives' developed in 2003 and 2004.[133] Considerable attention

---

[127] Concluding Observations of the Human Rights Committee – Tunisisa: CCPR/C/TUN/CO/5 (23 April 2008), [11]–[13].

[128] Ibid., [15].

[129] Another reference to 'offences dealt with under a similar juridical regime' was also removed from art. 2. These amendments were made by Law no. 2009–65 of 12 August 2009. Texts in French are available at www.jurisitetunisie.com.

[130] OHCHR, 'UN expert on human rights and counter-terrorism concludes visit to Tunisia', 26 January 2010.

[131] Ibid. Scheinin also noted 'the existence of serious discrepancies between the law and what was reported to me as happening in reality', choosing to speak out in advance of a full report on issues similar to those that concerned the Human Rights Committee in 2008.

[132] Amnesty International, 'Release of political prisoners in Tunisia is a welcome first step', 20 January 2011.

[133] The Greater Middle East Initiative was not, as originally planned, announced at the G8 Summit of June 2004, although some Arab states did attend to discuss an apparently less ambitious 'Broader Middle East Initiative'. For a critique of the first for failing to establish 'a basis for genuine partnership', see Marina Ottaway and Thomas Carothers, 'The

was paid to the findings of the set of Arab Human Development Reports by those seeking to formulate policies in the 'global war on terrorism', and in particular to extremely high levels of joblessness as well as lack of participation in social and political development. That different governments in the region (and their international allies) have not mobilised to address these serious challenges has been highlighted by the events of January 2011. Different bodies in the United Nations have considered the role of the organisation beyond the CTC in combating terrorism, including through 'norm setting, human rights and communication'.[134]

In a number of Arab states, new albeit limited human rights mechanisms have been instituted by governments, and certain other moves towards social, economic and political 'opening' (or 'reform') have been noted. Nevertheless, there is clearly a tension between these developments and the threats to core 'democratic' rights posed by legislation introduced or legitimated by the 'war on terror'. Fenwick observes that '[d]emocractic governments are perfectly entitled to take extraordinary measures if faced with a threat of atrocities' and explores the tension that necessarily arises between such measures and 'democratic values', with a view to proposing that such measures 'be subjected to the most rigorous tests for proportionality'.[135] The lack of space for public dissent and criticism, especially in the second half of the decade, was a particular obstacle facing those in the Arab states who would agree with this statement, and who would seek to constrain within a similar principle of proportionality the reaction of their governments to serious domestic and international threats.

A further obstacle is the apparent endorsement of legal and extra-legal practice by the United States in particular. In Yemen, a visiting delegation from Amnesty International, bringing up the mass arbitrary arrests and detentions that had taken place there since 9/11, allegedly with FBI involvement, reported as follows:

> The authorities, while recognizing that they were in breach of their international human rights obligations and their own laws, argued that this was because they had to 'fight terrorism' and avert the risks of a military

greater Middle East initiative: off to a false start', Carnegie Endowment for International Peace, Policy Brief 29, March 2004.

[134] Report of the Policy Working Group on the United Nations and Terrorism, UN Doc. A/57/273 S/2002/875.

[135] Helen Fenwick, 'Responding to 11 September: detention without trial under the Anti-Terrorism, Crime and Security Act 2001', in Lawrence Freedman, *Superterrorism: Policy Responses* (Oxford: Blackwell, 2002), pp. 100–1.

action against Yemen by the US in the wake of the 11 September events. The authorities said that they had 'no option' but to continue the practice of detention without charge or trial of those held contrary to their laws and international obligations, and that they had no plans to offer them an opportunity of access to lawyers or the judiciary to challenge the legality of their detention.[136]

Amnesty International has since reported on similar statements around the detention of three Yemeni nationals returned from US custody in CIA secret detention sites in 2005: 'Yemeni officials say they were instructed by the US Embassy to keep the men in custody until their case files were transferred from Washington. No files or evidence were ever received.'[137] Such deftly frank admissions of responding to pressure cannot excuse the state actor in such cases. Nevertheless, support – or pressure – for such measures from the United States sits uneasily with public promotion of reform in the Middle East as critical in its future engagement with the region. It was also in Yemen in 2003 that a CIA-controlled drone aircraft was reported to have launched a missile killing six men in a car in a suspected extra-judicial execution. Although Amnesty International reported receiving no response to its letters raising its concerns, Yemeni ministers later confirmed that the government co-operated with the US in this operation within the 'global war on terrorism'.[138]

Human rights activists in the region report an increasing perception of the hypocrisy of the international discourse of human rights and international law, in a region where it is already complicated by long-standing perceptions of selectivity, and where indeed the term 'international' is being increasingly read as meaning either US or US-driven. This is a concern not only for those who wish to see domestic reform initiatives take shape and continue rather than be interrupted or undermined. It needs no particular insight to suggest that such a development is of dubious

---

[136] Amnesty International, 'Yemen: united against rights', AI Index 31/011/2003, 24 September 2003. See also '200 held in Yemen to placate US', *The Guardian*, 24 September 2003.

[137] Amnesty International, 'Below the radar,' 15–16. See also Amnesty International, 'Yemen: cracking down under pressure', AI Index: MDE 31/010/2010 13 July 2010.

[138] Amnesty International, 'Yemen: the rule of law sidelined in the name of security', AI Index MDE 31/006/2003, 24 September 2003. Amnesty reported the US as arguing that such actions did not constitute extra-judicial killings but rather 'military operations against enemy combatants' and therefore as governed not by Yemeni police procedures but by 'the international law of armed conflict'. For US involvement with counter-terrorism operations in Yemen currently, see Amnesty International, 'Cracking down under pressure', 6.

efficacy in the effort to build international peace and security and to combat the phenomenon of terrorism. The protests that ousted Tunisia's President Ben Ali and shook Egypt's President Mubarak in January 2011, as well as troubling a number of other governments in the region, stand to challenge powerful Western states on what it is that they promote in the region as well as challenging Arab governments on how to address the tensions underlined by the protesters.